The Peasantry as the Lifeblood of the Nordic Race

The Peasantry as the Lifeblood of the Nordic Race

Richard Walther Darré

ANTELOPE HILL PUBLISHING

Richard Walther Darré (1895–1953)

Contents

Prefaces

Preface to the Fifth Edition

Due to typographical errors that have crept their way into the text, it has become necessary to undertake a revision of this work. I did this myself when my other work left me time to do so.

However, I was unable to commit to a major overhaul of the content, partly because of lack of time and partly because of a few fundamental considerations.

Taken as a whole, *The Peasantry as the Lifeblood of the Nordic Race* was tailor-made for its time as a polemic about the peasantry and for the peasantry. This book has completely fulfilled its purpose and has largely served as the forerunner of our present-day National Socialist conception of the German peasantry. Consequently, this book is a product of its time and for its time. If I were to rework the content, it would undergo a fundamental structural change—not because it has since been proven incorrect, but because, conversely, new evidence for its correctness could be brought forward today and would have to be included. The work would become a scholarly reference book, losing the vibrant freshness of the original composition. Above all, the work would have nothing to offer to intellectually curious *volksgenossen*[1] outside academic circles, since both the language and the content would have become too scholarly.

---

[1] Translator's note: The word *volksgenosse* (from: *volk*, meaning people or nation, and *genosse*, meaning comrade or companion), sometimes abbreviated as VG, was a term used by National Socialists to refer to fellow Germans. It is sometimes translated as national comrade, people's comrade, or even racial comrade.

This word's lack of a direct translation to English is related to the fact that the German word *volk* is hard to accurately communicate in modern English. In a nutshell, *volk* refers to a group of

I cannot, in principle, agree with the often-expressed opinion that this work, if it were to be reprinted again and again without changes, would necessarily lose its value in terms of content; it is a great mistake to think that the question of the peasantry as such has reached its conclusion with the recognition of its importance for our people. Peasantry[2] in the Germanic sense is not a matter of belonging to a certain occupation, but a matter of ideology, and since all ideology comes from the blood, it is also a matter of blood. Specifically, we are dealing with an ideology that stands in fierce opposition to any ideology born of Jewish spirit and blood. As far as the details are concerned, this remains true regardless of which area of human life is considered in relation to the premise of its Jewish ideology. The mighty struggle and mighty confrontation between the Germanic and Jewish spirit has only just begun today and will continue to leave its mark on the times to come. And so long as this confrontation remains at the beginning of its development, this work will still find its readers, because after all, it is not so much the problem of the peasant as such that is brought to the fore, but rather his contrast to the problem of nomadism—and Jewry is nomadism!

---

humans who share a common language, culture, and history due to a common descent. While modern German academics and writers would like to de-emphasize the aspect of consanguinity implied by the word, the echoes of its true meaning can still be heard by most with a good ear. The English word "nation" in its more original sense is pretty much a one-to-one equivalent. According to the Oxford English Dictionary (OED), nation is defined as "an extensive aggregate of persons, so closely associated with each other by common descent, language, or history, as to form a distinct race or people, usually organized as a separate political state and occupying a definite territory." However, this is not what most contemporary readers think of when the see the term; rather, they think of a group united by politics, not blood. This change is noted by the writers of the OED, "In early examples, the racial idea is usually stronger than the political; in recent use the notion of political unity and independence is more prominent." While this change is also happening in the German language, this was not the case in Darré's time and context. *Volk* and associated terms will be translated on a case-by-case basis, according to the context in which it is found.

2 Translator's note: The word bauerntum (from: bauer, meaning peasant or farmer, and –tum, equivalent to the English suffix -dom,) is used regularly in this text and may give the wrong impression to English readers. The German suffix -tum is cognate with the English -dom and works in essentially the same way—that is, it takes a more concrete noun (in our case, bauer) and abstracts it to denote the quality, state, or domain associated with the derived noun, like the English suffixes –ness and -hood (thus, peasantness and peasanthood). Additionally, it can also refer to a rank or status derived from the noun, as well as to a class of people associated with the word, including their customs and attitudes (in this case, the peasant class and their customs and attitudes). Because of this it is impossible to provide the same single-word translation for bauerntum in every case. Although mostly translated as peasantry in our text, a little bit of meaning can be lost when that is done. To ameliorate this, other words will occasionally be used instead (peasanthood, peasant character, peasant class, peasant community, etc.).

There are other -tum words used throughout this text. For example, the word herrentum (from: herr, meaning master or lord), which, given what was said above, can mean the quality or state of being a master or lord (lordliness), the rank of lord or master, or the class of lords and masters.

At this juncture it is also important to provide a detailed explanation of the term bauer. Although translated as peasant in this text, it must be pointed out that this translation may give the wrong impression to some readers. In English, we tend to contextualize the peasant exclusively in medieval society and associate him with qualities such as poverty. This is sometimes true of the German term bauer, but in most situations that would be a false view. As Lothrop Stoddard notes in *Into the Darkness* (1940), "The German *bauer* is an independent landowner, self-respecting and proud of the name. We can best visualize him as like the old English yeoman." Despite this, the translation "peasant" is still used as to best preserve the author's intent—almost all literature dealing with our subject translates *bauer* as peasant.

The SS Marriage Order and the Hereditary Farm Law (*Reichserb-hofgesetz*) represent the current state of this intellectual confrontation. These laws are so antithetical to all ideologies emanating from Judaism, whether of an economic or legal nature, that the SS Marriage Order and the Hereditary Farm Law can effectively be used as a litmus test for determining whether a person thinks according to a Germanic-German or a Jewish worldview. My experiences in this field have clearly demonstrated to me the correctness of this perspective. Anyone whose mind is influenced by Jewish thinking, or whose genealogical table bears the stain of Jewish blood, must and will always oppose both laws. For this reason, it seems right to me to reproduce both laws here, so that everyone who reads this work can, on the basis of the content of both laws, gain for themselves a clear understanding of the fundamental state of the confrontation as it stands.

— Berlin, the Month of Yule, 1934. R. Walther Darré.

Preface to the Second Edition

Given that I am in the middle of the struggle to preserve the German peasantry, I do not have the leisure to revise the new edition of this work myself. So I asked my longtime fellow combatant for the idea of Blood and Soil, Mr. Karl Motz (engineer), to take over this task for me. At this juncture, I would like to thank him sincerely and warmly for the work he has done.

— Berlin, August 1, 1933, R. Walther Darré.

On behalf of Mr. Reich Minister R. Walther Darré, I present to the public the new edition of his work *The Peasantry as the Lifeblood of the Nordic Race*. Due to recent political events, the author has not been able to carry out the revision himself. Upon review, however, it was determined that no major changes were necessary, especially in light of the significant shift in the German public's thinking since the first edition was published in 1928. All that was required were minor additions and small changes in very small numbers.

However, an important note must be made at this point, namely that there is a direct connection between the body of thought first proclaimed by the author in this work in 1928 and new German policy. This law of life, the inseparability of "blood and soil," is not only the basis of the political struggle of Reich Peasant Leader (*Reichsbauernführer*) Darré, but is an insight that (through the efforts of the author) has been so widely disseminated among the German people that it can unequivocally be characterized as the foundational idea of the new state and of the German future as a whole. Providence had placed the right man at the side of the Führer. And it is not by chance that under this new agrarian philosophy (*bauerngedanken*), based on the clear insights of this work, a historic achievement has taken place in a short time—the unification of the German peasant class.

The new Inheritance Law (*Erbhofgesetz*), in the development of which Darré played a leading role, is so directly based on the insights of this work that excerpts from this law are included at the beginning[3] of this new edition of *The Peasantry as the Lifeblood of the Nordic Race*. It is perhaps liberalism that has been most profoundly affected by this law, displaced by the agrarian philosophy of the German people.

— Berlin, July 1933. Karl Motz.

Preface to the First Edition

This work arose from what was for me a necessary rebuttal to Kern's *Stammbaum und Artbild der Deutschen* (English: *Family Tree and Breed Pictures of the Germans and their Kin*), published in 1927. In this book, Kern attempted to integrate race science into the field of history. His book is the first comprehensive work in this field.

In my research on the phylogeny of domesticated animal breeds, I arrived at the conclusion that a solution to these questions will only be possible when race science has uncovered the underlying structure of man's prehistoric migrations. In terms of evolutionary development, domesticated animals are an extension of humans and, like humans, are subject to certain scientific (natural) laws. Both are involved in a mutually reinforcing interaction with the environment. The correct assessment of these interactions must therefore be an essential tool in any research on human racial science. This is how I transitioned from the history of domesticated animals to human prehistory, and specifically to race science. By employing concepts from the history of domesticated animals, agriculture, and more recent developments in biology, I managed to identify a certain prehistoric framework from which it is possible to partially unravel the phylogeny of domesticated animal breeds.

While I was working on this, Kern's work had been published. I was obliged to realize that—as far as the Nordic race is concerned—his research results and assumptions do not coincide with my views. However, based on my own documents, I found it impossible to acquiesce to Kern's line of argumentation. As a result, the plan hatched in my mind to work out the essential points of difference between our conflicting views of the Nordic race in as clear and unambiguous a manner as possible. I do not intend to refute Kern in this endeavor, but rather, by presenting the stark contrast between our views, I would like to contribute to the clarification of these issues.

---

[3] The Hereditary Farm Law (*Reichserbhofgesetz*) mentioned in the Preface to the Fifth edition replaced the Peasant Inheritance Law (*Bäuerliches Erbhofrecht*) of May 15, 1933.

For these reasons, and in the interest of maintaining a coherent perspective, I have decided to not abandon the viewpoint of an agriculturally-trained researcher in the present work. This way, it was easier to maintain a consistent line of thought throughout the investigation—it also made it easier to introduce into these cultural-historical issues newer agricultural perspectives that had probably been considered little or not at all. Inevitably, the research spanned several academic domains and had to be incorporated into a unified observational framework. To avoid getting lost in such an approach, there is simply no choice but to limit oneself to certain basic principles. Therefore, I would like to characterize my work less as an investigation per se and more as an outline for a racial-scientific framework analysis. What I mean by this is simply that this work approaches the basic principles of various fields of knowledge from a clearly defined standpoint, brings them into a unified structure, and thereby establishes a framework that allows for further exploratory research at a later stage. In light of these considerations, I have on occasion not hesitated to express my own thoughts when they have seemed appropriate, to serve as a research bridge to gain a foothold into academically uncharted territory.

I must assume a certain familiarity with human races on the part of the reader, although it is not required to have knowledge in the field of genetics to follow my explanations. Where I have used technical terms or refer to the field of genetics, this is intended primarily for the expert and is always phrased in such a way as to not interfere with the layman's understanding of the arguments being developed. On the contrary, based on experience, it can be assumed that today there is already a certain level of familiarity with human race science. However, if I were to recommend a book for the layperson in the field of race science that delves into the issues explored here, then I would suggest the twelfth edition of Günther's *Rassenkunde des Deutschen Volkes* (English: *Racial Studies of the German People*). In order to facilitate the understanding of the reader who is not trained in biology, the book is written clearly and concisely, and contains a very detailed list of further racial-scientific literature, so that any educated person who wishes to study these matters in any way can easily find his way around.

As indicated by the title of the work, the present investigation primarily focuses on the Nordic race. I have endeavored to approach this matter with as much objectivity as possible, refraining from any excessive admiration of the Nordic race. However, I have not been deterred by any fears of public backlash from crediting the Nordic race with what I believe it should be credited with. I found this objective approach to be the right one to resolve the question as such. My hope is that I have contributed in some way to clarifying the nature of the Nordic race.

I am particularly grateful to Mr. R. Eichenauer, Study Counsellor in Bochum, for his kind assistance in proofreading.

— Wiesbaden, in the autumn of 1928.

I
Nomadic and Settled Peoples

I

In recent times, it has become popular to regard the Nordic race as purely a master race (*herrenrasse*).[4] It is believed that this race dominated other races and peoples during its migratory journeys, and then, on the basis of its martial master-nobility (*herrentum*), compelled those it conquered to embrace civilization. In a similar vein, it is often inferred that a master-nobility of this kind could only have emerged in an environment filled with warfare, with the Nordic race developing the fighting spirit and chivalrousness that accounts for its "nobility," but also making it more or less unfit for rough manual labor. This generally results in a particular perspective when it comes to the evaluation of human races. While this perspective does not deny the importance of the Nordic race in the past, it regards the modern Nordic race merely as a kind of necessary political evil, leaving the real productive work to other races. In the following chapters, it will be shown that dividing human races between those suitable for productive labor and those suitable exclusively for warfare and leadership is unfounded, though only matters directly related to the Nordic race will be considered in detail.

Günther has repeatedly pointed out that the Nordic race should not be portrayed exclusively as a race of warriors, for ancient Nordic records do not merely relate feats of warlike heroism, but also detail just as many

---

[4] Translator's note: Darré is mentioning Fritz Kern's use of the word *herrenrasse* (from: *herr*, meaning lord or master, and *rasse*, meaning race) here. Kern believed members of the Nordic race to be natural masters who were too noble to engage in "lowly" activities such as agriculture and farming. Thus, in this case, *herrenrasse* refers to a race of natural masters or lords.

deeds of a peaceful peasant nature.[5] It is obvious, however, that Günther's analysis has had little impact. This can be seen, for example, in the work of Kynast,[6] who builds on Günther's ideas in a one-sided manner. Despite his reliance on Günther's ideas, there is a recurring motif throughout his whole book that suggests that the "intellectually ambitious, noble" Nordic and the "earthbound peasant" should not be placed on equal footing, for the peasant belongs to a class of people suitable only for heavy labor.

Yet, there is no denying the fact that the Nordic race first appeared in world history with a substantial peasant class or, at the very least, with a clear and demonstrable peasantry of its own. For some reason, modern man finds it difficult to believe that a single race can be both truly peasant and truly martial in spirit. But since the realities of world history cannot be simply brushed aside, people attempt to find explanations that maintain the dichotomy between a martial master-nobility and a submissive peasantry, all the while attempting to make sense of their proven convergence when the Nordic race emerges on the world stage. Today, two schools of thought exist to explain this discrepancy.

The first seeks to identify a common ancestor for the long-headed, tall races of the Earth and sees these races as making up the mobile and warlike elements of humanity. The leading proponent of this view today is certainly Kern.[7] He imagines that these races, which include the Semites and Hamites, as well as the Nordic race, were part of the same warring pastoral people that departed from a common ancestral homeland somewhere near the steppes of southeastern Europe. They then dispersed throughout the world, with the part that now belongs to the Nordic race spreading into Europe. Here, this branch of the pastoral people from Eurasia merged with the existing local population to form a kind of symbiotic community. In heavily forested central Europe, these Eurasian nomads became accustomed to a somewhat settled existence, at the same time instilling their martial spirit in the subjugated settled population.

Some time later, there is then a return migration, with the now Indo-European master-nobility flooding the lands of ancient history. However, according to Kern, a remnant of these Indo-Europeans (who had by then transformed into the Nordic race) remained in the northern part of central Europe, destined for the most enduring future. This was the original Germanic stock. They would develop into a distinct people by the end of the Stone Age and the beginning of the Bronze Age. Kern writes, "The agrarian way of life began to take hold; starting from the Bronze Age, the plow is attested in the north." Kern identifies the large and sluggish "Dalian race" as the true core of this original Germanic stock, which Gün-

---

[5] Günther, *Adel und Rasse* and *Der Nordische Gedanke*.
[6] Kynast, *Apollon und Dionysos*.
[7] Kern, *Stammbaum und Artbild der Deutschen*.

ther[8] perhaps more accurately refers to as the Phalian race.[9] Thus, according to this view, the ancient Germanic peoples were actually primarily Phalian peasants that had in a sense been made mobile by a racially Nordic ruling class. Kern calls such a mixture noble-peasantry. He then contrasts this Germanic noble-peasantry with a class of servile laborers (see chapter twelve of Kern's *Artbild der Deutschen*). But Kern is neither clear nor logically consistent in either his explanations or the structure of his arguments. At any rate, it is very difficult for an agriculturalist to get an idea of what Kern actually envisions to be a "peasant." Agriculturally speaking, his noble-peasantry is not at all properly delineated, an issue that we will explore in more detail below.

The second school of thought puts much less effort into overcoming these difficulties. It regards the racial characteristics established by race science as more or less insignificant, expanding the concept of race into a kind of wellspring out of which, metaphorically speaking, a variety of waters can flow. At the same time, it limits racial characteristics to a few specific markers. Fortner, for example, expresses this view very clearly in *Süddeutsche Monatshefte* (*South German Monthly Magazine*; 1927, page 265):

> It is easy to see why the dolichocephalic (long-skulled) individuals come to the fore, particularly during this restless and combative age. This is because, according to racial-psychological law, the dolichocephalic individuals within a racial group always constitute the enterprising, adventurous, wanderlust-driven, conquering part of the population, while the brachycephalic (short-skulled) individuals represent the resilient, protective part of the population.

Unfortunately, however, Fortner does not disclose the source of this "racial-psychological law." I have to assume that Fortner is building upon K. F. Wolff,[10]

---

[8] See Günther's *Rassenkunde des Deutschen Volkes* [Racial Studies of the German People]. For further examination of this question, see *Grundriß der Menschlichen Erblichkeitslehre und Rassenhygiene* by also Erwin Baur, Eugen Fischer, and Fritz Lenz, as well as Fritz Paudler's *Die Hellfarbigen Rassen*.

[9] Translator's note: The Phalian (*fälisch*) race is a proposed sub-race of the European race commonly discussed in late nineteenth and early twentieth century racial science. According to Günther (*Rassenkunde des Deutschen Volkes*), this race is "very tall, with a long to medium head, broad face with a pronounced chin and broad lower jaw, nose of medium width (by European standards), light hair, light (blue or gray) eyes set in low sockets, and light skin." Paul von Hindenburg was considered an example of a predominantly Phalian type. It was originally described as the Dalian race by Fritz Paudler (1882–1945) due to its claimed prevalence in the Dalarna region of Sweden. Günther, however, argues that this type is no more prevalent in Dalarna than anywhere else in Europe. Rather, Günther contends that this type is more common in Westphalia, hence his renaming of the Dalian race to the Phalian race. Günther believes it to be the remnant of a Paleolithic Cro-Magnon race.

[10] Wolff's claims in *Rassenlehre* [Racial Doctrine] regarding the capacity of the Nordic peasantry should be approached with the utmost caution. In the forty-eighth chapter of his work, he shows a distinct lack of sensitivity to peasant thinking and feeling, indeed to the organic essence of any peasanthood. His views on the peasantry and settlement as expressed in this chapter would today probably find few adherents even in communist Russia. K. S. Wolff is not to be confused with Prof. H. Wolf (Düsseldorf), who also writes on race and racial questions.

whose work establishes the law mentioned by Fortner as the "law of cranio-logical polarity." Now, there is no doubt that the concept of "race" is initially nothing more than a scientific description of the hereditary and phenotypic characteristics of the human species, established by expert consensus for pur-poses of classification. As such, the concept of race can be interpreted more narrowly or more broadly. The field of animal breeding, for example, has adopted such a view and consequently regards the concept of race, or breed, merely as a preliminary classification stage for finer distinctions, then referred to as "types." What is claimed by Fortner-Wolff, however, is a complete up-ending of all our knowledge regarding the laws of inheritance, at least in the opinion of this author, who emerged from the strictly Mendelian school of animal breeding under Frölich (Halle). But it is not even necessary to have undergone any training in the laws of inheritance to recognize this "racial-psychological law" as inaccurate, if not downright incorrect. To this end, I recommend Gustav Frenssen's novel *Jörn Uhl*. Frenssen describes the exact opposite of what Fortner and Wolff claim. He speaks of the transient, itiner-ant, commercially-minded, round-headed *"kreien"* and contrasts them with the sluggish, land-bound, purely Nordic, long-headed *"uhlen,"* who are deeply rooted in their farms.

Kern's aforementioned view of a common ancestral root for all of today's tall, long-skulled races is far more problematic. Unfortunately, it must be pointed out that proponents of this school of thought do not always follow their views out to their logical conclusion. For instance, if one assumes a shared ancestral root for all of these races and still adheres to this view de-spite the significant differences in the expressions of life that exist among these races today, it does not seem very logical when, in such discussions, a few pages later it is claimed that only a completely uninformed judge would entertain the idea of excluding a living person today from the Nordic race due to a characteristic that deviates from the typical racial image (*rassenbild*). The last statement is certainly correct, and no one is more convinced of it than the author himself. Without in any way stepping outside the tangible reality of inheritance laws, it is safe to say that a race consists of a bundle of bloodlines (family traits) that are quite diverse.[11] Therefore, it is incorrect to use the characteristics of a few bloodlines as distinguishing features for the

---

[11] In animal breeding, the term "bloodline" refers to the phenomenon where, after a certain level of pure breeding is achieved, a family-specific trait (a distinct type) is consistently inherited. In prac-tice, this fact can be extremely useful, although from a genetic point of view, the situation is not completely straightforward. This is because it requires a linkage of genetic factors that are not affected by separation during cell division. Perhaps further developments in the understanding of the linked localization of genes in the chromosome could also provide a genetic explanation for the phenomenon of bloodlines. One might imagine, as it were, that the smallest hereditary units are not always jumbled up during inheritance, but rather are passed on in discrete packets. Only spe-cial circumstances and exceptions are able to divide one of these packets, leading to a re-arrangement. It is important to note that this is a metaphor of how this works, not a definitive statement. See in this regard: Friedrich von Wettstein, *"Wie Entstehen Neue Vererbbare Eigen-schaften"* [How Do New Inheritable Traits Arise], *Züchtungskunde* [Breeding Science] (1927), 2: 241. Also see: Friedrich von Wettstein, "Lecture Presented before the German Society for Breeding Science" (Göttingen).

entire race. The proponents of such views must remain true to their convictions and not draw overly ambitious conclusions about prehistory on the basis of present-day similarities in the skeletal structure of individual races.

To the extent that I possess an understanding of these scientific assumptions concerning the emergence of a dolichocephalic ruling class, particularly Kern's assumptions, they are all based on the aforementioned idea that, in a steppe environment, a dolichocephalic ancestral race evolved into a race of mobile warriors because only warriors could survive the struggle for existence that prevailed upon the steppe. This ancestral race then migrated from its place of origin, spreading across the earth and forming different branches. Wherever they encountered settled communities leading peaceful lives, they established themselves as the master caste. It is believed that settled life fosters industriousness and tenacity, but rarely provides the foresight necessary for statesmanship, a foresight that these nomadic races developed as they wandered the steppe. According to this assumption, the basic structure of a state emerges from the harmonious combination of a settled people and a racially nomadic master-nobility, the former being hard-working and constructive, but somewhat short-sighted, and the latter having a broader vision.

This interpretation is certainly based on proven historical observations. However, it is very doubtful that such observations have always been interpreted correctly. There are, in fact, several rather broad counter-arguments that can be raised concerning, on the one hand, the always presumed "pastoralist warriorship" of a nomadic race, and, on the other hand, the relationship between nomadic races and settled peoples. Of course, when it comes to nomadic races or nomadic pastoralist peoples, it is obvious that their way of life can result in a highly mobile race, but, mind you, it does not always have to, as demonstrated by some nomadic peoples in the north of Europe and Asia. But even the nomadic pastoralist, bred for maximum mobility, does not just aimlessly roam around in search of prey, but rather follows his flock quite slavishly. Herd animals are the foundation of the nomadic pastoralist's diet. The nomadic pastoralist really has no choice but to slavishly follow his flocks, for the natural instincts of these animals adapt more readily to the harshness of the desert or the steppe than those of man. Hence, the nomadic pastoralist never looks after his livestock but merely follows it, leaving the animals to fend for themselves. This is the hallmark of nomadic pastoralism. As soon as this is no longer the case, one is no longer dealing with nomadic pastoralists; this will be discussed in more detail shortly. Unless there is a particularly dire time of need that naturally causes the cattle to migrate of their own accord, thus leaving the nomadic pastoralist with no other choice but to undertake the extended migration with them, he will not even consider driving his animals through unfamiliar terrain. Otherwise, he runs the risk of completely losing his livestock in this attempt. Even lower on the nomadic pastoralist's list of priorities is the thought of doing this in order to encounter a settled people in some unknown distant land that would allow themselves to be subjugated by the nomads. In these instances of "subjugation," it is essential to recognize that settled peoples also have a say. This is a very important aspect, but it seems to be overlooked by most.

2

It must be said in general that the cultural-historical and racial-scientific assumptions about the origins of nomadic pastoralism often stand in stark contrast to what scientists understand regarding the phylogeny of domesticated animals. It may be advisable to cite here Ritter's (Berlin) summary of the very latest research findings in this regard.[12]

In the past, people were of the belief that pastoralists also originated from hunters. However, it is highly unlikely that the roaming hunter found the means to domesticate wild animals. A far more plausible assumption is that pastoralists owe their origins primarily to the earliest agricultural encampments. At these encampments, once humans recognized the utility of animals, they would have been anxious to preserve and increase their livestock. This is probably how domesticated animals (defined as animals that reproduce regularly in captivity) gradually appeared. Under the primitive circumstances of the time, the living conditions of the captive animals underwent relatively little change at first. Even today, in the interior of New Guinea, near human settlements, one can find female pigs that have been blinded to prevent them from roaming freely. Reproduction is then facilitated by feral boars. The young piglets are raised with care near the stilt huts and nursed at the breast by Papuan women alongside their children.

It is likely that small livestock was domesticated before larger livestock. As animal husbandry expanded, it was much easier to search for new grazing areas, especially because the primitive agriculture of ancient times naturally required the frequent relocation of settlements. In regions where the conditions for animal husbandry were particularly favorable, the availability of fodder was now the determining factor in choosing new settlement locations, while crop cultivation was limited to what was absolutely necessary.

In modern times, there are only a limited number of nomadic pastoralist peoples. Their grazing areas are very large, amounting to approximately one tenth of the Earth's land surface. These true nomads are distinct from herd owners who engage in regular migrations, since the nomads do not have permanent dwelling places. The latter (herd owners who are not considered nomads) can be found, for instance, in Persia, where they move to cooler mountainous regions during the summer. Even the seasonal migrations of herds in Europe, particularly in the Mediterranean region during times of summer drought, have nothing in common with true nomadism despite spanning considerable distances. True nomadism is primarily observed in the Old World. Nomadic livestock raising represents the sole form of land utilization in earth's arid regions, particularly in deserts and desert steppes. Nomads then migrate to areas where rain has triggered the growth of fresh grass, or they engage in regular migrations to seek out areas most favorable for fodder (such as in Algeria, from the Sahara to the Tell). Due to drought and their reliance on wells, the Kyrgyz people are forced to migrate periodically, moving northwards in the

---

12 Ritter, "Geschichte der Landwirtschaft der Welt."

summer and southwards in the winter. As a result of the unpredictability of fodder availability, nomadism is often associated with significant attrition. Frost and drought can occasionally cause extensive damage, as there is typically a lack of accumulated fodder reserves for times of need. Furthermore, the no-mad exchanges his surplus animal products for other goods that appear benefi-cial to him. In northern China, for example, millet is still cultivated for export to nomads. In coastal regions of Algiers and Tunis, during the months of abundant rainfall most beneficial for the growing of crops, nomads migrate with their large herds of camels and sheep southwards. The camels, which are averse to rain, can still find sufficient vegetation to sustain themselves in the drier inland areas. During the crop harvest season, they then return to the fer-tile coastal areas where sheep wool is sold, and at the same time, dates are trad-ed for the palm products of the oases. Thus, alongside natural conditions, an economic factor can also be identified as a motive for nomadic migrations—the need to exchange goods.[13] In the far north as well, the availability of fodder is the decisive factor for these migrations. Reindeer moss, for instance, is valu-able as a food source only when moist. Therefore, during the dry summer, reindeer primarily rely on grass and herbs, necessitating the search for summer pastures in areas more abundant in grass.

On page 198 of his book *Artbild der Deutschen*, Kern explicitly refers to the pastoralist warriorship of present-day nomadic races, primarily the Semites, as an example for his prehistoric hypotheses. He then uses this as evidence to argue that the Nordic race originated from itinerant nomadic pastoralists. However, it is not entirely clear which particular Semitic groups Kern had in mind during his analysis. The author, in any case, is aware that there are varying opinions regard-ing the warriorship of Semitic pastoralists. While further research may be re-quired on this matter, it is still important to highlight here that Kern explicitly relies on contemporary nomadic pastoralism to substantiate his claims about the Nordic race's origins.

It is suggested by Kern that immediately after the Ice Age, the Nordic race migrated into Europe as a group of itinerant warrior pastoralists. To reiterate, according to Kern, the Nordic race is just one branch of a primordial nomadic race that retreated from Eurasia into the steppes of southeastern Europe and southwestern Asia during the glaciation period of central Europe. Kern assumes an "Atlantic" climate for these regions. His assumption, however, already contra-dicts nature's laws. If Kern understands an Atlantic climate as one with abundant precipitation, then there would have necessarily been forests rather than steppes in the regions he refers to. Conversely, if there is proof that steppes did exist there, then there is no getting around the fact that the climate was continental, not Atlantic. These two elements are directly related to one another and are un-doubtedly true, at least as far as long-term climate is concerned, a timescale that Kern naturally assumes to allow for the formation of a mobile race. Otherwise, one might as well be talking about icy sunbeams and snowflake embers.

The term "Atlantic climate," originating in technical terminology used by

---

13 As one can see, nomadism is much more peaceful than cultural historians often imagine!

geographers, should in fact disappear. It can easily lead to misunderstanding. For example, it tends to lead to the misconception that the presence of a nearby sea automatically results in a climate with abundant precipitation. However, the amount of rain we see in central Germany, for example, depends on the Gulf Stream rather than, say, its proximity to the Atlantic Ocean or the Baltic Sea. As long as Europe has had the Gulf Stream, northwestern Europe has had a climate with high precipitation, regardless of ice ages, interglacial periods, and postglacial periods. Both the Mediterranean basin and the Guano Islands in South America, which, of course, are the very result of a lack of rainfall, are excellent examples of the fact that the presence of an ocean does not necessarily lead to increased precipitation. Therefore, either southeastern Europe had a climate with abundant precipitation during the Ice Age (the author agrees with this view), indicating that there were no steppes present, or if there were steppes, there simply was not a rainy climate. These questions are not entirely meaningless for a race such as the Nordic whose skin lacks pigmentation, especially in view of the fact that the steppe lacks the moderating effect of sunlight diffused by clouds.

We can also question why central Europe is supposed to have been uninhabitable during the Ice Age—or more accurately, during the advancement of the northern glaciers. Without in any way wanting to go into the scientific theories about the origin of the northern European glaciation known as the Ice Age, we can still make certain definitive statements about the conditions that prevailed in central Europe at that time. It is necessary to point out that no one has ever witnessed the spontaneous growth of glaciers on roads or in the open country when frost sets in. A glacier is formed only by snow pressure, never through freezing. For this reason, geologists no longer speak of an Ice Age, but rather only refer to various snow ages and their associated glacial advances. However, snowfall and extreme cold are not necessarily interrelated phenomena, meaning that glaciation in central Europe is not evidence of an exceptionally cold climate during this period. Furthermore, in central Germany, despite their massive size (with heights estimated at three to four hundred meters in some areas), the glaciers melted away instead of being halted by mountain ranges. Glacier termini form exclusively under warm conditions—not cold ones. While the weather in the glacier-free regions of central Europe during the snow periods may not have always been particularly pleasant, it was not more severe than the typical foggy, damp, and cold November days that we experience today. The exodus of large numbers of people from Europe at that time was probably not caused by weather conditions alone, but rather by an abrupt reduction in the available food supply, the "dietary space" (*ernährungsraum*). These are not mere assumptions or conjectures, but conclusions that can be clearly deduced from the discovered remains of plant and animal life. The author will revisit this point in a later chapter.

If one considers Kern's theory of a post-Ice Age invasion of Europe by nomadic pastoralists, the question arises as to what kind of herd animals these pastoralists would have actually brought with them. Horses are definitely out of the question. The domestication of horses can be placed with almost absolute certainty between 2500 and 2000 BC (we will come back to this subject later). Kern himself rejects cattle, as he sees them as a sign of a population engaged in agriculture. However, he is mistaken here because cattle in particular are very often found among nomadic pastoralist populations. We can certainly exclude pigs as well. Nomadic pastoralists never own pigs.[14] Therefore, only sheep remain, as reindeer are also not an option. Kern's claim that reindeer serve as evidence for the arrival of nomadic pastoralists in Europe after the Ice Age lacks justification. Reindeer are quite closely associated with the glacier's edge or the Arctic climatic belt in terms of climate, along with reindeer lichen, which relies on these specific conditions. During glacial periods, we can always assume the existence of reindeer in central Europe wherever reindeer lichen found its habitat along the edges of the glacier. With the shifting of the glacier's edge, the reindeer inevitably migrated as well. Thus, the presence of reindeer does not at all prove the validity of the Eurasian pastoralist theory because reindeer have always been present in central Europe. The presence of reindeer could just as well be used as evidence for the development of a native form of nomadic pastoralism in the region. But even if we were to assume that the Eurasian branch of pastoralists entering Europe already had sheep and cattle as herd animals, a second difficulty immediately arises. In the same way that Kern assumes a shared origin for the relevant human races, a similar assumption would have to be true for their cattle and sheep. To the extent that the phylogeny of our domesticated animals can be provisionally surveyed, the connections that are supposed to exist between the Nordic race, the Semites, and the Hamites cannot be readily established between their cattle and sheep.

On the contrary, particularly in the case of the Nordic race and the Semites, it can be said that their domestic and herd animals quite obviously never had anything to do with each other. The religious customs of the Nordic race show that the pig was one of their most ancient sacrificial animals.[15] If the Nordic race had been an itinerant nomadic race, it could never have adopted their sacrificial customs involving the pig. As we have already stated, all nomadic peoples completely reject pigs—this is very understandable, since nomads cannot drive or carry pigs over long distances. Today, all researchers of the phylogeny of our domesticated animals agree on this point.

What von Ihering observes in the oldest laws of the ancient Roman patricians is also relevant to the questions dealt with here.[16] We will get to know Ihering's investigations very thoroughly later on. However, it is worth emphasizing and demonstrating here that Ihering highlights quite stark contrasts between the laws of the patricians

---

[14] Darré, "Das Schwein als Kriterium für Nordische Menschen und Semiten."

[15] Ibid.

[16] The author's work is based in part on the following two publications by Rudolf von Ihering: *Vorgeschichte der Indoeuropäer* [Evolution of the Indo-Europeans] (Leipzig: 1894), which unfortunately remained unfinished, and *Entwicklungsgeschichte des Römischen Rechtes* [History of the Development of Roman Law] (Leipzig: 1894). These two works should not be forgotten by the Nordic movement. Ihering's basic framework and racial views are, of course, no longer tenable today. However, he has compiled so much valuable information that any researcher in the field of racial science—provided they have a sufficient background in biology, so as not to be confused by Ihering's sometimes advanced biological jargon—will turn to him again and again. In what follows, the author relies heavily on Ihering in order to make his work more widely known, but also because Ihering has much to offer researchers in the field of race science.

and the legal customs of the Semites. Semitic law can never hide the fact that it originated in a treeless desert. For example, the Semites stone criminals when they want to kill them—Herodotus[17] reports that the Carthaginians stoned prisoners of war. Conversely, among the patricians of Rome, punishments, including death, were always carried out with wood. However, wood and abundant forests are found only in areas of high precipitation and are thus the clear biological counter-evidence to the hypothesis of a steppe or desert origin of the Nordic race. Therefore, the legislation of the ancient Roman patricians must have originated in a wooded area, while, conversely, the Semites' fundamental avoidance of wood in their legal system clearly characterizes them as native inhabitants of the desert or steppe. Ihering aptly states that of all the ancient customs of a people, the customs related to legal practices can survive the longest and often continue to play a role even in later times because they are usually associated not only with the customs of the people but also with their ancient religious beliefs. To illustrate this claim, he points out that this is true for both Semites and Nordics. For example, Jews continued to practice circumcision with a flint knife well into historical times, and similarly, the idea of replacing wax lighting in our German churches with a more modern and better alternative faced great resistance for the longest time.

Just how pivotal a role wood played in the legislation of ancient Rome and how much it can be used to understand the patricians of ancient times is extensively detailed in Ihering's work. For example, he writes,

> In the early days of Rome, the rod was commonly used for the death penalty. In later years, since custom dictated that the death penalty for a person holding religious office could not be carried out by beheading with an iron axe, it was instead carried out like in ancient times, by means of flogging the condemned to death. With time, this type of death penalty remained in place only in the hands of the high priest, for the most severe religious offenses of his subordinates.[18]

According to Ihering, further punishments of the Aryans (we might as well say the Nordic race) include being tied to a stake, whipped with sticks or rods, and the scourge:

> The scourge (*stûpe*), which evolved into the pillory that was later used to publicly humiliate criminals, was the *drupada* of the ancient Aryans, as well

---

[17] Herodotus, *The Persian Wars*, Book 1, chapter 167, trans. A. D. Godley, Loeb Classical Library ed. (Harvard University Press: 1920), "As for the crews of the disabled ships, the Carthaginians and Tyrrhenians drew lots for them, and of the Tyrrhenians the Agyllaioi were allotted by far the majority and these they led out and stoned to death."

[18] See: Livy, *The History of Rome*, Book 22, chapter 57, trans. Benjamin O. Foster, Loeb Classical Library ed. (Cambridge: Harvard University Press, 1929), "Lucius Cantilius, a secretary to the pontiffs—one of those who are now called the lesser pontiffs—had been guilty with Floronia, and the Pontifex Maximus had him scourged in the Comitium so severely that he died under the blows." Original Latin, "*L. Cantilius scriba pontificis, quos nunc minores pontifices appellant, qui cum Floronia stuprum fecerat, a pontifice maximo eo usque virgis in comitio caesus erat, ut inter verbera exspiraret.*"

as of the Germanic and Slavic peoples, and the *arbor infelix* of the Romans. From the Latin word for tying or strapping (*ligare*) is derived the name of the official (lector) responsible for tying the guilty party to the stake. . . . We have been able to trace the penal stake back to even the earliest stages of Roman criminal law. However, we search in vain for the corrective stake (*schuldpfahl*) among both the Romans and other Indo-European peoples.

The following passage from Ihering also very clearly proves that patrician customs must have emerged from a water-rich region:

In the Latin language, the pontifices[19] are those whose duty it was to build bridges (*pontem facere*). The relationship between bridges and the pontifices is also indicated by the fact that their office in Rome was located at the Pons Sublicius,[20] and that the axe was part of the insignia of their office. Accordingly, the pontifices were the technicians of bridge construction— they were the bridge-masters.[21]

He continues,

In the mountains, man does not need stone to build a road, the only work that is necessary is to remove rocks in places where they obstruct the way. But on the plains, the swampy and marshy ground makes roads an absolute necessity even in the most rudimentary of civilizations. The construction of roads originated in the plains, not in the mountains; only after it was developed there did it make its way up to the highlands.

The most readily available material on hand for the building of paths was wood. Man built his house out of wood and he built his road out of wood. He laid tree trunks side by side in the swampy terrain. Where wood was more scarce, he made fascines out of bunches of logs and interwoven twigs (wickerwork). For many centuries, this was how the ancient Germans

---

Also see: Livy, *The History of Rome*, Book 28, chapter 11, trans. Cyrus Edmonds (London: 1850), "...the vestal, who had the guarding of it for that night, was scourged..." Original Latin, "*Ignis in aede Vestae extinctus, caesaque flagro est Vestalis...*"

[19] Translator's note: Pontifices is the plural of pontifex, a member of the Roman priest class and the *Collegium Pontificum* (College of Pontiffs), the most important of the four Roman colleges of priests. The pontifices of ancient Rome played a crucial role as religious officials and were responsible for overseeing the practices of the Roman state religion, including the maintenance of sacred rituals, calendars, and the proper conduct of ceremonies.

[20] Editor's note: The Pons Sublicius (in modern Italian, Ponte Sublicio) is the earliest recorded bridge in Rome, believed to have been built during the early Roman kingdom. It spans the Tiber River and was originally constructed entirely out of wood.

[21] The derivation of the word "pontifex" from "bridge builder" (*pontem facere*) attempted here by von Ihering—a derivation which still has some adherents—is widely disputed. For example, Ludwig Kuhlenbeck in *Entwicklungsgeschichte des Römischen Rechts* [History of the Development of Roman Law] (Munich: 1913) strongly opposes it. However, anyone who suggests a connection between the ancient Roman patricians and the Nordic race, and therefore relocates their proposed origins to north-central Europe, rich in water, and also considers the significance of traditional wooden bridge construction in this region through to the present day, would be inclined to agree with von Ihering's derivation of the word "pontifex."

built paths through their forested homeland—this was their celebrated "log road." He did the same with bridges that crossed rivers—they were made of wood. Among the Romans, we still find wooden bridges such as the Pons Sublicius, which survives to this day as a reminder of ancient times.

It is unlikely that Rome would have been so damaged by flames during the Gallic invasion had it not been for the predominance of wooden houses. It is evident that stone masonry was at that time already in use for private houses from the fact that all citizens were granted the right to erect stone houses and that the state provided them with bricks for this purpose.[22] The incineration of the city at that time will have marked the turning point for the transition from wooden construction to general stone masonry.

However, more important for our present analysis is the use of wood in another context. Ihering writes,

> For the slaughter of sacrificial animals during the conclusion of international treaties, the *fetial* (a type of Roman priest) was only allowed to use a flint axe (*silex*). At the Pons Sublicius, entrusted to the care of the pontifices, no iron nails were allowed, only wooden ones. For the *fetiales*, as for the pontifices, the customs of ancient times were authoritative. The same applied to the Vestal Virgins. When, at the beginning of the new year, the fire in the Temple of Vesta had to be extinguished and replaced with a new one, or if it had gone out at some other time due to carelessness and needed to be rekindled, it could not be done using iron and flint, but only by igniting a special piece of flammable wood (*materia felix*) by rubbing it (*terebratio*) against a hard wood. This act could not be done in the temple itself, but only outdoors, after which it had to be brought into the temple in a brazen pot.[23]

It is also very significant that ancient patrician marriages had to be confirmed with a pig sacrifice, therefore indicating that this institution cannot possibly be related to any kind of nomadic pastoralism. Furthermore, the boar slaughtered during the marriage ceremony had to be killed with a flint axe (*silex*). From this, we can conclude with almost absolute certainty that, historically speaking, both the custom of marriage and its customary pig sacrifice must date back to the Stone Age—in other words, the ancestors of the patricians had already developed customs during the Stone Age that clearly identified them as a settled

---

[22] Livy, *The History of Rome* Book 5, chapter 55, trans. Benjamin O. Foster, Loeb Classical Library ed. (Cambridge: Harvard University Press, 1924), "The state . . . granted everybody the right to quarry stone and to hew timber where he liked." Original Latin, "*Saxi materiaeque caedendae, unde quisque vellet.*"

[23] Sextus Pompeius Festus, *De Verborum Significatu* [On the Meaning of Words], 106. Original Latin, "*Ignis Vestae . . . tamdiu terebrare, quousque exceptum ignem cribo aeneo virgo in aedem ferret.*"

people. We will eventually delve into the topic of ancient patrician marriage in great detail in the penultimate chapter of this work. However, it is still worth mentioning here that the patricians identified themselves as peasants, particularly because other customs they observed during marriage ceremonies also distinguish them as such.[24] At a patrician wedding, the bride entered the husband's house with the words *ubi tu gaius, ego ibi gaia*, which seems to have been correctly translated by Ihering, citing Servius' commentary *ad Aen*, as "where you plow, I plow with you."

Tacitus also reports in chapter eighteen of *Germania* that among the Germanic people, the *juncti boves* (yoked oxen) was a symbol indicating that the woman was a *laborum socia* (partner in labor). In this context, it should also be mentioned that a so-called "wedding plowing" tradition is still practiced in Styria. On the third day after the wedding, the young couple harness themselves to a plow and then plow a field in front of their friends and relatives.[25]

The following, however, is also highly significant. When the plebeians had forced the patricians to recognize marriages with plebeians as fully valid marriages, the patricians still continued to adhere to their old marriage customs among themselves, alongside those that emerged from mixed marriages. The older (ancient patrician) form of marriage was done through *confarreatio* and could only be separated through the act of *diffarreatio*. The word *confarreatio* is related to the Latin *far*, which means "spelt," a type of grain that was a food staple of the patricians as well as a sacrificial grain on the altar of Vesta. All those hypotheses in which the Nordic race is only able to be viewed as a ruling class above a peasant underclass are likely to be met with their greatest difficulties at this point. The patricians would never have used peasant symbols for their ancient and sacred institutions, which they later maintained in contrast to the plebeians, if they themselves were not peasants by nature. But least of all would they have acted this way if the patricians, say, originated from an itinerant nomadic pastoralist society while the plebeians belonged to a peasant population. It is worth seriously asking whether the situation was just the opposite—that is, the patricians were the peasants, and the plebeians were either at a more primitive level of agriculture or could not be considered a settled people at all. Whatever the case, a quite similar development is happening right before our eyes in South Africa, where the ruling population is descended from Dutch peasants, while the indigenous population constitutes only an insignificant fraction of the settled population. Originally, the Boers literally kept the natives as serfs on their farms.[26] Nowadays, these South African coloreds have

---

[24] Undoubtedly, such a view aligns with the somewhat pointed but arguably accurate depiction by Theodor Birt in *Römische Charakterköpfe* [Distinctive Features of the Romans] regarding the original appearance of the ancient Roman patricians, "In fur and cap, unkempt and rough, and quite unclean—this is how we imagine that old type—with dirty nails and large ears, always reaching for the sword or pitchfork. With the spear, livestock was herded, and with the spear, battles were fought. They possessed tough, rugged natures, devoid of a sense of beauty, lacking any trace of fantasy, and also entirely unmusical, but energetic and swift in approach, and the antithesis of harmless."

[25] Buschan, *Das Deutsche Volk*.

[26] Valentin, *Kolonialgeschichte der Neuzeit*.

begun to fight for social and economic equality with their former masters, the Dutch Boers.[27] Why should we not assume similar—albeit less racially divergent—developments in ancient Rome? The author takes the liberty of postponing the answer to this question until later.

But if, on the basis of their sacrificial customs, we must regard the patricians of ancient Rome as an agricultural, settled people going back to the Stone Age, then we can draw the following conclusion with absolute certainty—if Kern is right that all long-headed, tall, slender human races descended from a common root, then the Nordic race split off so early that it is utterly useless to try to derive any valuable implications for the present from such a racial-scientific conjecture. Alternatively, Kern is wrong, and the Nordic race is an ancient settled race, in which case the racial similarities between the Nordic race and other races must be explained in some other way, if there is even any relationship between them at all.

As far as etymological research is concerned, it has already been determined that the knowledge of agriculture among the Nordic people dates back to prehistoric times. Schrader states the following on the topic: "There is no historical evidence to suggest that there ever was a time in which the Indo-Europeans of Europe were ever unfamiliar with agriculture, and the same can be said regarding the earliest Indians and Iranians." [28]

But even if we want to accept the scientific assumptions suggesting that the Nordic race entered Europe as nomadic pastoralists immediately after the Ice Age, we still face further difficulties. We have already seen that the most we can assume for these herders is sheep, and at best cattle. But why should those livestock-rearing herders have been so remarkably capable in war? And why, at the same time, should the indigenous settled population have been absolutely unfit for warfare, despite the abundant presence of bears, lynxes, wolves, and other formidable wildlife? Kern's argument, at least, is certainly not very persuasive.

3

In general, all assumptions about the martial character of nomadic pastoralists seem to be based on rather generalized premises. The assertion that nomadic pastoralists are self-evidently warlike "precisely because of their herds and the sparseness of their homeland" ought not to be so much asserted as proven. Colonial history, for example, demonstrates the exact opposite of such claims. Only one striking example will be mentioned here, and it comes from German colonial history. Before the seizure of German Southwest Africa, there was constant fighting between the warlike pastoral tribes of the Herero and the Hottentots.[29]

---

[27] Breune, *Süd-Afrika*.
[28] Schrader, *Reallexikon der Indogermanischen Altertumskunde*.
[29] Translator's note: The Hottentots, which are today known as the Nama or Namaqua people, a subset of the Khoekhoe ethnic group, are a historical rival of the Herero. They inhabited what would become German Southwest Africa (modern day Namibia). The German colony was founded when Maharero, a Herero chieftain dealing with constant Hottentot attacks, signed a protection treaty with Heinrich Ernst Göring (father of Hermann Göring) in 1885.

As far as martial prowess was concerned, the Herero were far superior to the Hottentots, and as a result there were concerns on the German side that the main difficulties in asserting German sovereignty would come from the combative Herero. Surprisingly, however, the exact opposite occurred, and the Herero were happy to come under German sovereignty. Major General Leutwein explains the phenomenon in the following way:

> In the battles between the Herero and the Hottentots, the former usually had the upper hand. But the Herero had one weakness, and that was their magnificent herds of cattle, which the propertyless Hottentots were particularly keen to seize. Therefore, despite their many victories, the Herero tended to suffer most of the war damage.[30]

Thus, the superiority of nomadic pastoralists in warfare (a popular belief today, considered by so many to be quite compelling and self-evident) is proven to be an unjustified generalization by colonial reality. But this becomes even more apparent in the context of prehistory when you consider that the settled inhabitants of Stone Age central Europe, living in an environment teeming with predators, could not exactly have been wimps—at the very least, they may well have rivaled the Hottentots in this respect.

In general, it is unjustified to always assume, without nuance, that nomadic pastoralism inherently implies a desire to roam around, let alone a desire to roam in a warlike manner. Nomadic pastoralists themselves never have such intentions in mind. Anyone who takes the trouble to walk across a desert or steppe will soon understand the reasons behind it—only dire need prompts actual migration. As we can observe with the Tatars and Arabs, nomadic pastoralists can only actually roam around in a warlike manner if they have access to riding animals. These allow them to cover great distances in a short period of time and to move away from their food source (their herds) without endangering their own lives. Accordingly, riding camels, reindeer, oxen, and horses are present among very many, but by no means all, nomadic pastoralists. With the recognition of these facts, we now confront the truly weakest point of all those scientific assumptions that want to simplistically, and without clear evidence, derive the Nordic race from a warlike pastoralist or nomadic race. What kind of riding animal would these warlike steppe herders have used to invade central Europe? Reindeer and camels are excluded for climatic and temporal reasons, and it is unlikely that one would assume riding oxen. Therefore, only the horse remains. But if there is one thing we can conclude with absolute certainty from the phylogeny of domesticated animals, it is the fact that the horse was tamed and domesticated by the Nordic race. The horse only appears when we can already quite clearly recognize the Nordic race as such. It has long been established archaeologically that the Nordic race was present in central Europe around the time in question. The history of horse domestication can be seen quite clearly in the various works of

---

30 Leutwein, *Die Kämpfe mit Hendrik Witboi.*

Kraemer, Hilzheimer, and Antonius.[31] However, even without these facts, an assumption that associates the riding horse with the influx of eastern nomadic pastoralists is untenable, simply because horses were not by any means originally domesticated for riding, but for driving. The concept of riding a horse is a comparably recent human achievement,[32] with the use of cavalry for warfare being less than 3500 years old. We have historical records to prove this last point, which can be consulted in the works of the aforementioned researchers—we are not limited to mere speculation here.

Furthermore, it should be added that there was at least one epicenter of horse domestication in northwestern Europe, and this epicenter is most likely the oldest in the world. Europe is home to a native forest horse (equus robustus), from which today's cold-blooded[33] horses originate. Such a horse has a different physique than the warm-blooded steppe horses of Asia. As a result, it is often possible to trace exactly where the waves of Nordic conquerors went with their cold-blooded horses.

Kern does state very emphatically on page 177 of *Artbild*, "The introduction of the horse from the west is out of the question." Unfortunately, however, he fails to provide evidence to support this claim.

Antonius's works, however, provide significant insights in this regard. Antonius personally examined the horse breeds of northwest Africa and determined that there could not possibly have been an evolutionary link between the horses of the Berber people and those of the local Arabs. According to his findings, the Berber horses must have somehow migrated from northwest Europe to northwest Africa, as the Arabian horses clearly demonstrate their Asiatic origins. Such observations hold particular value, as Antonius approached the question not through the lens of human race science, but rather through his studies on horses, which inadvertently led him to explore the field of human race science without explicitly addressing it.

These findings in the history of domestic horses, gained independently of race science and ethnology, also align with corresponding etymological research. Metzger (Helsinki) reports on this matter in the 1927 issue of *Deutsche Landwirtschaftliche Tierzucht* (Journal of German Agricultural Animal Breeding),

> Chariot racing, on the other hand, is an ancient and indigenous sport in the region, as are the winter trotting races that bring together the rural population every year on the frozen surfaces of

---

[31] Kraemer, *Allgemeine Tierzucht*; Hilzheimer, *Natürliche Rassengeschichte der Haussäugetiere*; Antonius, *Stammesgeschichte der Haustiere*.

[32] In Homer's *The Iliad*, for instance, riding is mentioned only in a single instance, notably in an escape scene, "So spake she, and he knew the voice of the goddess as she spoke, and swiftly mounted the horses; and Odysseus smote them with his bow, and they sped toward the swift ships of the Achaeans."

[33] Editor's note: Horse breeds are loosely grouped into hot-blooded and cold-blooded categories, with the warm-blooded category containing crosses between the two types. Hot-blooded horses are said to have lively personalities, and are bred for speed and endurance. Cold-blooded horses have more docile personalities and are bred for strength and for pulling.

lakes, which make excellent tracks. It is significant, therefore, that in the Finnish national epic Kalevala,[34] the enamored youth Lemminkäinen does not appear on a saddled horse to abduct the beautiful Kyllikki. Rather, he steals her away on a sleigh from a flowery meadow, amidst her companions. You see, in ancient times, people exclusively and originally traveled in sleighs, even during the summer. This holds true not only for Finland but for all northern forested countries, and perhaps even more broadly. This is supported not only by the folkloric tradition of winter trotting races that is observed throughout the north, but also by linguistic evidence. Linguists have known for some time that "riding" originally had a broader meaning than just *equitare*, namely that of *proficisci*, meaning "to travel" or "to move." In the Russian language, riding still means "traveling on horseback." Conversely, the English use the verb "to ride" for traveling in a carriage, and they also apply the related verb "to road" to movement on a ship, a carriage, or a horse. The Dutch even "ride" on their skates, and in Switzerland *reiten* (riding) has retained the meaning of "sledding" without any further addition. Therefore, it is not unjustified to compare "riding" with the Lapp and Finnish terms "*raiddo, raide, raito*" for reindeer sleigh caravans. These words, and perhaps even more obviously the Finnish word *ratsas* (ride), suggest to me an onomatopoeic root that likely mimics the "ritsch-ratsch-rutsch" sounds of a sleigh gliding over rocks and stones. This root probably underlies the whole group of semantically related and similar-sounding words in different languages. The proud horseman, of course, is unlikely to find the idea of originating from a "sledder" appealing and so would probably not find this illuminating.[35]

This research by Metzger (Helsinki) is perfectly consistent with findings in cultural history. Initially, man's understanding of horsemanship was limited to the driving of horse-drawn wagons or carts, with this development likely originating from sleighs in the wood-rich regions of central Europe. Riding on horseback was developed some time later.[36] This chronology leads us to consider two differ-

---

[34] Translator's note: The Kalevala was assembled by Elias Lönnrot (1802–1884) from age-old Finnish ballads, lyrical songs, and incantations that were originally transmitted orally. The term "Kalevala," meaning "the land of heroes," represents both the dwelling place of the epic's main characters and is occasionally used as an alternative name for Finland itself. The tale of Lemminkäinen is just one of the many stories making up the Kalevala, including an account of earth's creation.

[35] With the author's permission, we include the following interesting observation by Wilhelm Böcher (Grünberg-Hessen), "In the Upper Hessian dialect, specifically in the region of the Vogelsberg and the Wetterau, older individuals still use the word *reiten* (riding) to mean *fahren* (driving) a wagon, even today. As evidence, consider the following humorous scene: A pastor, who hails from the city, encounters an old lady from his village parish far out in the field. Surprised, he asks, "How did you get here, dear lady?" She replies, "I rode here." The clergyman exclaims in astonishment, "What? You can still ride?" To which he receives the response, "Yes, on the wagon!"

[36] See Gustaf Kossinna's various works on this subject.

ent possibilities, either the steppes of eastern Europe inspired the waves of horse-riding Nordic people, who entered them to engage in horseback riding, or the vast expanses of these steppes simply provided the ideal conditions for the proper development of equestrian skills.

4

In addition to this, the question arises as to what is actually meant by the term "pastoralist" in the field of cultural history. One often gets the impression here that cultural historians lump nomadic pastoralists, who are itinerant, and sedentary pastoralists in the same category in order to create a convenient framework for their cultural-historical classifications.

However, looking at the phenomenon of pastoralism globally from an agricultural perspective, it can be seen that this term, despite its apparent clarity, actually contains significant contradictions. When a settled population migrates and then settles in a steppe, it must engage exclusively in livestock raising due to environmental constraints. However, the mostly indigenous nomadic pastoralists of these steppes also engage in livestock raising. But while the nomadic pastoralist leaves it entirely to chance or the natural instincts of his herds to find food or overcome times of need, the sedentary pastoralist in the same area is compelled to sustain his herds during times of need through his own resourcefulness, foresight, and proactive measures.[37]

The nomadic pastoralist parasitizes on his herds; therefore, he subordinates himself and his comfort entirely to the living conditions of his herds. On the other hand, the sedentary pastoralist of the steppe must subordinate the living conditions of his herds to his fixed place of residence. Accordingly, he must also watch after them, especially since the given circumstances present additional difficulties. Thus, his herds, in a sense, parasitize on him. The nomadic pastoralist is dependent on his herds, while the situation is exactly the opposite for the sedentary pastoralist. One can hardly imagine clearer contrasts than those manifested by the ways of life of the settled person, that is, the sedentary pastoralist, and the itinerant nomadic pastoralist in the steppe. Under the same environmental conditions, this superficially identical way of life fosters in the nomadic pastoralist a kind of endurance to withstand hardships, while in the settled person it develops resourcefulness and a sense of responsibility toward his livestock and enterprise. These are by no means simply dull scholastic considerations. These differences can be substantiated by comparing genuine nomadic pastoralists and livestock-rearing, settled peoples living in the same area. The easiest way to provide evidence for this would be to refer to the colonial history of the last two centuries, particularly in regard to the settlements in Russia, as well as Australia, Africa, Texas, and South America. The previous existence of a type of pastoralism among the Nordic race in and of itself does not prove anything—it must be made abundantly clear whether this was an itinerant nomadic pastoralism, or

---

[37] Compare with section 1 above.

whether it was merely a type of sedentary pastoralism which preceded a truly settled form of existence.

However, there is yet another important aspect that is almost never given any consideration when assessing these questions. Throughout all of colonial history, it has been the case that nomadic races and nomadic pastoralists are incapable of adopting a settled form of existence. This is an undeniable fact, and therefore, in ethnology, much more attention should be paid to this fact than is currently the case. By itself, it would seem plausible that nomadic pastoralism should transition first to semi-settled pastoralism and then to fully sedentary pastoralism. However, experience has certainly shown us that nomadic pastoralists never even consider giving up their itinerant way of life in this way. This becomes easier to understand when one realizes that the crucial point in the transition from nomadic pastoralism to sedentary pastoralism by no means lies in the will of the nomadic pastoralist, but rather in whether he can give up his parasitic tendencies regarding his livestock— whether, out of natural inclination, he can assume responsibility for the care of his animals. While the transition from nomadic to sedentary pastoralism on the surface appears to be a barely perceptible change in their way of life, it is in fact a change that cuts deeply into the nature, way of thinking, and behavior of the nomadic pastoralist. This helps to explain why, throughout colonial history, we have yet to observe a transition from nomadic pastoralism to sedentary pastoralism, let alone to a settled form of existence. The opposite, which, of course, is definitely more in line with man's desire for comfort, is much easier to demonstrate. The author, who originally became aware of this contrast between nomadic pastoralists and settled peoples through his investigation of the phylogeny of domesticated animals, has not yet found any solid evidence that would indicate that it is possible for nomadic peoples to adopt a settled way of life.[38] Later, we will discuss a single exception suspected by the author. While the field of cultural history attempts to make such a transition plausible through a number of assumptions, the breeding history of domesticated animals raises legitimate doubts. Whereas domesticated animals can provide clear evidence for cultural-historical research, the field of human racial history unfortunately falls short for the time being. Outwardly, settled peoples and nomadic pastoralists living in the same environment may resemble each other so closely (especially in terms of hunting tools and other cultural artifacts) that even the discerning cultural researcher may find the differences practically imperceptible. But, in many cases, the herd animals of the nomadic pastoralists and the domesticated animals of settled peoples allow us to differentiate between populations where the environment forced a sedentary people into a pastoralist existence and populations that have always led a purely nomadic pastoralism.

However, often one can be confronted with contradictions that are difficult to resolve. For example, there are some Lappish (Sami) tribes where the men follow the reindeer to the pastures during the summer, while the women,

---

[38] Mucke, *Urgeschichte des Ackerbaus*.

children, and older men engage in simple grain farming. In winter, the reindeer are then brought back to the villages and fed with hay. Since light skin and hair are particularly common among Lappish people, one cannot help but suspect that this type of economy is that of a formerly settled people who, due to some circumstance, chose to use reindeer instead of cattle as a source of food and profit. However, under no circumstances can one readily draw the opposite conclusion and assume that these Laplanders are nomadic pastoralists who have turned to agriculture. The hallmark of nomadic pastoralism—living parasitically on one's herds—is completely absent in this case. It would be more plausible to assume that this peculiar way of life is the result of past racial mixing or conquest. Aereboe writes,

> What meadows and pastures have in common is that they begin to grow as soon as the weather in the spring allows for any kind of plant growth. This becomes even more important the shorter the growing season becomes. Here in Germany, winter crops also grow on arable land in the spring as soon as growth begins. However, winter crops have long since disappeared in the far north, where the use of meadows and pastures, along with the cultivation of summer crops on arable land, constitute the most important branches of agriculture.[39]

Needless to say, the contrast between settled and nomadic races is as old as time. It is entirely justifiable to ask the question: Where, in fact, did humans first make the transition to sedentism? This question will continue to occupy us a great deal in our discussions.

5

We can also now consider the fact that pastoralism is not dependent on the presence of vast grasslands, as one might simply assume. There is also a form of livestock raising that is based on the utilization of forest pastures. In this type of livestock raising, the animals have access to the foliage of trees and shrubs in the summer and are fed with dried leaf hay in the winter. This form of livestock rearing requires a sedentary way of life, but without needing agriculture or a large amount of space. Aereboe writes, "In the far north, the keeping of livestock is ultimately the only thing that the farmer engages in besides forest utilization; he becomes a part-time livestock farmer and a part-time forester. The situation is similar in high mountain regions."

It is very likely that this was originally the only available way of life, particularly in the northern deciduous forest zones of Europe. It has survived somewhat in Scandinavia, and in Finland it was almost exclusively used until 1918. In 1927, the author undertook a study trip to Karelia (eastern Finland), during which he paid special attention to this particular form of live-

---

[39] Aereboe, *Allgemeine Landwirtschaftliche Betriebslehre*.

stock raising, based on forest utilization without meadows or pastures.[40]

This agricultural way of life, which was quite self-evident and wide-spread in Germany until the late Middle Ages, has completely disappeared from our country to the extent that it is hardly mentioned in books on agricultural management, if at all. In Finland, however, it was so widespread that, until a few years ago, larger estates wishing to introduce modern farming methods with non-Finnish livestock breeds were forced to produce hay on their farmlands. The hay harvest had to be incorporated into the crop rotation through artificial turfing of the fields. In Germany, this method of hay production has been mistakenly called "regulated field grass farming," because the two methods have a very similar outward appearance. However, there is no grounds for equating the two, as Finland never had the wild field grass farming that existed in Pomerania, for example. The author was able to investigate this on site. It was not until 1926 that the Finns became officially acquainted with German meadow and pasture farming as a result of a study trip to East Prussia. The author has investigated these matters in such detail because methods of livestock raising based solely on forest pasture—likely unknown even in many German agricultural circles—are of vital importance if we want to shed light on our prehistoric Nordic life.

The Nordic race undoubtedly belonged to the races of man engaged in livestock raising. Ihering writes,

> The Roman and Germanic concept of wealth is derived from livestock. In Latin, the term for wealth is derived from *pecus / pecunia* (the wealth of the head of the household) and *peculium* (small livestock, children, and slaves). The Gothic *faihu* and Old English *feoh* mean both livestock and wealth. The word "sheep" has also been used to refer to money. I recall the same phenomenon from my homeland of East Frisia, where, even in my era, the lease contracts of the settlers in the *Moorkolonien* (*fehnen*)[41] still referred to "guilders and sheep."

According to Ihering, even in the most ancient of times, when there were no tools for branding animals, paint was applied to the skin of the livestock animal,

> This action of applying pigment is the basis of the meaning of the word *literae*. Marking on the skin leads to writing on the hide of dead animals. We find this usage among the earliest of Romans. This was the hide shield that Paulus Diaconus reports, citing Festus: "The ancient shield was also called, on account of its roundness, the

---

[40] For further details, refer to the author's articles in *Deutsche Landwirtschaftlich Tierzucht* [German Agricultural Animal Breeding], volumes 1926 and 1927.

[41] Translator's note: *Moorkolonisierung* refers to the extensive historical policy in East Frisia aimed at clearing and cultivating bogland (*moor* in German, meaning bog or marsh). The term *fehne* is a generic designation for settlements established in marshy areas as a result of this colonization effort.

skin of an ox, upon which the treaty of the Gabines with the Romans had been inscribed." The earliest tablets used by the Romans were made of oxhide, and international treaties were the first documents recorded on them, until copper took its place later. Later, in Pergamon, this first crude writing material gave rise to the refined form of parchment.

It is highly noteworthy that both sedentism and the presence of livestock raising can be quite clearly inferred from the legal traditions of the patricians mentioned so far. This means that, in the case of the patricians, we find an agricultural economic system that is native to the northern regions of central Europe. One can see how easy it is to jump to conclusions about the nomadic-pastoralist nature of a race when all relevant aspects are not kept in mind.

Therefore, the existence in history of a race whose agricultural activity was limited to livestock raising does not necessarily provide definitive proof that this race originated in a steppe region. The only way to find this out is by investigating the domesticated animals that accompanied that race. The presence of a sedentary, purely forest-based pastoralism throughout north-central Europe proves that there is hardly a characteristic more unsuited for establishing a steppe origin for the Nordic race than that of pastoralism in particular.

To reiterate, contemporary racial science is attempting to establish a common root for the long-headed, tall human races of the earth, and it believes that this root is a common pastoral existence in the southeastern European steppes. However, after a thorough examination of the term "pastoralist," which turned out to be a catch-all term for the opposite, and in view of the observable contrast between settled and nomadic peoples in colonial history, this pastoralist theory must be regarded as a scientific assumption that lacks sufficient foundational evidence.

On top of this, the assertion that the Nordic race developed a martial master-nobility through their itinerant pastoralist way of life presupposes notions about the nature of nomadic pastoralists that can by no means lay claim to universality. In order to get a clearer picture, one must first separate nomadic pastoralism from everything that is clearly sedentary pastoralism or makes one strongly suspect that they are dealing with a settled people who have adopted a nomadic pastoralist way of life. Additionally, one must study nomadic pastoralists and their way of life.

6

What stands out among all nomadic peoples is their marked sense of tribal belonging. This is quite natural because life in steppes, tundra, deserts, or the icy far north leaves individuals without a fixed abode vulnerable and helpless. The preservation and survival of each individual member is anchored in the preservation and survival of the tribe. The struggle for existence has, without exception, fostered in nomadic pastoralists a natural instinct that fundamentally avoids the development of an awareness of one's own personhood, because, simply put, any kind of "standing out" by an individual simply means death. The tribe becomes one's personhood. However, since every tribe needs leadership, no one person embodies the role of "being the head" more flagrantly than the person of the chieftain, especially among nomadic peoples. At the same time, outside of these nomadic peoples, it is quite rare to find such an absolute subordination of all tribal members to the commands of the chieftain—this should not be confused with superficially similar phenomena observed in the case of conquest.

It is reasonable to assume that the "Byzantism" that developed in Asia and the Orient had its beginnings under the rule of warrior-nomadic peoples. There is at least some evidence that it began with the infiltration of Semitic and Asiatic nomadic blood into existing forms of government. This could be supported not only by various events in the history of the Roman Empire, but also, more recently, by similar developments in Bolshevik Russia. Lenin, the great Tatar, lies in the Lenin Mausoleum in Moscow's Red Square. In a glass coffin, some ten meters underground, in a room kept at the same temperature all year round, lies "the Greatest Man of Russia." The tattered red flag that was first hoisted over the Tsar's Winter Palace in St. Petersburg (Leningrad) hangs on the wall behind him. The mausoleum is constantly guarded by four military guards, a post of honor. The starkest contrast to this personality cult of the leader or ruler is the kingship of the Germanic peoples and, as far as can be determined historically, of the Nordic race as a whole. This is the case at least as long as there is a healthy Nordic ruling class. In his book *Gottes Gnadentum und Widerstandsrecht* (God's Grace and the Right of Resistance), Kern mentions how Emperor Frederick Barbarossa expressed his contempt for the Byzantine forms of the imperial cult with sharp derision.

A nomadic people's strong sense of common belonging is the natural product of matrilineality; this is quite comparable to what certain herds of animals develop under similar living conditions. In the animal world too, patrilineality only makes sense when the father can be held responsible for the upbringing of his children, or must be held responsible because of environmental conditions—but this very responsibility is lacking in the case of a nomadic people.[42] The care of the tribe is entrusted to all men, or to put it another way, the responsibility for the lives of the children always rests with the entire tribe. This logically leads to a situation where the entire tribe (meaning all the men), make use of the female members of the tribe as they wish and have no connection with the child that may be born. It took some effort for Muhammad to introduce something like marriage to the Semites through Islam; nevertheless, he allowed up to four wives for each man. However, the husband can legally give his wife the boot at any time, so it can hardly be called marriage in our sense. The only requirement on the husband is that he must give his wife a

---

[42] All of the questions raised in this section will be addressed and substantiated in greater detail in the subsequent chapters. The first chapter is intended, in a way, only to provide the reader with an introductory overview of the significant contrast between settled and nomadic peoples.

three month notice period, which the husband must adhere to in order to not expel a pregnant woman from the household. However, if this requirement is rarely seen in reality, it is because the Prophet allowed for exceptions. Verse 28 of Surah 4 (4:24) in the Quran explicitly states, "This is a commandment, but it shall not be a sin if you go beyond the commandment by mutual agreement." In pre-Islamic times, women had a very low status among the desert nomads. Through marriage—if one can even call the cohabitation of a man and a woman in this way marriage—women became part of the husband's family property and had no rights. The husband could sell her at will. Accordingly, women were excluded from inheritance rights. The reason for this is of great relevance—only those within the tribe that participated in raiding expeditions were entitled to inherit. This is logical, because, well, the non-working Arab only knows how to acquire wealth through plunder. There is no property in Arabia (meaning "arid land," from the Hebrew *areb*, meaning "desert"), and therefore the desert nomad has never made the distinction between property and robbery. Although the Quran did indeed elevate the status of women, it has not been quite able to free them from the inferior position of the pre-Islamic era. Today, a woman can only claim half the inheritance of a male family member, and in legal matters, a woman's testimony is considered half as valuable as a man's.

While Muhammad very clearly stood up for women, nowhere does one find any special respect for women in his teachings. According to him, there is a bit of the devil in every woman, and in hell they are the majority. The same low and contemptible position of women can be observed among the Tatars. This can be seen among all other authentically nomadic peoples as well.

If one compares the Semitic view of women just mentioned with the position of women among the Germanic peoples or the ancient Roman patricians, one can immediately recognize quite striking contrasts. Bridging such contrasts is virtually impossible. Still, it would not hurt to convince oneself of these striking differences by referencing Ihering. Therefore, we will cite some provisions attributed to Romulus regarding marriage,

> A man who sells his wife shall be punished with death. He may kill her for adultery or if she becomes intoxicated. He may only divorce her for certain legally specified reasons. If he repudiates her without legal grounds, he shall forfeit his entire fortune, with half going to the wife and the other half to her *gens*.[43]

To the ancient Roman, the woman was considered his equal—the wife was his equal-born companion, his life partner who shared everything with him, divine and human. And precisely because their relationship is healthy, he finds no reason to mistrust her. He does not

---

[43] Editor's note: A *gens* was a family or clan that shared a common *nomen* (family name) and claimed a common ancestry.

forbid her from interacting with other men or appearing in public. The wife does not have this position because she is a wife but because she is a woman, due to the respect that the Roman accords to the female sex as such. In inheritance law, the Roman woman stands on an equal footing with the Roman man.

If Kern (*Artbild der Deutschen*) would at least confine himself to assuming an itinerant pastoral warriorship for the Nordic race only to the time of their postglacial incursion into central and northern Europe, and if he would then further elaborate the development of the Nordic race separately from the Semites, then there would at least be a certain developmental consistency in his argumentation. But Kern explicitly refers to present-day Semites to prove his assumption, stating on page 199, "The pastoral culture nurtures and safeguards the natural sense of modesty in the female sex." As is well known, Muhammad used to herd camels before he began his climb to success by marrying the owner of those camels. As such, there is no doubt that he was a nomadic pastoralist, because camels are the domesticated breed of choice for nomadic pastoralists in the desert. Thus, one would expect Muhammad in particular, who was nurtured in a pastoral culture, to have a special respect for female modesty (it seems, however, that he was not at all familiar with Kern's line of thought). Muhammad had such a weak will when it came to the female sex that he could not be left alone with a virgin. Although he limited the number of wives for Muslims to four, he exempted himself from this restriction, as can be read in the thirty-third Surah of the Quran in Hennings' Reclam edition.[44] This exemption, however, applies only to his wives, it does not even include his concubines. Despite this abundance of women, which by our standards is certainly more than enough, Muhammad apparently could not trust himself. To be sure, he also obtained an exemption from God from the Ramadan commandment which forbade believers from any sexual activity during fasting days. The reasoning behind this is quite amusing—he explained that God exempted him because, as a prophet, his kisses were free of any sensual passion. Once again on page 199, Kern refers very extensively to the sexual instincts of nomadic pastoralists, speaking of "pure religion and chaste women," explicitly mentioning the Bedouin in this context, and linking them to the nobility of the Nordic race. Compare this to what the author has outlined above about the position of women in pre-Islamic Semitic civilization. It must unfortunately be said that Kern, in tracing the origins of the Nordic race, employs a scientific assumption about Semitic pastoral culture that is in sharp contrast to the historical reality regarding both the Semites and, for that matter, the Tatars. Perhaps it is good to mention Ihering once again as a key witness for the differences between the Semites and the Nordic race. He writes,

> The form that marital life took among the Aryans stood far above that which otherwise was the rule among the peoples of Asia. The woman did

---

44 Translator's note: Reclam Verlag is a German publishing house founded in 1828 widely known for its iconic yellow-covered pocket-sized paperbacks known as the Reclam *Universal-Bibliothek*, specializing in affordable editions of literary classics.

not occupy the degraded position that she did among these peoples, where she was little more than a slave and a mere servant of the man's sensual pleasure; rather, her position was as an equal born companion to the man. Although she was legally subject to the authority (*manus*) of the man, as with the Romans, this did not in the least diminish her position in life. She was considered the mistress of the household, and even the husband's parents and younger siblings were to respect her as such after the governance of the household had passed to her. . . . Our conclusion is that matrilineality was completely alien to the Aryan people by the time that daughter nations like the Romans had separated. . . . All adhered to the Aryan family structure founded on marriage.

7

Among genuinely nomadic peoples, we also find a quite distinct attitude toward property. Within the tribe, everything is fundamentally communal, resembling what we would now call communism. While there may be some degree of individual ownership rights recognized, the concept of personal property as such is denied. Schultze is quite correct in seeing the Bolshevism of Russia as merely a Tartarization of Marxism.

Besides, it cannot be emphasized enough that the life of a nomadic people is always one of pure parasitism. This parasitic attitude toward the whole world explains why a nomadic person never wants to work, anywhere or anytime, except, of course, for the certain manual skills that he needs and must know in order to support himself. During the colonization of America, the importation of slaves was only necessary in regions where the climate prohibited the "White man" from working and where there was no sedentary Indian population. The latter easily and without difficulty entered into a working relationship with the White man.[45] If a member of a nomadic tribe wants to acquire something, the only thing he can do is loot or plunder. This is also the case in the animal world. In keeping with their nature, these rootless individuals resort to plunder, either through theft or looting. This appears to have fostered the view that among nomadic peoples, particularly among nomadic pastoralists, a martial spirit has been cultivated that has made these nomadic pastoralists capable of true nobility. An excellent way to study warrior-nomadic rule and government is through historical examples; later on, this very question will be examined in detail and compared with the master-nobility of the Nordic race.

8

The life of nomadic peoples is always tough. When food and fodder become scarce, tribes must fight for life and death. Survivors from the opposing side hold no value. Consequently, one can observe a bestial cruelty among all nomadic peoples—prisoners are ruthlessly slaughtered without mercy. Just

---

[45] Mucke, *Urgeschichte des Ackerbaus.*

examine the abundant literature on this subject, especially books that describe wars with Arabs. One can find references to this with almost absolute consistency in the accounts of escaped Foreign Legionnaires. The nomadic pastoralist only takes prisoners when he can gain something from them (slave labor, human sacrifices, etc.). In this regard, all nomads are the same; it makes no difference whether one is examining Tatars or Arabs, Herero, or Indians.

Schultze tells of the Tatars and their method of conducting raids as follows:

As early as the sixteenth century, it was reported that every winter, the Crimean Tatars of the army of the Khan would gather at the Tauric Isthmus of Perekop.[46] Each Tatar had to bring two or three additional horses, tied to leather straps, in addition to his riding horse. Some years, eighty thousand men would march out with two hundred thousand horses. This immense cavalry mass, up to six miles in width, would set off westwards. The usual target was Volhynia. There, they formed a large square to enclose the area to be plundered. Nothing escaped, neither human nor animal—those who resisted were slaughtered. In this encirclement, people and livestock were herded closer and closer, eventually bound and captured, and then driven away. The provisions they brought along with them did not last for more than fourteen days, but this period of time was enough to completely devastate an area of thirty square miles and often captured up to fifty thousand people. This was referred to as "fishing out the lands with a dragnet." The captured prisoners were sold as slaves in the ports of Crimea. From a single incursion in the Balkan Peninsula, the Avars are said to have captured three hundred thousand prisoners.

If one wants to get to know the natives of North America as they really are, without the exaggerated enthusiasm that has characterized their representation in Germany, and if one does not have the time or the opportunity to delve into the history of the settlement of the United States, one should refer to the various books by Friedrich Pajeken. Pajeken himself was a frontiersman and a settler; he owed his existence to the misguided enthusiasm caused by the *Leatherstocking Tales* in his homeland.[47] He is, in part, known for the educational campaign he conducted in Germany through youth literature that portrayed the situation in North America as it really was.

It is undoubtedly true that certain individuals among the Native Ameri-

---

[46] Tauric refers to the historical region of Taurica, which was an ancient Roman name for the Crimean Peninsula.

[47] Translator's note: The *Leatherstocking Tales*, a series of five historical novels by James Fenimore Cooper, takes place in the early days of the United States and revolves around Natty Bumppo, alias Leatherstocking, a frontiersman and pathfinder. These books were quickly translated into German and had a lasting popularity among German youth.

cans towered above their people in terms of personal courage, and it is equally certain that some tribes were more fierce and warlike than others. However, the Indian was never "noble" or even "magnanimous," but inherently cruel and underhanded like any other genuine nomad. The Indian only knew how to burn down and destroy painstakingly built settlements. Even if the methods used by the White settlers to eventually defeat the Indians were not always perfect, one must by no means feel pity for the "poor" Indians, as is currently very popular. Otherwise, one is behaving just like those types of people that cannot get worked up enough about the barbaric callousness of the German troops on account of the "poor" Belgian *franc-tireurs*.[48] When you must deal with thieves and robbers all the time, you frankly lose any sense of the morality or immorality of putting scoundrels in their place.

The massive slave hunts conducted by the North African Arabs, which lasted until the late nineteenth century and left horrifying devastation in their wake, are of course still fresh in our memory. As we all know, before German occupation, the Arabs were in control of German East Africa. They plundered and devastated the land as they pleased. It has been estimated that around one hundred thousand slaves were abducted from their homeland each year, transported on ships, and sold in Arabia, Persia, and Anatolia. But before that, the Arabs used cruel torture to force the natives to reveal where their treasures lay (gold, ivory). It is said that in those days, human life was worth very little. These circumstances played no small part in the reasoning that led the natives to voluntarily place themselves under German protection and free themselves of Arab rule.

It is also significant that Muhammad never dared to take action against slavery. Like a very good businessman, he confined himself to tolerating the enslavement of only those prisoners of war who were infidels. As a result of this measure, the nomadic pastoralist culture of the Semites and other peoples, eager for slaves, spread to neighboring lands under the banner of the Prophet. This allowed the desire for plunder to be combined with the pleasurable thrill of performing a godly deed.

As bloodthirsty as the nomad is, he is essentially a coward, for he places no value on fighting as such. For him, fighting is always theft through violent means. Thus, for the nomad, freedom means either being able to do as he pleases (to serve himself as he pleases), or, in light of the other side of nomadism, the ability to survive a time of need in order to be there for the better times to come. Reflecting a truly nomadic way of thinking, one man of letters, who should be quite familiar to most, once called out to the German people: "a live dog is better than a dead hero."

Of Lenin the Tatar, Schultze reports with amazement that this cruel Bolshevik ruler never committed the slightest infraction of the house rules, or any other transgression, during his entire student life at the Latin School educa-

---

48 Editor's note: *Francs-tireurs* ("free shooters") were irregular military formations in Belgium and France who engaged in unconventional guerrilla warfare against invading German forces, notably during the Franco-Prussian War and World War I.

tional institution in Simbirsk, notorious for its petty strictness. He was an exemplary teacher's pet. In this context, Schultze mentions that other great revolutionaries were also teacher's pets during their school days. For example, he names Robespierre and Saint-Just. The author is not informed about the ancestry of these two individuals, but in the case of Lenin, this behavior is undoubtedly an expression of the personal cowardice of the nomad, that is, a member of a nomadic race (the same is also historically proven for Mohammed). Lenin's behavior here is characteristically nomadic—he meekly resigns himself to his fate as long as he believes he cannot change it. Calmly, he awaits better times—he awaits the moment when he can unleash the beast of prey hidden within his breast. This trait is just as indicative of his Tatar heritage as the fact that he remained in power at the Kremlin till his death.

Henrik Witboi, the Hottentot chief in German Southwest Africa, also displayed a similar dual nature. As long as he believed that the time had not yet come to strike, he was the most considerate friend of the Germans, to the extent that the German side trusted him unconditionally. Then, when he suddenly launched an attack, they were reluctant to believe it, so much so that Captain von Burgsdorff, an old veteran of Africa, rode out alone to meet him, assuming it was all just a misunderstanding. However, Burgsdorff was ambushed and immediately paid for this trust in the form of a bullet; Witboi generously rewarded the murderer. Such a sudden shift from peaceful person to bloodthirsty tyrant is characteristic of all nomads. This fact was not the least of the reasons for the negative reputation of the infamous "Punic faith" (*fides Punica*) in antiquity.

9

The member of a nomadic race, of a nomadic people, always believes in the inevitability of his fate. We shall see later that this view is not alien to the Nordic race either, although it manifests itself in a fundamentally different way, especially in comparison with the Semites. The most striking aptitude shared by all nomadic races is their ability to accept the inevitable with patience. Those who are familiar with steppes or deserts, or the natural conditions of both, can definitely understand that in these places the forces of nature arbitrarily determine the fate of rootless nomadic tribes. In such an environment, only tenacious perseverance in enduring hardships and an unconditional will to live secure the hope of happier days. This predisposition is reinforced, especially among nomadic pastoralists, by the fact that in times of need they must rely entirely on the ingenuity of their animals. It is often only the immediate recognition of the opportune moment that saves one from certain downfall. Therefore, among all the nomadic races of the world, one will find a remarkably quick perceptive faculty, however, it is primarily focused on perceiving one's own advantage. In addition, constant wandering and the continuous foraging for available food resources requires a keen eye for utilizing what is at hand. The member of a nomadic race must act quickly everywhere to find what is suitable for him and to distinguish the useful from the useless. Consequently, nomadic migration is always characterized by its focus on untapped resources; in the wake of such migrations, the land is left barren and empty.

At this point, it may be useful to clarify the etymology of the word nomad. It is related to the Greek word *nome*, which essentially means pasture, from *némein*, meaning "to graze" or "to feed around oneself." Hence, in medicine, *noma* refers to a self-devouring ulcer; recall here the aforementioned raid of the Tatars. As clear as the word nomad expresses the essential nature of all nomadic races, especially all nomadic pastoralists, it seems that in race science, these connections have not been sufficiently recognized. Otherwise, people would have probably been more cautious in equating nomadism with the Nordic race.

We can now understand a very peculiar aptitude of the nomads. The nomad fundamentally adapts to the things that come his way and tries to exploit them according to his needs. Among other things, this gives rise to a rather peculiar statesmanlike talent for handling issues related to a state system based on the exploitation of what is already at hand. However, this aptitude is essentially nothing more than the instinct of the nomad to graze a pasture transferred to the exploitation of human labor power. What clearly distinguishes such a statesmanlike aptitude for the exploitation of what is available from the state-building forces of the Nordic race is its barren attitude toward the value-creating work of the subjugated population. It is the same contrast that can be seen in the relationship between late Roman law, with its principles that stifled creative work, and ancient German or Germanic law, with its provisions that encouraged creative forces. We will discuss these contrasts later on.

Among the Punics, Seljuk Turks, Tatars, and others, one can very clearly observe this incredibly flexible statesmanlike ability to exploit, adapted to their specific circumstances. Schultze writes,

> It will be remembered for all time how Genghis Khan managed to transform his wild hordes, armed only with wooden sticks, into a warrior class that, within only a few years, completely mastered all the military-technical achievements of other peoples to the point that they could not be defeated in either open field battles or sieges. Perhaps even more remarkable is how this crude people, using the knowledge of others, could establish a state whose accomplishments in administrative techniques, as well as in many other areas, greatly astonished Marco Polo.

The empire of Genghis Khan covered an area that far surpassed even the territory Napoleon I held at the height of his power. There is no reason to deny Genghis Khan his position as an administrative statesman of the highest order.

In East Africa, the organization and structure of the trade caravan routes used for slave raids, as well as all related arrangements, were fabulously and amazingly developed by the Arabs and their associated warrior nomads. Their achievements in this regard were matched by the aforementioned Tatar statesmanlike aptitude for exploitation. In the face of such impressive achievements, it was initially difficult for Germany to assert its administrative skills and gain the confidence of its native population.

Despite this, however, there is no reason to consider the exploitative talent of the nomad as a general aptitude in governance or even to equate it with the state-building power of the Nordic race. Both aptitudes were grown on different soil, consequently manifested themselves in different ways, and must be clearly distinguished from each other. The most striking difference between the political aptitude of the nomads and that of the Nordic race is that every form of nomadic rule has led to the decline or complete intellectual sterility of a previously flourishing human community, while every form of Nordic rule has always produced a genuine cultural flowering out of nothing, or at least out of inferior civilizations. Just compare the cultural achievements of tiny Athens with the intellectual forces that emerged from the vast empire of Genghis Khan. The latter have yet to be found. Lenin, with his Bolshevik state creation, is the faithful heir of the great Genghis Khan. Therefore, one should be cautious about expecting an imminent collapse of Bolshevik rule in Russia. At the same time, one should also not anticipate that it will produce more great intellectual or cultural achievements than were produced by the empire of Genghis Khan.

All nomads are also strikingly similar in that they have a certain mental agility that allows them to quickly grasp and distinguish the essential from the unessential. For example, it is fascinating to read the letters exchanged between Witboi[49] and the German authorities. Earlier, of course, the author already attempted to provide an explanation for this peculiar mental aptitude of nomads, based on their itinerant way of life. Despite this mental agility, however, one will search in vain among all nomads for a creative force that further develops an object or concept on the basis of its nature. We will discuss this point in more detail later, but it can already be said here that the Nordic race has such a fundamentally different impact on the world that the author cannot be convinced that this race has nomadic roots.

When one recalls, for example, the way of life of a livestock-raising settled person in the steppe, for whom adversity only stimulates a greater exertion of his drive, it becomes clear that such a settled person cannot solve his life's questions through merely "staying alive" or through the predatory existence of the nomad. For such a settled person, the concept of freedom is therefore associated with the idea of being able to do what benefits his existence. The freedom of the sedentary pastoralist is not a boundless individual freedom, as with the nomads, but is in all ways a freedom of action that is tied to productive work. If this freedom of action is taken away from the sedentary pastoralist, the very foundation of his existence is destroyed. He will either become uprooted (made into a nomad), or he will simply perish. The Herero fought the German settlers for their ancient grazing lands. The Boers fought the English for their freedom of action. It was by no means the mindset of itinerant nomadic pastoralists when, before one of the battles of liberation, the leader of Dithmarschen's women called out to the men, telling them to remember, "Living freedom,

---

[49] Leutwein, *Die Kämpfe mit Hendrik Witboi.*

what great glory and noble jewel!" (Original in West Frisian: *Welk grote Her-lichkeit und edel Kleinot de leve Friheid is*).

To prevent any confusion regarding the terms used in the following chapters, it is important to briefly explain here what is meant by "settled person" and "nomad." The author considers a settled person to be any person who has a permanent dwelling, is rooted to the soil, and uses their own manual labor to tap the natural resources of their surroundings. The way the dwelling is built and the way of life chosen by the settled person, or the stage of development expressed in his way of life, is irrelevant in this context. Even a semi-nomadic pastoralist existence with summer tents and huts is included, as long as the winter is consistently spent in the same place and in a genuine village. It is completely irrelevant whether the settled person, rooted to the soil, lives as a hunter or fisherman and does not practice livestock raising or agriculture, or whether he practices livestock raising alone, or whether he practices both livestock raising and agriculture. The least important thing is whether a settled person conducts his agriculture using a hoe or hoe plow, a swivel plow, or a motorized plow. While these may be useful means to differentiate between and identify levels of civilizational advancement within agricultural development, they must be rejected when establishing levels of civilizational advancement within humanity. The extent to which discerning cultural historians often completely miss the mark with their classifications can be seen in the following words of Privy Councilor Aereboe, the founder of contemporary agricultural science:

> When I arrived as an economic officer at a farm in Mecklenburg in 1885, I expressed my surprise at the complete absence of plows on the premises. Instead, they were relying solely on the old Mecklenburg hook for cultivation. In response, the white-haired senior inspector, Mr. S., then explained that the hook was actually more effective than the plow in preventing very risky overtillage, especially in the absence of sufficient fertilization. He mentioned that he was no longer able to obtain manure from the stables and was unfamiliar with how to use artificial fertilizers. . . . Even today, on all naturally nutrient-poor soils, the German farmer must be cautious not to plow his soil to excessive depth beyond what his budget allows for procuring manure.

The author considers all parasitic ethnic groups as nomadic. In this regard, it does not matter if they appear as roaming hunters without fixed abodes, or if they follow their herds as pastoralists, or if they ultimately parasitize as a ruling class of warriors over a settled substrate (like the Moors in Spain).

The nomad always necessarily subordinates himself and his culture to the environment, which, of course, he is forced to do by his parasitic way of life. Since the environment dictates the nomad's lifestyle, one might say that he is also the born advocate of a doctrine that expects all salvation to come from the environment and does not grant man himself any chance of shaping it. On the other hand, the settled person tries to fundamentally subordinate his environment; therefore, his culture always emanates from his own abilities and predispositions, along with the given environmental conditions. Certainly, there is a vast difference between Negroes who engage in hoe cultivation and the proud *uhlen* clans described by Gustav Frenssen; yet they stand together opposed to nomadic peoples simply because, throughout world history, experience has shown that the nomad—regardless of whether he is at a high or a low level of civilization—is incapable of settling down. It can of course be observed that nomadic tribes can "settle" among a settled people, for instance, as traders or overlords who have superimposed themselves in an imperious manner. However, nomadic races never become deeply rooted with the land. As soon as the settled nation has been leeched dry and dies out, the old urge to wander resurfaces, and the tribe moves on with its previous mobility (perfect examples of this are the Moors and Turks, especially the former). If, after observing a settlement history now spanning over two thousand years, we come to the conclusion that a nomad cannot become rooted to the soil, then there is actually no justification, without providing very serious evidence, to assume such a thing for prehistory, as Kern does. However, since it is possible to uproot a settled person and turn him into a nomad, but not vice versa, it is undoubtedly reasonable to speculate that the ability to settle was evolutionarily acquired by the human race after the acquisition of manual skills, since nomads and settled peoples share these skills. Furthermore, it can be said that part of humanity did not participate in this transition to sedentism, or later lost their settled form of existence by being driven into inhospitable areas, forcing them into a state of homeless wandering. Ultimately, however, it can also be assumed that both possibilities have coexisted throughout the history of humanity. The ability to settle is a human characteristic that is still (for the time being) an evolutionary puzzle, even in light of the many "plausible" assumptions that have already been made about it. In any case, it would be good to attempt to trace the beginning of sedentism step by step in terms of evolution. Under no circumstances should evolutionary leaps be made for which there is no evidence, just to achieve a convenient scientific classification in the field of ethnology and race science.

II
Nordic Nomads? A Study of Recent Settlement History

I

There are those in the field of race science who feel justified in taking the risk of drawing far-reaching conclusions about prehistoric conditions on the basis of present-day similarities between human races. Those who advocate for such an approach will hardly be able to object if, following this logic, the demand is made to group all present-day long-headed races in their present-day cultural manifestations into a single category. This would mean that if the Nordic race is nothing more than a race of nomadic pastoralists who have grown pale under the cloudy skies of northwestern Europe, then the study of the Nordic race would surely reveal certain characteristics that this race shares with the other nomadic races. Conversely, deriving the Nordic race from a nomadic race in this way must be regarded as questionable if the Nordic race manifests itself differently from present-day nomads—in fact, such a derivation would have to be incorrect if it is found that all nomads share common characteristics that we in turn cannot detect in the Nordic race.

In its fifteen hundred year history, the German peoples have had plenty of encounters with genuine warrior nomads. Recall how the Moors attempted to advance from the southwest into the heart of the Frankish Empire, or think of the storms of Mongols led by Balamber against the Goths, as well as Attila and Genghis Khan. One can also bring to mind the time when waves of Turks, under the leadership of the nomadic Seljuks, pounded on the gates of Vienna. Here we are dealing with phenomena that anyone can verify in German history. Above all, we have nomads of such pronounced warrior spirit and intelligence that no one would consider any comparison between them and the

Nordic race as being in any way one-sided or unjustified.

Although all of these nomadic peoples belong to quite different racial groups and ethnicities, they still have always had one thing in common—namely, throughout history, their raids have always been directed toward settled land. This is very natural, of course. After all, we have already familiarized ourselves with the hallmark of the nomad, his parasitic way of life. This way of life inevitably drives him away from the wretchedness of his land of origin to prosperous, settled agricultural lands. For the past two thousand years, we have been able to observe the repeated emergence of the Arabs from the Arabian Peninsula with great precision. It could almost have been predicted with certainty when they would invade North Africa. The ancestral homelands that nomads originate from are quite clearly operating like the radiating hubs of a centrifugal force (a force fleeing from its center), a phenomenon that absolutely indicates the presence of a geographic regularity within human migrations. This observation seems to correspond with the phylogeny of our domesticated animals. Unfortunately, however, this phenomenon has still not been sufficiently studied by ethnology for it to be readily used as a clear foundation for understanding the phylogeny of domesticated animals. Nevertheless, the existing material on the subject is more than enough to designate the Nordic race as a settled race, unrelated to these herds of nomads.

Nomadism, as we have already seen, is conditioned by a steppe or a desert environment, which are the product of a lack of rain in an area. While neither the steppe nor the desert is completely devoid of plant growth (as is sometimes portrayed), these areas still rarely contain genuine tree or shrub species in significant quantities. At most, there is vegetation at a few watering holes, but even then there are very limited numbers of species that could be even considered for timber use. Of course, we already saw in the first chapter that Ihering points out a contrast in the use of wood in Semitic and Nordic criminal law. It is worth noting that these different approaches to the use of wood—or, more precisely, water—are already so deeply rooted in the oldest legends of both groups that it is impossible, according to our present knowledge, to discover any connections that would indicate an earlier common ancestral root. While we can observe water in abundance in all legends of the Nordic race—not to mention in the Nordic belief in the kingdom of souls, e.g., Hades—no such thing is found in Semitic traditions. Due to the plentiful availability of wood in their native lands, the Nordic race adopted the practice of cremation at a very early stage. Of course, we should not expect to find this practice among the Semitic peoples. For the Semite, who has no access to wood and, due to being a member of a nomadic race, also lacks the means to create special burial sites, his options for honoring the deceased are limited. He has no choice but to dig a grave and then place a stone on top to protect the body from being disturbed by jackals or other animals. Interestingly, it was actually only through the influence of Christianity that the Germanic peoples acquired the practice of burial ceremonies and the use of gravestones. This remark should not be interpreted to mean that the Nordic race was never familiar with the burial of unburned bodies. These contrasts are only presented to stimulate thought.

It is also very noteworthy that the Semites envision paradise as being a garden. Of course, a garden always requires the presence of water in an otherwise arid region, whether naturally occurring or provided through artificial means. Ihering draws attention to these matters in his research on ancient Babylonian legal documents. Most of these documents quite undoubtedly date from periods when the existence of Semitic dominions can be demonstrated, or when the influence of Semitic blood on the local Nordic dynasties can be assumed. He writes,

> Only the fruit tree and the date palm, which paid for their place through their yield, were sustainable. But when it came to timber, which only the forest could provide in sufficient quantity, there was a great lack, as there were no forests in the area. Oil and dates are mentioned several times in Babylonian documents as the subject of legal transactions. The role that the fruit tree must have played in the imagination of these peoples in ancient times can be seen in the Old Testament legend of Paradise, where the first humans subsisted on fruit. The archetype of paradise is the fruit and ornamental gardens of the Babylonians.

It should be added here that when the desert sons of Arabia saw the plantations of the racially-alien settlers in the lowlands of Mesopotamia, they must have thought that they were witnessing paradisiacal conditions with ideal cool and shady splendors; in Arabic, *farâdîs* means pleasure garden.[50] Such ideas are completely alien to the legends of the Nordic race. For example, consider the role of the wild boar in Nordic legends. It is well known that this is a wild animal that needs to live in an area with an abundant presence of water.

With such things in mind, one should seriously begin to doubt Kern's hypothesis that the ancestral homeland of the Nordic race was in a steppe region. But if the Semites and the Nordic race had only separated in the postglacial periods of Earth's history, and if the Indo-Europeans were in fact the warrior-nomads that Kern sees them as, then there should absolutely be tangible similarities in the folk-

---

[50] The understanding of water as the originator of shade-giving places can quite undoubtedly be observed among the Semites from the very beginning; it goes without saying that they had sufficient observational material in the oases to give them this impression. Insofar as the Semites, especially the Arabs, have ever achieved anything in the field of agriculture, it has always been by encouraging the subjugated population to build irrigation systems. It is true that in Spain, the true art of gardening and the construction of fountains can be traced back to Arab rule. However, as we will see later with Rohlfs, this tendency to establish shade-giving places has nothing to do with agricultural talent per se. The much-praised "great" agricultural prosperity of Spain under Arab rule, although it can be attributed to the Arabs as the initiating cause, is not the result of Arab creativity in the field of agriculture. All the evidence cited for the alleged agricultural talent of the Arabs is about as convincing as saying that because a nurse breastfed a child, she must have also given birth to it. On the other hand, while the Nordic race has always shown outstanding aptitude in fields related to the practical use of water (shipbuilding, bridge building, canal construction, etc.), they have always learned the art of true urban gardening from other peoples.

lore of the two races. According to our present knowledge, this is not the case.

The same contrasting views of wood between the Semites and the Nordic race can be found in other contexts. When migrating, the nomad never carries wood—for fuel, he relies on the carefully collected dung of his herd animals. The nomad always rests on the ground. The "squatting" position is of course familiar to all travelers who have ever been to the Orient and Asia, although it is not always comfortable for Nordic limbs. For added comfort, wealthy nomads will, at most, have pillows and cushions, and, in the best-case scenario, they may have a kind of low divan.[51] It goes without saying that the nomad is completely unfamiliar with wooden chairs. It is interesting to note that in the history of antiquity, we can accurately observe how chairs or benches held a place of honor in the home only when the country was ruled by a Nordic ruling class. However, both forms of seating immediately disappear as soon as the racial composition of the state, at least as far as its upper classes are concerned, is upset. This is to make way for the Oriental custom of comfortable lounging. In the case of Rome, this point of transition can be identified rather accurately as the years 300 to 200 BC. The throne as an expression of sovereign dignity is a thoroughly un-nomadic notion. Such a view is only natural to a people accustomed to the forest. The peculiar emphasis on the "precious cedar of Lebanon" begins to make sense only if one remembers that the imagination of these people was not used to the sight of wood.

In fact, when warlike nomads have emerged victorious over settled peoples, we can observe two things. Either the nomads, driven by their highly developed sense of exploitation and predatory greed, simply plunder what they find, leaving behind a dead and desolate desert, or the nomads are wise enough to preserve the working capacity of the subjugated settled population, in which case they simply position themselves as a parasitic ruling class. In fact, it is widely believed in ethnology that the "cleverness" of such warlike nomads quite "self-evidently" leads them to establish themselves as a benefiting ruling class, sparing the subjugated sedentary peoples. While there is no doubt that this observation is true from time to time, in reality it is very rarely the case. It can in no way be considered as, say, the hallmark of nomadic rule. By his very nature, the nomad has no sense whatsoever of the interconnectedness of life, which forms the foundation of any sensible state structure. He knows how to exploit and plunder what already exists, but he never knows how to build anything. One only has to observe the terrible devastation caused by the Arab storms in Africa or the Tatar floods in Asia to immediately see that in these cases the nomad demonstrates his original nature and lives up to his name (noma from *némein*, meaning to devour). The few cases

---

[51] *Diwan* or *divan* (Persian *dîvân*, Arabic *daiwân*), which an Arabic scholar explains as deriving from *dêwan*, Persian plural of *dêw*, meaning devil, and *div* or *dîw*, meaning spirit or demon who guards hidden treasures. This has a similar etymology to the *Divan-ı Hümayun* of the Turkish emperor (known more commonly as the Ottoman Imperial Council) and the Turkish tax register.

where he "seems" to behave differently, such as the Moors and Seljuks,[52] are the exception rather than the rule and can be attributed to other causes. The author here relies on introductions to these questions written by the geologist Walther (Halle). For many years, Walther (Halle) was able to observe first hand in Africa how the Arabs transformed once thriving settler lands into barren deserts that were irreversibly ruined and could never be restored. This is because once the agricultural or natural vegetation in these regions has been destroyed, desertification can no longer be stopped, or can only be stopped with great difficulty. The reason for this is that the sun, shining down on the soil without an adequate plant cover to serve as an intermediate layer (insulating layer), draws up the ground water by means of capillary action. The water, which constantly rises and evaporates at the surface, inevitably carries the dissolved salts of the soil upwards, where they crystallize by evaporation, resulting in a severe salinization of the soil. Contrary to what is often claimed, such salinized soils cannot simply be repaired through irrigation. First of all, for irrigation to be successful, the soil needs to be prepared by leaching out the salts in the soil in order to reduce the amount of salt to a level at which plants can thrive. Secondly, desert winds usually blow a layer of dead desert sand—which, of course, is nothing more than weathered desert rock—over the soil in a short period of time. Under such circumstances, the reclamation of the soil can then only be done at quite enormous costs. It is quite certain, therefore, that the spread of the desert in North Africa can be attributed in part to the nomadic Semites; non-climatic factors are the primary drivers of desertification in North Africa. For as long as we have been able to observe them historically, Semites have always appeared together with camels, and since camels have only ever been animals of the desert, there can certainly be no doubt that the ancestral homeland of the Semites was located in the desert.

In Asia, the reasons for desert formation are similar— it is very easy to correlate the expansion of desert herd animals with the expansion of local nomads. This means that the Asian steppes also owe their expansion to the nomads, although from a meteorological point of view they were formed due to slightly different reasons than those of the desert.

In the context of recent colonial history, however, it is by no means necessary to focus solely on Arabs and Asians in order to recognize nomads as a purely destructive element of humanity. On the contrary, it is also very important to remember the terrible cruelty with which the Herero fell upon our compatriots in German Southwest Africa during the Herero uprising, how they razed everything to the ground. It is also instructive to recall the brutal killing of Whites by Native Americans. If ever there was a story that had nothing to do with reality, it

---

[52] A very curious piece of evidence in support of the nomadic origins of the Seljuk Turks is the "horse tails" of the Turkish Pashas. These horse tails actually have nothing to do with horses, but are the long-haired tails of the yak (*poêphagus*). The yak, a black, long-haired wild bovine, stands at about 1.6 meters tall and is found exclusively in the most inhospitable highlands of Tibet, between four thousand and six thousand meters in altitude. The yak has only ever been domesticated in this specific area, serving as a riding animal and a beast of burden. Its historical distribution elsewhere extended from this ancestral homeland to other locations where it was later replaced by the camel or reindeer.

is certainly the sentimental myths spun in Europe about the "noble" redskins.

But when the nomad is at least wise enough to not destroy everything and instead tries to parasitize, as can be observed more often with the waves of no-mads that have crashed into Europe, then the principle can be established that nomadic rule of this kind can only be upheld by the use of the sword. The nomad's sense of tribal belonging, rooted in his blood, and his keen sense of channeling the individual forces within his tribe outward against outsiders (but never inwardly), combined with the necessities of keeping subjugated peoples in check, give rise to quite distinctive political institutions. When warlike no-mads conquer new lands, they must first keep their army together and establish a secure base for their military leadership. This then leads to the establishment of large military camps, as exemplified by Attila's Tokaj (Hungary) or Genghis Khan's Karakorum. When the political situation stabilizes, or when the subju-gated population is too weak to defend itself, the nomads then gladly start building coercion castles[53] among the settled population. This strategy allows the ruling class to disperse and more effectively collect tribute from the subju-gated population.[54] Quite excellent examples of this can be found in the "kremlins" that arose during Tatar rule in Russia. Similarly, one can also con-sider the Moorish fortresses that appeared among the Berber population. The term "Berber" comes from the Arabic *berberei*, which refers to the land of the Berbers, quite simply meaning country dwellers, in contrast to the Moors who only inhabited the cities.[55] Another Arabic term with a similar connotation is *fellah*. Derived from the Arabic verb *falah*, meaning to split, plow, or cultivate, *fellah* thus serves as a collective term for the rural inhabitants of Egypt engaged in agriculture.

However, in addition to these fortresses, there were also certain key centers of authority where all the threads of power converged, these were seemingly more common in regions where the subjugated population was inclined to violent uprisings. A lot is revealed by these key centers of power. In essence, they are nothing more than the old tented military camps that gradually estab-lished themselves and developed into increasingly secure fortresses. If the no-mads had at their disposal a subjugated population with creative architectural skills, structures could be created like the Alhambra in Granada and the Moor-ish Royal Palace in Cordoba, which we can still admire today. Since these were not merely courtly encampments simply serving as residences for the ruler, but rather permanent dwellings for many people, it is not surprising that the

---

[53] Translator's note: Coercion castles, in German *zwingburgen*, refers to a type of fortress con-structed by a hostile force within a community where loyalty was uncertain or not guaranteed. The castles' primary roles were to assert authority, enforce their rule, and suppress the local population.
[54] It is good at this point to remember that the term "*divan*" encompasses both the Ottoman Imperial Council and the tax register.
[55] Similar connotations are expressed by the word *kaffir*. In essence, the *kaffirs* are a warlike and cruel tribe in South Africa. The word *kaffer* originates from Arabic and roughly translates to "infi-del" or "non-Muslim." In our German student slang, we also find the term *kaffer*, which is used to refer to an inept or uneducated person. The student slang adopted the word from criminal jargon, where it is derived from the rabbinical term *kaphri*, meaning villager or peasant. *Kaphri* itself is derived from the Hebrew term *kaphar*, meaning village.

builders of these complexes often characteristically constructed rather spacious buildings. Continuous residence within the fortified enclosure forced designers to, of course, make these structures as comfortable as possible. A prime example of this is the Old Saray built by Mohammed II in Constantinople. The word *saray*, known to us in its Italian form *seraglio* (*serail*), quite literally means a space that provides accommodation for many people. These fortresses, built among a subjugated population, are not to be confused with the defensive fortresses of a settled people. The latter are always found on the outskirts of settled lands or in locations that can be easily defended. This will be discussed in even more detail further below. However, the difference between a coercion castle and a defensive fortress can be clearly seen when one considers the old Moorish fortresses in Algeria, built among the settled Berber population, and compares them to the defensive outposts that were erected by the French Foreign Legion against the Arabs in the Sahara.

Another characteristic of nomadic rule is its view of property, especially land. As communistic as the view of property within the tribe is, the nomadic view of property outside the tribe is ruthlessly non-communistic. The proceeds of the labor of the subjugated settled population are channeled to the tribe and then collected in the main camps. This then creates a kind of reserve of accumulated power. This power is available at any time for any number of purposes, especially for the purpose of recruiting mercenaries when war is looming on the horizon. It is here that the connection between the tax registry and the Ottoman Imperial Council in the word *diwan* becomes quite clear. Just as the nomadic tribe does not care about the pastures of the steppe, by nature, it also does not care about the land of the settled population. Because of this, in warrior-nomadic societies, one will never see individual tribal members with an attachment to land. Even if the nomads' religious doctrine does not explicitly forbid them from allowing individual members of the tribe to develop a connection to the land (as with the Arabs), the most attachment to the soil that one can expect to find among them is a large-scale landowner that tends to his property only on the condition that it brings in a satisfactory income.

This sharp contrast with settled peoples (we might as well say to working people in general) is the natural consequence of the nomad's evolutionary history. In the course of his development, the nomad has only been taught to live parasitically and the only occupation he knows is "grazing" a pasture. The Arabic word *sûchra* means "forced laborer," and it is also used to refer to any object deserving of contempt. Inherent to nomadism is also the ability to easily abandon a people who have been sucked dry as soon as the nomads can no longer benefit from them. The nomad himself is not deeply affected by the downfall of a subjugated settled people that perished from excessive exploitation.

With great stubbornness, the nomad transforms the subjugated civilization without adding anything of his own. Thus, it can be said that the flourishing of a nomadic culture depends on the vitality of the subjugated settled population. Yet, if one takes the time to study Moorish rule in the Iberian Peninsula, it is amazing to see how, despite centuries of residence in a single location and access to the most advanced universities, the Moor still retained his nomadic characteristics. Gerhard Rohlfs writes,[56]

> Let us finally begin to assess a people according to their achievements in craftsmanship and, above all, according to their intellectual achievements! The Arabs have always been and will always remain parasites. Spain can be glad that it expelled these nomads long ago. It is true that Spain is not in the most splendid condition, but if it would have retained this dreadful gang, it would then be pretty much on par with Morocco and Tunisia. Compare the state of civilization in Spain with that of Morocco, Tunisia, and Tripolitania, and you will be astonished at the tremendous differences. If the Arabs were really the capable people they are too often made out to be, they would have, in fact, achieved the same thing in Morocco, Algeria, and Tunisia that they are said to have accomplished in Spain before their expulsion. Instead, all they accomplished in North Africa was the destruction of what remained of Roman civilization. In Spain, the conquerors found a more favorable field. They already had black slaves to work the land, and they also had many Christians to work the intellectual fields. Work themselves? Arabs never worked, here or anywhere else—they had others work for them. They did not invent—they had others invent for them.

How thoroughly the Arab excels in destruction is perhaps best illustrated by the popular saying in Sudan that "wherever the Arab treads, even the grass must wither."

Because of the Tartars' exploitative views toward settled peoples, the once-thriving lands of Russia eventually collapsed, resulting in the desolate steppes we see today. As already mentioned above, the devastated areas of Mesopotamia owe their existence solely to Asiatic and Arab nomadism.

Privy Councillor von Rümker, one of our most important scholars in the field of agronomy, appropriately concludes a chapter in his book titled *Current Issues in Modern Agriculture*,[57] which addresses the issue of weed proliferation in our fields, with the following words,

> The time of carefree irresponsibility toward the weeds of Germany has come to an end and will hopefully never return—that

---

[56] Gerhard Rohlfs was an explorer of Africa. In 1855, after serving as a doctor in the Foreign Legion, he studied the desert conditions in northwest Africa in great detail. From 1874 to 1886, he published numerous books on the desert and its inhabitants. He also served as the German Consul General in Zanzibar in 1884. Therefore, Rohlfs can be considered an expert, and his opinion on the nomads can be considered here.

[57] Rümker, *Tagesfragen aus dem Modernen Ackerbau.*

is, unless the ongoing dismantling of our peasant civilization reaches its culmination. This process, which has been taking place gradually since November 9, 1918, is accelerating as more racially-foreign ideologies and worldviews gain dominance. The goal of this process is to ensure that the absolute dominance of the weeds on Germany's soil is secured again. The eastern nomads, who can only take but not produce, will then be forced to abandon the deserts they have created and pitch their tents on other grounds that still possess a civilization worth dismantling.

Despite the ethnic and racial diversity that may exist among warrior-nomads, they are all the same in the way they rule over a settled population and in their exploitative views toward the labor of the settled population. It does not matter whether you study Arabs or Indians, Tartars or Huns. They are all the same in this regard. But where can it be shown that the Nordic race behaves in this same way?

There are those who would reply that simply by virtue of its special intellectual gifts, the Nordic race has always known better than to destroy the settled population that they have subjugated. It is worth reminding those people that, first of all, in arguing this they are already situating the Nordic race apart from other nomads. Secondly, they should draw their attention to the Arabs, whose intellectual flowering in the Middle Ages did absolutely nothing to induce them to transition from the innate, purely exploitative urges of the nomad into the constructive mentality of the settled person. To give an example, Semitic thinking has never understood the value of the peasant class in any period of world history. The nomad is simply incapable of doing this—he cannot do this just as, say, an unmusical person cannot become musical by will or intellect alone, no matter how much they may have recognized and understood the value of music.

There are also those who would object by saying that the Nordic race had already merged with the native settled population of northern Europe, and thus cannot be considered entirely nomadic, these individuals should refer to what has been said above, specifically that evidence for a prehistoric nomadic-pastoral way of life for the Nordic race has still not been sufficiently substantiated. Moreover, certain physiological reservations must also be raised against tracing the Nordic race back to an eastern European steppe region. In a steppe, with its intense sun exposure—a defining characteristic of the steppe—the pigment-less skin of the Nordic race and its characteristic inability to store pigment would never have developed. A more detailed study would probably also reveal very particular and unique characteristics in the subcutaneous connective tissue and dermis of the Nordic race. Plutarch, for example, said of the Cimbri at Vercellae, "Accustomed to enduring cold, they were completely weakened by the heat, broke into heavy sweat, panting, and had to hold their shields in front of their faces."

Instead, the atrophied remnants of resistance to cold exposure can still be seen in the skin of the Ostic race,[58] as well as resistance to the Winga, the icy, dangerous northern and northeastern storms of the Russian steppes.[59]

2

Throughout the history of mankind, wherever the Nordic race has appeared, it has always been creative and has never had a civilization-destroying effect. One could almost call it a stroke of luck that a book as magnificent as Mielke's *Die Siedlungskunde des Deutschen Volkes*[60] has entered the debate about the Nordic race. The work is undoubtedly an achievement for Mielke, and not only points out the connections between peasant settlement patterns and the Nordic race (as many have, of course, done since Kossinna), but also reveals the dependence of Nordic life on the peasant or manorial form of settlement. While race science still generally holds the position that Nordic blood in the Mediterranean and Asia has steadily dwindled away since prehistory due to disproportionate losses in wars, Mielke, on the other hand, very clearly argues that it was primarily the turning away from the land and the abandonment of the peasant way of life that struck an axe to the roots of the Nordic ruling classes. In the final chapter, the author will provide evidence that Mielke is absolutely correct in this judgment.

In Germany, we are plagued by the legacy of past centuries; we have developed the habit of erecting barriers between the nobleman and the peasant, between the peasant and the warrior. But we do not realize that this introduces something unnatural into the German character. The swordless peasant was entirely alien to the ancient Germanic peasantry.

Even in the modern era, it was still common in some peasant regions for people to appear at assembly armed. In the Middle Ages, the practice of training and sparring with weapons was by no means limited to the nobility—it was equally common among the peasantry. In G. Freytag's *Bilder aus der Deutschen Vergangenheit* (Images from the German Past), it is written that around the

---

[58] Translator's note: The Ostic (*ostische*) race, more commonly known as the Alpine race, is one of the proposed European races. The name (*ostiche* literally translating to "eastern") reflects Günther's belief that the race had Asian origins. According to Günther (*Rassenkunde des Deutschen Volkes*), this race is "short, short-headed, broad-faced with an unpronounced chin; short, blunt nose with a flat nasal root; stiff, brown or black hair; forward-set brown eyes; yellowish-brownish skin." Günther considered most of the German population to be racially Alpine (especially in Austria). Adolf Hitler reportedly described Benito Mussolini admiringly as a typical member of the Alpine race.

[59] The author has not done an in-depth analysis as to whether accurate studies have been done regarding the skin of the individual human races—his judgment is based on the excellent compilation that Zorn has written in the context of animal breeding: *Haut und Haar als Rasse- und Leistungsmerkmal in der Landwirtschaftlichen Tierzucht* [Skin and Hair as Breed and Performance Characteristics in Agricultural Animal Breeding] in the German Society for Breeding Science's pamphlet. There is no doubt that the society is willing to provide information upon request about recent developments in animal breeding related to this issue.

[60] Mielke, *Die Siedlungskunde des Deutschen Volkes.*

time of the first Crusades, the entire lower nobility (which today partially claims to be of ancient noble descent) ranked below the free peasants in terms of authority. For example, the history of the Netherlands is dominated by Westerwald peasants under the House of Orange—the House of Orange's linden trees on the slopes of the Westerwald have survived longer than the gratitude of the Netherlands to Germany.

The free peasant is undoubtedly the most perfect expression of the settled form of existence in the entire world. Our German language has preserved a sense of this distinction by very clearly differentiating between *bäuerlich* (peasant-like, rural, agrarian, rustic) and *bäuerisch* (boorish). *Bäuerlich* relates to *bäuerisch* as *kindlich* (child-like) relates to *kindisch* (childish). Freedom belongs to the peasant like the crown belongs to the king—without it, the peasant is no longer a peasant, but a steward or a servant. The free peasant must also be able to defend his freedom, otherwise he will not remain free. This is ultimately the basis of Kern's misunderstanding—he tries to deny the presence of a peasantry within the Nordic race simply because this race was brave.

Today very strange ideas about the peasantry are beginning to take hold. For those who wish to separate the Nordic race from the peasantry, perhaps it will be a good idea to point to an example where we can examine this issue very closely. A good example to refer to would be the settlement of North and South America, which were originally opened up and settled by the Nordic race. America is particularly valuable in clarifying this question because it shows how a race will adapt its modes of settlement according to the climatological conditions and available natural resources. The situation today can be roughly summed up as follows. In the north, in the vast primeval forests of Canada, trappers and fishermen still live in their log cabins—they build log cabins and do not simply adopt the wigwams of the Indians as a model. To the south is the main agricultural region. Further south, heading toward Mexico, on the vast prairies, we come across Nordic people exclusively functioning as herders. Soon the tropics begin to appear. Here, the "White" man is unable to do any physical labor. In places where he was unable to utilize the labor of sedentary Indians, the slave trade consequentially flourished. As one goes further south from tropical Central America, one finds the same ways of life just described, only in reverse order or shifted, due to slightly different climatic conditions than those in North America. Aereboe writes, "In the pure pasturelands of Argentina, even grain is a luxury because people can produce meat much more cheaply there, especially meat from animals that can be raised solely on pasture without supplemental feed. Therefore, even pork is considered a luxury good there."

Those who want to understand sedentary pastoralists should take a look at the gauchos of the Argentine pampas and the cowboys of Texas. Also of particular relevance are the views that these people have toward property. While stealing is not only allowed for nomads, but a fundamental part of their existence, the honesty of the gauchos used to be proverbial. In Texas, for example, despite the fact that all kinds of riffraff gathered there, people ruthlessly dealt with horse thieves and protected themselves against thievery in general through the enacting of lynching laws.

Nomads, on the other hand, only have property and (most importantly) a sense of ownership only to the extent that they exclude other tribes from their grazing lands. In the nomadic imagination, ownership is merely a matter of grazing (of consumption). Their other possessions, such as huts or tents, clothing, weapons, tools, and jewelry, are exclusively the products of their own craftsmanship, as the owner has either made these things with his own hands or exchanged them for other handmade items. Thus, nomads always have movable property, while immovable property, like the word *besitz* (property) itself, which, of course, is related to *setzen* (place), is alien to their conceptual world. The settled person, on the other hand, absolutely retains his sense of immovable property even when he lives as a true pastoralist on the steppes. If one carefully observes sedentary pastoralists, one can see how their life of herding has made them tough men—think of the "Rough Riders" of Roosevelt—and yet, the characteristic cowardly banditry and predation of the nomads is nowhere to be found among them.

Similarly, a Nordic man who settles in tropical Brazil and who, because of the climate, can only clear the forests and farm with the help of slaves, can hardly be equated with an Arab who owns slaves due to his unfitness for work and a deep hatred of any kind of sedentary activity, simply because both happen to be slave owners. Here it should be quite obvious that one can arrive at disastrously erroneous conclusions if one only takes a surface-level look at the agricultural operations of a people or a race and then uses that to identify defining characteristics in order to make ethnological distinctions.

If those race researchers who see the Nordic race as a non-peasant, mobile master race are correct, then their academic conclusions should be reflected in the colonization and settlement of the Americas. Following their logic, this development and settlement would have unfolded in such a way that pure representatives of the Nordic race would have been the true developers of the country and trailblazers of the culture. Or, according to the above-mentioned "racial-psychological law," it would have been those "enterprising, adventurous, wanderlust-driven, conquering dolichocephalics." Behind these trailblazers and pioneers of the frontier, however, the "resilient, conserving brachycephalics" should have then acted as the actual "maintainers" and "protectors," that is, as the peasants responsible for tilling the land. In any case, if this hypothesis is correct, the "restless" Nordic component would be less or not at all present among the peasant population after the complete development of the country. The Nordic race would instead be found among the soldiers, frontier guard, and in the leadership of cities and state-owned enterprises—in short, wherever there is "something going on."

What is the reality? Well, it is just the opposite! In the United States, the Nordic race, in its purest expression, sits as a peasantry in the countryside, while the other races are mainly concentrated in the cities. This is exactly what Grant emphasizes in the seventh chapter of his book *The Passing of the Great Race*. This is as certain as the fact that in the eighteenth and early nineteenth centuries, Europe contributed its best Nordic blood to the United States, a selective process that would undoubtedly fill any advocate of "racial-psychological laws" with delight. It is equally just as certain that these daring men were driven not so much by adventure but by the desire to clear a piece of land through hard work and to become farmers (peasants) on their own soil.

Anyone who still doubts whether this is really Nordic blood in the United States should read the following excerpt from Stoddard's work, where he clearly states that "the old 'Native American' stock, favorably selected as it was from the races of northern Europe, is the most superior element in the American population" and that "subsequent immigrants from northern Europe, though coming from substantially the same racial stocks, were less favorably selected and average somewhat less superior." [61]

In studying the settlement of the United States, it is simply remarkable how thoroughly the Nordic race has almost exclusively formed the basic peasant element of the population. In fact, one can even observe that in areas where the climate permits clearing and settling by one's own physical labor, only the Nordic race seems to have possessed the necessary tenacity, foresight, and prudence to initiate settlement and see it through against all odds, especially in the face of challenges from Native Americans and scoundrels within their own ranks. Other races always seem to come later—and that is only after the primary clearing work has been done.

But you by no means have to stick just to the United States. The same could be demonstrated in former German Southwest Africa, as well as among the Boers in South Africa and later the settlers of Australia.

In the United States, one could even observe that the free Nordic settler looked down with contempt on the soldiers and officers of the frontier fortifications. He chided them as lazy. In fact, he more or less put them on the same level as the so-called frontier riffraff.

These are far from the only observations that can be made in the United States that do not fit the usual hypotheses regarding the Nordic race. Grant definitely did not write his book *The Passing of the Great Race* because Nordic Americans were bleeding themselves to death in wars, but because they were being "uprooted." It has become customary today to speak of denordification through wars. However, this claim, which can be legitimately doubted on the basis of German settlement history, does not even begin to apply to the United States—unless one wants to argue that Nordic blood was depleted in battles with the Indians. It is easy to provide clear counter-evidence for this very claim. The actual history of settlement in the United States begins more or less one hundred and fifty years ago, which means that it can be very closely followed and observed. Grant, therefore, in his study of the causes of denordification, comes to the same exact conclusions as Mielke[62] in his studies on early-historical settlement. Both researchers find that abandonment of peasant life was the real cause of the decline of the "Great Race," with wars only serving to accelerate this process of uprooting. The same conclusion, reached by two different researchers with different objects of study, should really give us something to think about!

It is nothing short of astonishing how, when we delve into honest literature dealing with the life and activities of the first North American settlers, a number of commonalities with the Icelandic sagas emerge again and again. The moment an environment challenges the Nordic race to fight in its ancient way, it appears before us in its old form as it was centuries ago. Thousands of years ago, it was the spear and sword that the peasant knew to keep by his side as he plowed the land, but now it is

[61] Stoddard, *The Revolt Against Civilization.*
[62] Mielke, *Die Siedlungskunde des Deutschen Volkes.*

the rifle and the broad knife that makes peaceful settlement possible. As recently as fifty years ago, there were still regions of the United States where settlers could not plow their soil without a rifle strapped to their shoulder. No wonder, then, that among the soldiers of the American military whom we met on the frontlines in 1918, we encountered warriors who were in no way inferior to those ancient Icelandic sea-farers who once sailed toward Thule. Equally remarkable, however, is the fact that the Nordic race also regains its traditional chivalry toward women amid the harsh life of the frontier.[63] At first, the lack of women may have been the actual cause for this, as well as the need to protect the women who were there with them, but, to give a counter-example, it would certainly be impossible to find a similar display of chivalry toward women among the Arabs, even if they were to experience a shortage of women.

Those in intellectual circles that wish to regard the Nordic race solely as a kind of warlike master race can convince themselves of the inaccuracy of their view by examining the example provided by the settlement of North America. It was the peasantry who set out from Germany, Scandinavia, England, Holland, and other places to settle America. The evidence shows that it was the finest Nordic blood that migrated there. This peasantry made their way over there without the leadership of the nobility or any other warrior caste. This racially Nordic peasantry transformed the United States of America from a wilderness into a global empire within a few generations—barely one hundred and fifty years (compare that to antiquity!). Quite simply, this North American peasantry bears a quite striking resemblance to the German nobility of the Middle Ages who colonized Prussia under the Teutonic Cross.

Treitschke writes the following regarding the Teutonic Order of Knights:

> It was only because the Order was constantly replenished from the ranks of the German nobility that it possessed a multitude of great talents. Countless masterful swordsmen flocked to it—among them were those whose success was limited by the expanding power of princes and cities, those profound souls filled with religious fervor, as well as those men of daring ambition, without retainers, who still dared to hope to rise from the lower nobility to the princely throne. [64]

---

[63] We are referring to the chivalry of the old frontier families in early America, which has nothing to do with the modern "girl frenzy" in American cities. When assessing such questions, Germans tend to overlook the often rapid development of American cities, which mostly absorbed the dregs of the European population and created racial chaos of the worst kind. In 1789, for example, the clearing of land on the site of present-day Cincinnati began. By 1802, the city had only 950 inhabitants. By 1830, it had already grown to 24,831—today it has about 300,000 inhabitants. American cities are now in the process of swallowing up the surrounding countryside and "denordifying" it, even in moral terms.

[64] Heinrich Gotthard von Treitschke, *Das Ordensland Preußen* [The Order-State of Prussia] (Insel-Bücherei), 182.

One should look into the reasons that led the peasants to emigrate to America in the eighteenth and nineteenth centuries. They are the same reasons that Treitschke ascribes to the German nobility in the Teutonic Order, namely, to escape the oppressive confinement of their homeland into a freer atmosphere where the merit of one's ability and resourcefulness was rewarded. To be lord on one's own land or in one's own enterprise, these are the driving forces that compel the Nordic race to emigrate. It has nothing, absolutely nothing, to do with nomadism, and one must have very little understanding of the fundamental nature of nomadism to confuse the striving of Nordic man toward independence with the itinerant, rootless instincts inherent in the blood of nomadic races.

It would be fascinating to use genealogical research to determine the origins of today's leading Nordic family lineages in the United States. The author has attempted to achieve some sort of understanding in this area, but has failed for the time being due to the confusing nature of the material and its mostly inadequate treatment so far. Despite this, the author wishes to share his impressions, if only as suggestions. Without in any way wanting to claim any degree of scientific certainty in this judgment, it does seems possible to assert that the peasantry of northwestern Germany and the Netherlands primarily provided the "raw material" for the leading family lines of the United States today. The often overlooked peasants of the Palatinate region seem to come in second place, and actual Anglo-Saxons in third.[65] In the United States, there is currently an emphasis on emphasizing Anglo-Saxon ancestry, an attempt that would hardly withstand rigorous scrutiny. In any case, one is always amazed to discover that people with seemingly "authentically English" names, such as Ford, Upman, and others, are quite certainly descended from Low German peasant family lines.

Even more astonishing, however, is another fact that also deserves mention at this point. Every victorious country has a habit of spreading some of its peculiarities throughout the world as "fashion." Thus, thanks to the victory of the United States in the last war, we have, among other things, "knickerbockers" here in Germany, a style of sports pants. However, few people will know that these knickerbockers were a type of clothing worn by the kings of Wall Street, especially the old-established patrician families of New York. The name "knickerbockers" is said to be derived from Diedrich Knickerbocker, the alleged author of Washington Irving's *History of New York*, in which he humorously portrays an archetype of Dutch immigrants and peasant settlers in New York.[66] The latter wore loose knee breeches and tenaciously clung to this style of dress. As the old Dutch settlers in New York kept their blood very pure and,

---

[65] The actual emigration of Anglo-Saxon peasants from England to the United States of America did not begin until about 1820; we will discuss this more in chapter three. In the sixteenth century, a westward migration of peasants did begin in England, but initially occured in such a way that the primarily Nordic peasants began to displace the Celts, forcing the latter to emigrate. The main emigration from the United Kingdom itself, however, did not begin until the mid-eighteenth century, when large-scale land-holdings in England began to expand.

[66] New Amsterdam, the origin of present-day New York, was founded in 1612.

as New York developed, increasingly formed a distinct and true patriciate, their old derisive nickname "knickerbocker," based on their pants, slowly became an honorific. The old style of dress of the first Dutch peasants in New York has now become the iconic attire of the princes of the dollar.

The German nobility in the white cloak with the black cross and the simple Nordic-German peasant masses who built the United States are blood of the same blood, branches of the same tree. The history of settlement in the United States should be used much more than it currently is to understand the formation of states in the ancient Mediterranean.

Those who wish to disassociate the Nordic race from authentic, hardworking peasanthood simply overlook its settlement history over the last two centuries. In this context, a comment made by Riehl[67] half a century ago should be quoted verbatim,

> Even to the eye of the naturalist, the genuine German peasant is the historical archetype of German humanity. Nevertheless, the physical characteristics of peasants differ according to social class and region. In one region, we find a rather long-legged, tall figure, while in another we find a rather broad-shouldered, stocky type of humanity. These features have been handed down through the centuries unadulterated. Thus, in certain areas of Hesse, for example, one can still almost exclusively find those elongated facial profiles with a high forehead that widens slightly upward, a long straight nose, and small eyes with strongly arched eyebrows and large eyelids. These features were immortalized by the genre painter Jakob Becker and his numerous disciples, dispayed as standing figures in the popular painted village scenes of these artists. If one compares these peasant faces with the sculptures found in St. Elizabeth's Church in Marburg (built in the thirteenth century), one will discover that the same old Hessian facial type has remained unchanged for almost six hundred years, with the only difference being that the sculpted heads in these works of art belong to princes, lords, and noblewomen, whose features show the unadulterated characteristics of their lineage. Today, these same features can only be found among the country's peasants. If anyone wants to draw historically authentic medieval figures, all they have to do is use peasants as their models. This quite naturally explains why the old German artists, who worked in a time when people generally tended to think and create with far less conformity than in our days, gave heads in their works such a typical and uniform treatment—the race as a whole had not yet developed more individualized facial features.

---

[67] Wilhelm Heinrich Riehl, *Vom Deutschen Land und Volke* [From the German Land and People], ed. Paul Zaunert (Jena: 1922).

It should be noted that Riehl made his observations around the middle of the previous century. During his time, there was not yet a description of race as precise as we have today. Therefore, it would be pointless to scrutinize his words too closely in an attempt to determine whether there might perhaps be any "Phalian" features among the Hessian peasants he described. Those who are familiar with the old-established Schwalm peasants, likely the ones Riehl was referring to, also know that they are Nordic, not Phalian. The most important point in Riehl's observations is the fact that this keen observer noticed the resemblance in appearance between medieval nobility and your average present-day Hessian peasants—he even considered these peasants to be the epitome of medieval man. Unaware of the notion of "denordification," Riehl therefore came to the sincere conclusion that the nobility in the Middle Ages was simply more natural, that is, more uniform and similar to the contemporary peasantry. As Riehl saw it, the development of the nobility diverged from that of the peasantry over the course of the centuries.

3

Colonus means peasant. *Kultur* refers to agriculture, cultivation of the land, and care of plants. Only on a secondary level does it mean the development of man's natural predispositions, particularly in terms of his intellectual gifts. All throughout history, only the peasant has ever been able to colonize and spread *kultur* in its truest and most genuine sense. The nomad can merely spread *zivilisation*, which, of course, originally meant nothing more than the purely superficial affiliation of a citizen to a community.[68] But regardless of who we are discussing, it has never been possible to cultivate virgin land or maintain cultivated land in a troubled region without the sword. The word "Tannenberg" should, in fact, reveal the relationship between the plow and the sword sufficiently.

If race scientists today want to adopt the viewpoint that it was Nordic blood that gave birth to the individual civilizations of ancient history, and that this blood is still among us today, active and creative, then these same race scientists should hardly be able to object to us concluding that the behavior of the Nordic race in the settlement of North America sheds light on the darkness of European prehistory and quite clearly demonstrates that Nordic man must have been a peasant and a settler—never a nomad.

Have those who would like to separate the Nordic race from the peasantry completely forgotten the tremendous struggles for freedom waged by the Ditmarsians, Swiss, Tyroleans, and others, just to name a few examples? After all, these peasants simply wanted nothing more than to defend their peasantry—they had absolutely no intention of invading and conquering other lands in a "restless,

---

[68] Editor's note: The German words *kultur* and *zivilisation*, while cognates with the English words culture and civilization, respectively, have substantially different implications to their English counterparts in anthropological and sociological contexts. *Zivilisation* refers primarily to the superficial trappings of civilization, while *kultur* refers to the deeper intellectual, moral, and artistic elements of civilization—the "being" and national character of the German.

mobile, or warlike" manner. And yet, these peasants were adept at wielding the sword, as experience has shown. Riehl writes,

> But may it not be forgotten that it was the most capable farming communities, the true exemplars of the German peasantry (such as the classic Westphalian *hofbauern*),[69] that were the freest of their kind during the Middle Ages. At that time, they stood as imperial patricians over the other peasants, had a free municipal constitution regulated according to ancient custom, their own jurisdiction, and paid moderate taxes. And these successful peasants, who have been free since time immemorial, are quite conservative in appearance and are essentially the archetypes of historical German peasants. They serve as a testament to what our peasant class could have become if it had been granted free and independent development everywhere. One example of this is in Prussia. There, the Teutonic Order passed the so-called "Kulm Law," creating a free class of peasants, something that was entirely unknown in other parts of Germany. The descendants of these fortunate peasants, who have distinguished themselves through to our present day under the names of "Kölmer" or "Prussian Freemen," were for centuries the epitome of capable and traditional peasant stock. The heroes of German peasant history, the Stedingers and Ditmarsians, were free peasants who fought and died for their freedoms and ancient rights. With them, the characteristic peasant defiance heightened into heroism. In the lands they inhabited, a highly capable and staunchly perservering type of peasant still exists even to this day.

Arnold Winkelried is an example of peasanthood,[70] and the many Scharnhorsts[71] and Henniges von Treffenfelds[72] found in German history do not exactly indicate that the Nordic race has ever separated sword from plow. From President Kruger (Uncle Paul) in Transvaal, who hailed from German peasant blood,[73] to the

---

[69] Editor's note: In Medieval Germany, the *hofbauern* were free and successful peasants who owned medium- or large-sized farms. While they had more rights and liberties than standard peasants, they also had more duties and obligations to their lord.

[70] Editor's note: Arnold Winkelried was a Swiss peasant who sacrificed himself at the 1386 Battle of Sempach, fought between the nascent Swiss Confederacy and Austrian Habsburg forces. Tradition states that in the midst of the battle, Arnold grabbed a bundle of Habsburg pikes and impaled himself, opening a breach that permitted the Swiss to emerge victorious. The battle is considered a key event in the development of the Swiss nation and identity.

[71] Editor's note: Gerhard von Scharnhorst was a Hannoverian peasant that rose to the rank of lieutenant-general in the Prussian army and played a key role in both the Prussian resistance to Napoleon and Prussia's military modernization reforms.

[72] Editor's note: Joachim Henniges von Treffenfeld was a Brandenburgian peasant who was regarded as a war hero for his exploits in the 1672 Franco-Dutch War and 1675 Scanian War.

[73] Editor's note: J. Paulus Kruger was a South African Boer leader of peasant ancestry. He staunchly defended Boer independence against the encroaching British Empire, leading the Boer nation during the Second Boer War. Following the British victory, he fled into exile, where he died. He is the subject of the 1941 German film *Ohm Krüger* [Oh, Krüger].

"werewolves" described by Löns,[74] down to the famous *bauerntreck* (peasant trek) of the Cimbri and Teutons, the Nordic-German peasantry has always demonstrated its ability to wield both the plow and sword. The Cimbri and Teutons, both noble peasant peoples whose love of swordsmanship the Romans clearly felt, in fact perished during their migration in search of farmland. After the Battle of Arausio, Italy lay open to the Cimbri and Teutons, but they did not exploit their advantage and did not place their foot on the neck of defenseless Rome. Instead, they renounced conquest and preferred to acquire the land diplomatically—through good will with the Romans instead of their swords. Based on this example alone, anyone familiar with colonial history and the purposeful, predatory nature of warlike nomadic peoples would find it simply impossible to ascribe any bit of nomadic blood to the Germanic Cimbri and Teutons tribes, whose behavior was distinctly un-nomadic, particularly for their time.

One should indeed be a little more cautious when making hasty judgments about the belligerence of the Nordic German nobility and the peaceful languidness of the German peasant, allegedly of different racial blood. In any case, the Brandenburgian peasants under the Great Elector[75] showed far less torpidity and far more pride and martial enthusiasm than the high-noble and high-born Rhein dynasty in 1802. Regarding the latter, Treitschke writes, "In the frenzy of fear, all pride and shame were lost." He continues with biting sarcasm, "Like a swarm of hungry flies, Germany's high nobility pounced on the bloody wounds of their fatherland. The high-born opponents of the revolution begged for the grace of Talleyrand, courted his mistress, lovingly carried his lapdog in their arms, and zealously ascended to the small garret where his assistant Matthieu resided."[76] These are not the only examples from German history that can be juxtaposed in such a manner.

Of course, an unanswered question remains: what has triggered the many waves of Nordic peoples that the world has witnessed for millennia? Today, many are quick to provide explanations such as the presence of nomadic blood (a view on which we have already expressed ourselves sufficiently), Nordic expansionism, the spirit of the Vikings, an innate sense of heroism, and so on. However, these explanations do not touch upon the most important aspect of the whole question. In fact, this core aspect can be easily understood by examining the settlement history of Germany, which I will briefly outline. One will be able to recognize that thus far, cause and effect have apparently been confused.

In any case, it is certain that the key to understanding the expansion of the Nordic race after the Migration Period lies with the Germanic people. Our

---

[74] Hermann Löns wrote *Der Wehrwolf* in 1910. The book follows a band of peasant guerrillas that viciously defend their communities from marauders and plunderers during the Thirty Years War. It may have been the inspiration for Operation Werwolf, which attempted to organize a guerrilla resistance to the Allied occupation in 1944.
[75] "The Great Elector" refers to Frederick William of the Hohenzollern dynasty. The Elector of Brandenburg and Duke of Prussia from 1640 until his death in 1688, he greatly developed the duchy through his political, economic, and military achievements.
[76] Treitschke, *Deutsche Geschichte im Neunzehnten Jahrhundert*.

German civilization is built entirely on a Germanic foundation. Given that the Germanic people have always been regarded as representatives of the Nordic race in its purest form, the Nordic Movement emerged in response to the accelerating decline of German civilization. Influenced by Günther's work, the movement's aim is to restore our civilization to its ancient Germanic foundation. However, it has since been suggested that the Germanic people consisted of two races. Kern (*Artbild der Deutschen*) attempts to defend the idea of two races within Germandom (*Germanentum*) with the following explanation on pages 203–204:

> Alongside the peasant masses, founded on a fair and peaceful village structure, the various Indo-European peoples enter history with a wealthy landowning nobility and its dependents. The nobility engages in annual feuds; they maintain and employ a retinue to secure their possessions and maintain their power. They invest the earnings from serf labor in the maintenance of men who will, in turn, earn them new income. . . . Thus, in the ancient lordly culture, if a generous noble did not want his authority to be torn to shreds, he was compelled to engage in warlike activities with the assets he possessed that yielded him profit.

Kern's explanation ultimately leads to his view that this society is divided between the nobility, of nomadic Nordic race, and the serfs, who he mainly suspects belongs to the Phalian race.

Firstly, Kern's explanation suffers from the fact that it is not quite clear what he actually means by "peasantry." When Kern, for example, speaks of the "bone-breaking" work of plowing and sees this in particular as the main proof for excluding the Nordic race from the peasantry, it is hard for a farmer not to amusingly smile at such opinions on agricultural work. However, what is actually even worse is what K. F. Wolff does in his discussions on the peasantry.[77] Plowing, like any manual skill, gets easier with practice and once you have learned the "ins and outs" of it—a task that is certainly no challenge whatsoever for any country boy—it is rather difficult to see where the "bone-breaking" aspect comes into play. Exceptional or particularly austere times in which the peasant does not have any draft animals at his disposal cannot be made the basis for cultural-historical considerations.

Furthermore, Kern's two-race arrangement for the Germanic people is entirely ahistorical, at least with regard to the role he assigns to the Germanic nobility. We will return to this point later.

4

However, before attempting to gain an understanding of the Germanic people and their relationship to agriculture, let us first briefly discuss German settle-

---

[77] Wolff, *Rassenlehre*.

ment history, from which we can draw very important conclusions about the Germanic people.

When the Germanic tribes destroyed the Roman Empire, they found a population within its borders that, in spiritual terms, was utterly decayed and had been totally degenerated under the rule of a financialized system centralized in Rome. In this civilizational swamp, Christianity held an officially recognized position but was neither inwardly nor outwardly capable of addressing or overcoming the rot. What is noteworthy for us is the fact that within this Roman Empire, the total destruction of the peasantry had already taken place. Only large slave-holding estates existed. This was the moral chaos that the Germanic peoples had burst into. They came as peasants—not as semi-nomadic warrior-pastoralist groups with peasant attendants, an arrangement that has never been seen in terms of settlement history. The Germanic tribes ruthlessly cleared away the existing disorder and bestowed upon the Latin lands a new peasant class. This Germanic peasant class served as the lifeblood of the Roman lands for a millennium, all to the detriment of the Germanic motherland, Germany.

To the extent that Germanic law has survived, it is based exclusively on the peasantry and appeals to a peasant way of thinking. There is no evidence of any laws that make exceptions or accommodations for a nomadic nobility. The Germanic peoples, upon entering world history, appear fundamentally different from any nomads known to us thus far. In the future, when describing the racial make-up of the Germanic peoples, it will be advisable to not overlook their finely elaborated land law, nor attempt to whitewash the warlike nature of the nomads to such an extent that it no longer corresponds to reality.

We have become accustomed to concluding the so-called Migration Period with the formation of the Frankish kingdoms. This historical division is obviously arbitrary, if one keeps the later settlement history of the Germanic peoples in mind. The ensuing calm of this period is actually only illusory. If one delves beneath the seemingly tranquil surface into the life of the Germanic tribes after the formation of the Frankish kingdoms, it becomes evident that the unrest previously manifested externally had been replaced by industrious activity internally. Clearing and cultivating new land is taking place everywhere, providing an extensive field of activity for the surplus Germanic population. As these new settlements gradually fill up with people, the surplus population once again flows outwards, beyond its borders. Soon, the migration eastward begins, kicking off a glorious chapter of our history (the reconquest of ancient Germanic soil) that will always be a source of pride for all Germanic classes and tribes. The chapter comes to a close when this eastern settlement activity unintentionally comes to a halt (Tannenberg 1410!) and the Holy Roman Empire fails to or, rather, is unable to revive the colonization of the east due to powerlessness. To fully understand the end of this chapter, one must delve quite far back into history. The Germanic peoples originally organized around land cooperatives (*markgenossenschaften*) of free peasants.[78] Feudalism's emergence in the tenth and eleventh centuries interspersed a different a kind of land ownership in with the old land cooperatives. These large landowners, who probably corresponded to the dynastic nobility of the Middle Ages, granted land to serfs, eventually succeeding in bringing even the free peasants under their control. It is still not entirely clear how this development began or how it was carried out—it appears more or less out of nowhere as a given fact.

Since the surplus Germanic population could no longer be accommodated in the east and, simultaneously, a partial transformation of the free peasantry into unfree serfs was spreading rapidly within the Holy Roman Empire, both pressures converged and slowly but surely pushed the Empire toward disaster. In the Peasants' War, the old sense of freedom inherent to the Germanic people attempted to make space for itself forcefully once again. The result is of course well known, but it must also be emphasized that people have not given enough attention to these Peasants' Wars so far. One could also consider these sixteenth century peasant uprisings, whose religious or spiritual motives need not concern us here, as a cautionary example for the present-day German people—for the "*volk ohne raum*" (people without space).[79] In reality, however, this danger does not exist, because the rural inheritance laws within our BGB[80] contain arrangements that will effectively throttle any overpopulation of the peasant class.[81] In fact, the Germanic peasant class of Germany may soon be a thing of the past. In this respect, many people are blind to the fact that while a few ancient rural communities maintain closed inheritance customs, closed inheritance customs (*anerbensitte*) are not synonymous with closed inheritance law (*anerbenrecht*), and this distinction cannot be emphasized strongly enough. To prevent any misunderstandings and to counter the widespread mistaken beliefs about this issue, let me quote Dade word for word:

> Only closed inheritance guarantees that the peasant farm remains both at a productive operational size and within the same family, thus preserving a population class that can serve as the foundation of the

---

[78] Translator's note: A *markgenossenschaft* (from: *mark*, meaning borderlands, and genossenschaft, meaning cooperative) was a type of local association in rural areas with a shared economic and legal system, underpinned by a sense of common ownership of agricultural land, the "mark." This use of the word mark is related to the original English meaning of mark, meaning a boundary, frontier, or limit. As a cooperative, its land and assets is jointly managed by all of its members, not by a single landlord as was common in the Middle Ages. These associations typically had their own assemblies and courts and reflects the independence and communal-peasant heritage of the Germanic peoples. It is translated as "land cooperative" in this text.

[79] Editor's note: "*Volk ohne Raum*," literally "people without space," was coined by Hans Grimm in his novel of the same name, published in 1926. It struck a cord with the German public and became a popular nationalist slogan during the Weimar Republic and continued to be popular in the National Socialist era. It was connected with the desire of National Socialist leaders to acquire *lebensraum* (living space) for their nation.

[80] Editor's note: The *Bürgerliches Gesetzbuch*, known simply as the BGB or the German Civil Code, is the central codification of German private law. The BGB regulates the legal relationships between private individuals and is thus distinct from "public law."

[81] Darré, "Innere Kolonisation."

entire state structure. This societal foundation would enable the transmission of traditions, customs, and practices from one generation to another on family farms, maintaining cultural persistency in a large segment of the population and serving as a healthy counterbalance to the modern tendency of destroying and eroding the old social structures and traditions, particularly in the face of the incoming tide of urban and industrial populations. This was the reason why the majority of agricultural associations in Germany in the 1880s and 1890s demanded that the Civil Code codify closed inheritance law for all peasant property. It did not happen. Rather, in accordance with Roman legal principles, no distinction was made in the Civil Code between the bequeathing of movable and immovable assets. Therefore, it is no longer possible, not even through state legislation, to introduce a legally-codified closed inheritance law whereby the peasant farm is in all cases inherited in a closed manner upon the death of the farmer. Although Article 59 of the Introductory Act to the Civil Code affirms that state laws on family fideicommissum, feudal tenures, and hereditary estates remain unchanged,[82] and Article 62 similarly states that state-level closed inheritance laws remain unchanged, the articles also state that the testator can no longer be deprived of the authority to divide the farm through a will or voluntary determination. Accordingly, state legislation can only introduce closed inheritance law in cases related to intestate succession, where the state can implement closed inheritance in the event that the owner or testator does not have a will or has not made any other disposition. But even within these restrictions, previous efforts by Prussia to provide a legal foundation for closed inheritance have failed. While the Prussian province of Westphalia (and some adjacent districts of Prussia's Rhine province) were able to codify closed inheritance law through the Law of July 2, 1898, this law came with the caveat that ancestral property was passed down to an heir (the *anerbe*) only "in the absence of a contrary testamentary provision." Undivided inheritance remains a legal obligation only in the federal states where state legislation has secured peasant property through fideicommissum-like institutions. This is the case with hereditary estates in Bavaria, Hesse, and Mecklenburg, as well as with hereditary estates or farm estates in the Kingdom of Saxony, Baden, and some smaller federal states.[83]

Accordingly, the closed inheritance of peasant property is nowadays largely based on custom and precedent. The tenacity with which, in vast areas of German agriculture, the peasant class has held onto this custom from generation to generation (up to the

---

[82] This is no longer true.
[83] The reader must not forget that Dade wrote these words before November 9, 1918. Since then, these laws have already been partially repealed, and the whole issue is in flux, albeit rarely in a favorable direction for the German peasantry.

present day) is worthy of the highest admiration. In fact, approximately five sixths of agricultural land in Germany is still inherited in a closed manner. While large estates easily change hands like speculative goods without the support of fideicommissum or *majorat*-style inheritance, closed inheritance has persisted in many peasant properties of different economic strata thanks to their own efforts and deeply-held customs. Without the support of law, these farms have remained within the same family for generations and centuries, up to the present day. [84]

That's it for Dade! However, the author must add to the above that since 1918, the circumstances have changed rather significantly. The preservation of the closed inheritance of farms by the peasantry is only partially achieved by having fewer children. If there is only one heir, there are simply no inheritance disputes. Biologically speaking, this approach is as destructive to the peasantry as the abolition of closed inheritance law itself. However, we will discuss these matters in the final chapter.

The Germanic peasantry recovered surprisingly quickly from the bloodletting of the sixteenth century Peasants' War and the seventeenth century Thirty Years' War. While Russia had already absorbed many of the peasant settlements in the east, new developments in maritime navigation now allowed for the settlement of newly discovered parts of the world. As a result, the surplus population of the Germanic countries flowed across the world in enormous numbers. It has been quite rightly stated that the Germanization of the world in the eighteenth and nineteenth centuries far eclipsed the original Migration Period of the Germanic peoples. Therefore, those who argue that, even today, the Germanic Migration Period has not reached a conclusion are not entirely wrong. The form of migration has indeed changed, but not its essence. And now once again the old fateful reckoning of a "*volk ohne raum*" looms threateningly on the German's horizon.

It was not until the nineteenth century that some new reasons emerged for the migration of peasants—the effects of this in Germany will be briefly outlined below. In East Elbia, the so-called Stein-Hardenberg reforms did not bring about peasant emancipation and only resulted in the uprooting of peasant communities. While the reforms freed the peasants from feudal burdens, they exposed the peasantry to the merciless predations of the financial powers. Reichsfreiherr vom Stein is not necessarily to blame for this; firstly, the idea of peasant emancipation was an age-old favorite of the Hohenzollerns, and Stein only carried out what the Hohenzollerns had long been striving for, and secondly, Stein relied on research into English history as well as his experiences as chamber president of the County of Mark in Westphalia, where the old communal freedoms of the peasants remained preserved. Unfortunately, his successors did not consistently car-

---

[84] Dade, *Arbeitsziele der Deutschen.*

ry out the development he had initiated and are responsible for most of the damage done to the peasantry in the nineteenth century. The financial powers remained in control of the situation. Soon, in the German Empire, wherever the German language resounded, that callous process of uprooting and the destruction of ancient, old-established peasant family lines progressed; future generations will likely view this as the darkest point in German history. Like a vampire, usury wreaked havoc among the peasants in some rural areas. Disaster was only averted when the rural population, in their despair, rallied and broke the tyranny of the rootless financial powers by establishing the rural cooperative system. These facts are indisputable, in all their horrifying reality. For this reason, among others, the best German peasant blood was driven across the pond in droves during the first half of the nineteenth century. However, such conditions affected different German peasant regions in very different ways. In areas where the ancient German—we might as well say Germanic—custom of closed inheritance could be enshrined into law, and where the mortgaging of farms was thus made more difficult (for that is the crux of the matter), the financial powers could not easily exert their influence. It is quite significant that the very regions of Germany where the custom of closed inheritance has persisted the longest are also considered by race science to have the most purely Nordic population, even today.

Perhaps the conditions described here would not have had such devastating effects if it were not for the industrial boom that occurred with the founding of the German Empire in 1871, which, it goes without saying, many of us personally witnessed. Industry's demand for workers relentlessly sucked the rural labor force away from the countryside. Small-scale peasants and large estates were the least affected by this phenomenon. The former could usually operate without laborers or relied on family members, while the latter, although unable to replace the quality of the departed rural workers, could at least compensate with regards to quantity by employing migrant workers. However, the situation was completely different for large-scale farmer and smallholders, many of which could still be found on ancient inherited land and came from ancient German peasant family lines that continued to clearly exhibit ancient Nordic physical traits. This type of owner is always in the greatest predicament due to a shortage of workers or the presence of subpar workers. Their operations are often not large enough to employ supervisors to oversee unreliable workers, but are also too large for the owner to handle all the necessary tasks alone. The ownership of such a farm then either becomes a wretched burden or a nerve-wracking struggle with unreliable workers. In that case, if market conditions also deteriorate (meaning the farming operation is not profitable), the owner or their son may become disheartened with the whole affair and decide to sell the farm, seeking an easier livelihood in the city. This development can be observed quite clearly today in countries like Sweden and Finland, for example, as they are only now beginning to experience an industrial boom. Furthermore, it is perhaps the only scenario where long-established peasant lineages willingly relinquish a property that has been handed down since ancient times. Aside from the direct impact of industrial growth, industry in Germany has also had an indirect effect that has been destructive to the peasant class. This is true wherever the massive growth of individual cities, as well as of mining and industrial facilities, have downright forced peasants to abandon their old inherited land.[85] Germany's 1871 to 1914 industrial boom sacrificed hecatombs of peasant lineages—it can make a biologist's hair stand on end to witness this mass suicide be hailed as "progress."

Thus, since the founding of the German Empire, for economic reasons, a significant percentage of our finest Nordic blood has been driven away from the countryside and into the infertility machine known as the city. Of course, it is clear that it is precisely Nordic blood that seeks out a certain noble independence (even within the peasantry) and is therefore most inclined to abandon the drudgery of a farm without workers and seek employment in a city where he can utilize his intellectual aptitude to its maximum potential and establish a more independent life for himself. It is possible that in addition to this independence-seeking impulse, nomadic tendencies have also pressured Nordic blood into leaving farms that have been in families for centuries, but those who advocate for this as the primary motive must first provide evidence. If one lacks clears evidence yet still believes that the most devastating destruction of our Germanic peasantry ever witnessed in German history can be sufficiently explained away by references to "Nordic expansion into the distance," or even to nomadism, then history may hold him responsible for distorting the harshest period of adversity the Nordic race has ever faced—or even for making it out to be some kind of nomadic virtue. Furthermore, one may also be burdened with the guilt of diverting the public's attention from the roots of the real evil.

In examining these questions, one must not forget that certain intellectual currents, let us just call them fashion trends, have played an equal part in the peasant population's migration to the city. In the previous age, with its ignorant affirmation of purely physical and materialistic views of life, it was considered a sign of "enlightenment" for the person of "reason" to break with old family traditions, give away or sell the family's hereditary property, and participate in the general pursuit of money. As late as the middle of the previous century, almost every educated person came from the countryside or was at least familiar with rural life—in pictures from around 1870, many present-day cities still resembled villages. By contrast, even before the World War, the wealthy sons of landed gentry that studied agriculture in Halle were ashamed to have "stud. agr." printed on their visiting cards. Others preferred to serve a few years in the military and then be addressed by their achieved rank on their home estate for the rest of their lives, as if they wanted to prove that they were valuable to society in something other than agriculture. This generation had lost all pride in its farming profession (in being a peasant). By contrast, Bismarck remained

---

[85] Kerckerinck zur Borg, *Beiträge zur Geschichte.*

devoted to it completely, heart and soul, and Frederick the Great always gave it his chief attention, once stating, "Agriculture is the foremost of all arts. Without it, there would be no merchants, poets, or philosophers."

The idea of separating oneself from rural life was originally so absolutely alien to the Germanic peoples that the founding of cities north of the Alps nearly failed because of this fact. One had to resort to the dangerous — and at that time deeply hated — measure of granting freedom to all serfs who were willing or able to move to the city. The phrase "city air makes you free" emerged during that time. In order to obtain a patriciate (a ruling class) for this confused urban population, medieval rulers often simply designated every tenth free person by lot. Note the contrast between the Nordic nobility of the Germanic peoples, who did not want to be brought into the city, and the Moors, who regarded any rural population as fundamentally oppositional to them (see the etymological explanation of the word Berber in chapter one). Unlike all nomads, who seem unaffected by centuries of residence in cities (Kremlin, Seraglio, Moorish palaces, etc.), the Nordic race has never been able to survive as an urban ruling class for very long. For example, the Bismarcks, originally a noble urban dynasty from Stendal, owe their present prosperity solely to the uprising of the guilds in Stendal and the fact that they were expelled from Stendal as a result. They subsequently retired to a country estate and continued to live as landed gentry. The Bismarcks are by no means the only medieval urban dynasty to have survived by transplanting themselves to the countryside. This chapter, which has given us a brief survey of nomadic and Nordic settlement history, and which was intended to serve as a bridge to the actual study of the peasant civilization of the Nordic race, can therefore be concluded in no better way than with the following words of Wilhelm Heinrich Riehl: "The history of ancient Germanic civilization physically extends into the modern world through the peasant class alone. To study peasant conditions is to study history; the customs of the peasants are a living archive, a historical sourcebook of inestimable value."

III

The Germanic Peoples and Agriculture

I

In the previous chapter, we established that the Germanization of the world in recent centuries is only a small part of the settlement history of the Germanic peasantry. The question now arises as to the racial classification of the Germanic peoples and their level of agricultural development when they entered world history. Nomads have always considered it beneath their status to learn agriculture from a subjugated population. As such, it should be possible to deduce quite clearly and unambiguously from the Germanic peoples' relationship to agriculture whether or not we can justifiably suspect them of being nomadic. This means that the agricultural practices of the Germanic peoples are much more than a cultural phenomenon that might interest a cultural researcher, they also hold significance for a racial researcher. In fact, agriculture is nothing short of the key to clarifying the racial situation of the Germanic peoples. Of course, no one today doubts that the Germanic peoples practiced agriculture per se. What is disputed, however, is how important it was to them. But if it is impossible to understand the racial circumstances of the Germanic peoples without first understanding their agricultural circumstances, then we cannot help but investigate whether the Germanic peoples were directly or indirectly involved in agriculture. In other words, whether the Germanic peoples worked the land themselves or simply had others work it for them. Of course, the author has already taken a very clear position on this issue in the previous chapter, in the discussion regarding Germanic land rights. Here, however, it may still be worthwhile to try to establish certain agricultural facts about the Germanic peoples that can be used as indirect evidence (circumstantial evidence) to then clearly determine the place of agriculture within Germanic society. As an agriculturalist, the author is not very interested in what forms of agriculture were developed by the Germanic peoples—far more important to him is whether agriculture can be established as the natural foundation of Germanic life, or whether it was merely a secondary task that could be left to serfs.

But before we delve deeper into the agricultural practices of the ancient Germanic peoples, it is still worth addressing the alleged nomadism of the Germanic peoples during their first encounters with the Romans. E. M. Arndt writes,

> Such annual rotations and exchanges of fields as described by Caesar is inconceivable under normal circumstances. It also appears impossible when considering the climate and natural characteristics of a land rich in rivers, streams, lakes, swamps, marshes, and forests. Imagine how foolishly crude it would be to plow and cultivate new fields every year, and so on. [86]

Professor Fleischmann (Göttingen), today one of the most knowledgeable experts in the history of ancient Germanic agriculture, provides just as clear a stance on the matter:

> And finally, regarding the wandering itself—believing that, year after year, the Germanic peoples roamed the land with women and children, harvested crops, households, and farming tools (in short, with all their movable possessions) in areas that, at that time, were still predominantly covered with swamps and primeval forests—let anyone believe that who can. [87]

In more recent times, the view that the Germanic peoples were nomads primarily goes back to Meitzen.[88] Meitzen goes to considerable lengths to support his claim of Germanic nomadism with "convincing" reasoning. Nevertheless, his assumption is completely baseless. After providing a detailed exposition, Fleischmann dismisses Meitzen's argument as follows:

---

[86] Arndt, "Einige Leichte Bemerkungen."

[87] Wilhelm Fleischmann, *Cäsar, Tacitus, Karl der Große und die Deutsche Landwirtschaft* [Caesar, Tacitus, Charlemagne, and German Agriculture] (Berlin: 1911).

[88] Meitzen, *Siedelung und Agrarwesen.*

Kern, by the way, explicitly refers to this book by Meitzen on page 203 of his work, and in connection with it says the following about the Germanic nobility, which he in turn believes must be assumed for the Indo-Europeans as well, "Alongside the peasant masses, founded on a fair and peaceful village structure, the various Indo-European peoples enter history with a wealthy landowning nobility and its dependents. The nobility engages in annual feuds; they maintain and employ a retinue to secure their possessions and maintain their power. They invest the earnings from serf labor in the maintenance of men who will, in turn, earn them new income. The lord who does not convert his wealth into labor with the sword is a poor economist, a poor lord of his retinue, and a poor politician at the same time. The dormant capital of the little lord is his undoing, for it belongs to the lord who knows how to turn it into martial power. Thus, in the ancient lordly culture, if a generous noble did not want his authority to be torn to shreds, he was compelled to engage in warlike activities with the assets he possessed that yielded him profit, in order to prevent them from remaining unused." We cannot deny that the position of the Germanic and Indo-European nobility within their respective peoples as theorized by Meitzen aligns quite well with the financially-oriented thinking of many inidividuals today. However, his analysis fundamentally and thoroughly misses the essence of the Germanic nobility, this will become more evident as we progress through this chapter.

So much for Meitzen's presentation. Imagination is undoubtedly indispensable to guide the progress of your research, but it must not wander unrestrained into the immeasurable. . . . Nomads, otherwise only found in oases and sparsely populated steppes, are transplanted into the forested and swampy regions of Germania, which, according to Meitzen, was relatively densely populated. The transition from nomadism to permanent settlement is said to have taken place in less than a hundred years. To explain this rapid transformation, it is suggested that the common freemen had come to the conviction that it was now high time for them to finally settle down. Regarding this and many other things in Meitzen's work—that which is based on itself awakens the thirst for fresh water from the sparsely flowing springs.

It will perhaps be easier for an agronomist to arrive at a clear judgment about the agricultural conditions of the Germanic peoples. Even so, Kern, with his two-race theory mentioned in the previous chapter, has completely undermined the foundation of all previous research into this matter. This was surely not his intention at all. But in reality, he has in a sense created two levers that can be used at will to flip this or that switch when difficulties arise and the smooth operation of his scientific narratives are in danger of being hampered. With his two-race theory, every researcher is free to pick and choose from the Germanic sources whatever they see as particularly appropriate for their preferred race. Kern has failed to provide any insight into the situation and has only confused it more. Therefore, we have no choice but to examine his view more closely.

Above all, it is the position that Kern assigns to the Germanic nobility that calls for criticism. The Germanic peoples never possessed such a parasitic nobility. In all that has been handed down to us, the Germanic common freemen and their nobility differed only in the most insignificant of ways. Under no circumstances can one speak of a strict racial stratification (like the assertion that the nobility belonged to the Nordic race and the common freemen to the Phalian race).

However, we must still address the question of whether it is possible to include both the nobility and the freemen as belonging to the Nordic race, but counting the serfs as belonging to the Phalian race. That may well have been possible, but it is not directly related to the task at hand. Namely, a nomadic nobility does not drag agricultural serfs along on its military campaigns. Of course, there is no denying that the Germanic peoples transplanted their peasantry into the depopulated Roman territories, establishing Germanic land law. As a matter of fact, from a cultural-historical point of view, the establishment of this land law is one of the most significant achievements of the Germanic peoples. Ultimately, history tells us that nomads would never even think of creating a new legal system for a subjugated population, so in this particular case we can also say that the Germanic peoples settling the former Roman territories were undoubtedly free. Whether we like it or not, we will have to count the Lombard and Frankish peasants among the freemen of these tribes. In any case, an assertion that would consider the Lombard and Frankish peasants as Phalian serfs should ultimately be rejected as completely unfounded. If it was not well known just how few peasants there were in the lands of the Roman Empire before the incursion of the Germanic peoples, then we might not be able to make such a definitive judgment on these matters. But there is absolutely no getting around the fact that the free Lombards and Franks must have been genuine peasants. This observation brings us back to the starting point of our discussion. The Germanic peasantry quite unquestionably consisted of freemen. Von Amira quite clearly states,

> The Germanic people of historical times are sedentary; their legal associations require a territory within permanent boundaries. Even when such a legal entity embarks on a migration, it does so solely to seek out a new territory of a similar nature. It is due to rather exceptional circumstances that the oldest polity in Iceland is non-territorial by nature. [89]

We can also tackle this question from an entirely different perspective, namely the agricultural history of Scandinavia. Neither Sweden nor Norway has ever experienced peasant serfdom or genuine agricultural forced labor in their history. Instead, there has always been the distinction between free peasants and what are known as *adelsbauern* (noble peasants), a distinction that was also reported among the early Germanic tribes. There is no doubt that it was from these Germanic noble peasants that the old German nobility of the Middle Ages emerged. Interestingly, however, the Scandinavian noble peasantry did not go down the same path as its German counterparts. Instead, toward the end of the Middle Ages, alongside the free peasants, it entered into a potentially dangerous relationship of dependence with the newly emerging non-Scandinavian nobilities, mostly of German origin. In Sweden, particularly during the first quarter of the seventeenth century, this trend took on particularly threatening forms, primarily due to the economic difficulties faced by the crown as a result of its involvement in the turmoil of the Thirty Years' War. At a *riksdag* (Swedish legislature) in 1650, the peasants' resistance to the increasingly influential, and increasingly foreign, nobility led the crown to take countermeasures against the nobility. From 1680 onwards, the economic superiority of the nobility was shattered, and the old noble peasantry began to recover relatively quickly. In Norway, developments were consistently more favorable for the peasantry. However, there were occasional attempts, originating from Denmark, to subjugate the peasants, but these only ever found temporary success.

In this brief outline of the development of the ancient Scandinavian peasantry, one fact of decisive importance emerges—from the very beginning, we find the distinction between free peasants and noble peasants, something also reported among the early Germanic tribes. The Scandinavian noble peasantry,

---

[89] Amira, *Grundriß des Germanischen Rechts*.

however, did not break away from the peasantry or develop into a parasitic nobility devoted solely to martial pursuits. Instead, this noble peasantry increasingly became tied to its land, even in some cases relinquishing leadership to a foreign nobility. The behavior of the Scandinavian noble peasantry, as illuminated by history, seems to be quite instructive in gaining clarity regarding the nature of the Nordic race. Ultimately, Scandinavia must certainly be recognized as playing a significant role in the debate surrounding the Nordic race.

But why should we assume anything different for the Germanic peoples than what the agricultural history of Scandinavia tells us regarding the local Swedish and Norwegian peasants? Why, when everything fits so well (common freemen, noble peasants, and other institutions) and can be traced back well over a millennium? Why complicate the early history of the Germanic peoples with forced explanations when the living reality of the Germanic peoples is still unfolding before our very eyes, practically in broad daylight?

In any case, one thing should be clear—if, on the one hand, archaeology unequivocally tells us that the Germanic peoples originated in Scandinavia, and, on the other hand, we can still observe the same ancestral Germanic characteristics reported by Tacitus among the North Germanic peoples today, then it is undoubtedly permissible to use the Scandinavian North Germanic peoples to gain an understanding of the German-Germanic peoples of the Migration Period.

To prove the validity of this comparison, the author will present information on the early historical migrations of the Germanic peoples, drawing from the latest research findings summarized by the esteemed pioneer of Germanic prehistory research, the archaeologist Kossinna.[90] According to Kossinna, during the early Iron Age (from 750 BC to the birth of Christ), the situation was roughly as follows. The Germanic peoples, advancing from Scandinavia, conquered the Illyrian region of eastern Germany and all of Poland, as well as the Celtic territories of northwestern Germany, which extended into Belgium, and eventually the Middle Rhine region as well. At that time, they still lacked the territory that today consists of Austria and southern Germany. The Germanic peoples exhibit an evident cultural contrast between the larger population that settled in western and north-central Germany and the smaller population that settled in northeastern Germany and Poland. These two major tribal groups, with the lower Oder River serving as the dividing line, are referred to as the East Germanic and West Germanic peoples.

The East Germanic peoples consisted of six larger tribes, listed from south to north. The first consists of the original Silesian Vandals that lived east of the Oder, in southern Posen, and in southern and eastern Poland, including Galicia. They are grouped together with the Silingi Silesian Vandals who lived west of the Oder. The second is the Burgundians of central and northern Posen and northwestern Poland. The third is the Gothic Gepids, who dominated West Prussia and eastern Farther Pomerania. The fourth is

---

[90] Kossinna, *Ursprung und Verbreitung*.

the original Goths of the Vistula Lagoon and in the East Prussian Samland. The fifth is the Rugii of western Farther Pomerania. The sixth is the Lemovii of western Pomerania and Rügen.

Among the West Germanic peoples, according to Kossinna, three major tribal confederations can be clearly distinguished in the historical record through archaeological findings—the Irminones, the Ingvaeones, and the Istvaeones.

The Irminones are the Germanic peoples of the Suebian Elbe, and they extend from the Leitha Mountains in Lower Austria, over Moravia and North Bohemia, down the entire Elbe region, up to Ostholstein. They are clearly divided into five larger tribes, listed from south to north. The first is the Quadi of Moravia.

The second is the Marcomanni of Bohemia. The third is the Hermunduri, who resided in southern parts of today's Province of Saxony and in northwestern parts of today's Free State of Saxony. The fourth is the Semnones of Altmark and northwest Brandenburg. The fifth is the Langobards in northeastern Hannover, eastern Holstein, and western Mecklenburg.

According to Germanic convention, a wasteland area in Holstein divides the Irminonic Langobards of East Holstein from the Ingvaeones, who start here. To the Ingaevones belong to the following tribes. The first is the Saxons of western Holstein. The second is the Angles, whose ancient territory in southern Schleswig is still called Anglia; they are separated from the Saxons by a deserted area north of the Eider River. The third is the Warini of northern Schleswig, southern Jutland, and Funen. The fourth is the Jutes of central and northern Jutland. The fifth is the Chauci of the North Sea coast, west of the Elbe up to the mouth of the Ems; their territory boasts dense settlement both in the first century BC and in the third and fourth centuries AD, but, rather conspicuously, it is sparsely populated in the first and second centuries AD, apparently as a result of the tribe's strong westward push. The sixth is the Angrivarii, whose name lives on in today's Angria, who settled south of the Chauci and west of the Weser.

Further southwest begins the westernmost of the three West Germanic groups, the Istvaeones. The Bructeri, who lived on both sides of the upper Ems, must have belonged to this group, although history says nothing about them. The Istvaeonic tribes living on the right bank of the Rhine cannot be marked on a map as they abandoned their settlements often due to the constant disturbances caused by the Roman occupation of areas along the Rhine. Nevertheless, archaeological discoveries of weapons from the first and second centuries AD show that a number of Germanic sites did exist on the right bank of the Rhine and in the Moselle region. Larger Germanic settlements, however, are found only on the Middle Rhine, where they can no longer be described as Ingvaeonic tribes, but Suebian tribes. These Suebians of the Main had already separated from the main Suebian tribe of the Elba by 100 BC, having first moved through Thuringia and Kurhessen to Upper Hessian Wetterau and then immediately expanding into Rhenish Hesse, Hesse-Starkenburg, Rhenish Palatinate, and Lower Alsace. The Suebian prince Ariovistus, a dangerous opponent of Caesar, made a name for himself in world history by uniting all the Germanic tribes on the left bank of the Upper Rhine under his rule.

It is therefore no coincidence that we see so much of what Tacitus describes about the Germanic peoples in the peasant structure of the Scandinavian countries in the Middle Ages. Although cultural differences might have developed among the individual Germanic tribes over time after they left Scandinavia, it is undoubtedly justified to assume that the Germanic peoples of the Migration Period had a "racial foundation" that was more or less uniform among all of the tribes.

However, the question raised by Kern still requires us to explore whether the free members of the Germanic tribes behaved like warlike nomads or rather like robust, sword-wielding peasants.

Anyone who examines the early stages of the Germanic Migration Period in any detail, while at the same time thoroughly and objectively examining the available historical records, will very soon come to the conclusion that not a single case of genuine, imperious conquest can be identified. Least of all will you find anything that even remotely resembles the raids of plunder and conquest typical of warlike nomads. We have already discussed the search for farmland of the Cimbri and Teutons.

Ariovistus crossed the Rhine in order to establish settlements, not to invade Gaul out of greed for booty. The Usipetes and Tencteri also requested settlement land from Caesar, as did the Goths from Emperor Valens in 378. It can generally be stated that apart from the Lombards, who invaded Italy in 568, not a single Germanic tribe had any intention of destroying the Roman state. With nothing short of a childlike innocence, the Germanic peoples clung to the hope that the Romans would voluntarily grant them a share of the amenities offered by the Roman state. In return, they were willing to take over its defense. Even back then, there were instances of what might be called "policies of rapprochement," examples of which can be found throughout the fourteen hundred years of German history. Theodoric the Great, for example, can undoubtedly be called the father of a Germanic-Roman policy of rapprochement and understanding. Unfortunately, the German people have always paid a lopsided price for this policy. Tacitus even observed the *stultitia* of the Germanic peoples, which we may politely translate as a "lack of talent for questions of higher politics."

As a matter of fact, Caesar also did not, by any means, see the Germanic peoples as hordes of conquering, semi-nomadic warriors, but as people eager for settlement. This may not be directly apparent from his writings, but it can be inferred indirectly. Namely, nomadic warrior peoples are relatively easy to hire as mercenaries. While they may be unreliable as soldiers, as we will see in later chapters, the Romans nevertheless did not hesitate to use them. If the Germanic peoples were still semi-nomadic or, as Kern assumes, peasants with a nobility of racially Nordic nomads, then it should have been easy for Caesar and his Roman successors to recruit this nobility as mercenary auxiliaries, separating them from any connection to an agricultural background. Due to the Germanic freeman's concept of loyalty, they naturally did not have the unreliability typically associated with nomads, and due to their nomadic nature, they would have been easily moved from one theater of war to another. Kern's Germanic peoples would have been exemplary auxiliaries. In reality, however, the Germanic never separated himself from his homeland. He may have entered Roman service as an individual, but his sentiments nevertheless remained rooted in his tribe along the Rhine. This circumstance made the Germanic Question a primary political concern for the Romans, for the "bloc" of Germanic peoples along the Rhine did not dissolve and could not be dissolved.

In fact, in all the historical accounts that discuss the Germanic peoples and their relationship with the Roman Empire, there exists a still unresolved historical contradiction. During the period of the Germanic Question, the Romans had already been suffering from a long-standing depopulation of the countryside and were striving to revive their peasant class. At the same time, the Germanic peoples were asking for land in a truly peaceful manner. Additionally, their exaggerated concept of loyalty made them domestically harmless in the eyes of the Romans, otherwise the Romans would never have employed Germanic individuals as their personal bodyguards. Despite these circumstances, however, the Romans did not invite the Germanic peoples in as peasants, nor did they disperse them throughout their vast empire. Instead, the Romans did everything in their power to keep the Germanic peoples away from the borders of the empire. At times it almost seems as if the *līmes* were not so much a defense against the "sword" of the Germanic peoples, but rather against certain Germanic character traits. The Germanic peoples had views that are never compatible with a completely financialized state—and at this very moment in history, Rome was becoming just that.

2

Contrary to today's unfortunately widespread view that the Germanic peoples possessed a simple and primitive legal system, they actually had a remarkably sophisticated and morally distinctive system of law.[91] Germanic jurisprudence, completely based on personal responsibility, stands in stark contrast to the mechanized jurisprudence that is produced by completely financialized economies. Such an economy inevitably does away with any awareness of personhood and reduces human beings to mere objects. Thus, one might suspect that the financial lords of Rome feared not so much the swords of the Germanic tribes, but rather their concept of morality, which could not be swayed by wealth. While individual Germanic mercenaries posed no threat, a collectively settled population of Germanic peoples within the borders of the empire had the potential to become a source of constant domestic unrest.

The law of the Germanic peoples is indeed remarkable. As von Amira puts it, "it emanates from the common man, lives in his consciousness, and, even more, in his feelings." Germanic law is quite capable of either provoking the ridicule of a financially-minded man who calculates only in terms of numbers

---

[91] Amira, *Grundriß des Germanischen Rechts*; Merk, *Vom Werden und Wesen*.

and things (if he is able to afford such ridicule), or of filling him with horror, if it is the Germanic man who has power and not he. Namely, the most remarkable aspect of Germanic law is the unity of law and God. According to the Germanic view, the two cannot be separated; God himself is law. For the Germanic person, law is simply the manifestation of his very existence. Thus, to name an example, there are no statutes of limitations among the Germanic peoples. An old Germanic legal concept puts it bluntly: "One hundred years of injustice are not made right by one hour of justice." This is quite logical, since any statute of limitations necessarily presupposes human intervention in the law. It is probably for the same reason that Germanic law was not written down, but only guided by oral traditions (*weistümer*). This too is logical, for a living thing can only be guided, explained, and directed—not made static in writing. Thus, when Kern believes that he can resolve the difficulties between his nomad hypothesis and the attested agriculture of the Germanic peoples by postulating the existence of a "strictly fair agrarian legislation," he misunderstands the very essence of the matter. Namely, that a strictly fair agricultural system presupposes either the voluntary bestowal of this system by the nobility upon the serfs or an agreement between the nobility and the serfs. In both cases, however, this system would then be the work of man, and would stand in stark contrast to the divine origin of the legal concepts peculiar to the Germanic peoples.

In general, the Germanic legal system operates like the naturally evolved skeleton of a living, healthy organism. In fact, it always functions as the support system of a living form of expression. The divine origin of this legal system helps explain the peculiar relationship between the nobility and the common freemen among the Germanic peoples. Compared to the common freemen, the nobility's hands are often bound in a way that is, by no means, always to the benefit of the Germanic peoples. Even Tacitus noted that among the ancient Germanic kingdoms, the power of kings was not unlimited, but legally bound by duties to their people. Von Amira gives an example,

> The original Germanic system of governance left no room for the power of individual rulers. The head of state was the *Landsgemeinde* (Rural Assembly). Apart from it and the *Hundertschaftsversammlung* (Assembly of Hundreds), there were no other state organs or officials— indeed, apparently the only officials were those who were elected by the *Landsgemeinde*. The *Landsgemeinde* appointed a permanent, albeit removable, official to lead the state, choosing him only from the noblest lineage. The selection of individuals of only the noblest lineage was done with the same reasoning that distinguished the ancient hereditary nobility, for it is the leader's relationship with the divine that determines the people's welfare, and so the people hold him responsible for it. Such a leader is called king because he is the highest official, whether as the leader of the tribal polity, as the descendant of a noble lineage, or as the "*volksführer*" (people's leader). . . . Certain basic features recur uniformly in the character of Germanic kingship, for example, the king's personal responsibility for his functions, no matter

the nature of those functions. Examples of the functions of the ancient Germanic king are the upkeep of the army and the maintenance of law and order, in short, to keep the peace. Even in Tacitus, the king is described as a collector of *friedensgeld*[92] and is often called *judex* (judge) by the ancient authors. Additionally, the ancient Germanic king lacked any and all independent legislative power—he had no greater right to vote in the *Landsgemeinde* than the next best free peasant.[93]

In this respect, the law is so uniform and consistent that no foreign racial stratification, influence, or interference can be detected in it. You will not find such a thing among any nobility in the world that owes its origins to conquest by warrior nomads. This alone should be more than enough to invalidate Kern's view of a racially Nordic nomadic nobility and a racially Phalian peasantry.[94]

For our analysis, it is particularly crucial to recognize the fact that this uniformly applied law, obviously the result of natural evolution, originates in peasant thinking and is quite clearly speaking exclusively to peasants. In the Middle Ages, ancient Germanic law transitioned into the *Sachsenspiegel*, a codified set of laws based on Saxon oral legal traditions (*weistümer*) that was authored by the Saxon nobleman Eike von Repgow between 1215 and 1235. The land law of the *Sachsenspiegel*, which was based on and is simply a continuation of Germanic land law, remained in effect in the old Prussian territories until 1794, in the Kingdom of Saxony until 1863, and in the Saxon and Thuringian duchies, Holstein, and Lauenburg until the enactment of the German Civil Code in 1900. Consequently, when investigating Germanic land law, we are by no means solely reliant on the scarce Roman sources or on ingenious deductions and conjectures. The *Sachsenspiegel*, the land law of Germanic people extending into modern times, is perhaps the best place to find tangible facts that shed light on the darkness of ancient Germanic prehistory. Anyone who is

---

[92] Editor's note: *Friedensgeld* was a payment of restitution paid to both the victim and the king for a criminal offense.

[93] In this respect, the Germanic king is thus the polar opposite of the nomadic chieftain who alone and exclusively determines the state's course of action.

[94] In studies of the racial conditions among the Germanic peoples, scholars often fail to distinguish between the various degrees of free individuals. The true Germanic individual was the fully free or "common" free man. Above this category was the noble fully-free individual, while below this category was the so-called "semi-free" individual. This hierarchy primarily played a role in breeding rather than having legal or racial significance. The semi-free individuals were the so-called "freedmen," and their racial divergence from the fully-free and noble fully-free individuals, as pointed out by von Amira, can be observed on several occasions. Further down this hierarchy of semi-free individuals were those who were "alien to the tribe" and of non-German descent (although these are often conflated with the semi-free individuals in historical accounts). Among these were individuals that the Germanic peoples encountered during the Migration Period, on the occasions that these tribal aliens were even granted legal rights. Therefore, in the Frankish and Lombard realms, such tribal aliens were the Romance peoples, while in England they were the Britons. Both groups were collectively referred to as *wälsche*, meaning speakers of foreign languages (Anglo-Saxon *wealas* and Old High German *walaha*). Interestingly, the serf, or unfree dependent peasant, was below the semi-free individuals in the Germanic social hierarchy. Thus, racial stratification permeated between all free individuals on the one hand and the serfs on the other, but it never delineated between the fully-free and the noble fully-free.

reasonably acquainted with it and then compares it to the complete intellectual and spiritual sterility found in the land rights of any ancient Semitic people should question their assumptions regarding a nomadic nobility for the Germanic peoples. At the very least, they should refrain from placing the Nordic race on the same level as the desert nomads of Arabia, as Kern does.

However, there has been opposition (from agricultural circles specifically) against using the Saxon oral legal traditions as evidence for the existence of a peasantry among the earliest Germanic peoples. It is deemed inappropriate to directly apply the conditions reflected in the oldest Saxon documents to the earliest conditions in Germania. Even if we agree with this point, we cannot ignore the fact that it is still very possible to derive valuable information from these documents, at least for the purpose of assessing the likelihood of various assumptions regarding the agricultural conditions of early times. For example, if it could be proven that a significant portion of the Germanic people were still free peasants during the period of the early Middle Ages when the manorial system (manorialism) was beginning to emerge, then it would be highly probable to assume that in the earliest of times only free peasants existed. However, Wittich emphasizes that according to his research, the existence of a population of free peasants among the Saxons during the time of the Carolingians cannot be demonstrated.[95] But it may have been different elsewhere. The oldest Saxon documents, in fact, testify to a dependent (partially personally dependent and partially materially dependent) but undoubtedly peasant population of such a size that the transformation of originally free peasants into materially dependent peasants cannot be easily explained.

Before we can address this question, however, we first need to clarify what manorialism actually is. Von Amira writes,

> Manorialism (court or manorial rule, lordship, *dominium*, known as *senioratus* or *senioria* in Frankish times, later on *seigneurie* in French) is the embodiment of all the powers associated with the possession of a *fronhof* (from *vrônhof* or *salhof*, meaning manor or center of a jurisdiction and seat of the authority exercising judicial power). This authority is partly under public law and partly under private law. . . . The power of the lordship under private law is partly the product of full ownership over the properties beloning to the manor (forest, pasture, wasteland, bodies of water) and partly from the so-called upper ownership of peasant farms and their attachments through reserved rights (privileges to the soil, game rights, trade monopolies, veto power over a tenant's disposition of their farm). Vassals (clients, *homines subjecti*, subjects) could belong to different social classes, however, they were all under the responsibility, command, and jurisdiction of their lord, in a similar vein to members of the lord's household; together they thus formed a household cooperative (Latin *familia*, Old High German *hîwiski*). This household cooperative also

---

95 Wittich, *Die Grundherrschaft in Nordwestdeutschland*; *Die Frage der Freibauern*.

resulted in the duty of the lord to protect his vassals, ensure their safety, and support those who became impoverished. The household cooperative is essentially a personal association.

Therefore, it seems that what we have here is what Kern (Artbild der Deutschen) understands as noble peasanthood and what prompted Wittich to challenge the idea of an original free peasanthood among the Saxon peasants. According to Kern, the manorial lords would belong to the Nordic race, while the vassals would belong to the existing subjugated population, for which Kern suggests the Phalian race. However, such an explanation is incorrect for multiple reasons. Firstly, it can be demonstrated that the institution of manorialism, as it has been transmitted to us from the early Middle Ages, is not convincingly of ancient Germanic origin, or at least does not date back to the time of the Migration Period, developing only in the early Middle Ages, evidently under the influence of Frankish notions of administration and governance. Von Amira comments on this matter,

> The authority of the outgoing ancient Germanic hereditary nobility is initially assumed by, and its remnants incorporated into, a service nobility or (according to Latin sources) *optimate* nobility that develops among the South Germanic peoples after the Migration Period. . . . The Visigoths and Burgundians, after adopting the late Roman system of *possessores*, with its *patrocinium* (patronage) over vassals, designated the large landowners to be *optimates*, placing them on the same level as the service nobility. . . . Visigothic and Frankish law are based on the post-Roman system of private contract patronage and guardianship (*patrocinium, mithio*), which, unlike kingship and immunity, was non-territorial and understood by the Germans as *munt* (protective subordination, which gave the patron the power of representation and command). The *tabularii* (clerks) of the *Lex Ripuaria* were subjected to the jurisdiction of their ecclesiastical *munt* lord's immunity court. The feudal jurisdiction of the Middle Ages seems to have originated from the *munt* of the feudal lord over his vassals.

From this, we can already see that manorialism, in the form in which it is understood by Wittich—and perhaps more generally today—is not entirely Germanic. However, it is also not entirely Roman, as it was not directly adopted from the model of the Roman bureaucratic state. Therefore, it is perhaps best to say that while medieval manorialism must have Germanic origins, in all other respects it is primarily a Roman administrative concept adapted by the Germanic peoples.

But what exactly should be understood here as "Roman" and what as "Germanic"? Without clearly distinguishing between these two concepts, the entire early history of the Germanic peoples cannot be clearly detailed. Roman conceptualization first and foremost denotes unrestricted individualism without regard for the collective good. When the Germanic tribes encountered the Roman state, it had already evolved into nothing more than a colossal institution aimed at exploiting all known production centers of goods. Thus, the Roman state at that time had essentially implemented the modern concept of a global economy. In this state, there was no sense of community among citizens beyond that of mutual advantage. Simply put, whoever managed to ruthlessly ascend into the wealthy strata was considered a made man—the "how" or the suffering inflicted on those destroyed by his rise was of no consequence at all.

The Germanic individual approached the concept of the state from a fundamentally different perspective, he was entirely unfamiliar with limitless individual freedom. The free individual was fundamentally integrated into the collective of the free community and evaluated solely on the basis of his value to the collective.[96] Individuals were evaluated on a hierarchical scale, and those who had the highest standing were those who were of most value to the collective. This hierarchical evaluation encompassed not only the individual, but also the clan to which he belonged. Through this hierarchical evaluation, the Germanic peoples created human communities in which members interacted in a highly interconnected and lively manner, without ever working against each other, as long as the idea of service to the collective remained alive. As a result, Germanic forms of community always manifest themselves as living organisms. Despite the adoption of some Roman institutions, the German Middle Ages retained this basic Germanic idea of evaluating the individual in a social context. Accordingly, the state was always regarded as an organism extended to a larger scale. Of course, in this medieval state, the individual was bound to the role assigned to him by his origin (clan evaluation). At the same time, however, the community also ensured that the individual was provided with the highest degree of personal happiness and domestic peace within his designated sphere of influence. It is not a particularly easy task to detail the basic ideas underlying the late Roman state and the medieval Germanic state. In his biography of the English statesman Disraeli, the English historian Froude paints a picture of the contrasts between the Germanic and non-Germanic conceptions of the state, which Günther cites.[97] Although Froude is describing English conditions, they are applicable to any country led by Germanic peoples in the Middle Ages. He writes,

> Liberty in the modern sense, liberty where the rights of man take the place of the duties of a man—such a liberty they neither sought nor desired. As in an army, each man had had his own position under a graduated scale of authority, and the work was

---

[96] Unfortunately, contemporary racial-scientific literature largely overlooks this characteristic of the Germanic people, which is obviously a product of a Nordic racial heritage.
[97] Hans F. K. Günther, *Ritter, Tod und Teufel* [Knight, Death, and theDevil], fourth edition (Munich: 1934).

hardest where the rank was highest. The baron was maintained in his castle on the produce of the estate. But the baron had the hardest knocks in the field of battle. In dangerous times he was happy if he escaped the scaffold. He maintained his state in the outward splendour which belonged to his station, but in private he lived as frugally as his tenants, sleeping on a hard bed, eating hard, plain food, with luxury unheard of and undreamt of. The rule was loyalty—loyalty of the lord to the king, loyalty of lord to peasant and of peasant to lord.

In the towns the trades were organised under the guilds. The price of food, the rate of wages from household servant to field labourer and artisan, were ordered by statute on principles of equity. For each trade there was a council, and false measure and bad quality of goods were sharply looked to. The miller could not adulterate his flour. The price of wheat varied with the harvest, but the speculator who bought up grain to sell again at famine price found himself in the hands of the constable. For the children of the poor there was an education under the apprentice system, to which the most finished school-board training was as copper to gold. Boys and girls alike were all taught some useful occupation by which they could afterwards honestly maintain themselves. If there were hardships they were not confined to a single class, but were borne equally by the great and the humble. A nation in a healthy state is an organism like the human body. If the finger says to the hand, 'I have no need of thee; I will go my way, touch what pleases me, and let alone what I do not care to meddle with,' the owner of the hand will be in a bad way. A commonwealth, or common weal, demands that each kind shall do the work which belongs to him or her. When he or she, when individuals generally begin to think and act for themselves, to seek their rights and their enjoyments, and forget their duties, the work of dissolution has already set in.[98]

Froude then contrasts this with the un-Germanic view of the state, or to be more precise, he contrasts it with the modern view of the state as it developed and spread in England. As we proceed below and in the next chapter, we will find that the conditions in modern England, as described by Froude, are in fact quite similar to those of the late Roman period.

From the Restoration downwards the owners of land began to surround themselves with luxuries, and the employers of labour to buy it at the cheapest rate. Selfishness became first a practice and then developed boldly into a theory. Life was a race in which the strongest had a right to win. Every man was to be set free and do

---

[98] Froude, *The Earl of Beaconsfield.*

the best which he could for himself. The Institutions remained. Dukes and earls and minor dignitaries still wore their coronets and owned the soil. Bishops were the spiritual lords of their dioceses, and the rector represented the Church in his parish. The commercial companies survived in outward magnificence. But in aiming at wealth they all alike forfeited their power. Competition became the sole rule of trade; a new ideology was invented to gild the change; artisans and labourers were taught to believe that they would gain as largely as the capitalists. They had been bondsmen; they were now free, and all would benefit alike. Yet somehow all did not benefit alike. The houses of the upper classes grew into palaces, and the owners of them lived apart as a separate caste; but the village labourer did not find his lot more easy because he belonged to nobody. As population increased his wages sank to the lowest point at which he could keep his family alive. The 'hands' in the towns fared no better. If wages rose the cost of living rose along with them. The compulsory apprentice system was dropped, and the children were dragged up in squalor upon the streets. Discontent broke out in ugly forms. . . . They were told that they must keep the peace and help themselves. Their labour was an article which they had to sell, and the value of it was fixed by the relations between supply and demand. Man could not alter the laws of nature, which political economy had finally discovered. Political economy has since been banished to the exterior planets; but fifty years ago to doubt was heresy, to deny was a crime to be censured in all the newspapers. Carlyle might talk scornfully of the 'Disraeli science. Disraeli might heap ridicule on Mr. Flummery Flum. But Mr. Flummery Flum was a prophet in his day and led the believers into strange places. The race for wealth went on at railroad speed. Vast fortunes were accumulated as the world's markets opened. The working classes ought to have shared the profits, and they were diligently instructed that they had gained as much as their employers. . . . 'The wealth of the nation,' the Free-Traders of Manchester said, depends on its commerce.

So says the English historian! In impressive style, the Englishman Froude has elucidated for us the basic ideas distinguishing the Germanic and non-Germanic view of the state. Now, we will encounter a similar distinction between Roman and Germanic law as presented by a German jurist. Merk states the following,[99]

Roman law is individualistic, German law is cooperative and socially responsible. When it came to private law, the Romans early on (and with the utmost consistency) separated the individual

---

[99] Merk, *Vom Werden und Wesen.*

from all natural and social bonds and left him completely on his own; the cohesion of these atomized individuals was based solely on the coercive bond of an all-powerful state. Despite thousands of years of gradual growth in individualist sentiment, German-Germanic law has always emphasized the position given to the individual based on his blood and family ties, as well as his membership in a professional community and other cooperative and feudal associations. Compared to the Roman, the German is much freer vis-a-vis the state, while at the same time being legally bound by these natural and social ties.

Roman law always looks to the individual. The starting and focal point here is the unattached individual and their subjective entitlement. The individualism of Roman law, combined with the omnipotence of the state and the slave economy, prevented the development of cooperatives in Roman life. The few collective associations of persons recognized as independent legal entities (juridical persons) are legally given fictitious personhood. Just as the state is the creator of objective law (legal principles), the individual is the creator of his subjective rights. In Roman private law, the individual's personal sovereignty is, in principle, the only factor relevant in granting him legal rights and shapes his subjective rights. The idea of the self-importance and boundless power of the rightsholder permeates all of Roman law. The will of the rightsholder to rule is as unrestricted as possible—in public law the will of the head of state, and in private law the will of the owner and the other holders of subjective rights. Roman law tends to contrast the purely one-sided rights of the entitled person, divorced from any obligation or consideration, with the equally one-sided duties of others. Only the influence of tradition and public opinion had any restraining influence. These counterweights were generally effective so long as Romans of the old, hearty stock continued to hold influence, as they had typically been through the iron discipline of the army, were animated by a love of country and respect for the traditional, and embodied the spirit of order and legality. During the decay of the late Roman Empire, when these moral forces had waned, this freedom inevitably degenerated into licentiousness and shameless exploitation of the nation's economically weaker classes. This mechanism of Roman law, when applied to peoples with different worldviews and customs, was bound to have an equally damaging effect. In the hands of modern economic liberalism and capitalism, it became a powerful weapon for shattering medieval social bonds in civil and economic law.

Whereas the idea of community is anathema to Roman law, it dominates Germanic law. The entire history of German law is marked by the tendency to form associations and cooperatives. Until the introduction of liberal-individualist economic legislation in the nineteenth century, the norms of German economic life were cooperative. The main pillars of the economic order in the countryside were the land cooperatives (*markgenossenschaft*), and in the cities, the guilds and trade associations. The community, not the unattached individual, therefore forms the basis and focal point of German-Germanic law. The individual is always evaluated as a member of a community, whether large or small, whose collective necessities and needs take priority over his own rights and free will. He does not have unlimited power as a rightsholder, but is merely a member of a community order based on reciprocity. "The common good takes precedence over individual gain." Even according to the Visigothic legal code (Book 8, 4.29), no person should act against the common good while pursuing their own self-interest.[100]

According to the Germanic view of law, subjective rights are not unlimited, they are morally and socially bound legal power. In medieval law, the concept of property was primarily social, as opposed to the individualistic concept of property in the *Corpus Juris*. Land ownership among the Germanic peoples was bound with far-reaching obligations to the community (especially for the good of the family), the land cooperative, and the state. Unlike late Roman law, land under Germanic law could not be freely squandered and sold off like a commodity—it formed the basis of a family's economic, social, and public legal position and was to remain in the family. Therefore, the owner could not freely dispose of the property upon death. Instead, a member of his family would inherit an irrevocable right to the property. The landowner

---

[100] About the origin and age of the oldest Germanic legal documents, von Amira says the following, "The legal codices of the South Germanic regions emerge around the time that the so-called Migration Period comes to a halt. The reason for this lies in the profound transformation of legal conditions brought about by the relocation of tribal seats, the merging of highly diverse ancient peoples into new 'tribes,' the establishment and demise of states, the adoption of Christianity, and the evolution of the economy during these centuries. As the increasingly complex structure of society and the accentuation of social inequalities disrupted the uniformity of the population's traditional legal systems (a circumstance the author wishes to emphasize), customary law now required written documentation. The oldest legal codices belong to East Germanic legal traditions, especially the Gothic and Burgundian. Among them, the Western Gothic was developed first. According to an absolutely reliable statement by Isidore of Seville, the earliest written laws of the Visigoths came from King Euric (466–485); fragments of this monarch's legal code exist in the Paris Codex (*rescriptus*), line 12161. The capacity for abstraction necessary for the formulation of legal principles is fostered by the study of classical and sacred literature. Thus, the task of formulating and recording legal principles fell to those who had received such an education—rhetoricians, clerics, and the laity trained by them. They used their literary language, Latin, attesting to the substantial influence of their social class in matters of jurisprudence and legal development. Nevertheless, these authors recognized that Latin was inadequate for expressing certain Germanic legal concepts. Consequently, they infuse it with Germanic terminology, either by Latinizing these terms or by inserting them into the text with explanatory notations. Alternatively, they could modify the meaning of Latin expressions by translating Germanic terms literally. Limiting our understanding, however, is that the entire body of legal documents in Germanic languages is known only within the Anglo-Saxon source history of the period."

and the artisan, according to the medieval view, should consider his position at the head of his enterprise as a kind of public office in the service of the community.

Since every entitlement is subject to moral and social limitations in Germanic law, the exercise of rights for the sole purpose of harming another (such as the erection of "spite houses" solely to block a neighbor's view) has always been prohibited as an abuse of rights under German law; see the corresponding prohibition of abuse in the German Civil Code, section 226. Roman law, on the other hand, takes a fundamentally different approach, as evident by the Roman legal maxim "*Qui iure suo utitur, neminem laedit*," which can be translated to mean, "He who exercises his rights does not harm anyone." The shylock[101] practice of rigidly enforcing formal law even in cases where enforcement appears indecent and unethical would not gain a hearing before a tribunal under Germanic law.

All Germanic rule is simultaneously a relationship of duty and obligation. One can identify a primacy of duties in Germanic law (as opposed to the primacy of subjective rights in Roman law) where rights appear as a means to the fulfillment of duties rather than as an end in and of themselves. While the ancient Roman system finds it challenging to reconcile the notions of power and duty within a single person,[102] the Germanic view, in contrast, sees an inherent connection between law and duty. No rights without duties, and no duties without rights! Likewise, there are no privileges without obligations, and vice versa. Indeed, duty is seen as an inherent constraint within the law, rather than outside it. This basic idea appears everywhere in the Germanic relationships between husband and wife, parent and child, guardian and ward, feudal lord and feudal man, lord and servant. The *munt* of the husband, father, and guardian, as well as the position of the employer, is not a one-sided tyranny that gives rights to the one wielding power while imposing duties on the person subjected to power. Rather, the *munt* is a protective power infused with duties of care, with the person subjected to this power possessing independent rights within the private-legal community that both the person with power and the person subject to this power are members of.

The same reciprocity of rights and duties exists in the relationship between a lord and servants. The duty of the lord toward the servants is endowed with particular power. The lord is obligated to care for the well-being of his subordinates, to support and sustain them in times of need and illness. Thus, in medieval maritime law

---

[101] Shylock is a cruel and greedy Jewish-Venetian moneylender in William Shakespeare's *The Merchant of Venice.*
[102] Ihering, *Geist des Römischen*, 296.

documents, extensive provisions can be found regarding the duty of the shipowner to provide suitable accommodation for his crew and to care for any seamen that fell ill aboard the ship. In mining, miners' funds were established, and in the craft industry, journeymen's funds were formed, to which the employer was obligated to contribute. The long-standing miners' funds of the mining industry served as a model for the workers' insurance introduced by Bismarck. In the medieval manorial system, the duties of bonded peasants (serfs) were counterbalanced by their real rights to the farm's leased property and other claims on the landlord, such as the right to gather building materials and firewood from the landlord's forests and to graze livestock on the landlord's pasture. In return for paying rent and performing labor services, serfs were usually given a small favor, such as bread, a piece of cake, a drink, or even a meal. According to the rural oral legal tradition, the landlord is also obliged to host his serfs, servants, and their wives and children on certain occasions. The whole of Germanic law is imbued with a high moral spirit, and above all it strives to make the life of the serf as easy as possible.

In Prüm Abbey, for example, the bailiff was therefore expected to collect the bailiff's fee amicably, ensuring that he "does not wake the child in the cradle nor frighten the one in the crib." When the lord of the court and his friends take shelter in a peasant's farmhouse, they are supposed to remove their swords and spurs at the door so as not to frighten the woman. If a representative of the lord enters a house to demand a *zinshuhn* (chicken payment) and finds a woman who has just given birth, he should break the head of the chicken as a token for the lord and throw the chicken backwards into the house, so that the woman can enjoy it. When a serf receives the news that his wife has given birth, according to the Wendhag oral legal tradition, he is immediately relieved of his labor service and should quickly unharness his horses, head home, and do whatever the woman needs so that she can adequately nurse his child and raise his young peasant better. According to Article 45 of the Bern Charter, a married son should give the best place at the hearth and table to his elderly widowed mother. One would search in vain for such heartfelt gestures in Roman legal sources. While Roman law treats the employment contract as a mere contractual exchange of labor for money, according to the Germanic view, the lord and servant, employer and employee, are not bound merely by a loose contractual bond, but their relationships are elevated to the status of a personal-legal obligation. The lord and servant, employer and employee, together form a professional community consisting of a head and its members, a community based on personal rights with a lordly leadership. The lord acts as the leader of this community and as its representative to the outside world. However, within the community, the serving members are granted a cooperative participation (to some extent) in the resolution of communal matters. For instance, the peasant landholders serve as judges in the feudal lord's court, while the vassals (*ministeriales*) act as judges in the vassal's court.

The core Germanic idea that rulership is not so much about the right to exercise power but rather about the duty to provide protection also applies to the relationship between public polities and their members. Unlike the law of the Roman Empire, Germanic law does not recognize boundless and arbitrary rule by public authorities nor the duty or defenseless submission of subjects to this arbitrary rule. The Germanic state is not an impersonal apparatus of coercion based solely on command authority and an obligation to obey, but rather a personal association of loyalty built on the reciprocity of rights and obligations. The Germanic kings and princes were not absolute rulers, but personally responsible leaders and trustees of the people. Tacitus observed that in the ancient Germanic kingdoms, the power of the king was not unlimited but legally bound in relation to his fellow countrymen. The people's kingship of the Germanic world stands in stark contrast to late Roman imperial rule and its repugnant imperial cult, the result of the general Orientalization of its civilization in late antiquity. Even the medieval German emperors, even at the height of their power, were never absolute rulers—they were always bound by law and custom and did not have the authority to unilaterally interfere with the traditional legal status of their subjects.

And that's it for Merk! Now that we have become familiar with the fundamental differences between the Germanic and non-Germanic views of the state through the works of Froude and Merk, it becomes immediately clear that the structure of the medieval German state must have been inherent to the essence of the Germanic peoples. Otherwise, the complete replacement of the Roman system by the Germanic peoples of the Migration Period cannot be explained, especially in view of the fact that the Germanic peoples had been trained in Roman administration and estate management for centuries. Therefore, we can state with absolute certainty that medieval manorialism could not have been developed as an institution explicitly for the exploitation of labor, but was merely a theory of administration that, though non-Germanic, was apparently necessitated by the new conditions of the conquered lands. The Germanic peoples could only come to terms with these new conditions by adapting the familiar concept of household rule to a larger scale. Indeed, von Amira has written on how medieval manorialism first emerged from an evidently peasant conception of household rule.[103]

Our free medieval peasant communities did indeed emerge as political

---

[103] Amira, *Grundriß des Germanischen Rechts*.

entities from a system of manorialism. But to conclude that this is evidence that before they achieved independence by developing into a political entity, the peasants had always been serfs is to oversimplify things. Early medieval manorialism arose in part due to shifts in property relations within communities. Furthermore, it also occurred as a result of the transfer of sovereignty from one Germanic tribe to another during times of warfare—this can be easily demonstrated in part by the case of the Franks and the Lower Saxons. Therefore, while the medieval manorial system provides evidence for many things, it unfortunately provides very little evidence for the assertion that a serf family in the Middle Ages was already at that station during the sixth or seventh centuries. On the contrary, the remarkably rapid abandonment of manorialism in the Middle Ages by many rural communities in Lower Saxony and the reintroduction of the ancient Germanic practice of political self-government actually proves the opposite, namely that manorialism was never able to gain a very firm foothold in such regions. But let us hear what von Amira says on this matter:

> A division within the free community was brought about in most Germanic states due to the nature and manner of land ownership. This becomes particularly evident among the Anglo-Saxons. In Wessex, the Germanic landowner was part of the "six hundred" (Anglo-Saxon *sixhynde*) class, with a wergild of six hundred shillings, above the "rent-payer" (*gafol-gilda*) or the "peasant" (*gebúr*; Norman *villanus*) as "twohundreders" (*twyhynda*). The latter should not be automatically considered serfs simply because they may be obligated to perform weekly labor. Indeed, in the later period of Anglo-Saxon law, the *gebúr* (peasant) is at least equal to the "cottager" (*cot-setla*; Norman *bordarius*) in terms of fines. However, even the cottager is explicitly counted among the free in the *rectitudines*,[104] despite his obligation to perform weekly labor on his lord's land. . . . The German laws on the mainland at the beginning of the Early Middle Ages partially stem from similar ideas. Additionally, the form of public service required becomes a decisive factor.

That the manorial system only rather loosely overlaid itself over the existing structures of medieval peasant law is demonstrated by von Amira in section nine of *Grundriss des Germanischen Rechts*.[105]

---

[104] The *Rectitudines Singularum Personarum* (Rights of Individual Persons) is an Anglo-Saxon legal document dating to the early eleventh century which details the rights and duties of different classes of people.
[105] Amira, *Grundriß des Germanischen Rechts*.

3

We may perhaps make the following conclusions with regard to the significance of medieval law in understanding ancient Germanic history. First, medieval law, in its structure and application, is as un-Roman as possible and must therefore be considered inherent to the essence of the Germanic peoples, since it is by no means Celtic. This means that it is undoubtedly permissible to use the Saxon oral legal tradition to shed light on the legal relations of the Germanic peoples during the Migration Period. The similarity between the Saxon oral legal traditions and the legal codes of the Goths and Burgundians—which appeared in the fifth century and are undoubtedly purely Germanic—is so evident that there is no doubt whether they have a common root, which must lie within Germandom. Second, even if medieval documents seem to indicate that, for example, the Saxon peasants were not free, this does not prove that they were not free during the Migration Period. Third, the concept of medieval serfdom should not be confused with later interpretations of the word "serfdom" that became known during the era of peasant emancipation and is now used as a political catchphrase. Medieval serfdom was a matter of division of labor rather than a unilateral relinquishment of rights on the part of the serfs or the result of military conquest. To gain a clear picture of these relationships, it is better to think of subordinates and superiors in the military, where an increase in authority brings an increase in personal freedom of movement along with the assignment of tasks that are free of physical labor and exertion. At the same time, however, this higher position entails a greater sense of responsibility to the whole and to subordinates. Fourth, medieval manorialism indeed reflects an ancient peasant way of thinking among the Germanic peoples, otherwise the Germanic peoples would never have derived the concept of manorialism from the concept of household rule. However, manorialism, in its administrative sense, is not completely Germanic, but rather a Roman administrative institution that was adopted and further developed by Germanic ideas. Organizations established for the exploitation of labor were absolutely foreign to the Germanic peoples, and any attempts to extrapolate something similar from the manorial system of the Middle Ages are based on decidedly non-Germanic notions regarding the concept and implementation of authority.

With that, we can now address the question of what Germanic agriculture looked like since, based on the Germanic legal traditions, there is no doubt about the original peasanthood of the Germanic freeman. This initially leads us to the question of how exactly to define a "peasant."

If we want to shed light on Germanic agriculture, the answer to this question is of fundamental importance. Unfortunately, however, many researchers have overlooked this question in their studies of the Germanic peasantry, often unconsciously projecting modern-day interpretations of the term "peasant," attributing to this term characteristics that may be familiar to us today, but which may not have been entirely valid as far back as the Migration Period.

What is this modern-day interpretation of the term peasant? In general, it refers to a farmer who has free disposal over his land and derives benefit from his property through agricultural activities. When the owner of an estate no longer works the land himself, he is then called a landowner or a large-scale farmer. If the landholding is below a certain size, we primarily use the term smallholder, and for even smaller landholdings there are specific terms that we do not need to busy ourselves with here. Hardly anyone will claim that this definition provides a straightforward account of the term peasant, since what we now call a peasant could just as well be called a farmer. However, our current understanding of peasantness is the product of a very specific historical development. Before the emancipation of peasants, which took place about one hundred years ago, there was a fairly well-defined and graded classification for all human activities related to the land. In this context, however, the historical development of the term peasant does not initially give us much guidance, for what German history has made of the concept of peasant over the course of a millennium may have been far removed from its original meaning among the Germanic peoples. With this, however, we are already at the source of most misunderstandings that can arise when studying peasant issues within Germanic civilization. The leadership of our late medieval German state was predominantly held by three estates—the nobility, the clergy, and the bourgeoisie. However, these three medieval estates are of little use in studying the agrarian conditions of the Germanic peoples. Neither the nobility nor the early medieval clergy can be flawlessly traced back to the Germanic nobility or the Germanic common freemen. On the contrary, precisely during the Carolingian period, for the sake of a more unified and reliable administration, unfree servants of the king—especially those who proved reliable as officials on royal estates—were often elevated to positions of great influence.[106] Of course, this does not imply that we know for sure that these people would have been of non-Nordic blood. However, it should be pointed out that we cannot reliably use the relationship between the medieval nobility and the peasant class as evidence of the relationship between the nobility and the peasants/common freemen at the time of the Germanic Migration Period. The bourgeoisie, on the other hand, are too much of a medieval innovation in Germany to be relevant to the question at hand.[107]

Now the question arises as to what the ancient Germanic peoples understood by the term peasant. Perhaps the development of early Icelandic gover-

---

[106] Our German term *minister* clearly reflects this aspect; *minister* comes from the Latin *minus*, meaning lesser, similar to how *magister* is derived from *magis*, meaning more. During the Roman imperial era, *ministeriales* were household servants of the emperor's court who wielded significant power. It is obvious that the Franks then adopted this practice.

[107] In the political struggle of the years 1931–1932, the following definition emerged, "A peasant is someone who, in hereditary connection to the land, cultivates it and views this activity as a duty to their lineage." This definition contrasts this the more liberal *landwirt*, "A *landwirt* is someone who cultivates land without a hereditary connection to the land and views this activity solely as a means of earning money." These definitions assisted with the development of population and hereditary health policy and brought it into the forefront of public interest, impacting agricultural policy as well.

nance can provide us with a good introductory example in this regard. For in Iceland, authority and state were tied to the ownership of a *hof*, a pagan shrine *"unter dach und fach*," meaning "under roof and shelter." The owner is the sole authorized priest (*gode, hofgode*) and, in that sense, the natural head of the religious community. The power of jurisdiction, including the power of execution, also rested in the hands of such a *gode*. From this, a later chieftaincy subsequently evolved. Of particular relevance to us here is the importance of the shrine, or *hof*, being "under roof and shelter." This, in fact, leads us to a commonality with the etymology of the German word *bauer* (peasant). Heyne explains,

> *Bauer*, from Middle High German *bûre*, originally referred to someone settled in a *bur* (corresponding to Old High German *bur* or *pur* as well as Middle High German *bur*), meaning dwelling or house; now only used in this sense in the word *vogelbauer*, meaning birdcage. The word is also related to *gibûre* (Old High German *gibûro* or *gebûr*), which denotes a member of a settlement cooperative. *Bäuerin* is the term for the wife and mistress of the peasant household.[108]

Perhaps even more enlightening is the etymology provided by Weigand:

> *Bauer*, from Middle High German *bûr*, previously *gebur* or *gebure* (genitive *geburen*, also *gebures*), from Old High German *giburo* or *gibur*, meaning inhabitant, fellow citizen, or rural inhabitant and formed from *gi-*, meaning "with," and Old High German *bûr*, meaning dwelling, thus essentially meaning "co-dweller," fellow villager, or *nachbar* (originally *nachbaur, nachtbaur, -bar*; in fourteenth century Middle High German *nâchbûre* or *nâchgebûre*, in Old High German *nâchgabûr*, and in English, neighbor).[109]

Therefore, the concept of peasant is closely connected to the idea of dwelling. In German, we also refer to a dwelling as *haus* (house). For us, the term *haus* now has the dual meaning of a constructed dwelling for humans as well as (particularly in Old High German) a noble lineage (such as the House of Habsburg). Understanding this, we can see that the German word *haus* is therefore connected to the aforementioned Icelandic term *hof*, denoting a shrine situated "under roof and shelter." This connection becomes even more evident in the Gothic term *gudhus*, meaning house of God. It can be assumed that the sacredness associated with the concept of the home is directly related to the worship of fire, which is observed among all Indo-European peoples. The fire—the hearth fire—served as the focal point of the home and was never allowed to go out. In the evening, ashes were carefully placed on top of the fire, and in the morning, the embers under the fire were carefully rekindled. It is clear that maintaining a fire in the rainy northern regions of central Europe would have

---

[108] Heyne, *Deutsches Wörterbuch.*
[109] Weigand, *Deutsches Wörterbuch.*

been challenging without shelter. The Icelandic sacred place of worship, the "house," located "under roof and shelter," thus makes sense as a way to facilitate the preservation of fire. Originally, the fire likely burned quite simply on the ground. According to Weigand, the Old High German word *herd* specifically referred to the hearth as merely the soil or "ground for the fire."

In the next chapter, when we discuss the Indo-Europeans, we will see how marriage and procreation was directly intertwined with the obligation of the head of the household, as the priest of the sacred fire, to father a son who would succeed him in maintaining the sacred fire after his death. Since the fire was directly connected to the ground, or soil, the maintenance of the sacred fire required a completely sedentary way of life. After all, it is practically impossible to carry an open fire for days on end. If the owner of such a household fire wanted to fulfill the task of maintaining the fire, he inevitably needed enough land to sustain himself and his "house" (family), since, of course, he was tied to one place due to his responsibility for maintaining the fire. Thus, in order to maintain a domestic fire, the land had to provide adequate sustenance for the family responsible for maintaining the fire. In fact, we can now demonstrate from Germanic law that the size of land holdings was determined by the land's capability to provide subsistence for a family (household). As a result, the size of individual family landholdings among the Germanic peoples of the Migration Period varied depending on the type of land. Von Amira writes,

> Units of measurement for land ownership are the *hufe* (Old Saxon *hôva*, Old High German *huoba*, possibly denoting a share of yield), *los* (*sors*, Anglo-Saxon *hluz*), *wohnland* (residential land), or *pflugland* (plowland). Everywhere, these units were understood to denote the average amount of agricultural land needed to support a family, and for this very reason they could not have been the same size everywhere—they could only have been a local measure of land area. The common land shared by members of a cooperative not subject to cultivation were usually factored in as well.

This makes another Germanic tradition more understandable. Namely, in ancient Germanic times, the acquisition of land was tied not only to the establishment of boundaries, but also to the act of kindling a hearth fire. When land ownership was transferred from one family to another, the original owner had to extinguish their household fire, an act that was accompanied by a rather elaborate ceremony. Subsequently, the new owner would then kindle their own household fire with equal ceremony.[110]

The concept of the Germanic household therefore consists of a peculiar trinity in which the hearth serves as the focal point, the roof protects the fire

---

[110] Incidentally, such customs persisted well into the nineteenth century. For instance, Gustav Kohne's *Jugendsehnen: Ein Scharnhorst Roman* [Youthful Yearnings: A Scharnhorst Novel] charmingly depicts how, during the acquisition of an estate, Mother Scharnhorst solemnly lights the hearth fire and carries out various ancient rituals.

from the weather, and the land provides sustenance for the family maintaining the fire. In this way, the Germanic house becomes an entirely organic entity, a living structure (organism) that can hardly be understood in more complete terms. However, the most self-evident prerequisite for establishing such a structure around a fire is arguably that the family lineage maintaining the fire be sedentary. Any kind of itinerant way of life would make it impossible for such structures to be preserved. Our German language actually confirms this. As we saw above, the inheritance of such a "house" was of great importance in terms of the maintenance of a household fire. Heyne explains that in the ancient languages, the word *erbe*, which today simply means heir, meant a member of a hereditary land cooperative (Gothic *arbja*, Old Norse *arfi*, Old High German *erpeo* or *erbo*, Middle High German *erbe*). Weigand explains the ancient meaning of *erbe* as hereditary real estate or inherited ancestral property. If one was already convinced of how clearly Germanic concepts related to important aspects of life are connected to the land, the etymology of the next word (which is unexpected in this context), serves as further proof that assuming any kind of nomadism for the ancient Germanic peoples is nothing less than a complete falsification of the actual facts. Furthermore, according to Heyne, our word *adel* (nobility) originally meant nothing more than a cooperative of landowners (Middle High German *adel* and Old High German *adal*, an ablaut of the Old High German *uodal*, meaning ancestral seat). The connections are even more explicit in Weigand, with Old High German *uodil* or *uodal*, Old Saxon *odil*, Old English *adel*, and Old Norse *odal*, all meaning hereditary estate or homeland. The same is confirmed by von Amira:

> Words for hereditary or ancestral properties included the Old Norwegian *ódal* (otherwise used in the north to denote genuine ownership in general), the Anglo-Saxon *édél* (until approximately 900), the Old Saxon *ôdhil*, the Old High German *uodal*, probably the Frisian *ethel* in its early medieval form (also referred to as *statha* in West Frisian), and finally also the Old Swedish *byrb*. In some of these cases, not only was the owner's power of disposition limited, but the right of first refusal was also granted to the male lineage, as seen in the Norwegian *ódal* and the Anglo-Saxon *édél*. What is more, indivisibility and inheritance of the hereditary estate by the eldest male relative (*schwertmage*) was also characteristic of those forms of hereditary property that emerged in the Early Middle Ages in Upper Germany as *hantgemahele* (contracted as *hantgemâl*) among fully free and typically knightly-born individuals. In addition to the legal guidelines, the Anglo-Saxons also had a type of endowed hereditary property (a kind of familial fideicommissum) since the eighth century. . . . Again, Norwegian law—particularly West Norwegian law—in the Early Middle Ages even makes a distinction between the person who inherits a hereditary estate (*ódal*) or has a claim to it (*holdr*, meaning hero or capable man) and the ordinary or common freemen.

So, if we take the etymology of the words *adel* (noble) and *bauer* (peasant) quite literally, the Scandinavian word *adelsbauer* (noble peasant) expresses that the person to whom this designation of nobility was applied to was also a peasant with an inherited property. The most essential component of such hereditary property was its inalienability; moreover, it included a sacred hearth fire and, in its overall form functioned as a genuine organism. The particular advantage of such a noble estate clearly lay in its undivided inheritance, while the peasants—who were communally organized in the farming communities—did not possess such unconditional indivisibility of their farms. In fact, based on their "cooperative association for the working of the land and ensuring sustenance," they redistributed the land among the families on a case-by-case basis, depending on the size of the family. The member of such a Germanic cooperative was called peasant. Therefore, the difference between the Germanic noble peasants and the Germanic peasants consisted mainly in the different ways of inheriting the land necessary for sustaining a family.

With this in mind, the Germanic concept of the peasant—including both the cooperative peasant and the self-sufficient noble peasant—was defined as the head of a family or, in other words, the owner of a "house." However, as we have observed earlier, for the Germanic people, the term "house" represents a sacred trinity encompassing three essential elements: fire, shelter, and the land necessary for a family's sustenance. As a result, the Germanic family becomes a cohesive living entity whose sustenance is provided by the treasures of the land. It is incumbent upon the man to represent this organic unity to the outside world, but it is the woman who has supremacy over the actual internal affairs of the house; in chapter nine we will return in detail to the distinctive way labor is divided between the sexes in the Germanic peasant household.

In summary, we can say that the Germanic peoples considered a peasant to be the leader or head of a family unit organically tied to land ownership.

As we saw above with von Amira, the peasants were grouped together in the *bûrschaft* or *Landsgemeinde*, and this *Landsgemeinde* had legislative power. The nobility did not have any privileges at all, only possessing the advantage of being considered first when choosing and appointing officials.[111] The fact that the Germanic peasants were freemen can therefore no longer be denied in light of this. Thus, it begins to make sense why, as the author already mentioned at the beginning of this chapter, the Germanic peoples bestowed a new peasantry and a new land law on the Latin countries that had been emptied of peasants.

But anyone who now wants to make racial conclusions from this must be quite clear as to whether or not he counts the freemen of the Goths, Lombards, Franks, Vandals, etc., as belonging to the Nordic race. From all we know so far,

---

[111] The relationship between the Germanic nobility and the Germanic freemen can be vividly imagined by drawing a comparison with our volunteer soldiers during the World War. The volunteer soldier with higher education had an advantage over the volunteer soldier without special education when it came to being appointed to be an officer by the officers of his regiment, provided he was deemed suitable for such a role. However, as long as both wore the uniform of the common soldier, they were treated equally.

a racial stratification between the nobility of these tribes and the common freemen is neither expressed in their imagery nor in their law. Additionally, it is certain that these Germanic tribes did not bring with them Phalian serfs, but rather, in the case of the Franks, gradually transformed into a manorial nobility over centuries, eventually becoming the Frankish nobility of France.

Given the importance of the house—the dwelling place—to the Germanic peoples, it is clear that we can indeed determine the spread of the Germanic peoples through the spread of Germanic architectural style over the course of settlement history. By simultaneously studying the linguistic boundaries of the German or Germanic language, the striking correlation between architectural style and language becomes striking. Combined with the ancient rural customs preserved in the oral legal traditions (*weistümer*) and their surviving remnants, such as in closed inheritance law and other customs, we gain far more ir-refutable clues regarding the peasantry of the early Germanic peoples.[112] These sources offer us much more valuable insights than the medieval rights and du-ties of social classes, which often depict a completely altered relationship be-tween peasants and the nobility, clergy, and bourgeoisie. Therefore, interpreting medieval historical materials (especially when contemporary notions regarding peasant life and serfdom are also erroneously present) can lead to misunder-standings about the nature of the serfdom of medieval peasants and their an-cient relationship to the Germanic free community.[113]

It should be clear that the free Germanic people's conception of the peas-antry discussed here does not have anything to do with agricultural work in the strict sense of the word. For the nature of the Germanic peasantry did not lie in how they exploited the soil, but solely in the fact that they had the right to use it for the sake of their families (houses). As a comparison, one can think of the German military officer—belonging to the officer class was connected with

---

[112] Professor Beckmann (Bonn) once said, "The German rural estate, whether a peasant farm or a knight's manor, practiced a particular type of marriage; that is, a son or daughter always stayed on their estate once married. This has been a Germanic custom for thousands of years. As a result, the other siblings were obligated to either remain unmarried or leave the farm after marriage. From this we have known for centuries the practice of the uncle—the uncle, unclehood—a waste in terms of biology but an economically valuable asset which is becoming increasingly rare due to the industrial and communal development of Germany providing more and more opportu-nities for the uncle to make an independent living." The core essence of this system of inheritance is to avoid weakening the productive capacity of the farm through continuous division of inheri-tances. In other words, it aims to preserve the farm—and consequently the soil—as a means to sustain a family with a brood of children. This form of peasant inheritance, therefore, regards the farm merely as the land necessary for the sustenance of a family so that its genetics may be passed down from generation to generation.

[113] In this day and age, even among the educated, one encounters the most distorted notions of Germanic culture. For these people, a Germanic person is still nothing more than a club-wielding, bear-fur-clad semi-barbarian with swelling biceps. Lest there be any misunderstanding, it should be noted that there indeed exists a Germanic architectural style that serves as a guide where excava-tions fall short. Specifically, the so-called "Romanesque" architectural style is not Romanesque at all, but Germanic. It is simply the adaptation into stone of the architectural arcades found in Ger-manic wooden houses. For those seeking further insights into the civilization of the Germanic people, I refer them to: Friedrich Behn, *Altgermanische Kunst* [Ancient Germanic Art] (Munich: 1930) and Gustaf Kossinna, *Altgermanische Kulturhöhe* [Heights of Ancient Germanic Civiliza-tion] (Munich: 1927).

the performance of tasks and duties that did not necessarily apply to the officer's daily activities; it did not exempt the officer from mastering the craft of the common soldier, in the event that the officer needed to replace the common soldier in battle. Therefore, at its core, the nature of the Germanic peasant did not at all depend on whether he plowed his fields himself or whether he delegated all field work to a married servant, all that mattered was the manner in which he utilized his property. In fact, this ancient Germanic view of peasantry has been with us for much longer than is commonly believed. In fact, it is not at all the case that every peasant in Germany drives his plow with his own hands. There are still many parts of Germany where the peasant or farm owner does not even consider doing more farm or field work than is necessary. In some places, he limits his work only to what falls under the category of so-called "peasant work," in fact, in some cases the peasant almost believes that he would lose face if he took on work that a farmhand could do just as well. In these places, it is still very common for a married farmhand to live on the peasant's farm—often the farmhand's family has lived on that farm for generations. The farmhand manages the actual farm work quite independently, either acting as foreman when work is being done, or enjoying the privilege of choosing an activity that best suits him. In various parts of Germany these head farmhands are common, though they go by different titles in different parts of the country. In some areas of southern Germany, they are usually allowed to drive the peasant's best horses and are therefore also in charge of the stables. Although plowing is generally considered to be peasant work (meaning work that belongs to the peasant and is part of his labor privileges), it is more often the case that the peasant does this work only when required or when circumstances force him to do so.

With these examples, the author should have sufficiently clarified the nature of the Germanic peasantry, as well as the fact that it is not difficult to draw parallels between our long-established peasantry and the common freemen of the Germanic people.

4

We can now proceed to examine agriculture itself among the Germanic peoples. As we have analyzed the legal relationships of the Germanic peoples and established that they were sedentary (in other words, peasants), all that remains is to determine the nature of their agriculture. The main purpose of Germanic agriculture was a familial-economic one. Therefore, when dealing with this topic, one must first ensure that today's economic ideas about agriculture are not used as a yardstick for evaluating the agriculture of the Germanic peoples of that time; unfortunately, this is very frequently not the case. Since today we judge how successful a farm is by the value that the owner is able to extract from the land, some researchers of Germanic conditions make the mistake of applying the same standard to Germanic agriculture, without considering that Germanic man did not need to extract more value from his land than was necessary for himself, his family and his servants, in a word, for his whole household. During the Migration Period, the Germanic peoples had virtually no grain trade, so there was no incentive to grow more grain than could actually be consumed. When this fact is fully understood, and when one also considers the tremendous abundance of wildlife and fish provided by the Germanic forests and waters (which played a substantial role in their diet), it becomes clear why researchers should avoid demanding more from Germanic agricultural practices than is justified under the conditions prevailing at the time.

The first truly reliable source that we obtain regarding the agricultural practices of the Germanic peoples is from Charlemagne the Saxon Slayer, particularly his estate ordinance, which was issued around the year 812. Emperor Charlemagne's estate ordinance is certainly not evidence of agriculture among the Germanic peoples during the Migration Period; however, we do get a coherent picture of the Carolingian period and a glimpse into an advanced system of animal husbandry, thus gaining a deep understanding of the agricultural practices of the time, both in farming and horticulture. It is undoubtedly worthwhile to describe this agricultural approach, if only to give the reader a comprehensive picture of the agricultural conditions of our ancestors in the eighth century. For a description of Charlemagne the Saxon Slayer's estate ordinance, it is best to read Fleischmann's account:

They have ceased limiting the income from their estates (*fenus servare*, as Tacitus says) and are happy to do so. Emperor Charles never tires of exhorting his officials to not miss any opportunity for profit on their properties and to work constantly to increase all yields (*fenus agitare*), thus bringing about an increase in the peasants' taxes. What has already been achieved informally can be clearly seen in the estate ordinance. Forestry and fish farming begin to develop, meadows and pastures are cultivated and hay is produced, hunting is regulated, and the number of domesticated animals and useful plants increases due to the introduction of previously foreign species. In addition to cattle and horses, pigs, sheep, and goats are also mentioned, as well as chickens, geese, ducks, pigeons, pheasants, peacocks, and even beekeeping. The list of plants recommended for cultivation in the gardens of the manor houses includes seventy-three different plants, among them culinary plants (including all kinds of vegetables, several types of onions, and spices), a number of medicinal plants, ornamental plants (including flowers, shrubs, and trees), and a large number of pome and stone fruits, including precocious and perennial apples, dessert and cooking pears, cherries, peaches, almonds, nuts and berries. Craftsmen of various kinds had their own plots of land and lived among the peasants in the villages, supplying products for the manor farms. There was also no shortage of spinning rooms, baking ovens, wine presses, and weaving facilities for linen and wool. In the household pantry, various products are prepared, including sausages, brawn, cured meat, smoked meat, bacon sides, lard, tallow, butter, cheese, liqueurs, wine, beer, mead, malt, vinegar, and mustard. Additionally, honey, eggs, vegetables, herbs, spices, and fruits are collected and stored. Among the supplies found in warehouses, storerooms, and barns, the following are mentioned: wax, soap, beets, grain, flour, legumes, millet, hemp, flax, wool, raw and processed dyes, whiteware, blankets, bed feathers, beds, household and farm utensils, wool combs, teasels, hand tools, barrels, war chariots, firewood, pine and timber, torches, hides, skins, horns, etc. Special care is given to wine making and horse breeding. [114]

This shows that the agriculture of the Germanic peoples in the eighth century was highly developed. But—and this must be explicitly pointed out— Carolingian agriculture already had a feature that must have been fundamentally foreign to Germanic agriculture only a few centuries earlier, something that Fleischmann naturally points out in the first few sentences. In Charlemagne the Saxon Slayer's estate ordinance, we can already see an economic approach to agriculture that breaks with the idea of a self-contained household economy oriented only toward satisfying the needs of the family. By the eighth century, Germanic agriculture had already become a revenue economy, going well beyond satisfying family needs and aiming to make a profit. It makes no difference whether the surplus profit directly or indirectly benefited the peasants themselves or whether the Frankish state authorities and bailiffs were the primary beneficiaries.

When it comes to the agriculture of the Germanic peoples during the Migration Period, we have only limited information. Nevertheless, what we do know is certainly more than enough to arrive at clear ideas about it. But, as Fleischmann once sharply remarked, we must finally start to banish ideas of "prehistoric Germanic forest and marsh nomads" from our own minds.

What must be kept in mind above all else—or at least should be remembered—is the fact that before the arrival of the Germanic tribes, the Celts had already inhabited the Rhine and possessed a highly developed system of agriculture. For example, Schuhmacher reports that plowshares with an iron point were already known in these areas in the later Iron Age (La Tène period), as well as iron sickles, scythes, shovels, field hooks, etc. He writes,

In one of these farms, belonging to the early La Tène period, near Heilbronn, evidence of a milk chamber has been identified based on the shape of vessels. Moreover, in the manor at Gerichtstetten in Baden, which dates back to the second or first century BC, not only is the purpose of each building discernible, but also the fact that the estate was originally an open settlement, fortified only around 100 BC. [115]

---

[114] Fleischmann, *Cäsar, Tacitus, Karl der Große*, 1911.
[115] Schuhmacher, *Der Ackerbau in Vorrömischer*.

When the Germanic tribes arrived, more words would have to be added to those of Schuhmacher.

And now a question. Is it really possible to believe that the Germanic peoples—if they had really been those "prehistoric Germanic forest and marsh nomads" that some people still like to see them as—would have refrained from simply exploiting the highly developed agricultural system of the Celts as an exploitative ruling class? Of course, in that case, all they would have had to do was plant their fortresses among the Celts, just as the Tartars did with the kremlins in Russia.

But the fact that the Germanic tribes simply did not do that, but transplanted their form of settlement to the Rhine and either wiped out the Celtic settlements or pushed them into areas they did not want (this can be clearly inferred from the settlement history on the Rhine) proves that the Germanic tribes did not conquer the Rhine region to form a parasitic ruling class, but merely conquered new farmland as peasants. The history of the first Germanic invasions definitely confirms this idea. In fact, archaeology would have clear evidence if a foreign migration came into the Celtic settlement area on the Rhine and formed a separate ruling class, namely through the sudden appearance of Germanic fortresses in the midst of Celtic villages. No such evidence exists. In chapter eight, the author will give a brief introduction on the history of the Cimbrian migrations and Ariovistus's conquest of Alsace. In essence, anyone who portrays the land-seeking peasant treks of the Cimbri, Tigurini, Helvetii, and Teutons as an adventurous expedition of a non-agricultural master race devoted exclusively to warfare is completely falsifying the historical record. Despite four victories over the Roman legions, they did not dare to break across the Roman border into Italy. Since we have historical documents on the subject, it borders on a falsification of history to present Ariovistus's peasant state in Alsace, which reigned in peace for fourteen years and which Caesar did not dare attack without reason, as a non-peasant conquest—more on this in chapter eight.

But back to the agricultural practices of the Germanic peoples. Schuhmacher, for example, states quite clearly:

> In the cultivation of cereals, the Germanic peoples were even ahead of the Romans, for they had long cultivated wheat, various kinds of spelt, barley, millet, oats, and rye—the Romans would adopt these last two kinds of cereals from the northern peoples.[116]

The Germanic love of oatmeal reported by Pliny is the same as what we see today among Scandinavians, the English, and in many Low German regions, where morning oatmeal is never absent from the breakfast table (the "porridge"

---

[116] Schuhmacher's view that rye and oats were introduced to the Romans by the Germanic peoples is controversial and has been challenged. However, there is evidence to support it, such as the fact that oats, for example, are a cereal crop that thrives in humid conditions, and the focus of its cultivation remains in the rain-rich regions of northwestern Europe.

of the English).[117] The obvious love shared by Germanic lands for oatmeal in the morning, coupled with the fact that non-Germanic peoples are the least likely to understand this oatmeal consumption, undoubtedly establishes clear connections linking Germanic civilizations with the cultivation of oats.

The first truly tangible account of Germanic agriculture comes from Caesar. Unfortunately, however, Caesar's account must be taken with a grain of salt. Müllenhoff has shown that Caesar was quite obviously not afraid to tell outright falsehoods from time to time.[118] These things are also pointed out by Fleischmann, who summarizes Germanic agriculture as described to us by Caesar as follows:

> During Caesar's time, it is evident that agriculture and livestock raising was practiced among the Ubii, Sugambri, Usipetes, Tencteri, and Suebi, with livestock raising likely being more dominant. It is simply impossible to sort what is true or even what is probable from what Caesar states about Germanic agriculture.

In spite of this, some things can still be determined from Caesar's report. We follow Fleischmann:

> During Caesar's time, grain cultivation must have been widespread in Helvetia, all of Gaul, and in Britannia. This can be inferred from the fact that Caesar did not encounter any difficulties in provisioning his army with grain in these lands. Since Caesar, in his comparison of the characteristics of Gaul and Germania, emphasizes that the Germanic peoples practiced very little agriculture, it may seem justified to assume that the situation was better in Gaul. However, grain cultivation was by no means absent in Germania. During his initial visit to the right bank of the Rhine, Caesar destroyed the grain fields of the Sigambri,[119] and during his second visit, he procured grain from the Ubii.[120] It is also mentioned that the Usipetes and Tencteri were unable to cultivate their fields for several years because they were heavily pressed by the Suebi.[121] Caesar's personal experience therefore testifies to the practice of agriculture among the four Germanic tribes living on the right bank of the Rhine. All the other tribes also practiced it,

---

[117] Pliny the Elder, *Historia Naturalis* [Natural History], Book 18, chapter 44, trans. John Bostock (London: Taylor and Francis, 1855). "...so much so, in fact, that tile oat has become an equivalent for [grain]; for the people of Germany are in the habit of sowing it, and make their porridge of nothing else."

[118] Müllenhoff, *Deutsche Altertumskunde*.

[119] See book 4, chapter 19 of Caesar's *Commentaries on the Gallic War*: "Caesar, having remained in their territories a few days, and burned all their villages and houses, and cut down their [grain], proceeded into the territories of the Ubii..."

[120] Ibid, Book 6, chapter 10: "Having learned these things, he provides a supply of [grain] . . ."

[121] Ibid, Book 4, chapter 1: "The motive for crossing was, that having been for several years harassed by the Suevi, they were constantly engaged in war, and hindered from the pursuits of agriculture."

but they generally did not put great effort into it;[122] in fact, in another passage it is even said that the Germanic peoples in general had very little enthusiasm for agriculture.[123] However, there seems to have been a particular reason for Caesar's increased emphasis on the Germanic contempt for agriculture. A few days after the start of Caesar's second visit to the Ubii, he received information from his scouts about the Suebi's behavior, which seemed somewhat suspicious to him. Even though he had only recently collected grain a few days earlier, and even though he was situated in the vast and flourishing territories of the Ubii[124] and was directly connected to grain-rich Gaul via his Rhine bridge, and despite the fact that the grain in the fields had already begun to ripen,[125] he suddenly feared a shortage of grain. As a result, he turned around and crossed the Rhine again. The Romans' somewhat conspicuous fear of a grain shortage is justified by assertions that the Germanic peoples were particularly inept at growing grain. Perhaps Caesar's testimony about the agricultural practices of the Germanic peoples were not always entirely free from the influences of strategic considerations. Even if Caesar's account that the Suebi were constantly engaged in warfare and could only engage in agriculture to a minimal degree were true,[126] it would still be inappropriate to apply the conditions of the Suebi to all Germanic tribes without further consideration, as Caesar does. Whether the Suebi were actually at such a low level of cultural development at that time, as Caesar would have us believe, seems questionable.

The fair-minded reader of the *Commentarii de Bello Gallico* is left wondering why Caesar applies the conditions of the Suebi, which he only learns of through hearsay (he briefly outlines this in book four), to the entire Germanic people in book six. It would be more logical for him to base his account on the social and economic conditions of the Germanic tribes on the right bank of the Rhine, whom he had actually encountered. It seems to have been different with the Usipetes and Tencteri, whose territory Caesar did not enter, and these two tribes are mentioned in the same chapter in

---

[122] Ibid, Book 6, chapter 22, "They do not pay much attention to agriculture, and a large portion of their food consists in milk, cheese, and flesh . . ."
[123] Ibid, Book 6, chapter 29: "As we have observed above, all the Germans pay very little attention to agriculture . . ."
[124] Ibid, Book 4, chapter 3: "On the other side they border on the Ubii, whose state was large and flourishing . . ."
[125] Ibid, Book 6, chapter 29: ". . . when the [grain] began to ripen . . ."
[126] Ibid, Book 4, chapter 1: "The nation of the Suevi is by far the largest and the most warlike nation of all the Germans"; chapter 3: "They esteem it their greatest praise as a nation, that the lands about their territories lie unoccupied to a very great extent, inasmuch as [they think] that by this circumstance is indicated, that a great number of nations can not withstand their power; and thus on one side of the Suevi the lands are said to lie desolate for about six hundred miles"; chapter 4: "In the same condition were the Usipetes and the Tenchtheri . . . who, for many years, resisted the power of the Suevi, but being at last driven from their possessions . . ."

which the life of the Suebi is described as something out of the ordinary. Perhaps the incredible things he was told about the Suebi seemed more captivating to Caesar than what he had seen in the land of the Ubii and Sigambri. In his account of the Suebi, he mentions that they regularly sent one thousand men on the warpath every year, and that all the others stayed at home to feed themselves, as well as provide supplies for those in the field. As a result, neither agricultural nor military operations suffered any interruption.[127] He also says that there is no private ownership of individual plots of land, and that no one is allowed to live on a plot of land for more than one year so that it can be developed. His story describes the following as standard for the Germanic peoples: individuals do not have private ownership of land, rather, authorities and princes allocate land year after year to families, clans and tribes at their own discretion and in whatever quantity and location they desire, they then force them to emigrate elsewhere after a year.[128]

If we take these words as they are and do not distort their meaning, they imply that the Germanic people were subject to substantial abuses by their authorities and rulers. Those who are not on the battlefield are led around like a flock of sheep and forced to be content with the land allotted to them, no matter how much or where the authorities choose to give it. They are forced to cultivate it and must agree to be resettled elsewhere at the whim of the authorities after one year. And so this cycle goes on year after year. Directly following the description of the Suebi's way of life, Caesar remarks on the Suebi's character, stating that they are free of obedience and discipline from an early age, doing only what they want and nothing else.[129] Caesar terribly contradicts himself with this statement. As far as agriculture at this time is concerned, we are expected to believe that all the freemen of the Germanic tribes split their time between warfare and peaceful farming, all of their own free will and conviction. Simultaneously, we are expected to believe that those who went to war one year would not return to their former homes and regions the following year—that they would have to settle in different homes in a different place not of their choosing. Likewise, those who stayed at home were supposed to be sent else-

---

[127] Ibid, Book 4, chapter 1: "They are said to possess a hundred cantons, from each of which they yearly send from their territories for the purpose of war a thousand armed men: the others who remain at home, maintain [both] themselves and those-engaged in the expedition. The latter again, in their turn, are in arms the year after: the former remain at home. Thus neither husbandry, nor the art and practice of war are neglected."

[128] Ibid, Book 6, chapter 22, ". . . nor has any one a fixed quantity of land or his own individual limits; but the magistrates and the leading men each year apportion to the tribes and families, who have united together, as much land as, and in the place in which, they think proper, and the year after compel them to remove elsewhere."

[129] Ibid, Book 4, chapter 1, ". . . for having from boyhood been accustomed to no employment, or discipline, they do nothing at all contrary to their inclination..."

where from year to year. It is a well-known fact that the land never repays the effort and labor devoted to it within just one year, rather, it does so over the long-term, over the course of several years. Among the ancient Germanic peoples, it was said that the fruits of all diligence are never gathered by the diligent individuals themselves, but by strangers in their place. The notion that free men, voluntarily working the land, would have permanently tolerated such a situation defies all economic sense and age-old experience. Agriculture has never failed in its peculiar effect—it has always tied those who continuously practice it to the soil.

There is not much to add to Fleischmann's words. However, the author would like to make just one point. The Germanic peoples of the Migration Period, like the Suebi here in question, were in a state of migration; this is evident not only from historical sources, but has also been revealed to us by archaeology, which has found ample evidence regarding the origins of the Suebi. It is therefore possible to assume from the outset that Caesar had correctly observed something and that the conditions he described among the Suebi referred to migratory conditions—perhaps Caesar did not even mention the non-migratory Germanic tribes because he probably did not think that their sedentism was anything out of the ordinary, in other words, sedentism was the natural state of the Germanic tribes. There was nothing for him to notice in this sedentism, while the unusual behavior of the Suebi was a source of surprise to him.

It could also be assumed, for example, that the Germanic tribes did not travel in a single continuous procession, but rather moved from stage to stage, so to speak, stopping and resting from place to place, and in this way covered only a certain distance each year. In fact, it could be assumed that the Germans completed their actual migration around May, settling somewhere and possibly establishing a camp to practice agriculture for one summer. Of course, in this case, one should not imagine a proper plow-based agriculture with thorough soil preparation, but rather something similar to what we understand and still recognize today as Hauberg agriculture. In this method of agriculture, forests are cleared, the wood is used, and the branches are burned. The soil and ashes are then thoroughly tilled and the summer crops are sown. We will discuss this type of agriculture in more detail in a later chapter. Such a method of agriculture does indeed entail forest depletion, especially if it is carried out in high forest. However, it is still feasible wherever forests are abundant and wood scarcity is not an issue. As a result, the practice is still occasionally found in wood-rich regions such as Scandinavia and Finland. During the World War, it experienced a revival even here in Germany, as areas devastated by the logging of high forests were used to feed the population by introducing single-summer grain cultivation.

If the author's assumption is correct, Caesar's words begin to be more easily understood. Such a Germanic peasant trek in the process of migration would find a resting place and remain there during the summer, dividing the land between the clans present. They would then clear the forest, use the wood, burn the branches to ashes, sow crops into the ash-covered fertile forest soil, and harvest in the fall. Presumably, they would remain in their established camp through the winter and resume their journey to another area the following spring, resting again in May to repeat what they had done the previous year. In fact, this assumption is very likely, mainly because of timing considerations. If one imagines the Germanic tribes as a highly mobile pastoral people (which, by the way, contradicts their entire hearth fire cult) or, to use Fleischmann's words, as ancient Germanic forest and swamp nomads, then it would have been quite possible for them to move from the easternmost regions of Europe to the westernmost regions within the span of a year. Attila was capable of doing so. Even if one were to consider the Germanic migration as a slow-moving peasant trek, then such a trek—no matter how slow-moving it may have been—would never have taken longer than one or, at most, two years to travel from the farthest eastern regions of Europe to the farthest western regions, assuming it moved continuously and without interruption. These considerations can be conclusively deduced from the historical accounts of the Cimbrian migrations, where their carts are precisely described, and their marching speed can be verified by measuring the distances they covered in Gaul.

The Germanic tribes, however, advance so slowly toward the Roman frontier that the gradual progression of such a tribe from winter camp to winter camp, with intermittent single-summer agriculture in between, becomes an almost unavoidable assumption.

With this, however, Caesar's reports become quite understandable. One can see why the distribution of land in the newly occupied summer camp was carried out by leaders, and it could even be argued that it was necessary to do so in order to avoid disputes, which, of course, was quite in keeping with the general cooperative philosophy of the Germanic peasantry. Furthermore, one can see why the organization of a migratory peasant trek required a constant state of readiness for warfare, which in turn necessitated a rigid division of labor. The most skilled and reliable warriors were therefore assigned to defend the trek, while their remaining comrades worked to provide food for the entire group. It is likely that the thousand-man unit emphasized by Caesar was actually a temporary functional organization during the period of migration, separated from the overall migrating population for the sake of maintaining order. That would be consistent with another consideration. According to von Amira, the *hundertschaft* (group of one hundred) had the following significance:

If the spatial and transportation conditions of the territory require it, it is divided into districts (*bezirke*) for the purposes of orderly jurisdiction, military and police administration, and in more recent times, also for financial and ecclesiastical administration. The small Germanic state typically only uses one type of district. At the time of the creation of the legal codices, this concept appears among the Germans and Scandinavians as *hundertschaft*

(Old Alamannic *hundari* or *huntari*, Old East Norse *hundari* and perhaps also *hundina*). This was translated from Latin by the Franks as *centena*, hence Middle High German *zent*, which probably originally referred to a social division, and was not to be understood as a numerical unit of one hundred or one hundred and twenty, but rather simply as a collective grouping of people. This could represent a purely private association, a military contingent, or a judicial assembly, later (probably in prehistoric times) evolving into a geographic concept denoting the location of this association.

Now, at another point in von Amira's work, we come across a mention of *zehn hundertschaften* (group of ten hundred):

The legal document written in Småland around 1300 belonged solely to the legal district known as *zehn hundertschaften* (*tiuhaerap*), of which only the section pertaining to ecclesiastical law is fully preserved. It belongs to the group of Swedish legal documents that utilize records of foreign land laws. At present, the legal documents from Östergötland and Upland serve as templates. We are relatively well-informed about the origins of these legal documents.

The name of the legal code, "*zehn hundertschaften*," would hardly have become established if it did not accurately encompass and designate a higher administrative concept situated above the ordinary *hundertschaft*. So we are already dealing with a mass of people that, while not exactly one thousand, is still roughly equivalent to one thousand.

After all, one must also consider that during the migration of such huge masses of people, a certain level of order had to be maintained. This was necessary for strategic reasons of defense (tactical considerations) alone. It ensured that in the event of a battle, the warriors would not be easy prey for the enemy by being helpless and scattered. Perhaps the explanation for this lies in the fact that all Germanic migrations, like those of the Indo-Europeans in general, were led by kings. It seems that these kings had a military authority (military command) during the period of migration that was not subject to the will of the people, even if it could be challenged by this will. Perhaps we can also assume that, during the Germanic migrations, the *tausendschaft* (group of one thousand) was an independent migrating group that moved in coordination with the other *tausendschaften* (thus continuing to act in concert with the people as a whole), but which formed a totally autonomous unit as far as summer settlement and food supply were concerned. A thousand men roughly constitutes the strength of a modern infantry regiment. Anyone who has ever examined the rations list of such a regiment will readily admit that feeding such a large number of people—especially in the absence of a permanent residence or access to supply depots—is an organizational feat of the highest order. We have no reason to believe that the Germanic peoples of the Migration Period were more skilled in the art of provisioning than the quartermasters of the former Imperial German Army. However, if we assume that a Germanic *tausendschaft* was sourced from about one hundred migrating clans or families, Caesar's remarks start to sound more realistic. The assumption that a Germanic family could provide around ten swordbearers is not implausible, considering the historical evidence of the Germanic people's high birth rate. In this case, the provisioning of the *tausendschaft* would be distributed between the one hundred families. For a migrating Germanic peasant trek moving in the previously described yearly patten and establishing fixed winter encampments while also engaging in single-summer grain cultivation during their rest periods, this arrangement should not have presented significant difficulties.

The author's assumption is further supported by the fact that Caesar explicitly mentions such conditions for the Suebi, who, as we know, were in a state of migration and in search of virgin territory. This would not be inconsistent with the fact that Ariovistus, after settling on the left bank of the Rhine, did not immediately disband the military organization of his people, but rather kept the warriors armed, presumably in anticipation of possible resistance from the Celtic tribes in the region. Caesar's remarks would have to be understood in this context—on one occasion he is discussing the migration of the Suebi, and on another occasion he is describing the martial organization employed by Ariovistus for defending the newly conquered territory.

It follows, then, that the accounts of the agricultural conditions of the Suebi that have been passed down to us through Caesar do not indicate this tribe's primitive agriculture, but, on the contrary, are evidence of an outstanding talent for designing and structuring a Germanic peasant trek that was on the move and had a vast number of people. What Caesar tells us about the Suebi now becomes entirely comprehensible, and we may consider ourselves justified in assuming similar conditions among the Cimbri and Teutons as well. However, since we have a fairly good and historically authenticated account of the Cimbri and Teutons migrations, including the distance and duration covered, we can, in turn, draw conclusions about the Suebi who appeared on the Roman frontier about a generation later.

Thus, the Germanic migrations emerge out of the darkness of Germanic prehistory with the first arrivals of huge treks of peasants at the borders of the Roman Empire. The historical behavior of these treks resembles that of a peasant people in search of land, and this aligns entirely with the events previously described in this chapter as told through the study of archaeology and Germanic legal history.

The next testament to Germanic agriculture is Tacitus, given that Pliny's twenty-volume work *Bella Germaniae* (The Germanic Wars), which was published around 60 AD, has been lost. Considering that Pliny served seven years with the Roman cavalry in Germania, made many forays throughout Germania, and therefore knew the Germanic conditions from his own experience, one can only regret the loss of this work.

By the time that Tacitus wrote *Germania*, the Germanic tribes had already been in direct and continuous contact with the Roman Empire for one hundred and fifty years. Thus, whether Tacitus himself was in Germania or not (which remains a matter of debate) is essentially of little consequence. In any case, he had access to highly knowledgeable individuals in Rome who were well-versed in Germanic affairs and could assist him in an advisory capacity. Nevertheless, this circumstance requires that we take Tacitus's words with a certain degree of caution. For example, when Tacitus recounts the warlike nature of the ancient Germanic peoples and their disregard for agriculture and peaceful occupations, this may indeed seem to contradict the notion of a peasantry among the Germanic peoples. But, to give a concrete example about the value of such non-German reports about Germany—anyone who has any familiarity with foreign countries today, especially as a German living abroad before the war, and who has had to experience the downright nonsensical ideas that foreigners have about the fencing culture, the *mensurwesen*,[130] of our students and the bloodthirsty "militarism" of our active officer corps will always find that the views held abroad about the German people never even have the smallest connection to reality. In fact, anyone who has attentively followed any of the atrocity propaganda spread by our enemies during the World War can see this clearly. What was said abroad about the German officer corps was unprecedented—and today this nonsense has indeed even made its way to the German people. And don't forget the foreign view of German students! To many foreigners, the German student was seen as an idle, gluttonous, and excessively drunk individual who occasionally thrashed around with his saber without any sense or understanding, and who basically lived without any real purpose in life. Foreigners never noticed the contradiction inherent in portraying the same student community as semi-barbaric savages while, at the same time, acknowledging that it produced some of the world's most eminent scholars, whose diligence and expertise were revered. The lesson we can learn here, in any case, is that it is apparently impossible for a non-German to have an accurate perception of Germans. When one compares today's foreign whining about our "drinking, brawling, lazy German students" with the words of Tacitus about the free Germans who supposedly loved the sword more than work, and the mead jug more than moderation, then one is almost forced to take the words of Tacitus with a grain of salt.

There is yet another aspect to consider. If we compare the agricultural conditions in Scandinavia at the end of the nineteenth century, where agriculture was still limited to meeting the needs of a somewhat large family (purely family-based farming), it becomes clear that agriculture here took up relatively little space. Large farms exclusively devoted to agriculture where more grain is grown than is needed by the family (either to meet the nation's

---

[130] The *mensur* is a traditional form of German fencing typically practiced by student associations. It is still practiced by some organizations today.

needs or to make a profit in the market) are worthwhile only from the point of view of a national economy. When family-based economic principles dominate an estate or farm, it becomes meaningless to cultivate more land than is strictly necessary. Rather, the surplus land is used as pasture for livestock, as woodland, or for some other purpose. In this way, the owner derives personal benefit from it without the need for additional labor. These conditions have persisted in Scandinavia until recently, and can be compared to the legal traditions of the Germanic people (see above), where a family was only allotted as much "plowland" as necessary to sustain the family's livelihood.

In this type of small-scale agriculture, all the plowing work takes place in a very small period of time. Aside from spring and fall plowing, there is little else to plow, and these tasks can be completed in a matter of days during the spring and fall. The author personally witnessed this in Finland, when a large-scale Finnish farmer (whom the author was visiting and whose horse breeding he wanted to study) first had to look for and fetch his horses from the forest pasture in order to be able to harness them to pull his carriage. In response to a question, the author was told that it was customary to also leave the field horses in the forest during the summer, since, of course, they were only needed for plowing for "about two to four days" in the spring and were then not needed until late summer when the harvest was brought in. Very similar agricultural practices are still observed today in remote regions of Scandinavia.

Such plowing can easily be accomplished by one or two farm hands. The farmer and owner of the land do not really need to operate the plow themselves, and they usually do not. This circumstance is clearly pointed out by the historian von Below, for example,

> If Tacitus seems to portray the free Germanic tribes as people who, when not engaged in hunting and warfare, lay on bearskins and depended on unfree agricultural laborers for their sustenance, it is essential to consider the pointed nature of his portrayal, which contrasts sharply with the fact that agriculture was practiced quite extensively at the time. This Germanic agriculture, however, required very little labor, therefore, the peasant (who remained so for a long period of time) engaged in intensive agricultural work for only a few short periods a year, in stark contrast to the bustling activities of Rome.[131]

We can, with absolute certainty, assume that such an ancient Nordic agricultural system, which can still be observed today, also existed during Tacitus's time among the Germanic peoples. We are justified in doing so precisely because the Germanic peasant (the head of the family) always had enough workers at his disposal, whether they were farmhands, bonded servants, members of his clan, or his sons. In fact, it would be nothing short of contradictory to as-

---

[131] Below, *Der Deutsche Staat des Mittelalters.*

sume that the head of a Germanic house (the peasant), in view of the important position he held in public life, would have done any work that was not
absolutely necessary. After all, the public legal capacity of the entire family was
derived from its head alone. But does this prove that the Germanic peasant
who did not drive his own plow therefore despised plowing or did not know
how to plow at all? Such an assumption would be about as convincing as suggesting that because the infantry lieutenant in 1914 went into battle equipped
with a sword, and was instructed by the combat manual to not pick up a rifle
and shoot alongside the common soldiers, in order to better oversee the troops
under his command, this is proof that the infantry lieutenant "despised" the
rifle, the weapon of the common soldier and non-commissioned officer, and
did not know how to use it.

Tacitus tells us that Germanic agriculture was determined by family-
based economic considerations, which we have already mentioned above in
connection with the estate ordinance of Charlemagne the Saxon Slayer. To
the Romans at the time of Tacitus, who had long been accustomed to purely financial thinking, it was rather incomprehensible that the Germanic
people only used their land to meet a family's needs and did not maximize
its output. For the Romans, the only way to understand the value of world-
ly things was in terms of how much money you could get out of them. To
use a modern buzzword, the Roman could not quite "get" the non-eco-
nomic way of thinking of the Germanic people of that time, which priori-
tized spiritual imponderables and the quiet comfort of one's home over the
financial exploitation of the treasures of this world. If the Germanic people
had not adhered to this principle throughout the Middle Ages and consistently ensured that the economic activities of their guilds and estates did
not become dominated by egocentric, selfish, financialized perspectives
(while also prioritizing the domestic peace of the head of the household),
we would not be able to make such confident judgements about these matters. But such a view—that the common good takes precedence over self-
interest—was so deeply ingrained in the blood of the Germanic peoples
that the Roman Empire did not succeed in stripping them of their basic
worldview like they did with the Celts. The opinion that "I can do what I
want with my money" is thoroughly un-Germanic and therefore un-German and, for that matter, un-Nordic. The Germanic people managed to
completely extinguish the thoroughly unethical and financialized worldview of the vast Roman Empire,[132] leaving their Germanic mark on the
Christian world for well over a millennium—at least until the eighteenth
and nineteenth centuries, when this basic Germanic philosophy begins to

---

[132] Theodor Birt writes in *Römische Charakterköpfe* [Distinctive Features of the Romans], "The
decline of morality in Rome had grown considerably through the period of civil wars since the
time of Sulla; it was founded on the egoism of individuals who wanted everything, strove to own
everything, and who gained everything through bloodshed and cunning. Even during the period of
peace, when Oriental luxury had triumphed, this selfishness only increased, this time directed
toward baser and more ignoble ends. Rather than inherit heroism, the likes of Lucullus, the
supreme hedonist, and Julius Caesar inherited only adultery."

recede.

The late Roman and Germanic views of the economy and of economic relations are so fundamentally different from each other that we should not hesitate for even a moment to insert context into Tacitus's descriptions of Germanic life.

Regarding specific details provided by Tacitus, we first refer to a passage from Fleischmann:

> The existence of villages (*vici*) is repeatedly mentioned as something self-evident in chapters twelve, sixteen, and nineteen. However, considering the diversity of life everywhere, it is unlikely that only village settlements existed in Germania at that time. Rather, it can be assumed that in certain places custom, soil conditions, and climate led to settlement in the form of individual farmsteads (*einzelhöfe*). It should be noted that even in the villages, the houses did not adjoin one another but stood alone, and each house was surrounded by a farm.

This is also confirmed by von Amira:

> The Germanic people of historical times are sedentary—their legal associations require a territory within permanent boundaries. Moreover, when such a legal association embarks on a migration, it does so solely to seek out a new territory of a similar nature. . . . The settlement or dwelling place (Gothic *haims*, Old Norse *heimr*, Old High German *heim*, Scandinavian *bygd*) itself had no political significance in the earlier period of Germanic law. It mattered little whether it was an individual farmstead (Old Norse *ból* or *gardr*, Middle High German *einôte* or *einoede*, and possibly Old High German *sedal*) or a village (Old Norse, Old English, and Old Saxon *thorp*, Old Franksih *thurp*, Old High German *dorf*, Old Swedish *byr*, Old Danish *by* and possibly *bóer*, Anglo-Saxon *tún*, Low German *wîc*, and Gothic *veihs*).

Comparing the oldest surviving legal customs and the state structure of the Germanic tribes (which can be reconstructed on the basis of the surviving legal principles), with the village settlement described by Tacitus, the Germanic peoples of early history are quite clearly free peasants residing on individual farms and in villages. However, it must be taken into account that at that time, agriculture was practiced only from the point of view of a family economy, and therefore, quite naturally, the records do not report very extensive agriculture. However, the presence of a Germanic peasantry is not contradicted by examples of Germanic freemen having their fields tilled by serfs or accepting tribute from land worked by serfs. As the Germanic people encountered servile populations along the Rhine, they probably became increasingly less inclined to have agricultural work done by their own kin, and instead adopted the proto-feudal mindset that would prevail for a millennium thereafter—they were content to live off the fruits of the serf's labor. Nevertheless, it should be noted that the settlement history of the Germanic people provides no evidence to suggest, for instance, that the Franks kept the pre-existing population in place as bound serfs tied to the land. However, it is reasonable to assume that the manorial system, which had become necessary in non-Frankish settlement areas, eventually spread to the Frankish areas and resulted in a division within the population.

With this, we have indeed demonstrated that the individual Germanic person was a free peasant engaged in agriculture. However, the level of cultural development of Germanic agriculture at that time has not yet been made clear. This, however, may not be as difficult to determine as is commonly believed.

5

The historical agricultural practices of the Germanic people exhibit a distinctive feature of great cultural-historical importance. From the earliest mentions of Germanic agricultural practices, we encounter the three-field system. This system is practiced consistently by the Germanic peoples and we are able to trace it throughout Germanic history, only being replaced within the last century. Tellingly, the origin of this replacement was England, where financialized economic development displaced traditional agrarian economic relations (in other words, the land was now seen from the perspective of financial exploitation). We will see below that England destroyed its peasantry with its thoughtless approach and in the course of only one hundred years denordified itself so thoroughly that the leadership of today's English state can no longer be regarded as being Nordic.

The three-field system is a rather distinctive Germanic practice that seems to have been deeply rooted in Germanic community life, much like Germanic law. One could almost argue that in Germanic history, the decline of the three-field system and the ultimate abandonment of Germanic legal concepts always went hand in hand to a considerable extent. What is remarkable is that, in a sense, the Germanic three-field system seems to have appeared rather suddenly in history. Equally remarkable is the fact that the land laws of Charlemagne the Saxon Slayer simply failed to address the manner in which field cultivation should be managed. Whether one likes it or not, this must be interpreted as follows—for centuries, field cultivation must have been practiced in such an unchanged and well-established manner that the idea of changing the method of field cultivation did not even occur to them. If the Germanic peoples had not possessed the three-field system at the time of Charlemagne the Saxon Slayer, and if Charlemagne had believed that the three-field system could enable a more profitable agricultural economy, then, based on all the other provisions outlined in his estate ordinance, one would absolutely expect to find detailed instructions for the bailiffs aimed at encouraging the peasants to adopt the three-field system. This is not the case.

Therefore, one must assume that at the time of Emperor Charlemagne, no one would have thought to expect anything other than the three-field system when it came to agriculture. Such an assumption would be entirely consistent with the persistence of the three-field system in Germanic-influenced regions a millennium after the time of Charlemagne the Saxon Slayer.

First of all, what is the three-field system? The three-field system divided farmland into three parts, with one serving as a rotating pasture, the second cultivated with winter cereals, and the third with summer cereals. In summer, the pasture is plowed once to prepare the land for seed sowing. The winter and summer fields are used for grazing after the harvest, until the arrival of winter. The pasture and stover fields were collectively grazed by the entire village's livestock. All owners of land in each area were obliged to utilize it according to the principles of the three-field system (known as *flurzwang*).

However, when it comes to explaining the three-field system, these are all essentially superficial aspects. Namely, the three-field system contains cooperative principles of unparalleled importance. This aspect has been rather excellently pointed out by Fleischmann:

> In the eighth century AD, a remarkable agricultural system arises seemingly out of nowhere and from obscure origins, already fully developed and wide-spread—a system that later justifiably gains fame and recognition under the name of the three-field system. It is completely unique and without precedent in agricultural history before it appeared in Germany. Its defining characteristic is that it is not designed for the individual operation of farmland but, rather, for communal operation by a group of peasants organized into a labor association—a peasant community. The three-field system should not be equated with other agricultural forms or "operational systems" described in agricultural textbooks. It is not merely a type of grain farming on three fields, which could also be implemented by an independent farmer on three adjacent plots, a practice that was likely implemented in other places, particularly in Italy and the Orient. The three-field system has much greater significance than this. It a societal institution of the utmost importance, comparable to a formidable machine of perfect simplicity. Sustained by the absolute necessity of agriculture, it operates with the certainty of a natural law, protecting the cultivated land from diminishment while simultaneously ensuring the careful supervision of the labor of individual community members with iron strictness. It satisfied the fundamental needs of earlier developmental stages of agriculture to such a remarkable extent that it completely dominated German agricultural practice for more than one thousand years—perhaps even for over two thousand years—persisting well into modern times. Through the agrarian legisla-

tion passed at the end of the eighteenth and in the first half of the nineteenth century, it was stripped of any political or economic significance. It disappeared as a system, but its traces are still clearly evident everywhere and are unlikely to completely fade away anytime soon.

The three-field system necessitated certain internal organizational elements, namely the labor association, the division of the land belonging to each *hufe* into three parts, the separate positioning of these three parts, and finally, the *flurzwang* (the communal and uniform manner of field cultivation enforced on all *hufen)*. This system prevented a reduction in grain availability by ensuring the yearly cultivation of approximately two-thirds of the total arable land across all parts of Germany. It also made it impractical to grow other crops alongside grains on the same farmland. Moreover, it compelled every peasant, whether he wanted to or not, to cultivate his fields and perform all necessary agricultural tasks in a timely manner. Moreover, the obligation to perform similar tasks simultaneously in full view of everyone initiated a spirit of competition among the community members, which effectively enhanced the execution of the tasks.

The annual cultivation of two-thirds of the land belonging to each *hufe* appears to have been the most that could be demanded in the times from whence the three-field system originated. Under the organization of the three-field system, the cultivation of each *hufe's* arable land was carried out in such a way that each field had to bear crops for two consecutive years and were then "rested" the third year. In fact, a rotation of winter and summer crops—one sown in the spring and the other in the fall—was consistently and universally practiced. The winter crop was cultivated after the fallow year, resulting in an efficient distribution of all field tasks and allowing for careful attention to be paid to the cultivation of fallow land and the eradication of weeds.[133]

Under the structure of the three-field system, a *hufe* was comprised of a house with a farmstead or farmland, the plowland, usually some meadowland, and the rights to utilize pastures and access timber resources. As mentioned earlier, the plowland of each collective *hufe* was distributed into three separate sections located in three different areas within the communal farmland. This arose from the fact that when establishing an association, comprised of, say, twenty peasants, the association designates an area as communal plowland that is approximately twenty times larger than the plowland allocated to a single *hufe*. The entire area

---

[133] The author kindly requests that this sentence be read with particular attention, as further down we will extensively delve into the favorable distribution of labor inherent in the three-field system in relation to the seasons.

was then divided, taking soil quality into account, into three roughly equal-sized parts called *gewanne*. Each *gewann* was further subdivided into approximately twenty roughly equal-sized sections. As a result, the entire communal plowland consisted of three sets of twenty fields, totaling sixty fields. In the end, each of the twenty *hufen* received three sections, with one section allocated in each of the three *gewanne*. The three *gewanne* were jointly cultivated by the twenty peasants in a three-year rotation. Each year, a single winter crop was cultivated in one *gewann*, a variety of summer crops in another *gewann*, and a third *gewann* remained fallow or "rested." This well-established arrangement compelled each peasant to cultivate two-thirds of his plowland annually, precisely following the prescribed pattern of sowing with grain. For the execution of all necessary individual tasks, the peasant leader of the collective, known as the *bauermeister*,[134] determined the specific timing, which each peasant had to strictly adhere to. Any failure to comply resulted in disruptions to the work of neighboring farmers—and even of the entire association—leading to the imposition of fines to provide compensation for damages. In this system, it was hard for the slow and lazy to fall behind and, simultaneously, it was also not possible for the ambitious to extract any yield from the resting field or even to extract extra yields from the cultivated fields. This was because every peasant had the right to graze their livestock on the resting *gewann*, and, in fact, on any field as soon as it was harvested. This highlights the fact that the three-field system is not an institution primarily intended for the benefit of individuals, rather, it places the labor of peasants in the service of the general public.

That covers Fleischmann! In a truly brilliant way, Fleischmann has eloquently conveyed the cooperative philosophy at the heart of the three-field system. Unfortunately, he later uses the three-field system to try to prove the existence of manorialism among the Germanic peoples during the Migration Period. In other words, he claims that the three-field system was, in a sense, an invention of manorialism aimed at more effectively exploiting the labor of peasants. Firstly, it would never have occurred to the Germanic people—or indeed, to Indo-Europeans as a whole, as the following section will elaborate on—to exploit the labor of individuals or

---

[134] *Bauermeister* literally translates to "peasant master" and is roughly equivalent to bailiff in English.

establish institutions that organized the exploitation of labor power.[135] Secondly, based on the knowledge we have gleaned from Germanic and ancient German legal traditions, we have a clear understanding of the significance and implementation of the cooperative principle, as well as the fundamental curtailment of any exclusively individualist authority. Therefore, we must reject Fleischmann's attempt to explain the three-field system in this way. The manorial concept, particularly when it involves the exploitation of the labor of serfs, is not of ancient Germanic origin (we discussed this in detail earlier) and a labor system designed to exploit the labor power of peasants would be thoroughly un-Germanic. It was only in modern times that the Germanic nobility adopted these types of concepts, when the notion of taxation—which was referred to as *bitte* (petition) during the Middle Ages because the landlords had to "petition" the necessary funds from their subjects—was employed to establish a state structure (and rightfully so). It was then only under the influence of French absolutism that the concept of taxation became corrupted. This is a contemporary ailment that must not be attributed to the German Middle Ages, let alone the Germanic peoples.[136]

From such a perspective, it becomes clear that the three-field system

---

[135] One should be cautious about projecting onto Germanic or Old German conditions contemporary notions of a financialized economy, Frederick Taylor's "scientific management," and all those euphemistic slogans that aim to extract as much monetary value as possible from a thing or a person. While this approach may provide quite "plausible" explanations in terms of the modern mindset that recognizes rights but lacks a sense of duties (especially those duties rooted in voluntary and moralistic origins), it actually misrepresents the realities of the Germanic and Medieval German contexts.

[136] The current popular conflation of slavery, feudalism, and serfdom is nothing short of a detriment to the burgeoning field of race science. The limited extent to which the Germanic peoples understood the concept of slavery can be gathered from the following words from von Below: "Those who were materially unfree, technically known as serfs, constitute a considerable class of the unfree in the Middle Ages. Counterposed to them were those who were personally unfree, the *leibeigenen*. It is difficult to fully grasp the ancient arrangements in terms familiar to us. For the sake of simplicity, let us refer to them as materially unfree and personally unfree—these terms should, for the most part, characterize the differences. The personally unfree are the *proprii de corpore*, which expresses the contrast with material bondage. These personally unfree individuals should not be compared with Oriental or African slavery. It is also erroneous to think of the personally unfree as enslaved individuals, consisting only of domestic servants or agricultural laborers. Occupation alone did not define the personally unfree. We find these people in a variety of economic positions—they could manage the estates of their lords or those of other lords, work on a free basis as rural laborers, pursue various professions in the cities, and hold various offices. Their only distinguishing feature was a personal unfreedom, as opposed to material bondage. They paid a *kopfzin* (personal tax), which distinguished them from the serfs who paid a *grundzin* (basic rent). From our previous observations, it is clear that the unfree individuals of the German Middle Ages were not subject to absolute bondage. In fact, we can go so far as to say that economically, they were essentially free. Legal 'unfreedom' was accompanied by considerable economic mobility. Both materially and personally unfree persons were subject to rent, death duties, a modest amount of corvée labor, and some obligatory domestic service (of only local application). Additionally, they had the obligation to attend the manorial court if the lord possessed one, as was usually the case. Because these obligations were legally or de facto limited and not comprehensive, the unfree individuals had little room for unrestricted movement. Serfs were subject to minimal economic regulations, and the personally unfree were generally free to choose their occupations." From: Georg von Below, *Der Deutsche Staat des Mittelalters* [The German State in the Middle Ages].

established on the basis of cooperative principles must have been inherently characteristic of the Germanic peoples.

There are a few more ways to turn this assumed high probability into something closer to certain. When the Saxons and Angles, led by their legendary leaders Hengist and Horsa, conquered England in 445 AD, they did away with the old Celtic family structure and settlement pattern. Although the Celts had been under Roman rule for the last four hundred years, the old Celtic system remained unchanged—a fact that does not speak well to the cultural fertility of the Roman Empire of that time. In its place, the Saxons and Angles introduced the *haufendorf*, or clustered village. In such villages, the arable land was divided into the *gewanne*, of the three-field system and the *flurzwang*. Mielke also states,

> The structure of the English village is of ancient Germanic origin, partially featuring scattered land plots, three-field cultivation, complaints courts, large plots of land, and the later introduction of the Danish *bol* system,[137] to which some weak Norman influences are added.[138]

Do you really believe that the Anglo-Saxons would have introduced three-field cultivation to England if it had not already been deeply rooted in their flesh and blood? No Germanic tribe in history has become so proverbially famous, or one might even say infamous, for its tenacious adherence to traditions and customs handed down from generation to generation, more than the Lower Saxons. Therefore, we can assume that the Anglo-Saxon three-field system was known to these Low Germanic peoples long before the year 445.

There is no reason to doubt that the Anglo-Saxons who migrated to England were anything more than a free peasantry seeking new agricultural land by way of the ancient Germanic process of *landnahme*, the conquest and settlement of new land. For several centuries the Anglo-Saxons lived in England not as lords, but as free peasants, until William the Conqueror (1027–1087) appeared with an entirely different system of agriculture, the so-called feudal system. William the Conqueror distributed land to his Norman followers as crown estates, and, incidentally, it is from these crown estates that

---

[137] The once common term "*bool*" in Denmark and Schleswig-Holstein means "gathering place." *Bolsbroder* and *rainbrüder* refer to kinship companions within an inherited estate. The *bol* system developed as a response to the tribal migration from the region of Skåne into the islands of Denmark in the first centuries AD, encroaching on the individual farmsteads and confining them to the heathlands of Jutland. These individual farmsteads (known as *torpe*) always passed to the eldest heir, thus ensuring uninterrupted ownership within the clan. In the midst of the above-mentioned tribal migration, the *bolverfassung* (*bol* charter) established legal safeguards for land ownership and privileges were granted to the landowning families (known as the old and venerable families) over other tribal members; the latter is not strictly within the legal framework, but rather in accordance with custom. The clan remained in the region, possibly even building separate houses for independent family members, until the individual farmstead evolved into a small hamlet-like settlement.

[138] Mielke, *Die Siedlungskunde des Deutschen Volkes.*

the English *latifundium* system of later centuries originated. It is revealing, however, that William the Conqueror did not manage to completely implement his feudal system in the eastern counties. In these counties, the peasant class was composed predominantly of pure stocks of Anglo-Saxon peasants. In short, the relationship between the Normans and the eastern counties was comparable to the relationship between the original peasant cantons (*urkanton*) in Switzerland and the feudal system of the House of Habsburg. But one can also think of the similar relationship between the Scandinavian peasantry (in Sweden and Norway) and the non-Scandinavian nobility that came from Germany. The development in England of the relationship between the Anglo-Saxons and the Normans is of great relevance to our understanding of the Germanic peasantry. If the Anglo-Saxons had not been true peasants, then it is unlikely that they would have rather ruthlessly transplanted their peasant form of settlement to England—they probably would have imposed a similar arrangement on the local Celts that the Normans who subsequently came to England attempted to impose on them. They certainly would not have thought of transplanting their Low German form of agricultural settlement to England. It is more likely that they would have attempted an imperious exploitation of the existing Celtic peasant culture, as the Romans had already been doing in the country for four hundred years. It is significant that not only did the Anglo-Saxons not have this approach, but also that half a millennium later the Normans were unable to implement their feudal system in the very areas most densely and exclusively settled by Anglo-Saxons.

In this connection it is particularly noteworthy that, for example, according to Beddoe, the county of Yorkshire is the area most purely populated by the Nordic race, with the "Yorkshireman" being the most pureblooded Nordic type in England. What is even more important, however, is the fact that the denordification of these eastern counties of England is due to mundane agricultural reasons, and not to those reasons which today are considered to be the main causes of denordification. Specifically, it was the high price of grain that drove the so-called "yeomen," who made up the actual Anglo-Saxon peasant population of the eastern counties, away from the soil between the years of 1795 and 1815. Warfare, which would have diminished this Anglo-Saxon blood, hardly played a role at that time. Due to the increase in net income from rising grain prices, it seemed advisable for yeomen to take out high-interest loans to improve their estates or farms. But once the Napoleonic wars had ended and grain prices fell again, most of the peasants could no longer meet their obligations and were forced to sell their farms, many of which had been in their families for more than a millennium.[139] The destruction of the traditional, soil-bound Anglo-Saxon peasantry in the eastern counties, brought about by the emergence of the financialized global economy, led to the massive wave of Anglo-Saxon emigration to North America in the years following 1820. The

---

[139] We are currently experiencing this phenomenon in Germany, so it is not necessary to use one's imagination to comprehend the situation as it was then.

remnants of the peasant population remaining in England were then subsequently forced to relinquish their agricultural livelihoods in the years after 1870, when England sacrificed its domestic grain cultivation in favor of its overseas grain trade. It has been calculated that of England's old-established peasantry that was dispossessed at that time (before 1820), about 65 percent went to the United States. England, however, ensured that this peasantry was not lost to English civilization by the exemplary introduction of a basic right. England granted land free of charge to these peasants from the state-owned lands in its colonies and decreed that this land became the private property of the peasant who took possession of it to work it; this principle was then later retained in the United States. The granting of permanent land tenure as private property to peasants expelled from their homeland, together with the guarantee of personal freedom and independence through legally protected implementation, is the key to understanding the enormous Anglo-Saxon colonial success in the nineteenth century, including in the countries of Canada and Australia.[140]

These aspects are all important for gaining an understanding of the agricultural conditions of the Germanic peoples. After all, on the basis of English agricultural history we have come to know the Anglo-Saxons (whom Beddoe explicitly describes as the purest representatives of the Nordic race in England) as peasants from the very beginning. Furthermore, over the course of a millennium and a half, we see them linked and associated with the peasantry in a way that quite convincingly demonstrates the peasant core at the heart of Anglo-Saxon existence. In fact, it becomes simply impossible to believe that there was any non-peasant influence among them. Otherwise, the history of the Anglo-Saxon yeomen in the eastern counties of England would probably have been a little simpler and less tragic. Therefore, it is undoubtedly justified to regard the three-field system brought to England by the Anglo-Saxons in 445 AD not as an accidentally acquired cultural phenomenon of these tribes, but as an agricultural manifestation inherent to the Anglo-Saxons, which we can then assume to be the case with the other Germanic tribes as well.

Having quoted Mielke earlier, it is also very instructive to read his description of Scandinavian settlement history, for this settlement history can perhaps provide us with a very simple explanation for the emergence of the

---

[140] Nevertheless, the old adage holds true here as well, "God's mills grind slowly, but they grind exceedingly fine." It is no doubt a cruel twist of fate that the descendants of those peasants who were callously expelled from England a hundred years ago are now helping to shape the destiny of the very country that is currently challenging England's position as the world's superpower— namely, the United States. Without Australia, South Africa, and Canada, which were settled and led by Germanic peoples, England would probably have been removed from the list of influential nations as a result of the World War. It is a mistake that we in Germany perceive the United Kingdom as merely a commercially-oriented branch of a global trading company! In reality, the situation is quite different. Further reading on these questions can be found here: Augstin, *Die Entwickelung der Landwirtschaft*; Darmstädter, *Die Vereinigten Staaten von* Amerika; Demangeon, *Das Britische Weltreich*; Skalweit, *Die Englische Landwirtschaft*; Valentin, *Kolonialgeschichte der Neuzeit*; Williamson, *A Short History of the British Expansion*; Caldecott, *English Colonization and Empire*.

three-field system. He writes,

> In addition to the individual farmstead, known as the *torp*, a larger settlement type also emerged in very ancient times, most likely exclusively inhabited by members of the same clan. This is evident from the suffix *by* (from *bu*, meaning to build) that frequently appears in this context. Such a "*by*" settlement is essentially a village compared to the *torpen*. In the thirteenth century, the former was still referred to as a *haugedorf* (from *haug*, meaning hill or barrow), of pagan origin, and contrasted with the *fullbyr*, meaning full-fledged village. The contrast between the individual farmstead and the village is also reflected in the Swedish terms *torpekarlar*, meaning common peasant, and *odallbönder*, meaning noble peasant. . . . Between the settlements and their estates, there were unused areas, mostly wastelands and heathlands, which belonged to no one and were often later utilized for establishing daughter settlements. The Swedish kings, who themselves originated from the class of estate owners and ascended to their authoritative positions through deeds and personal qualities, initially had no entitlement to these types of estates. However, in conquered territories, such as the subdued Götaland, they were granted one-third, and in Denmark, the entire borderland. Consequently, the settlements established on this territory became the property of the kings, significantly bolstering the dynastic position of the Merovingian and Carolingian rulers in later times. By controlling unclaimed lands, state authority was subsequently empowered to organize significant Germanic colonization across vast regions of Europe. . . .
>
> In 1327, when King Waldemar ordered the registration of all rights, tax sources, and ownership status in his property registry, many individual farmsteads (with their extensive land holdings) were associated to numerous villages. These villages, however, were not the result of communal land reclamation, but of the division of clan property. In these irregularly arranged farmsteads, clustered around a central square, the North Germanic spirit prevailed unabated and attempted to challenge the aforementioned Jutish law. The clan cooperative would continue to dominate settlement patterns for years, and the cultivation of the land would continue to be carried out through the combined efforts of the villagers. It seems that the great North Germanic eight-furrow plow, drawn by eight oxen, was a key factor here, as it required a large amount of resources to operate, leading users to form a plow cooperatives. These cooperatives, consisting of four to eight members, would own the land, which was then later divided. With the introduction of Christianity in the ninth century, ownership began to consolidate, and the land started to be apportioned to individuals in smaller parcels.

The indigenous population would engage in large-scale clearings, but only with the consent of all those who had rights to the land. "If some wanted to clear the land, but others did not, the latter were to be summoned to a public assembly known as a *ding*—if they failed to appear, they would forfeit their claim." This provision is from an ancient Scanian law and reveals a strong sense of communal interest, where distribution of profits—and clearing the land promises such profits—is reserved for everyone.[141] However, the individual is also protected in their rights. If a person owns a lawful farmstead in the village, along with the associated land, meadows, and shares in the communal property, he is then also entitled to all the rights associated with this ownership. Here we have a political cooperative based on land cultivation that protects and supports the individual members while also imposing obligations on them for the collective good. The strength of the sanctity of ownership is demonstrated by the fact that the homestead is exempt from regulation.[142] Even in the case of someone who has moved away but still maintains his homestead in the field, this cannot be confiscated until the owner has freely chosen another plot of land.

In Scandinavia, ancient conditions have been preserved for a longer period compared to other cultural regions in Europe. Particularly noteworthy are the settlement patterns, which, due to geographic conditions, have remained almost unchanged over time. . . . It was through the individual farmstead that the Germanic peoples asserted

---

[141] Here, the prospect of profit may not have been the only reason for cooperative clearing efforts. As in the settlement of America, settlers banded together either as families or as cooperatives to clear forests and convert them to farmland. Indeed, the individual faces considerable difficulties in dealing with the roots of trees while preparing land for plowing; one can imagine the labor involved in cutting down a colossal tree several feet in diameter. Thus, the settlement of America also demonstrated through experience that cooperative clearing remains the most efficient approach for rapid progress.

[142] In this passage, Mielke speaks of something that has received insufficient attention in the field of Germanic prehistory and warrants a more thorough investigation. For example, when the Vandals crossed the Strait of Gibraltar and established their Vandal kingdom on the site of Carthage (a kingdom that was to have a relatively short existence), they did not relinquish their claims to the lands of their German homeland. Curiously, this was fully recognized in their original ancestral seats. However, as the Vandals who remained in Germany faced a shortage of land, a diplomatic mission was sent to Carthage to ask the North African Vandals to relinquish their rights to the lands.

The North African Vandals were indeed inclined to agree to this request, until an aged, white-haired Vandal stood up and said something like the following, "Fate smiles upon us today, but we remain uncertain about the fate of our grandchildren. It is wise for them to know where they have a home." In light of this, the Vandal delegation from Germany returned home empty-handed. As history shows, the Vandal empire eventually collapsed, and as a result, the North African Vandals' claim to the lands of their ancient Germanic homeland could no longer hold political sway. As a result, we are left to speculate on the possible legal and political ramifications that might have ensued. In any event, the conduct of the Vandals underscores not only that they must have been considerably settled before departing from their original ancestral seats but also that, for the Germanic people, the connection with land and territory was markedly more profound than what we are typically inclined to presume.

their homeland. Where this individual farmstead prevailed, foreign racial influences were unable to interfere. In the case of the clustered villages, however, this changes, as these villages were often established in a different racial environment or accommodated foreign migrants. In fact, over time, such elements could infiltrate any mass settlement. The individual farmstead, on the other hand, is able to preserve not only national character, but also the two opposing poles—strong individualism and subordination to the will of the collective. What was already inherent in the bond between the individual farm and the peasantry, namely the firm commitment to order and organization that became the basis for labor distribution within the clan, was condensed into a political notion of the state. The pure peasant state, however, has not yet matured to completion among any of the Germanic peoples.

What is particularly important about Mielke's remarks here is that in Scandinavia we can observe a fully legal relationship between individual farmsteads and village cooperatives. In both instances, the focus is on the idea of the clan. In one scenario, the clan restricts itself to one farm by handing the farm over to one heir, in the other scenario, the clan expands its available resources by founding new farms—by establishing subsidiaries and settling them. In the individual farmstead, all unmarried clan members remained under the manorial authority of the farm's heir, a practice that persisted in the good peasant regions of Germany until the late nineteenth century. They were accustomed to collectively employing their labor and resources in order to maintain the land necessary for the sustenance of their clan (the individual farmstead). It is only natural, therefore, that with the branching out of the clan and the establishment of multiple households, the basic "all for one" idea inherited from the individual farmstead remained intact. This cooperative idea continued to apply and the property belonging to the clan, as well as the land necessary for the sustenance of the clan-based clustered village, continued to be collectively managed. However, it is likely that the heir who remained on the individual farmstead still retained a kind of authoritative supremacy over the new establishment, which essentially manifested itself as a demonstration of respect by the younger members of the clan toward him. This respect extended to subsequent heirs as well, given their position as direct descendants of the original head of the clan. Thus, in a sense, after the clan had branched off, an amount of reverence remained for the branch that remained on the individual farmstead (similar to the respect that would have been owed to the eldest brother regardless), as these were the farm's heirs before the clan split into separate settlements. This would quite easily explain the peculiar position that the Germanic nobility held compared to the Germanic freemen—the Germanic nobility was entitled to a priority of respect, but not a priority of rights. Additionally, the basic idea of the three-field system, namely the cooperative cultivation of the land necessary for the clan's sustenance, can be most naturally derived from the ancestral homeland of the Germanic people, which, according to the above words from Kossinna, we may presume to lie in Scandinavia.

However, if we may assume that the three-field system existed among the Germanic peoples even before they arrived in Germany, it leads to a conclusion of the most far-reaching importance. Tacitus writes that, "They distinguish and name winter, spring, and summer, but they do not know the names and gifts of autumn."[143] Anyone traveling to central Sweden in the second half of August, the harvest month of the Germanic peoples, may be surprised to find that harvesting and sowing takes place simultaneously. The reason for this is very simple. Due to the relatively early winter, winter crops (grains that must be sown before winter and must sprout before the onset of frost) must be planted as early as August. As a result, our autumn planting coincides with the harvest in central Sweden—or, in other words—agriculture in central Sweden still does not recognize autumn the way we do. Such a simultaneous occurrence of harvest and planting leads to a considerable accumulation of work in the short time available in the closing days of August. The Swedish farmer compensates for this drawback through the use of the black fallow technique. This allows for the plowing of fields to be postponed to a less labor-intensive period. The winter crop is sown in the previously fallow field, and the harvested field is used for the new fallow period. There is then ample time between the completion of the harvest and the onset of frost to plow the field. The Institute of Agricultural Management at the University of Göttingen examined this central Swedish technique during a study trip in 1927. The author relies on this report, which does not describe exceptional or particularly backward or outdated farmers. In the past, the central Swedish technique was said to have been common throughout Sweden. If one looks for the areas in central Europe that correspond more or less to southern Sweden in terms of climate, one finds the regions of Lower Germany east of the Elbe. Perhaps it would be more accurate to specify between the Elbe and the Vistula, although some isolated climatic enclaves east of the Vistula have similar conditions. The regions west of the Elbe belong to milder climate zones, some of which hardly experience winters. Due to the significant cloud cover attributed to the Gulf Stream and prevailing westerly winds, the temperature differences between winter and summer are quite balanced in these areas; in some places one could say that autumn merges into spring without a clear winter. Only a brief mention can be made here of the climate zones in Germany, of which we have approximately twelve within the boundaries of our empire, some of which exhibit quite notable differences.

This leads us, first of all, to the rather surprising observation that the lack of a specific term for autumn as a season is a natural consequence of traditional Swedish agricultural practices. Now, if the Germanic people also appear in history without a term for autumn, the most plausible conclusion is that they were farmers originating from Sweden, who, due to the natural conditions of the region, had no reason to develop a term for a concept that was quite unfamiliar to them. Since these cli-

---

[143] Even in Old High German, the term *herbst* (autumn) does not yet signify a season but rather solely refers to the act of harvesting (*herbsten*).

matological considerations coincide exactly with Kossinna's archaeological findings, we can confidently assert that these are not mere coincidences, but rather consistencies that quite indisputably indicate a Swedish ancestral homeland for the Germanic peoples and just as indisputably characterizes them as farmers. Furthermore, we can even say that the way of life of the Germanic peoples was so profoundly agrarian that it even influenced the development of their temporal concepts. Just consider the great significance that the autumn season would have had in the life of a hunter in the heavily forested, wildlife-rich regions of southern and central Scandinavia. One will be astonished to discover that this splendid time of autumnal hunting apparently had no discernible effect on the Germanic people's conceptual development of seasons in the whole of north-central Europe, at the very least taking a back seat to their peasant existence.

But that's not all. In this Swedish system of agriculture, fallow cultivation is important because harvesting and cultivating in the fall is an absolute necessity. Regarding the fallow fields of the Germanic people, the following has already been acknowledged by Aereboe,

> The fallow field, therefore, serves to achieve a more favorable distribution of labor and reduces operating costs. As the fallow can only be allocated to newly broken land, this results in a particularly advantageous distribution of labor. This is the ancient Germanic agricultural system (*arva per annos mutant et super est ager*) where the fields are changed each year and there is still enough land left for cultivation. In this regard, one need not concern oneself at all with the fertility of the soil, as land that is reused after grazing becomes virgin land anew. The utilization of pastures especially helps combat weed growth, as weeds require a certain level of soil disturbance for their proliferation. Turnip, radish, poppy, wild oats, and couch grass are nowhere to be found on the pastures. Only thistles seem to resist for a bit longer in these fields. Under the conditions of the three-field system, it is unwise to fertilize, but it is wise to cultivate a considerable amount of land under the plow.[144]

Since clan settlement, as an offshoot of single-farm settlement, did not recognize individual ownership of land by individual clan members, but only communal clan ownership, it follows quite naturally that fallow, summer crop farming, and winter crop farming were also managed on a "clan" basis. In this three-way division, which is influenced by the climatic conditions of Sweden, the further subdivision of land into plowland or *hufen* (which provided a family within the clan with sustenance and a comfortable livelihood) is merely a natural progression of established agricultural practice. The use of fallow land as pasture for livestock seems to have arisen more or less by accident, with the grazing of this land helping to control the growth of weeds in the fields. Dur-

---

144 Aereboe, *Allgemeine Landwirtschaftliche Betriebslehre.*

ing these early historical periods, and as was the case in Scandinavia until recently, the primary source of food for livestock was forest pasture, which we will explore in more detail in chapter six.

Now, consider the aforementioned conditions of Swedish agricultural practices where the harvest and autumn tilling is compressed into the waning days of August, approximately fourteen days in total. When juxtaposed with the evolution from single-farm settlements to clan settlements depicted above, one cannot help but acknowledge that under such climatic and agricultural conditions, a cooperative settlement pattern can only ever be viable if the members rigorously ensure that all participants strictly adhere to the short period of harvesting and cultivation. This gives us a better understanding of the development of the *flurzwang* in the three-field system, both in its beginnings and in its expansion.

In summary, we can say that the three-field system provides us with a highly significant clue as to the origins and agrarian conditions of the Germanic peoples. We can now assume with a high degree of probability that the Germanic peoples were already familiar with the three-field system long before their appearance in recorded history. Moreover, we can perhaps assume that the Germanic three-field system served as the nucleus of all later cooperative existence.

Knowing this, when we look back at the Germanic Migration Period, the image of the land-hungry peasant treks of the Germanic peoples become so vivid in our minds that it is quite a feat to not assume the presence of agricultural practices among the Germanic peoples.

The Franks and Alemanni exhibit remarkable sedentariness in the sense that they are never displaced from their settlements by the Vandals, Suebi, or Alans. Instead, the migrations of these groups pass over them or occur in the spaces between them. The Alemanni did not extend beyond the Upper Rhine basin—this is significant because the Voges Forest and the Jura Mountains were not attractive for peasants. On the other hand, the Franks found a way to access the source of the Sambre, which allowed them to expand on both sides of the Scheldt.

Only the Burgundians, the only tribe that established a state along the Rhine, failed to establish roots anywhere, which proved to be very detrimental to them. They were disconnected from any strong ties to the land, placing greater value on the sound of hunting horns, the clinking of goblets, and the clashing of swords than the hard work of a settled person. In fact, they had diverged so significantly from the way of life of other Germanic tribes that their unique condition was perceived with complete amazement by the other tribes. In any case, it is remarkable that the history of the Burgundians, their kingdom, and their downfall garnered such extensive attention, as it allowed for the preservation of their story in legends and heroic songs that have endured until modern times. Only the Normans, who emerged half a millennium later, established states on the mainland similar to those of the Burgundians on the Rhine. According to Kossinna's findings, the Burgundians migrated from Bornholm to the mainland just before the birth of Christ. This leads one to suspect that not only were they closely related to the Normans, but that they likely had been a coastal population engaged in seafaring and fishing on Bornholm, rather than traditional rural inhabitants (peasants). Because of their coastal lifestyle, they may have either forgotten the traditional agricultural practices or, as a coastal people since time immemorial, never really learned them. Consequently, Burgundian rule on the mainland had to be based on different principles than the other Germanic tribes, who were peasant by nature. It is therefore highly advisable to leave the Burgundians and the Normans out of the picture when studying the agricultural conditions among the Germanic tribes, as their conditions are likely outside the norm and will mislead the researcher.

Significantly, the Burgundians stood quite alone among the other Germanic tribes; they are recorded as being fiercely hostile even to other Germanic tribes such as the Franks and Alemanni. This circumstance played no small role in allowing the Roman commander Aetius, in alliance with Hunnic mercenary bands, to bring the Burgundian kingdom of Gundicar to its knees after a heroic resistance in the year 436 AD. Aetius settled the remaining Burgundians on the high plateau of Lake Geneva, at the Jura passes, and along the Saône. He placed them within Roman settlements as part-owners, or "serfs" according to the understanding of that time, with the specific purpose of putting a stop to the increasingly land-hungry Alemanni. The Burgundians were to be used as a bulwark or protective buffer for the Roman Empire. The approach taken by Aetius would have hardly been feasible without fundamental differences between the natures of the Alemanni and the Burgundians. Although Aetius handed over numerous Burgundian nobles to his Hunnic allies—who were then taken by these Mongols as slaves to the tent of King Attila in Hungary—the Burgundians who remained along the Rhône River and in the Savoy Mountains earned a high reputation. Perhaps this was due, in part, to the fact that this non-peasant Germanic tribe had been forcibly accustomed to the soil by the strong, victorious hand of Aetius.[145]

---

[145] Aetius did not bask in his victory for long and bitterly gained first-hand experience of the unreliability of nomadic auxiliaries, as discussed previously. In keeping with previous discussions, it would be interesting to acquaint ourselves here with the military tactics of the nomads. Attila appeared in the regions along the Rhine, which had been left unprotected by the Burgundians, quite unexpectedly. He built two bridges over the Rhine near the mouth of the Neckar. All the cities of the Palatinate and the Moselle were reduced to ashes and ruins, churches and chapels were destroyed, men slaughtered, and women kidnapped—see earlier descriptions of Tatar raids. Attila's advance quickly penetrated the heart of Gaul, and those who did not seek refuge within the walls of Troyes, Soissons, and Orleans met their doom. Attila ruthlessly plundered and ravaged the open countryside until no grass grew under the hooves of his horses. His wagon fortresses amassed simply astonishing amounts of gold, silver, and female slaves. Whenever resistance threatened the spoils, Attila knew how to effectively wield the swords of his Germanic auxiliaries (Gepids, Ostrogoths, Heruls, Thuringians). Attila accomplished all this in the short span of a single summer campaign in 451.

It is indeed a challenge to identify any nomadic migrations or other nomadic characteristics within any of the Germanic peasant treks at the onset of the Migration Period. This is especially true for anyone who makes the effort, even just once, to peruse Hunnic and Saracen military history, particularly its intersections with Germanic-inhabited central Europe during the first half of the first millennium AD.

Finally, it should be noted in this context that the western boundary of the Germanic settlement area that formed after the year 400 AD has remained largely unchanged for one and a half millennia. It stretches from Dunkirk through Brussels, Metz, the crest of the Wasgau region, and down to South Tyrol. This would not have been possible without the pure peasanthood of the Germanic peoples.

As this chapter ends, we have conclusively ascertained that the freemen of the Germanic peoples must have been peasants. This, however, places the Germanic peoples within the framework of the settlement history of the German people. Or, stated differently, the Germanic peoples merely constitute the precursor of the peasant movements observed in Germany for the past one and a half millennia. If we want to gain a clear understanding of the racial identity of the Germanic peoples, we must first examine whether the predecessors of the Germanic peoples, the Indo-Europeans, manifested themselves as peasants or as nomadic warrior pastoralists. For this is clear—if we also establish that the Indo-Europeans had been peasants, then we can remove all doubt and unambiguously assign the Indo-European peasantry to the Nordic race. According to all available information, the Phalian race is far too underrepresented among the Indo-Europeans to be relied upon for an understanding of the Indo-European peasantry.

IV

The Indo-Europeans and Agriculture

I

In this chapter, we seek to answer the question of whether the Indo-Europeans were peasants or warrior-nomadic peoples. To do this, it may be advantageous to present a line of argument that attempts to arrive at the clearest, most authentic, and most likely conclusion possible. Therefore, a simple summary of previous research on Indo-European agriculture will be of no value. Rather, we will attempt to build upon existing research to paint a complete picture that either vividly presents the Indo-Europeans as peasants or quite clearly indicates them as being a nomadic people.

The previous chapter will have undoubtedly raised questions in the minds of every thoughtful reader. It is likely that these questions primarily have to do with the Germanic household and its peculiar significance as a living cell within the body of the Germanic community. To reiterate, the Germanic household is a self-contained organic entity that consists of the following elements: a hearth fire, which acts as its central point, a "roof" that provides shelter for the hearth fire, the land necessary for the household's sustenance, and, finally, the family lineage who maintain said fire and land. This organic entity is so profoundly natural and healthy, so clearly the result of natural development, that the gradual formation of this "house" must have been deeply connected with the developmental path of Germanic civilization in prehistory. Therefore, in an attempt to understand the fundamental nature of the Indo-Europeans and their civilization, we will begin with an investigation of whether this basic Germanic family concept (where fire, house, and sustenance-providing land are united to form a living entity both internally organized and clearly demarcated) can also be found among the Indo-Europeans. In the following, the question will be examined by studying the customs and traditions of the ancient Roman patricians and the Hellenes.[146]

To begin, we will follow Kuhlenbeck as he describes the ancient Roman household as it appeared among the patricians,

It is incorrect to regard the ancient Roman patricians as a pastoral people, and it is certainly incorrect to regard them as a migrating nomadic people. They were conquerors who were sedentary from the very first places they lived, and although they may have primarily raised livestock, they were already familiar with agriculture and were looking for a new home in a new land. Their economy was a mixed system of agriculture and livestock raising. A strictly monarchical family structure, based on regular monogamous marriage, was the foundation of their legal system. The people (or lineage) were, above all, the product of procreation and the blood community (*blutsgemeinschaft*) derived therefrom.

For the ancient patricians, the family served as the foundation upon which law was formed. Its true focal point, however, was the household. The concept of family in those times was fundamentally different and broader than what the present-day understanding suggests. It approximately corresponded to the concept of the household-community. It encompassed everything that belonged to the ancient Roman household, including individuals and objects, as well as all of its wealth, with the exception of the so-called *pecunia*, which originally referred to livestock. It denoted the permanent wealth that was inseparable and inalienable from the person—or family in the modern, more narrow sense—and contrasted with the alienable property that could be separated from the individual. The legal language of the Twelve Tables faithfully preserved this meaning when it referred to the estate, and inheritance as such, as *familia* (*proximus agnatus familiam habeto, actio familiae erciscundae*).

The structure of this household-community was strictly monarchical as it was under the unrestricted power of the head of the household, "under his hand" (*manus*) in Roman parlance.[147] Therefore, the *pater familias* is not merely the father of the family in the modern sense—the word *pater* does not mean progenitor, the Romans used the word *genitor* for that—rather, it is a word that reoccurs in all Aryan

---

[146] During the printing of this book, the author was referred to the new work by Hans F. K. Günther, *Rassengeschichte des Hellenischen und Römischen Volkes* [Racial History of the Hellenic and Roman Peoples], which provides further detailed evidence for the Nordic origin of the Greeks and Romans.

[147] Ihering states, "The Roman house is a small self-contained world that is solely subject to the rule of the lord and into which no one may interfere." The authority that the head of the household holds over the family is called *manus* (hand). The hand as it appears in ancient Roman law is a natural symbol of power, it too appears in ancient Germanic law, derived from the same root (*munt*).

(Nordic) languages, including Greek, Latin, German, and Sanskrit, whose Sanskrit root *pâ* means "to nourish, to protect, to preserve," synonymous with *rex* (king). The family unit is concentrated in his hand (*manus*). Therefore, *manus* is the primordial right out of which every other right in the private sphere develops, branching off into family law and property law.

Accordingly, the following two aspects can be distinguished in household rule. The first aspect is the power over the individuals belonging to the household-community. This includes the wife under the authority of the husband (*uxor in manu mariti*),[148] the children (the *manus* over them is later referred to as *patria potestas*, meaning paternal authority), the so-called *mancipia* (*qui in causa mancipii sunt*),[149] and slaves or, more accurately, servants. The second aspect is the power (*manus*) over things. *Dominium* (lordship or ownership) is derived from *dominus* (lord or owner), in turn derived from *domus* (household). The original identity of the primordial right of the *manus* over persons and things is attested in language itself—*res mancipi*, *mancipium* and *vindicatio* (claim) in the case of persons and things.[150]

So says Kuhlenbeck! Since, in the previous chapter, we learned about the importance of the hearth fire as a sort of spiritual center for the Germanic household, we are now in the position to recognize the same importance placed on the hearth fire in the ancient Roman patrician household. Every ancient Roman home had an altar on which a sort of perpetual fire was maintained, similar to the so-called eternal flames found in Catholic churches and chapels. It was carefully covered with ashes every evening and rekindled the next morning. It was considered to be a most alarming sign for a family to allow the fire to go out due to negligence. This fire was lit and maintained in honor of their ancestors, who, in the earliest of times, were probably even buried beneath the hearth. If it went out, a special solemn ritual was required to rekindle it. The altar of the Lares or Manes was located here and, in later periods, the images of the Penates.[151] This domestic religion transformed each house into a chapel—in a sense, every meal

---

[148] "*Uxor in manu mariti*" translates to "wife in her husband's hand."

[149] "*Qui in causa mancipii sunt*" roughly translates to "who are in conditional servitude." *Mancipium* is a unique type of temporary Roman debt-slavery where a person is placed in the service of another due to a debt or an offense. Freemen under this type of conditional servitude had more rights than the typical slave, and retained their citizenship. Once the debt was paid, the person would be *emancipium*. *Mancipium* formed a part of a special category of Roman property law known as *res mancipi*, which covered property of particular importance (slaves, animals, buildings, land, etc.) to an owner. Transferals of this property required the ceremonial act of *mancipatio*.

[150] Kuhlenbeck, *Die Entwicklungsgeschichte des Römischen Rechts*.

[151] Lares in ancient Roman religion were guardian deities associated with the hearth and the home. Penates are associated with Lares but are distinct, functioning more as household deities responsible for the prosperity and well-being of the household. Manes were ancestor deities, representing the spirits of deceased relatives. Lares, Penates, and Manes were considered lesser (personal) gods when compared to the traditional pantheon of Roman gods, but nevertheless played a central role in household worship, persisting well into the Christian period.

was a sacred affair accompanied with prayer and libation. Rarely did a man leave his house without invoking the gods of household and hearth.

The veneration of the dead was intimately connected with this hearth fire cult. Mielke writes,

> This courtyard, which in its name atrium, meaning "black room," still testifies to its origin as a hearth room, where families in primordial times placed their household hearth.[152] Behind it and in front of the sleeping quarters was the location where ancestor worship took place. This meant that each house was intimately connected to the family, and this remained the case even after the Laws of the Twelve Tables forbade burial of the dead in or near the house. The intimate connection that the Romans had to their native soil is manifested in the cult of the household gods, the Lares and Penates, and in ancestor worship.[153]

Out of this mixture of hearth fire cult and ancestor worship arose the moral duty to marry. Kuhlenbeck writes,

> The deceased wanted to be honored only by his descendants—only from them could he receive offerings, and the presence of strangers disturbed his rest. Therefore, the most unfortunate fate that a house (family) could experience was for a *pater familias* to die without leaving children. This was uniquely intertwined with the equally ancient idea of reincarnation. Leist[154] writes, "As the son is the matured seed of the father in the mother, so the father continues to live, even after his death, in the son and so on in the grandson and great-grandson." As a result, the primary obligation of the male was to get married, the duty to *matrimonium liberorum quaerendorum causa*—to produce children who can maintain the hearth fire and continue making offerings to the dead.[155]

This type of hearth-centered religion requires a settled existence (the Latin word *vesta*, ultimately personified as the goddess Vesta). Consequently, it is

---

[152] The Latin word *atrium* comes from the word *ater*, meaning black. The connection between the Roman *atrium* and "black room" comes from the location of the hearth in prehistory. In these earliest of times, the hearth would be located in the middle of the dwelling, ventilated by a hole in the roof. This left large amounts of black soot on the surrounding ceiling, making the room "black." This central hearth room gradually transformed into the Roman atrium, an open air courtyard in the center of the home. Like the hearth room of the Indo-Europeans, the Roman atrium was also the most important room of the house, where the family gathered, shared meals, and worked.

[153] Mielke suggests the following for further reading on the sacred hearth—Hesiod, 679; Thucydides, *The Peloponesian War*, Book 1, chapter 136; Cato, *De re Rustica*, 143; Cicero, *Pro Domo*, 40; Virgil, Book 2, 512; Ovid, *Fasti*, Book 2, 651–633 and *Fasti*, Book 6, 291.

[154] Leist, *Alt-Arisches Jus Civile*, 190.

[155] Cicero, *De Legibus III*, 2.

linked to the most ancient form of land ownership, which in its earliest manifestation was strongly influenced by ancestor worship. Kuhlenbeck writes,

> The Penates, not the respective head of the household, own the hearth
> and its surroundings, as well as the territory on which the family has
> its house, its fields, and its pastures. This leads to the conclusion that
> the ancient Romans originally lived in individual farmsteads, as
> Tacitus also found among the Germanic peoples of his time.[156]
> The entire territory of this family settlement was inalienable. The
> alienability of landed property was later codified by the *jus civile*. . . .
> It was customary for the master of the house and his family to take a
> solemn walk along the perimeter on certain days, while singing
> hymns and offering sacrifices.[157]

An analogous custom, the so-called *schnatgang*, has long been preserved in
German property cooperatives. He continues,

> Landed property and inheritance were essentially one and the same
> for the ancient Romans. In fact, Lower Saxon peasants still refer to
> landed property as inheritance. An inalienable closed inheritance law
> arose naturally out of this concept. The right of the firstborn was
> authoritative. After the head of the household had passed, the eldest
> simply continued his rule (*morte parentis continuatur dominium*),
> meaning that the eldest was in a way already considered co-owner,
> even when the master of the house was still alive (this is still the case
> in Germanic peasant custom). The daughter—and the female
> descendants in general—was excluded from the right of inheritance.
> If someone died without male descendants, the inheritance went to
> the nearest agnate. If there were no agnates, the closest gens were
> identified.

The reader has certainly noticed the absolutely astounding similarity between
the Germanic and ancient Roman households. However, this similarity
becomes even more apparent when we closely examine the social relations
of the ancient Roman patricians (in other words, their relationship with
the subordinate population). This fact is particularly important because,
as we have already seen in chapters one and two, all nomads have quite
distinctly impersonal and purely parasitic views toward the population
that they have subjugated. Therefore, we have something unmistakable to
look out for in the legal relationship between the patricians and the sub-

---

[156] From Tacitus' *Germania*: "...they do not permit houses to touch each other: they live separated
and scattered . . . they lay out their villages not, after our fashion, with building contiguous and
connected; everyone keeps a clear space round his house, whether it be a precaution against the
chances of fire, or just ignorance of building."
[157] Mielke suggests the following for further reading: Cato, *De re Rustica*, 141; Cato, *Scriptores
rei Agrariae*, Goez ed., 308; and Ovid, *Fasti* Book II, 639.

ject population which will allow us to identify the potential presence of nomadism among them. We follow the words of Kuhlenbeck:

> Hugo had valid concerns about the translation of *servus* as "slave," since this word can immediately lead to false ideas about the social position of slaves in ancient Rome, especially in light of the historical context of Negro slavery. Although the slave was deprived of all personal freedom because he had, in a sense, forfeited his life (and was thus on the same level as an object), ancient Roman slavery did not have the same inhuman, cruel character that slavery had in later times, when a global slave trade resulted in the selling of slaves from inferior, distant races. The *servus* became a member of the household community (*famulus*, derived from *familia*). He was accepted into the family through a special ritualistic act—he was made to stand before the hearth of the Penates and was incorporated into the household religion through a form of baptism (sprinkling with holy water).[158] The servant could even stand in for the master in performing religious acts. The *servus* participated in the communal prayers and festivals and was under the protection of the Lares, just like any other member of the family. Hence, the relationship with the family was entirely patriarchal. At the beginning of the year, the slaves were served by the household's mistress, and during Saturnalia, by the master at the table. They ate together with the family at the same table. When freed, the servant or slave entered the broader circle of clients.

If the relationship of the ancient Roman patricians to their slaves has nothing that could even suggest the influence of nomadic blood, then the institution of clientship does so even less. Kuhlenbeck continues,

> Niebuhr has acknowledged that the institution of clientship dates back to the so-called pre-Romulan period, and that the oldest clients were the subjugated original inhabitants of Italy. They were probably distributed to each family when the land was divided. They possessed personal freedom, but being former *hostes* (enemies), they were only guaranteed this freedom through a protective relationship with a *pater familias*, who for this reason was called their *patronus* (patron, defender). The contract establishing this protective relationship was called *applicatio*. The entire relationship was, in turn, under the protection of their

---

[158] Further reading can be found in Aeschylus, *Clytemnestra* 1055–1038 and in Cicero, *De Legibus II*, 8 and 11–12, "Nor is the religion of Lares to be repudiated by those who were betrayed by the elders, both masters and servants." Original Latin, "*Neque ea, quae a majoribus prodita est cum dominis tum famulis religio Larum repudianda est.*"

religion, specifically that of the hearth and was a relationship of mutual trust (*fides*). The similarity between *patria potestas* (paternal authority) and patronage also impacted the legal position of clients regarding property. Although similar to the son of the household in that he himself had legal capacity, the client had only de facto property, not property in the legal sense, no *patrimonium* or *dominium*. The patron had to represent his clients to the outside world, and that is why *patronus* also meant 'advocate' even in later times. However, he was also held liable for their behavior toward third parties, just like he was for other household members, children, and slaves. The client was closer to the patron than *cognatus* (relatives).[159] In contrast to the servant, who was unfit for military service, the client was required to perform military service. He was obligated to provide his services to the patron whenever they were needed, and he was, among other things, to assist him financially upon assuming public office, when endowing his daughters, when being bought out of captivity, or when being sentenced to fines. The client relationship was hereditary unless explicitly terminated through a contract.

This concludes our description of the structure of the ancient Roman household. However, before we proceed to evaluate the Roman relationships presented here, it would be wise to first learn a little more about the Hellenic concept of the family. Hellenic relationships—particularly the Spartan—will continue to interest us a great deal because they provide us with quite excellent insights into the nature of the Indo-Europeans. Here, however, are some preliminary remarks on ancient Hellenic family relationships. These will allow us to make a comparison with those of ancient Rome. The author relies here mainly on Busolt:

> The first migration clearly indicates the existence of family-based legal associations. The form and organization of these associations evolved significantly over time, taking different forms in different states. But the core of their character and functions largely go unchanged and go back to very ancient times. . . . In all respects, the community had an essentially peasant character—its prosperity depended on the strength and stability of land ownership. The plots of land allotted to each member of the community provided them with a means of subsistence and enabled them to be productive. It was of great interest to the

---

[159] Aulus Gellius, *Noctes Atticae* [Attic Nights], Book 20, section 1, trans. John C. Rolfe, Loeb Classical Library ed. (Cambridge: Harvard University Press, 1927), "...a client taken under a man's protection should be held dearer than his relatives and protected against his own kindred." Original Latin, "*clientem tuendum esse contra cognatos.*"

community that the lots were handed down to the descendants of the recipients and that their number did not decrease. Therefore, a connectedness to the land was widespread, especially among those who had ownership of the "first" or "old" lots, as these were the plots of land allotted to individuals by the community at the time of settlement and land division; these were subject to legal restrictions. While the estate economy of the nobility differed from the peasant economy of their subjects, the economic and social position of the nobility was still based on agriculture. The natural economy, therefore, continued to be prevalent. Despite the extraordinarily high regard placed on property and acquisition, the agricultural activities of the nobility did not go beyond the production necessary for the needs of their own households. The autonomous economy of the individual household appears to be the prevailing type of economy. The needs of the house members in terms of food and clothes are to a large extent met by this individual household economy. Just as the women produced clothing at home, the head of the household by and large also crafted farming equipment with his servants. . . . [160] According to Aristotle, a complete household cooperative consisted of the head of the household, his wife, children, and slaves. Aristotle compares the position of the head of the household in relation to the other members of the household to that of a king; he commands the slaves as a master, he rules over the children as a kingly father, and he leads his wife. He was the family's natural guardian, as well as their representative to men and gods—the cult of the domestic gods rested upon his shoulders. He represented his slaves, his wife, and underage children before the court. . . . The slaves were originally members of the household, even retaining the household name later on. The slaves participated in the domestic religious services. . . . The serfs, or bonded peasants, were fundamentally different from these slaves. This system of serfdom and manorialism arose as a result of the subjugation of the older indigenous population and the confiscation of the land by the conquerors. While slaves were subjected to the will of their lords, it was the community that fundamentally ruled over the serfs. The right of disposition of the serf's immediate masters—the owners of the *klêroi* (hereditary estates) which the serfs served—was also restricted by law

---

[160] During the Homeric era, the individual farmstead with a residential house, farm buildings, and an enclosing fence was the norm. See: Homer, *Odyssey* Book 6, 291–295; Book 14, 5–17; Book 17, 182–183 and 261–268; Book 23, 137–139; and Book 24, 148–149 and 204–209. Mielke, as cited previously, writes, "The ancient Indo-European individual farmstead, the seat of the *anax* (tribal chief) in the Homeric age, consisted of a farm surrounded by a wall, upon which stood the owner's residence and those of the household staff, along with the hearth and the stable for horses. The cattle stables and other agricultural spaces were situated farther from the main farm."

with regard to their person and property. The bonded peasantry was therefore an entirely homogeneous mass, much more prone to rebellion than the slaves, who came from every diverse corner of the world. Serfdom was common in earlier times among the rural population, but with the development of democracy, they gained their freedom. This, however, was when true slavery begins to first establish itself. It was a common belief that in the earliest times, the Greeks had no slaves whatsoever.[161]

These brief descriptions of the ancient Roman and Hellenic "houses" ought to have been more than enough to prove that these two institutions, despite being from different periods of ancient history, were quite similar in nature. For that matter, the Germanic house (*haus*) can also be placed alongside these two institutions, allowing us to make the initially surprising observation that, despite being separated by a period of at least fifteen hundred years, the fundamental nature of the Indo-European and Germanic family structure has remained unchanged.

2

With this, however, we are brought to a rather important observation—we find that the Germanic and Indo-European family is so rooted to the land and is so based on the idea of attachment to the soil, that we are possibly observing here the final stage of a long prehistoric development. This flies in the face of those who believe that this is the first stage of a new development—those who claim that in pre-Indo-European times, a nomadic people adopted a sedentary way of life by establishing themselves parasitically above a stratum of serfs (conquered peasants) and from that point on established for themselves a hearth fire cult.[162]

But now we are confronted with a clear either/or situation. Either the Indo-Europeans were nomads (or nomadic pastoralists, if we want to continue to use that awkward and inaccurate term from cultural history), in which case they simply would not have had a "house," an eternally burning fire, or a soil-bound inheritance system with ancestor worship and monogamy, or, simply put, they were not nomads, in which case they would have logically been able to develop all of the things that we have learned are characteristic of the Indo-European concept of the family.

Quite simply, it is impossible to see anything in the ancient Indo-Eu-

---

[161] See: Herodotus, *The Persian Wars*, Book 6, chapter 137; Timaios, *Athens*, Book 6, 264c and 272a. Compare with: Albert B. Büchsenschütz, *Besitz und Erwerb im Griechischen Altertum* [Ownership and Acquisition in Ancient Greece] (1869).

[162] Certainly, if a nomadic people were to take this step toward sedentism, it would (at most) be evidence of how thoroughly that nomadic people had shed its nomadism—this possibility can never be invoked to prove a nomadic disposition for a sedentary people. An example of this logic would be the following: since penguins, known to be incapable of flying, have wing stubs, they must have once been able to fly—therefore, penguins still belong to the category of flying birds today.

ropean family structure that could even remotely suggest the instincts or influence of nomadic blood. The whole notion of ancestor worship and its associated eternal hearth fire compels the kinship group (the clan) to be tied to the soil to such an extent that this institution is inherently the complete antithesis of any kind of nomadism. The author has so far tried in vain to find anything in the accounts of historical or modern warlike nomads that could be even remotely compared with this Indo-European family structure. Considering that land ownership by individuals and families is religiously forbidden among both the Arabs and the Tatars, the difference between the Germanic-Indo-European family structure and the nomadic one becomes all the more strikingly apparent. In fact, the either/or situation here is so absolute that no thinking person could possibly reconcile the structure of the Indo-European family—so dependent as it is on the soil—with the so-called Indo-European campaigns of conquest. One is forced to look for a special circumstance that would allow one to make a reasonable connection between this attachment to the soil and the Indo-European migrations. The author will try to resolve this problem below.

After all, this much is clear—the Indo-European considered his purpose in life to be the devotion of all of his energies to the clan and its cult —he would not just suddenly get the idea, out of some feeling or desire, to simply leave his family and his home and wander off into the distance. But if he were able to do just that, then everything that has been handed down to us about the Indo-European family structure must be wrong.

If, for reasons of racial systematics, one were compelled to include the Nordic race among the nomadic races, then it must first be explained how the Nordic race came to have this soil-bound family structure, which is completely beyond the scope of any kind of nomadism. It goes without saying that, by this point, the reader will have realized that the Indo-European concept of family is not a parasitic system based on the exploitation of serf labor. For good measure, we will also demonstrate shortly that the Spartan warrior state cannot be taken as an example of such a system, even though it is always portrayed as particularly "imperious."

The author has already pointed out in detail in chapter two that all nomadic rule is essentially the same—fortresses are built among the subjugated (largely peasant) population, with the nomads frequently being an exclusively urban population in a primarily peasant country (see the earlier explanation of the etymology of the word Berber). Since the Hellenic takeover of Greece is reasonably accessible to us, it is in our interest to examine it and see whether we might find something nomadic about it, in other words, we will seek to identify whether the Hellenes established themselves as a parasitic, fortress-dwelling warrior caste.

Of particular relevance to this question is the fact that the pre-Hellenic population had already been living under governmental structures very similar to historically attested nomadic governments, and that these pre-Hellenic principalities were quite clearly distinct from the Hellenic principalities.

If the Hellenes had only sought conquest, all they would have had to do was overthrow the existing ruling families and then establish themselves in the fortresses. But the Hellenes never thought of doing things this way. Instead, they did exactly what we previously saw with the Germanic peoples during the Migration Period—the Germanic peoples simply avoided Roman cities, settling in individual farmsteads and clustered villages. The Hellenes, too, simply disregarded the existing cities and settled instead in camp villages. It is significant, therefore, that Busolt speaks of a "peasant architecture" appearing in the Greek Middle Ages in the wake of the Doric migrations (circa eleventh century BC).[163] The immigrating Hellenic tribes wanted to own land. Therefore, everywhere, they settled close to the land. Just like the ancient Germanic peoples, the Hellenes also chose to settle on the most fertile soils. While the native population remained in their cities, the Dorians and Eleians settled in open camp villages, in *kômai* or *dêmoi*. Thucydides considered residence within unfortified villages as "the ancient mode of settlement" in Hellas. Strabo,[164] citing Apollodoros, states that almost all the places in the Homeric ship-catalog must be regarded not as towns but as districts, comprised of village associations. In the regions that had lagged behind in economic and social development, such as those of west-central Greece and many in Arcadia, "the ancient mode of settlement" was preserved as late as the time of Thucydides. Sparta was a unified entity of open *kômai* (villages), a type of settlement that had an entirely non-urban character.[165] Busolt writes,

---

[163] Just like the Germanic tribes, the Dorians migrated to Greece under the leadership of kings. Busolt writes, "The kings, like lower officials, were fundamentally subordinate to the community and limited to a certain sphere of duties. These duties were strictly subject to the legal order, constantly supervised, and subject to accusations and judgments from elements of the community. The two Spartan royal houses, like other princely families, traced their lineage back to Heracles. Nevertheless, their power was not unlimited. Even in the time of Herodotus, they possessed only the formal rights of a sovereign military leader." It probably needs no special emphasis here that Busolt's words could just as well have been a description in the previous chapter of the Germanic kings and their relationship to Germanic freemen. To compare, see section two of chapter three.

[164] Strabo, *Geographica* 8.3.3: "But Coelê Elis was distinct from the places subject to Nestor, as is shown in the Catalogue of Ships by the names of the chieftains and of their abodes."

[165] At the head of a community was usually the *basileus*. The outward symbol of their authority was a staff or scepter. The office of *basileus* was a lifelong one and was passed down within the family; if there were several sons, the eldest had the privilege. An important honor of the *basileus* was the possession of a *temenos*, a piece of land that (like crown land) was passed down to the successor, was inalienable, and was distinguished by its quality and size when compared to the land lots of the free community. However, these *basilei* had the same social status as the other freemen; indeed, the latter could easily marry the daughter of a *basilei*. An ordinary nobleman, on the other hand, could only rise to the status of *basileus* if he married the wife or daughter of a *basileus* and there was no heir left to the *temenos*. This, incidentally, is the point of the entire Odyssey, where the suitors attempt to disinherit Telemachus and elevate themselves to the position of *basileus* in place of Odysseus. Penelope's "faithfulness" is based primarily on a sense of responsibility to her royal status and her husband's claim to the throne, as the twenty-year absence of his military expedition certainly would not have deprived him of his privileges as *basileus*.

Regarding the distinctive legal obligations of these *basileis* to the other free Greeks, which strikingly resemble the relationship between the Germanic nobility and the Germanic common freemen, refer to: Georg Busolt, "*Griechische Staatskunde*" [Greek Civic Studies], *Handbuch der Klassischen Altertumswissenschaft* [Handbook of Classical Antiquity]1, (Munich: 1920), 321.

According to Greek custom, the conquest of land was immediately followed by its division and distribution. Among other things, the Odyssey has the settlement of the Phaeacians on Phaeacia (Skhería) begin with the division and distribution of the fields. This was standard practice when founding colonies. According to Plato, the Dorians divided the land when founding their Peloponnesian states.[166] A particularly special estate that stood out above the rest was set aside for the king as a crown estate. The otherwise normal allocation of land-shares generally presupposes a fundamental uniformity in the yield capacity or value of the shares.[167] This means that only in a plain or in hilly corridors with soil of homogenous quality could the lots be of the same size; Plato writes that soil quality is taken into account in the division of land, resulting in lots of different sizes.[168]

In Homeric times, Ionia's economy was still based on agriculture and livestock raising. Busolt writes,

> At the beginning of the Greek Middle Ages, the economic and social foundation of national and communal life thus had an entirely peasant, rustic character. As such, agrarian cults and festivals played a significant role in society. Agriculture was always regarded as the most reliable foundation for state life, and the land-owning peasant population as the most capable citizenry. Land was to be owned by citizens; non-citizens were allowed to own landed property only as a special privilege.

People today would like to frame the Nordic "master and conqueror" race as hostile to agriculture—however, the Hellenes were clearly not like this at all. The sons of princes took part in the tending of flocks. Odysseus boasted to the suitors that he was able to plow straight furrows. Priam's sons harness the chariot, Nausicaa's brothers harness the mules, Laertes works in the garden, and both princes and nobles slaughter, skin, and roast animals for their meals. Queens engage in spinning and weaving alongside their slaves, the princess Nausicaa goes with her maidens to do the laundry.

3

Thus, upon closer examination, the Hellenic takeover of Greece turns out to have been a deeply peasant affair. It is an injustice to transform the Hellenes

---

[166] Plato, *Nómoi*, Book 3: "But the Dorians had this further advantage, that they were free from all dread of giving offence, so that they could divide up their land without dispute…"
[167] Compare to the Germanic division of land in chapter three.
[168] Plato, *Nómoi*, Book 5: "Some districts are ill-conditioned or well-conditioned owing to a variety of winds or to sunshine, others owing to their waters, others owing simply to the produce of the soil, which offers produce either good or bad…"

and their sword-wielding peasantry into a non-peasant master-nobility (*herren-tum*) built exclusively on the sword. However, the idea that peasantry and the Indo-European nobility are mutually exclusive has become so strongly ingrained in the minds of many friends (or enemies) of today's racial movement that it is simply impossible for them to even imagine that the Spartan military state could have been founded by Doric "peasants." Sparta in particular is used again and again as an example of a master-state (*herrenstaat*), supposedly established by the sword and eventually undergoing gradual denordification through wars, ultimately to the point of its own destruction. For these reasons, we will present the rise and fall of the Spartan state informed by historical reality—it will be shown that the truth is far different from what is usually believed, particularly by those who equate the Nordic race with an exclusively non-peasant warrior class. In volume two of Busolt's *Griechische Staatskunde* (Greek Civic Studies), we find a wonderfully clear and comprehensive introduction to the structure of the Spartan state, which we will paraphrase here in a strongly condensed—but essentially unchanged—form:

Around the eleventh century, the Dorians, most likely coming from Argolis through the Thyreatis, invaded Laconia. They arrived as a cohesive group. The country was inhabited by a South Achaean population related to the Arcadians; the main town was Amyklae, an important principality in the upper Evrotas plain. The Dorians reached the Evrotas via the road that descends into the Oinus valley; after crossing the river, on the northern edge of this low plain (in the last foothills of a chain of hills advancing from the north), they found a natural base for further advance. There, on the site of Sparta, they set up a camp, and from this grew a settlement. When they had conquered the whole low plain up to the coast, they divided the conquered land among themselves using the customary method—they broke it up into plots of land with yields as equal as possible and then drew them by lots. For this reason, the plots of land that went to each person were referred to as "lots." Particularly special estates were set aside, or "cut out," for princes and gods. The native population that remained behind on the confiscated land became serfs (peasants bound to the soil). These land plots were referred to as "citizen's land" and were legally different to the land that remained in the hands of the neighboring subject peoples (*períoikoi*). Unlike the individual crown estates, the owners of "citizen's land" were essentially landless people as they had a bound right of ownership. This meant that the Spartans were not allowed to sell their *kleroi* (hereditary estates), as they were not the owners and had no free right of disposal over them. Gustav Gilbert describes the *klêroi* as state fiefs (*staatslehen*); the owners were merely enfeoffed with the property, whose formal ownership remained in the hands of the state. Furthermore, the hereditary estate (*klêros*) was impartible. It was bequeathed to one son, or, in the absence of legitimate sons, to an adopted son. If the testator left behind only daughters, it would be bequeathed to an heiress daughter, who was to propagate the family and mediate the further inheritance of the hereditary property within the family line.[169] The inheritance of a hereditary estate to several legitimate sons is not attested but possible, with the stipulation that one of them (usually the eldest) would be considered the recognized head of the household. He would also be considered the lord of all helots residing on the hereditary estate and had to provide for any brothers who were not provided for.

Initially, the plains of the Evrotas Valley abundantly satisfied the conquerors' need for land and they settled in the previously mentioned "camp villages." Locations "lying low among the hills," that is, places that were "citizen's land," appear in the ship's catalog of the Iliad.[170] Places like Pharis and Bryseae, the latter of which was lost to time except for its temple, are listed next to Sparta and Amyklai. In the surrounding mountainous regions, productive arable land could only be found in a few places.[171] It was not attractive to seize such a territory, which was, in addition, vast and difficult to survey. Also, asserting ownership would not have been easy to achieve. Furthermore, given these conditions, it was obviously unwise to subjugate the entire population of the region, thereby hardening native interests against the foreign intruders. Nevertheless, the conquerors in Laconia, as well as in Argolis, Elis, and Thessaly, had to bring the surrounding mountainous areas under their control, at least as far as the region's natural borders. Otherwise, their estates in the valley would have been threatened by the inhabitants of the mountains. Their slaves, anxious to throw off their yoke, would have found dangerous support in these mountain inhabitants. The mountain dwellers living in or around the area were therefore subdued, but they were not enslaved. They were kept in their villages, which were originally somewhat fortified, and which, in contrast to the open camp villages of the Dorians, resembled small country towns. For this reason, and because of their nominal autonomy, these were called *póleis*—the economic character of the population was not a factor.[172] Their demonym *períoikoi*, meaning "surrounding inhabitants" was determined by

---

[169] Gilbert, "Der Staat der Lakedaimonier.": "The reluctance to let a house (lineage) become extinct is expressed, among other things, in the fact that in Sparta, those who had not yet left behind children were spared in war (Herodotus, *The Persian Wars*, Book 7, chapter 205)."

[170] Homer, *The Iliad*, Book 2, lines 581–583, trans. Samuel Butler, (London: Longmans, 1898), "And those that dwelt in Lacedaemon, lying low among the hills, Pharis, Sparta, with Messe the haunt of doves; Bryseae, Augeae, Amyclae, and Helos upon the sea."

[171] Isocrates, *Panathenaicus*, section 179: "while to the mass of the people they apportioned only enough of the poorest land so that by working laboriously they could hardly gain their daily bread."

[172] *Póleis* is derived from the Sanskrit *par*, meaning a fortified place, castle, or city and from the Lithuanian *pilis*, meaning fortress or castle.

their relationship to the ruling Spartan community; they lived in the surroundings of Sparta and on citizen's land. Constitutionally, they occupied a middle ground between citizens with limited rights and subservient allies who were required to pay taxes and provide services. There were approximately one hundred *póleis* and the names of about eighty of them are known. Its inhabitants were partly peasants but predominantly tradesmen. They understand their origin as belonging to the ancient Achaean population that had been conquered by the Dorians. The *póleis* of the *períoikoi* were subordinate communities that had limited autonomy—each pólis stood on its own, each had its own community citizenship, its own administration, and its own festivals. Their self-governance, however, was limited to communal affairs, subject to supervision, and was consolidated within the framework of the Lacedaemonian state. These *períoikoi* polities were under the supervision of a Spartan *harmostaí* (supervisor) and the *éphoroi*, or ephors,[173] who were permitted to forcibly intervene in the interest of state security. The primary obligation of the *períoikoi* was to support the Spartans in the event of war. However, according to Greek custom, the only people who could serve as hoplites (*hoplítai*) were landowners that could afford to provide themselves with hoplite armaments.[174] This was the only standing (regular) branch of the Lacedaemonian army until the year 424. While the *períoikoi* communities did not have to pay regular taxes to Sparta, the crown estates of the Spartan kings were worked by a certain, unspecified number of *períoikoi*. The *períoikoi* effectively monopolized the operation of trade and commerce throughout the territory. Their favorable economic situation and the fact that their land was better protected against hostile invasions than the land of other Greek states more or less made up for their lack of political rights.[175]

---

[173] The ephors were a board of five officials elected annually that were responsible for a wide array of judicial, military, and religious tasks. Considered to be among the most esteemed and capable Spartans, they were the only individuals in Sparta that did not kneel before the Spartan king.

[174] This is highly significant! While all nomads instinctively, without fail, turn against the rural population, the peasant Dorians evidently felt so connected to the existing settled landowners that they placed the most trust in them and granted them the honor of standing alongside them as equals in times of war. Moreover, it can be assumed that the pre-Dorian landowners were not very racially distant from the Spartans.

[175] During the great helot revolt of 404, only two *perioikian* cities joined the insurgents, despite the critical situation of Sparta (Thucydides, *The Peloponnesian War*, Book 1, chapter 101). It was only the subsequent prolonged wars—which disrupted *períoikoi* trade and demanded a disproportionate toll of *períoikoi* blood—that led to increased tensions. This caused them to withhold military support during Epaminondas's invasion of Laconia, providing assistance to the enemy. Nevertheless, they returned to their former relationship after the enemy's departure. After the defeat of the Spartan king Nabis by T. Quinctius Flaminius in 195–194 BC, the relationship between the *perioikian* cities and Sparta was finally severed. The combative *períoikoi* had been indispensable to Sparta's position of power.

The helots (*heílōtes*), like most of the *períoikoi*, belonged to the ancient Achaean population that had been dorianized. Unlike the *períoikoi*, however, they were not considered Lacedaemonian. They remained on the lands occupied by the Dorian conquerors. This land was divided by the conquerors into plots (hereditary estates) of essentially equal yield. Each hereditary estate (*klêros*) had several helots who lived there with their families; they were bound to the land of the *klêros*. The lord of the hereditary estate did not have a free right of ownership, but had rights limited in the interest of the community—just as he was forbidden to sell or divide the manor, so was he forbidden to sell or release the helots. Only the community had the right of release, a right which was constantly exercised.[176] Helots were obliged to accompany their masters on campaigns as armor and baggage bearers, and in earlier times also as light soldiers. It was typical for each Spartan to take one helot from his hereditary estate as his armor bearer. In some cases, the helots had to provide personal services to their lords at home, though the Spartans had special slaves for actual household chores. Economically, it was of fundamental importance that each hereditary estate formed a self-sufficient unit; this remained unchanged even if several hereditary estates were brought under the same ownership.[177] The helots of each hereditary estate cultivated the land independently at their own expense. In earlier periods, they collectively handed over one half of all the crops cultivated from the soil to their immediate lord, the owner of the hereditary estate. In later periods, the fixed rate of eighty-two Aegean *médimnoi* of barley (about 59.1 hectoliters) and a corresponding quantity of oil, wine, fruits, cheese.[178] They saved whatever was left over from farming; when conditions were optimal, they could save a modest fortune for themselves. The only thing that was poor was the security of their person. It was forbidden to kill a serf without a judge's decision in Thessaly, and the same was true of slaves in Athens—the helots, however, did not have this legal protection. It was said by Thucydides that, fearful of the rashness and sheer size of the helot population, the Lacedaimonians always made their arrangements cognizant of the need to defend themselves against the helots. According to Aristotle, the helots were constantly waiting for misfortunes to befall the Lacedaemonians and for a favorable

---

[176] Among the various classes of freedmen, the *mothakes* held a distinctive and favored position in the sense that they had grown up in close association with the sons of Spartans and had undergone a civic education. They were most likely the illegitimate offspring of Spartans, who had them educated at their expense.

[177] This did not occur until the time of Sparta's decline, which we will come back to.

[178] Editor's note: A *médimnos* (plural *médimnoi*) was a unit of volume in ancient Greece used primarily to measure grain. The exact size of one *médimnos* varied greatly depending on the region in question. Busolt estimates that the Aegean *médimnos* was approximately 72.07 liters.

opportunity to strike. Thus, distrust naturally grew, as did the intensity of surveillance, the ruthlessness of the proceedings against helots suspected of organizing, and the harshness of their general treatment. In turn, there was rising hatred against the state and a desire to throw off the yoke. The *Krypteia* (*krupteía*), a secret police and gendarmerie service, was a defensive measure taken by the Spartans against the helots and their clandestine machinations. Young Spartans affiliated with this service were occasionally sent out into the countryside to kill suspected helots. It is said that during nocturnal patrols, they killed anyone that they encountered on the road, apparently because these people were suspected of facilitating secret, dangerous communications with the helots. However, since the mere killing of a slave carried with it the stigma of blood-guilt, the ephors formally declared war on the helots year after year upon taking office, thereby allowing them to be treated as enemies who could be killed without process.[179] As a result, the country was always officially at war, and the helots became a very sore point in the Lacedaemonian political system.

That's it for Busolt! He paints for us a picture of a well-thought-out state structure under the authority of a peasant clan which, as a result of the right of the victor, transformed its peasant system into a manorial one (manorialism). In this amazingly clear and simple Spartan state, there is nothing that might suggest the existence of a parasitic nomadic nobility, devoted solely to warfare and wasting their days without any sense of responsibility to the land. If one analyzes things clearly and fairly, then we can summarize this as follows—a group of Nordic peasants conquered the land surrounding Sparta in search of arable land. In other words, this was a "peasant trek" similar to that undertaken by the Suebi under Ariovistus. Since they were peasants, the conquerors did not simply exploit the labor of the population they found, but rather, after their victory, stipulated by treaty that the victorious side (the Spartans) would share in the proceeds of the agricultural labor of the conquered. This is essentially the reason why the community, and not the individual head of a Spartan family living on a hereditary estate, had the right of disposal over the helots, even though the collection of the proceeds (as determined by the community) directly benefited the individual owners of the hereditary estates.

We can naturally assume that before the Dorian conquest, the pre-Hellenic inhabitants, who sat on the best arable land in the country, were not exactly inept or incompetent. However, these very same peasants were turned into helots by

---

[179] This annual declaration of war against the helots proves that the Spartans were by no means a people for whom war was an informal affair. These measures seem to reveal the truest essence of Nordic peasant blood, which affirms struggle but employs collective warfare only in exceptional circumstances. No nomadic people in the world has ever entertained the idea of dealing so elaborately with a subjugated population that posed as many challenges as the helots did—and, it must be admitted, with an astonishing sense of responsibility toward human life. This is further discussed in chapter eight.

the Spartans, who also wanted arable land. The other subjugated inhabitants, the *períoikoi*, more or less walked free. This must have created a very dangerous powder keg among the helots from the start, for the *períoikoi* served as a constant reminder to them that there were other forms of servitude in Laconia besides helotry. The helots, therefore, never resigned themselves to their fate. We can perhaps hold this circumstance responsible for the entire military structure of the Spartan state. In his conquest of the left bank of the Rhine, Ariovistus kept a large part of his population permanently under arms and in military service among the rebellious Celts, while the rest of the population proceeded with settlement. Transferring the Suebian situation to Sparta, and then taking into account the helot population—which was undoubtedly very disobedient and often a threat to Spartan farms and villages—we can now rather effortlessly explain how it was possible for the remarkably well-disciplined Spartan warrior state to emerge among a peasant people. The military training of youths and their constant readiness in the capital of Sparta was obviously a product of the ancient migratory organization of the people adapting to the special conditions that prevailed during the conquest of the Spartan lands. Once established, this structure was maintained, expanded, and strengthened over time. Consequently, in Sparta we did not have a warrior class whose members, like nomads, assembled in a few coercion castles in order to be ready to repress the population at any time or to raid neighboring territories at opportune moments. Rather, the militaristic structure of Sparta would be the defensive system of an authentic peasant state, a military defense organization similar to that developed by Prussia right before our eyes in German history.

This explanation, however, does not seem to be consistent with a hypothesis that has recently become more popular in racial research circles. What I am referring to here is the theory that the ancient Indo-European states were constantly losing their best and noblest blood as a result of casualties sustained in the battles they fought for the purposes of conquest or assertion. Due to this, these states underwent "denordification," inevitably leading to the downfall of their state. After all, Indo-European states were only viable as long as there were enough Indo-European (Nordic) people to maintain, protect, and lead the state. Since Sparta in particular appears in history as a state that experienced quite a lot of war-related losses and eventually disintegrated due to the decreased number of Spartan family lines, it is always given as definitive proof of the theory that it is possible for a state to undergo denordification as a result of war-related losses. Furthermore, this example is used to support the claim that, among the Indo-European peoples, the Spartan warriorship was the best at preserving the fundamental nature of the original Indo-European civilization, which was not peasant in nature. But we will soon see that this book's claim of the peasanthood of the Spartans does not contradict the claim that Spartan family lines decreased due to war-related losses, which is a truth that can be verified in light of Spartan history. In fact, we will see that these two claims are directly related to each other.

4

The theory that Indo-European states underwent denordification due to wars has already become academic dogma that no one is allowed to call into question. Nevertheless, the author must confess that he does not believe in this doctrine and considers it an intellectual fallacy. Instead, the author believes that the key to understanding the enigmatic denordification of Sparta lies in land issues (the land question) and in the original peasanthood of the Nordic race.

In fact, it is clear that when it is claimed that a state can undergo denordification due to war-related losses, some kind of biological miscalculation is made. In the following example, one will very quickly recognize the root of the whole issue and immediately identify the logical error that has gone unnoticed until now.

If one hundred pea seeds are sowed in a seedbed and pigeons fly by and pick fifty of them, then the seedbed is 50 percent less pea—instead of one hundred plants, now only fifty will grow. But if one were to draw a conclusion in line with the theory of denordification, one would have to say—because only fifty plants remain, only fifty seeds can be sown again the next year. To believe that war-related losses caused an Indo-European civilization to undergo denordification assumes, quite simply, that a person who dies in battle cannot be replaced by his descendants. And therein lies the basic calculation error! This miscalculation is readily apparent in the pea example mentioned above. The fifty pea seeds saved from the pigeons should, the following year, be readily capable of producing plants on their own whose yield easily compensates for the loss incurred—this is because each pea plant can produce a manifold of pea seeds. If, however, the pea plants fail to do this and the harvest is so small that each plant can only supply a single pea seed for next year's sowing (which means that the pea bed can no longer be fully planted with one hundred pea seeds), this is surely not the fault of the pigeons but of the peas themselves—there is then something wrong with the peas. According to the eternal laws of nature, the fertility rate among a generation of offspring should always be enough to maintain the biological equilibrium in a species-appropriate environment, even in the face of a ruthless culling. In nature, the number and strength of a species or race declines only when this equilibrium is disturbed and the number of living beings who have fallen victim to the culling begins to outnumber the offspring produced.

This means that the moment it is suggested that an Indo-European state underwent denordification due to warfare, every trained biologist immediately wonders why the governing Nordic family lines were no longer in the position to make up for these war-related losses by producing more offspring. This is the most crucial aspect of the whole question for the biologist, not whether wars had caused denordification, a fact which can only be demonstrated through historical analysis. Just as the pigeons are not to blame if the descendants of the pea seeds they spared turn out to be so small in number that the necessary quantity of seeds for the bed is no longer produced, the war-related losses of the Indo-European people are not to be blamed as the cause of the diminishing number of Indo-European family lines, and thus also of individuals.

If the loss of Nordic blood among the Spartans is approached from this perspective, it is surprising to see that this Indo-European military state "par excellence" did not lose its Nordic blood through wars, but through economic issues related to land rights and other related biological causes. In fact, particularly in the case of the military state of Sparta and the abundant historical records available on the subject, we perhaps have no historical example better suited to both prove the absurdity of the theory of denordification through wars and, on the other hand, mark the land question as nothing less than the most consequential question for the Nordic race. For this reason, the history of Sparta's "denordification" will be treated here in more detail, albeit in a condensed form.

In order to properly approach this question, we must investigate the basic idea at the heart of the Spartan state, the Spartan hereditary estate tied to the family, and therefore to marriage. It remains an open question whether, as Plutarch claims, the Spartan state truly began with nine thousand lots (hereditary properties). Only half of this amount would have been sufficient because every hereditary estate at the same time implies a marriage. Due to how things worked on the hereditary estate, these marriages did not have to worry about the economic aspects of child rearing. Therefore, 4,500 healthy Spartan marriages bearing children should have been a sufficient biological source of regeneration for the Spartan state, capable of compensating for even severe wartime losses. This is especially true in the case of the Spartan state, which emphasized the idea of the hereditary estate as a family's sustenance, to the point of demanding that the mistress of such a hereditary estate bless it with a brood of children. This was a genuine legal obligation for the mistress and proprietress of such a hereditary estate; if her own husband had passed, a "procreation assistant" (*zeugungshelfer*) could take his place. A war could cause quite a bit of damage to the hereditary estate before the losses became biologically noticeable (in terms of offspring), since in addition to the heads of the families (whose numbers equaled those of the hereditary estates), the head of the household also had a slew of unmarried and younger brothers not entitled to inherit. If the lord of such an estate was killed in battle, the younger brother took the place of the spouse and continued to produce children for the hereditary estate with the estate's mistress, and in most cases also became the house master of the hereditary estate. If all the male members were killed, the mistress of the house was obligated to immediately marry another Spartan related to her spouse, or else resign from the hereditary estate or retire for good. Thus, as long as hereditary estates were available and could be occupied with the daughters of Spartans, and as long as these women remained fertile, the male Spartans could still provide the hereditary estates with sufficient children even if the male Spartans had been reduced to a small number in a war. One can even understand this at a theoretical level. In fact, it is not until the fifth century BC—after Sparta had already ruled in the same place for about six hundred years, having endured bloody wars, rebellions, and other calamities—that we even hear something about the number of Spartan family lines decreasing (and not just of the Spartans, as it is always portrayed). Suddenly, the drop is so rapid that it can only be described as torrential. Busolt writes,

> In 418 there were still approximately 2,100 to 2,500 Spartans. When the defeat at Leuctra was delivered, the Spartans numbered 1,400—of whom four hundred were left on the battlefield. Within forty-seven years, therefore, the citizenry had decreased by 40 to 45 percent, on average almost 1 percent per year. It decreased by almost the same percentage between 480 and 418 BC, when Herodotus reports that there were just over seven thousand citizens counted in Sparta at the time of the Persian Wars.[180]

Every reader must admit to themselves, after some reflection, that this sudden and devastating decline among the Spartans cannot be attributed solely to the events of the war. But what were the causes of this phenomenon?

Undoubtedly, war-related events partially played a role—this is certain and should not be denied at all. Above all, the helot uprisings (which generally receive less attention) and the fierce battles with the Arcadians and Argives resulted in bloody losses. But the earthquakes also played a role in the denordification of Sparta, particularly the one of 464. According to Diodorus Siculus,[181] twenty thousand Lacedaemonians are said to have perished.[182]

However, all this would never be enough to truly reduce the number of family lines to a significant degree, only being enough to perhaps temporarily reduce the total number of citizens or perhaps leading to the extinction of a few family lines.

For the question under investigation here, it is therefore very revealing that, rather suddenly, there are complaints in the historical records about the decline in the number of children in Spartan marriages. Suddenly, lawmakers lament the new practice of having only one or two children. Busolt writes,

---

[180] Gustav Gilbert *Handbuch der Griechischen Staatsaltertümer* [Handbook of Greek State Antiquities], as cited earlier, provides slightly different numbers: "While we have evidence that at the time of the Persian Wars there were eight thousand Spartans, by the year 371 there were hardly more than 1,500. Aristotle calculates the number of Spartans in his time at just under one thousand, and at the accession of Agis III (244–243), there were only seven hundred left. In the Battle of Leuctra, the four Spartan regiments used in the battle contained seven hundred Spartans, encompassing age groups up to 55 years old. This totals 1,050 Spartans between the ages of 20 and 55 across all six regiments."

[181] Diodorus Siculus, *Library of History* 11.63: "During this year a great and incredible catastrophe befell the Lacedaemonians; for great earthquakes occurred in Sparta, and as a result the houses collapsed from their foundations and more than twenty thousand Lacedaemonians perished."

[182] This is certainly an exaggeration. However, the Spartans' losses must have been quite high, otherwise the earthquake—not an uncommon occurrence in Laconia—would hardly have triggered the great helot uprising in the same year. When the rebellion suddenly broke out, all Spartans who found themselves alone were killed.

Legislation sought to encourage families to have more than two children. Fathers of three sons were exempt from military service, and fathers of four sons were exempt from all civic burdens. However, such premiums were unable to halt what was now an irreversible development.

Thus, we are quite clearly dealing with internal damage within Spartan society, which may give biologists a clue as to why the Spartans were suddenly unable to compensate for war losses. This is undeniably a similar situation to the pea example given above, a situation which could be described as chronic genetic damage or disorder, which was our conclusion in the pea example when the pea seeds spared by the pigeons were no longer able to produce plants that could guarantee a large number of genetically healthy offspring.

If we try to get to the bottom of this peculiar phenomenon in Sparta, we find, surprisingly enough, an underlying economic cause, in particular the land question. Sparta's legislation was entirely peasant in nature and forbade, among other things, any accumulation of wealth. Only the hereditary estate was permitted as property and as the source of a family's sustenance or livelihood. As long as Sparta's political reach did not extend beyond the functions necessary to defend the peasant state, the internal condition of the state remained healthy, as did the citizenry. However, from the moment that an expanded foreign policy forced individual Spartans to make greater expenditures, the absence of financial compensation began to make itself felt. The Spartan, as a participant in military campaigns—that, of course, ultimately imposed significant costs—was often faced with the question of where he could acquire resources without stealing. He was not allowed to enrich himself with the spoils of war, and he could not exploit the labor of his helots at home since their contributions were determined by the community council and not by the landowner. If his brood of children of children consumed his bread at home, he soon found himself in a very disadvantageous economic situation. This is initially why Spartans were urged to limit the number of children—for the sake of personal security. The one or two child system was encouraged by the system of inheritance, where indivisible hereditary estates were passed on to a son. However, as there was never a shortage of illegitimate children born to helot women (who had no right of inheritance), it is clear that the Spartans did not lack procreative power.[183]

This placed Sparta at a turning point in its history. From the moment that the peasant closed inheritance law, for economic reasons, had to rely on a one or two child system, degeneration very easily set in. This was due to the simple fact that the small number of children born no longer allowed for a healthy culling, and the heir became whoever just happened to

---

[183] Herodotus, *The Persian Wars*, 6.61: "Once Cleomenes returned home from Aegina, he planned to remove Demaratus from his kingship, using the following affair as a pretext against him: Ariston, king of Sparta, had married twice but had no children."

be there, instead of selecting the healthiest and most respected son, as was customary and demonstrably practiced in Sparta when there was a larger number of children born.

In the historical records, we also suddenly hear about Spartan marriages becoming increasingly barren—a king reportedly marrying three women in succession until he finally succeeds in conceiving a child with the third one. People want to make inbreeding—which was quite undeniably present—responsible for this infertility. While this could have been true, it may not necessarily have been the case, as we will see in chapter nine when we discuss inbreeding. Instead, it is more likely that several causes were acting together here. Perhaps it is advisable to first familiarize ourselves with the political developments in Sparta during this period.

In sharp contrast to the continual decline in the number of citizens, the Spartans continued to expand their political and military enterprises. Prior to the fifth century BC, they had only ventured beyond the Peloponnese a select number of times—during their campaign against the tyrant Polykrates and for their military expeditions against the tyrants and democracy of Athens. However, when all of Hellas was threatened with subjugation by the Asiatic potentates, Sparta's hegemony of Hellas began, a task that their state was not biologically equipped to withstand in the long run. Money and gold became increasingly important to the Spartans with nothing less than disastrous effects over time. Given the changed circumstances resulting from Sparta's regional political hegemony, the prohibition of private ownership of gold and silver only served to intensify the desire and greed to possess them among the Spartans. Their wars were expensive, and this fact, despite some old Spartans fighting tooth and nail against it, led to the adoption of money for political and military purposes in Sparta. But once Sparta became accustomed to using money in its public affairs, desiring its use for the individual's own needs was not very far off. Eventually, it was believed that all Spartans were greedy and corruptible. It was prophesied that greed, and nothing else, would overcome Sparta—the ephors and gerontes were considered particularly corruptible.[184] In short, a "feudal plutocracy" was formed among the formerly peasant Spartans, similar to what we witnessed in England in the last century.

Additionally, another circumstance intervened disastrously in this general development. Since the Spartans were not permitted to accumulate movable property alongside their hereditary estates, but still had to pay for their personal political obligations, family lines were practically forced to consolidate their hereditary estates under one person in order to

---

[184] Editor's note: The gerontes (elders) were members of the Gerousia, or Council of Elders. Also known as the Spartan Senate, it consisted of twenty-eight elders and the two ruling kings. Gerontes had to be over the age of sixty, were elected for life, and had a primarily judicial and advisory role. The Gerousia served as a panel of judges in legal situations of particular significance, such as in the case of capital crimes. It could present legislation to the Ecclesia (Spartan Citizens' Assembly) for consideration and could also veto any legislation originating there.

provide the heir with a livelihood appropriate to his status. They accomplished this through their inheritance policies and by refraining from having multiple children. The Law of Epitadeus (Epitadas) at the beginning of the fourth century BC is thought to have emerged as a result of this crisis; this law granted the owner of a hereditary estate the power to dispose of the estate at will through gift or testament. This right of disposal may have already existed in earlier times, but was limited cases of childlessness. Its unlimited expansion had such disastrous consequences because it not only called into question the inheritance of children, but also provided an opportunity to conceal what was in fact a sale. Gradually, the majority of hereditary estates passed into the possession of wealthy Spartans through purchase or as gifts or dowries for the numerous heiresses, or through testamentary dispositions. While each hereditary estate always had only one lord, the consolidation of several hereditary estates into the hands of one lord was no longer prohibited.

This was the beginning of Sparta's descent into the abyss. If it had been willing to adopt a sensible and socially-bound economic system like the German state managed to do in the Middle Ages, or, if it had acted like Prussia during its period of political ascendancy and protected its landowners and peasant class within the existing economic system, then there would have been a chance to save much of Sparta. Unfortunately, it was now possible to consolidate several hereditary estates under one hand.[185]

In terms of marital law, this measure had quite a drastic impact. Gilbert writes,

> Full citizenship in Sparta depended not only on birth but also on other conditions. In Sparta, full citizenship could only be obtained by those who received a Spartan education, and of these, only those who regularly contributed to and participated in the *syssitia* could maintain full citizenship.[186] Those who failed to fulfill these two obligations lost the political rights of full citizenship, but likely retained civil rights.

---

[185] Due to its unique circumstances, the development of *latifundia* estates did not occur in Sparta. The Spartans continued to adhere to the concept of the hereditary estate as a self-contained economic unit, with internal affairs that were fundamentally regulated by the community. If a Spartan combined several inherited properties under his control, he could not manage these properties as a single unit from a central location for profitable cultivation. Instead, the economic unity of each inherited property had to remain intact. For example, they could not even dictate to their helots how and what work was to be done—they had to be content with whatever came their way from the estates under their supervision.

[186] Editor's note: The Spartan *syssitia*, also known as common messes or dining clubs, were social institutions central to Spartan society. Within these groups, male citizens dined together daily, fostering camaraderie and solidarity among them. Participation in a *syssition* was mandatory and served to reinforce the values of discipline, loyalty, and military readiness. Membership began in adolescence and continued throughout a Spartan man's life. A comparable modern institution would be a military mess hall or dining facility.

In Sparta, a fully valid marriage could only be contracted on a hereditary estate. Only children conceived in this way would be able become the fully Spartan parents of a new generation of Spartan citizens. It was not necessary, however, for the father of a fully Spartan child on a hereditary estate to also be the head of the household. That being said, the Spartan descent of this parent had to always be faultless.

As long as the number of hereditary estates matched the number of marriages, the numbers of Spartan offspring still remained somewhat in balance, despite the encroaching one and two child system that reduced the total number of citizens. Nevertheless, there was always a certain equilibrium in the fact that daughters, as heiresses or spouses on hereditary properties, remained highly sought after, and the number of girls born never actually fell below the number of hereditary estates. However, even when the number of full-citizens and eligible spouses fell below the number of hereditary estates, the number of children on these estates did not necessarily decrease, as the institution of the procreation assistant existed. Politically, this situation was initially not dangerous because it was customary for Spartans to father illegitimate children with helot women as they pleased. These children received a full Spartan education and stood politically and militarily on equal footing with their fathers (except in terms of their ancestry, as they never qualified as heirs for a hereditary estate). Until its downfall, Sparta quite relentlessly maintained the principle of blood purity among both the male and female citizenry eligible to inherit.

The situation described here initially ensured that the overall birth rate of fully legitimate children did not fall below a certain number. One may estimate that, on the average, there were twice as many children born as there were hereditary estates. As long as the ancient principles of physical education and training were still in force—in short, as long as the ancient Spartan spirit still animated the family lines—there was unlikely to be a decline in the genetic quality of the Spartan offspring, even in spite of the one or two child system, which, of course, dangerously reduced the choice of available heirs.

But the situation took a turn that was nothing short of disastrous the very moment that the practice of consolidating several hereditary estates under a single person began. Each time estates were consolidated, the number of fully legitimate marriages was reduced by the number of merged estates. From that moment on, the number of Spartan lineages plummeted. The turning point was the law of the ephor Epitadeus (Epitadas). This law severed the vital connection between the Spartans and their land. Around the middle of the fourth century BC, it had already come to the point that most of the citizen's land that had been divided into *klêroi* (hereditary estates) had come "into the possession of a few family lines," two fifths of which belonged to women (heiresses who inherited the property because no male heirs remained). Of course, this is not to say that only a few hereditary properties were occupied by "lords," since it can be assumed that the family lineages still in possession of hereditary properties provided their sons with such properties whenever possible, even if they did not allow the sons to redistribute the jointly inherited family estate among their own children. However, the fact that two fifths of the inherited properties were in the hands of heiresses speaks volumes.

These heiresses, however, were to exert a fateful influence on the decline of Sparta. By virtue of their possession of hereditary estates, the heiresses were quite wealthy. Thus, they stood somewhat separate and privileged compared to their female counterparts, as Spartan women were otherwise not entitled to inheritance. Throughout world history, it has always led to disastrous consequences when the girls or women of the ruling class begin to accumulate wealth and independence. The same held true in Sparta. All of a sudden, well-to-do heiresses found life much more pleasant when it was enjoyed as much as possible, instead of being troubled by "barbaric fertility," as childbearing was referred to in those days. These young Spartan women believed that they could fulfill their duty of bringing one or two children into the world (and giving them their hereditary property) just as well at the age of thirty as they could at twenty. The physical exercise of girls, which Lycurgus had introduced for patriotic reasons and for the benefit of the collective, and which was supposed to shape them into fertile mothers, was now transformed into "sport." Instead of seeing physical training as an aid in making them more fit for childbearing, they now viewed it as a pleasurable component of "beauty care." They no longer considered jeopardizing their youthful figures through "barbaric fertility." Since these young Spartan women had fortunes at their disposal thanks to the income of their hereditary properties, and because nobody really kept a close eye on them (as male Spartans had to engage in politics and were very frequently abroad), they also began to adorn their beautiful, well-toned bodies with all sorts of luxurious items. In other words, they rather abruptly introduced a culture of luxury, thereby widening the gap between the rich and the poor citizens even further. They found support from those Spartans who had acquired a taste for a luxurious lifestyle abroad. Before long, it reached a point where the owner of merely one hereditary property was considered poor. Eventually, there were even reports of impoverished female citizens personally selling vegetables or other agricultural products in the market to eke out a living.[187]

But that was not even the worst of it. When young women are wealthy, beautiful, and independent, with nothing else to do but focus on themselves, then they often entertain all kinds of foolish ideas. Moreover, in a society like Sparta, where sexual intercourse itself was not subject to any sort of moral judgment (unlike the production of inferior children or children whose ancestry was not faultless), it was only a matter of time before sexual licentiousness took hold, along with its inevitable corrupting effects. This is indeed what we see in the Spartan historical record. Spartan women eventually became notorious throughout Greece for their sexual promiscuity. However, one should not assume that because of this, the lineage of children born to female Spartan citizens on hereditary estates was somehow flawed. Spartan women during the period of Sparta's downfall—the women who had given themselves over unhesitatingly to many

---

[187] This is evidence that, unlike all nomads, the Spartans, even at the time of their greatest political ascendancy, still always considered farming the most appropriate occupation for their status—even in the face of adversity.

men before their marriage and ensured that no children were born from these prior relationships—these Spartan women—who did not have a second thought when it came to this sort of premarital sex—even they would have considered it quite a grave sin against the gods and the spirit of their ancestors if a child conceived in a legitimate marriage had not been completely faultless in its origin and descent by not actually belonging to her husband or to the husband-approved or community-approved procreation assistant. However, these facts may nonetheless provide the key to understanding something in the history of Sparta that has yet to be fully understood, namely the rather sudden and striking prevalence of infertility among Spartan women. The author discovered in a medical journal a highly informative article that demonstrated how continuous contraception, especially when employed from an early age, easily leads to complete infertility in females.[188] The previously attributed cause of the infertility of Spartan women, inbreeding—an issue that quite undoubtedly existed—is not sufficient to explain the issue, as we are familiar with incestuous marriages, particularly from antiquity, that were anything but barren. Chapter nine provides further details on this matter. However, the common practice of premarital sexual relations among Spartan women during the era of decline, coupled with the use of contraceptive methods (the specific methods are unknown, but we do know they were employed), can reasonably be considered the cause of the enduring infertility of Spartan marriages.

In summary, we can say that the internal and actual reasons for the denordification of Sparta are partly economic and partly biological in nature. It was economic in the sense that the old Spartan idea of marriage, linked to a hereditary estate and rooted in peasant thinking, was abandoned for the sake of satisfying economic needs. The Spartan state no longer ensured that hereditary estates would be able to sustain a large number of children regardless of the father's personal wealth. It was biological in the sense that the widespread system of having only one or two children limited the choice of heirs to the estates. Furthermore, the moral decline resulting from the successes of Sparta's foreign policy killed the sense of responsibility among Spartan women, and the spread of immorality led to infertility among them.

These are, broadly speaking, the internal (biological) causes of the decline of Sparta. They are the causes that we sought in the example of the peas, in order to find, as biologists, the conditions that could lead to the extinction of a race when the proportion of births to deaths decreases.

Under the conditions we can observe for Sparta, it is evident that wars naturally had a highly devastating impact, but this is an effect and not a cause. The cause was the abandonment of their previous connection with the land, which had allowed the Spartans—originating from a peasant background—to rise to a powerful manorial power.

Moreover, the decline of Sparta in particular proves that even under such circumstances, devastating wars need not necessarily cause the leading Nordic family lines to diminish.

---

[188] *"Die Schwangerschaftsverhütung als Sozialmedizinisches."*

The political and economic development of Sparta led to the situation where the Spartan family lines residing on hereditary estates gradually distanced themselves from peasant customs and life on the land. Thus, we see the arrival of what inevitably occurs when the Nordic nobility keeps the scents of earth and stables out of their clothes and begins to seek world domination through gold—namely, revolution from below.

The first conspiracy was suppressed in the year 398. At that time, there were about 1,500 to 2,000 Spartans (the entire citizenry) against approximately 15,000 to 20,000 *períoikoi* and 50,000 helots. Under such circumstances, the state could hardly endure the defeat at Leuctra, which resulted in the loss of four hundred able-bodied citizens (that was 33 percent of the citizenry). Epaminondas's invasion of Laconia in 370–369 BC had brought the state to the brink of collapse. But the Spartans did not give in. With ruthless energy, they suppressed every revolutionary movement, and although they had to relinquish some border territories, they maintained the independence of their state and control over almost the entirety of Laconia. The old Spartan family lines firmly retained control of the state. Despite constant wars, lack of money, and insufficient mercenaries, they held their own. They even defied the Macedonian King Philip, who ravaged all of Laconia but failed to subjugate Sparta. The political tenacity and uncompromising will to prevail demonstrated by these Spartan family lines is astonishing and admirable. This can, of course, only be explained by the fact that the Spartans, amidst the general dissolution of the values of their old state, at the very least did not make the mistake of carelessly mixing their blood with others. As lax as their sexual morals became, when it came to what children were eligible for full citizenship, they seemed to adhere strictly to blood purity to the very end. This held true under all conditions for the families residing on the hereditary estates, so while the Spartans diminished in number, they did not lose their aptitude for political leadership and mastery of political issues.[189] This is the most remarkable aspect of these family lines—despite all the moral decay, they never abandoned the principle of maintaining their thoroughbred lineage. We will dedicate a more detailed examination to the thoroughbred question in chapter nine. Here, the author would only like to point out that contrary to the frequently expressed view in racial-scientific literature regarding the inevitable miscegenation of the Spartans due to their losses in war—losses they supposedly replenished with non-Spartans—the Spartans themselves never considered such actions. In fact, the author would even argue that it was precisely this staunch position of blood purity that explains why these family lines, abandoned by the entire world, did not waver in their noble will-to-power or their political determination despite the immense war-related losses they incurred.

In the year 243–242 BC, it is said that no more than one hundred Spartan

---

[189] As a matter of fact, the extent to which the Greeks considered aptitude for politics and political affairs to be a distinct characteristic of their own race can be seen in the fact that the Greek word for a person who had no sense or understanding of matters of statecraft, namely "idiot," has persisted as an insult among us to this day. Idiot comes from the Greek *idiotes*, which referred to a private citizen that lacked knowledge of state affairs or was excluded from them due to being of a lower social class.

families possessed hereditary estates and political rights, and it was during this time that the youthful King Agis IV attempted a reform. Although the impoverished or less well-off Spartans stood behind him, he achieved practically nothing. The division of the jointly inherited hereditary estates back to their original number and their allocation to impoverished Spartans—which would have been the key to saving the state—did not occur. Instead, small and large landowners were released from their debts, which was generally perceived as a good thing but was ultimately only a temporary measure that missed the true heart of the issue. In the year 235, Cleomenes III then implemented the necessary division and reinstated the ancient Spartan constitution. However, he seemed to forget that these matters are fundamentally a question of blood and, as the English say, it is men who make history, not measures. Although Cleomenes generally took positive measures to save the state, it appears that he did not allocate the hereditary estates to the right people.[190] Throughout the period following Cleomenes's measures, the newly created status quo only served to drive a constant state of civil war. Eventually, Nabis, supported by the proletariat and foreign mercenaries, restored peace by expelling or executing those who stood above the rest in terms of property or origin, distributing their properties to the proletariat and to the mercenaries, and making their wives and daughters available to them and the freed helots. It was the typical picture of an authentic ancient revolution.[191] Finally, in 195 BC the Romans put an end to the whole affair, subjugated Sparta,

---

[190] Unlike Cleomenes's inadequate reforms, Miklós Horthy, the current regent and head of state of Hungary, seems to be effectively implementing similar reforms. Horthy has revived the ancient Spartan concept of rural state fiefs by reestablishing a version of them in Hungary. Veteran enlisted soldiers and officers are accepted into a so-called "heroic brotherhood" and endowed with land—the land is completely free and thus without interest-bearing obligations. In return for the allotted land, the soldier is required to have impeccable character, impeccable conduct, devoted loyalty to the fatherland, marriage to an impeccable woman, and so on. Such an "heroic domain" or "noble domain" is inherited by the son of the recipient, if the son (usually the eldest) is deemed worthy of succession by the "noble chapter," as the "noble title" is associated with the noble domain. Noninheriting younger brothers may apply for newly established noble domains as descendants of an "enfeoffed person" if they desire and if there are no objections to their conduct or character. The sons of fallen frontline soldiers from the previous World War enjoy the privilege of preferential consideration when applying for a noble domain. The cost of acquiring and endowing these noble domains is borne by the noble chapter, which collects donations. To donate, it is required that the donor be a person of impeccable character, thus making it an honor to donate anything to a noble chapter. Horthy's intention with this whole system was "to bring into being a new class from the stratum of the nation which was undoubtedly the most valuable and the healthiest, which could serve as a model for everyone, and which would continue to cultivate the traditional virtues of the Hungarian race."

Horthy thus avoids the mistake made by Cleomenes III in Sparta, who allocated land without any selection requirements for the applicants. Horthy essentially imposes a kind of moral performance test on all applicants before the opportunity to apply for a noble domain. In essence, Horthy merely reiterates what the Germanic people already possessed, encapsulated by the terms "nobility" and "hero"—see chapter three.

Compared to the frequently expressed contemporary notion of allocating hereditary agricultural leasehold estates on state lands to Germans seeking land, the fundamental difference with Horthy is that the expectations of the enfeoffed are not made in monetary values but in moral terms. Based on the experiences of antiquity, it can be said that Horthy will likely achieve a positive outcome in his endeavors.

[191] See also: Polybius, *The Histories*, 13.6–8 and 16.13; Livy, *The History of Rome*, 34.31.17–18.

and imposed cruel terms of peace on the country. According to Busolt, Sparta subsequently became "a quite prosperous free city, which, because of its glorious past, its antiquities, and its maintenance of ancient institutions, enjoyed no small reputation and was considered a sight to behold."

Let us summarize the outcome of our brief analysis—wars did not "denordify" Sparta, and the ruling Spartan families, until the very end, never once entertained the idea of mixing their blood. If we want to name the causes of Sparta's downfall, we would have to say that although this state originally had a brilliantly thought-out structure that took into account issues of genetics and possessed a healthy peasant foundation, Sparta did not have the insight to flexibly adapt the internal development of the state to the changing circumstances of its foreign policy successes. Instead of leaving the ancient Nordic closed inheritance laws untouched and opening the door to a sensible, socially-bound economic policy (which, with suitable protective measures for hereditary estates, would never have been able to undermine the idea that the hereditary estate was the foundation of a family's sustenance), Sparta took the fateful step of using the ancient Nordic closed inheritance laws to bring about family-bound large-scale land holdings, thereby continuously reducing its number of family lines with valuable blood.

The explanation for the rise and decline of the Spartan family lines lies in the closed inheritance laws and is rooted in a peasant way of thinking. The Spartans paid the price for deviating from the developmental path determined by their peasant origin, leading to their downfall.

5

Unfortunately, when it comes to the founding of other Indo-European states in antiquity, we cannot in every case trace the connections that led to denordification as clearly as we can in the case of Sparta. This is due to the fact that Sparta understood how to maintain its original conditions for a remarkably long period of time.

On closer examination, however, one also notices that, when it comes to the state foundations of other Indo-European (and, for that matter, Germanic) peoples, there are certain phenomena which are undoubtedly similar in their nature and which only differ in the timing of their development. Often, these phenomena also show local variations conditioned by the nature of the landscape or of the subjugated population. Let us attempt to very briefly outline the fundamental aspects of this development, as it leads the researcher right into the heart of the issues we are concerned with.

With very few exceptions—some of which will be addressed in chapter seven—Indo-Europeans appear in history as peasants or manorial lords. Indo-European manorial rule, however, was never a simple superimposition over pre-existing cultures; rather, it represented a highly distinctive enhancement of the existing peasantry toward an organic division of labor and leadership. Even so, the conquerors held on tenaciously to the culture they had brought with them, so that in terms of cultural history one can speak of a superimposition. The Indo-European "lord" indeed experiences a reduction in workload in terms of agricultural work, but in turn, also assumes social responsibility for his "serfs." This is a fundamentally important factor that clearly separates Indo-Europeans from any form of nomadic governance, a factor that has unfortunately been largely overlooked by many modern researchers in the field of race science. The lack of attention to this factor is just one of the reasons that the question of Indo-European and Germanic nomadism was even raised in the first place.

All forms of Indo-European manorialism derive their soundness from their land laws, which were designed to preserve the family unit as a whole while subordinating individual family members to the overall idea of the family. For this reason, the ability of an Indo-European family to survive was largely rooted in its family law, which had an organic connection to the land and made the family the most basic living unit within an Indo-European community.

History, as observed among the Indo-Europeans, seems to begin with communities vying for dominance among themselves until one community emerges as the recognized leader. The ruling community is eventually constrained in the range of its rule by geographic boundaries. The course of this development follows a consistent pattern, visibly influenced by the nature of Indo-European civilization.

However, soon a new chord begins to resonate, at first nearly imperceptible, but then increasingly audible. The larger the territory controlled by a leading community, the more noticeable the economic and administrative challenges become, requiring solutions. Alongside the manorial estates of the leading family lines (which are peasant in nature), trading centers begin to flourish—slowly but surely influencing the Indo-European landed nobility. The previous subsistence economy based on its foundation of self-sufficient household economies, which had until then satisfied the needs of families, proves to be too cumbersome to meet all their long-term demands. The increasingly powerful trading sector demands monetary regulation. The initial measure of value, livestock (bartering), proves to be too cumbersome. Soon, people look for simpler means of payment. Inevitably, in the history of all Indo-European states, a moment arrives that quite clearly marks a crucial turning point in its development—precious metals become the means of payment. The original source of this idea lies in the Orient, where precious metals have been used in trade since their earliest recorded history. In the Orient, the reign of money began its triumphal march around the world.

At first, the penetration of a monetary economy triggers a surprising flourishing of cultural affairs. In principle, of course, it is natural that this occurs—trade expands, creating more employment opportunities, which in turn places greater demands on their management and provides an opportunity for the creative forces of the people to express themselves freely. The hallmark of such times is the flourishing of cities, which are always the seats of commerce and thus are always directly connected to its destiny.

It is well understood that trade always flourishes best when the mobility and freedom of goods can be extensively realized and when the merchant (although it is better to refer to him here as the trader)[192] is subjected to as few constraints and limitations as possible. In antiquity, however, this fact inevitably clashed in a hostile way with the whole concept of Indo-European soil-bound family law. Because trade felt restricted by this family law at every turn, purely driven by instinct, it opposed it vehemently and attempted to undermine the foundations of this law in a protracted small-scale war. In this struggle, trade has always emerged victorious.[193] The stages of this struggle, which almost always extend over several centuries (in Greece, for example, from the seventh to the third century BC), are characterized by certain phenomena that repeat themselves with a nearly clock-like regularity. An outline of the three main stages will be mentioned here. The first stage is the proclamation of individualism, that is, the glorification of the individual that is responsible only for himself and who stands exclusively on his own two feet. The second stage is the liberation of the peasantry (the abolition of serfdom), an act that usually serves the interests of justice, since an initially socially-responsible manorial system can still degenerate into oppressive feudalism under the pressure of an emerging plutocracy. Such a development has long made serfs out of peasants whose ancestors came to the land as equal conquerors alongside the ancestors of the ruling noble class. The third stage is the rise of democracy, with its fall from estate-bound kingship to unrestricted ruling plutocracy.

It is usually not until late within this developmental trend, however, that the connectedness to the land is severed. The peasant class, left to fend for themselves due to peasant emancipation, will for some time continue to stubbornly defend Indo-European closed inheritance law, a system that was either inherent to their race or a system that had been instituted by their Indo-European lords. But soon the fate of the closed inheritance law is sealed, and land is turned over to trade and commerce as a commodity to be sold at will. Interestingly, one can observe time and time again that trade, in its struggle against peasant closed inheritance law, resorts to a distortion of terms that is highly illuminating from the perspective of cultural history.

Namely, trade portrays the question of closed inheritance law exclusively from the perspective of ownership and presents property as an undemocratic institution that only serves to enrich individuals. However, this perspective overlooks the fact that this closed inheritance law was not the result of economic expediency but merely a part of ancient Indo-European family law. Therefore, with the abolition of the closed inheritance law, the idea of the soil-bound Indo-European family structure was also abolished. Consequently, the concept of the Indo-European family virtually collapses, and with it, very quickly and logically, all those moral val-

---

[192] The distinction between a merchant and a trader will be further elaborated upon by the author in chapter seven.
[193] Only the Germanic peoples were able to bridge these contrasts; however, since the time of Hardenberg and the liberalism of the nineteenth century, trade has once again emerged as the undisputed victor.

ues that had been nourished at the wellspring of the Indo-European marriage.

At first, the trading sector seems to have been correct in its measures against the inalienability of land, for the penetration of a monetary economy into rural conditions brings about a flourishing of agriculture. But the liberated peasants quickly fall into interest bondage under the urban financial lords; they are subsequently forced to leave their homes and farms and migrate to the city. While the countryside is stripped of its people, the cities begin to swell. Although the peoples of antiquity usually experience a cultural blossoming at this moment and produce their noblest and most valuable cultural creations, upon closer examination, this "blossoming" proves to be less an expression of a lively interplay of forces within the healthy body of the people (*volkskörper*), and more a phosphorescent symptom of decay produced by uprooted Indo-European creative power—the best part of the people consumes itself in a bright but brief flash. The interested reader may verify the accuracy of these statements for Greece with Gilbert, Busolt, Lübkers, and others, and for Rome with Mommsen, Ferrero, Kuhlenbeck, Ihering, and others. The author would like to add that the history of agriculture as well as modern, racially-oriented historical research indicate that the same process seems to apply to all other Indo-European state formations (including China). In any case, this historical process in the life of an Indo-European state—this period which brings with it the illusion of cultural heights—already carries within itself the seed of its own decay, and therefore, in spite of all the political power of the state, often ends in a terribly rapid descent into the darkness of history.[194]

In their soil-bound family law, the Indo-Europeans possessed a biological counterweight that could compensate for all war-related losses. Under reasonably healthy conditions, all the sons of a peasant or landowner would never—or at least very rarely—die in a war. In most cases, at least one son would remain who could perpetuate the family line on his father's farm.[195] When individualism prevails, however, the founding of a family becomes a private matter, leaving the maintenance and sustenance of a family to the individual; each death on the battlefield now brings an end to the further perpetuation of a family and gives no opportunity to any offshoot of the family lineage (brother, cousin) to keep the paternal family line alive by taking up the vacated position. These matters will receive a more detailed analysis in chapter ten. Ferrero absolutely correctly illuminates this in the following about Rome:

---

[194] One should not be deceived by the seemingly divergent trajectory of Rome's development. Directly following the Punic Wars, the history of a Rome led by Nordic lineages came to an end, and the history of an entirely un-Nordic plutocracy began. This plutocracy, decade after decade, progressively eradicated the last traces of Nordic blood in Rome, eventually culminating in the establishment of the Caesarist regime. While the regime created by G. Julius Caesar discovered a means to forestall the collapse of even the most decayed state, this Caesarist regime bore no resemblance whatsoever to an Indo-European state.

[195] Münchhausen, "Die Grafen von Beaumanoir.".

This is how Rome, in the fourth and third centuries BC, was able to ever increasingly spread not only its influence and laws but also its race and language, founding eighteen powerful Latin colonies between 334 and 264. As a result, strong Latin farmers were scattered over the various regions of Italy. These peasants alternated between the toil of rural life and the craft of war; their pay and the gifts received from generals after victories provided a desirable supplement to their agricultural profits—warfare practically became an auxiliary industry to agriculture. With these farmers, who were at the same time soldiers, the Roman nobility in their first military encounter was able to defeat Carthage, the mighty trading power, whose commercial expansion eventually clashed with Rome's military and agricultural expansion. . . . If such military achievements and conquests were able to be continuously accomplished for centuries, it is solely due to the fact that Rome, thanks to its inherent moral discipline and the conservative mindset of the aristocracy, always remained a peasant-aristocratic and martial polity. At the end of the day, even in times of barbarism, a land is conquered only by the plow; it does not belong to those who soak it with blood in fierce battles, but to those who, once they are lords of the land, cultivate it, sow it, and populate it. By the end of the third century BC, Rome became the master of Italy because the virtues held highest by all the classes of Roman society were those unique to the well-ordered peasant communities, virtues of the kind that we find again today among the Boers.[196]

One can see that as long as the ancient Roman patricians remained faithful to their ancient Nordic peasanthood, wars not only did them no harm, but even enabled their growth, thereby turning warfare into an "auxiliary industry to agriculture." Denordification began the very instant that Rome, after their victory over Carthage, abandoned its peasant foundation and became a mercantile nation engaged in world trade, with all the downsides of a state structure centered on capitalism.

Even racial mixing is never the result of war-related losses, as it is often portrayed today. Rather, this only ever begins when the economic foundation of the noble families ceases to be landholding and becomes money. This is quite natural. When money, rather than skill, carries value in a state, the Nordic race must compete with other races in a field for which it is developmentally ill-prepared. Under the protection of a socially irresponsible financial economy, personalities rise to the top who, apart from cunning and cleverness, bring no other significant intellectual gifts with them, but who, through their daughters, can still give the increasingly impoverished old Nordic Indo-European nobility the appearance of ruling splen-

---

[196] Guglielmo Ferrero, *Größe und Niedergang Roms* [Greatness and Decline of Rome] (Stuttgart: 1922).

dor, albeit at the expense of the blood-value of their offspring.[197]

This picture of the rise and fall of Indo-European states, sketched here very briefly, reappears with a (please forgive the expression) virtually mindless regularity when one takes the time to examine the history of these states from this perspective. With this same mindless regularity, we also see repeated attempts to save the state shortly before its decline. At this critical juncture, it is recognized that the original peasantry is, in some way, causally involved in the health of the state, and very earnest attempts are made to save the remaining peasantry and/or to establish a new peasantry. But the crux of the whole matter is typically completely overlooked—it was the soil-bound family law of the Indo-European peoples that made the peasantry of the previous centuries so healthy. Attempts are made to save the peasantry by economic or other legal measures—without success, of course, because no peasantry can assert itself in the long run in a state devoted to an unaccountable financial economy. This is rooted in the nature of the peasantry and cannot be further elaborated here.

One can see that peasanthood was the destiny of the Indo-Europeans! With this understanding, we have the key that allows us to unlock and penetrate the fundamental nature of all Indo-European civilizations, as well as their rise and fall in the light of history.

6

When clarifying the Indo-European question, Ihering's research into the legislation of the patricians of ancient Rome (before the introduction of the Twelve Tables) will likely always remain one of our most valuable resources.[198] Therefore, when trying to answer these questions, we should start with Ihering's findings. From the outset, the most revealing fact is that the patricians did not have a specific term for autumn as a season. Ihering finds, much to his surprise, that this is generally true for all Aryans; he bases this opinion on Kluge and Daniczek. This can be compared to some etymological research done by Schrader (*Reallexikon*), who states verbatim, "There is, therefore, no historical evidence to suggest that there ever was a time when the Indo-Europeans of Europe were unfamiliar with agriculture, and the same can be said of the first

---

[197] The evidence for this has been clearly and unequivocally elaborated by Busolt for Greece and by Ferrero for Rome. Busolt writes, "The character of the ruling class also underwent a change. The social preeminence of the old aristocracy was based on wealth of land and cattle and was associated with noble lineage. The importance of this, however, was greatly diminished by the exponentially larger profits that could be made in trade and industry. The aristocracy was caught up in the tide of the new era, not only leading colonial ventures (originally agrarian in nature), but also engaging in large-scale trade in the major maritime cities. The phrases 'money made the man' and 'wealth mixed the blood' come to mind! The dominant aristocracy evolved into a plutocracy based on wealth as measured by the census." By the way—when Solon the Athenian turns against the ruling class, he never fights the blood-nobility itself, but always targets the wealthy, who in his time belonged largely, though not exclusively, to the old aristocracy.

[198] Rudolf von Ihering, *Entwicklungsgeschichte des Römischen Rechtes* [History of the Development of Roman Law] (Leipzig: 1894) and *Vorgeschichte der Indoeuropäer* [Evolution of the Indo-Europeans] (Leipzig: 1894).

Indians and Iranians." According to Schrader, agriculture, along with animal husbandry, must have been the basis of the economic life of the inhabitants of Europe as early as the Stone Age. In the previous chapter, we established that the absence of a specific term for autumn in Sweden's agricultural communities is not coincidental but can be very naturally explained there. This points to an Indo-European ancestral homeland that we may speculate to be southern and central Sweden. However, it will perhaps be best to not fixate on Sweden as the Indo-European ancestral homeland; any reference to Sweden should be regarded more as a geographic point of reference within north-central Europe. Even if the weather in the Baltic region after the Ice Age was not nearly as unpredictable as is often claimed (this is arguable on the basis of observable flora), there certainly still were climatic variations that should make us cautious about theorizing where hubs of civilization might have been in the postglacial period, especially those of an agricultural nature, given that they are inherently tied to the weather.

Nevertheless, merely on the basis of the fact that they did not have a term for autumn, it is fair to say that it is very likely that all Indo-Europeans were peasants and that they came from an ancestral homeland centered on what we can reasonably assume to be southern Sweden. Conversely, it is highly unlikely that they inhabited central Europe as pastoralists or hunters. For pastoralists and hunters in particular, the autumn of these regions would have been of special importance and would have necessarily led to the emergence of a term for this season.

Therefore, it is only natural that Ihering—whose contemporaries believed with absolutely certainty that Aryans were an Asiatic nomadic people—could not help but observe that the patricians must have already adopted agriculture in a very early period and that the occupation of the land along the Tiber occurred under agrarian circumstances. He writes,

> From the very beginning, Roman legend depicts the Roman as a peasant. When Rome was founded, Romulus allocated two yokes of arable land to each citizen, and his successor, Numa Pompilius, did away with animal sacrifices and replaced them with bloodless ones. Since a sacrificial offering is essentially equated with a household meal, this serves to illustrate that Roman tradition, even in the most ancient of times, had already made the transition from a primarily animal-based diet to a primarily plant-based one. This fact is also evident in the worship of Vesta, known to be one of the most ancient cults of the Roman people. The altar of Vesta represents the domestic hearth, and offerings placed upon it represented the ordinary food of the common man, which consisted of a cooked porridge prepared with the oldest grains known to the Romans (farro and spelt, the latter appears in bread form when entering into a Roman marriage, *confarreatio*) along with some salt. Even the name for a soldier's pay in later times is derived from grain (*stipendium*, from *stips*, meaning cereal grain, and *pendere*, meaning to weigh).

The spelt mentioned here by Ihering is a species of wheat (*Triticum spelta L.*) that is better known in German by the names *spelz* and *dinkel*, but also as *fesen* and *veesen*, and internationally as *épeaudre* and *spelta*. Spelt comes in both summer and winter varieties, with the latter being highly resistant to winter conditions. Nowadays, spelt is limited only to the Eichsfeld region of southern Germany and the countries in the northern Alps region.

But a far stranger proof of the agricultural nature of the Indo-Europeans can be found in a most unexpected place—India. If we consider southern Sweden as our geographic orientation point for the ancestral homeland of the Indo-Europeans, it becomes clear that the Indo-Europeans must have been a people of the forest, for Sweden has always been a country of forests. The author had previously come to this conclusion based on purely evolutionary and nutritional-physiological reasons in an earlier study.[199] What is frankly quite astonishing is the fact that India's Indo-European ruling class used the same root word in Sanskrit to refer to a steppe that the Greeks and Romans used for a field. In an absolutely clear-cut manner, this indicates that the Nordic conqueror class in India originally had knowledge of treeless terrain only in the form of a field—in the form of cleared land. This quite indisputably indicates that the conquerors of India were formerly forest peasants. Such a derivation is also consistent with Kossinna's findings, which demonstrate that the Indo-Europeans in India simply transferred the names of central European forest trees (oak, beech) to local trees. Oak and beech, importantly, are only found west of a line connecting Königsberg in Prussia to Odessa. For those who may find such evidence insufficient, another quite different proof can be presented of the original peasanthood of the Indo-European ruling class in India. According to Schrader (*Reallexikon*), these conquerors of India had a word that originally meant "agricultural settlement," and this word was synonymous with the concept of plowing. It was from this root word that the term for *volk* and for people in general was later developed. This word was explicitly used in contrast to the pre-Indo-European population, who, according to Schrader, engaged only in livestock raising and worshiped different deities. We must document this fact here very precisely, and therefore must be emphasized—the first Indo-European conquerors of India referred to themselves as peasants. They employed the root word for plowing as a way to distinguish their own race (*volkstum*) as distinctly as possible from the subjugated population, who were exclusively pastoralists and unfamiliar with agriculture.

For more details on this matter, please refer to Schrader. Very important for us here, however, is the fact that the ancient Indo-European conquerors of India quite clearly opposed being associated with nomadism. We should then not think of their migration as a mobile military campaign led by conquest-minded warriors, but rather as a trek of peasants in search of land, a genuine Boer trek. For those who find it difficult to comprehend the idea that genuine peasant peoples can become a genuine master race, consider the Dutch peasants who arrived in present-day New York (United States of America). They

---

[199] Darré, "*Das Schwein als Kriterium.*"

cleared the land and settled it, and their descendants, now Wall Street royalty, currently demand annual tribute in the form of Dawes' burdens.[200]

It had already been recognized by Ihering that the key to almost all questions about the Indo-Europeans must lie in their migrations. He observed that an understanding of where the Indo-Europeans came from and why they migrated would naturally resolve many questions. He observed that the Indo-Europeans never spread out organically in the sense that they never really emanated from a particular central point like flowing lava, so to speak, spreading out in all directions. The Indo-Europeans spread out quite differently from what we have seen of the nomads in chapters one and two. It has been emphasized by Ihering that Indo-European peoples do not spread, but rather emigrate. He observes quite accurately that emigration is always the fate of peoples or individuals who are denied what they need in their homeland, for "only hardship puts the wandering staff in both their hands." Ihering writes, "Emigration of the whole nation or of one of its parts in a time of need is an idea as familiar to all Indo-European peoples as it is foreign to all other peoples (Ihering is referring to the Semites)." The patricians called such an emigration *ver sacrum* (holy spring).

Since there are still some surviving records regarding the customs of the *ver sacrum*, it is only natural that Ihering started here in his mission to solve the mystery of the Indo-European migrations. What Ihering manages to collect in this regard is highly remarkable. However, he fails to find an adequate solution because in his time (the 1880's) he did not have the benefit of contemporary racial science and the idea of searching for the ancestral homeland of the Indo-Europeans in north-central Europe was not widely accepted at that time.

Nevertheless, the author must note here that Ihering's depiction of the *ver sacrum*, which will be presented below, will in some places lead to contradictions. Generally, the *ver sacrum* is understood as the custom of dedicating offerings to Mars or Jupiter during times of hardship with the goal of bringing forth an abundance of crops, livestock, and people during the spring season, and with the intention of them later emigrating.[201]

The author must honestly admit that he has not yet been able to come to a satisfactory conclusion regarding this explanation of the *ver sacrum*. In the event that ancient Rome experienced a period of hardship so severe that it was decided to designate the children born in a particular spring for emigration, practically speaking, the actual emigration could not take place until twenty-one years later. For, as we shall soon see, the minimum age for participation in the *ver sacrum* was twenty-one years. Of course, it should be obvious that agricultural products (cattle and crops) produced twenty-one springs earlier would no longer be fresh

---

[200] Henry M. Dawes was an American banker and the developer of the 1924 Dawes Plan, which restructured Germany's impossibly large post-war reparation payments in a more manageable manner.

[201] Livy, *The History of Rome*, Book 22, chapter 10, section 3, trans. Benjamin O. Foster, Loeb Classical Library ed. (Cambridge: Harvard University Press, 1929), "...the Roman People, the Quirites, offer up in indefeasible sacrifice to Jupiter what the spring shall have produced of swine, sheep, goats and cattle—which shall not have been consecrated to some other deity—beginning with the day which the senate and the People shall have designated."

by the time of the emigration. But if one were to assert—and here we are much closer to the heart of the matter—that in that particularly difficult year, only children born in the spring would be chosen for emigration, with a community obligation to provide these children with an adequate amount of livestock and grain for their migration, this would introduce a more reasonable rationale behind the entire tradition, but it would still contradict other facts. As long as one understands the term "people" (*volk*) to mean simply a large mass of individuals—that is, what we mean by the term "people" today—then the idea that a single spring could produce a sufficient quantity of children to make a *ver sacrum* expedition possible seems plausible. But this view does not particularly apply to the circumstances of the ancient Roman patricians. As we will see in chapter ten, the patricians strictly defined a legitimate child as one conceived on a hereditary estate within a legally contracted marriage. Consequently, the largest number of children that could be hoped for in the spring during a time of hardship is limited to the number of hereditary estates. That is as clear as day. Such a number of children, considering the somewhat hazardous travel conditions of that time, was not sufficient for a *ver sacrum* expedition. To this consideration is added another limitation—one cannot simply suppose that a child was born every year on every hereditary estate, if only due to the fact that each woman could only have a limited number of births in her lifetime.

Before the author attempts to provide an alternative explanation for the origin of the *ver sacrum*, let us first briefly outline Ihering's thoughts on the matter. In order to avoid misunderstandings, however, the author would like to say beforehand that Ihering was certainly aware of the common interpretation of the *ver sacrum*, which sees it merely as a promise of sacrifice in times of need. He does not recognize this interpretation, however. Ihering holds the view that all religious customs must have originally had a tangible and practical meaning, and that a better understanding of it is only a matter of discovering this original purpose within the historical record. He expresses himself quite clearly in this regard,

> There are certain Roman traditions for which the assumption that their later purpose was also the original one can be most strongly objected to. These are bound to raise questions in the mind of any impartial observer—how could they have resorted to such a peculiar means of realization if they had the later purpose in mind from the outset? As an example, I mention the Roman augury (auspices). What an odd idea it was to project the approval of the gods into the belly of an ox or the beaks of chickens! How could a people think up such an idea? Faced with this dilemma, I came to the conclusion that it must have originally had another objective —not a religious one, but something thoroughly practical, linked to the circumstances of the migration.[202] This leads me to distinguish between two purposes of one tradition—an original

---

[202] Here, Ihering is referring to the tradition of the *ver sacrum*.

purely practical one and a later exclusively religious one. Brought into being for a purely practical purpose, the tradition (like so many others) has been conserved superficially and its original purpose was subsequently replaced with another (religious) one.

This is a view that the author fully endorses, and it is also the reason why the author relies so heavily on Ihering, in the belief that only by following Ihering's approach can one arrive at a natural explanation of primeval conditions. Now, as far as the *ver sacrum* is concerned, Ihering first states the following:

> The external cause of the *ver sacrum* in Rome was general adversity . . . [203] and an overpopulation of the land. Even well into historical times, Celts and Germanic peoples resorted to emigration—everywhere a demand for land resounded. These peoples were even willing to lay down their arms if this demand was granted to them. . . . The Romans and Greeks created breathing space through colonization.

Just how little *ver sacrum* had to do with setting out on a war of conquest is shown, among other things, by the fact that the youth had to first reach the age of twenty-one, even though they were already eligible for military service at the age of seventeen.

Of Ihering's various studies on the *ver sacrum*, only the following will be mentioned here, so as to not digress further. From the traditional sacrificial customs associated with the *ver sacrum*, he deduces that an apportioned tax was levied on the entire population in order to assist the departing colonists. The rules for the *ver sacrum* only mention livestock, not the people accompanying them. This leads Ihering to assume that participation in the *ver sacrum* was voluntary in nature. But since provisions had to be secured, a tax was levied on those who stayed behind. The author suspects that this tax was not related to provisions, but rather to the need equip the colonists with everything they needed to establish a settlement in a new, unfamiliar homeland; this will be discussed in more detail below. Ihering writes,

> Even in Rome, despite the rich development of the sacrificial system up to that time, the sacrifice associated with the *ver sacrum* remains unparalleled. Alongside the sacrifices incumbent upon individuals (*sacra privata*) and on all citizens (*sacra popularia*), there are also those that the entire people (*publica*) or the gentes (*gentilicia*) must offer—these are done from their available wealth and are not a tax imposed specifically for that purpose. The mechanism of the *ver sacrum* contradicts the entire structure of

---

[203] Described by Festus as "*magnis periculis adducti,*" or "brought about by great dangers."

Roman religious practices so blatantly that there is no other explanation than the one I have given—that it is the replication of a primeval process. . . . It is noteworthy that the collective sacrifice to the dead offered by the entire population (the festival of *Feralia*) occurs in the penultimate week of February. This is followed by a joyous festival called *Caristia*[204] and later by a farewell celebration from the neighbors (*Terminalia*).

These final references bring us to the most peculiar aspect of all the customs associated with the *ver sacrum*. The migration begins on March 1 and ends no later than May 31. The patricians divide the year using this as a reference, obviously to commemorate the time when they migrated to the Tiber. In any case, they speak of the migration period (March to May) and refer to the remaining months as the resting period. Ihering fails in his attempt to find a natural meaning for these migration periods; he refrains from proposing a solution because he does not understand why the migration period is observed during the three months of March to May. Nevertheless, we can attempt to explain this from an agricultural point of view by making use of the traditions surrounding the *ver sacrum* at that time to help us prove that the entire *ver sacrum* of the patricians must have been a true peasant trek.

As long as one clings to the notion that the Indo-Europeans were originally nomadic pastoralists (assuming one still wishes to retain that misleading term; see chapter one), one will not be able to make sense of the traditional March-May migration period. If we hold that central Europe is the ancestral homeland of the Indo-Europeans, it is hard to see why the Indo-European nomads would not have preferred the months of May to September for their migrations instead. Any soldier who fought on the front lines of the World War will still vividly remember how much more comfortable mobile warfare was in the summer months when compared to late fall or winter, to say nothing of the damp conditions of February through April (March 1918!).

But if we assume that a peasant population in southern Sweden or Lower Germany wanted to emigrate, or that some of its young men had to be sent out because of overpopulation, then the traditional migration months of March to May become practically self-evident. During a peasant trek (a march of emigrating peasants with wives, children, and all their belongings), people tend to bring with them everything they think they'll need to maintain their peasant way of life in a new and unknown destination, as informed by the ideas and beliefs of their old homeland. It is worth noting, for example, that any visitor to the German colony of Blumenau in Brazil will repeatedly point out with amazement how peculiar their German farmhouses, village layouts, and village customs appear in the Brazil-

---

[204] This is correctly interpreted by Ihering as those remaining behind bidding farewell to those departing.

ian jungle terrain; the peasant simply plants his familiar culture down in his new homeland.[205]

This is indeed one of the most natural things in the world. Despite today's brilliant travel books, as well as the ability to present these accounts vividly through impeccable photography, it still takes a certain amount of training to truly understand the conditions of a foreign country if you are not familiar with it yourself. For the vast majority of people, it is impossible to free themselves from the mindset of their home country and accurately assess foreign conditions without ever actually being there. Every German living abroad will probably have had similar experiences after returning home. But even the old frontline soldiers may still remember the days at the beginning of the World War when the most absurd things were sent to the front in care packages, at least until the military leadership intervened and issued guidelines for such packages. It was simply impossible for those at home to properly conceptualize the conditions at the front. A person's conceptualizations simply exist within what he has experienced, and he who has never ventured outside his four walls will always have his understanding confined within the realities of those four walls. This is a rather self-evident fact, and the few extraordinary minds that can defy it are the exceptions. The English, for example, take this fact very much into account when educating their youth. Now just consider those prehistoric times when no one could venture outside of their own community without risking life and limb—extensive individual travel was hardly possible. Consequentially, a peasant people in this time would have imagined the new homeland as exactly like the familiar one; thus, they would have taken with them everything that seemed important and necessary in their old homeland to the new one. Nomads, on the other hand, are fundamentally characterized by a noticeable lack of baggage.

A peasant trek cannot simply set out for conquest, but must organize its migration according to certain geographic preconditions. First of all, the presence

---

[205] This is elegantly illuminated by a brief note in the *Königsberger Allgemeine Zeitung* [Königsberger National Newspaper] No. 135 dated March 21, 1929: "The Historical *Schlackwurst*." A highly respected philologist from Hamburg, Professor Gr. (who passed away just a few years ago), embarked on a study trip to Brazil shortly before his death. There, in a store, he bought a *schlackwurst* sausage with a very unique taste. It immediately reminded him of a type of sausage that he, having traveled extensively throughout Germany, had found exclusively in the Spessart region and which had made a deep impression on him. As a diligent researcher, he promptly inquired whether the seller's family hailed from Spessart. "No," came the reply, "we are Russians, or rather Volga Germans. We departed from Russia right after the World War and have been here since." But the scholar was not content with this. He proceeded to ask whether they possessed any other old family souvenirs. Of course they did! The man immediately lugged in a large crate.

Our professor went through the crate and eventually discovered an old German hymnal. This hymnal had been printed in 1724—in Spessart! In such a relatively short time, the memory that the "Volga Germans" had of their ancestral homeland had completely vanished. The only constant among their disappearing memories had been the *schlackwurst*, which now served the German professor as a genealogical tool through which he could demonstrate to the family their origins. It was as if he had traveled to Brazil specifically for this purpose. "Never," the elderly scholar declared upon his return, "in all my extensive travels have I felt such satisfaction from a discovery as I felt from this historical *schlackwurst!*"

of heavy baggage (the baggage train) limits the trek to specific roads. These roads should not be imagined in the modern sense, but rather, in the sense that regardless of terrain, only a relatively limited number of paths allow for a fleet of wagons. Furthermore, a peasant trek will always be forced to choose between either forcing their way through enemy territory—the wagon fortifications of the Indo-Europeans are quite excellent evidence of this—or obtaining a safe passage by paying tribute. The latter can be clearly proven historically in the case of the Celts, and we do have historical evidence of it in the case of the peasant trek of the Cimbri and Teutons. But since it is relatively difficult to feed everyone on a peasant trek (literature on recent colonial history might also provide excellent proof of this), there really is no other way of migrating other than migrating in stages. A long break is taken at each stage, ensuring grain for the next winter through single-summer agriculture. The expedition of the Cimbri and the Teutons also provides rather clear evidence in this respect.

If we now consider the time of year that must have been the most suitable for the migration of a peasant people in north-central Europe, in particular Sweden, the following considerations arise. Winter is out of question. It is difficult to make progress with a peasant trek during winter's ice and snow. For example, as long as the German mercenary armies of history possessed a baggage train, winter campaigns were almost always avoided, with winter camps being established instead. It was only in more recent military history, with the transition from professional armies to a people's army that did not possess baggage trains, that winter campaigns became possible. Nevertheless, many frontline soldiers will be able to vividly imagine the difficulties of moving wagons and teams during such a winter journey, especially when a solid road is not available. Additionally, a winter journey is much more physically demanding for both man and beast, and accordingly presents a completely different set of logistical challenges when compared to a journey in warmer seasons. In the case of Sweden, winter typically takes place between September and February, hence these months are excluded as start dates for a peasant trek. Additionally, we also have to consider that such a peasant trek would be forced to stop along the way to sow and harvest. In Sweden, the harvest occurs near the end of August. Therefore, from the perspective of a Swedish peasant, such an expedition must be conducted in a manner that allows for the sown grain to ripen by the end of August. As there is no central European grain variety that takes less than three months to grow, anyone who wants to harvest by the end of August must have sown by no later than the beginning of June. Following this reasoning, since the months of June to August must be used for agriculture, and the winter is taking place from late September to February, only the months of March to May are available for the actual journey. This gives us the exact traditional migration period for the *ver sacrum*.

A farmer may still object to this conclusion, questioning which cereal crop would be suitable for the short growth period of June to August, considering that most summer grains require far more time. The objection is valid, but the solution to this question is also particularly enlightening in this context. Only one grain variety is initially suitable, namely the small four-row barley, which takes seventy to eighty days to mature. Of course, one could also consider buckwheat, which has the same maturation period, but buckwheat is said to not be indigenous to Europe and is therefore not relevant here. Barley, due to its aforementioned short growing period, is often the only cereal grown in the short Nordic summers. It even occurs as far north as the North Cape, located below the seventieth parallel of latitude. In northern countries, therefore, it is the main bread crop and, as a result, is just called "grain" in Sweden. We have evidence that barley was known to the Greeks and the Romans. The role of spelt among the patricians mentioned by Ihering is not something that the author has yet drawn decisive conclusions about. However, the author would like to emphasize that spelt and barley are not necessarily mutually exclusive. There are several ways to engage in double cropping with these two cereals, but a detailed discussion of this topic is beyond our scope here.[206]

Very important for our investigation is Schrader's observation that even in the earliest times of Indo-European existence, a certain amount of agriculture was present alongside animal husbandry. The linguistic correlations are so striking that it must have been a uniform and subtle evolution. Schrader's finding is very much in line with our view that, for agricultural and meteorological reasons, both the absence of a term for autumn and the conventional migration period of the Roman *ver sacrum* point rather clearly to Sweden as the ancestral homeland of the Indo-Europeans. In chapter one we noted that the patrician custom of sacrificing a boar during marriage ceremonies with a stone axe (*silex*) clearly identified the patricians as a settled Stone Age people—this aligns with Schrader's conclusion that agriculture was practiced throughout northern and eastern Europe during the later Stone Age. If we consider these facts together with our discussion of the patrician *ver sacrum* and the lack of a term for autumn among all Indo-Europeans, we can quite indisputably directly link them to the Stone Age farmers of north-central Europe (Sweden!).

This leads us to the conclusion, perhaps surprising at first, that the Indo-Europeans can be quite clearly integrated into the phenomenon of the Germanic peasant movements of German history; we have described these in more detail in chapter two. We now have an entirely continuous thread running from the Stone Age to our era, a thread that runs through both the Indo-Europeans and the Germanic peoples, as well as the Germanic peasant movements of German history. It appears that as long as there has been a peasantry in the north of central Europe, a "people without space" (*volk ohne raum*) seems to have been the fundamental problem for its entire history.

And yet, the logic deducing that the Roman *ver sacrum* took place due to overpopulation has a flaw in its argumentation. Namely, that the patricians had a closed inheritance law which would have naturally regulated the population,

---

[206] Without wanting to go into this question in detail here, the author would like to point out at least once that a thorough study of the traditional historical zones of grain cultivation could provide further insights into the Indo-European and Germanic tribal migrations. For reference in this regard, see: Robert Gradmann, "*Der Dinkel und die Alemannen*" [Spelt and the Alemanni], *Württembergisches Jahrbuch für Statistik und Landeskunde* [Württemberg Yearbook for Statistics and Regional Studies].

since only the heir would ever marry. This means that it was essentially irrelevant if his brother was killed in a war, or tended pigs at home, or contributed to the economy in some other useful way. All that really mattered was that he did not get married. However, if the patricians were suffering from overpopulation, this would indicate that there must have been problems with the effective implementation of closed inheritance law. What was probably the case was that their closed inheritance law included the possibility of occasionally designating some of the younger sons for settlement. In the previous chapter, Mielke noted that the Germanic clustered village emerged from the individual farmstead, which in itself was indivisible. If Mielke's idea is placed next to the similar customs known to have been in place in Greece (and Rome, for that matter) then the following picture emerges—the land must have originally been divided into individual farmsteads. Mielke writes, "A lot of evidence points to the Roman individual farmstead. The hills on which the city later developed were owned by families who had built their farms there and let their herds graze in the marshy lowlands." Alongside and between these individual farmsteads, new hearths would have been lit on recently cleared land and given to younger sons for cultivation—this was done ensuring that the ability of the existing farmsteads to sustain a family was not reduced.[207]

Thus, any given area must have been gradually filled with settlements. At the same time, the proportion of children born annually in relation to the total population increased. It can be assumed that, for this slowly but steadily increasing number of families, the ability of their territory to sustain the families eventually became insufficient. One can imagine a valley area being gradually occupied by settlements and then eventually becoming so densely populated that, if there ever were a sudden emergency, the grain grown in their territory would not be enough to feed the entire population. The first thing they might try would be to invade the neighboring valley, if it was possible. However, if this was not possible, either because the locals could successfully resist the invasion, or because the neighboring area was also overpopulated or experiencing other hardships, then they likely would have moved forward with an expulsion of a portion of the families (not of individuals, as there is no evidence to support this notion). The idea of limiting the number of children was, of course, an entirely foreign concept to the early Indo-Europeans, so this way of compensating for insufficient land (in terms of its ability to sustain families) is not relevant to our present investigation. One can imagine, then, that in times of dire need, a community could decide to embark on an expedition that was open to anyone who had reached the age of twenty-one and, of course, the children of participating parents. The married heirs of the old original settlements were presumably excluded. The following picture would then emerge— as a territory gradually fills with settlements, a fraction of the families are expelled, much like a beehive occasionally releases a swarm from the main colony and sets out on a migration. On the basis of Ihering's above-mentioned expla-

---

[207] August Baumeister, *Denkmäler des Klassischen Altertums* [Monuments of Classical Antiquity], volume 3, 1447.

nations, we can assume that such an expedition took place in the form of an orderly peasant trek and was equipped with everything necessary for the new settlement, according to an understanding shaped by their old homeland. In that case, it is likely that a special leader was chosen for this journey and was given absolute punitive and commanding power during the migration. Apart from the fact that all the records of the Indo-Europeans do indeed confirm this hypothesis, it also gives a more tangible form to the legendary primeval founder-kings that played such a decisive role in the establishment of various Indo-European communities. We can probably assume that the widespread custom of granting the king a particularly large piece of land as a crown estate in the newly conquered territory represented a kind of gift (gratuity) or recognition of successful leadership. It should be borne in mind, however, that leadership among the Indo-Europeans was always based on the leader's sense of responsibility, and that the leader, upon assuming leadership, could only choose between leading well or losing his head. In fact, it would be understandable if, before emigrating, the leader had even been assured that he would be given a large estate in the newly conquered land. In any case, the practice of granting a crown estate to the leader occurs so consistently among Indo-Europeans and Germanic peoples that the phenomenon can no longer be considered a mere coincidence.

This would also explain another fact, namely that these leader-kings initially retained leadership temporarily. Obviously, the experience of the migration—since it certainly involved resting for several years in one or more places—revealed that a newly founded settlement, even after subduing the conquered population and distributing the land lots, was far from secure. They had to be prepared for uprisings from the subjugated population, and it took a considerable number of years before a political equilibrium could be established with neighboring communities. For example, it took several generations for the Spartans to truly dominate Laconia. Thus, it may have happened that the military organization under the supreme command of the leader (king) initially persisted and was also passed down to his sons according to the Indo-European concept of primogeniture. However, as soon as a state of equilibrium was achieved, or when the new settlement was no longer threatened by hostile neighbors or rebellious serfs, the ancient Indo-European idea of legal equality among all free individuals resurfaced and manifested itself in the desire to curtail the privileges of the king. At least in this way, it would be very easy to explain the fact that all Indo-European and Germanic traditions tell us about founder-kings, whose reign, however, is always closely connected with ongoing turbulent times and warfare (which is quite natural and connected with the conquest of new lands). Likewise, it explains why there was always an attempt to quickly eliminate the dominance of these kings. Only in cases where the situation did not improve and the citizens' military defense structure had to remain intact (as in Sparta) were the kings able to remain in power longer than usual. The Frankish kingship was originally maintained for reasons very similar to those of Sparta—on the one hand, the kings had very tangible economic support in the allotted royal estates of newly conquered Gaul, and on the other hand, the political situation at the time of the establishment of the Frankish kingdom prohibited the disbanding of the army. Taken together, these two circumstances then contributed significantly to the development of the Frankish kingdom, which was, after all, the original seed of our present-day German Empire. The other Germanic tribes did not need to keep their armies constantly armed because of the protection of the western flank provided by the Franks. Therefore, the political structures of these tribes often developed entirely differently, at the very least not forming such absolute kingships as with the Franks.[208]

For the time being, the motives that led to the actual Germanic Migration Period are still admittedly unclear, for the number of peoples who were "on the move" in this period obviously exceeds all previous Indo-European migrations by far. As we saw in chapter three, however, it could not have been a simple desire for conquest. Even the Norman (Viking) invasions,[209] which are often attributed to "Nordic expansionism," cannot readily cite conquest as a motive.[210] Recent studies by E. Almquist (Sweden) have convincingly argued that the Vikings were merely conducting massive retaliatory campaigns in response to the cruel methods of conversion imposed on the Saxons and the suppression of the worship of Wotan. It was only with the collapse of the Frankish Empire that the actual Norman (Viking) invasion could begin, eventually surging into the affected lands like a flood. More details on this matter will be found in chapter eight.

7

The author has already mentioned that we should consider south and central Sweden more as a point of orientation or a broad geographic reference point for the ancestral homeland of the Indo-Europeans, rather than as an absolute fact. We must also refrain from adopting a mechanical "wave theory" to explain these events. The fact that all Indo-Europeans emerged from a relatively small area does not prove that they all reached the places we find them at the beginning of history in uninterrupted waves. Even less likely is envisioning this migration process as a continuous, lava-like flow. Even if the migrations from the ancestral homeland did occur in "layers," we should nevertheless imagine these migrations more as individual streams following the terrain. At the endpoint of the migration, we need not immediately imagine a superimposition over what came before, rather, one might imagine it as a mosaic-like jumble of a displacement. It is also conceivable that each settlement, over the course of generations, forced the emigra-

---

[208] The Franks also resemble the Spartans in the sense that the cultivation of the king's crown estates were not carried out by free Franks, but rather by trusted individuals from the subject population. For further discussion on this topic, refer to Busolt and Gilbert, as mentioned before. In the case of the Franks, these circumstances famously led to elevating of the *Hausmeier* (in Latin *maior domus*, in English, Mayor of the Palace) to such an influential position that they could seize political power, indeed, it is well known that the Carolingian dynasty ascended to prominence in this manner.

[209] Clauß, *Rasse und Seele.*

[210] Almquist, "Die Nordische Rasse."

tion of a portion of its inhabitants, thus forming Indo-European daughter colonies, which would, with time, send out their own emigrants. Examples of this would include the colonizing activities of the Greeks and Romans in the Mediterranean basin. Such considerations make it impossible to assume from the outset that we will find the same agricultural conditions among all Indo-Europeans. Not only did each later instance of migration from the ancestral homeland necessarily bring with it somewhat more advanced agricultural techniques, but, due to differences in weather, soil, and irrigation, the natural conditions of the new homeland necessitated modifications to the familiar forms of agriculture they brought with them. If such a new homeland also becomes a hub of Indo-European civilization, the young people who migrate away from there will quite naturally carry with them their now modified Indo-European agricultural techniques. Such migrations would then necessarily reveal some sort of evolutionary deviation from the old agricultural techniques. The author was originally led to this possibility through the history of domesticated animals, as some ancient Indo-European peoples possessed domesticated animals that were contradictory to their theorized origins or that could not be explained. For example, it is often suggested that useful breeds of domesticated animals discovered in the new homeland would be incorporated into the existing domesticated animal stock. However, it appears that no one dared to sacrifice these new domesticated animals to the old gods. To go into these matters in detail would require a separate investigation, and only brief allusions can be made to it here.

Something similar is also suspected by Schrader. He explicitly emphasizes that despite the common origin of all agricultural terminology, these terms often show a shift in their meaning as they continue to evolve. Schrader assumes that due to the diversity of geographic and meteorological conditions, certain terms became further developed while others correspondingly withered away. The correctness of Schrader's assumption, which should be self-evident to any agriculturalist, can be proven from the history of German pig breeding. For example, Hoesch[211] points out that among the Germanic peoples, pig breeding played a leading role in animal husbandry. Accordingly, Germanic pig breeding led to the development of a refined and sophisticated catalog of necessarily specialized technical terminology that can only evoke admiration today. This Germanic pig breeding was based on the utilization of forest pastures (beech and oak). When deforestation began in Germany in the Middle Ages and the modern era, German pig breeding also necessarily declined, eventually dwindling into insignificance by the end of the eighteenth century. In this process, our pig breeding also lost all of the related refined technical terminology created by the Germanic people. Today, as the pig has regained its position in the German economy as a waste recycler for industry, we as animal breeders can only lament the loss of the old German linguistic heritage in the field of pig breeding.

If Schrader (*Reallexikon*) states that agriculture must be considered a proven fact among the Indo-Europeans, we can agree with him based on purely agricultural considerations. We are not surprised, then, when Schrader, to pick

---

[211] Wilhelm Hoesch, *Die Schweinezucht* [Pig Breeding] (Hannover: 1911).

an example, emphasizes the cultivation of onions, beans, garlic, millet, and wheat among the North Pontic Scythians, who, of course, could very well be considered nomads, as mentioned by Herodotus.[212]

In this context, however, let us consider some ideas mentioned by Ihering that should not be forgotten. The concept of the slave, as we have already seen, was originally alien to the Indo-Europeans.[213] These early people originally only knew the serf (*hörige*), or the dependent. *Hörig* (serf) is related to *gehorchen* (obey) and primarily denotes a dependent relationship. However, the concept of the slave (*sklaven*), a word of Germanic origin and related to the Slavs, includes the notion of abolished personhood. The slave is an unpersoned object, a commodity. Europe only came to know of the concept of slavery through Asia and the Orient, historically primarily through the latter. Since the slave is a prized piece of plunder among all warlike nomads and often the most significant motivation for military campaigns, we may well assume that the world first acquired the concept of slavery through the nomads.

Ihering also points out that our concept of Sunday was in itself quite alien to Indo-European culture. Among the Germanic peoples, the introduction of Sunday through Christianity encountered strong resistance. Sunday, in the sense that it was a day of unconditional rest from work, must have simply seemed alien to the Germanic peoples. We will soon see why the Germanic people resisted a prescribed period of rest. Sunday (as a day of rest from work) has Jewish origins and can be traced back to the Jewish Sabbath. But even the Jews adopted the Sabbath from elsewhere. According to Ihering, it derives from the Assyrian word *sabbattu*, meaning rest or celebration, and thus is of Babylonian origin. Ihering then connects a very insightful observation to this finding. Every day of rest necessarily presupposes work. However, the concept of work can evoke fundamentally different notions depending on whether the work is done voluntarily or under compulsion. In other words, it is not work itself that ultimately shackles personal freedom, but rather the compulsion to work. A slave must work, while a free person can choose for himself the manner and nature of his work or activities. In the case of a free peasant, the distribution of work and rest time is determined by the necessities of his agricultural operation. The peasant works when the circumstances require it and celebrates when there is a reason to celebrate. He organizes his celebrations and festivals according to the conditions of the seasons. However, the concept of an unconditional and mechanically occurring day of rest every seven days, namely Sunday, fundamentally lacks meaning for him. Observing a Sunday rest could potentially cost a peasant his harvest. For these very natural reasons, the peasant Indo-Europeans did not possess the concept of Sunday as a

---

212 Herodotus, *The Persian Wars*, 4.17: "in other ways they live like the Scythians, plant and eat grain, onions, garlic, lentils, and millet. Above the Alazones live Scythian farmers, who plant grain not to eat but to sell..."

213 This fact must be emphasized again and again. If the Nordic Movement does not take an unequivocal stand on this fact, and if it does not see to it that this truth becomes common knowledge among the German people, it will essentially be digging its own grave. Otherwise, it will allow the Oriental concept of the ruler (the limitless position of authority without obligations to subordinates) to be applied to the Nordic race. This would divert the focus of the German people from the noblest and most valuable characteristic of the Nordic race; see chapter three.

day of unconditional rest from work. They only have celebrations and festivals that are within the framework of an agricultural way of life and are often related to the weather conditions of a particular region. Therefore, the Indo-Europeans also calculate the day based on the sunrise and sunset, as the work of the farmer is determined by these circumstances. The peasant does not really have any use for dividing the day into hours. Even today, our rural population still determines their daily schedule on the basis of the conditions of their agricultural work; breakfast, midday, snack, and dinner are natural rest periods in this work. The agricultural land measurement called *morgen* originally referred to the area a peasant could plow or mow in a morning—it literally means morning or half day. Accordingly, the *morgen* is not an absolute size in Germany but varies depending on the region, which is why the standardized term "quarter hectare" has been agreed upon today. In Bavaria, one doesn't speak of *morgen* but rather of *tagwerk* (literally meaning day-work) to indicate the size of an area, which emphasizes the connection between work and time even more clearly. What all these terms ultimately have in common is the peasant idea that the division of time must orient itself according to the work of the peasant and not the other way around—this is what a mechanical, inorganic division of time presupposes (eight-hour day!).

We owe the division of the day into equal halves (day and night) to the Babylonians. Each of these halves is then further divided into exactly twelve hours. In contrast, the Indo-Europeans calculated the day based on the sunrise and sunset, as we mentioned before. Ihering writes, "The ancient Romans, during the time of the Twelve Tables, also followed this practice, concluding their legal proceedings at sunset (*sol occasus suprema tempestas esto*)."

In this context, Ihering points out that in the Babylonian empires, we have clear evidence of a pronounced slave economy and the use of slaves. It remains anyone's guess why the use of slaves was particularly common in Mesopotamia (and Egypt, for that matter), however, the fact is that civilization in those lands could only be developed through a highly sophisticated utilization of slaves. In any case, the nature of the land itself fostered a highly developed system of forced labor. Ihering presents the compelling idea that this Babylonian labor plan, detached from any agricultural or natural organic basis, necessitated an economic division of labor in order to preserve the health and productiveness of their slaves. Otherwise, slave owners would be shooting themselves in the foot by prematurely exhausting their workforce. Ihering attributes the practice of working for six consecutive days to the fact that workdays were measured in sets of three, and humans cannot sustain mechanical labor for nine or twelve consecutive days, while three days were insufficient.[214] Ihering writes,

---

[214] According to Ihering, the number five was not originally known but rather derived from three and ten. Three persisted for a significant period in declarations of war, while ten remained present in the so-called witnesses of *confarreatio* marriages. Ihering's assertion is supported by Hildebrand Bodemeyer's work, *Die Zahlen des Römischen Rechts* [The Numbers of Roman Law].

So, the day of rest among the Babylonians was merely a socio-political institution whose entire significance lay in ceasing work on the seventh day for the purpose of recovering from the efforts of the six day work week. We encounter the commandment to cease work on certain days among other peoples as well. Among the Greeks and Romans, work had to be suspended on public festivals and holidays, not for the sake of the worker himself but rather out of religious sentiment. To prescribe a periodic day of rest for the sake of the worker did not occur to these two peoples, nor to any other people of antiquity except the Babylonians, the Egyptians, and the Jews, who borrowed it from them. . . . Based on what has been discussed so far, the entire Babylonian division of time can be attributed to a single idea—the organization of forced labor for public construction projects by the state. . . . The concept of equal measures for day and night is thus a thoroughly civil institution, and equally so is shifting the beginning of both to 6 o'clock in the morning and evening, respectively, instead of the astronomically correct noon and midnight. . . . Babylonian timekeeping was developed for the purposes of labor, particularly forced labor, whom the state had to keep in mind. . . In any case, the Babylonians deserve credit for being the first in history to solve the difficult problem of bringing time and space into a fixed measurable relationship with each other.

If we continually observe that the Indo-Europeans were originally peasants and that, for these reasons, the exploitation of human labor was initially quite alien to them, the question begins to arise as to whether this peasanthood of the Indo-Europeans can be reconciled with their actual conquests, which can be clearly traced archaeologically and historically. The author believes that there is no need to reconcile any contradictions here, but rather that one is conditioned by the other.

To answer this question, it is best to begin by becoming acquainted with the items that warlike pastoralists and other nomads carry along with them when traveling. It can perhaps be said that, with the exception of weapons, all things carried by nomads are made of organic material and limited in quantity. One can be convinced of these facts even today by observing any nomadic people living under primitive conditions. The early or prehistoric migration of a nomadic people would not be archaeologically traceable at all. It would take a very fortunate coincidence for such organic material to have been preserved unweathered over the millennia. The only things that could be expected are perhaps human skeletons and weapons, as well as tools, as long as they were made of inorganic material (stone). However, given that nomads very rarely stay in one place for long periods of time, it is unlikely that these remains will be found in large numbers in a single place. Rather, it is more likely that they will be found scattered over a wide area.

On the other hand, archeologically speaking, a peasant trek will appear markedly differently. When peasants take possession of new land, they simply push aside the pre-existing population—they do not always subjugate them. Peasants are quite uncompromising in implanting their culture into the conquered territory. Archaeologically speaking, this creates a rather stark superimposition over the preceding culture. In that case, the old and the new cultural layers overlap, much like the hanging and underlying layers in geological stratification. One only needs to examine the peasant colonization of the United States or of South Africa for evidence. In these cases, it can be seen that the Germanic peasant culture terminates the preceding Indian or *kaffir* culture as if it had been cut off. An archaeologist studying the Germanic settlement history of the United States and South Africa thousands of years later, assuming they approach their work with present-day concepts, would likely assume that an "imperious, warlike" conquest had taken place. In reality, however, a truly imperious and warlike (non-peasant) conquest can only ever be proven archaeologically by indirect evidence, never by direct evidence. This will be easily understood, for example, by comparing the position of Anglo-Saxon culture in the United States with that in India. The Englishman brought his peasantry to America and planted a true Anglo-Saxon offshoot that will always remain archaeologically traceable there. In India, however, the Englishman appeared from the beginning only as a conqueror and master. From an archaeological point of view, it is hardly possible to identify an Anglo-Saxon conquest of India, and archaeologists would be even more perplexed if they were asked to determine the date of the English conquest of India on the basis of excavations alone. This could only ever be indirectly determined archaeologically, either by demonstrating an English modification of Indian architecture or by identifying English cultural hubs that can be proven as foreign to Indian culture. This fact becomes even clearer when considering, say, the current occupation of the Rhineland, which, of course, is based purely on military conquest—archaeologically, this occupation would be almost impossible to detect.

Therefore, as far as archaeology is concerned, the nomad does not leave any evidence whatsoever of his existence. If he leaves any evidence at all, it is only in places where he has destroyed everything without replacing it with anything new, that is, where he has left behind steppes or deserts. Otherwise, he can only be recognized by his modification of existing architectural norms. Think of the Hagia Sophia in Constantinople, which was originally a Christian church and is now a mosque. Another example is the church of San Giovanni degli Eremiti, built in Palermo in the year 1132, which was built with five domes in the Byzantine style, but with pointed arches in the style of Saracen architecture. Similar examples were constructed in large numbers in Spain during the period of Moorish rule and can be easily found by any cultural historian.

Therefore, we come to the realization that the archaeological evidence of Indo-European conquest, manifested as a blatant superimposition over pre-existing cultures, is in fact evidence of a peasant takeover of the land. Even the castle construction of the Indo-Europeans, highlighted by Schuchhardt, does not contradict but rather supports this assumption, as we will eventually see in chapter eight when discussing Nordic warriorship in more detail.[215]

---

[215] Schuchhardt, *Alteuropa, eine Vorgeschichte unseres Erdteils.*

8

But having recognized that the Indo-European migrations were certainly peasant treks, yet another observation can be made. This observation could potentially have fundamental significance for the entire field of prehistoric research. As we saw in the second chapter, the nomad's attention is always directed toward untouched civilization. Geographic barriers, be they mountains or rivers, do not prevent the nomad from reaching his destination. After all, he takes little with him, or at least does not place an exaggerated value on doing so, and can therefore literally worm his way through terrain. A nomadic raid thus always strongly resembles a swarm of locusts that sweeps over a land, stripping everything bare (as discussed in chapter two).

A peasant trek, on the other hand, is subject to entirely different parameters. The cumbersome baggage they carry limits the types of terrain they can traverse. Mountains and rivers can only be crossed at certain points, resulting in the establishment of migration routes by the Indo-Europeans over time. Let's look at a map of Europe and Asia and ask ourselves the following question: suppose a peasant trek in Lower Germany (such as in the Oder and Vistula regions) wants to migrate southward by land, what paths can or must they take, and where might they end up? Soon, one will realize that this trek will naturally come across routes that align with the ancient Indo-European migratory routes. As such, it can be stated—quite superficially, of course—that following the course of the Oder River leads to the Danube lowlands, which in turn provide an open path into the Balkans; the Italian peninsula, by contrast, is not readily accessible by this route. However, if you follow the course of the Vistula River, you will first encounter the Carpathian Mountains and, continuing along the Dniester River, you will eventually reach the Black Sea. From here, one can either head south across the Danube and continue toward the Balkans or travel eastward along the northern edge of the Black Sea. In the latter case, one can either attempt to cross the Caucasus Mountains and proceed through Armenia and Kurdistan to reach Mesopotamia, or alternatively, head eastward through the lowlands between the Ural Mountains and the Caspian Sea to penetrate into Asia. Now India is accessible to such a peasant migration, and it is also important to note that Mesopotamia becomes accessible once again, albeit in a rather cumbersome and roundabout manner, entering Mesopotamia from the northeast—a fact that the author deems it very necessary to draw special attention to.[216] Therefore, based on very simple geographic considerations, it is evident that it is much more natural for a trek of Nordic peasants to reach Mesopotamia by way of the Caucasus or

---

[216] The Babylonians and the Assyrians called the horse "the donkey of the mountains," or the "donkey of the east." Since the Semites were not originally familiar with the horse and therefore could not have originally domesticated it, various animal historians have long suspected that the peoples who introduced the horse into the Mesopotamian region did not come from Anatolia or Arabia, but rather migrated over the plateaus of Iran.

the Turanian lowlands than through Asia Minor, as the Dardanelles and the Bosporus would have posed quite insurmountable obstacles for such an expedition.[217]

There is never a need for nomads to stick to these migration routes. In the case of the Huns, we can prove this quite well in the opposite direction. Thus, when looking at a map, it is clear that the Indo-Europeans must have migrated in the form of a peasant trek.

To obtain a clear understanding of the potential duration of these migrations, it is advisable to consider the following. While the Huns, for example, rushed from east to west in an incredibly short time, and the Arabs covered immense distances in Africa at an even faster rate, the waves of Nordic migration seemed to flow at a leisurely pace whose noticeable slowness (even compared to the duration of the medieval crusades) can only be explained by assuming that this migration took the form of a laborious peasant trek. When considering such questions, it is important to bear in mind that during the World War, many German batteries and squadrons managed to reach the Black Sea from their German garrisons without using railroads, both on horseback and by vehicle. They returned to their homeland in the same way. Even at the time of the crusades, the roads to the Orient could not have looked much different from the roads of the Indo-European migrations. If the crusaders were able to cover this distance in a few years with a very cumbersome and unwieldy baggage train, and if our troops were able to reach the Black Sea and return in just under four years (with interruptions due to major battles and conflicts), then perhaps in the future we will be able to assume that the Indo-European migrations also took place within very natural and narrow limits not exceeding a human lifetime.

Of course, one might wonder why peasants in Sweden or in the lowlands of northern Germany between the Elbe and the Vistula would choose to migrate up the Oder and the Vistula instead of directly east or west. The answer may be quite simple. A peasant people in the lowlands east of the Elbe (in the Baltic Sea region), which year after year witnesses migratory birds leaving in the fall and returning in the spring, will naturally tend to move in the same direction as the migratory birds. Such a people can observe quite clearly how well the winter in the distant south suits the migratory birds. Think of storks, for example, which always return to their old breeding grounds and are therefore always very familiar to the local peasants.

This brings us to an aspect that has received little attention in previous Indo-European research. When it has been possible to trace the migratory routes of birds that spend the central European winter in Africa, they are found to take two main routes. One of the routes goes from north-central Europe through France, across the Pyrenees, and through Spain, crossing the Strait of

---

[217] In 1927, a small group of *Wandervögel* from Nerother (Rhineland) embarked on a journey to India on foot and is expected to return in the spring of 1929. The analysis of such expeditions, particularly the conditions of routes and the duration of the journeys, holds immense significance for prehistoric cultural research.

Gibraltar into Africa. The other route passes through Eastern Europe, across the Balkans and Asia Minor, eventually reaching Egypt. Could it be that these two ancient migratory routes perhaps served as guiding paths for the northern peoples? In any case, peoples who migrated toward the birds coming from the direction of Asia Minor and the Balkans in the spring by travelling up the Oder and Vistula rivers, would have found themselves on the previously described Indo-European migration routes for geographic reasons—after all, they could not fly. The other route taken by migratory birds into northwest Africa will be discussed in more detail below.

It has been suggested by Ihering that the augury of the patricians could not have arisen from some simple childish notions of divine worship, but must have originally had a practical meaning. The word "augur" is derived from *avi-gur*, combining the Latin *avis*, meaning bird, and the Celtic *gûr*, meaning *vir* (man). The word "auspex," meaning bird observer or diviner, is derived from *avi-spex*, a contraction of *avis*, meaning bird, and *specere*, meaning to observe. To auspicate, from the Latin *auspicari*, means to interpret the flight of birds and the telling of fortunes in general. Ihering tries to connect this augury with the ancient Aryan migration of the patricians, believing that the leaders of this migration observed the movements of birds to gather information about travel routes and other related matters. If one considers what uses a migrating people might have for observing the routes of migratory birds, then Ihering's assumption here may be correct, rather surprisingly. In the case of an itinerant nomadic people with no fixed destination, observing the flights of birds would serve no purpose. At most, one could imagine it having a superstitious purpose. However, since warlike nomadic peoples such as the Tatars, Huns, and Semites roamed vast territories, each containing quite different bird populations, any superstition based solely on bird observation would quickly collapse due to the nomads' ignorance concerning the patterns and behaviors of newly encountered bird species.

However, if we look at these Roman bird interpreters from the perspective of whether bird migration might have had special significance for a peasant people in the southern lowlands of Sweden, the situation is quite different. The fact immediately emerges that these peasants had no better tool for accurately determining the seasons and other necessities of rural life than the observation and knowledge of the avian world in particular. Perhaps some day a skilled ornithologist will comment on these matters. At this point, however, it is safe to say that while bird watching is of little to no importance to nomads, at best serving as general wildlife observation, it is of great value to agriculture in north-central Europe. Consider, for example, the well-known "rain calls" of certain bird species in the deciduous forest zone of central Europe.[218] Considering the great diversity of bird species in central Europe and the fact that an

---

[218] The recently deceased zoologist Valentin Haecker (Halle), who introduced the author to the basics of ornithology, possessed an almost uncanny accuracy in deducing the seasons, weather, sunrise, and sunset from the behavior and expressions of birds. For example, Haecker was able to tell the time in the morning to the minute, even without a clock, by observing the order in which the birds' songs began during the morning chorus and converting this to the time of sunrise.

understanding of their characteristics requires detailed study, coupled with the inherent complexity of bird observation, which requires a certain level of observational skill, it is conceivable that in earlier times, specific individuals were entrusted with the task of observing the avian world. Therefore, thanks to their predisposition and education, certain families may have emerged that were particularly gifted in these matters. Their historical traditions have been preserved for us in the augurs of ancient Rome. Von Amira writes,

> Divine lineage is ascribed to Germanic noble families; in other words, their forefathers demand and enjoy constant worship. Hence, popular belief attributes extraordinary powers to noble lineage that surpass those of ordinary people. For instance, in the Rígsþula (stanza 45 and 47), there is mention of their understanding of the language of birds.[219]

By way of example, let us briefly indicate the illuminating results that may be obtained from a thorough exploration of these questions for the fields of cultural history and race science. One notable migratory bird in the Swedish lowlands is the goose. Regarding the goose, two aspects are essential—that the goose practices strict monogamy and that the farmer can infer weather conditions from the behavior of geese (for example, when geese run into the water honking, it indicates rain). Among the ancient Roman patricians, the goose was the sacred bird of Juno. Such a connection between Juno and geese actually points quite clearly to Sweden or Lower Germany as the place of origin for this religious custom. For it was only here that both of these things could have been observed together and merged into a single concept in the imagination of a people.

As we conclude this discussion, however, we should leave room for one more thought. To the extent that we can form an opinion in this field, it may perhaps be said that the Phalian race is rarely, if ever, to be found among the Indo-Europeans. In any case, we are yet to find surviving sculptures of the Indo-Europeans that bear the characteristic traits of a Bismarck or a Hindenburg. Previous explanations of this phenomenon have been somewhat simplistic, assuming that the peasant Phalian race did not have the inclination for long-distance migration (a trait supposedly exclusive to the Nordic race), while the mobile, non-agricultural Nordic individual moved into the distance and conquered foreign lands.

But now that we have established the Indo-Europeans as true peasants, there is unfortunately not much that can be done with this explanation. In fact, it contains an inherent contradiction. For peasant peoples, overpopulation and emigration have always been the natural challenges of their existence; a failure to send out emigrants leaves only the choice between deliberate infertili-

---

[219] Also see the Norwegian fairytales of Asbjørnsen and Moe.

ty and progressive Sinicization.[220] It is only among nomadic peoples that the problems of overpopulation and emigration are unknown, since the surplus population either perishes out of necessity or forms a daughter tribe that splits off from the main tribe and continues to migrate on its own.

Based on these considerations, the following problem arises. Either the Phalian race was a peasant race, in which case, like all peasant peoples, it must have occasionally reduced its overpopulation by means of emigration, or the Phalian race was not a race of peasants, meaning that it was not originally indigenous to Europe at all. The assumption that the Phalian race is a nomadic one may well be considered impossible—with all probability it may also be assumed that this race is indigenous to central Europe. But then why don't we have any evidence of Phalian emigration? Perhaps the migratory bird routes discussed above can bring us closer to solving this mystery.

First, it is necessary to determine where the Phalian race can reasonably be assumed to originate. Paudler[221] and, along with him, Kern,[222] believe that the region of Dalarna in Sweden can be considered the origin point of the Phalian race and therefore refer to it as the Dalian race. Günther prefers to draw a connection to the contemporary region of Westphalia instead, and therefore considers the term "Phalian race" to be more accurate.[223] The author would like to align himself with Günther for several reasons. The Phalian race is undoubtedly more prevalent in Westphalia than in the Dalarna region, moreover, it is also certain that Westphalia was settled before than Dalarna following the Ice Age. Furthermore, the literal translation of Dalarna is "the valleys," so the proposed name "Dalian race" suggested by Paudler and adopted by Kern actually means nothing more than "valley race." First of all, the term "valley race" is very vague, and secondly, it easily conjures up the idea of a lowland race. Adding to the confusion, cattle breeders refer to breeds that are large and heavy as lowland breeds. Therefore, the term "Dalian race" could potentially evoke the opposite idea of what Paudler and Kern intend to convey; namely, not a race but a location-specific modification.

If we agree with Günther that the lands surrounding what is now Westphalia constituted the ancestral homeland of the Phalian race, we could consider the Weser River as a geographic point of orientation. However, we are now in the low-lying areas west of the Elbe. In these lands, the birds do not migrate in the direction of the Balkans and the Black Sea. Instead, they migrate toward Spain, Gibraltar, and northwest Africa. And what do we know about the history of those regions so far? If we are honest, the answer is practically nothing. While we are well aware that vast empires must have existed in northwestern Africa, and we may even speculate that the legend of Atlantis will find its answers here, we currently lack any precise knowledge of the history of these regions. In fact, we must ask the thought-provoking question

---

[220] We will get to know the meaning of this term below. What is meant here is the continuous breaking up of landed property during the division of inheritance.

[221] Paudler, *Die Hellfarbigen Rassen.*

[222] Kern, *Ursprung und Artbild der Deutschen.*

[223] Günther, *Rassenkunde des Deutschen Volkes.*

of why we still know nothing about these cultures and why we seem to have difficulty reconstructing them. After all, we have long since brought to light the most deeply buried Indo-European civilizations of Asia and the Middle East. Might the solution perhaps be found in the possibility that in these regions there did exist Phalian civilizations, but we have not been able unlock them with an Indo-European key, so to speak? Why do we find it so difficult to determine the origin of the Guanches of the Canary Islands, whom Paudler and Kern would be absolutely correct in associating with the Phalian (Dalian) race? On page 34 of *Artbild der Deutschen*, Kern mentions Löher, who once remarked that "when he ventured from the coast of Tenerife into the interior of the islands and met the villagers, he often saw a face so purely Saxon, that it was as if he were looking over his farm fence onto the West-phalian heathland."

In this context, and to some extent as an amplification of the assumption expressed here, it is also worth mentioning an observation from the field of domesticated animal history. The author already noted in chapter one that the indigenous European forest horse (equus robustus) was the root ancestor of our present-day cold-blooded horses. These horses are distinctively heavy and often have a slightly long back, heavily feathered fetlocks, and a deeply set tail that they either let hang loosely or tuck in tightly like dogs (their most remarkable characteristic). The preferred gait of these horses is a walk or a trot, and less commonly (and usually reluctantly) a gallop. By comparison, the Asiatic steppe horses prefer to walk or gallop and are reluctant to trot. Interestingly, as demonstrated by Antonius, Berber horses are descended from our European forest horse, while the Moorish horses clearly betray their Arabian-Asiatic origins.[224] Interestingly, the horses of the Fula people are also of the same origin as those of the Berbers, while the so-called Togo horses are in turn related to the Arabian horses. Since we have yet to identify a wild horse in Africa that could serve as an ancestor to our domestic horses, all that remains is to assume that the horses of the Berbers and the Fula came to their present location from western Europe. They could not very well have migrated on their own—some form of human migration must have been the cause.

According to Antonius, the now extinct Dongola horses of Nubia are also related to the Berber horses. In fact, Hagenbeck's "Nubian Caravans" found this horse even as far as Abyssinia and Shewa.[225] Typically, this type of horse is found alongside the Hamitic tribes of inner Africa, but this does not suggest that the Hamites originated in northwestern Africa or that they are an Africanized Phalian race. The convergence of the Hamites and Berber-type horses can be explained in several other ways.

Curiously enough, however, a similar pattern can also be observed among the other domesticated animals of the Hamitic people. For instance,

---

[224] Antonius, *Stammesgeschichte der Haustiere*.
[225] Carl Hagenbeck, one of the fathers of the modern zoo, was a German wild animal merchant from Hamburg. He pioneered the development of zoo enclosures without bars and in some cases controversially displayed indigenous people alongside wild animals. His Nubian Caravans toured Europe displaying animals and people from East Africa 1878–1879.

Antonius (page 180) states the following regarding the origin of Hamitic cattle:

> At least one thing is certain—there is a remarkably close relationship between southern primigenius cattle[226] and the Hamitic ethnic group, to which I have already alluded to elsewhere,[227] and which has recently been extensively explored by L. Adametz.[228] Somatically pure Hamites, such as the Fula of western Sudan and the Tutsi and Wahinda of the Great Lakes region, frequently breed the purest primigenius cattle. This cattle is also found among the Negroids who have been influenced by the ancient pastoral culture of the Hamites, as is the case with the Bantu peoples of southern Africa. Furthermore, modern anthropology suggests a very close relationship between the Hamites and the indigenous Iberian population of Spain, suggesting that these Iberian waves reached as far as England (here we also find an ancient breed of primigenius descent). Even the cattle of the ancient Egyptians exhibited the primigenius type quite clearly, as my most recent research on osteological material has confirmed. . . . The aurochs continue to exist today in the fighting bull breeds of southern Spain, as demonstrated by the exemplary research conducted by S. Ulmansky.[229] We do not know how old this breed is, but it can be assumed with certainty that there was an ancient breeding population of primigenius stock in the western Mediterranean region, as evidenced by Bronze Age rock drawings. The significant similarity between certain cattle breeds in Great Britain—especially the Welsh Black and Devon—and Andalusian cattle (to which a reference has already been made) suggests an ancient domestication and a very early spread to England.[230]

The author would like to add here that the African primigenius cattle that appear together with the Hamites should not be confused with the humped African cattle of the Zebu type. These Zebu cattle spread out from northeastern Africa, often quite clearly interbreeding with the primigenius cattle of Hamitic origin. We even find these humped cattle in Somaliland, among the Maasai, and southward to the Wahehe, as well as among the southeastern *kaffirs*. The author suspects that these cattle belong to the Semitic nomadic pastoralists.

We cannot delve too deeply into the field of domesticated animal history research here. But it was nevertheless quite useful to contrast research results from this field with Kern's assertion that the domestication of animals came to Europe from abroad and that, for example, the domestication of the horse

---

[226] He is referring to the domesticated cattle breeds descended from wild aurochs.

[227] Antonius, "Die Abstammung der Hausrinder," 7.

[228] Adametz, "Herkunft und Wanderung der Hamiten."

[229] Ulmansky, *Die Andalusische Rinderrasse.*

[230] See also: Saborsky, *Das Wallisische Schwarze Rind*; Weisheit, *Devons und South Devons.*

in Europe is inconceivable.[231] By the way, just to cover all the bases—the wild ancestral form of the horses of the Indo-Europeans, which undoubtedly traces back to an Asiatic steppe homeland, is already present in Europe as early as the penultimate stage of the Upper Paleolithic period (Solutré) in such quantities that at one site, the remains of approximately seventy thousand specimens were discovered.[232]

But back to the Phalian race. It should not be claimed that only Indo-Europeans inhabited the right bank of the Elbe, while only Phalian-related peoples resided on the left bank of the Elbe. Nor should one believe that only Indo-European people migrated in the direction of the Balkans and the Black Sea, while the Phalian race exclusively moved toward Spain and northwest Africa. Such a sharp division is impossible for geographic reasons alone. But it is at least conceivable that the basic outlines of these migrations may have unfolded in such a way. We should then not be surprised by the absence of the Phalian race in the cultural sphere of the ancient Indo-Europeans.

With this, we are once again in the position of having to draw racial-scientific conclusions. Having indisputably established the Indo-Europeans as farmers (peasants in the truest sense of the word), we are now faced with a choice—either the Indo-Europeans belonged to the Nordic race, in which case the Nordic race was a peasant race without any itinerant nomadic pastoralist tendencies, or we adhere to current notions and continue to separate the Nordic race from the peasantry. In the latter case, however, one must then make the effort to discover a new race for the Indo-Europeans. At any rate, according to our present knowledge, the Phalian race is not a viable candidate for the Indo-European peasantry.

The Nordic race and the Phalian race may not have played the same role, but they have certainly played a role of equal importance in north-central Europe. Just like the greatest German statesmen of the past two centuries have been predominantly Nordic (Frederick the Great) and Phalian (Bismar-

---

[231] See Kern (*Artbild der Deutschen*), chapters twelve and thirteen. Kern often contradicts himself in these two chapters, sometimes even developing points of view that are quite consistent with the ideas presented by the author in this chapter. Unfortunately, Kern's book simply lacks a consistent logical progression in its conceptual structure, he twists and turns within it to preserve (at all costs) the notion of a former nomadic pastoralist-warrior culture among the Germans and Indo-Europeans. Kern even goes so far as to suggest that true agriculture is only possible when a formerly nomadic pastoral-warrior culture transitions to a sedentary lifestyle. On page 201, he begins with the telling statement, "Indo-European peasanthood thus arose from a true fusion of herding and plant cultivation; yet, as the whole structure of the Indo-European world shows, the pastoral culture was the creative and dominant component." As an aside, compare this with what Ritter says about nomadism in chapter one.

If anthropology, for the sake of classification, wants to trace the Nordic race and the Semitic Hamites back to a common root at all costs, and believes that it has found the key to this assumption in a "pastoral-warrior culture," then it will also have to come up with a plausible explanation for why the domesticated animals of these three human races have no connection in their phylogenic roots. Based on Kern's assertion, the author has so far unsuccessfully attempted to identify a common ancestral domesticated animal root for the camels and donkeys of the Semites, on the one hand, and the pigs and horses of the Nordic race, on the other. After all, domesticated animals play a major role in the context of the "pastoral" warrior culture!

[232] Kraemer, "Zur Ältesten Geschichte der Pferde."

ck), so too do we find both races represented in the two greatest military leaders of recent times, the Nordic Moltke and the Phalian Hindenburg. Therefore, the author is of the opinion that the previous descriptions of the two races (Lenz, Kern, Paudler, Günther) have not done them full justice. Both races are undoubtedly genuinely peasant master races, and both are fit for leadership. Now that public attention is focused on the existence of these two races, perhaps additional evidence will soon be available that will allow for a better assessment. After all, there is still a lot that remains unsettled in our German history, especially with regard to the Nordic and Phalian races. Likewise, the centuries-old animosity between the Franks and the Saxons must have included, among other things, certain racial tensions that could not be easily overcome. Curiously enough, several centuries later, the same animosity existed in England between the Anglo-Saxons and the Normans. These contrasts within the Germanic people should at least be mentioned here.

However, this work deals exclusively with the Nordic race. The author states that, on the basis of his research on the Indo-Europeans, there can be no doubt about the peasant nature of the Nordic race, at least during the period of the Indo-European migrations. Nevertheless, on the basis of certain considerations, it would be worthwhile to attempt to make a few observations as to whether the Nordic race was settled or nomadic during the pre-Indo-European period. This will be attempted in the following chapter.

V

Thoughts on the Pre-Indo-European Era of the Nordic Race

I

In the first chapter, we established that the emergence of the settled form of human existence is a development whose beginnings and individual stages might still be unknown.

When modern ethnologists attempt to classify mankind's oldest known civilizations, and then attempt to bring their findings to life, so to speak, by means of scientific assumptions, this is often vividly reminiscent of the time when, say, geologists considered the gathering of fossils to be their most important task, and tried to explain geological prehistory by means of assumptions alone. But just as geologists were forced to recognize that the fossil record is nothing more than a manifestation of the biological life cycle, which in turn must have been dependent on other, quite specific biological determinants (communities of life—biocoenosis!),[233] so too must ethnologists choose to consult not just the discovered remains of a civilization, but also the symbiosis of the environment to which they once belonged to, particularly if they want to shed light on the most ancient history of mankind. There is not a single living being that is not intimately interwoven into a community of life—the mutual interdependences inherent to the entire natural world. Any time there is a

---

[233] Biocoenosis, first coined by German biologist Karl Möbius in 1877, refers to a community of interacting organisms living together in a specific habitat or ecosystem, encompassing their roles in maintaining ecological balance.

change in the body design or life course of one species, it inevitably brings about changes in all others. Therefore, it must be possible to clearly establish both the origins of mankind and its individual races using indirect evidence from the life sciences (biological circumstantial evidence). For no other race in the world, however, will this circumstance be as essential as it is for the Nordic race; after all, we are investigating the possibility of naturally deriving this race from the natural conditions of its ancestral homeland.

As far as the author can tell, ethnology and race science have so far given little to no consideration to such a biological approach in their research. There exist a number of prominent hypotheses about the origin of man that always seem to lack a biological point of view. We hear, for instance, that the evolution of man from a great ape can be roughly imagined as follows—the great ape, originally a forest dweller, was forced by deforestation to inhabit the steppes. In this environment, it became necessary for him to adopt the mobile existence of the hunter, which is how upright walking (bipedalism) was able to develop. What this scientific hypothesis has in its favor is that it is consistent with the evolutionary history of the human skeleton. But looking at it physiologically—that is, regarding the human body and its expressions of life—this hypothesis still raises some doubts. First of all, against this hypothesis, it can generally be said that nowhere in the animal world can we find a tendency for animals to simply abandon a food source that they depend on. Even the most mobile and adventurous predator remains parasitically bound to its accustomed diet (the diet of carnivores is derived from herbivores, who in turn depend on highly localized vegetation). Therefore, from a geographic perspective, even the most mobile of animals are still immobile—they only migrate when their food source also begins to migrate. When the plant life of an area changes due to geologic factors, the changed plant life attracts animals into the area that depend on the newly forming plant growth. The movement of animals behind a food source is often incredibly fast when climate or other changes cause plant life to change. Even here in Germany, some species of animals from the Russian steppes appear during very dry summers. Conversely, however, the previous animal life of an area also disappears rather quickly when there are changes in this area's plant life; the animals migrate to places where the old living conditions have been preserved or where similar ones have arisen. As of yet, there is absolutely no evidence of readaptation to another food source. It seems that readaptation only occurs when the ability to migrate is inhibited by some sort of constraint and the new food source gradually changes. Thus, the "disappearance of the forest" alone cannot be assumed as the initiating cause for the development of upright walking in humans. For this hypothesis to be true, there would have to be at least one other constraint that did not allow humans to leave their original homeland. From a biological point of view, the problem should already be quite apparent here, because, first of all, the change in the environment must be geologically verifiable, and, secondly, the radical transition from life in the forest to life in the steppes naturally affects not just man alone, but also the whole circle of animals that co-existed with him in the forest. Therefore, it should be possible to identify a focal point in the animal world whose animal forms clearly indicate the transition from forest life to steppe life, where man would only be "one of many." The author currently knows of no such focal point.

Additionally, this hypothesis would also have to be supported by the evolutionary history of the human stomach and intestinal structure. The evolution from herbivore (which is certainly what a tree-dwelling forest animal is) to carnivore (as a hunter of the steppes) would have to be demonstrable via comparative anatomy. But when we try to do just that, we are faced with an insurmountable difficulty—when we look at the human stomach and intestinal structure, we can certainly see the step from carnivore to omnivore, but not the step from herbivore to omnivore/carnivore. In other words, the step from carnivore to omnivore is provable, whereas the step from herbivore to omnivore is by no means immediately ascertainable.[234]

It has been argued by the archaeologist Schuchhardt that man must have originated in Europe as a cave-dwelling animal and that it is easy to trace him from there.[235] It was out of Europe that man then poured out over the world in uninterrupted waves. Among experts, Schuchhardt has been attacked heavily for this hypothesis. These are controversial issues that archaeologists and anthropologists must solve among themselves. Here, however, we are very much captivated by the fact that Schuchhardt's hypothesis at least transfers Nordic man into a biological environment that is in many ways appropriate to Nordic man. Schuchhardt has been criticized for relying too heavily on the caves of France to derive his cave hypothesis for the history of human evolution. But what is overlooked with this criticism is the fact that almost all predators living in north-central Europe—assuming one does not include the Arctic region—have also adapted to living in burrow-type dwellings (including caves) in a manner very similar to the human cave dwelling of the Paleolithic. It was just claimed a little while ago that humans evolved from carnivores to omnivores rather than the other way around. Interestingly, we observe that the same development has occurred with very few exceptions in the previously mentioned world of central European predators. All one has to do is study the expressions of life—above all the dentition—of badgers, foxes, bears, etc., and one will not be able to deny that the same developments have taken place in them as in the human

---

[234] To the extent that the author understands, humans lack a stomach or intestinal arrangement capable of breaking down plant cellulose. In any case, it is a fact that the introduction of the potato in Europe and the flourishing of the sugar industry in Germany have, at present, provided humans with the means to more extensively exploit plant carbohydrates for purposes of national nutrition.
[235] Schuchhardt, *Alteuropa*.

being.[236] If in the past we studied anthropoid apes in order to draw conclusions about human prehistory, in the future we might also want to take a closer look at the habits of brown bears to study their amazing resemblance to humans. Even the plantigrade walking of bears and badgers, at the very least, did not arise randomly or independently of the plantigrade walking of humans. In short, if one simply makes the effort to explore the animal world of central Europe, the human being is so well integrated into this world from an evolutionary point of view that, while the archaeologist Schuchhardt may have made some errors in detail, he did not err in his basic idea of central Europe as the ancestral homeland of the human race. This, of course, also grants us the possibility of establishing Europe as the origin of the Nordic race. It may only be a matter of time until we have sufficient indirect evidence (circumstantial evidence) from biology to uncover the developmental path of the Nordic race out of the north of central Europe.

Having pointed out above that the beginning of sedentism is still, for the time being, an evolutionary mystery (sedentism in the sense of the self-sufficient settled man who exploits the natural resources of his environment), I would now like to draw attention to the fact that almost all of the predators of central Europe have undergone an evolutionary step quite similar to the one undergone by mankind on its way to sedentism. Consider the territorial hunting practices of brown bears and how they live in caves. We also have the first signs of self-created individual dwellings in the badger's sett (den), with its elaborately positioned chambers and its arrangement of tunnels that branch out in all directions (similar to Reynard the Fox's Castle Maleperduis),[237] certainly suggesting an evolutionary proximity to a form of human cave dwelling observable in early history. But one could also think of the elaborately designed otter's holt (den), or even look to the masters of hydraulic engineering, the beavers, for some concrete examples that could explain humanity's transition to a settled form of existence in a natural way, all without making

---

236 The author would like to emphasize here that he is indebted to Professor Metzger (Helsinki) for these insights. In the course of his research into the phylogeny of domesticated animals, the author encountered a clear contrast between settled and nomadic peoples. He found himself compelled, on the basis of the domesticated animals found among the Nordic race, to trace the origin of the latter back to a settled existence. The author happened to cross paths with Metzger, who, as an agricultural and forestry expert for the German Embassy in Helsinki, had spent three decades professionally traversing the region from Denmark to the Urals. Out of scholarly enthusiasm, Metzger seized the opportunity to amass an extensive collection of materials on agricultural customs and hunting practices in the north. With considerable insight into Professor Metzger's collections, the author can only express the hope that this remarkably unique material will be made available to the public in the not-too-distant future. It should be emphasized here that there is absolutely no reason to postulate a non-European ancestral homeland for the Nordic race. And least of all did this race originate in a steppe environment.

237 Castle Maleperduis is the fictional stronghold of Reynard the Fox, a central figure in medieval European fables, particularly popular from the twelfth to the fifteenth century. The castle serves as Reynard's refuge in these allegorical tales, which satirize human society through the adventures of anthropomorphic animals.

any assumptions. It is very important to note that this is a primitive form of sedentism common to nearly all predators. All of these predators transitioned to a way of life based on gathering without immediately adopting a plant-based diet as a result, an assumption that ethnologists today tend to make to explain the beginning of human sedentism. "Meister Petz" is a hermit, and a tough one at that, but only in emergencies is he content with an exclusively plant-based diet.[238]

Naturally, not much can be said here about the individual stages of development that led from sedentary cave dwelling to the settled form of existence typical of the Nordic peoples, since it is still the case that there is not much research available in this area. Nevertheless, we should still try to see if we might not perhaps track down a few clues. For the present, however, it is quite sufficient to note that there is no biological contradiction in assuming the existence of an ancestral homeland for the Nordic race in Europe, and in further presupposing that the development of a settled existence in this area was natural. If this assumption is correct, then it is also reasonable to suppose that all those peculiar qualities that we recognize in the Nordic race can be easily deduced from its history of settlement. Or, expressed differently, the settled form of existence typical of the Nordic race, which is age-old in terms of evolution, must be the best possible way to understand both the physical and mental expressions of this race. This and the following chapters will attempt to provide proof of this, at least to the point where the reader will find it worthwhile to continue along this path with curiosity.

In order to avoid any possible misunderstandings, when the author refers to the influence of the environment on breeding or on certain cultural institutions, I declare firmly that what I mean by environmental breeding is in no way what Lamarckism understands by this concept. For Lamarckism, race is like a kind of putty in which each new environment erases the old breeding conditions and embeds new ones. This means that in Lamarckism, races only differ in terms of the material used in the different kinds of putty. For me, environmental breeding is the selective culling of unsuitable individuals. This results is an accumulation of favorable hereditary traits in the survivors, which ultimately leads to the homozygosity of these predispositions and the consolidation of the racial appearance. If a race finds itself in a new environment, the interplay of race and environment begins anew, building upon earlier deviations—these can always be traced back in terms of their phylogenesis.

The Edda assumes that Búri, the primordial father of the gods, was "licked out of the ice." If the Edda is to be credited to the Nordic race, it is highly improbable that the Nordic race, living in the steppes, would ever

---

[238] Meister Petz is a German folkloric figure and anthropomorphic bear often depicted as a wise but sometimes bumbling character in fables and stories. The name "Petz" is a colloquial term for "bear" in German, and "*Meister*" (meaning master) emphasizes his anthropomorphic qualities, portraying him as a respected (though occasionally clumsy) figure within animal tales. Stories involving Meister Petz typically highlighted is love of honey and nature.

have had the idea of supposing such an origin for the primeval father of the gods. One always suspects that a compressed version of the phylogeny of a race or people is revealed in their myths and tales. For these reasons, the story of how Búri came to be has been placed here first, before the following analysis.

Working on a purely hypothetical basis, the evolution from Ice Age cave men to Nordic peasants living on individual farmsteads might be thought of in the following way. We will present it in a broad outline. Humans, who were accustomed to Ice Age cave dwelling, followed the retreating ice northward. It would be simplistic to think only of reindeer hunters in this context. The central European deciduous forest belt advanced northward, following the retreating flora and fauna native to the Arctic. This was only possible when the soil of what is now Lower Germany, which had been killed off and rendered infertile by the ice cover, was once again able to support suitable vegetation. All the animals who depended on this vegetation, which formed part of a temperate forest belt in central Europe, naturally followed it—we have a very precise understanding of the animal and plant life of this climatic belt during the Ice Age.[239] Now, while humans in particular are relatively independent of their dietary space, we may still assume that this deciduous forest area—even when it was at its most restricted—held on to a group of wandering hunter-gatherers who were dependent on the local wildlife and would not willingly abandon it. When the central European deciduous forest area began to expand, the animals belonging to it also followed—but so did the human beings, who, as game hunters, relied on these animals. Since the vast majority of these animals still prefer to live in burrow-type dwellings, we can assume that as the glaciers advanced, the associated cold climate of the snow ages apparently forced these animals to adapt to living in the numerous caves of central Europe. Be it out of habit or out of necessity, the fact is that these animals did not give up their burrow-type dwellings once they were no longer necessary. In the caveless lowlands of central Europe, they retained this burrow-type dwelling way of life by transitioning to the construction of self-created caves (dens). Here, almost all of the animals that belonged to this climate zone took the first steps toward the sedentary existence of a settled human being and, in part, turned quite decisively toward a simple foraging existence. This step is of great importance for the evolutionary history of mankind because it could explain how the human race became sedentary, providing a natural explanation. Now, if we assume that this group of game hunters followed the native wildlife of the central European deciduous forest area northwards, it is entirely possible that these humans would have adapted to the living habits of these animals, or, to put it more plainly, imitated what the bears, foxes, badgers, otters, beavers, etc., showed them—that is, they dug out caves or dens in which they could live.

---

[239] The author relies on many theories that he owes to his teacher, the geologist and paleontologist Walther (Halle).

It will be difficult, however, to pinpoint the exact time when this development began.[240] But since it is tied to a particular development that also occurred in the animal word, and since these animals in their modern form become quite clearly recognizable after the great interglacial period, it will probably not be so difficult to answer this question quite accurately by means of indirect evidence from the life sciences. The author, however, would rather not venture into this area of anthropological research; he is content with the conclusion that the glaciers, which retreated after the great interglacial period, forced adaptations not only in the wildlife we are considering here but also in Cro-Magnon man.

At this stage, the whole process that led mankind to begin to make use of fire is unclear. This is also true for the further development of this concept, which encouraged mankind to preserve it and make use of it. From a geologic perspective, however, it is important to note that charcoal serves as a distinct index fossil for determining particular stages of cultural development. In and of itself, the geologic layer in which charcoal fire first becomes apparent should be completely distinguishable.

In purely conceptual terms, if we want to deduce what the further development of these humans looked like, following the development of living in self-created "caves," then the following can perhaps be assumed. The next stage of development was the transition from self-made caves to the covered dugout. Of course, it is also possible that the covered dugout existed from the very beginning, and mankind transitioned directly from natural caves to the covered dugout. The winter campaigns of the World War proved that, even in severe frost, a man in a self-dug trench (which looked like a small grave covered by a tarp) could generate enough heat on his own to survive a cold and frosty winter night. During the first winters of the war, before the use of heaters became common in the military dugouts (due to the lack of heaters and the fear of observation balloons), the author himself lived for months in unheated foxholes (military dugouts at the time were nothing more than that) next to gun emplacements. Life was not always pleasant, but it served us extraordinarily well—when heaters were introduced in December 1915, the first flu symptoms began to appear among the men. We can, of course, safely use this experience from the World War to say that the humans living in the postglacial period were more than capable of surviving the central European winter in covered pit dwellings. In any case, by assuming the existence of covered pit dwellings, we hold in our hands the seeds from which genuine house construction

---

[240] Recently, Schuchhardt has made the assertion that the Nordic race must have had its ancestral roots in Thuringia. Without wishing to express an opinion on this anthropological debate, the author would like to point out that Schuchhardt's thesis is quite compatible with the lines of thought developed by the author. This is due to the fact that during the Ice Age, Thuringia was demonstrably a refuge for the central and northern European deciduous forest (*Alteuropa*, page 250). One could imagine that a ruthless selection process determined who could survive in this densely packed habitat, facilitating the cultivation of proven families and bloodlines (*Alteuropa*, pages 244 and 269).

could develop over the course of generations. But for this to make sense, a brief meteorological analysis needs to be included here.

As long as Europe has had the Gulf Stream, it has had a climate abundant in precipitation, extending from the northwest to the Baltic Sea region. In the true north of Europe, we can observe that the cold weather and winters did not prompt man to become sedentary or to start building dens or caves. This was not possible due to the frozen ground. In fact, among the wildlife of the Arctic region, only the fox knows how to construct storage chambers. It stores food for emergencies in crevasses and the like, which act as a kind of artificial cold storage. The other predators of the north, however, live more mobile lives, something that can be easily verified by comparing the neck of the polar bear to that of the brown bear. By comparison, we see that the animals of the deciduous forest region of central Europe tend to be sedentary without exception. The deciduous forest is both directly and indirectly a consequence of precipitation. As such, it is reasonable to assume that the sedentary nature of animals native to this region is directly related to the amount of rainfall that occurs. Perhaps some of those who took part in the military campaigns during the war still remember how different life could be in rainy conditions, compared to dry and cold conditions. Cold can be tolerated quite well in foxholes by a healthy person who is engaged in reasonably healthy activities and dressed in appropriate fur clothing, even without a fire. We discussed this in more detail above. In the dry cold, diet (especially a high-fat diet), seems to be more important than actual housing conditions. This is supported not only by the way of life of the people living in the Arctic (which is still a nomadic way of life), but also by the way of life of the animals living there.

But the situation is fundamentally different with rain. While rain may not have an immediate impact on the wildlife itself, prolonged cold rain mixed with snow would have undoubtedly forced the local wildlife to adapt to these conditions. We can safely assume that these weather conditions were prevalent during the snowy seasons of central Europe (the legend of the flood!). In any case, man had no choice but adapt to it, for no human being can withstand prolonged exposure to rain out in the open. Former frontline soldiers will certainly agree with me on this point. It is also entirely possible that the rain was the real catalyst for the maintenance of natural fires that humans found by chance. The presence of abundant rain always leads to an abundance of forests and wood, thus creating the perfect conditions for a person to come into contact with a fire during a thunderstorm by means of a lightning strike. Maintaining a fire is therefore no longer difficult given the abundance of wood in a forest. Once a fire is burning steadily, it can be maintained even with wet or green wood. Why should it not have occurred to man from time to time to place a piece of wood on a fire that happened to be burning, so as to obtain the pleasant warmth radiating from it? Beavers use wood for even more elaborate things, and marmots even know how to make hay from grass so that they can have a reasonably warm place to dwell for the winter.[241] One can assume that Ice Age man was just as capable as these animals in putting the same level of thought into how to survive the central European winter as comfortably as possible. In the end, it must not be forgotten that the human being, as a bare-skinned animal, benefited most from being brought into contact with the comfort of a warm fire. Additionally, with his hands, man had at his disposal a very useful means of grasping, which made it possible for him to handle a burning fire and add more wood to it. The fact that man can use his hands as a gripping tool is something that he, of course, shares with the brown bear, who uses its hands and fingers exactly like a human. However, by virtue of its fat and pelt, the brown bear is not so restricted by cold weather and, therefore, has no reason at all to engage with fire.

But let us return to covered pit dwellings. It makes absolutely no difference what materials are assumed to have been used for the actual covering of the pit. Whether made of hides or twigs, the supports for the roof would have certainly been made out of wood (branches). But the use of wood in the construction of dwellings necessitates a quadrangular or rectangular floor plan, something that has been pointed out by Schuchhardt.[242] This results in a roof form that corresponds approximately to a small soldier's tent, since heavy rain necessitates that a roof is sloped sideways. In the field, when we were forced to bivouac for a long period of time in a constant cold rain—as was often the case in the French winter—we dug small pits, which we covered with tarpaulins and surrounded them with gutters to prevent water from flowing in. In the winter of 1914–1915, outside of the primary combat zones, these pits partially developed into a sort of dugout that looked like small log cabins set into the ground up to the edge of the roof. This construction form then continued to develop later on in the "camps" located well behind the front. Over time, however, the need to make the roof bulletproof made it stunt-

---

[241] An interesting observation was made in the ancient village of Ellenberg in the Altmark region while processing a massive poplar tree at the local sawmill. After the sturdy trunk had passed through the saw's gate several times, a sudden discovery was made—a cavity about one meter deep within the trunk. This cavity was further exposed by additional cuts, revealing a longitudinal cross-section of the hollow. The entrance to the cavity was just large enough for the body of a weasel to pass through. The cavity itself served as a winter storage chamber for the weasel, and the collected supplies were layered within the hollow.

At the bottom, there were forty-four mice, still as fresh as the day they had been caught. The layer of mice was covered with sand and humus, which served as a hermetic seal, and is what preserved the mice so well. On the layer of humus and sand there were two wagtails, followed by a quantity of acorns that filled the storage chamber up to the entrance of the cavity. The supplies themselves had not been tampered with, leading to a reasonable assumption that their owner had perished shortly after filling the winter storage with provisions. Within the same poplar, there was yet another cavity, filled with a squirrel's winter supplies.

Such observations are exceedingly valuable, as they allow us insight into the winter diet of animal species generally labeled as pests. As the weasel's storage chamber demonstrates, however, these species can also exhibit beneficial traits. In this regard, the operations of sawmills could yield many valuable insights.

[242] Schuchhardt, *Alteuropa*.

ed and flat. These observations from the past war demonstrate the development from the bivouac to the pit dwellings (which, by the way, the Frenchmen knew to insulate with foliage) to the comfortably constructed dugout—this is something that we may perhaps also assume for those Ice Age people living in pit dwellings. The only difference is that they did not need to flatten their roofs and could even allow them to rise more steeply out of the ground with advanced construction techniques. In any case, it can be said that in the rainiest part of Europe (the northwest), the roofs would have had the steepest gables. It can at least be assumed that in these regions, where roofs are made of reeds and straw, rain must be drained quickly to prevent the roof from deteriorating.

As a matter of fact, these purely conceptual considerations coincide with etymological research into Indo-European languages. Schrader (*Reallexikon*) states that "house" in the Indo-European languages apparently means little more than "to hide or conceal." In addition to providing detailed justifications for this claim, he also mentions Meringer, who directly asserts that the original etymology of the Indo-European "house" derives from "hiding place" and "animal den." Scrader states, "The Sanskrit word *gṛhá* (गृह), meaning house, is related, for example, to the Avestan word *gereda*, meaning cave or pit. Perhaps one could also associate the Old High German word *hof* with the Sanskrit word *kûpa* (कूप), meaning cave."

Once one understands the development process of pit dwellings, it is not difficult to see how Nordic pit dwellings were able to develop. Once these ancestral Indo-European people began lining their pits with wood, then, as was already mentioned, the rectangular architectural form was necessary due to natural constraints. However, in a snowy and rainy climate, it is also necessary to ensure proper water drainage on the roof. The gabled roof was a natural result of this need. One could say that that this roof form gradually evolved and emerged from pit construction over the course of its development. Even today, Icelandic farmhouses are built into the ground, with only the roof sticking out. It is likely that this architectural form was originally more widespread in the northern part of central Europe than is generally believed. Fehrle[243] writes that Xenophon[244] notes of the Armenians, "The houses here were underground, with a mouth like that of a well, but spacious below; and while entrances were tunnelled down for the beasts of burden, the human inhabitants descended by a ladder." Strabo reports of the Illyrian Dardanians, "The Dardanians are so utterly wild that they dig caves beneath their dung-hills and live there . . ." [245] He also reports, "Ephorus, in the passage where he claims the locality in question for the Cimmerians, says: They live in un-

---

[243] Fehrle, *Archiv für Volkskunde* 26:260.
[244] Xenophon, *Anabasis* 4.5.25.
[245] Strabo, *Geographica* 7.5.7.

derground houses."[246] Incidentally, the Greeks also had a name for such subterranean dwellings, and the ancient Germanic peoples had pit houses with only the ridge sticking out, similar to those still existing in Iceland (Schrader). The fact that the roof of a house dug into the earth protrudes from the ground is probably the main reason why the Nordic peasantry attaches so much importance to the roof and links the name of the house and its owner to it, along with related aphorisms and the like. Any other part of the house would be out of the question, since only the roof and the back of the house project from the ground.

Mielke writes regarding the oldest identifiable Indo-European dwellings:

> In northern Europe, their simple rectangular-roofed huts were sunken, but in the classical regions (where they probably only arrived in the early part of the second millennium BC), they were ground-level dwellings. Although the excavations and observations have not yet provided enough evidence to provide a definitive and clear picture of the ancient Indo-European house, they do show that the rectangular house, accessible from the gable end, has dominated architectural development up to the present day. The hearth was placed in the open on the sunken floor, sometimes next to a bench made of earth or clay, or even in front of the entrance. However, it has not yet been established whether there was a projection of the roof on the gable side to protect the fire.

The extent to which the gable has always had a special significance among the Indo-Europeans can be seen in the following words by Mielke:

> The mythical importance of the gable, which is also expressed in proverbs and legends, appears to be an inheritance from the Nordic vorhallenhaus.[247] An intriguing connection is evident in the Old Norse verse, "a wolf hangs at the front gate, and above him, an eagle looms," as well as the Greek word for the upper tympanum, aëtus (meaning eagle). This connection is emphasized by the fact that the gable, or pediment, was reserved exclusively for temples dedicated to gods. The Roman people recognized Caesar's extraordinary importance by having a pediment installed.

---

[246] Ibid, 5.4.5.

[247] Translator's note: The *vorhallenhaus* (literally meaning entrance hall house) was a type of house with a particularly large entrance hall strongly emphasized by its gable. This type of architecture was more prominent east of the Elbe.

2

The realization that in the deciduous forest area of central Europe, man underwent a similar development to that of the local animal world is very revealing. To be more precise, humanity's cave-dwelling clearly evolved from the animal world. But that is not all. Strangely enough, human gender relations and customs also evolved in a similar way to those found in the animal world. Once the animal world had adapted to living in caves or nests, the relationships between the sexes took on forms that we also find among the Indo-Europeans. The animal world, for example, has also developed monogamy, and we can also identify extended families among them. Among individual animal species, customs take the form of either lifelong monogamy or the so-called "extended family." The term extended family here refers to the cohabitation of a kinship group that obeys a male figure and lives together in one place. To give an example from the animal world, we can mention the marmots of our alpine region. The fox, on the other hand, prefers monogamy.[248] The explanation for this similar phenomenon being observed in both animals and Indo-Europeans lies in the fact that cohabitation of genders in a single confined space leaves no other options. In the animal world, whenever animals live in herds, there is always a phenomenon comparable to human matrilineality. This is quite natural, because the living conditions in a steppe or in a desert make very different demands with regard to the preservation of a species than, for example, in a forest. Under such circumstances, matrilineality, as well as the collective behavior of mother animals to secure sustenance, becomes a necessity dictated by nature. Therefore, wherever animals have developed a sedentary way of life and live together in a single space under unfavorable weather conditions, they prefer lives based on extended families or monogamy (or forms that lie between the two). In a similar vein, we find echoes of human matrilineality when a mobile way of life becomes necessary for the preservation of a species and when animals live in herds or packs. The author does not fully understand why research in cultural history assumes the op-

---

[248] This circumstance also explains why the fox has not been domesticated—only herd or pack animals accustomed to social interaction have entered human service. Conversely, the solitary existence ingrained in the fox has nurtured a very pronounced sense of self-awareness and freedom, making it highly unlikely for the fox to contemplate willingly submitting to captivity. Thus, we observe on the one hand, the fox adapted to a territorial solitary existence and possessing both monogamous tendencies and a strong sense of personal liberty, and on the other hand, the wolf, adapted to roaming freely in packs and engaging in a kinship-based social structure for its entire reproductive life. The latter readily became a companion of humans and relinquished its independence.

The author should not be faulted for using such examples from the animal kingdom to make scientific assumptions about prehistoric wandering pastoral tribes, as these comparisons are far from self-evident, as they are often presented today. This comparison between the fox and the wolf is not the sole instance where the animal world provides insight into this matter. For instance, it is a well-known fact to animal handlers that bears are more difficult to train than lions, as bears never truly come to terms with their captivity and hence remain unpredictable. Refer to the preceding discussion.

posite for human beings, (matrilineality for early sedentism and patrilineality for itinerant pastoralism).

In places where the brown bear has not yet come into contact with modern weapons technology and is therefore not yet afraid of humans, the male bear reigns as an absolute king in his own territory. He is thus very sedentary and knows how to masterfully maintain his supremacy in his hunting territory. Bears and humans are surprisingly similar. When it comes to their diet, at least, they are practically the same. This means that humans and bears are well-matched rivals when it comes to the search for food. Therefore, the bear generally attacks any unfamiliar male bear that enters his territory, and does the same to any unfamiliar human male; however, it generally leaves women alone. The natives of such areas know "their" bear very well and completely acknowledge its supremacy, and in return, the bear leaves them alone. However, the bear can clearly distinguish a foreign face from one he is familiar with. The bear's behavior would not make sense if one did not look at the whole question from the point of view of its ability to secure its food source. A sedentary animal only makes sense in nature if the environment can provide it with all the food it needs. When this is the case, another factor comes into play, namely, that this food source must be defended against intruders. Here we come to the fact that dependence on territorial ownership demands assertiveness and therefore engenders an affirmation of struggle (*kampfbejahung*).[249]

Of course, sedentism's affirmation of struggle implies a special reason for conflict. In places where nature sets the table generously, such as in the warm areas of the tropics, the conflict-prone predisposition of sedentary animals recedes entirely. It is revealing that animal tamers do not consider the training of lions and tigers to be as difficult or as dangerous as the training of bears. As such, the behavior of the male brown bear with respect to other male bears and with respect to unfamiliar human beings in its territory is completely natural. The male brown bear leaves females alone because it only has to fear males as equal competitors for food in its territory, since females under primitive conditions (the bear's worldview still functions at this level) are only perceived as subordinates to males.[250]

As a further consequence of these conditions, the uniform distribution of the food source necessitates the dispersal of offspring, since the territory can provide food for a generation of growing children, but not enough for a generation of adults, less so once they have children of their own. As a result, these biological circumstances necessitate subordinating family formation to the

---

[249] The concept of *kampfbejahung* translates to "affirmation of struggle" or "embracing conflict." It is often associated with a philosophical or ideological stance that emphasizes the importance of struggle, conflict, or competition as a means to achieve growth, development, or a higher state of being. Proponents of the philosophy encouraged embracing struggle as a vital component of life, promoting the idea that conflict can lead to positive outcomes and transformation.

[250] The author wishes to reiterate that he is following the insights of Professor Metzger (Helsinki), who originally drew the author's attention to the anthropomorphic characteristics of the brown bear. In general, the author would even go so far as to consider himself a student of Metzger in the study of the deciduous forest area of central Europe!

available dietary space, which means either dispersing the adult offspring or abstaining from forming families altogether. This is a fundamental biological law in the deciduous forest region of central Europe, and it can be observed more or less clearly in all of its native animal life.

The fact that forms of cohabitation developed by cave and burrow-dwelling animals native to the deciduous forests of central Europe are also found among Indo-Europeans is of great importance for our understanding of their evolutionary history. Indo-Europeans practiced two family forms, namely the nuclear family and the extended family. In the case of the nuclear family, the son would leave his father's house when he married, lighting his own hearth fire, and consequently managing his own farm and household. In the case of the extended family, however, the sons remained on the paternal property even after they married and often after the father's death, usually under the authority of the eldest brother. Here they formed a household and an economic community. It is likely that the extended family is the original form, and over time, the nuclear family evolved from it. The nuclear family is most pronounced among the Germanic peoples. Therefore, they clearly represent a sort of final stage in this development.[251]

The natural, or biological, idea behind this development is that, on the one hand, living together in a confined space demanded an orderly structure and family leadership (for internal organizational reasons), and, on the other hand, the environment demanded that someone be held responsible for maintaining and protecting the family. Whatever the case, at the heart of this development is a dependence on the available dietary space, conditioned by the original cave-dwelling lifestyle. Conversely, whenever there is no such attachment to a particular territory, and when the rearing of the young can or must be provided by the herd or pack, matrilineal conditions are found among animals, where the males essentially serve only as the initiators of a fertilization process.

We see, then, that the peasant inheritance laws of the Indo-European and Germanic peoples—the subordination of family formation to the conditions of the available dietary space—can be derived just as naturally from the laws of nature of the deciduous forest region of north-central Europe as it can from the Nordic race's attested affirmation of struggle.

It is worth noting that, according to Schrader, the original Indo-European language did not have a word for marriage. On the other hand, even before the word "marriage" appeared, other terms can be identified that refer to long-term cohabitation between a man and a woman, as opposed to a temporary relationship with a concubine. For example, in Sanskrit, while there is no specific word for marriage, a term for "spouseship" can certainly be identified and already had the meaning of "head of household" and "mistress of the house." The connection between the living space and spouseship is already clear here, and it

---

[251] To understand how the Nordic individual farmstead evolved into village settlements in southern and central Germany, one can refer to Mielke's work *Siedlungskunde des Deutschen Volkes* [The Settlement History of the German People], published in Munich in 1927.

becomes even clearer in Old High German. In Gothic, we have *heiwa*, meaning house, and in Old High German, we have *hîwo* (meaning husband), *hîwa* (meaning wife), and *hîun* (meaning spouses). Compare with what the author has stated previously concerning the evolution of the Nordic house from the pit dwelling, and it will become undeniable that the Nordic forms of marriage resemble those observed among the animals of the deciduous forest area of north-central Europe.

It is quite natural that forms of pairing associated with a single living space and a single food source produce characteristic phenomena in both the animal kingdom and the Nordic race. The female departs from her circle of relatives and enters the sphere of influence of her husband through the marital union.[252] This process leads to a relationship that is patriarchal in every sense of the word. But it is a mistake to equate this relationship with the Semitic patriarchal system of pre-Islamic times. The patriarchal system of the Semitic people cannot hide its matrilineal origins—fundamentally, it cannot hide the fact that it developed out of the pastoral way of life of a nomadic people who were not dependent on the land. During the patriarchal era of the Semitic peoples, women did not leave the kinship context of their own families. Accordingly, in Arabic, the term for husband is *abu rahim* (*rahim* meaning both mother's womb and relatives), indicating that he is the head of a community united through the mother's womb. The sense of belonging of the woman and her children to the woman's family likewise remained so strong that the man had to show consideration for it. The woman herself had no rights whatsoever in relation to her husband. The man could send his wife back home or even sell her, entirely at his whim. But due to the matrilineal bond between the woman and her family, the husband had to fear potential revenge from her family. Thus, despite the woman's actual lack of rights, in reality there existed an indirect protection for her. Compare this to the complete withdrawal of the ancient Roman patrician woman from her own family and the extensive rights she had in relation to her husband, despite fully entering into the husband's family circle (discussed in chapter one). It must be acknowledged that while there may be certain external similarities between the patriarchal system of the Semites and the marital rights of the patricians, closer examination does reveal profound evolutionary differences going back to primeval times. These differences would be inexplicable if one did not take into account the original settled form of existence of the Nordic race in the deciduous forest area of north-central Europe and the original nomadic lifestyle of the Semites in the Arabian Desert.

Significantly, the ancient Germanic settlement pattern—in addition to the aforementioned individual farmstead—is the formation of village communities through land cooperatives. These are probably nothing more than the result of a fragmented kinship group that distributed the originally unitary living space of the clan into multiple individual spaces (see chapters two and three). Schrader concludes that the origin of the Indo-European household was the

---

[252] The reader can also verify this by observing any stork's nest in their vicinity.

cohabitation of the family in a single space. He emphasizes that in Indo-European, the words for "house" originated from words denoting a burrow or pit, with two things to consider—first, the root of the word "clan" refers to such underground living quarters, and second, the same root also refers to a living space for domesticated animals, which very clearly indicates that the kinship group and their domesticated animals lived together in the same space. One only has to think of the Lower Saxon farmhouse to see the final development of these conditions. By the way, it should be very clear by now just how inadequate the claims are of those who would like to trace the beginnings of Indo-European animal domestication back to a nomadic way of life. It is not typical for nomads to bring their animals into their tents or living quarters.

Ihering also determined that, based on the marriage laws of the patricians, the Indo-Europeans could never have been nomads. It is worthwhile to quote him verbatim here:

A fixed place of residence and settlement in a specific location is the beginning of all civilization. It requires stability and permanence, so that something that comes into being can endure. The German language vividly illustrates this with words such as *sitte*, meaning custom, *satzung*, meaning statute, *gesetz*, meaning law (derived from *sitzen*, meaning to sit, and *setzen*, meaning to put, place, or set), and *gewohnheit*, meaning habit (derived from *wohnen*, meaning to dwell or live). In Latin, too, the basic concept of private law is taken from the idea of dwelling (the *familia*). *Familia* linguistically corresponds to "dwelling place" and is derived from Sanskrit *dhâ*, meaning to set, and *dhaman*, meaning dwelling place and later denoting residence; also *fam-ulus*, meaning household member or servant.[253] Thus, it refers to the household, not in the natural sense of *domus* or *aedes*, but rather in an economic and legal context. It refers to the foundation of all economic and private legal existence, the household, along with everything it includes and encompasses (the spouse, children, slaves, farmland, etc.), in essence, the entire domestic household. As will be expounded below, this specifically pertains to the domestic household of the peasant. *Familia* was a legal concept on which virtually all ancient civil law was based, with only a negligible part falling under the concept of *pecunia*. *Familia* represented what was firm, lasting, and enduring, while *pecunia* representd what was transitory, changing, and fleeting. Thus, *familia* was meant to endure, which could only be achieved if a woman bound herself to the man and shared in the concerns of the household with him. With the wife, the *familia* expanded from things to persons, encompassing first the wife, then the children she bears for the husband, and their children in turn, all the way out to the circle of agnates united by common descent from the same man. This represents the broadest extension of

---

the concept of family—the extension of agnation beyond this circle no longer falls within the scope of the term. Likewise, it does not extend to relatives through the woman (cognates). Logically, *pater-familias* refers to the person to whom the *familia* belongs (from Sanskrit *på*, meaning to nourish, protect, or maintain).

The primary guiding principle for all Nordic marriages was the space available for housing and feeding the family. It is therefore logical that these two basic concerns, as if brought together through the focal point of a lens, constitute the core essence of the ancient Nordic marriage and form the Nordic hearth fire. Every ancient Nordic marriage involved lighting a hearth fire. Ihering writes,

> The hearth, the local focal point and symbol of the domestic community, is also the altar at which offerings are made to the domestic gods. What the hearth signifies for the individual family, the hearth of Vesta signifies for the entire people. However, the hearth offering is not an offering for the dead—such an offering is presented at family graves only on certain days, which the Romans called *parentalia*. . . . Domestic worship corresponds to public worship of Vesta. According to Livy, the worship of Vesta was established by Numa, who also established the religious character of the vestal virgins (*virginitate aliisque caeremoniis venerabilis ac sanctas fecit*). But the strength of this argument for the origin of the vestal virgins' religious character is weakened by the note added by Livy alleging that Numa took the worship of Vesta from Alba (*Alba oriundum sacrificium et genti conditoris haud alienum*).[254]

This age-old custom, in which the hearth serves as the center and sanctuary of the family, has partially survived to this day in the placement of the matron's chair, which is always behind the hearth in old German farmhouses. Von Amira writes,

> In the earliest of times, the occupation or *landnahme* (literally land-taking; from the Old Norse *nema, land,* and *landnam* and the Old English *niman* and *land*) of unclaimed land not only involved the establishment of its boundaries but also the lighting of a fire on the property, an act of taking possession that appears in a weakened form in the Icelandic expression "*fara elldi um landit*" (to encircle the land with fire) and perhaps has also left a trace in the German term *sonnenlehen* (sun fief).

---

[254] Ihering, *Vorgeschichte der Indoeuropäer,* 148.

In summary, we can conclude that from ancient times, the Nordic race has presented us with the trinity of the hearth fire, household, and permanent marriage.

Now we come full circle in the most natural way. The Nordic race's ancient sedentary way of life is entirely consistent with the possibility that this race, because of the spare time resulting from their engagement with the environment, eventually advanced toward land use (agriculture) for a variety of reasons. However, this development should not be seen as sudden, and perhaps began simply as a methodical exploitation of forest products (such as hazelnuts, etc.).

It is certainly no accident, therefore, that the Nordic race should have elevated the domesticated animal most characteristic of sedentary life and of life in a deciduous forest region—the pig—to a particularly sacred status. It is also not surprising that during the later clash between the Nordic race and the Semites in the eastern Mediterranean, it was the pig in particular that caused the most intense disputes. The pig represents the antithesis of the desert climate in animal form.[255] Furthermore, it is natural that the patricians emphasized the cultivation of grain in their marriage ceremonies (see chapter one) and sacrificed a boar, which had to be killed with a stone axe (*silex*). Both practices clearly identify the patricians as Stone Age farmers. It is now understandable why upon marriage, the patrician woman entered her husband's house with the words "*ubi tu gaius, ego ibi gaja*," as noted by Servius. Ihering aptly translates this as "where you plow, I will plow with you." It is also not surprising that the erotic cults of Venus and Aphrodite, which came from the ancient Orient, were never associated with pig sacrifice.

We have now proved that in all likelihood, the Nordic race, through the environmental pressures of the central European deciduous forest region, underwent a continuous development from an originally animal-like cave-dwelling existence to the possession of domesticated animals and the inhabitation of pit dwellings. Moreover, the later peasanthood of the Nordic race is clearly shown to be the natural and also necessary progression of a developmental trajectory that had already been set during the Ice Ages.

3

The phylogenesis of the human races still remains shrouded in complete darkness, and any attempt at explanation leads the researcher into unfamiliar and uncertain territory. Therefore, the primary goal of prehistoric research must be to find a foundation that can withstand rigorous scrutiny. With this goal in mind, one can either establish firm links to a known field of research or try to explore new and unexplored fields of prehistory. It is in this sense that the author requests that the following remarks be considered only as thoughts that may provide inspiration for future research into European prehistory. So far, the author has (for good reasons) deliberately focused on the developmental

---

[255] Darré, "*Das Schwein als Kriterium.*"

path of the Nordic race from cave-dwelling hunter-gatherers in the deciduous forest region of central Europe to peasants in the same region. The intention was to first highlight these two biological factors separately (the Nordic race and the central European deciduous forest) and then proceed to link them together. If it is indeed possible to establish with some degree of certainty the connection between the Nordic race and the central European deciduous forest area, then we have a tool of the utmost value for uncovering the phylogenesis of this race. With this observation, we not only identify the deciduous forest as the native environment of the Nordic race, but also consider all the biological, geographic, and meteorological factors that are related to or influence this forest. This includes not only the clearly identifiable flora and fauna, but also elements such as water conditions, humidity, cloud cover, illumination, temperature levels, wind conditions, hunting practices, way of life, etc. It is also important to note that we can, for example, rather accurately say how this moist air affects the available amount of sunlight, which in turn allows us to draw conclusions about human skin.

These last words touch upon a very important area of race science. The human organism is subject to the requirement that it must maintain a constant level of body heat, regardless of the nature of its life activities. But since humans can engage in very different activities and, furthermore, the caloric power of the ingested food is not constant, the body, like any steam-powered machine, must also have valves to release excess heat. It is clear that a body that passes from a rest state into an active state generates more heat through this activity than it did before. The body must be able to get rid of this excess heat, and the pores of the skin are available for this purpose (the body begins to sweat). The main purpose of sweating is to bind the body's internal heat to the body's surface through evaporative cooling. But the heat of the environment on the earth's surface varies greatly. The human body therefore faces the challenge of having to take this into account as well.

Essentially, the human skin becomes an organ that acts as a mediator between the body's internal temperature and that of its environment. In other words, environmental pressures must always primarily affect the skin. Thus, once we have identified with certainty the environment of the Nordic race's ancestral homeland, we also know (since we will also know the diet) all the internal and external factors impacting Nordic skin. Since skin plays the role of thermal mediator for the organism, it is unambiguously the product of natural selection. For that matter, it is not only heat regulation that is relevant here. The lighting conditions also play a role. Furthermore, it should be noted that the human skin is an excretory organ, and gas exchange through the skin should therefore be mentioned (cutaneous respiration).

To some researchers of human racial conditions, the author's suggestions will seem somewhat bold. From a zootechnical point of view, however, the case is actually simpler. For centuries, animal breeders have long been accustomed to evaluating the quality of skin and hair when judging their breeding animals; this, of course, requires practice and special talent. However, one only has to discuss these factors with experienced sheep breeders—they will provide nothing short of astonishing analyses on the constitution and life story (nutrition, fertility, etc.) of any given animal. As a result, scientific animal breeding has recently returned to this area and has already conducted and published highly informative research on skin and hair.[256]

Finally, an essential point in all these questions is certainly the fact that skin, including that of humans, is directly related to other bodily character-istics via the evolutionary history of its germ layers. In the outstanding work by Zorn (Breslau), we find the following noteworthy passage:

Pigmentation therefore depends on the physiological condition of the organism, to which specific environmental pressures must be added. As far as nutrition is concerned, the tendency of all highly bred breeds of domesticated animals (Shorthorns, Simmentaler) to lose their coloration is attributed to a more ample and water-rich diet, especially during their youth, namely due to a weakening of their constitution, resulting in less or no skin pigmentation.[257] Adametz also attributes the occurrence of many piebald and tiger patterns among the old Pinzgauer (Noriker) horses to their ample and water-rich diet, which had a weakening effect. Similarly, J. R. Robertson and Bunsow point to a phenomenon that they describe as one of the most fascinating in heredity, namely that the personality type (and even the skeletal formation) of the animal carrying the color is very often inherited along with the color to such an extent that the offspring of a stallion of the same color resemble him completely in both personality and in their overall appearance, while differently colored offspring do not.[258] This observation also absolutely corresponds to my own practical experience in a West Prussian breeding farm. Many professional breeders may have made similar observations, about which I would be extremely grateful to hear about.

Lang rightly states, "Attention is drawn here to phenomena that could potentially be of great significance." This phenomenon would indeed be worthy of more extensive large-scale scientific observations. Wilckens has also pointed out such correlations when he states that, as a rule, the horse that inherits its coat color also inherits its body shape. This is reportedly particularly noticeable in cases of chestnut colored English horses and gray colored Arabian purebred and half-breed horses. Wilckens also regards the black coat as a valuable characteristic indicating mass and bone strength. . . . Returning to the starting point of our discussion, one must surely acknowledge that,

---

[256] Refer to the works published in the Kühn Archive by the Animal Breeding Institute at the University of Halle-Wittenberg (under the direction of Professor Frölich), as well as the publica-tions from the German Society for Breeding Science, Göttingen.

[257] Adametz, Österreichische Molkerei-Zeitung, 318.

[258] These observations, however, refer to phenomena within a specific race or breed.

although unrecognized, there are systematic connections between color, markings, and the health, performance-capability, resilience, etc., of animals. However, it is still necessary to observe the skin and hair texture in order to draw conclusions in many other respects. Hair, like the skin, is alive and is to some extent closely dependent on the skin, and therefore the overall organism. Thus, as Henle already stated, it is indeed possible to draw conclusions about the degree of skin health from hair texture. If the hair is soft and shiny, it indicates well-hydrated and perfumed skin, whereas dry and brittle hair suggests a collapse of the bodily surface due to an inadequate circulation of fluids. Hair as such is a mirror of health.[259]

Only a few particularly relevant passages have been selected and cited here simply to demonstrate that skin and hair can be important factors in the study of a race or breed. However, we will never be able to obtain a reliable basis for research into the development of human skin if we know nothing about the environmental conditions in which it developed.

But once one has contemplated these interactions, it becomes very clear that the question of whether the Nordic race originated in the water-scarce, light-rich environment of the steppe or in the water-rich, light-deficient environment of the central European deciduous forests is by no means a secondary question but rather becomes the key to the entire problem. The author wants to at least draw attention to such connections.

It is possible that some readers may agree with the basic idea of these explanations, but may still object to the fact that we lack conclusive evolutionary evidence for the Nordic race from the point in time when we clearly identify a deciduous forest area in Europe. This objection is justified. But must the Nordic race be non-European simply because we happen to not have in our hands every single link in the chain of evidence? Or because we do not yet have the unbroken phylogenesis of the Nordic race? In the field of race science, it seems to be a foregone conclusion that a race can only emerge through prolonged isolation and continuous selection (culling) by the environment. However, the developmental history of our domesticated animal breeds proves that there are also other means and methods to bring about changes in a race or breed. Sometimes it is enough for a natural mutation to occur that proves to be particularly advantageous and is inherited across the board. For example, the renowned Russian breed of Orlov trotters traces back to a single stallion (Bars I), and the even more renowned English beef cattle breed of Shorthorns, spread all over the world today, can be traced back to a single bull (Hubback).[260] But let us now hear what one of our most successful practitioners in the field of cattle breeding, Dr. Peters, Director of Animal Breeding in Königsberg, has to say about such mutations:

---

[259] Zorn, *Haut und Haar als Rasse*.

[260] In the case of the two sires mentioned, however, the particularly fortunate coupling of homozygous hereditary factors also played a role.

So far, at least some of the researchers in the field of heredity have doubted the success of selection. However, breeders of large livestock have been able to counter this view with the fact that they were able to modify their breeds in the desired direction through selection within purebred populations (in other words, without crossbreeding with foreign breeds). Deviations are much more pronounced in large animals compared to small animals because they can be observed more easily by the eye. One should not underestimate the observational ability of breeders. They have an extraordinary sensitivity when it comes to assessing animals, and they can perceive deviations that remain invisible to the less initiated. This is the talent of the breeder. Therefore, I tend to believe that mutations have played a major role in the formation of breeds. It is conceivable that the small and most subtle deviations, captured by the livestock breeders in their breeding selection, have greatly contributed to the changes that livestock breeds undergo over time. Those who have observed the development of a type of livestock over a long period of time and reflected on how changes have occurred will likely come to the conclusion (in light of the recent advancements in heredity science) that some modifications can be attributed to mutations that were previously explained differently. German Black Pied cattle, whose main strains I am familiar with and whose development I have had the opportunity to observe for twenty-seven years, has undergone a particularly typical change in thigh formation during this time (among others things). The change was brought about by two bulls, Prinz and Poseidon. Before their time, the Black Pied cattle in East Prussia had thighs that were slightly too narrow. The breeders sought to eliminate this deficiency but did not want the round pig leg shape; instead, they wanted to maintain the beautiful, elongated lines of the thighs that indicated high milk yield. Suddenly, Prinz and Poseidon appeared with a thigh formation that fit the breeders' ideal. These two bulls were therefore highly valued and were the highest-priced bulls bred in Germany at that time. Prince and Poseidon were cousins, having been descended on their father's side from the two full brothers Junker and Kammerherr. Junker and Kammerherr were sons of Winter out of Ernestine, an Adda daughter. Since Winter did not possess this characteristic himself, nor did his parents, but Adda had similarly well-shaped thighs, I attribute this characteristic to Adda. I am not aware of where Adda obtained this trait. However, this body part had never appeared so beautifully before. Through the widespread distribution of the bloodline of Adda (through Prinz, Spinoza, Quinzow, Teufel, Anton), this characteristic has become a significant attribute of East Prussian Dutch cattle.

Breed development clearly shows that a change in type in the desired direction by breeders is always achieved, even in breeds that are not bred through crossbreeding but rather through selective breeding. The only variable is the time required, which can vary depending on whether one is more or less fortunate. The occurrence of influential sires such as Prinz and Poseidon was a stroke of luck for German Black Pied cattle breeding, and allowed them to bring about the desired modification. But even if this stroke of luck had not occurred, the breeders would still have achieved a strengthening of the thighs. They would have invariably preferred animals with broad thigh formation and built upon that foundation until the desired outcome had been achieved, albeit over a much longer period of time. This example only serves to illustrate the way in which a desired characteristic can be established within a type of cattle. Breeding work primarily involves scouting for animals that possess the desired traits to the greatest extent possible. When such an animal is found, breeders seize the opportunity and great investment is made.[261]

The author would like to emphasize that the examples presented here have been chosen completely at random from available literature on the history of our domesticated animal breeds.[262] Thus, the insights provided by Peters are particularly significant because he offers them as practical complements to the discussions by H.J. Muller and E. Baur (Berlin), who lectured on the frequency of mutations at the recent International Congress on Genetics, held in Berlin. The ideas developed by Peters demonstrate in a particularly impressive way that we need not necessarily only consider migration and geographic isolation when establishing assumptions about the formation of human races. Therefore, we can confidently maintain the standpoint that the Nordic race is indigenous to Europe and originated solely through particular circumstances—as of yet un-known—from another race by intra-racial displacement (by mutation). Whether this occurred through a single mutation or the sum of various muta-tions is irrelevant. Cro-Magnon man could be considered a precursor to the Nordic race. In this context, it could be of importance to note that the shift in racial image from Cro-Magnon to the Nordic race is also reflected in the ani-

---

[261] Peters, *Deutsche Landwirtschaftliche Tierzucht* 32.3: 53.

[262] In recent years, it has often been argued that there is no justification for applying experiences from domesticated animal breeding to the field of human racial studies. In the author's view, this objection is not valid. On the contrary, while it is true that one cannot directly apply experiences from domesticated animal breeding to human races, one can still use the breed history of our domesticated animals under all circumstances, just as knowledge gleaned from peas and corn can be used to explore the genetics of human heredity. Three essential categorizations can be applied from animal breeding: the quantity of offspring in a litter, the interval suitable for the repetition of births, and the duration of sexual maturity. Some examples may illustrate this claim: 1) The aver-age litter of a sow consists of ten piglets, while a mare gives birth to one foal; it is understandable that with ten offspring, a different genetic selection occurs than with one; 2) The sow repeats the litter after half a year, while the mare repeats the litter after a full year. In the same time that a mare produces two foals, a sow produces forty piglets; 3) A female piglet is capable of reproducing after one year, while a filly reaches maturity only after four years. By the time the second generation of horses is born, the fourth generation of pigs is born.

Thus, breed change in pigs will be faster than in horses to the extent that the three factors mentioned above provide an advantage in terms of time and genetic selection. In the case of hu-mans, even slower temporal conditions are at play. Five generations of successive mothers in im-mediate succession would theoretically take five years for pigs, twenty years for horses, and one hundred years for humans—and this is without even considering the possibility of difficulties, setbacks, and other contingencies. However, the essence of the matter concerning the emergence of breeds does not lie in these aspects, but rather in the time within which the process unfolds.

mals of the central European deciduous forest region; it is certain that these animals exhibit parallel phenomena. The enormous cave bear of the Ice Age has evolved into the smaller, more agile brown bear that we see today. The giant deer of that era has become the common deer we know today. The massive Ice Age wild boar (sus scrofa ferus antiquus) had to give way to the present-day wild boar (sus scrofa ferus). Here it is important to note that this transition obviously did not occur suddenly; instead, the smaller, more agile forms grew alongside the old, larger, more sluggish ones and later displaced them. In any case, the giant deer existed in our region until early historical times, and Pira[263] conducted enlightening research into the giant pig of the Ice Age, whose smallest discovered representatives still always surpass the largest living wild boars in size.

Therefore, it is entirely possible that Cro-Magnon man is the stock out of which both the Phalian race and the Nordic race emerged. The Phalian race would then be the branch that, most closely resembling the Cro-Magnon, managed to survive due to particularly favorable circumstances, while their counterparts in the animal world have since disappeared. For a researcher trained in animal breeding, it is in any case remarkable that the Phalian race has been observed precisely in areas that are known to animal breeders as habitats for certain heavy animal breeds. This is not to suggest that the Phalian race is necessarily the result of these particularly fertile regions, which promote exceptional growth in domesticated animals. However, there is a possibility that after the Ice Age, Cro-Magnon man encountered in these areas the very favorable living conditions necessary to sustain its physical power (massiveness) and, as a result, was able to persist. It then gradually transitioned into the racial image of the present-day Phalian race.

While on the subject, the shortened facial features of the Phalian race seems to be indicative of this fact. We have in the domestic pig an animal whose physical structures are remarkably similar to those of man. In fact, if one is looking for points of reference for the digestive processes of man in comparison with those of the animal world, one can most easily refer to the manifestations of the pig's body. It is quite curious that those breeds of domestic pigs which have been bred for heavy bodies have also developed broader, bulkier heads, while at the same time having shortened facial features. The English, by means of exaggeration, have bred pigs with veritable pug heads. Nathusius demonstrated that these changes in the pig's facial features were directly related to diet. He was able to produce completely different facial profiles (one straight, one concave) in purebred pig littermates simply by changing their diet. While these experiments initially only affect the appearance of the animals, the history of domestic pig breeds has shown corresponding phenomena. Nevertheless, one must be careful not to readily attribute these changes in facial features as evidence of fundamental changes to the skull. Facial features are undoubtedly closely related to the internal secretions of the body, which is not necessarily true of the skull (or at least has not yet been proven). The author

---

[263] Pira, *Studien zur Geschichte der Schweinerassen.*

has presented these examples from pig breeding to only show that, from the point of view of evolution, the Phalian and Nordic races may not be so far apart physiologically as one might think due to their skeletal differences. In any case, it would not be biologically impossible for the Nordic and Phalian races to have descended from Cro-Magnon man, but this should not be taken as a fact, only as something to think about.

In chapter four, the author had indicated that the greater part of Phalian emigrations apparently moved in the direction of Spain and northwest Africa, and we may obtain greater insights into the culture of the Phalian race there in the future. In the case of the Germanic peoples at least, both races, Phalian and Nordic, occur together, standing side by side on equal terms, rather than in a stratified manner. The following references will provide evidence for this. Apollinaris Sidonius portrays the Visigoth Theoderic II as being of a remarkably pure Nordic type, albeit of medium height. He states, "the crown of his head is round." He certainly did not mean this in the sense of round-headedness but rather in the sense that a particularly high curving line could be viewed from the side. Conversely, the Wilkina saga depicts Dietrich von Bern as being of tall build, broad and strong, albeit with black eyebrows, indicating mixed blood. In contrast, the Volsunga saga describes Siegfried as practically Phalian:

> He had a high nose and a broad and strong boned face. . . . His shoulders were broad—as though you were looking at two men. His hair was brown, but his eyes were so piercing that few dared to look beneath his eyebrows.

Remarkably, Turpin and Angilbert speak of similar eyes when referring to Charlemagne the Saxon Slayer, and also mention his towering stature. Eginhard even depicts him as very similar to the aforementioned Frankish Siegfried, "Charlemagne had a broad and strong bone structure, of great but not exaggerated height, with very large and lively eyes[264] and a slightly oversized nose." Widukind also emphasizes Otto the Great's "mighty physique that displays royal dignity."

In these descriptions, it is not of very much importance whether one can detect foreign blood influences or not, or whether one wants to attribute one characteristic to the Phalian race and another to the Nordic race. What is more important, however, is the fact that among the Germanic leaders, racial characteristics from both appear in a mixed manner. If the leadership of the Germanic peoples had been uniformly in the hands of representatives of the Nordic race, all the accounts would have also emphasized the Nordic appearance of the leaders and covered over or suppressed Phalian features. The descriptions would never have endowed Germanic heroes with Phalian traits. Of course, one can argue about what can be attributed to the Nordic race or the Phalian race in the above examples, but it must be conceded in fairness that a clear delineation between the two races is not possible.

---

[264] Hence the characteristic "Bismarck" eyes.

The very same impression arises when one objectively compares the surviving sculptures of Germanic people. Certainly, they are all distinctly Germanic or, as an animal breeder would say, "typical" of Germanics. But these Germanic individuals do not all look exactly alike. Such uniformity should not be expected, even if we were dealing exclusively with Nordic Germanics. Even in animal breeding, where the most selectively bred breeds possess "typical" breed characteristics, certain family differences (bloodlines) always persist so tenaciously that experienced experts of a breed can immediately identify the likely ancestors of an unspecified animal when presented with it.

Some researchers in the field of race science like to mention the famous passage in Tacitus' *Germania*, where, regarding the appearance of the Germanic peoples, he states that Germanic peoples are "a pure tribe of its own, equal only to itself." Some people like to use this as proof that the Germanic people must have been completely pure representatives of the Nordic race. But those who examine more closely what Tactius wrote at the beginning of this sentence will be a little more cautious in their judgment. Tacitus begins this sentence with the following caveat, "For my part, I agree with the opinion of those who . . ." Only then does he claim that the Germanic peoples are all the same. It is probably reasonable to conclude here that during Tacitus' time, there were apparently different views on this point, and Tacitus, based on his observations of some "typical" characteristics among the Germanic peoples, deemed it justified to assume a uniform descent.

Thus, in conclusion, the author would like to affirm that both the Phalian race and the Nordic race originated in the central European deciduous forest area. It is likely that both races can be traced back to Cro-Magnon man. Both races largely carried out their early historical migrations independently, and only in the Germanic period did they appear together and on an equal footing. In view of the fact that the Roman Empire collapsed under the onslaught of the Germanic peoples who had formerly lived on the right bank of the Elbe, it is perhaps not surprising that during the Migration Period the Nordic race predominated among the Germanic peoples.

4

However, it would be beneficial to conclude this section with a brief consideration of the weather conditions during the snow periods (Ice Age) in order to avoid any misunderstandings regarding the possible presence of deciduous forests in central Europe during the Ice Age. It is important to realize that previous discoveries of animals, humans, and plants of that time can be interpreted in any number of ways, and both nothing and everything can be deduced regarding the phylogenesis of a race. During this period, the animal and plant life of three continents (Africa, Asia, and Europe) occasionally converged in Europe. There were constant changes in the weather, which altered plant conditions and consequently the associated wildlife too. Often one species was replaced by another and everything simply became whisked together in a haphazard manner. For example, Walther notes:

Especially in times of significant climate change, terrestrial animals are driven to rather arbitrary migrations, losing any connection to the soil of their natural habitat. . . . The fauna of the Rabutz basin clays, a long-known site for diluvial mammals, was recently reexamined by Soergel and consists of the following species: Equus sp., Rhinoceros Mercki, Sus scrofa ferus, Alces cf. palmatus, Cervus capreolus, P. euryceros, P. elaphus, Bos primigenius, Bison priscus, Elephas antiquus, Cricetus, Canis cf. lupus, Ursus arctos, Felis leo, birds, Emys orbicularis, Esox lucius. Of these species, sixteen are relevant for the assessment of sedimentary conditions, namely all the terrestrial animals (even turtles are not decisive, since they are air-breathing animals). Therefore, the discoveries of *Esox*, which undoubtedly lived in the water where its remains were found in the mud, are all the more significant. The pike is a predatory fish that depends on other feeder fish, which in turn can only thrive in a water environment rich in aquatic plants. Therefore, the Rabutz clay could not have been formed in the cold meltwater of an ice tongue, nor could it have been a confined reservoir. Instead, it must have been connected to the general hydrographic river system. Any conclusions drawn from the hypothetically assumed lifestyles of the sixteen land animals that were found in the Rabutz basin as carcasses or hunting remains are invalid if they contradict the lifestyle of the only indigenous fossil.

If we have proven in this way that a temperate forest climate can be established for central Europe during the snow periods, then the same should be the case for Siberia. Even the most indisputable evidence that the Nordic race temporarily resided outside of central Europe during the snow periods is still by no means proof that they must have lived in a steppe during this time. Walter writes,

Experiments conducted in St. Petersburg (Leningrad) with the coagulated blood of a mammoth, as reported by Pfizenmeuer, revealed a blood relationship with the Indian elephant. The discoveries in eastern Siberia, according to von Toll, are post-diluvial, and he reports that the presence of willows, birches, and alders with large trunks and branches in the vicinity of mammoth carcasses is so characteristic that any attentive ivory hunter can expect lucrative prey in the vicinity of such subfossil plant remains, especially when he sees tree trunks of such plants protruding from a riverbank collapse. The same picture of a mild climate is presented by the plants found around the Borna mammoth, and also by the flowering plants found in the stomach of a mammoth as an unswallowed bundle of grass. This animal must have been trapped and quickly drowned while grazing in a swampy forest meadow.

On the other hand, even here in central Europe, there were times when conditions were favorable for steppe life. Walther writes,

> Since there is not a single German profile in which a more significant loess deposition has been observed between glacial till, I conclude that the actual loess is postglacial. Additionally, considering that in Inner Asia, lithologically identical loess is observed far from any glacial till in its largest distribution and greatest thickness, we cannot classify loess as formations necessarily associated with the glacial advances of large ice sheets. It was not the steppe that generated the loess; on the contrary, the lining of the late glacial hills by mud-laden rain showers created numerous flat areas of permeable loess soil and facilitated the establishment of steppe vegetation. Eventually, under its influence, the upper layer of loess deposits became blackened and transformed into chernozem, marking the end of the eventful history of the late diluvial period. If the formation of black soil were a simultaneous process with loess formation, thick loess deposits on the primary deposit should always exhibit horizons of black soil intercalation. However, along with the steppe vegetation, the grass-eating saiga antelopes migrated from Siberia to Germany, France, and even reached England via the land bridge that existed at the time across the Channel, where undeniable remains have been found in the Thames Valley."

It is probable (at least the author would like to assume) that Asiatic hunter-gatherers of the steppes also came to Europe with this Saiga antelope. Since it is believed that remnants of these hunter-gatherers survived in central Europe, it is likely that the racial image of these hunter-gatherers can be found among today's Europeans. It can be assumed, however, that these itinerant hunter-gatherers of the steppes, accustomed as they were to the steppe's relentless sun exposure, could never have brought the skin of the Nordic race (which is so sensitive to the influence of the sun) with them to Europe. The skin of such nomads must have been tough and resistant, capable of easy pigmentation, protecting its owner not only from the sun's rays, but also from the icy cold storms of the steppes, which often carry enormous quantities of sand, and which would not allow the development of delicate, easily inflamed skin. In short, such skin must be the opposite of the easily inflamed skin of the Nordic race. But what should we expect from such a postglacial nomadic invasion in terms of archaeological remains? What insight into the culture of such people would be gained by these remains?

As we saw in the previous chapter, nomads do not leave much behind during their migrations, so, at most, we can expect a few skeletons and perhaps an occasional weapon or two. With this in mind, we must consider the possibility of assuming the Ostic race as the hunter-gatherers who followed the Saiga antelope. This race "seeped" into Europe (in the archaeological sense), thereby showing characteristic nomadic behavior. The author is also convinced that the Ostic race was originally a nomadic race. When the steppe disappeared from Europe after a short time, the Ostic race seemingly got left behind in Europe. Exposed to a climate unfamiliar to their kind, this race underwent a modification of its original racial characteristics. It is certainly too narrow a focus to simply rely on the pigmentation ratios of the Ostic race to answer this question. More important would be a thorough study of the structure and characteristics of their skin and hair, for these would undoubtedly reveal the nomadic heritage of the Asian steppe, which this race once crossed in its ancestral history.

When considering such matters, one must always remember that the interactions between environment and race always occur within the framework of pre-existing (antecedent) racial characteristics, and do not simply cancel them out. When two races are exposed to the same environmental conditions, they will inevitably show similar, but never identical, characteristics because of the divergence that once occurred in their evolutionary history. If we consider the formation of races as a preliminary stage to speciation, we can see the playing out of the relevant biogenetic law. Once a divergence has taken place, no matter how insignificant it may be, it simply can never be erased from the record of phylogenic development.

We have enough examples in the phylogeny of our domesticated animal breeds to explain "intra-racial" shifts in a racial image without having to refer to crossbreeding or deliberately-guided breeding. Therefore, the author believes that the current phenotype of the Ostic race has been selectively bred through its prolonged presence in central Europe. Over time, the Ostic race came into contact with the indigenous settled population of Europe, who were Nordic and Phalian. Eventually, over the course of millennia, they adopted a genuinely settled form of existence. However, the author strongly disputes the notion that the Ostic race originally played a special role in the peasantry of central Europe. Had there been a clearer distinction, in statistics and the like, between the rural population and the actual peasantry, one would likely never have entertained the idea of considering the Ostic race as a characteristically peasant race, as is often done today. German villages where the Ostic race makes up the actual peasantry are likely to be rare, even today. Often, it can be observed that while the village may be populated by Ostic people, the long-established, genuine peasant family lines (the peasants of the "better farms," as they are often called in southern Germany) quite clearly belong to a different race—Nordic blood usually predominates quite conspicuously among these peasants. Among the other races, only the Phalian and Dinaric races may still be relevant to the old peasantry in the German-speaking countries, while the Ostic and East Baltic races probably originally constituted only a negligible fraction of our German peasantry. Whether the Western race might still be relevant to our peasantry somewhere, perhaps in a scattered enclave, the author does not venture to decide.

How little the Ostic race can be taken into account for our actual peasantry is, by the way, demonstrated by a factor which race researchers easily overlook. The main places of settlement of the Ostic race are always described as distinct "retreat areas," meaning areas to which a village community (or any other kind of human community) can retreat to when it is no longer able to defend itself against the enemy by force of arms. Retreat areas usually allow for an easy defense that a militarily superior enemy cannot quickly overcome. Such areas are most commonly found in the mountains of central Germany, which in earlier times provided even greater security for those pursued. These areas were even more impregnable for the attacker since the inherent ease of defense was further aided by particularly impassable primeval forests.

Such regions are generally precluded from engaging in actual agriculture, however, as they only allow for forestry and animal husbandry. Based on the history of settlement in Germany, it can be shown that there are areas (particularly in the Black Forest, the Lake Constance region, and the Alps) where there is still little to no agriculture, even today. Now, the author does not want to claim that these areas coincide with the main settlement areas of the Ostic race. But the author must point out the contradiction that arises when, on the one hand, the Ostic race is presented as a typical peasant race, but, on the other hand, settlement areas are assigned to them that are particularly known for their lack or insignificant practice of agriculture.

For years, the author has observed peasants in assemblies during his occasional professional travels. However, he has rarely encountered truly Ostic peasants, though in some regions a certain degree of Ostic admixture in old peasant families is not to be denied. When one comes across villages inhabited entirely by Ostic people, the village usually immediately stands out from the rest, at least in the eyes of an agriculturalist.

If one wishes to evaluate the rural population of a village in terms of racial history, it is necessary to also consider the settlement history of the village in question, especially the role that agriculture once played or continues to play in the village. This last remark is by no means meant to imply that all villages without agriculture belong to the Ostic race. On the contrary, there is plenty of proof of purely Nordic settled areas without agriculture (such as the region around Eiderstädt). However, the question of agriculture is important in determining whether the area in which the village is located was formerly an established retreat area. Occasionally, it may also be possible to determine, on a case-by-case basis, the era in which the village in question was introduced to agriculture. Only by considering the settlement history of a village can race science identify or understand the racial conditions of a particular village. Above all, one should pay attention to the movement of blood within the peasant families of a village. If the peasant families (a category which does not include all of the families living in rural areas) of a village today belong to the pure Ostic racial type, this does not prove that this was the case, say, one hundred or two hundred years ago.[265]

The infiltration of Ostic blood into our peasantry may not even have taken place all that long ago. The author would even speculate that it was only with the general introduction of the potato to our region that the Ostic race had the opportunity to take root among the German peasantry. The German peasantry originally fought the potato tooth and nail. The potato was the quintessential crop of small-scale farmers and settlers, and its cultivation was therefore originally considered a sign of poverty. Accordingly, the potato became the foundation of the so-called dwarf holdings (*zwergbesitz*). Without potatoes (relying solely on grain and live-stock raising), it becomes difficult to divide farms into smaller plots if one intends to support a family on them. The Ostic race appears to have infiltrated the old peasant population through these dwarf holdings made possible by potato cultivation. At first, it probably established itself geographically among the old peasant family lines; later, the occasional opportunity arose to also marry into the old family lines. This is supported, for example, by the fact that the peasant refers to an un-Nordic (Ostic) face as a "potato face," and that he calls a very ignoble nose shape a "potato nose." The term "potato farmer" was considered a dirty word for a long time. The proverb "The dumbest peasant always harvests the biggest potatoes" is quite revealing, because the peasant, who otherwise would never think of mocking a bountiful harvest, is suggesting that in potato farming, even a non-peasant without agricultural skills can achieve a good harvest. With this, the peasant is simply saying that people with potato faces and noses do not belong to him and his kind. Needless to say, these views no longer apply to modern potato farming.

It has already been repeatedly pointed out to the author that it is impossible to use the term "potato nose" in a racial sense, as it clearly appears to be nothing more than a good-natured, comedic designation for a different or unattractive nose shape. However, in the author's opinion, this objection is hardly justified. There must have already been "potato noses" in Germany before the introduction of the potato to Europe. Our peasants had plenty of examples of such noses in turnips or in tubers of other plants, and they certainly did not have to wait for the introduction of the potato in the seventeenth and eighteenth centuries to come up with such a term. Furthermore, the popularization

---

[265] Such matters are often relatively easy to verify through church records. The appearance or disappearance of surnames is a strong indication of racial rearrangement. The same is true of the appearance of foreign surnames by intermarried women, with particular concern arising when the wife's maiden name suddenly appears among the peasants and replaces an old surname. The latter phenomenon always indicates an influx from outside or, more importantly for race science, the economic advancement of former servants or other individuals of lower social status. Only when it can be demonstrated in a village currently inhabited by Ostic peasants that there has been no change or influx of surnames in that village for one hundred or two hundred years, and the records of the settlement history of the village do not report anything to the contrary, can such villages be used as evidence of the peasant nature of the Ostic race. However, until such evidence is presented to the author, he reserves the right to doubt the existence of an original Ostic peasantry. However, he does not doubt that we have some Ostic settlements in Germany who originated from peoples who knew only animal husbandry and not agriculture.

of a catchphrase requires that it is understood by everyone and that the humor behind it is universally appreciated. Therefore, the emergence of the potato and its apparent favoritism by individuals with non-Nordic nose shapes during the time when the witty expression "potato nose" emerged indicates that this was a widespread phenomenon that caught general attention.

Moreover, it must not be forgotten that the interbreeding between the Ostic and Nordic races (which can spread from the *instleuten*[266] within a peasant population) quickly works to the advantage of the Ostic race, especially if it is allowed to enter into equal marriages with the old-established Nordic peasant lines. By making this connection, the author is not so much concerned with the so-called "birth victory," a concern that is certainly relevant for races living next to each other—but rather with what might be more aptly described in zootechnical terminology as "displacement crossing." Displacement crossing is a breeding strategy that displaces a breed by deliberately crossing it with another breed; this is the cheapest and most common way to change the genetic traits of a herd or to replace one breed with another. In this case, breeding is continued only with the blood that is desired; among the resulting offspring, only the best suited blood is used for further breeding.

In crosses between the Ostic race and the Nordic race, the end result of this breeding is similar in nature to the displacement crossing of animal breeding. This is likely to occur unintentionally because of the racial correlations between the female pelvis and the shape of the skull. Under simple conditions (meaning without modern obstetrical assistance), a Nordic woman would probably never be able to give birth to a child with an Ostic head shape, while the reverse is undoubtedly possible. Perhaps gynecologists will one day express their opinion on this point, ensuring they assume simple conditions (without considering the possibility of specialized obstetrical assistance) to bring further clarity to this question. But if the author's suspicions are correct, the transformation of a Nordic peasant population into an Ostic one through replacement breeding must have proceeded at an almost frightening pace.[267]

---

[266] *Instleuten* was a common term for a rural population of lower social stature. This term typically referred to day laborers contractually bound to a specific farm or property. The term used to describe this population differed greatly by region, with *instleuten* being popular in northern Germany.

[267] Before finalizing this text, the publishing house received a letter from Dr. Liek of Danzig, stating, "One of my friends (unfortunately deceased two years ago), Dr. Herbert Krüger of Budwethen (Tilsit Lowlands), himself a thoroughly Nordic individual both inwardly and outwardly, wrote to me many years ago that the Nordic race in his rural district was being eradicated through childbirth. Nordic women could only give birth to Ostic children with the utmost difficulty. Either they perished during childbirth (as this was a rural area with very challenging road conditions, especially in winter) or only one child survived. Krüger himself was deeply affected by this recurring observation."

VI

The Central European Forest Peasantry of the Nordic Race

I

So far in our investigation, which began in modern times, we have descended deeper and deeper into prehistory. The probability of a peasant origin for the Nordic race can be proven without any gaps. Logically, it also follows that we may be able to learn more about the Nordic race from its peasant heritage. In other words, the peasantry of the Nordic race must be the most sensible way of gaining a better understanding of this race. The following chapters will attempt to offer evidence for this possibility. However, before we can embark on this task, this chapter will provide a brief sketch of the Nordic forest peasants of central Europe and their environment. The author knows from experience that it is difficult for many modern city dwellers to even imagine a free genuine peasantry, let alone the Nordic peasantry of prehistoric times.[268]

But before we can do just that, let us briefly address the question of what assistance archaeological prehistory can offer us in relation to these matters. In accordance with the aim of this book (to present arguments from a purely agricultural perspective), the author will refrain from consulting previous archaeological works. The value and achievements of archaeology in this area are undisputed. As such, it might still be useful to include a few basic remarks about such research aids. Anyone convinced that, in the field of pre-

---

[268] In this context, the author would like to recommend the novels by Sigrid Undset, which readers can refer to in order to gain an understanding of the ancient Nordic peasantry. These novels are published by Sandmeier and are available through Rütten and Loening, Frankfurt-Main.

historic research, only those who limit themselves to existing findings can claim to be scientifically rigorous may, among other things, be giving themselves over to a very gross fallacy. There is no field in which it is as easy to be unscientific as in archaeology, as researchers in this field can rigorously adhere to the preliminary results of an excavation without taking into account surrounding circumstances and the context in which the remains once lived. This has been demonstrated in an example from the history of domesticated animals, where Antonius is quoted as saying,

> I myself found, at the foot of a mound north of Aleppo, in close proximity to a Neolithic artifact, recent sheep bones that were clearly only a few weeks old! There should be no doubt in anyone's mind that if these sheep bones were covered with sand or debris next to the stone artifact, no one, not even the most skilled researcher, would be able to definitively determine the difference in age after the passage of several centuries.

An additional difficulty one must wrestle with when evaluating the subfossil remains of domesticated animals is their numerical ratios; these depend on all sorts of circumstances in which the remains of individual forms are found, and can very easily lead to misinterpretations. A particularly instructive example in this regard are the remains of domesticated animals that have been found on Dutch terps, dating from the beginning of the present era (AD) to the period of Frankish dominance in central Europe, thereby making them perfectly tangible in terms of history. Looking at the impressive collections of E. E. van Giffen at the Zoological Laboratory in Groningen, one might easily conclude that the ancestors of today's Dutch almost exclusively bred dogs along with large domesticated animals such as horses and cattle but possessed rather limited numbers of sheep and pigs. While there are several hundred complete skulls of the other animals available, the remains of sheep and pigs can be counted on the fingers of one hand! Even if one assumes that this abundance of dogs is indeed accurate, given that these mostly large and robust animals were primarily used to protect the homes, farms, and livestock on isolated homesteads during those tumultuous times, it becomes difficult to accept that sheep and pigs were less common by comparison! Consequently, there must be other reasons for the striking proportions found in the surviving remains, but it is not yet possible to do more than speculate about them. One possible reason may be that dead dogs were not exploited and used for cooking like slaughtered pigs or sheep. This very case, relating to a time and culture with which we are very familiar, clearly shows how a rash conclusion can be drawn from the rarity or complete absence of one animal form and the frequency of others.[269]

---

[269] Antonius, *Stammesgeschichte der Haustiere.*

Everyone will likely agree that we could easily apply these observations from the prehistory of domesticated animals to the prehistory of humans in Europe. Perhaps it will also be appropriate to mention here a phrase coined by the paleontologist Walther. Although it was coined for geologic research, it still has its relevance for us, "It will always remain our goal to point out the bionomic connections of different circumstances and to draw attention to the polydynamic interplay of natural forces instead of the one-sided monodynamic explanation."

In view of these things, the author wants to assert that we will never be able to flawlessly reconstruct the peasant culture of the Nordic race on the basis of archaeological evidence alone. In this field, everything can only be made plausible—never completely proven. The more one affirms the connection between the central European deciduous forest area and the peasant culture of the Nordic race, the less one can actually count on finding supporting archaeological remains. In Helsinki's open-air museum, an ancient Finnish farmhouse has been reconstructed and preserved, complete with all of its stables and outbuildings. One thing very noteworthy about this farmhouse is that apart from four axes and a few pots, nothing, absolutely nothing, in the entire extensive complex is made of artificial, inorganic materials. Not even the hearth, as it consists only of cleverly assembled natural stones. In order to even imagine such a farmhouse, you have to see with your own eyes how organic materials have been used to create the most incredible things—things that modern people can hardly imagine were made from organic materials (wood, bark, etc.), such as nails, farming and hunting tools, fishing equipment, and other things. However, if we ask ourselves what archaeological remains this farmhouse would leave behind, a surprising fact emerges—it would likely be limited to four axe blades, some pots, some charcoal and some sooty natural stones. Complicating matters further, it would be a particularly fortunate coincidence if archaeologists were able to find these few objects together in their original location during excavation, rather than scattered and found independently. What archaeologist would even dare to deduce the layout of such an extensive farm from a few broken potsherds, four axe blades, some charcoal, and a few soot-covered stones? Hardly any! And since everything in a central European forest area (similar to the Finnish farm in Helsinki's open-air museum) was surely made of organic material, we should not expect archaeology alone to provide us with conclusive insights—it can contribute nothing more than skeleton fragments to the investigation of the prehistory of north-central Europe. Only the biologist will be able to breathe life into this skeleton by integrating these prehistoric humans into the natural conditions of their existence.

So let's start by imagining the lives of these Nordic forest peasants in the most natural way possible. Vast deciduous forests covered north-central Europe west of a line that starts roughly in Königsberg (Prussia) and runs southwards to Odessa. Even in the Germanic period, these forests were incredibly abundant in wildlife. Thanks to the damage caused by browsing animals, these forests were not impenetrable like the jungles of the tropics, but were rather a more or less dense savanna forest.[270] It is important to emphasize this point because misconceptions about the nature of the forest can lead to misconceptions about life in the forest. In Scandinavia and Finland (although in Finland the true deciduous forest starts to recede), you can still experience the old Nordic primeval forest in their pristine state, provided you make the effort to venture off the usual tourist routes. But even here in Germany, remnants of the ancient Nordic primeval forest can still be found in the Harz Mountains (Brocken area), the so-called Bavarian Forest, and several other places where it has remained relatively untouched and true to its original form. Unfortunately, some of the old deciduous forest areas have since been replaced by other types of woods. Unwise water management practices and the obsession with evaluating forests solely from an economic perspective have led to the clearance of many old deciduous forest reserves.

In such a true forest area, animal husbandry was originally the standard agricultural way of life. Cattle are driven into the forest in late spring, where they remain until autumn (around mid-September), when they are herded and brought back to the stables. The author personally witnessed this ancient Nordic way of life in its original state during a short study trip to southwest Finland in 1926, and during a longer trip through Karelia (eastern Finland) in 1927. In Finland, winter fodder for the animals consists of birch leaf hay and pine bark, supplemented (if necessary) with a small amount of concentrated feed made from ground grains. According to Finnish farmers, the birch leaves must be broken in June to produce the best quality hay.

Although it is not possible to raise animals from highly specialized breeds in this way, native Finnish livestock still performs amazingly well on this diet. Thus, when investigating Finnish horse breeding conditions, the author was able to observe that despite their meager diet, the medium-sized Finnish horses are capable of achieving quite incredible performance.[271] The Finnish peasant often travels one hundred kilometers on two-wheeled carts to get to a market, on country roads whose actual surfaces are nothing more than rocky ground that has been rutted and weathered into a path over centuries. On these old country roads, with their arbitrary bends and even more arbitrary climbs and descents, the Finnish peasant travels the one hundred kilometers to the market at a more or less brisk trot and, equally important, makes his way back as soon as possible. During his trip, the author wrote about the Finnish horse:

---

[270] From a personal note from Metzger (Helsinki) to the author. Additionally, the publishing house received a letter from Dr. Liek (Danzig): "A year and a half ago, I spent several days at the estate of Privy Councillor Bier-Sauen in the Brandenburg region. He showed me the following in his approximately three-thousand-acre forest—several hectares at various locations were enclosed with fences, and no game was tolerated within the enclosures. Right beside them, on the same soil and in the same area, there were zones without fences. The difference was astonishing within just a few years. On one side, there was a thick and proper brushwood, and, on the other side, a young high forest. This was not even a particularly game-rich area. As a layperson, I would never have believed that such differences could occur in a short period of time."

[271] Darré, "Das Finnische Pferd."

During stays along a country road or during forestry work, the horse must make do with what the circumstances offer. It must be able to withstand the hardships of the Nordic winter night without additional protection and occasionally be satisfied with frozen feed. Moreover, the latter is often quite meager, as Finns in more remote areas (who even cut their bread flour with pine bark flour in lean years) can provide their animals with no more than what they have. If the Finnish horses can still perform well under these conditions at an advanced age, they are certainly giving themselves the best possible testimony.

Moreover, the performance of the cattle—which, by the way, are small (approximately 112 centimeters tall) hornless breeds of cattle, as described by Tacitus regarding the Germanic peoples—is quite satisfactory in terms of milk production for household needs, without receiving anything other than what the forest pasture provides for fodder in summer and winter. Even the sheep yield profits with this feed; lambs born in spring reach a slaughter weight of thirty kilograms after three and a half months of forest grazing. In winter, the sheep feed on birch leaf hay, which is harvested in June and then dried. As supplementary feed, a felled pine trunk was traditionally placed in the farm and stripped of its branches and bark, the latter of which served as food. The author has gone into these things in detail, because otherwise it would be difficult for the reader to get an idea of what livestock raising based on the exclusive use of forest pasture looks like.

In the Swedish language, the specialized terms for this method of ancient forest agriculture have been remarkably well preserved and have even entered modern technical agricultural terminology.

When one considers the enormous wildlife population of the ancient north and the abundance of predators within it (such as lynxes, bears, and wolves), it becomes understandable that the ownership of domesticated animals could not originally be safeguarded by each owner individually. Undoubtedly, the herds of a tribe were grazed together, which of course facilitated their defense. Such an explanation may solve the mystery of the ancient Nordic common land (*allmende*). Because of the original need for collective care of domesticated animals, the custom simply continued even after the forest and its predators had disappeared. This should not be taken too literally, however, for as late as 1817 some one hundred and fifty wolves were still being killed annually in the area around Trier. Nevertheless, this assumption is likely to be accurate because the legal concept of agricultural land has undergone a different development. It is important to note that farmland has always been family property. Arable land is never as vulnerable as livestock, as it is protected from wild animals by fencing. These fenced fields are still a common sight in Finland today. Von Amira writes,

> In the early South Germanic period, individual clans were allocated arable land for their exclusive use, while the grazing and forest land remained under communal usage. The unit of land ownership was the *hufe*, or lot, the *wohnland* (residential land), or the *pflugland*

(plowland). Everywhere, these units were understood to denote the amount of agricultural land needed to support a family, and for this very reason they could not have been the same size everywhere—they could only have been a local measure of land area.

Nothing, by the way, demonstrates the peasant origin of the Nordic race more convincingly than Indo-European land law in particular.[272]

At this point, it would also be beneficial to become acquainted with the results of Ihering's research on the ancient property law of the patricians:

The pasture-land was common property; private ownership of land was unkown in antiquity (all land was public property). The Germans and Slavs clung to this institution long after they had transitioned to agriculture, while Roman legends trace the introduction of private ownership of pasture-land back to Romulus, who allocated a *heredium* (meaning property, from *heres* in Old Latin, meaning owner, as still seen in the *Lex Aquilia*) to each citizen. The communal ownership of pasture-land nevertheless persisted among the Romans for centuries; *ager publicus (populi)* denoted public or common land, and was distinct from *ager privatus (privi)*, meaning private land, and therefore also with *proprietas (quod pro privo est)*. This was equally true among the Germanic and Slavic peoples. Thus, there can be no doubt that pasture-land was public property in the mother nation (which, according to Ihering, was the people of the ancestral Aryan homeland).

The driving together of herds belonging to different owners on a single pasture is unfeasible unless measures are taken to differentiate their ownership. Among the Romans, this was done by marking them

---

[272] To avoid any misconceptions, I will state the following. The socially-connected and communal aspects of Indo-European-Germanic (Nordic) land rights has nothing to do with modern communist notions of nationalizing land. *Communism*, in all its considerations, begins with the individual person—the mass is superior to the individual. When a certain territory is available to such a mass, it becomes the responsibility of its leadership to ensure that each individual within the mass, in enjoying this land area, does not suffer a deficit, in accordance with a general principle of equitable distribution. Essentially, this is nothing more than the simple transposition of the primitive nomadic grazing instinct to modern circumstances.

In contrast, the Nordic view of soil connectedness does not start from the unconnected individual person, but rather considers the *family* as the smallest unit within the collective. It employs the land precisely to sustain this unit.

Certainly, in both cases, the individual person is not able to dispose of land according to their own discretion. Nonetheless, these two perspectives (communist and Nordic) are the polar opposites of one another. Nordic soil connectedness fosters the family (marriage), while communism shatters the family and marriage, because communism, due to its nomadic grazing instinct, recognizes no intermediate unit between the individual and the whole herd. Consequently, communism quite logically fosters unconnected males and females, leading inevitably to matrilineal conditions, just as they naturally arise in wild animal herds.

One should not be mistaken. From a biological standpoint, both perspectives have an entirely *equal* right to exist. Viewed from the perspective of cultural evaluation, however, there should be hardly any doubt for any German about which perspective to choose.

(*signare*), with each animal being branded with the mark of their community as well as that of the individual owner.[273] In the case of sheep and goats, where the mark would be concealed by the growth of wool and hair, it was applied with paint. This explains the reference in Gaius[274] to *pilus* being brought into court to demonstrate ownership. *Pilus* in this case does not mean tuft of wool, or hair in general—this would have served no purpose in the statement of formal claim which was to take place at the hearing. Rather, it referred to the special portion of wool upon which the mark of ownership was painted in colors, and which could be cut off without having to bring the animal before the court of justice. With animals which had the mark branded into their skins, there was no other option aside from bringing the animals themselves before the court.

The brief summaries provided so far should have made it clear that a robust system of livestock raising and agriculture (as reported among the Indo-Europeans) can be quite naturally derived from the conditions of Nordic forest grazing and farming. Once again, the deciduous forests of north-central Europe appear to be the nucleus of Indo-European culture, or, from the standpoint of racial science, the cultural-foundational elements (*kulturunterlage*) of the Nordic race.

2

If a peasant is completely self-sufficient, agriculture will always play a lesser role, particularly if an abundance of game and livestock guarantees the main food supply. Until recently, it was possible to observe and study this agricultural way of life, most likely of ancient Nordic origin, in Finland. Part of the forest is cut down, the timber is used, and the rest is burned. After an adequate tilling of the soil, the summer crop is sown in the ashes. When the soil is exhausted, it is left to itself, and reverts back to forest. In the Swedish language, the connection between fallow land and reforestation has been preserved quite distinctly, as fallow land is called *träda*, and tree is called *träd*. The Swedish word for plowing is *plöja*, which has the same root word as our *pflügen* (meaning to plow). Additionally, the term *bruka* is or was commonly used to mean plowing, and also means to plow, to use, and to cultivate; *bruk* means to use and to cultivate. While the connection between clearing woodland and agriculture may not be explicitly evident from the last words, it is nonetheless probable. A cleared piece of forest land temporarily used for cereal cultivation is simply referred to as "in use." It is worth mentioning here the development of another word—as mentioned, *bruka* not only means plowing, but also "to cul-

---

[273] Virgil, *Georgics*: "at once they brand them with the marks of the owner and that of the community." Original Latin, "*continuoque notas et nomina gentis inurunt.*"
[274] Gaius, *Gaii Institutionum Iuris*, 4.17: "If it was a flock of sheep or herd of goats, a single sheep or goat, or a single tuft of hair was brought." Original Latin, "*...ex grege vel una ovis aut capra in ius adducebatur, vel etiam pilus inde sumebatur.*"

tivate a field," however, this expression can also be translated as *odla* in Swedish. *Odla* means to cultivate and nurture in the sense of education (in other words, what civilization actually means). *Odlare* refers to cultivation, and *odling* means both cultivation and the reclamation of new land, while at the same time implying civility or civilization in the broader sense. It is also important to note that the German word *adel* (nobility) derives from this term.[275] Here, the chain of evidence comes full circle—nobility, civilization, and peasantry are considered to be of equal importance, thereby proving the peasant origin of the Nordic race.

The utilization of forests for agriculture has also persisted in Germany through so-called Hauberg agriculture. In this form of agriculture, coppice forests of oak and birch are allowed to grow for a period of sixteen to twenty years. Afterwards, the trees are cut down and the ground is cleared using a *hainhacke* (a specialized type of hoe). The grass and small branches are then burned to serve as fertilizer. This newly reclaimed land is cultivated for two years and then left fallow for another twenty years, allowing it to be covered by new forest growth (the connection between fallow land and reforestation becomes very clear once again in this context). Hauberg forest management, also known as Hackwald forest management, is still practiced in Germany, particularly in the Odenwald region, the Hauberg forests of the Siegen region, and the Reuteberge mountains in the Black Forest. For those cultural historians who have established a precise chain of development from the hoe to the plow, they must decide which hoe-cultivating Negroes they wish to place these German peasants next to within their ranking system. While we're at it, it would also be enlightening to learn the rank of the Frisian peasants from the Eiderstedt marshlands, who use neither hoe nor plow on their farms.

In this context, it is worth mentioning a remark by Riehl, who noted that in his time there were still farming villages in the Westerwald which, despite the fertile soil, concentrated primarily on intensive livestock farming and harvested only as much from their fields as they absolutely needed for their own households.[276]

Such a way of life, which places the main emphasis on livestock raising with a small proportion of agriculture, is so natural for the northern region of central Europe that it is hardly surprising that it has been able to persist there. Evidently, there has been no moment of economic deprivation to force an intensification of cereal cultivation, even up to the present day. It must be admitted that this form of peasant life, while capable of instilling all the peasant virtues, does not in any way produce an overworked population bent under the burden of labor. On the contrary, except for the short planting and harvesting seasons, nothing is done in the fields— the peasant does not tend his livestock personally, and forestry work is spread out over the winter. Thus, like the Finnish and Swedish peasants (until recently), they had plenty of free time, at least until the ambition or compulsion to adopt "modern" agricultural practices was awakened in them. As the cattle are brought in dur-

---

[275] Günther, *Adel und Rasse*.
[276] These forested areas have no connection to the retreat areas of the Ostic race mentioned in the previous chapter. The distinction lies in the fact that, in the retreat areas, due to the terrain, no agriculture can be practiced, while in the areas just described, the decision of whether and what kind of agriculture to pursue is purely a matter of economics.

ing September or October but are not driven out until mid-April, there were essentially seven winter months in the old Nordic times, which, apart from the forestry work, provided ample time to alleviate boredom by participating in hunting expeditions and sharing hunting tales.

When Kern writes in *Artbild der Deutschen* that "the soul of peasantry is work that makes use of every hour," he is correct in a moral sense. However, if Kern intended this statement as a description of labor relations—and the overall context of that passage suggests such an interpretation—he is greatly mistaken. Such notions concerning agriculture may be applicable to the land-working slaves of the Orient (see chapter four), or to an unnatural serfdom situation among the peasants, but they are not applicable to the ancient Nordic peasantry. It was only when Emperor Frederick Barbarossa granted *fehderecht*[277] to the nobility that peasant life became burdensome for the German peasantry. This marked the beginning of the struggles between petty dynasties and knights, in which the peasant—due to his vulnerable position—often bore the brunt of the consequences (this reality did not apply equally to all peasant regions in Germany).

However, for those who still cling to the idea that the Nordic peasantry could not possibly have had a warlike spirit, it is important to realize how much hunting was associated with personal danger in early European history. Even today, hunting bears, lynxes, elk, and black boar with modern firearms is by no means without risk. Therefore, back then, it was undoubtedly much more perilous and required considerable courage. If this explanation is still not enough to make you understand how such manly heroism could develop, then we advise you to go on a bear hunt armed only with a spear and without a firearm. Hunting in central Europe with simple weapons not only required nerves of steel and a steady eye capable of fearlessly facing danger, but also required a body of iron tendons and sinews, and a heart and lungs that would not falter in the face of adversity. In short, it required nothing less than a combination of strength and agility. The battle cry of these hunters was not a sound for cowardly ears.[278]

It would be instructive to insert here a physiological consideration that will show how, in spite of the sedentary nature of the Nordic race, there is no obstacle to extrapolating its noble build. Hunting and the constant threat of danger from wild animals and other surprises in the Nordic wilderness undoubtedly required a nervous system with both high resilience and a quick reaction time, even in situations of extreme peril. However, the nervous system can only react so quickly in a body that has a fast metabolism. Ultimately, every vital activity of the body origi-

---

[277] *Fehderecht*, literally "feuding rights," was the right of feudal lords in medieval Germany to engage in private feuds, which were often violent and indistinguishable from warfare. By legally recognizing these feuds, the emperor sought to bring these conflicts under Imperial oversight.

[278] In Egon von Kapherr, we find a modern writer who, in an engaging manner, introduces us to life and activities within a Nordic primeval forest. Reading such books is recommended for two reasons. Firstly, many ancient hunting customs have been preserved in the north to a greater extent than is commonly assumed. Secondly, one will never arrive at useful conclusions regarding the early history of the north without clear notions of how life unfolded in a Nordic primeval forest and what this Nordic primeval forest actually looked like. The cataloging of petrefacts has not propelled geology forward on this question, and there is no reason to believe that ethnology should achieve different success in this regard.

nates from its smallest structural units—its cells. A small cell, due to a larger surface area in relation to its size, is better equipped for robust metabolic processes
compared to a larger cell that inherently has a smaller surface area relative to its
size.[279] Consequently, in animal breeding, a fine constitution can be observed in
all animal breeds that are required to achieve high physiological performance,
thus necessitating an energetic metabolism within the body. This can be seen in
noble horses, cattle with exceptionally high milk yield, and sheep with very fine
wool. "A fine constitution, however, is always associated with a dry, noble appearance. Such animals exhibit a smooth glossy coat, a more slender, upright body,
well-defined bone prominences, expressive joints, and clearly defined, sharp tendons." This statement about the phenotype of an animal breed with a fine constitution, taken directly from a textbook on animal breeding, can also easily be used
to characterize the phenotype of the Nordic race.

Nevertheless, the author would like to present some additional evidence
from animal breeding to demonstrate that the formation of the Nordic race from
a more general racial background is quite conceivable without necessarily attributing it to geographic isolation. The following examples aim to highlight that
the distinction between free peasants and noble peasants, as shown in chapter
three, can also be attributed to a strictly performance-based type of breeding,
without the need to invoke racial superimpositions as an explanation for this
phenomenon.

Let us continue with the concept of a fine constitution here. A fine constitution is always developed through breeding as a result of the need for a strong
metabolism in the body. In the case of the Borzoi, a Russian breed of sighthound,
we have an excellent (if perhaps somewhat exaggerated) example of a body capable of withstanding the highest levels of stress on the heart and lungs. It is striking that while this sighthound still has the same skull length as its wild ancestor,
it has nonetheless clearly acquired a quite narrower skull due to the refinement of
the cellular structure of its body. For in some way, the refined cellular structure
must manifest itself, and if, for whatever reasons, the length of the skull cannot
decrease, then the width must simply accommodate. Hand in hand with this
cranial development, the sighthound exhibits a distinctly convex profile in the
bridge region of the nose, as well as remarkably long and finely articulated limbs.
As Hilzheimer[280] rightly states, "It is not the length of the skull that is the most
important characteristic, but rather its narrowness, as well as the steep position of
the side walls formed by the upper jaws, often accompanied by a convex facial
profile."

The striking correspondence in the direction of biological development between the human Nordic race and the canine sighthound breed is surely obvious.

But this does not yet prove that it was the environmental pressures of life in
north-central Europe that selectively developed the Nordic race in a specific direction. Rather, it only seems to show that the Nordic race (in keeping with
Kern's perspective) acquired its characteristics in some sort of steppe environ-

---

[279] Malsburg, "Die Zellengröße als Form."
[280] Hilzheimer, *Natürliche Rassengeschichte der Haussäugetiere.*

ment, though one cannot sensibly imagine why the ancestors of the Nordic people would have roamed the steppes so much that they eventually transformed into what is now the Nordic race with a sighthound-like phenotype. After all, the sighthound achieved its present genotype by being selectively bred in a manner that artificially exaggerated its innate predispositions and is not a product of the steppe per se. This, in turn, is related to the fact that the breed is very difficult to maintain through breeding and whose constitution has a tendency to coarsen.

In order to demonstrate that it is entirely possible to assume the development of the Nordic race locally on the basis of breeding selection criteria, the following research results are presented, which may be of utmost importance for understanding the formation of races or specific variations within a type. At the Institute of Animal Breeding at the University of Breslau, the director, Professor Zorn, and two of his assistants (Dr. Gärtner and Dr. Heidenreich) have carried out a very precise study of constitution and individual performance in a purebred flock of sheep.[281] The details of the study cannot be discussed in detail here. Only this much can be said—the Merino meat sheep herd of the Prussian Experimental and Research Institute for Animal Breeding in Tschechnitz has been there since 1925 and was purchased from the internationally renowned Wenig-Rackwitzer breeding stock, which has been in existence since 1806 and, during this time, has not only been meticulously bred, but has also achieved a remarkably balanced nature through systematic breeding toward a clear breeding objective. This is further enhanced by the fact that for decades, sires have been almost exclusively blood-related. In this way, the differences between individual constitution types within the herd were therefore minimized, and the variation range in terms of all characteristics and properties was naturally extremely limited. Consequently, a layperson in animal breeding would find it incredibly difficult to distinguish one sheep from another within this flock. However, during the experiment, certain notable differences were observed, which are presented here in excerpt. The author apologizes to readers who may not be trained in terms of biology or animal breeding, as he will not delve into explaining the technical terms used. It would almost be a separate task in itself to introduce a layman to this field. An explanation of the highly intricate and meticulously executed examination procedure must also be omitted here.

The first significant result of the research was that a pronounced early maturity (body weight after the completion of the first year of life) and relatively coarser wool was generally associated with a higher blood dry matter content, lower blood alkalinity, and longer blood coagulation time.

Additionally, the arranging and examination of the families of the bucks revealed that within these families, the aforementioned interrelationships are even more clearly pronounced than in the overall research.

Moreover, the research revealed that there are indeed positive interrelationships between the head width index and constitutional predisposition and performance. The wider the head, the more precocious the yearling is, with a correspondingly high blood dry matter content and low blood alkalinity. Con-

---

[281] Wettstein, *Züchtungskunde*, 3, no. 5.

versely, the narrower the skull, the later the respective yearling matures, with a lower blood dry matter content and higher blood alkalinity.

Furthermore, a corresponding family-based comparison revealed that within the herd, there was a concurrent relationship—on one hand, a high head width index correlated with higher blood dry matter content, lower alkalinity, thicker ears (indicating coarser skin), and a larger circumference of the cannon bone; on the other hand, a low head width index was associated with lower blood dry matter content, higher blood alkalinity, finer ears (indicating finer skin), and a smaller circumference of the cannon bone (indicating slimmer, finer bones).

It should be noted that in this case, we are not comparing different breeds, but rather observing these differences within a herd that has been purely bred for decades and is internationally renowned for its balanced nature and breed purity.

However, the other findings of the experiment are also quite revealing. The bodies of the animals were subjected to a state of hunger, and various environmental influences (including feeding) were then introduced. This measure aimed to disrupt the physiological balance of the body and induce so-called shock effects. The outcome was also such that the animals responded in varying ways, and it was quite evident that these responses differed on a familial basis. However, these shock effect experiments could not be carried out to completion due to economic considerations that had to be taken into account for the herd, which prohibited any health risks to the valuable breeding animals.

Nevertheless, this zootechnical experiment demonstrates that no biological contradiction arises when considering the development of a fine-featured, delicate-skinned, and narrow-headed performance type within a human race, which becomes the "nobility" and then seemingly creates the impression of a superimposed racial stratum. Conscious breeding toward the two constitution types, as observed in the herd, would result, for example, in bloodline divergence, potentially bringing out at least two distinct types. This would then correspond, in a metaphorical sense, to the assumption that among the Germanic noble peasants, the "finer" branch is seen, while among the free peasants, the coarser-built branch of the Nordic race is observed. In chapter nine, the author will demonstrate that in the Nordic race, there indeed existed a performance-based breeding that had to or could produce a noble type characterized by a fine constitution and physical agility.

Therefore, one sees that despite affirming the existence of a Nordic peasanthood, there would be not the slightest difficulty in assuming the formation of a noble race in the north of Europe. Agility, in any case, was significant among the Germanic peoples despite their stature. For instance, the Teuton king Teutobod, who surpassed the Roman triumphal insignia in height, could leap in full armor over the backs of four and six horses. Although we need not attribute excessive height to these horses, and many students at the Berlin College of Physical Education would attempt such a jump today, the agility displayed by the king, given his reported height, is nonetheless very noteworthy. Something similar to Teutobod can be found in the weapons skills of the Gothic king Totila, indicating his great dexterity.

In addition, it should be noted that the Nordic race was likely predominantly reliant on a protein-based diet, and it is even possible that this diet played a decisive role in the emergence of the Nordic race. Abundant protein intake coupled with ample physical activity results in larger bodies—this is a fundamental principle in animal breeding, grounded in empirical evidence. However, in our current understanding of human nutritional physiology, we undoubtedly suffer from a form of plant-based mental disorder (vegetarian psychosis). Many hold the view that a nearly pure protein diet is either impossible or at least detrimental to health. In this context, it may be enlightening to present the winter menu of a Finnish peasant, as recorded by the author. It includes bread, dairy products, meats (raw, dried, or smoked), and fish (either air-dried or that has turned sour in a weak salt brine, all of which are consumed raw). As a variation, roasted fish or wild game, as well as cereal gruel, are also consumed. It is worth noting that Finland no longer possesses the abundant wildlife that was once readily available to the Nordic race prior to the Germanic Migration Period. It would be quite odd if the high protein diet and the significant demands placed on the nervous system, coupled with an entirely healthy lifestyle, did not result in the Nordic race being as beautiful and noble as it is manifested today in its physical appearance. Besides, in Grant's book *The Passing of the Great Race*, he emphasizes that the Nordic individual is a hearty meat-eater, a viewpoint with which the author absolutely agrees with.

At this point, a brief remark on constitution must be inserted. In the field of animal breeding, as well as in human race science, the study of physical constitution remains somewhat untouched. However, a fundamental difference can already be observed in the approach taken by both disciplines. In animal breeding, only the healthy animal is considered, and all studies on constitution are based on healthy specimens. In contrast, influenced by medical science, human race science attempts to infer the healthy state from the diseased individual (Kretschmar).

For these reasons, animal breeding today resists adopting the methods and designations commonly used in human constitution research. Professor Walther (Hohenheim), the well-known champion of Mendelism in the field of horse colors, recently criticized attempts (primarily introduced by veterinary medicine) to apply such views to animal breeding. During the Spring Conference of the German Society for Breeding Science (which took place on February 1, 1928 in Berlin), he stated,

> While it is undeniable that the biological foundations for humans and domesticated animals are the same, one must still not lose sight of the fact that the attempts to impose order on the chaotic array of constitutional forms among civilized peoples by establishing habitus types represents a stage of primitive understanding that animal breeders in civilized countries have long since surpassed. The civilized

man, abandoned by both natural and artificial selection, is the most neglected mammal in the world from a breeding perspective.

Animal breeding has today established a relatively clear division of labor. It entrusts the care of sick animals to veterinarians and only concerns itself with healthy animals for breeding concerns. In the same vein, it has been Prussia's initiative for several years now to clearly separate the scientific and practical training of animal breeders and veterinarians, recognizing that they represent quite distinct fields of work. To avoid any misconceptions regarding the terminology, it is necessary to explain what animal breeding considers as "healthy." An animal is considered healthy by the breeder when all vital processes related to respiration, digestion, overall metabolism, and reproductive functions occur undisturbed and consistently.[282] Naturally, when assessing an animal's suitability for practical use rather than breeding purposes, different criteria apply. One will understand that animal breeding was, in a sense, endowed from the very beginning with a different approach to the question of constitution than the one that human race science (influenced by medical science) could adopt. Above all, animal breeding does not equate the concepts of breed and constitution, nor does it attempt to establish an equivalence. An example from horse breeding illustrates this very well. The Arabian and English thoroughbred horses do not differ constitutionally, but in zootechnical terms they belong to two different breeds. As a breeder, one must choose either the English or the Arabian thoroughbred. Considering why both horse breeds possess the same constitution unfortunately does not aid the breeder in making breeding decisions. This is not to say that the issue of constitution is completely resolved for animal breeders, on the contrary! The author merely suggests that animal breeders, first, do not confuse the question of constitution with the question of breed (although interactions between the two must obviously be considered) and, second, that they approach the study of constitution from the perspective of healthy animals rather than focusing on individual cases of disease. Constitutional deviations of a pathological nature are thus relegated to where they belong, in the hands of a veterinarian. The sharpness with which animal breeding distinguishes between the healthy and the sick may be illustrated by the words of one of our most outstanding horse breeders, Stable Master von Oettingen:

> The only flaw that should never be forgiven in a breeding animal is ill health and its associated weakness.[283] Being overly cautious about other faults, which ultimately cannot all be avoided, is the straightest path to inferiority.[284]

---

[282] Determining whether an animal is healthy or not is naturally the initial responsibility of a veterinarian, as is the case in any assessment of livestock, where a veterinarian is consulted as an advisor. However, once the animal's health has been confirmed, the subsequent actions lie within the purview of the breeder and are no longer within the domain of the veterinarian.
[283] Weakness in the sense of physical susceptibility to diseases and other physiological disorders.
[284] Oettingen, *Die Zucht des Edlen Pferdes*.

The author has delved somewhat deeper into these questions here in order to avoid any misunderstandings among proponents of human race science regarding the concept of constitution. Furthermore, the author hopes to have demonstrated in this chapter that there are no biological contradictions when it comes to deriving the appearance of the Nordic race from a settled existence in the deciduous forest regions of central Europe.

VII

The Peasantry as the Key to Understanding the Nordic Race

I

In this chapter, it is not the author's intention to provide a scientific justification for the peasant character of the Nordic race. Rather, he will attempt to derive certain qualities characteristic of Nordic man from his original peasant heritage.

To be a peasant means to be free. He who lacks the agency to freely manage his life and cannot make good use of the fruits of his activity as he wishes is not a peasant, but a steward or a tenant, a servant or a serf. When the Nordic race first began establishing its characteristic single-farm settlements, this was the moment when man's herd instinct, perhaps natural in itself, was broken. In this environment, man evolved to be self-reliant and confident in his own abilities. The term "unfree peasant" is inherently contradictory and should disappear from the German language. No other way of life in early history was able to instill such a marked sense of freedom than the way of life of the peasant, a lifestyle that was best exemplified by the Nordic individual farmstead. On the Nordic individual farmstead, you either have something to offer or you do not. If we recall the nomads, whose strength lay precisely in their ability to suspend awareness of individual personhood for the benefit of the tribe, we can see that the uninhibited awareness of individual personhood and personal freedom typical of the Germanic peoples is by far most easily and naturally derived from their peasant origins.

Merk[285] says of the Germanic people:

> In the lands they conquered, by means of their settlements and land laws, they did away with the depopulation of rural areas and the unhealthy dominance of cities, restoring a strong peasantry. To a world enslaved by the all-powerful Roman state, they brought back personal freedom.

It was only in those regions of Germany where the peasantry was subjugated in the late Middle Ages that the unfortunate saying first appeared, "Bend your back and God will help you." But it would cost rivers of blood before the German peasantry reached this stage in certain areas. After all, by no means were all regions subjugated, especially in northwestern Germany. The German Reich owes the loss of two of its most prosperous provinces (Switzerland and the Netherlands) to pernicious attempts to force our free German peasants into an un-German state of slavery.

To be a peasant means to know one's craft. The peasant must master every task necessary for his way of life, even if he does not participate in the work himself, in order to be able to instruct his workers and judge their work. No farmhand should have the opportunity to hoodwink their peasant employer, and no peasant should ever order his men to do something that he does not know how to do himself. It is precisely in Germany's oldest and freest peasant communities that the custom of sending farm heirs to other peasants as apprentices has persisted the longest, for "one who aspires to command well must have served well beforehand." Therefore, on rural agricultural operations, the relationship between employer and employee is fundamentally different than it is in the city. Among the peasantry, reality is absolutely separated from illusion, and one's vision is sharpened to spot the essential—incompetence is always recognized and put in its place. "Accomplish much, stand out little, be more than you seem," these words from Count Schlieffen, though coined for the German General Staff, definitely stem from a peasant mindset and is an embodiment of the ennobled peasanthood.

To be a peasant means working actively on one's farm, not to sit on it as a parasite. The peasant is the first and highest authority on the farm. Thus, the peasant attains a consciousness of self and a self-confidence. The uncorrupted peasant is not ashamed to be a peasant—on the contrary, it is much more natural for him to underestimate anyone who does not wear overalls. When the Transylvanian Saxon wishes to express his respect for a man, he says "he is one of us," and in Hesse, clear memories of the old glories of a free peasantry are preserved in the saying "a peasant requires four horses," meaning that the peasant is allowed to ride "four-in-hand."

A charming anecdote recounted by Riehl illustrates the characteristic pride of the peasant as he looks down upon urbanites:

---

[285] Merk, *Vom Werden und Wesen.*

An esteemed jurist, who is still alive today, was designated by his peasant father, as a late born son, to learn the butcher's trade. But since the somewhat delicate boy couldn't bear the sight of blood, the old man declared that he should study law, as he was "too weak" to learn something "proper."

Riehl then makes the rather sober observation that the peasant acted wisely in this case, for otherwise, the son would have only turned out to be an average butcher instead of becoming a skilled jurist.

The true peasant, who is invariably Nordic, Phalian, or Dinaric, harbors deep within his heart a profound and often silent contempt for the urbanite or non-peasant. Urbanites would likely have a different opinion of peasants if they did not insist on stumbling blindly through nature, failing to comprehend the thoughts hidden behind the brows of our peasants.

But let us return to the relationship between the peasant and his farm. The farming operation exists not only for the peasant but also vice versa. The peasant manages the whole operation—he is the head, and the others are the limbs. However, as a collective, they all clearly work for the benefit of the operation. Consequently, they all perceive the operation as a totality, in which the peasant is integrated as a part, albeit the main one. Being a peasant, then, means having an overall understanding of the organic interplay of forces at work. The peasant's self-confident sense of freedom and his sense of responsibility toward his work and his farm are at the heart of the freeman's sense of duty. Service to his work and way of life becomes the noblest act of the free individual. The phrase "I am merely the first servant of my state" is nothing more than the Nordic peasant's worldview elevated to royal lordship. The Nordic peasantry gave humanity that moral standard that measures the actions of a free individual by a standard higher than merely one's own self-interest. It was here that the Nordic race, while still in its cradle, kindly received from Providence a gift out of which its most remarkable trait may well have blossomed—the profound inner desire of the Nordic man to dedicate his life in service to a cause or a work, and deriving his own internal moral guidelines from the necessities that determine this work.

It is said that the peasant is tough because his emotions are directed toward what benefits his farm. But are not the renowned Prussian *staatsraison* and the Anglo-Saxon motto of "right or wrong, England first," tangible consequences of this peasant mentality?[286] It is perhaps worth recalling that it was the peasant Cromwell who laid the foundation for the British Empire,

---

[286] In the following, one will come across assessments of the English and England that may occasionally deviate from what is currently assumed in Germany. The author by no means claims to be an expert on England. However, having been raised alongside young Englishmen during his youth as an *auslandsdeutscher* (German living abroad), and having some firsthand familiarity with the English school system, he deems himself entitled to express his opinion on the English.

In Germany, the assessment of the English is often based too heavily on their foreign policy, without considering how greatly one would deceive oneself if one were to judge the Germans solely based on their foreign policy. This applies not only to the present but has been true since 1888.

and that his Prussian-trained counterpart Bismarck was dubbed by his opponents as the "diplomat in wooden shoes" for good reason. Riehl states the following about the peasant:

> The peasant is far removed from any modern sentimentality and emotional romanticism. The family is holy to the peasant, but we will search in vain for an affectionate love for parents, siblings, and spouses. Unfortunately, it is all too well known that in rural areas, for example, there is a lack of reverence among adult children for their elderly parents, especially when the parents, upon reaching old age, transfer all their possessions to the children in exchange for the duty of "supporting" them (providing them with food and care until death).

Perhaps it is here that we will find the key to understanding a peculiar tradition among the patricians of ancient Rome. Originally, the patricians disposed of the elderly by throwing them into a river from a bridge—this activity fell under the responsibility of the Vestal Virgins. Later, straw figures were used instead, and these were thrown into the river in place of the elderly. In this regard, Ihering mentions the following,

> Even to this day, in a region near the Elbe in Hannover, a saying in the Low German dialect has survived. Locals report that it was recited in ancient times as the elderly were thrown from a bridge into a river, "*Kruup ummer, Kruup ummer, de Welt is di gram,*" meaning "Crawl under, crawl under, the world bears you ill will."

In chapters two and three, we discussed the peasant nature of the Nordic nobility. However, a brief review of this topic is called for here. In addition to the etymology of the word "noble," which, as noted above, derives from property rather than blood, the fact that the term *hof* (the peasant's very way of life) is still used today to denote the residence of kings (*hof* meaning farm or court) may also serve as evidence of how fundamentally peasant in nature the nobility has always been. The concept of kingship was originally so peasant in character that the peasant identity of the king could not be separated from his person. Schäfer writes, "In all medieval states, court offices (seneschal, marshal, cupbearer, chamberlain) played a decisive role; they all originated from the Germanic household and had no connection with Roman institutions."

What if the whole secret of Germanic kingship could be easily traced back to the Nordic peasantry as an idea that originated in the peasant's worldview, was intensified to monumental proportions, and allowed no separation between the person of the leader and his ownership of the land? The question is by no means as absurd as it may seem at first glance. According to the Nordic view, a king's power extended only as far as his land, not the reach of his sword. Here again, the Nordic race drastically separates

itself from any form of nomadism. The people living within the king's borders were subject to him, but they were not serfs—only certain rights belonging to the subjects were transferred to the king, in return for which he
took on certain obligations. The Nordic race was at first completely unfamiliar with the concept of absolute power and only ever learned of it under
the influence of foreign races. The entire Nordic kingship is conceived of in
the most peasant way possible and stands in clear contrast to a nomadic
rule detached from the land.

Indeed, some aspects of German kingship seem to have been more
peasant in character than one might initially think. An example from the
history of domesticated animals will illustrate this. According to our understanding, the ermine mantle is the insignia of princely and royal dignity.
Upon closer examination, however, this royal garment reveals itself to be a
fairly peasant object. Today, the domestic cat, descended from the African
wildcat, has become a familiar and commonplace creature in every peasant's home—it is a faithful assistant to every farm and housewife in the
arduous battle against the armies of mice. But that was by no means always
the case. Germany only became acquainted with the domestic cat through
the spread of monasticism, around the tenth century AD. Its introduction
was initially met with strong resistance (it is certainly obvious that our domestic dogs have still not adjusted to this change). Prior to the arrival of
the domestic cat, Germanic peasant households kept tamed weasels instead,
specifically the European large weasel (*putorius nivalis*) and the ermine
(*putorius ermineus*), as well as some other animals for the same purpose,
although their presence is not as clearly documented as that of the
weasels.[287] Therefore, at that time, these creatures were as commonplace as
domestic cats are today. Just as no one today would consider a fur coat
made of cat fur to be particularly valuable, no one a millennium and a half
ago regarded the ermine as something extraordinary. The close association
of the ermine mantle with royal dignity can then only have been intended
to express something that everyone understood, much like the uniforms
worn by the Hohenzollern princes. Therefore, the only thing we can assume is that the ermine coat was a way of proving one's "peasantness" or, in
other words, this peasant insignia made one's affiliation to the most distinguished and highest estate clear, just as the uniform did for the kings of
Prussia.

In some places (including certain regions of France), it is customary
for the rural population to adorn images of saints with peasant garb on
certain festive occasions. The peasant's traditional garment was originally
the most precious ceremonial attire for the peasant. This practice can by all
means be brought into connection with the thoughts we have just developed about the ermine coat. The peculiar fate of the Dutch pantaloons,
which, through the rise to power and wealth of the original peasant settlers

---

[287] Ludwig Reinhardt, *Kulturgeschichte der Nutztiere* [Cultural History of Domesticated Animals] (Munich: 1912.

of New York (United States of America), are now returning to Europe as the "latest fashion," of course provides us with tangible proof that a peasant garment can attain the highest esteem. Once we embark on the task of unearthing our ancient German peasant culture, we may perhaps encounter many surprises in the aforementioned realm. Anyone who has ever seen the crowns worn by the bride and groom in Schwalmstadt will inevitably come to think of the crown as an emblem of princes and kings, which would definitely agree with the theories developed here.

To a contemporary urban mindset, which for decades has been accustomed to using the term "peasant" as something akin to a license for stupidity, describing the peasantry as the highest social class (as exemplified by the ermine mantle) may not make much sense. However, those who are willing to delve into ancient Nordic culture and also possess the ability to think and feel like a peasant will encounter peasantry in every aspect of ancient Nordic life, and will never encounter signs that a non-peasant master class parasitically ruled over a peasantry.

Rembrandt once said "Idealism is dangerous for rulers." By this he means to say that rulers who lose sight of reality can easily lose their thrones. This applies not only to all rulers but also to peasants. Working on a farm is an entirely real affair. It forces the peasant to correctly establish causal relationships between things; otherwise, they may soon find themselves reflecting on cause and effect in unfortunate circumstances. Genuine peasant life thus cultivates an ability to calculate "with given variables." But it also trains the peasant to accurately assess the impact of his actions in advance, in other words, as the saying goes, to apply the lever in the right place. In this way the Nordic race has received, in terms of its evolutionary history, the seed of that peculiar aptitude for genuine politics which so distinguishes it. It is no coincidence that deeply peasant peoples, such as the Romans, Prussians, and Anglo-Saxons, have also been masters of politics (the author hopes that we are only at the beginning of this development here in Prussia). It is worth mentioning here, however, that it is definitely no coincidence that the coup attempt in Vienna on July 15, 1927 collapsed due to the stance of the Austrian peasant communities.

The political thinking of the Nordic peasant extends from their way of life to the individual and their community, progressively encompassing wider circles, ultimately incorporating kingship as the pinnacle of peasant-hood in a grassroots structure. This can be quite clearly demonstrated in cases where Nordic peasant life was able to develop freely, as seen with the Dithmarschers of the Middle Ages.[288] The Dithmarschers had a strictly structured, free, cooperative existence that, for a long time, was able to assert itself based on its own capabilities, even without the support of im-

---

[288] The development from the Germanic peasant assembly (*thing*) to the modern state structure, evolving from the bottom up, has recently been elucidated through a brief examination of Swiss history by Dr. Fick of Küßnacht (Zürich). Refer to Fick's work *Deutsche Demokratie* [German Democracy].

perial charters. Regarding the land cooperatives of the Germanic peoples, von Amira states,

> Generally, a leader (bailiff, marchwarden, chief marchwarden, forest count) was responsible for implementing the decisions made by fully vested members of the cooperative's march or borough assembly. This was the natural organ for both self-legislation and jurisdiction within the cooperative, to the extent that they constituted a legal entity (often with their own criminal law), as is customary in Germany.[289]

Here, then, the appointed public official based on the principle of self-administration becomes quite apparent. This racially Nordic view of the state, emanating from the bottom up, stands in quite clear contrast to the nomadic view of the state, which always goes from the top down and is fundamentally hostile to its own subjugated population. The Nordic race, through a sort of step-by-step process of bottom-up selection, effectively identifies individuals deemed suitable for leadership and allows only the best of the best to make it to the top. This elite is consequently seen as a leadership class that has arisen through the free consent of its subordinates and can therefore be removed if necessary (the right of resistance in Germanic legal customs). Such a view is not only unknown but also completely incomprehensible to the nomad. The nomad would consider it a blatant revolt if the subjugated population dared to question his rule or publicly expressed their opinion about it. Fostered by his evolutionary history to value property only from a predatory perspective, it is perfectly natural that the nomad will perceive any freedom of expression coming from a subordinate as simply the beginning of a "counter-raid" directed against him and the property he has just stolen (see chapter two). Politically speaking, however, the nomads, driven by their need to exploit existing civilizations and the necessity of protecting their usage of these civilizations, have invented and developed something that was originally completely alien to the Nordic state concept (which was based on self-administration and the election of leaders), a firmly established bureaucracy responsible only to the state leadership. Of course, in chapter one, we already discussed the ingenious internal mechanisms of exploitation employed by the nomads in great detail. The fact is, however, that the Germanic peoples only came to know true bureaucracy through Emperor Frederick II. He took it from the Saracens and introduced it on a trial basis in Sicily.[290] This practice proved so successful in Sicily that the Grand Master of the Teutonic Order and confidant of the Emperor, Hermann von Salza, adopted an outline of this administrative body for his order. This circumstance was one of the main reasons for the power and colonial successes of that Order. The Teutonic Order in Prussia was the first Germanic state on

---

[289] Amira, *Grundriß des Germanischen Rechts*.
[290] The Frankish counts during the reign of Charlemagne the Saxon Slayer cannot be readily referred to as genuine government bureaucrats in the strict sense of the term—they were enfeoffed with land and were thus firmly rooted in place. Consequently, they are better described as trustees of the emperor rather than true bureaucrats.

German soil that was built on a purely nomadic basis. Its eventual downfall is partly related to the fact that the Order later failed to integrate into its un-German administrative body any sort of Germanic system of self-administration. The state of the Teutonic Order was never able to take root in the land it ruled, and it is only thanks to the peasants it settled that its legacy was not lost to the Germanic people. It was the Prussian state that first attempted to find a solution to these issues, namely by seeking to organically combine the nomadic idea of uniformly-managed governance with the ancient Germanic (ancient Nordic) concept of self-administration. One can assume that this attempt probably began with King Frederick Wilhelm I.[291] Treitschke writes,

> King Frederick Wilhelm I firmly established the fundamental principles of internal order in the Prussian state in such an unshakable manner that even the laws of Stein and Scharnhorst, as well as the reforms of our time, could not destroy it—they only served to further develop the work of this hard man. He is the creator of the new German system of administration, our bureaucracy, and the officer corps. His unglamorous and industrious endeavors were no less fruitful for German life than the military exploits of his grandfather, for he introduced Germany to a new form of government, the unified state entity of the modern monarchy. He gave significance and substance to the new name "Prussia," united his people into a community of political obligations, and instilled the idea of duty into this state for all future generations.

> As resolutely and systematically as William the Conqueror had once done in conquered England, Frederick Wilhelm I constructed a unified state over the ruins of his territories. But the unified state did

---

[291] For curiosity's sake, it should be noted that this monarch, who instinctively grasped and effectively implemented the inherently non-Nordic idea of the centrally-directed modern state, was not, in fact, entirely of purely Nordic blood. His mother, Sophie Charlotte, had a touch of non-Nordic blood from some side of her family. This first queen of Prussia consistently exhibited behavior not typically found in Nordic female figures of history—she never truly comprehended the responsibilities associated with the position of a ruler, even going as far as mocking such matters. Additionally, she neglected her maternal duties, despite having a strong emotional attachment to her only son. Instead, she relished engaging in free-thinking and irreligious discussions late into the night and indulging in an unrestrained passion for music. Her contemporary, Father Baule, described her as follows, "Her stature is not tall, yet she is quite robust. Her facial features are standard, but there is an exceedingly odd attribute— in contrast to her blue eyes and fairest complexion, she has jet black, curly hair. She combs it freely from her forehead and wears it without powder." From Friedrich Paulig's *Friedrich I* (Frankfurt an der Oder: 1907).

It seems, therefore, that Frederick Wilhelm I indeed had non-Nordic blood, which provided him with an aptitude for understanding the advantages of a unified and centrally-directed state, independent of any sort of self-governing constituents. However, the fact that he did not turn his monarchy into a nomadic exploitation institution (in other words, he did not perceive his state as a feeding trough), but rather, in a way, only established the framework within which the ancient Germanic idea of estate-based self-governance could continue to evolve to new life, can likely be attributed to his Nordic blood. One could argue that the non-Nordic blood component from his mother had been sufficiently mitigated within him, allowing it to act more like an "activating agent," influencing him and leading his abundant talents in the realm of state-building, bringing about a unique blossom.

not appear to him as an estate of his house, as it did to that Norman, on the contrary, the idea of the modern state was present in the mind of the unlearned prince in a remarkably clear and conscious way.

Through him, the centralization of administration was established earlier than anywhere else on the continent. Whatever remnants of traditional authorities remained were abolished or subjected to the command of the monarchical bureaucracy. Everywhere, the particularism of the estates, regions, and communities resisted the new uniform order in an antagonistic manner. The noble landowners reluctantly acquiesced to the dictates of the civil officials.

Thus, Prussia's new ruling class, the royal bureaucracy, was molded by its victorious struggle for state unity and equality before the law. The king gave his bureaucrats a respected position in civil society through a fixed hierarchy and secure salaries, demanding from each entrant proof of skill and knowledge. In essence, he established an aristocracy of education alongside the traditional hereditary social stratification. For many years, the Prussian bureaucracy became the foundation of the German concept of the state.

Only in Prussia was the nobility won over to embrace the duties of the modern state, becoming as firmly intertwined with the life of the state as England's parliamentary nobility.

However stern and authoritatively this kingship may have asserted its sovereignty as a *rocher de bronze*[292] against any insubordination, the work of unification actually proceeded with much greater tact than the violence of the French Revolution. The state could not hide its Germanic nature.[293]

Kayser states,

The struggle for the formation of the German state has also always been a struggle for the orderly interaction between professional groups and the state.

While in England the estates embodied the actual political leadership and power, rendering a state outside the estates superfluous, and while in France the estates were suppressed and also deprived of their social autonomy, in old Brandenburg-Prussia the three great Hohenzollern rulers established a balance of power between the estates and the state. This ensured that the state was the sole source of political leadership and power while permitting the

---

[292] Editor's note: *Rocher de bronze*, literally translated from French as "rock of bronze," was a popular saying during the time of King Frederick Wilhelm I. It described something of incredible strength.
[293] Heinrich Gotthard von Treitschke, *Deutsche Geschichte im Neunzehnten Jahrhundert* [Nineteenth Century Germany History], volume 1, (Leipzig: 1927).

estates to retain their social autonomy and integrating them into the service of the whole.[294]

Thus, the Prussian state has hitherto stood as a truly unique entity in world history, for although world history has witnessed many dominions and empires, it has not yet seen an attempt to conceive the state as an organic entity and a supra-personal organism. Jung writes,

> The Prussian state and its history embodies for us Germans the idea of devotion to a higher goal, to the state and the fatherland. This demands dedication and sacrifice from individuals and their self-interest, and for this very reason it becomes the most important and effective educator of ethical conduct.[295]

Following Bismarck's departure, the Prussian state had not yet succeeded in accomplishing its task of developing itself into an organism. This is quite natural, for an independent bureaucracy detached from the people and a robust self-administration emerging from below are two fundamentally opposing forces that can certainly be reconciled within a monarchy but are far from organically inevitable. Without an understanding of these contrasts, a state that aspires to become an organism will never find an optimal compromise between self-administration and bureaucracy. Perhaps the German people, as inheritors of the Prussian state, are called upon to solve this task and bestow upon the world a genuinely organic state. As the roots of this problem go back to the contrasts between the Nordic race and nomadism, a brief discussion of these aspects has therefore been included here.

But let us return to the peasantry of the Nordic race. Through this peasantry we can gain an insight into a characteristic which is deeply rooted in the blood of the Nordic race and which has often led to many unjust accusations against it. Living closely with family members and subordinates under the same roof, the peasant must always keep a certain distance in both joy and sorrow (especially the latter) so as to maintain the respect that can only (of course) be maintained with a calm demeanor. Every genuine peasant today still possesses this noble bearing. Through its peasant nature, the Nordic race evolved a unique and confident sense of maintaining distance and bearing, a fact that we can only admire in this race. This mentality is never lost in any situation and fundamentally prevents them from displaying emotions in front of subordinates. The education of the German officer corps was built upon this principle, just as it still is with the education of English youth today. The characteristically reserved character of the Nordic race, often criticized as arrogant lordliness, is possessed by every genuine peasant today. From this nuanced sense of distance, which is always linked to a refined sense of achievement, the

[294] Kayser, "Berufstand und Staat."
[295] Jung, *Deutsche Geschichte für Deutsche*. See also: Treitschke, *Deutsche Geschichte im Neunzehnten Jahrhundert*; Wundt, *Staatsphilosophie*.

sense for rank and title emerges, as long as they are expressions of true accomplishment, whether inherited by blood or earnestly acquired by the holder. In no estate other than this one can we clearly observe that genuine achievement and genuinely manly deeds receive unenvious recognition, particularly among true peasant and noble classes, even though both initially exhibit the greatest reserve toward strangers.

The author cannot help but provide a true story that happened recently as evidence of this assertion. After the end of the World War, a retired general purchased a property in a southern German state. This general, originally from East Prussia and a passionate horse enthusiast, brought along a four-horse team of East Prussian horses. However, as soon as the south German peasants discovered the junker-aristocratic inclinations of the noble general, they made it unmistakably clear to him that the horses would be promptly killed if he dared to drive a four-horse team through the village. Such views were new to the general, as in East Prussia every farmhand drove with four horses. However, being from a rural background himself, he knew peasants well and patiently waited for an opportunity. It happened faster than he had anticipated. The peasants faced great difficulties in spreading manure during the winter of 1918–1919. This was due to a shortage of horses, which meant that they did not have enough teams to remove the manure from their yards. The general offered his assistance, namely his horses, which was gratefully accepted. But the peasants were astonished when they saw their general, wearing work boots and a hunting jacket, personally harnessing the four-horse team of East Prussian horses to their manure wagons and driving each wagon to its destination himself. Since that day, the peasants have been proud of "their" general, and the general happily drives his four-horse team through the village.

In their strong sense of being, both the genuine peasant and the Nordic race cannot be deceived by appearance, that is, by semblance. At the very least, they themselves abstain from it.[296] For example, among the English, who, like no other people on earth, adhere to traditional customs and are absolutely willing to acknowledge an individual's rightful claim, one can witness an indifference toward meaningless titles and forms of address that always astonishes Germans at first. People (Germans especially) are quick to explain away such apparent contrasts in English culture by dismissing it as "cant." In reality, however, the only thing at play here is the ancient Nordic peasant heritage of the English. Likewise, a title-hungry peasant would appear amusing in this country, and an undignified German may perhaps come across as boorish and never truly peasant-like. Riehl nicely depicts how the peasant's sense for traditional and established forms often manifests itself in an exaggerated manner:

The peasant still clings to the historical even when it would be wiser to abandon it. In the Wetterau region, near Großen-Linden, a peasant

---

[296] Friedrich Rückert once wrote, "Appearance and being never unite, only being alone endures on its own. Whoever is something, does not strive to appear; whoever wants to appear, will never be anything."

girl is considered the finest if she wears the most layers of skirts. Going to work in the fields with seven layers of skirts, whether in wet grass or tall crops, is evidently very unreasonable, but it is historical.

Despite all medical concerns, in many regions, the peasant still refuses to give up fastening his trousers with the dangerous leather belt strapped across the stomach; one could more easily impose a new municipal law upon him than new suspenders.

Here the author would like to add that in England, and in Anglo-Saxon countries in general, it is still not customary to use suspenders.

2

It has been said that the Nordic race always displays creativity, no matter which field one examines or encounters them in. Such a claim fundamentally contradicts biological experience, which does not recognize organisms that are fully developed in all areas. However, since there is no doubt that all the cultural heights of humanity are associated with the Nordic race, one could rather suspect that the Nordic race possesses certain inherent abilities that enable them to creatively develop existing cultures and their own. The following will be an attempt to derive such inherent abilities of the Nordic race from their peasant background. The author requests that this attempt be understood as intended, namely as nothing more than an attempt to take a step forward on unfamiliar terrain.

The nomad traversing the steppe or desert evaluates things solely from his own perspective—he judges them based solely on whether they are useful to him or not. In the nomad's imagination, this "wandering over things" must be represented in a way similar to seeing the successive images of a film pass by in a movie theater. As the consecutive film panes pass by, we perceive a "movement," even though this movement does not actually occur in space. To the self-migrating nomad, the daily and hourly appearances also present themselves in his imagination as a stringing together of film panes. For the nomad, the connection between these images exists only insofar as he moves from one image to the next. Whether one recognizes the force responsible for the movement in the images (the wall projector or projection apparatus) and allows the viewer to remain in place, or whether one leaves the image fixed and moves the viewer over it, does not fundamentally change the fact that human consciousness only perceives images in each instance. The image is a "surface" and its dimensions are determined by two variables.

In any case, humans naturally have difficulty with depth when seeing with one eye, that is, they see things as an image. The relationships between bodies in space, as well as the relationships of the bodies themselves, cannot ever be determined directly with a single eye. Our ability to see or perceive objects in space as three-dimensional is based solely on the fact that our two eyes capture two slightly different images, as each eye has a slightly different viewpoint. We have long unconsciously accustomed ourselves to converting the error perceived through the two image transmissions into an estimation of distance and space, so that our consciousness properly places objects in space.[297] In this way, we see spatially, but strictly speaking, we still see in a flat manner because the perception of space itself is not an immediate fact but rather an experience-expression of our consciousness, which quickly and automatically eliminates sources of error. The further apart the eyes are, and thus the greater the differences between the two images transmitted to the brain (that is, the more obvious the differences in the two images becomes to consciousness), the easier it is for consciousness to associate the spatial dimensions of objects in the two images and correctly estimate them. For example, the artillery binocular periscope was built on this principle; its design allowed the eyes to be separated by folding telescopic tubes with angled mirrors to a distance of about one meter. The image captured by the eyes in this manner through the binocular periscope did not really appear spatial, that is, the way we are accustomed to perceiving space. However, the very pronounced differences that the two images conveyed to our consciousness made the objects in space appear as if they were arranged in consecutive backdrops; the location of the shots could be well integrated into these visual backdrops. Although we know from experience that things in the world are entirely determined by three dimensions, we do not initially perceive them as spatial and three dimensional, but rather as flat and two-dimensional. Nevertheless, we make no errors in seeing and estimating because this ability to compensate for the source of error has long been ingrained in our subconsciousness.

Thus, we can safely say that the thinking of the nomad, that is, the processes within his consciousness, is solely concerned with the succession of arranged images—his consciousness only perceives "images." Since each image is a two-dimensional surface, the nomadic consciousness or the nomadic perception initially only "senses" the "surface" of objects that it becomes "conscious of." The nomadic way of seeing is thus focused on the surface of things—authentic "surface-level perception." Consequently, this surface-level perception necessarily develops a thinking that remains fixated on the surfaces of things and perceives their true essence solely based on their appearance. Such thinking leads the consciousness to at most only perceive changes in the shifting of an image and tends to see the changes in things (and the essence of these things) solely based on their surface, that is, in their arrangement or rearrangement, in brief juxtaposition or succession. This thinking, however, never engages with the essence of things because the nomad has nothing to do with the essence of things. One could designate such thinking, given that it clings only to the surface and operates within a two-dimensional level of consciousness, as "two-dimensional thinking" or surface-level consciousness.[298] This two-dimensional thinking or surface-level con-

---

[297] The reverse test can be conducted by squinting one eye and then attempting to light a cigar—it will take a moment to bring the match and cigar together. Horses that have jumped well but have lost one eye due to war or cold can still jump, but evidently with incorrect distance estimation and must rely heavily on their riders as tournament horses if they are to achieve anything in this regard.
[298] As a stimulus to the reader, I would like to present a statement by Houston Stewart Chamberlain regarding art, which he expressed on one occasion, "Those who believe that the cinematographic portrayal of everyday life on the stage is naturalistic *art* are too firmly grounded in the most naive panopticon viewpoint to make discussion with them worthwhile."

sciousness will possess an aptitude in scientific fields that do not require spatial thinking or that can be exclusively accomplished on paper. This includes, for example, the entire field of mathematics, chemistry (excluding the latest atomic theories that require spatial thinking), as well as those fields that are content with the atomization of matter without utilizing analysis as a guide for reconstruction.[299] Astronomy can also be listed here. It is indeed interesting that during the Middle Ages, the Arabs, despite having access to the best-equipped universities in the world, were mainly engaged in these aforementioned sciences but otherwise gave humanity nothing truly new in other areas. Philosophically, this two-dimensional perception and thinking, this surface-level consciousness, will tend toward sophistry, exhausting itself in quibbles and oversubtle reasoning. This thinking, of course, is not concerned with the essence of things but rather with their relationships and juxtapositions, remaining fixated on their surface-level qualities. Consequently, it will eventually resort to "playing with concepts," that is, the continual rearrangement of concepts, in order to get at the essence of philosophy, thus ultimately—certainly without intending to do so—dissolving philosophy within itself.

Authentic peasant thinking is fundamentally different. The peasant does not move across things but remains rooted in a single place. The things that surround him in his life are entities that he constantly gets to know from the most diverse of perspectives. As a result, these things acquire a completely different significance for him than they would, say, for the nomad. For the peasant, the things establish a fixed relationship among themselves and—this is crucial—also establish a more or less fixed relationship with him. The simple cinematographic progression of things within the sensory world, as represented in the surface-level consciousness of the nomads condemned to two-dimensional thinking, is fundamentally brought to a standstill by the peasant.

Despite this, in its initial stages, peasant thinking also continued within the two-dimensional plane of a purely surface-level consciousness. Eventually, something new comes into play with the peasant. He, of course, not only sees things as they are (he does not merely glance at them), but he also observes their becoming and passing away. To grab a hold of this, it is not enough for him to see things. He must strive to grasp things according to their essence. As a result, he fundamentally turns away from a perspective that merely looks at things, and pivots to seeing into things. From a seed, a plant emerges for the peasant, and from the plant, he gains a harvest, which again yields new seeds. Suddenly, his very person feels integrated into the coming, becoming, and passing away of things. His grandfather passed the farm down to his father, who, in turn, passed it on to him, and he will one day pass it on to his son. His family lineage emerges from infinity, and it continues into infinity. Thus, a vertical dimension emerges alongside the two-dimensional plane of surface-level consciousness, opening up an understanding for the essence of things. Because the peasant must engage with

---

[299] Goethe characterized the Nordic analyst as follows: "To find yourself in the infinite, you must distinguish and then connect." Houston Stewart Chamberlain encapsulated this idea in a more concise formula: "To structure means, first differentiate and then connect."

the essence of things, this leads to the path of knowledge, as the two-dimensional thinking matures into an awareness of space as determined by three dimensions. It evolved so that the surface-level consciousness could be supplemented by the ability to grasp the essence of things in their becoming and passing; thus, a feeling for the organic connections of life was born.

Of course, various generations gradually worked on this development and eventually anchored such knowledge in the collective memory of their race. However, if anything can demonstrate the peasant developmental path of the Nordic race, it is their distinctive inclination to "get to the bottom of things," to build upon things in order to derive their natural laws in the service of their further development. Genuine peasant life, therefore, always also has a philosophical bent, and every true peasant is a philosopher by nature. The most essential characteristic of a philosophy emerging from a peasant foundation is precisely its engagement with the essence of things—with their organic connections and natural laws. A peasant philosophy is without a doubt always a philosophy of knowledge that never remains surface level. Here lies the key to understanding why it has only been the Nordic race that has advanced humanity in the genuine philosophy of knowledge. At any rate, this is the conclusion reached on the basis of the historical documents of the Indo-European civilizations. To what extent the Phalian and Dinaric races, as genuine peasant races, also take part in this talent, the author does not dare to decide, although he would like to assume it for the Phalian race and, with restrictions, for the Dinaric race. However, he must firmly deny it to the Western and Ostic races, although one might suspect that the East Baltic race still appears to be in an intermediate stage of development.

There is an infinitely subtle meaning behind the tale of the fall from grace. Man loses paradise when he tastes from the tree of knowledge. As long as man, always like an animal, lived only in the realm of two-dimensional thinking, simply seeking his sustenance and remaining subject to the laws of nature, his consciousness was never disturbed. Man lived without purpose, was born, experienced love, and died without feeling the need to engage with the organic connections of this world. But when a group of people began transitioning from surface-level consciousness to an awareness of organic relationships, thus not only acquiring spatial thinking but also, along with it, an awareness of their own existence as an organism within this space, they were inevitably damned to progress on the path of knowledge, that is, to move forward. Thus, it was precisely at this moment that man stepped out of paradise (out of the state of unconsciousness) and could no longer go back. Those who begin to study things and begin determining the laws that govern life must necessarily inquire until they have satisfactorily grasped the essence of things.

As the horizon of the Nordic race began to expand, and an increasing amount of new insights enriched their collective memory, this race had to follow its peasant pursuit of delving into the essence of all things new, whether it wanted to or not. While the race sat on ancestral soil and only had a vague sense of the existence of "far off" things (things that still eluded their understanding), there may have been a sense of tranquility. Frenssen and other rural poets have masterfully described such Nordic peasants in the past. Later, as Nordic migrations encountered environments that were foreign and unfamiliar to the Nordic race, the peasant drive for knowledge gradually engaged with what was new. Splendid blossoms of philosophy were thereby bestowed upon humanity, whether we think of the Indians, the Greeks, or the Germanic peoples. Later, when the world was opened up through transportation, the Nordic race's drive for knowledge broke free without restraint and surged inexorably forward along this path, following its inner compulsions as determined by its evolutionary history.

How often has the Nordic race been suspected of this drive for knowledge! One feels unsettled by these people. They are never satisfied with the surface of things and they do not simply accept things as they are, always striving to penetrate and develop them further. The two-dimensional-thinking individual, with his surface-level consciousness, can only sense the movements caused by the Nordic race among the things of his familiar environment. He infers—since his consciousness can only comprehend a change of image through the activity of his own locomotion—that the disturbance in his existence caused by the Nordic race must also go back to the same cause in the Nordic race. Thus, he transfers what would trigger a change in his conscious impressions, namely his own movement, to the Nordic race and (based on the laws of his sensory world) concludes quite unconsciously—since I experience a disturbance in my existence caused by the Nordic race, the Nordic race must be a particularly restless and mobile race. He does not seem to comprehend the idea that a change in a visual impression can also be triggered by an internal alteration of the appearance, without the observer needing to move from his place.

But one cannot alter an appearance from within if one has not previously examined it in terms of its essence. Thus, on the one hand, it is quite natural that any change in an environment caused by a Nordic individual presupposes a more thorough engagement of this Nordic individual with the essence of the altered things, while, on the other hand, this very fact is most incomprehensible to the individual with surface-level consciousness, for he would never think of exploring or wanting to change the essence of things. It is in this way that the individual with surface-level consciousness is most unsettled by the Nordic race in particular. Consequently, he comes to perceive the Nordic race merely as the race that triggers his restlessness, the race that sets in motion alterations of his familiar image of reality. Ultimately, this is the root of that tragic distortion that attempts to label the race most rooted to the soil in the world, which, through its peasant nature, bestowed upon the world the drive for knowledge, as a "restless, mobile race."

Under certain circumstances, however, the individual with only surface-level consciousness may also occasionally regard the person who thinks in terms of organic connections as particularly backward. This can be illustrated by way of an example. When Henry Ford came up with and built a people's automobile, the individual who thinks in terms of evolution and organic connections will perceive it as a contribution to the development of transportation and undoubtedly recognizes it as a new stage in its evolution. It is fundamentally meaningless to this person who in particular takes a leisurely drive in a Ford, as this question of course has nothing whatsoever to do with the essence of the Ford car itself.

However, the individual trapped in two-dimensional thinking will approach this question very differently. For example, if he sees a negro tribal chief driving a Ford today after, say, previously moving around in a sedan chair, he considers it to be progress in absolute terms. The word "progress" is very instructive in this regard. Surface-level consciousness, which can only think in images and necessarily remains stuck on the surfaces of things, is accustomed to experiencing a change in images solely through the activity of its own movement. Therefore, it does not ever consider the possibility of a change in image arising from the essence of the thing. For this reason, a change in image that appears valuable to a nomad is simultaneously seen as progress. This expresses quite literally that the concept of development is unfamiliar to him, but progression toward the object of his admiration is, of course, natural. It is fundamentally of little significance to the question of transportation technology whether Negroes or Native Americans can now drive automobiles, for they neither invented the automobile nor will they be able to further develop it. However, according to the two-dimensional thinking of the nomad, the fact that he experiences two different images—first a walking Negro and then a Negro driving a car, where it is apparent that Negro number two is better off than the Negro number one—is fundamentally considered progress. This is because, based on his nature, he can only experience such changes of image through progression.

But if the organic and historically minded individual still perceives a Negro tribal chief driving a Ford as merely a Negro and never considers viewing "driving" as one of the Negro's cultural achievements—since, of course, the African cannot be held responsible for the existence of the automobile— then the nomad perceives such thinking as highly backward. The same is true, for example, if an Indian chief today knows how to wear a tailcoat and attends an American university. To "surface-level" thinking, this is naturally seen as "progress," whereas in the essence of the matter, the Native American has nothing to do with the tailcoat or the university. However, a person with a surface-level consciousness will never comprehend this, as he only knows how to judge the surface and not the essence of things. According to him, when the surfaces of things become equal, their essence has also become equal.[300]

The nomad lives for the day, while the peasant lives for the future. For the nomad, there is no point in worrying about tomorrow, for the present, the today, the immediate is before them and must be taken advantage of.[301]

---

[300] Treitschke once said, "In all their great epochs, the Germanic peoples have valued content more highly than form."

[301] One only needs to consider what types of figures come to mind when one thinks of the term "Bohemian." Figures of the Nordic, Phalian, and Dinaric types are quite certainly not among them.

Conversely, there is no point for the peasant to overly concern himself with today, for it is always only the result of previous measures he initiated yesterday or in the past, and his mind must already shift from today to the forthcoming, which he must master and cannot leave it to "dear God" as the nomad can. The nomad is a fatalist, while the peasant must say "help yourself, and God will help you!" It is this "looking toward tomorrow" that is so contrary to nomadic thinking, the nomad hates this forward thinking in the deepest core of his being. Why should the nomad get worked up about tomorrow? They are truly people of reality and do not appreciate being disturbed while grazing. The nomad would consider anyone who wants to alter this reality as detached from reality, even crazy, and, based on their biological development, it is understandable why they do so. Of course, the nomad can simply continue wandering if something no longer suits him. But the peasant cannot wander, and tomorrow will be what he grasps and initiates today. This means that the true peasant, like any genuine sedentary person (even true for some colored tribes, to a certain extent), is always the person of tomorrow, with a forward-looking care for his entrusted property and, by virtue of his sense of duty, necessarily an uncomfortable and unsettling figure for all thoughtless individuals drifting through life. The lazy farmhand has always cursed the energetic peasant who has set him to work.

The person who thinks nomadically, therefore, is "ahistorical" through and through. However, a sedentary person, in particular a peasant, requires the experiences of the past in order to take steps into the future. If he fails to do so, he is fool. It is evidence of Goethe's profoundly peasant and organic thinking when he once said,

He who cannot give an account
Of the three thousand years gone by,
Remains in darkness, inexperienced,
May live from day to day.

What use does the nomad have for memories of grazed pastures or consumed meals? Indeed, it would be nothing but a biological irresponsibility if nature had endowed him with a backward-looking gaze. The nomad must move forward if he wishes to survive, and he would be a fool if he wanted to burden himself with the past.

The peasant derives his actions from the necessities of his way of life, that is, from knowledge. This knowledge then becomes the guiding principle for all his actions, and he is trained to sacrifice personal comfort when it is required by the necessities of his way of life.

The introspective peasant nature of the Nordic race is accustomed to testing actions through thought.[302] But once this Nordic peasantry has rec-

---

[302] Goethe once stated, "Thinking and doing, doing and thinking, that is the sum of all wisdom, acknowledged from time immemorial, practiced from time immemorial, yet not comprehended by everyone."

ognized the necessity of carrying out an action based on knowledge gained from thinking, they will go on with its execution, whether it is associated with personal inconvenience or not. The peasant, of course, is not deterred by factors such as weather from doing what he has recognized as necessary. Thus, on the one hand, the Nordic individual is absolutely a ruminating and ponderous individual, but on the other hand, he is also a person of action. Whereas the nomad, who moves from thing to thing, could more readily be called a person of activity, without aligning their activity with rational thought. Nietzsche once aptly characterized this type of activity:

> It is the misfortune of the active that their activity is almost always a little senseless. For instance, we must not ask the money-making banker the reason of his restless activity: it is senseless. The active roll as the stone rolls, according to the stupidity [of the laws] of mechanics.[303]

Thus, nomadic activity corresponds to Nordic action, while Nordic rumination would correspond to nomadic indolence. Often it is the case that the Nordic ruminator is only superficially idle and slow-moving, while the idleness that occurs in the nomad is always genuine.

Action always changes the conditions of things, but activity does not necessarily do so. This leads to a seeming contradiction, namely that the fundamentally sedentary person (the peasant) is the person who changes our conception of the world, while the mobile, active person of non-peasant origin can indeed destroy things and thus negatively alter our conception of the world, but he fails to fundamentally change or further develop things (compare this with what Frenssen states about the *uhlen* and the *kreien* in the first chapter). Moltke, who was stiff in appearance and demeanor, was a man of action through and through—indeed, the idea of a relaxed, friendly military commander would be a comedic character for us today. Attila, eagerly storming toward Europe, and the fair-haired, blue-eyed Columbus embarking for America out of knowledge and rumination (or Count Zeppelin attempting to conquer the skies for similar reasons) are complete opposites. They act for such completely different reasons that it is impossible to confuse their motives. Those who perceive the Nordic race as a nomadic race have not yet truly understood its essence. Jörn Uhl is a peasant and a very Nordic individual—but never a nomad.

Perhaps the reader will permit me to insert here a side note which may add some vivid color to this picture of the Nordic race. As mentioned earlier, it was in peasant life that the Nordic race received its education in spatial awareness and organic thinking. With this realization we may also be holding the key to solving the mystery of why only the Nordic race has been able to create truly harmonious, space-controlling, corporeal art. This applies both to sculptural art in space and to the composition of an image that dominates a flat surface. In

---

[303] Nietzsche, *Human, All Too Human.*

any case, the drying up of Nordic blood in art is apparently always easiest to detect in the fact that the mastery of space and its relations to the object wanes.

Could this also have something to do with the fact that here in Germany, creative animal breeders or rural areas with highly developed animal breeding always show a strikingly clear connection to Nordic (Phalian?) peasant blood? In England, which is still very Nordic, zootechnical questions receive as much general attention as they do in North America. They are discussed in the newspapers there as extensively as captivating issues in other fields are discussed in our own country. In fact, nothing demands such a keen eye for body proportions and the expression of movement quite like creative animal breeding. It was pointed out by a clever equine expert (hippologist) half a century ago that the ability to breed noble horses decreases in proportion to the decline of good taste in architecture.

3

As the peasant culture of the Nordic race provides us with an explanation for why this race is capable of creatively advancing in all the fields it engages with, the peasant origin of the Nordic race also provides us with the key to understanding a peculiar cultural phenomenon that is not always commonly associated with peasant culture or traced back to a peasant origin. Although the author has previously pointed out the peasant roots in Anglo-Saxon culture many times, the assertion that even the English merchant (*kaufmann*) cannot hide his peasant origins is likely to initially meet with opposition. We have unfortunately become accustomed to speaking disparagingly of the mercantile spirit of the English. Some Germans may already no longer even consider the English part of the Nordic race—indeed, some see the English Empire as merely a similar entity to Carthage. But nothing could be further from the truth, as English commerce (*kaufmannstum*) is the complete opposite of its Carthaginian counterpart.

In assessing this question, one must not overlook from the outset that the English merchant is merely the heir of the German Hanseatic League. Mielke has pointed out that most of the cities in our Hanseatic League on the North and Baltic Seas clearly exhibit the Lower Saxon influence of their founders, while Frisian culture either did not participate at all or only to a negligible extent. These may appear to be contradictions, as one would assume that the seafaring Frisians should have been the natural intermediaries of overseas trade. However, the contradiction is immediately resolved and the fact of the Lower Saxon origin of the Hanseatic League becomes evident when one considers the peasant background of the Lower Saxons (which, of course, also includes the Anglo-Saxons) and traces the history of sedentary commerce from this background. Mielke writes,

Most cities in the Lower Saxony region originated from agricultural settlements where no thought was originally given to a commercial or trade-oriented position, even when they had partially abandoned their agricultural endeavors. Later, when cities primarily became hubs of trade, agriculture was still not entirely displaced from their walls. . . . The peasant, who is the basis of the urban population in Lower Saxony, sacrificed the freedom provided by the layout of his farmstead only out of necessity, due to the demands of relatively limited building space. The old, simple farmhouse, unmistakable in its design, first manifests itself in its gable. The townhouses were placed gable to gable with a narrow space in between, which, together with the narrowness of the streets, imposed the dominance of vertical lines on the urban landscape. It is no coincidence that the flourishing of the Hanseatic spirit coincided with the Gothic period, which regarded all urban architectural elements—churches, town halls, city gates, and bourgeois houses—as assertive expressions of civic pride, an idea that also strongly influenced the Renaissance.

Regarding the Frisians as city founders, Mielke states,

All Frisian cities lie somewhere between a village and an actual city, only gaining significance when they became administrative or dynastic seats, or when a large number of Lower Saxons settled there. The Frisian is a sailor, fisherman, and a peasant of the marsh, not a city founder. Where he has taken root as a city dweller—in Meldorf, Heide, Schwabstedt, Husum, Tondern, and others—he has been absorbed into Saxon culture, which has always pressed upon him and in the foreseeable future will perhaps absorb the last remnants of this powerful and sympathetic tribe, as their language has already become extinct except for a few remnants on the islands.

As soon as it began to engage in trade, the Nordic race, having a peasant heritage, conducted its commercial affairs from a fixed location in accordance with its predisposition to sedentism. The Nordic race is not inclined to itinerant peddling, characterized by busy movement from place to place. However, when conducting trade from a fixed point, this does not imply that the merchant is immobile and stuck in one place. Rather, it merely signifies that they always operate with a stationary point serving as the base of their commercial activities. Inevitably, certain natural laws begin to take effect. Sedentary commmerce always begins in the homeland and only begins to flourish when the homeland establishes active connections with the outside world. Its tendency is to then establish its trading posts where the conditions for trade appear most favorable, leading to the emergence of locations with increased trade relations. Such places must be well-connected to trade routes and have a productive hinterland as self-evident prerequisites. The location of the homeland, the layout and condition of trade routes, the products of the hinterland, as well as the demands of the market are the forces and factors that more or less necessarily dictate the laws of conduct for the sedentary merchant. From these circumstances, certain common objectives emerge among all merchants in the same location, primarily focused on protecting the homeland, safeguarding the transportation of goods, and pursuing shared advantages. Thus, the foundation for building a commercial cooperative (such as the Hanseatic League) is already laid. Further development of the cooperative is merely a matter of time and experience. It should be noted, however, that the structure develops organically from the bottom up, from the small to the large.[304]

The peddler (*hausierer*) is not sedentary—by nature, he undoubtedly has nomadic origins. While the sedentary merchant merely facilitates and enhances the natural flow of goods in the trading process, thus being a genuine and necessary component in the organic course of a healthy production process, the peddler travels around with his goods and is not entirely dependent on the actual process of production. If peddlers also decide to establish a fixed location, they understandably do so where they can interject themselves into an already existing trade flow. This is most often and easily the case near trade hubs, because here the trader (*händler*) does not need to move, rather, a rich selection of goods passes by them. The term *zwischenhändler* (middleman) is familiar to us, while the term *zwischenkaufmann* (intermediary merchant) sounds foreign; the juxtaposition of these two terms sufficiently illustrates that the German language has still preserved a sense of distinction between a merchant and a trader.[305]

As we have seen, the naturally sedentary merchant depends on the conditions of his immediate homeland to enable him to engage in commerce on a larger scale. Consider the Knickerbockers of New York (United States of America) as an example. This is quite natural, as the sedentary merchant is, of course, merely a part of the production process of their homeland, and their own prosperity therefore depends on the prosperity of their homeland's own goods production. The shift in power within the territory of the German Hanseatic League from the Baltic Sea to the North Sea, as well as the rise of London, were significantly connected to the disappearance of herring shoals along the southern coast of Sweden in the sixteenth century.

In contrast, the peddler of nomadic blood (undoubtedly considered the

---

[304] Very informative in this regard is the work by Fritz Rörig, *Hansische Beiträge zur Deutschen Wirtschaftsgeschichte* [Hanseatic Contributions to German Economic History].

[305] The etymology of the German word *börse* (meaning stock market or stock exchange) is highly enlightening. *Börse* (from French *bourse*, Italian *borsa*, Old High German *burissa*, meaning pouch or purse; related to Dutch *beurs*, derived from Medieval Latin *bursa*, Greek *byrsa*, meaning stripped hide) originally referred to a bag or wallet. In a figurative sense, it denoted a public building where merchants gathered for their business affairs. Thus, the *börse*, in its contemporary sense as a financial institution, essentially serves as an accurate indicator for movements in the trade of goods. As long as the *börse* remains in this capacity, the institution is healthy. Formerly (not even half a century ago), it was well-known that only merchants who had an impeccable personal reputation as both businessmen and individuals were allowed to trade on the stock exchange. Those were the times of the "*royal merchants.*" However, it is quite revealing that nomadic intermediary trade found its stronghold precisely in the stock exchange, where it consolidated its power and eventually gave rise to the concept of a *börsianer* (meaning speculator, broker, or operator). When the stock exchange falls into the hands of speculators and becomes an end in itself, it inevitably leads to the impoverishment of the production of goods. This is because, under such circumstances, the lifeblood of the economy is drawn from the most inappropriate place. In Germany, in certain circles, many would not be so blindly up in arms against the institution of the stock exchange (and the banks) if one remained conscious of the distinction between a stock exchange in the hands of *merchants* and one in the hands of *speculators*.

true ancestor of the trader), by virtue of his mobility, migrates to the places where trade happens to be in a particular state of prosperity. The trader, therefore, already presupposes trade. The true merchant is at a disadvantage compared to the trader due to his settled nature. The merchant can only compensate for the disadvantage of being sedentary by attempting to exercise control over trade. This means that they must strive to keep the markets in their hands, since they are the true drivers of production in their homeland. As a result, a sedentary merchant cooperative very easily (and almost always) heads in the direction of employing a conscious market policy. Later, it also usually heads in the direction of a more or less clearly guided foreign policy, provided that the merchant cooperative, as in the case of the Hanseatic League and the Anglo-Saxon world, rises to political independence. The Hanseatic League followed this path,[306] and, obviously, there is no need to provide evidence for the Anglo-Saxon Empire. The Anglo-Saxon merchant's sensibility, which stems from a Nordic peasant sedentism, is clearly and aptly summarized in this phrase about market policy, "Trade follows the flag." By this, the English mean that the securing of political power in foreign trade must precede any commercial calculation, otherwise business cannot be reliably predicted in the long run and remains subject to chance, falling into the realm of pure speculation (like a stock exchange trader). The speculator, however, is to the merchant what the gladiator is to the strategist. The English view on this is evident from the statement published in the Fortnightly Review in 1893: "Trade either produces a navy strong enough to protect it or falls into the hands of foreign merchants who enjoy such protection." In Germany, Ballin famously held the opposite view: "Germany needs maritime influence but not sea power." However, the course of history has absolutely proven the English perspective right.

Such a development toward purposeful market policy is by no means inherent in the trader of nomadic blood. When trade routes change, the trader follows the trade, just as their ancestors once simply followed the natural instinct of their herds to richer grazing grounds. The trader follows the trade. In Carthage and its fate, history has shown us such a trading activity and its development. Carthage lacked a clearly directed market policy, but it did produce a brilliant organization for exploiting existing trade relations. With its keen sense for exploitation, Carthage absolutely demonstrates its nomadic blood-inheritance. Carthage merely limits itself, as one might say,

---

[306] A prime example of the deliberate market policy of the German Hanseatic League is the following. When England's King Edward III waged war on the continent, he brought with him his crown regalia—which at that time had high status as symbols of state power independent of their personal wearers—both to display the full splendor of royalty and to secure financial support. He was forced to pledge his crown to the Archbishop of Trier, as well as his wife's crown (along with a smaller crown and other jewels) to a group of Cologne capitalists. The archbishop then shifted his political allegiance from the English to the French side, and there was a risk that the pledged royal crown would be in peril. It was only with the assistance of Hanseatic merchants that the king was able to prevent the worst from happening. The compensation they received for this intervention was a sacrifice of state rights and a privileging of Hanseatic merchants in England. See: Hansen, "Der Englische Staatskredit."

to not being pushed away from the gold sources. No one has understood how to portray the nature of these Carthaginian traders, which stems from their Semitic Phoenician origin, in a more true-to-life manner than Flaubert in his novel *Salammbô*. The term "Punic faith" is of course a well-known historical concept, and even the Odyssey refers to the Phoenicians as "greedy knaves." In the end, Carthage perishes because of its nomadic sense of exploitation, which does not give way to the constructive sense of organic commerce. Cato, the ideal example of a political peasant,[307] knew very well why he let his words resound, "*Ceterum censeo, Carthaginem esse delendam.*" But just as a nomad in the steppe or desert does not think to implement perhaps the simplest measures in the world (such as establishing irrigation to provide lush pastures for their livestock), the Carthaginian likewise did not consider gradually expanding into specific market areas. Carthage had trading colonies, but not an actual colonial empire like Rome.

England is accused of perfidious (malicious) politics, and it is claimed that when the Englishman says the word "Christianity," what he really means is "cotton." But something is overlooked here. It may not be very nice, but this is certainly a deliberate marketing policy put in place by settled commerce to conceal their ultimate aims in order to achieve them. The "disloyalty" of the Carthaginians, on the other hand, was not the result of a deliberate marketing policy in disguise, but rather an example of "going with the wind" and refusing to be crowded out by competitors, thus becoming completely unpredictable, both for the individual concerned and for those who wish to form an opinion based on their behavior.

---

[307] Plutarch's *Cato the Younger* portrays Marcus Porcius Cato as quite Nordic: "As for his outward appearance, he had reddish hair and keen grey eyes, as the author of the well-known epigram ill-naturedly gives us to understand: 'Red-haired, snapper and biter, his grey eyes flashing defiance. Porcius, come to the shades, back will be thrust by their Queen.' His bodily habit, since he was addicted from the very first to labour with his own hands, a temperate mode of life, and military duties, was very serviceable, and disposed alike to vigour and health . . . Nay, he was far more desirous of high repute in battles and campaigns against the enemy, and while he was yet a mere stripling, had his breast covered with honourable wounds. . . . In battle, he showed himself effective of hand, sure and steadfast of foot, and of a fierce countenance."

Moreover, Cato worked alongside his servants in the fields and even shared meals with them at the same table. Significantly, Plutarch goes on to say about him, "...a man who wrought with his own hands, as his fathers did, and was contented with a cold breakfast, a frugal dinner, simple raiment, and a humble dwelling—one who thought more of not wanting the superfluities of life than of possessing them—such a man was rare. The commonwealth had now grown too large to keep its primitive integrity; the sway over many realms and peoples had brought a large admixture of customs, and the adoption of examples set in modes of life of every sort." See: Ibid, chapter 4, sections 1–2.

Two things emerge quite clearly from this. Firstly, the old patricians were still working peasants themselves (old school peasants, as we would say today) and secondly, the patricians only abandon agricultural work in the fields when their political successes begin to spoil them. Thus, it is precisely the same condition that we can observe nowadays in South Africa, Australia, and the United States of America, where the relentless industry of Nordic peasants opens up the land to civilization, and by this circumstance, the newly developed areas are drawn into the realm of world politics. Subsequently, the old peasant way of life gradually accustoms itself to life as a master class, losing its connection with land and soil. It is then only a matter of time until denordification completes.

It also worth mentioning that it was not customary in our army to loudly announce every operation in advance and make it known to the enemy. During the World War, the troops learned the value of camouflage. Perhaps it is advisable to consider such motives in the future when seeking to understand the English and their politics. The tenacity of English politics is nothing short of the tenacity with which Hindenburg-Ludendorff achieved victory at Tannenberg—both are based on a correct assessment of the situation and the resulting necessities, allowing German strategists as well as English politicians to patiently await the results of their measures. The root of both is undoubtedly of peasant origin and resembles the tenacity of a peasant who, for example, has chosen a piece of uncultivated land for development and then proceeds calmly with its development, being momentarily hindered by unexpected obstacles or incidents but never deterred, unless in the exceptional situation where it proves truly impossible to continue. Hence, both the English politician and the German strategist have never been men of theory. Both have always taken circumstances into account and resolutely pursued their will by carrying out a plan and swiftly adapting their desires as soon as they were convinced that the situation required a change in the direction of their will. Moltke writes,

> It is delusional to believe that one can establish a campaign plan far in advance and carry it through to the end. The first encounter with the enemy's main force, depending on its outcome, creates a new situation. Much becomes unfeasible that may once have been intended, and many possibilities arise that were not expected before. Properly grasping the changing circumstances, arranging the appropriate measures accordingly, and resolutely implementing them is all that military leadership can do.

The secret of this tenacity, which is nevertheless flexible, lies precisely in a North German peasant heritage that tests action against thought and knows how to act appropriately based on it. The peasant always evaluates action against thought, and the German strategist as well as the English politician have never done anything else. For this reason, English foreign policy always appears so logical. We, of course, only pay attention to the result without considering that this result is merely the consequence of long-established measures. By the time we, the non-English, can recognize the measures insofar as we can relate them to the actual goals of the English, they are usually already unstoppable, heading toward their objective. Therefore, Langbehn was undoubtedly correct when he claimed that there were no differences between the true merchant and the successful strategist. It is also no coincidence that the pure-blooded peasant region of Lower Saxony has given us so many outstanding merchants, strategists, and politicians.[308]

---

[308] In the booklet by Langbehn titled *Niederdeutsches, Ein Beitrag zur Völkerpsychologie* [Low German, a Contribution to Ethnic Psychology), there are a multitude of outstanding ideas pertinent to the topics being discussed here. While it may be challenging to determine what aspects of Langbehn's Lower Saxon identity are influenced by the Phalian or Nordic elements, it is likely that he masterfully captured the true character of Lower Saxony.

Generally speaking, it seems to the author that it is a remarkable fact that here in Germany we have the Nordic Anglo-Saxon (who is so deeply connected to his homeland) sitting right on our doorstep, in theory that would mean that we should know him for who he actually is. But in spite of this, we still speak of the nomadic blood instinct of the Nordic man. In fact, there is hardly any modern civilized nation that clings so tenaciously to the soil as the Anglo-Saxon (Nordic) Englishman. Apart from the fact that the Nordic Englishman still harbors a profound hatred for urban living in his heart and merely considers it a necessary evil, everything outside his home is fundamentally foreign to him. True, he engages in world politics, for England has since evolved into a global empire, and he recognizes the expediency of this fact. He also travels abroad to see the world for himself, he willingly and frequently sends his sons abroad, so that, as mature individuals with clear notions about the workings of the wide world, they can then sit at home and follow the necessities of English global politics with understanding. But that doesn't mean that the Englishman would consider questioning his outlook on life. If he must reside abroad, he prefers to transplant Old England directly into the world of his new existence—it matters little to him whether the part of the world he finds himself in at the moment is called India, South Africa, or China, and whether the culture of his homeland harmoniously or disharmoniously fits into his new environment. The main thing that matters to him—if he must stay outside of England, then he must stay in an environment that, to the best of his ability, replicates the familiar surroundings of his homeland.

The Nordic Anglo-Saxon recognizes only himself and his familiar homeland; anything else does not exist for him at all in the whole wide world, at least not initially. However, it is a great mistake to assume that this is, say, an expression of narrow-minded arrogance, a view which he can afford because of his filled purse and the British Empire supporting him. On the contrary, this characteristic is simply an inheritance from his original Low Saxon peasant background. Whether the Nordic Englishman utters the words "my house is my castle," with unmatched pride or whether a German marshland peasant, with the same pride, declares to his son, striving into the distance, the familiar phrase, "Here is the marshland, and out in the world is the heath. What do you want, you foolish boy, in the world?" is essentially irrelevant.[309] In both cases, the pride stems from an original peasant way of thinking that places all of its pride in preserving the soil inherited from one's fathers and can only respect the person who represents the legacy of his forefathers with the same pride.

This unconditional affirmation of the native soil and the associated peasant soul-dependency on the land of the homeland has been best preserved by the Hamburg merchant in particular. Mielke describes it quite nicely:

> Hamburg has always remained a small town in a positive sense. The well-traveled Hamburger sought and always found his way back and

---

[309] Original in Low German: "Hie is de Marsch, un buten in de Welt is man Geest, wat willt du dumme Jung in de Welt?"

was happy to be able to live modestly as a Hamburger among Hamburgers in his old age. Is it Hamburg's rootedness to the soil, loyalty to Lower Saxony, or the spirit of the peasant that keeps alive the love of his hometown even on the high seas and in branch offices on foreign continents? It is likely all three. . . . Even the modern metropolis, which stirs its wings on Jungfernstieg, on the Alster, or at the new harbor, which builds its country houses in a wide area from Bergedorf to Blankenese, which observes the rise and fall of securities at the stock exchange, has within itself this spirit of action and tranquility. His thoughts encompass all continents, but in the evening, the merchant prefers to dwell at home with his family. Therefore, Hamburg has relatively few theaters. That is Old Hamburg — not the new one that has spread around the Alster basin, which ruthlessly pushes aside what has remained from the earliest days.

Having arisen from Low Saxon peasant blood, the "royal merchant," as manifested by the Hanseatic League and the Anglo-Saxon, could not be more gravely misunderstood than when lumped together with the outwardly dazzling yet internally thoroughly corrupt trading class of the Carthaginians. However, today the royal merchants of England—at least insofar as the London Stock Exchange is concerned—should already belong to history.

VIII

The Warriorship of the Nordic Race

I

Of all the qualities that distinguish the Nordic race, its acknowledged love of the sword is undeniably the most disputed today. Love and hate, admiration and detestation, all wage a fierce debate over the warriorship of this heroic race. What both proponents and opponents unfortunately seem to agree on, however, is that this warriorship should serve as the starting point for evaluating the Nordic race. But what they fail to consider is that such a warriorship may just as well be the manifestation of certain inherent predispositions that do not necessarily have anything to do with war per se.

First of all, let us take the German people as a general example. Here, pronounced bravery coincides with utmost peaceableness—this has been the case now for two millennia. It hardly needs to be pointed out to a German that one will necessarily arrive at a completely distorted view of German identity if one takes German bravery as the starting point for their analysis.

During the World War, our troops from Baden fought with recognized bravery, as Ludendorff explicitly pointed out. However, Baden is not populated by a warrior nomad nobility, nor does it have the centuries-old military education of Prussia. Baden is home to a largely peaceful peasant population. Nevertheless, the Loretto Heights, the Champagne region, and the Chemin des Dames were witnesses to the heroic deeds of these peasants. One does not hesitate to compare these deeds with those of the ancient Germanic legends. Meanwhile, the history of the Great War does not record any heroic deeds on the part of the "spahis," who were recruited from a desert warrior nomad population. The French could not even deploy the spahis at the front because of their inherent ineffectiveness in actual combat.

One can perhaps begin to gather from this that the concept of bravery itself does not necessarily give us any insight into a people's relationship to warfare. The spahis of the French army, unfit for frontline combat and intense fighting, come from a predatory nomadic culture where the primary pursuit is to wait for opportunities for violent raids. By contrast, none are more peaceful than the peasant sons of Baden—yet they have been the world's finest soldiers. Just think of Albert Leo Schlageter, a peasant son from the Black Forest.[310]

In order to make proper use of this insight when forming a judgment regarding the Nordic race's role in prehistory, it would be a good idea to first describe the main aspects of nomadic warriorship and then compare it with the Nordic race's approach to military strategy.

The Arabs have a war game known as fantasia, and it is a good portrayal of the offensive tactics employed by desert nomads. The main theme of fantasia is the swift emergence—the bold and precisely orchestrated attack—which can be just as swiftly halted, allowing the attackers to vanish without a trace. It is all quite eerie. But once one recognizes the main idea of fantasia, the whole thing becomes very natural. The desert nomad sees warfare only as a means of gaining loot—in other words, theft by violent means. He is solely focused on taking spoils, on the outcome—definitely not on the struggle itself. Therefore, the nomad conducts his attacks with the utmost regard for his own safety. The idea of sacrificing oneself for the good of the collective is alien to the nomad's way of thinking. Whenever possible, they use ambush tactics, and where the terrain does not permit this (such as in the desert), they conduct lightning raids. In an ambush, success always depends on the degree of surprise and speed of execution. By the same token, however, continuing an ambush becomes pointless the moment it is determined that success is impossible. At that point, there is only one objective, and that is to avoid further loss of life. In this way, we see that fantasia is an excellent reflection of the predatory philosophy of the desert nomads.

When Charles Martel met the Saracen Abd al-Rahman at Poitiers, a battle unfolded that is highly illustrative for the present discussion. We shall now follow the words of Stegemann,

> Charles Martel did not dare to expose his slow-moving Frankish forces to the swift swarm attacks of the mounted archers in the open plain, so he remained in his advantageous position. On October 18, the Saracens appeared before Tours. They set up a fortified camp to secure their immense spoils and then attempted to lure the Franks into battle. However, Charles calmly stood his ground and repelled

---

[310] Albert Leo Schlageter was a combat veteran of the First World War. After the war, he led an armed resistance unit against the French occupation of the Ruhr. He was eventually betrayed by a comrade and executed by the French. His alleged betrayer was then killed by Rudolf Höss, a future SS officer, and by Martin Bormann, the future head of the National Socialist German Workers' Party (NSDAP) Chancellery. Schlageter would be memorialized and honored in many ways during the National Socialist era.

their skirmishers. On the seventh day, the Saracens resolved to launch a frontal assault against the army positioned between the rivers. The Franks withstood the onslaught, their shields pierced by arrows, and they greeted the approaching squadrons with heavy blows. The day passed with exchanges of attacks and counterattacks. The Arab superiority shattered against the defense of the small Frankish army. As evening fell, the Muslims ceased fighting and retreated to their camp. The exhausted Franks rested on the battlefield and prepared for the next morning. However, the enemy did not return. Instead, before daybreak, they loaded up their spoils and evaded a renewed battle. The Saracens swiftly retreated toward Narbonne and across the Pyrenees. They no longer dared to advance beyond the Garonne, but they by no means abandoned their conquests. They turned Narbonne into their operational base and resumed their incursions along the coast and toward the Rhône.[311]

Cabanis states,

> The purely nomadic peoples have always been, and still are, nothing more than hordes of predators and plunderers. In their wandering way of life they regard all the fruits of the earth as rightfully theirs. They have no concept of private property, which is the basis of almost all civil laws. In their imposed separation from other peoples, the nomads develop the habit of viewing everything alien to them as hostile. This general and everlasting hatred toward their fellow man inevitably generates in their hearts an unjust, cruel, and sinister mentality.[312]

The Arabs call this form of warfare (raiding) "razzia," and the Turkmen call it "*alaman*." This predatory view is so deeply ingrained in the blood of the no-mads that the highest ambition of their caliphs or emirs was to earn the hon-orary title of Gâzi (Râzi) through successful acts of plunder. The title of Gâzi is the highest goal a Muslim can aspire to, and it is worth noting that the main features of it are ambush, destruction, murder, and plunder. Freiherr von Kre-mer[313] provides an interesting account of these razzias:

> It is reported that Harun al-Rashid undertook a summer campaign against the Greeks with 135,000 mercenaries. Such a summer campaign was essentially nothing more than a large-scale *razzia*— they invaded enemy territory, laid it to waste, and returned home with as much plunder and captives as possible.

---

[311] Stegemann, *Der Kampf um den Rhein.*
[312] Cabanis, *Rapports du Physique.*
[313] Kremer, *Kulturgeschichte des Orients.*

For the nomad, this predatory way of life is simply a natural need, and a telling example can be given for this. The Sunni Turkmen, without hesitation, carried out their razzias against the Persians, who were also Muslim but of the Shia sect, and supplied the markets of Central Asia with numerous slaves. They would openly declare that if the Persians were to suddenly convert to Sunni Islam, they themselves would immediately have to become Shia in order to find a pretext for their razzias.

If one takes the trouble to examine travel accounts depicting battles with nomads, the theme of the Arabian razzia will manifest itself time and time again (see chapter one). The differences are only in the details, not in the essence. Sometimes the nomad's actions may be described as cowardly murder, while on other occasions the term slaughter may be more appropriate. However, whenever possible, the nomad painstakingly avoids exposing his precious self to any danger. Before a battle, everything is done to ensure that the prospects of winning are as secure as possible.

A study of the rules of warfare among desert nomads reveals a recurring pattern of sudden ambushes by one encamped tribe against another. These ambushes are usually carried out at night and involve the massacre of the men of the opposing tribe. If they are successful, they then seize the livestock and equipment and take the women and children into slavery. The sudden ambush by mounted troops, coming like a desert storm with no warning, is the primary form of desert warfare. Perhaps some readers will still be able to recall the Indian books of their youth and remember how the entire "heroic" romance of the Indians amounted to silently sneaking up on the enemy and attacking at lightning speed, accompanied by a piercing war cry to further confuse the senses of the victims. However, if the ambush was discovered in time by those targeted, they could just as quickly slither away. A similar pattern can typically be observed among all nomads, as well as the fact that an attack will only be carried out if the loot is considered secure and the expected resistance is deemed insignificant. The nomad shows no mercy to the enemy, except in extremely rare cases where he intends to use them as slaves. As a result, nomadism throughout the world is characterized by brutal cruelty and is essentially nothing more than predatory; they all steal like magpies.

In his book *Artbild der Deutschen*, Kern attributed the warrior and heroic qualities of the Nordic race to its original nomadic heritage, relying primarily on the example of Semitic nomadism to support his argument. In order to demonstrate the complete groundlessness of Kern's assertion, it is worth sharing the words of an Arab regarding his own religious and racial comrades. This judgment comes from the famous Arab historian Ibn Khaldun,[314] who documented it in a chapter entitled "How the Arabs Bring Rapid Decline to the Lands They Conquer."

---

[314] Abd al Rahman Ibn Chaldun was born in Tunis in 1332 and died in Cairo in 1406. He was a statesman and a historian.

The reason for this is that they are a wild people, to whom wild behavior is innate, akin to that of a rampaging beast, shaking off the yoke of wisdom's admonitions and defying political authority. Their entire essence is one of change and upheaval, which runs counter to the stability required for civilization. For instance, they employ stones for their basic life necessities, using them as supports for their cooking pots, and they extract these stones from buildings, subsequently demolishing the structures. They also do the same with wood, which they require for the supports of their tents and as stakes, dismantling roofs in the process. Their entire nature rebels against construction, which is the foundation of civilization. This mentality is widespread among them. Moreover, their inclination toward plunder is a guiding force. Their livelihood flourishes only in the shadow of spears. Their greed knows no bounds, and they plunder whatever goods and property their hands can reach. They employ artists and craftsmen without remuneration for their work. Their hands are against each other when it comes to collecting taxes. Their civilization is in decline, and their treasury is squandered. Look at the lands they seize in the name of the Caliph, how they strip them of all semblance of civilization, how they have plundered their inhabitants, and how the land itself has transformed completely. Yemen, the cradle of their power, has been devastated, except for a few areas cultivated by the Ansar. The same fate has befallen Arabian Iraq (Mesopotamia). The civilization of Persia has perished, as has that of Syria. The African coast and Mauretania have been laid waste since the Banu Hilal and the Banu Sulaym settled there in the fifth century of the Hijra and resided there for a quarter of a century. How the land between the Sudan and the Mediterranean Sea was once cultivated is evidenced by the ruins of structures and the sites of villages and towns. By God! He shall inherit the earth and its inhabitants, and He is the Best of Heirs.

With his final words, Ibn Khaldun is expressing that in these devastated places, there is only something left for God to inherit, while the civilized man no longer has anything to find there. Just like the Arab nomads (and in some cases, even worse), the Turkmen nomads also wreak havoc.

Like all predators, the nomad is also inherently cowardly. In Wiese's work *Gustav Nachtigal*, one can find excellent evidence regarding the so-called "heroism" of the Arabs during their slave hunts. Nachtigal, who had to participate in such a razzia for political reasons, describes the pitiful cowardice of the slave hunters with great humor, even though he nearly chokes with disgust.

Based on our analysis, we can therefore conclude that the war-loving nomad is by all means representative of a part of humanity that actually denies struggle. Now it may begin to make sense why the French were able to use the spahis to torture captured soldiers under their supervision and why the French had the spahis trample women and children on the sidewalks during the separatist riots in the occupied territories, but could not use them at the front where the enemy could actually fight back. Throughout military history, no-madic soldiers have always proven to be highly questionable, as our Asia Corps saw firsthand during the World War.

Even in those moments of history when the nomad appears in a seemingly different light (appearing personally braver), the author has not been convinced that the nomad was actually truly changed by those circumstances or became more struggle-affirming. Simply put, one must not forget that it is very diffi-cult for us to ascertain with certainty which auxiliary people's individual no-madic chieftains had at their disposal. In the case of some Asiatic nomads, we can prove the existence of mercenary troops of Nordic blood. For instance, tens of thousands of German *landsknechte* defended the Turkish sultans as janis-saries (renegades), and a Graz native even became Grand Vizier. Serbian kings and Wallachian voivodes almost always had German bodyguards. Records of isolated heroic deeds, therefore, do not immediately justify attributing them to the nomads themselves. Nomads are also not inclined to keep their blood pure —it is precisely in this respect that Kern (*Artbild der Deutschen*) has missed the mark in his argumentation. In this context we can refer to the Kriemhild saga involving the Huns. Mohammed's third wife was the fair-haired Aisha, and among the seraili (women of the imperial harem in the ancient Seraglio of Constantinople) there were several women from the Western world, such as Safiye, the kidnapped Venetian and wife of Murad III, whose connections with the Doge of Venice contributed to many pages of Turkish history. Therefore, we cannot readily attribute the heroism of individual nomadic princes to a struggle-affirming attitude in nomadic culture unless there is quite clear evi-dence that the individual is not influenced by Nordic blood.

In assessing this question, however, we must also keep in mind that, tacti-cally speaking, nomads always have an initial advantage over settled peoples due to their particular circumstances. Settlements are inherently characterized by dispersed living arrangements, with individual villages often scattered. In contrast, it is inherent to the nature of nomadism that the tribe remains tightly unified. First of all, when nomads attack a settled area, they have the benefit of being able to choose the exact timing of their attack. Second, they have a sig-nificant tactical advantage in that they can break through a loose or even un-prepared defense as a cohesive wedge and simply roll up the defense, rendering it more or less ineffective.[315] For those who find this difficult to imagine, the early history of the Herero uprising in German Southwest Africa (where the Herero initially achieved quick victories) is instructive. It still remains highly questionable whether the German presence could have ultimately prevailed against them in the long term without support from the homeland. Still, no one would argue that the individual Herero was in any way more intelligent or militarily superior to the individual German.

---

[315] "It is less about what one does in war, but rather that it is done with proper unity and strength," Gerhard J. D. von Scharnhorst. "In war, there is only one objective—the destruction of the enemy in the quickest and most decisive manner," Napoleon I. "Wherever the decisive outcome is sought, one cannot be strong enough," Count Alfred von Schlieffen.

By 1894, the nomadic Herero and Hottentots had brought the economic development of German Southwest Africa to a total standstill. When peace finally returned, Witboi launched his uprising in 1904–1905 with a mere five hundred men. It took the best soldiers in the world, the Germans, 128 battles to suppress the Herero and Hottentot uprising, resulting in the deaths of forty officers and three hundred soldiers, not to mention many more wounded, sick, and missing. The first sudden razzia led by Maherero (Samuel Maharero) on January 12, 1904 claimed the lives of 159 settlers and caused property damage amounting to seven million *friedensmark*. For that matter, it would not have taken much for the outcome of the uprising to have been even bloodier for Germany. In March 1905, former Colonel Berthold von Deimling, now an advocate of pacifism, narrowly avoided a bloody defeat at the hands of the Hottentot bastard[316] Morenga (Jacob Morenga) in the Karas Mountains. It was only due to the iron tenacity of the Kirchner detachment, which was initially attacked and pinned down by Morenga, that the Germans did not suffer an outright defeat.

The story of the Herero uprising of 1904–1905 is highly instructive and shares many similarities with other colonial wars involving nomadic peoples. Since the settled person has to cultivate his farm or agricultural operation, it is inevitable that he will have to separate from his comrades on many occasions. Meanwhile, the nomad can calmly wait at the border for an opportune moment and strike again. Thucydides reports that the inhabitants of northwestern Greece lived in scattered dwellings, greatly hindering the defense of their homeland. The settled man can protect himself only with a well-planned arrangement of defensive fortresses, an aspect that has been alluded to earlier.

One can now understand why the author claimed that the undeniable victories of the Tartars, Huns, Turks and Moors are still by no means proof of the military prowess of these peoples. However, we can now also understand why the settled Goths preferred to carry the fight westward to escape the unrest caused by the nomads (Huns), rather than engage in combat with them. Indeed, the settled man simply cannot readily predict the nomad. Either the nomad suddenly invades and succeeds, rendering the military prowess of the individual settled people useless (as in German Southwest Africa), or the attack is successfully repelled. In the latter case, if the settled people were to launch a retaliatory campaign, their intentions would likely be in vain. Tactically speaking, the nomad is always more mobile and can easily use the challenging terrain of his former desert homeland as an ally against the settlers' military expeditions. The history of the Herero uprising in German Southwest Africa provides a powerful example of this, and there is a plethora of other examples from colonial history as well. Erwin Rosen particularly emphasizes this point in his famous book on the Foreign Legion. Before volunteering for the Foreign Le-

---

[316] Translator's note: In German, the term *bastard* describes a person that is either an illegitimate child (as in English) or, in biology, something that is a hybrid or a half-breed (such as a hybrid plant or an animal cross-breed). In this context, the word is referring to Morenga's half-Hottentot, half-Herero ancestry.

gion, Rosen had served as an American soldier in the campaign against Cuba and then completed his one-year voluntary service in Germany. He thus had sufficient military training to assess the Foreign Legion from a military standpoint. Significantly, Rosen says that there is a legitimate reason for the Foreign Legion's harsh discipline, namely, that desert warfare against the Arabs can only be conducted by troops who are capable of covering incredibly long distances in an incredibly short time. We had the same experience during the war in German Southwest Africa, where we would have never been able to capture the Herero in their deserts without our old Prussian soldiering ethos. According to this ethos, one must devote every fiber of their being to the success of the mission. To truly appreciate the achievements of our colonial army in southwest Africa during the uprising, one must have been a soldier and experienced war. However, anyone can learn a great deal about the difficulties of warfare against nomads from such concrete examples. Lettow-Vorbeck took advantage of having such a disciplined force during the defense of German East Africa from 1914 to 1918, where his small, mobile, and independent group of troops were unable to be pinned down by the Entente armies in the rugged terrain. This becomes particularly clear when one realizes that in 1918, for every German rifle in German East Africa, there were a hundred enemy rifles, not to mention the vast array of automobiles, artillery, armored vehicles, aircraft, and other equipment that the Entente assembled against our small force.

Since we now know that the pressure the Goths were under at their eastern border was the cause of their westward migration, and since we are able to demonstrate this historically, and since, furthermore, the eastern nomadic invasions played a decisive role throughout the first millennium of German-Germanic history (until the first Saxon emperor, Henry the Fowler, finally succeeded in overcoming them), the author would like to align himself with those who see this nomadic pressure as the true cause of the Germanic Migration Period.[317]

However, several qualifications must be made. In the case of the Cimbri and the Teutons, their emigration seems to have been solely the result of major incidents of flooding, which were a cause of emigration throughout the Middle Ages.

What first led the Goths from the Baltic to the Black Sea was probably the same thing that drove earlier Indo-European peasant treks, the only difference being that we can attest to it historically. The same can be said for the Suebi, Usipetes, and Tencteri, although the question remains open as to why they migrated westward and not southeastward. Perhaps the reason was that the departure of the Goths left the eastern flank of the Germanic peoples vulnerable, or perhaps it was because the Goths, retreating from the Huns, inadvertently exerted pressure on some of their own people along the upper course of

---

[317] In the meantime, the author has been able to confirm the accuracy of his perspective unequivocally. However, in this context, he confines himself to mentioning only the short work by Robert Kohlrausch, "*Herrschaft und Untergang der Goten in Italien*" [Dominion and Decline of the Goths in Italy], published in *Deutsche Volkheit* [German Nationhood].

the Vistula and Oder rivers, due to the position of the Carpathians. In any case, the Germanic Migration Period gives many people the impression that the Germanic peoples on the right bank of the Danube and Rhine had allowed themselves to be driven into the Danube-Rhine corridor (around the relatively calm pole of Germanic peoples on the left bank of the Elbe), as if under pressure from the east, in a clockwise direction. The Alps and the Roman frontier apparently formed the insurmountable boundaries of this corridor.

However, this hypothesis is contradicted by the fact that the pressure on the Germanic peoples along the upper courses of the Vistula and Oder did not necessarily set in motion the Germanic peoples in present-day Lower Germany, between the Elbe and the Vistula. But since we do not know the connections that existed between individual Germanic tribes, such an improbability does not necessarily rule out the hypothesis. However, it is also conceivable that the southern Germanic peoples, who were compelled to move due to pressure from nomads, infected the northern Germanic peoples with a sort of travel fever—the nomads would then be the immediate cause in one case and the indirect cause in another. The latter option is supported by the fact that the Huns always closely followed behind the Goths, who were retreating through present-day Hungary (south of the Carpathians) as a result of the ongoing nomadic invasions, while Lower Germany was initially empty after the Germanic departure. The Slavs, who were hardly nomads in the true sense, slowly and hesitantly took possession of the depopulated land. The westward migration of the Slavs was by no means directly linked to eastern nomadic pressure. This is relatively easy to understand and deduce from a map. The Huns could only penetrate Europe in the depression between the Caspian Sea and the Ural Mountains. From there, their thrust had to proceed directly westward toward the Carpathians, through Ukraine, roughly between Kharkov and Crimea. The Carpathians, however, formed a peculiar bulge at the very point where they would have been hit by the eastern nomads, giving the eastern nomads the choice of either bypassing them to the south and entering the Danube Valley and Hungary, or bypassing them to the north. In the latter case, it meant moving up the Dniester River toward Lemberg (Lviv) and Krakow. North of the Dniester, we find the Rokitno Swamps, which today we may rightfully consider as the ancestral settlement location of the Slavs. These swamps put a natural end to the advance of the Asiatic nomads, just as it did our armies in the World War. Therefore, it is likely that the Slavs were not pestered by the Huns. Since the Huns also had to cross the Sudeten Mountains during their northern bypass of the Carpathians, probably on land already abandoned by the Germans, this action likely foundered on its own. However, south of the Carpathians, along the Danube, the advance of the Huns found more promising terrain. Once the western flank of the Slavs was freed of the Germanic peoples and no further Hun disturbances were expected from the south, the Slavs initially appear to have gradually started moving westwards.

However, it could be argued that this does not sufficiently explain the central aspect of the Germanic migration, namely, the emigration of tribes in Lower Germany between the Elbe and Vistula. For instance, one could object that these tribes could not possibly have known the fate that awaited the Goths at the hands of the Huns. However, this objection overlooks a significant fact, one that can be observed from our recent experiences, particularly in African colonial history. Even during the past World War, we had to acknowledge that the natives of Africa, despite all the diverse races, languages, and ethnic groups, were able to transmit messages rapidly through the use of palaver drums from South Africa to Egypt. At least in the case of the Germanic tribes, we need not dismiss as simply impossible what the African natives are capable of. We can safely assume that the Germanic peoples possessed similar methods of communication and that the fate of the Goths was generally known among the Germanic tribes. In any case, the whole way in which the Germanic peoples appear along the Rhine allows for many different possible conclusions—but not for the notion that a warrior-nomadic nobility sought to invade the Roman Empire. The Romans would have been no more able to stop a sudden and unforeseen Germanic attack than the German colonial army was able to stop the five hundred men led by Witboi in 1904. Anyone even remotely familiar with the military campaigns of nomads would find it impossible to identify anything among the Germanic peoples of the Migration Period that could be compared to this. This needs to be made very clear.

2

Let us closely examine the behavior of the Germanic peoples during their initial appearance in history. When the Cimbri first encountered the Romans in the Drava Valley, they did not think of simply overrunning the Roman borders and then invading the Roman Empire. Instead, they initially engaged in rather extensive negotiations with the Romans and were willing to take a detour if the Romans agreed to let them pass undisturbed and in peace. As is well known, the Romans agreed to their request but then lured them into an ambush. When the Cimbri realized their situation, they were overcome with fury and, in an intense assault, defeated the Roman legions. This victory opened up the passes of the Carnic Alps for them. However, instead of capitalizing on their triumph, the Cimbri turned their backs on Italy, pivoted westward, and journeyed along the northern edge of the Alps until they reached the Rhine. Any group of warlike nomads would have inevitably done the opposite, as their rapacity is far too pronounced to let an opportunity to plunder go to waste. After this, they disappeared once again into the obscurity of history, and no accounts have reached us about where this peasant trek of tall, blond people crossed the Rhine with their wagons. The only thing we do know is that the bread- and land-seeking people between the Alps and the Jura did not find suitable settlement land and, after some time, re-emerged, reinforced by a number of Helvetian polities and the belligerent Tigurini tribe. At this point, the Teutons join them. The power of this coalition was so strong that everything yielded before them. They flooded the Rhône Valley, broke through the Côte d'Or and the Faucille Mountains, and penetrated deep into the interior of Gaul. They did not find land for settlement—instead, they mainly sustained themselves by demanding tribute from the Gauls, as the land was fragmented by clan rule and could not refuse this demand.

In the year 109 BC, they once again encounter the Romans in the Rhône estuary, where a consular army had long been prepared to receive them. However, the Cimbri and Teutons, half of whom were enough to defeat the Roman legions in the Drava region, did not engage in battle but instead requested land and grain. An embassy carried this request to Rome. This is the first officially documented demand made by the Germanic peoples to the Roman state in history. When the Roman Senate refused this request for political reasons, the Germanic peoples challenged the Roman legions to face their blades and annihilated them. However, they did not exploit their victory and only saw it as making amends for the insult they received. Despite their victory, they preferred to acquire the sought-after settlement land by means of the voluntary consent of the Romans, rather than their swords. This may sound surprising but not if one knows how to think like a peasant. Peasants need peace in order to settle and cannot afford to have a constantly disruptive enemy at their borders. Thus, the Cimbri and Teutons turned westward again, passing through the flourishing Provence region along the southern foothills of the Cevennes and toward the Garonne. The consul Lucius Cassius Longinus was sent to destroy them, but things turned out differently than Cassius had anticipated. The Roman commander was defeated, and he and his soldiers survived only by leaving behind their war equipment and enduring the disgrace of the Caudine Forks. The entire coastal region fell away from the Romans, but the Germanic peoples yet again did not know how to make the most of this fact. After four years, they are back at the Rhône, and the Romans are ready to receive them. The Battle of Arausio ensued. Interestingly, the Germanic peoples fought this battle out as a divine judgment and, at great cost to themselves, annihilated the entire Roman army. Still, they do not consider politically exploiting their victories, something that would come naturally to any nomadic group. One only needs to think of Balamber and Attila, Genghis Khan and Lenin. The Cimbri and Teutons turn westward again, wandering aimlessly in the Seine basin and along the Loire for another three years.

Then they do something that is not only very non-nomadic, but also distinctly Germanic (one might as well say German). The Cimbri and Teutons quarrel among themselves. As long as they were united, the whole world at that time trembled before them. But they walked around with a political blindfold on that is quite incomprehensible and can only be understood as the lack of natural aptitude for foreign affairs that is often found among peasant peoples. The Cimbri and Teutons separate. Marching and fighting separately, they succumb to the Roman commander Marius. The Teutons are slain at Aquae Sextiae (102 BC) and the Cimbri meet their end on the Raudine Fields southeast of Vercellae on July 18, 101 BC.

For a long time, fair-haired Cimbrian boys fought as gladiators in the Roman arena. They serve as living proof that the Germanic peoples, from the beginning of their history, have displayed a struggle-affirming love of the sword, which, unfortunately, fate inexplicably forgot to accompany with a complementary sense for understanding the complexities of foreign policy, a natural instinct that every nomad receives with his mother's milk (so to speak). Warlike nomadic peoples have historically behaved in the exact opposite ways as the Germanic peoples. During their military campaigns, they devoted considerable attention to the political objective of the entire endeavor, eagerly striving to make the entire razzia profitable. However, they preferred to leave the actual combat required for such matters to others. Attila at least demonstrated exceptional skill in manipulating the Germanic peoples against each other.

In the year 72 BC, the Suebian leader Ariovistus crossed the Rhine at the mouth of the Neckar. He came to the aid of Celts who had called for help against their fellow Celts. Thus, at first, his crossing of the Rhine was by no means marked by any intention of conquest. However, he displayed a greater sense of purpose than the Cimbri and Teutons. Upon realizing the complete ineptitude of the Celts, he decisively defeated both warring Celtic factions, extending his rule from the Neckar to the Saône. Yet, he did not exploit his victories to establish parasitic rule—instead, he settled his warriors. He claimed two-thirds of the land as property for his warriors and secured it through the power of his sword. However, the Celts gnashed their teeth. In 59 BC, Ariovistus had to defeat a Celtic army once again. Nevertheless, he remained aware of the restless and rebellious Celtic population, and for this reason, he kept a part of his army under arms and under his control, preventing these warriors from dispersing to their homes and hearths. Thus, a firmly established Germanic peasant state emerged north of the Roman Empire. It is noteworthy that Ariovistus maintained peaceful relations with the Germanic peoples to the east and north of his realm, and with the Celts situated in the north and northwest. The latter, incidentally, explicitly boasted of their partial Germanic ancestry and sought to coexist peacefully with Ariovistus. These tribes absolutely regarded Ariovistus's political situation as a legitimate territorial acquisition for the purpose of establishing a peasant settlement for his Suebian people.

However, the southern and western Celts had a different stance toward Ariovistus. The pleasures that they had acquired through Roman trade and to which they had long grown accustomed were more appealing to them than the powerful sword hand of the Germanic peasant king and his sturdy retinue. Therefore, they sent messengers to Caesar. However, Caesar did not readily comply with their requests, despite the favorable nature of their message. He first sought a viable pretext for war. Unfortunately, it would be beyond the scope of this discussion to delve into the ingenious political strategy employed by Caesar in orchestrating this game against Ariovistus, leading the latter to have no choice but to confront Caesar on the battlefield. Yet, nothing quite demonstrates the peaceful peasant nature of Ariovistus as clearly and unequivocally as this political game initiated by Caesar. The sequence of events is as follows. The Helvetii had returned to their former territories after the expedition of the Cimbri and Teutons (which, by the way, is highly significant!), but continued to struggle to support their excess population on their meager soil. Caesar was aware of this, but he also knew that the Helvetii were planning a new emigration. Therefore, he prolonged negotiations with the Celtic envoys regarding Ariovistus until the Helvetii (who were hemmed in by Germanic tribes to the northeast, Ariovistus to the north, and the Roman Empire to the west) attempted to break through toward the Santones in the west, who occupied fertile soil between the Garonne and Loire rivers. Through a strategically and tactically astute military campaign—wherein the bravery of the Helvetii is as evident as the underhandedness and cunning of the Romans—Caesar succeeds in annihilating the Helvetii and subsequently achieves his strategic objective, namely, his confrontation with Ariovistus. Nevertheless, for his part, Caesar did not attack Ariovistus, and Ariovistus himself had even less inclination to attack first. But Caesar assessed the situation. His messengers initiated a clever game among the Celts, and eventually, the pro-Roman Celtic factions sought Caesar's assistance against the Germanic king. As one can imagine, Caesar very graciously accepted their requests and set himself up as the savior of the Gauls against Germanic aggression and Ariovistus.[318] Ariovistus was initially quite perplexed, emphasizing to Caesar that his claim to the land was at least as valid as the one Caesar purported to defend. Moreover, the Gauls had called upon him for help and called him into their land before Caesar. His claim, therefore, was older and stronger. But Caesar knew what he wanted. The negotiations fell apart, and Caesar skillfully manipulated the situation, ultimately placing the blame for war on Ariovistus. Both sides prepared for the summer campaign of 58 BC.[319] In this campaign, the strategically trained Roman dictated the course of action to the strategically untrained Ariovistus. Caesar decisively defeated Ariovistus, who luckily managed to escape across the Rhine. However, it is worth noting that directly before the battle, Ariovistus had requested a meeting with Caesar, during which he tried to convince him of the legitimacy of his claim to the newly established Suebian territories. Unfortunately, we only have Caesar's rather one-sided account of this meeting, which is undoubtedly presented in his favor. If the deeply indignant and agitated Germanic chieftain did not display a highly polished and composed demeanor during the meeting, this can absolutely be understood from a human perspective. It is unjustified to conclude from the cold-blooded and calculated composure of Caesar during the discussions that Ariovistus' indignation and agitation were evidence that he remained at a more barbaric level of civilization. Either way, the meeting is significant precisely because it clearly shows that Ariovistus's mind was preoccupied with concerns for his country, and therefore could not have been a purely militaristic king without any attachment to the land. A ruler of nomadic blood would never have acted in the same manner as Ariovistus. Ariovistus demonstrates a commendable sense of responsibility toward his country, and this ultimately becomes the main cause of his downfall.

Looking at recent colonial history, a situation has unfolded that bears a striking resemblance to Caesar's behavior toward the agrarian Suebi. I am refer-

---

[318] Analogies are known to be misleading, but in this case, one is clearly reminded of a similar phenomenon during the previous World War. The Anglo-Saxon world skillfully concealed its global political objectives by calling upon the sentimental slogan of the suffering of violated Belgium at the hands of the German barbarians.

[319] Ariovistus thus ruled the country in complete peace for fourteen years after crossing the Rhine.

ring to the conduct of the English toward the Boers. The Boers were the true pioneers of South Africa. However, the English, motivated solely by geopolitical considerations, constantly sought to take over the Dutch settlements in South Africa. Initially, the Boers simply tried to get out of their way. This led to their well-known emigration across the Orange River, known as the "Great Trek of 1836." But toward the end of the nineteenth century, the English finally succeeded in exerting control over this courageous peasant people.[320] The peasant state of the Suebi under Ariovistus and the peasant state of the Dutch in South Africa are undoubtedly the same in that they both demonstrate an attachment to the soil, which is quite natural because no peasant willingly abandons the labor he has invested in the land. But they also resemble each other in being oblivious to the purely geopolitically-motivated objectives of their adversaries and only engaging in war when they had no other choice.

Once one understands the true nature of nomadic warfare, one becomes immune to even the possibility of perceiving the warriorship of the Nordic race as nomadic. It is highly unlikely that anyone will be able to cite examples from the relatively well-researched history of the Nordic race that can be likened to the distinctively cowardly predation of the nomads.

Quite the opposite, the Nordic race from the very beginning holds views of warfare so fundamentally different from those of the nomads that it may be safely said that Nordic warriorship is as different from that of the nomads as the war record of the peasant sons of Baden in the World War is from that of the French spahis.

3

The first thing that stands out about the Nordic race is that, contrary to all nomads, this race unconditionally affirms struggle. In what we can see in the Germanic historical record, the purpose of a struggle or battle is practically a side issue, while its affirmation takes center stage. While the nomad gladly enters a battle based on precisely calculated prospects of winning, Hagen von Tronje,[321] without even batting an eye, consciously embraces his own death— indeed, he even invites it—even though there is not the slightest advantage to be gained for the Burgundians.

When one tries to trace the struggle-affirming nature of the Nordic race back to its basic ideas, the first thing one encounters is the value that the Nordic race allots to perseverance in battle. The man who is hailed as a hero is not the one who, like the nomad, slaughters many enemies, or the one who

---

[320] By the way, just as one cannot hold the Nordic patrician of ancient Rome accountable for Caesar's geopolitical strategy, one cannot blame the Nordic Englishman for the geopolitical strategy of nineteenth century politicians. However, this is not the appropriate place to discuss these matters.

[321] Editor's note: Hagen von Tronje, a central figure in the medieval German epic *Nibelungenlied*, is known for his loyalty to King Gunther and his cunning nature. As he was aware of the hero Siegfried's only vulnerability, he betrays and kills Siegfried on behalf of King Gunther. Despite this betrayal, Hagen remains steadfast in his loyalty and honor, ultimately accepting his own death with dignity as a consequence of his deeds.

recognizes the futility of a battle in time and, therefore, wisely and skillfully breaks it off with the opponent. Instead, the Nordic race holds in high esteem the one who sees the battle through to its end, regardless of the destiny that the goddesses of fate may have allotted to the warrior. The Nordic race certainly does not understand perseverance in battle as merely a senseless and stubborn "standing one's ground" that allows one to be easily defeated, but rather as the devotion of one's entire personality in the will-to-victory. This is particularly evident, among other things, in the writings of Tacitus, who explicitly mentions that among the Germanic peoples, retreating in battle was by no means considered a disgrace, as long as one resumed the fight later.[322]

But under what circumstances does perseverance (the just mentioned staying the course) hold value in combat? Well, whenever fighting becomes necessary, and this applies first and foremost to defense. If you do not want to be trampled on, you must be prepared to fight to the death. Considering the peasant character of the Nordic race, this idea becomes self-evident. When the peasantry is attacked, it is faced with the choice of either completely repelling the attack or submitting (perishing). Only a peasantry that can defend itself is free. Genuine military states have always grown out of exposed peasant states, as can be clearly seen in the cases of Sparta, Rome, and Prussia. There has never been a more peaceful peasant people than the Brandenburgers and their royal house, the Hohenzollerns. Anyone who claims otherwise must be met with Treitschke's famous reply, "That is simply not true." But rarely has a military state been so obviously shaped by its circumstances than Prussia in particular. The exposed border necessitates defense and requires that its citizens be militarily trained for the defense of their homeland, whether they like it or not. Paulus Diaconus writes, "It is better to risk one's life in war than to become a mockery to the enemy as a wretched slave people."

Across the whole span of modern colonial history, the weapon still remains the pride and joy of the Nordic settler. He cherishes and nurtures it like nothing else (see the Boer War). One is also reminded of the famous rifles of the Tyrolean peasants under Andreas Hofer,[323] and once again the World War!

For this reason, the peasant nobility of Rome has handed down to us the saying, *si vis pacem, para bellum*—if you want peace, prepare for war. For the constantly lurking nomad, who is always seeking plunder, this phrase holds no meaning, as they do not seek to preserve peace with the sword, but rather to destroy it and earn the honorary title of Gâzi (Râzi). Wieland once said, "Peace is always the ultimate intention of war." This perspective is absolutely Nordic and peasant. The nomad would say just the opposite: "War is always the ulti-

---

[322] From chapter 6 of *Germania*: "To retire, provided you press on again, they treat as a question of tactics, not of cowardice." The system of mobile defensive warfare as introduced by Ludendorff during the World War thus reveals itself to be a quite ancient German institution.

[323] Andreas Hofer (1767–1810) was a Tyrolean innkeeper and leader of the Tyrolean Rebellion against Napoleon's forces. He led the Tyrolean peasants in a notable uprising that initially achieved several victories. However, the rebellion was eventually suppressed and Hofer was executed. At his execution, he refused a blindfold, refused to kneel, and opted to give the order to fire himself. He is remembered as a national hero in Austria and South Tyrol for his resistance against foreign control.

mate purpose of my momentary peace." It may sound contradictory, but the tendency of the Nordic race to embrace struggle is very clear proof of its peasant and peaceful nature.

The Old Testament legend of Cain and Abel is, in its most basic elements, more than clear and unmistakable evidence of this. The peasant is Cain, and the nomadic pastoralist is Abel. The two are absolute and irreconcilable opposites. Cain, the peasant, cannot defend himself against Abel, the nomad, except by taking up arms and striking him down. This is the beginning of human fratricide. This is the right way to put it, because in the animal world, for example, no species knows organized intra-species fighting. Of course, it is true that male animals fight each other for females, and that one species fights another (organized hunting of lions, ants, and others). But fighting between groups within the same species is absolutely alien to the animal kingdom. This form of fighting, which we humans first developed and call war, presupposes fighting for something (ownership). In this respect, the legend of Cain and Abel is quite clear and, above all, it correctly marks the beginning of fratricide. However, it is incorrect to place the blame on Cain alone. He, who had worked for his possessions, had no choice but to affirm struggle in order to assert himself. Given the incapability of the nomad (Abel) for creative constructive work and his predatory drive to exploit the self-created civilization of the peasant (Cain), in practical terms, the peasant (Cain) simply has choice but to raise his hand against the robber and predator (Abel). It is essentially the same dynamic as Prussian militarism—it was born under the iron compulsion of defense and so has always stood under the banner of protection. Yet, it still faced the world's opposition for allegedly disturbing world peace. Simply put, such views arise from the primordial urges of nomadic thinking, and these views are on the same level as those of criminals who see the police (from the Greek *politeia* and Latin *politia*, meaning state administration or state) only as restrictors of their "freedoms."

This certainly does not answer the entire question regarding the attitude of the Nordic race toward warfare. Before attempting to answer this question, however, it is necessary to present some additional characteristics of the Nordic race in regard to warfare. These characteristics lend themselves to various explanations, but none of them points to a warlike and predatory nomadism.

This includes, for example, the shield and the significance attributed to it by the Nordic race. Returning from combat without a shield was considered a particular disgrace. The shield is the ultimate weapon of defense. A light, mobile nomadic people that prefers ambushes to actual combat never possesses heavy shields. In combat, one discards their shield only if they want to flee (in other words, if they do not want to persevere in battle). On the other hand, if the retreat is done solely for tactical reasons, one will be hesitant to discard their shield.

The chariot also falls into this category, as strange as it may seem at first glance. Originally, chariots were not used on the battlefield, but only to reach it. The warriors would dismount on the battlefield and take their positions in the battle line. At the very least, this is the best interpretation of the available historical evidence. Apart from the fact that this way of engaging in battle is the exact opposite of the ambush tactics used by the nomads, there are other instructive conclusions that can be drawn from this. First and foremost, both parties must have peacefully discussed and agreed upon the battlefield in advance, a practice confirmed by the history of the Germanic peoples. From this, however, it can be inferred that such battles must have been preceded by a formal declaration of war, which is also confirmed in Germanic history and in Indo-European history more broadly. In Rome, for example, a red war flag was raised when danger threatened or when a war was to be initiated. Nothing proves more convincingly that war was an exceptional situation for the peasant patricians than this very fact. Ihering writes,

> At a time spears tipped with iron had long been known in Rome, the *fetiales* were for centuries obliged to continue using the *hasta praeusta* in their solemn declarations of war, whereby a spear was thrown onto the enemy's land. This was a spear made entirely of wood, with its tip hardened in fire and then soaked in blood. It is also found in the *hasta pura*, which was granted as a reward for bravery, and in the *festuca* of the vindication process. The *hasta praeusta* also appears in the *cranntair* of the Gaels in the Scottish Highlands and in the *bodkefli* of the Scandinavians, in the form of a staff burnt at the ends and then dipped in blood, which was sent around a territory as a sign of impending war and involved an obligation to gather at a designated location. In Sweden, this custom persisted until the sixteenth century, and among the Gaels until the eighteenth century.

This is even more clearly expressed by Kuhlenbeck:

> Among no other people do we find such firm rules regarding the declaration of war, the initiation of hostilities, the conclusion of peace, and adherence to international treaties as among the Romans. Some of the Roman conventions of war appear to be of ancient Aryan origin. As part of the *fas*, a college of priests called the *fetiales* were entrusted to serve as *quia fidei publicae praeerant* (guardians of public treaty compliance). Without the approval and involvement of this priesthood of experts in international law, there could be no just, pure, or pious war (*justum, purum, piumque bellum*). Above all, Rome observed the inviolability of envoys with exceptional conscientiousness. Just as it, on the other hand, brutally punished those peoples who violated the dignity of the Roman people by harming their envoys. Rome was even known to extradite any of its own citizens without hesitation if they had transgressed against this principle and violated the *fides* of international law.

However, all of this is done only when a decision is sought in a conflict that cannot be reached without warfare. In other words, battle here is not like that of the nomads, which involves theft by violent means. It is not a razzia, but rather a continuation of politics through different means. This quite unmistakably assigns it a unique status, and is naturally the norm in all freedom-loving and militarily capable peasant societies. In fact, we know from the accounts of the Cimbri, Teutons, Ariovistus, and other surviving records that the Nordic race was not nearly as quick to draw the sword as is often portrayed today. On the average, extensive attempts at peaceful resolution preceded a conflict.

Even more peculiar, and yet also largely overlooked, are the accounts indicating that, if necessary, one would forgo the battle itself and settle the conflict by means of a duel between leaders or between a few select individuals. During the duel, the two armies calmly observed, and the defeated side did not ever entertain the thought of taking up arms in anger afterwards. In the entire history of nomadic warfare, one will not find a single instance comparable to this. This not only suggests that the Nordic race viewed battle only as a last resort, but also indicates their willingness to prevent unnecessary bloodshed if the circumstances permitted.

One may have varying thoughts about war, but it can hardly be denied that this manner of conducting warfare has almost nothing to do with a plundering conquest.

In the traditions of the Indo-European and Germanic peoples, the principle of defense in their military organizations can be demonstrated much more readily than that of a constantly lurking warriorship focused on conquest. It is said by Kern (*Artbild der Deutschen*) that the word *krieg* (war) derives from *kriegen* (to grab) and clearly demonstrates the nomadic mindset of the Nordic nobility of the Germanic peoples. However, Schrader offers an alternative explanation for the word *krieg*. Schrader writes,

The Middle High German *krieg* in its current meaning is new. Italian *guerra*, French *guerre*, from Old High German *wêrra*, and English war initially only meant confusion, dispute, and, according to Frisch and Adelung, even just the clamor or noise of quarreling.

On the other hand, *krieg* in the sense understood by Kern likely corresponded to Old High German *urliugi* (see also: *orlogschiff*).[324]

Similarly, the word *burg* (meaning castle, fortress, or citadel) among the Germanic peoples by no means refers to the fortresses of nomads (coercion castles), but rather to protective fortresses. Schrader suggests that *burg* is related to the Indian word *pur*, which simply meant a fortified refuge in times of danger. Furthermore, the word *burg* is likely connected to Gothic *baurgs* and Old High German *burg*, which can be traced back to the word *berg* (mountain), as all fortifications in earlier times were strategically elevated for defensive purposes. In this context, however, it is also worth mentioning the Old Norse *tun* (enclosed farmstead) and Old English *tun*, from which the word town (enclosed place, city, etc.) originated. Ihering, in his research, also

---

[324] Translator's note: *Orlogschiff* is an antiquated German term for warship.

concludes that cities were established by "Aryan" peasants for defensive purposes, and that they were always built with enough space in mind to permit
the rural population to take refuge in the city with their belongings. As an
example, Ihering cites Alesia, where Vercingetorix was able to accommodate
not only his numerous cavalry but also seventy thousand infantrymen, as
well as a large quantity of livestock and enough provisions for at least a
month.[325] Ihering continues,

> An interesting parallel to this (Alesia) is the Roman rite of city
> foundation borrowed from the Etruscans. It consists of yoking a bull
> and a cow to a plow, with the bull positioned on the stronger,
> externally threatened side and the cow on the weaker, internally safe
> side of the future city . . . where the gates should be, the plow is
> lifted. . . . . [Rome] is thus characterized as the work of peasants, and
> the walls and moats, which the founder restricted himself to in his
> work, reveal why he established them—for his own security. . . . If the
> city had been intended as a market, they would probably have first
> delineated the market.

Indeed, the full Roman citizen, originally a peasant living in the countryside,
only entered the city on special days such as market days, court days, public
festivals, or when a sudden enemy invasion forced him to do so.

Far more important, however, is another consideration of Ihering's. He
establishes that in Roman law, one can precisely observe the transition from the
ancient Nordic (Aryan, according to Ihering) law of the patricians to the mechanical law of later times (Twelve Tables). In doing so, he discerns two distinct sources of military organization:

> In my view, the appearance of military numeration establishes a turn-
> ing point in the history of civilization. It signifies the transition from
> the organic organization of the people to a mechanical organization.
> The former developed naturally, the latter was made. . . . The Latin
> language has two terms for the army, one of which, *exercitus*, is more
> recent, while the other, *classis*, belongs to more ancient times. *Exerci-*
> *tus* linguistically describes an armed band forcing its way out of a
> fortress (*ex arce*), yet the fortress itself, along with the surrounding
> city, does not date further back than the time of settlement. The term
> *classis* linguistically brings to mind an army summoned by word of
> mouth (*calare*). . . . The cogency of this argument is demonstrated by
> the fact that this primitive form of summoning people together per-
> sisted among the *pontifices* until late in the historical period. The as-

---

[325]From *Commentarii de Bello Gallico*: "The army of the Gauls had filled all the space under the
wall, comprising a part of the hill which looked to the rising sun, and had drawn in front a trench
and a stone wall six feet high. The circuit of that fortification, which was commenced by the Romans, comprised eleven miles."

semblies they convened were therefore called *comitia calata*. This should not be understood as a type of convocation that had been peculiar to them from the beginning, and that secular authorities had therefore always used a different one—it was the only method of convocation known in antiquity, predating even the working of metal. . . . The absence of bugles in primeval times meant that commands in battle could only be conveyed by shouting. This required the employment of "battle criers," individuals with far-reaching voices who did not necessarily have to be leaders. As mentioned earlier, the *pontifices* maintained the ancient practice of *calare*. Linguistically connected to this are the *calatores* (their servants), who were responsible for proclaiming the cessation of public work during sacrifices, the *calendae*, the first day of the month on which they orally announced the monthly calendar, and the *curia calabra*, the location from which this was done. The oral proclamation of the calendar is just as characteristic for them as the oral convocation was for the popular assemblies. They refused to make use of writing for the former just as they refused to use the bugle, which had been developed in the meantime, for the latter. With the advent of writing, secular authorities replaced their oral proclamation (*edicere*) with a written one, albeit retaining the term *edictum*, which is no longer linguistically appropriate, just as in the case of *classicus*. But the *pontifices* did not embrace newer technology in official applications, even though they were the ones who had actually facilitated its development. Just as they retained the use of wooden bridges when masonry appeared, wooden nails and spears when iron was used, scourging to death when beheading had become commonplace, and the oral convocation of the people after bugles had been developed, so too they retained the practice of orally proclaiming the calendar and orally imparting formulas for lamentation, even after secular authorities had replaced them with writing.

It is quite revealing that Ihering, who at first absolutely believed in the early nomadic character of the Aryans, abandons his view during the course of his investigation and attributes all Indo-European state formations to the consolidation of military power in response to a defensive situation. The author would like to fully endorse this view.

Besides, it is also entirely implausible that the highly advanced peasant civilization of the Nordic race in Europe, which is now gradually being revealed to us by archaeology, emerged during a time filled with warfare. No social class requires peace and tranquility for cultural flourishing as much as the peasant class. A time dominated by warfare would inevitably have destroyed the isolated farm settlements, as they might withstand a few hostile incursions (as seen in the Roman invasions of Franconia and Lower Saxony), but they would not have been able to maintain individual farmsteads during frequent invasions or continuous insecurity (as illustrated in "Der Werewolf" by Hermann Löns).

The author will even go a step further and claim that, in addition to this, the Nordic race initially did not exhibit any particular aptitude for military strategy. One should carefully reexamine depictions of the initial encounters between the Germanic peoples and the Romans with an open mind. One will then have to concede that while the Germanic peoples are indeed splendid and brave individuals, unafraid of death and danger, one can truly discern no trace of any military art nor even a moderately sensible military strategy among them. On the contrary, the Romans were able to hinder the Germanic tribes for centuries partly due to the lack of strategic awareness of the Germanic peoples. Certainly, throughout history, when the Nordic race has had the opportunity to train in the art of war and pass down what they have learned from generation to generation, their innate bravery and capacity for ordered thinking, derived from their peasant roots, helped produce strategists of great importance. However, without training, the Nordic race does not possess an innate aptitude for military strategy, although each individual is endowed with all the qualities valued in an honorable warrior.

To those who perceive this as a contradiction, they should refer to the English officers of the World War, who without exception fought with outstanding bravery but often exhibited a blindness in troop leadership that worked to our advantage on more than one occasion. If the English forces had been led by German officers on November 20, 1917, during the tank battle at Cambrai, they would have achieved markedly different results than they actually did. It was on this very day that, despite a desperate situation and being alone with a handful of men, the German officer, trained in military strategy, wrested the initiative from the numerically superior English officer, who was untrained in military strategy but displayed remarkable bravery. The English quite openly admitted this in their daily reports.

In order to fully appreciate the significance of this day for the glory of our army, one must realize that a single German division—the 54th Infantry Division under General of Artillery Baron von Watter—withstood the attack of eight English infantry divisions and three cavalry divisions, each of which had a multitude of guns at their disposal, as well as three hundred fifty tanks and five hundred aircraft (according to Royal Norwegian reports from Colonel Schnittler, it may have been as high as a thousand). Moreover, the English attack was so unexpected that the entire first and main defensive lines of the 54th Infantry Division were already overrun before the German side could fully comprehend what was actually happening. But the English did not know how to utilize their cavalry, nor did they know how to effectively eliminate the German small unit groups. Essentially, the English cavalry no longer had an adversary before them. It is hard to imagine what would have become of the German western front if the English commanders had simply unleashed their cavalry, as every German recruit would instinctively have done after half a year of training. The English, however, did not find the courage to make such a decision. Probably never in the history of the world has a troop of cavalry disgraced themselves more than the English cavalry at Cambrai. As a matter of fact, it received condemnation from its own infantry and has since been honored by being given the name "Purple Riders." It would be a good idea to directly quote here an expert opinion on the English cavalry to truly emphasize how little personal bravery aligns with the ability to effectively lead troops. From the second issue (year five) of "The Light Artillery":

> Here, at noon, for the first time, the English cavalry missed the opportunity to fulfill its mission and intervene decisively in the battle. By German standards, this is what should have taken place at that point. They would have had an easy task here against a shaken (at least initially shaken) opponent, before he had the opportunity to regain his composure and organize himself in his original undaunted manner. If the English cavalry had followed the old German rider's motto, it would have brought good fortune to England—charge and breakthrough! If thrown energetically together, all three of them would have made it through. They actually had the upper hand until dusk. In the afternoon, they missed the second and final opportunity, and thus, according to German cavalry concepts and principles, allowed themselves to be "coffined."
>
> The English cavalry divisions remained passive throughout the entire day. A cavalry must be active. Otherwise, it is not a cavalry but a useless and burdensome fixture among the troops, which serves no purpose anywhere and hinders everything. However, it would be misguided to solely blame them for the failure of that day, as perhaps the transmission of orders also failed to provide them with a clear top-down picture of the situation regarding the enemy and their own infantry. This, however, heavily burdens the command, as they needed to know what the cavalry divisions had at their disposal at the appropriate moment. On the other hand, if the cavalry divisions truly couldn't obtain the desired information from the command, then it was their responsibility to seek independent reconnaissance. As far as we can judge, they lacked in independent and responsible action, as well as in bold assertiveness. It must be assumed that the three cavalry divisions were under the unified leadership of a higher cavalry commander. This commander had to act with absolute independence —if he did not, he should be brought before a military court— because in such situations, the cavalry commander must not timidly depend on higher command. The history of the German cavalry is replete with examples where the independent action of cavalry commanders not only rescued the infantry from desperate situations, but also led to victory through such independent action and through the uncompromising advance of the standards into the enemy's ranks.

The same phenomenon was even more pronounced in 1918 among the Americans, who attacked with an incredible disregard for their own safety and often behaved so foolishly that as a soldier, one did not know whether to laugh or cry at the tremendous losses these magnificent characters had just incurred. The author himself witnessed on multiple occasions that the Americans, without being intoxicated in any way, would charge with rifles slung over their shoulders, shag pipes in their mouths, and hands in their pockets.[326]

In short, one may examine the Nordic race wherever one wishes and will undoubtedly encounter outstanding personal bravery among its members. However, it can also always be observed that only in a gradual manner do they acquire tactical and strategic experience; they by no means possess these qualities naturally.

This observation could be considered insignificant if it did not also provide us with revealing insights into Nordic prehistory. If the Nordic race was a brave but by no means warlike race, we hold in our hands further evidence that it grew out of peasant soil and can dismiss theories of nomadic origin for them.

However, in this case, one must be able to explain the bravery of the Nordic race without military training (in other words, excluding a constant state of war). Sufficient possibilities for this do exist, let us attempt to make them clear. We can consider the self-reliant personal awareness typical of the Nordic peasantry as a primary reason for this, as the harsh Nordic environment characteristically prevented any softening of character. The settled person has no choice but to confront the environment if he is to survive. This confrontation becomes as tough and stormy as the environment itself, whether this is because of animals, humans, or natural forces. This is an experience that the colonial history of the last one hundred and fifty years confirms for the Nordic race, and it is not a small part of why the entire active political life of the Germanic peoples since the Migration Period has played out in colonial territories (England, Prussia, Austria, and others). Faced with the harsh forces of nature, the settled person is presented only with the choice between submitting and "conquering the environment." The peasantry of the Nordic race followed the path of conquest, tempering their will in this struggle against the wild northern environment, and became accustomed to facing destiny with steady eyes. In north-central Europe, a settled form of existence necessarily ripened into heroism (heroism here is understood as a person who affirms their destiny in order to overcome it).[327] All the terrifying and edifying, all the gruesome and beautiful aspects of this Nordic heroic race find their entirely natural explanation in this self-reliant peasantry of the north. Those who do not want to believe this

---

[326] The author is by no means alone in his judgment of the Americans, nor has he generalized exceptional cases. Even French and English observers, while admiring the personal bravery of the American soldier, were horrified by his lack of tactical finesse in combat. Generally speaking, the American displayed no sense for the rational command of a military unit. One can indeed understand the words said by the English Admiral Lord Fisher (Records, 246): "In a newspaper article, a Cabinet Minister stated that the Entente was at the end of its strength when the armistice came, as if by a miracle. Even Marshal Foch was at his wits' end due to the incompetence of the American army and the inevitable consequences of the new army's lack of experience. Although the English army captured Mons, the German army was still formidable, not demoralized, and had enormous defensive lines behind it. This was not another Waterloo, Sedan, or Trafalgar!

[327] Frederick the Great was exceptionally adept at expressing this sentiment with the following words: "I know that I am a human being, therefore doomed to suffering. And in the face of twists of fate, only steadfastness can help."

should listen to the stories of the settlers in our colonies regarding the interactions between them and their environment—the heroic struggle of Lettow-Vorbeck, of course, did not arise purely by chance. It is understandable that a life in constant confrontation with harsh forces also brings forth a quite clear sense of purpose and determination. Eventually, a person comes to the conviction that it is only through action that they can ever master their destiny.

In the evolution of their mental faculties, the Nordic race's settled form of existence led to the development of spatial awareness and organic thinking. The moment that a person feels that they themselves are the bearers of destiny, fear ceases to exist for them. Hagen, who invites his own demise because this fate had been prophesied to him, is a perfect embodiment of the Nordic spirit. This self-evident willingness "to face death" has been demonstrated countless times in the history of the German army since 1813. Many participants in military campaigns may also be familiar with cases where comrades quite consciously anticipated their own death, yet cheerfully and naturally fulfilled their duty until their last breath. Rarely, however, has such a case been recorded with such certainty as in the following, and so it is worth mentioning here in brief. This is also done because, in a peculiar, albeit "modernized" form, it resembles the conscious willingness "to face death" demonstrated by Hagen von Tronje. The author takes the following lines from an obituary dedicated to Captain von Consbruch, Battery Commander of the third battery of the 25th Field Artillery Regiment, written by his senior officer in the unit's regimental memorial magazine:

I will skip the description of the first days and weeks with all their impressions and experiences and only start with the first day because it was from that day on that I got to know Captain von Consbruch and his downright fatalistic anticipation of death. Perhaps he expressed himself in this manner to me more because he had known me for years, or because he knew that I too was married and leaving behind a wife and child, or because I was his senior officer and he knew that I would be the one to make the call to replace him in the midst of battle. Yet, in this daily reminder of his death, there was nothing of fear, nothing of dread, nor anything that should somehow weigh on my heart. He was only concerned with constantly facing and arranging everything necessary for this destiny, which he firmly believed would soon and inevitably occur. Every night before going to bed, he would say to me as his senior officer, "Let's have a drink together, because it might be my last." Since there was nothing but strength in this anticipation of death, I had long since given up trying to respond to it, no matter how deeply it cut into my soul. I always carried this impression with me. When on August 22, 1914 we received our baptism of fire at Maissin and saw how our brave second battery was essentially covered by shrapnel without any casualties, I said to Captain von Consbruch, "Well, now you see, if the French continue shooting like this for the remainder of this war, nothing can happen to us at all." His response was, "That was today, wait until tomorrow!" And that "tomorrow" did come. It came for the third battery on the unforgettable, very difficult day of August 28, 1914. On this day, at 4:30 in the afternoon, near Raucourt, the first group (four shots) of a French battery struck, resulting in the loss of twenty four men from the 3/25, including Captain von Consbruch. Thus, his premonition of death had been fulfilled. He faced it fearlessly, finding the noblest death that a brave artilleryman can endure, an eternally painful and irreplaceable loss for us, but also an eternal example of the most faithful fulfillment of duty until death. Signed, W. Beck.

Such knowledge of fate and its nature has nothing in common with the fatalism of the nomad. The fatalist always resigns himself to fate as something absolutely given, while the Nordic individual confronts it and views it as a struggle in which the soul is tempered as it advances from stage to stage until reaching its highest and truest earthly mission. Hence, the Nordic race did not originally entertain the idea that one can purchase eternal bliss by "refraining from sin." The author does not intend to establish a philosophical theory here, but the ideas developed here can be discerned, to a greater or lesser extent, by any attentive observer of our frontline soldiers. At the very least, it justifies the application of these observations to our understanding of the Nordic race. If we want to draw conclusions about the Nordic race's struggle-affirming spirit from our German frontline soldiers, then we can say with certainty that the struggle-affirming spirit and fearlessness of the Nordic race must, at least in part, be intimately connected with its affirmation of destiny. This is true even if fearlessness is a veritable result of breeding and has become second nature to him —Nordic man need not first reflect on his destiny in order to be brave.

Now we can perhaps begin to understand the warriorship of the Nordic race. For them, war was not a razzia, a raid, but a fateful confrontation, a national duel that, when necessary, was initiated and conducted according to all the rules of an honorable duel. With this, the peculiar behavior of the Nordic race with regard to pre-battle discussions becomes clear, as well as why this behavior is never found among genuine nomads. But it also becomes clear that such fateful decisions were occasionally left to the leaders alone, in the natural and chivalrous conviction that there was not a coward on either side.

The flip side of this very noble view of combat, remnants of which have persisted to this day in our almost exaggerated emphasis on formal declarations of war and moral justifications for war (a concept entirely foreign to nomadism) is the assumption that one must never avoid a battle because it is always a test of fate. This has led to the fatal belief, so detrimental to the survival of the Nordic race, that every duel always carried a divine judgment. It need not be emphasized how devastating this belief has been for Nordic blood— nonetheless, it has not completely vanished even in the present day. While it may no longer take center stage in actual duels, it can still be found in the need to give thanks to God for victory in war. Such considerations are crucial for shedding light on Nordic prehistory. Namely, they quite convincingly demonstrate that an individual representative of the Nordic race could view the sword as an essential part of their human existence, while war itself was always regarded by the race as a rare and extraordinary occasion.[328] Anyone who believes that times of peace can corrupt a people's heroic courage should consider the small Boer colony in South Africa, where an entirely peaceful peasant population was still capable of waging an utterly heroic struggle for freedom. The forty-three years of peace had not diminished the fighting spirit of the German infantry in 1914, and the French were no more capable of calmly withstanding our assault than the Romans were against the Cimbri and Teutons two thousand years ago. Although the French have always been masters of defense, their resistance in the World War was never based on defense by bayonet, a tool that the English did not shy away from. This circumstance can certainly be considered a distinguishing racial feature. In open combat, bare steel quickly separates the brave from the faint-hearted. One must be aware of such matters when passing judgment on the heroism of the Nordic race.

Two phenomena in Nordic prehistory are relatively easy to understand from the perspective of viewing war solely as a divine judgement. The first is the recorded human sacrifices of some captives, while the second is the conviction, deeply ingrained within the blood of the Nordic race, that an equal born opponent should only be fought on an objective basis, and that their defeat affects them only in an objective manner (not personal). This is to say that once the conflict is settled, all enmity ceases. Only the Nordic race is capable of lowering their sword before an honorably vanquished opponent, just as it is only the Nordic race that can wholeheartedly extend a hand to the victor as a defeated party. In essence, both traditions, the human sacrifices and the objective attitude toward the opponent, are contradictions that can only be reconciled by viewing them within the context of the basic religious principles of the Nordic race related to warfare.

Excluding our own military tradition, it is arguably the English who have most traditionally preserved the sense of maintaining an objective attitude toward an opponent. In 1914, captured English soldiers congratulated our infantry on their victory in a completely impartial manner. The propaganda of the Entente quickly put an end to such behavior, but we should accustom ourselves to seeing through the artificially created fog and avoid the generalization of isolated cases of genuine malice among the English to all Englishmen. In order to make an objective assessment of the English soldier, we must not for-

---

[328] Perhaps the following example will vividly illustrate the distinction that can exist between personal bravery and an individual's understanding of warfare. As an Artillery Liaison Officer (*Artillerie-Verbindungs-Offizier*), the author observed a young infantry officer getting carried away by combat enthusiasm during an infantry assault. He became overly involved in the fighting on a personal level, causing him to lose control of the company that he had taken charge of due to the leader's absence. This momentarily led to a somewhat chaotic and uncomfortable situation. As a result, the officer received a reprimand from the battalion commander, who stated, among other things, the classic phrase, "Sir, you are not in the field for your own pleasure but to fulfill your duty as an officer." Imagine trying to explain the sense of duty demonstrated by German wartime officers to warlike nomads!

get that it was through the daily reports published by the English that we first became acquainted with many heroic acts of German frontline soldiers, who they quite openly and admirably mentioned by name and regiment.[329]

The view that one should not avoid a proposed fight or that it is cowardly to evade it has persisted, with some modifications, longer than one might initially assume. When an English gentleman is challenged to a boxing match by someone he considers to be of equal worth, he never declines the fight, even if he belongs to the most aristocratic element of society and expects a physical thrashing in the fight. The German party member (not a deputy) who defends his former position "upright" and "unswervingly" is carved from the same wood, although it should not be implied that both are equally great.

For that matter, in English culture, the Nordic sense of steadfastness has also been strongly preserved in another context—English sports. The Englishman understands sport (among other things) not merely as a physical game but rather as the ability to "stay the course," as an expression of will that engages every fiber of his being with the goal of achieving something. While in the context of everyday life, this primarily manifests itself in physical sports (aligning with our contemporary understanding of sports), the Englishman does not limit the concept to that area alone. The Englishman may perceive an academic research trip to a foreign land as sport, implying that he certainly does not undertake the journey for his own pleasure. Rather, it means that he will voluntarily devote body and soul to see it through and bring it to a successful conclusion. Therefore, for the Englishman, sport is linked to determination and, in rare cases, it is not exclusively associated with the notion of leisure. In this sense, we cannot directly translate into German the English word "sport," but if we rephrase it in a meaningful way, such as "doing something with all of one's soul" or "doing something wholeheartedly," the basic idea becomes clearer. Suddenly, we begin to feel kinship with an English popular expression that once seemed foreign to us but is nevertheless the product of our shared Nordic blood.

4

Let us recall a previously mentioned observation—that the Nordic individual farmstead shattered the sense of tribal belonging and fostered the development of a self-confident personality. Furthermore, let us remember that in Nordic peasant society, a sense of duty toward the farm had to develop, as well as the

---

[329] This includes, for example, the heroic death of Lieutenant Karl Müller, battery commander of Field Artillery Regiment 9/108, on November 20, 1917, at Flesquières (Cambrai). The English did not know his name, referring to him only as the "lone gunner of Flesquières." On the basis of the English daily reports, the Germans were able to determine, by means of a general inquiry in 1927, who the officer so highly praised by the English had been. Müller, as the only survivor of his battery, continued to engage tank after tank with his gun until he himself was hit and fell at the gun. Moreover, it should be noted that the attack at Cambrai was carried out by the English Guards, and it can be said that Lieutenant Müller's martial spirit was as noble and Nordic as the public and chivalrous recognition of his heroic deed by the attackers, whose officers belonged to the most illustrious English nobility.

notion that one's own emotional state had to take a backseat to the necessities of that way of life. By considering these factors, along with the aforementioned understanding of duels, we can perhaps learn that these elements, when combined, provide us with the key to understanding many gruesome incomprehensibilities in Nordic history. When well-established customs or the firm direction of a strong-willed monarch were absent, the Nordic race was quite naturally assailed by the inclination to engage in a struggle of all against all, tearing themselves apart in the process. After all, the line of sight of this race, with its peasant orientation, has always been directed toward the neighbor rather than the common enemy at the border. Examples of this are easy to find in German history, just as they are the exception among nomads.

In nomadic rule, nobility is based on tribal affiliation—it is derived from blood. Land ownership never plays an important role for individual nomads. Instead, conquered lands are, just like in the steppes or deserts, held in a communistic type of communal ownership. Interestingly, Dungern has demonstrated that the German nobility of the Middle Ages (until the thirteenth century) was also a closed nobility based on kinship.[330] An individual's membership in the nobility was determined by blood, and in this respect, this form of nobility corresponds to nomadic nobility. However—and this is very important— within the nobility, the individual attained their rank through land ownership, though not in the modern financial-economic sense. The entire imperial nobility was a manorial nobility, thereby standing in stark contrast to any nomadic nobility. The term "nobility" originally derives from ownership of land, not blood, although one's blood was a self-evident prerequisite.

For the Nordic nobility, land ownership was not just a prerequisite, it was the cornerstone of their integrity. Riehl aptly points out that our German custom of allowing all sons to inherit noble titles has contributed significantly to the creation of an aristocratic proletariat. In this respect, England has remained more in line with the old Nordic tradition, where names and noble titles are still linked to land ownership, allowing brothers to bear entirely different names.

The very manner in which German counts exercised their office in the Middle Ages, by being the first in their community and assuming responsibility only for specific delineated powers, clearly demonstrates that this nobility operated with a clear understanding of the needs of the peasantry.[331] They

---

[330] Dungern, *Adelsherrschaft im Mittelalter*.
[331] If the Nordic race had a nomadic way of thinking, for instance, the development from Carolingian county offices into feudalism would not have been conceivable. Such a progression presupposes that the Frankish counts had an awareness of the significance of land ownership. This awareness was so deeply ingrained that it took the full force of Charlemagne the Saxon Slayer's efforts to prevent the naturally-occurring Nordic concept of hereditary linkage between a public office and land from emerging among his counts. He pushed aside the notion of heredity within a count's office. "Perhaps the transformation of county offices into fiefs was linked to the property with which the office was endowed. For a considerable period, the records often differentiate between the count's properties, which undoubtedly included landed property, and the office. It seems, therefore, that property became a fief earlier than the office." See: Below, *Der Deutsche Staat des Mittelalters*.

thoroughly integrated themselves into the peasantry as its head, rather than simply superimposing themselves upon it. Thus, this nobility stands quite clearly outside of any nomadism and essentially reveals itself as nothing more than a nobility that evolved out of the peasantry—an ennobled form of peasantry—or as Dungern aptly remarks, a result of genuine high breeding. This nobility emerged from the people it led through rigorous performance-based breeding. Dungern explicitly refers to it as the "ideal of consolidated and highly-bred national strength." Dungern rightly points out that a freedom-conscious and freedom-loving people like the Germans could never have flourished under a nobility possessing such immense power (such as the medieval nobility) if this nobility had been in opposition to the people and the people had not seen in the nobility their own organic leadership and the fulfillment of their own yearning for individuality. It is only with the disintegration of the old true nobility in the thirteenth century that an unfortunate era begins in Germany, pitting the freedom-loving Germanic people against authority and ultimately triggering unrest that still shakes us to this day, and which now, quite unjustly, some suddenly want to collectively blame on the Nordic race.

If we closely examine our nobility from the beginning of the disintegration of imperial power in the thirteenth century, we cannot help but have the impression that this perpetual squabbling over rights, inheritances, and territorial boundaries bears a devilish resemblance to the behavior of lifelong peasant litigants. At the very least, both behaviors stem from the same source. It initially had little to do with a desire for conflict or martial activity or even "Nordic expansion," rather, it arose from a solid and inherently healthy peasant instinct for land ownership. Our nobility never went beyond a feudal peasantry. Nothing is more indicative of this than the fact that, on their own, the German nobility never even considered the idea of directing their gaze outward and pursuing nomadic conquest policies in foreign lands. Basically, the entire spectacle of late medieval sword clashing appears rather plain. The era of robber barons is clearly a symptom of decline and can be easily refuted by the colonizing Teutonic Order, leaving no grounds for any arguments against the peasant origins of the Nordic nobility.

At times, the Nordic nobility even appears fairly unwarlike. Many nobles who took part in military campaigns "to the Eastland" were (at least in part) motivated by the generous compensation they received and were more than willing to fight against pagans if it meant getting a fief. One will never find anything in this German medieval nobility that could be compared to the razzias of the nomads.

Even the famous the Vikings raids are always unjustifiably invoked as a defining characteristic of the Nordic race. A simple consideration tells us that these voyages cannot be readily considered as being characteristic of the Nordic race. If the Vikings were exclusively engaged in warlike piracy, we would have heard of these pirates even before the ninth century, which marked the beginning of the era of Norman (Viking) raids. But that is simply not the case. Tacitus even explicitly reports of a mighty Swedish king who dominated a vast trading alliance, similar to our medieval Hanseatic League, and had trading posts along all the major rivers of Europe, from the Rhine to the Volga. Such circumstances suggest well-regulated conditions instead of unbridled piracy. Additionally, such consolidated power would have absolutely been capable of emerging on the world stage even before the ninth century. However, it only appears in our historical record when Charlemagne the Saxon Slayer attempts to gain control of this consolidated Baltic Sea trading area. Professor E. Almquist (Västervik) of Sweden[332] has demonstrated in a very instructive exposition how it was the conversion efforts of Charlemagne the Saxon Slayer against the Lower Saxons that incited the Normans (Vikings) to sate their inflamed hatred via massive retaliatory campaigns. Let us follow the words of Almquist:

> It is *a priori* impossible to imagine that such extensive trade, which was carried out for centuries, was largely based on plunder. The maritime connection between the Baltic Sea and the western European Elbe, Weser, and Rhine rivers used to run along the Schlei to Hedeby (Schleswig), from where the boats would be pulled overland to the Eider. From there, they soon reached Cuxhaven, a port of call for the cogs or *kuggs*. In Stieler's Atlas, we find several important place names in the area between Schleswig and Eider— Stapelholm, Norderstapel, Süderstapel, as well as "Drage," which in Swedish refers to a place where boats were pulled overland. The trade between the Saxons and Scandinavians was very active there since ancient times, their kinship was close, and their religion was the same. Under Charlemagne the Saxon Slayer, this trade was endangered. Nevertheless, the Swedes and Danes managed to maintain this important connection for several more centuries.
>
> The conversion of the Saxons took thirty years. By the year 800, the work was almost completed. Charlemagne's methods are well-known. On a single day, thousands of men were beheaded on the lower Weser, Holstein was partially cleared, and a Wendish settlement was established. The aforementioned connection between the peoples along the Eider and their trade was threatened, Saxon brethren were being treated in an undignified manner, and their shared religion was in danger. There was indeed sufficient cause for a ruthless war.
>
> It may have even been the case that Charlemagne attacked the Scandinavians in their own land. The great Battle of Brávalla, where ten thousand warriors fell, must be relocated to Norrköping, according to recent research. Through studies of the many place names mentioned in the ancient accounts, Hederström has been able to clarify not only the course of the battle but also the march of the two opponents. Partly on foot and partly by sea, the Swedes and their allies from western Gotland and Norway arrived from the north. The attackers sailed from the south to Kalmar county. There were Saxons,

---

[332] Almquist, *Archiv für Rassen und Gesellschaftsbiologie* 19: 418.

Wends, Danes, and Latvians, presumably under the leadership of a minor king from East Gotland. The Saxons alone numbered seven thousand men. The Swedes emerged victorious. According to the annals of a Frankish monastery, this great battle was fought in the year 812. If the date is correct, we must see here an attempt by Charlemagne the Saxon Slayer to conquer the Swedes by force. In doing so, a main center of the Wotan cult and a key Scandinavian polity would have been destroyed. Naturally, a failure of this scale had to be concealed as much as possible. Ansgar gained great respect because he dared to go to Sweden as a missionary around 830. In spite of his distinguished and very kind personality, he and his successors failed miserably in the work of converting Sweden. It is likely that Frankish tactics were still too fresh in their collective memory. Only in the following century would any significant progress be made—but not from Hamburg and Bremen. The Anglo-Saxons carried out the conversion.

For a long time, the connection between the Roman Empire and the Baltic Sea ran along the Vistula River. This was severed after the establishment of the Polish kingdom; how this came about is not to be explained here. A new route was needed. It has been established that the Swedes of Kiev had eminent importance not only for Russia, but also for the Empire in Constantinople. They enabled the survival of the Eastern Roman Empire for centuries after the destruction of the Western Roman Empire. It is well known that the Russians invited a Swedish leader to organize their kingdom.

It appears that the Nordic race in general converted to Christianity without significant resistance or intense reactions. Higher religion and civilization is sometimes able to assert itself among Nordic peoples almost on its own accord, albeit gradually. As a result of the conversion of the Saxons, wherein methods that were hardly appropriate for these peoples were employed, a tremendously agitated sentiment arose among the Scandinavians in opposition. The war that ignited as a result had magnificent consequences for civilization. In Normandy, a polity was organized that would produce beneficial ripple effects throughout Europe. However, due to Charlemagne's cruelty, the spread of the new religion to the north was significantly delayed. We have already highlighted the close connection between Sweden and the Anglo-Saxons. The numerous English coins from the tenth century that have been found on our soil testify to this close connection. It is hardly a coincidence that the Anglo-Saxon kingdom declined at the same time that the line of Swedish kings died out. The ancient Swedish realm was of a completely different nature to the later states that emerged in the north, which had quite well-defined and fixed borders. Our realm primarily focused on organizing the extensive regional trade and fulfilling certain religious duties. Provinces were hardly conquered—even after the conquest of

Constantinople, provisions regarding reciprocal trade rights remained the main concern in the conclusion of peace agreements. We (remember that Almquist is Swedish!) established numerous colonies on the European continent, formed trade alliances with various peoples, defended them, and kept pirates at bay to the best of our abilities. Within this realm, the freedom of individual regions was considerably greater than it would be later on, and this often led to abuse and disputes. It is remarkable that under such a lax organization, the extensive trade of the Swedish kings could continue for a thousand years after the time of Tacitus. It was only in the late Middle Ages that this regional trade would fall into the hands of the Hanseatic League.

That covers Almquist! It is instructive to find in his writings, once again, an absolute rejection of all those views that seek to associate the combative nature of the Nordic race with the baseless warfare of the predatory nomads.[333]

If the Nordic race truly harbored those nomadic instincts that Kern so eagerly attributes to them, then the sword-loving warrior culture of that race would inevitably have burst out of the borders of the Holy Roman Empire once the empire began to decline, sweeping across its borders in colossal military campaigns, just as all nomads and semi-nomads do when their grazing lands become too restricted. But where in all of their history have the German people ever produced singular and mighty warrior figures like Genghis Khan of the Mongols and Attila of the Huns? Instead, the Germanic civilization of the Middle Ages never truly understood the Mediterranean policies of the German emperors, and during their only major military expeditions (the Crusades), the knights were guided by an "ideal," participation was a "duty," and alongside the crusaders rode homesickness and a longing for their loved ones. The legends do not mention the homesickness of the Moors in Spain, and upon closer examination, following the Prophet's banner in "Holy War" is a highly practical justification for predatory instincts. Such instincts cannot be attributed to the Christian crusaders in any way.

In their folk heroes, each people depicts its own ideal. But where has the Nordic race presented us with pure warriorhood as an ideal, as the nomads do, where the number of enemies killed often takes center stage, regardless of what was achieved or intended to be achieved thereby? Attila was a formidable martial figure, and to a people or nobility solely focused on war, he must have emerged as a kind of idealized figure. Interestingly, however, legends transmit him to us as Etzel or Godegisel, meaning "God's scourge." After the mighty Battle of the Catalaunian Plains in 451 AD, in which Attila unleashed his steppe coalition (the Huns, Gepids, Ostrogoths, Heruls, and Thuringians)

---

[333] When Lieutenant Joachim-Hans von Zieten, who had been discharged by Frederick Wilhelm I, was offered the position of captain (with his own squadron in the imperial army) by a landowner in Wustrau, Austria, he replied, "I do not wish to sell myself like a *landsknecht* to this or that person, I will remain where God has placed me."

against the West but ultimately had to retreat back to the east because his horse-riding hordes became depraved if they couldn't roam freely, Europe celebrated the grace of heaven and built higher walls and churches.[334] Rightly, Hermann Stegemann[335] states, "Public opinion celebrated the retreat of the Huns as a victory for the community of nations in western Europe, thus elevating the battle to an event of universal-historical significance."

The clearest evidence against the belief in the nomadic nature of the Nordic race, however, can actually be inferred from Germanic law, something the author has already pointed out. While in all forms of nomadic law, a strict superimposition over the subjugated population is unmistakably maintained, the exact opposite can be observed in Germanic law. Muhammad, for example, was able to induce a kind of common national feeling among the peoples of the Orient only by associating adherence to Islam with ideas of matrilineality—that is, by proclaiming that all believers must support one another as if they were blood relatives from the same womb. With the exception of the master-slave relationship, any form of human relationship between people who are not of the same tribe would be beyond a nomad's understanding. Conversely, Tacitus noted that in the ancient Germanic kingdoms, the power of the kings was not unlimited, but subject to legal constraints in relation to the citizenry. While all nomadic rulers are always despots whose official actions depend entirely on their whims, with rulers appearing as borderline divine to the people, the basic Germanic idea of rulership is always that it is not authority by force but a duty to protect. All Germanic rulership is built on a mutual relationship of duties, and no prince is granted rights without obligations—this conception also assumes the proud fact that there are no obligations without rights. Therefore, the subject did not owe the ruler obedience, he owed him loyalty. The disloyal ruler, however, forfeited his claim to the loyalty of his subjects. Obedience is only owed to the extent that loyalty demands it. Absolute obedience—that is, the mindless relationship of a slave and his master, or as a modern slogan says, "cadaver obedience"—was completely foreign to the worldview of the Germanic people and is of Oriental origin. It could be said that nothing could more clearly prove the improbability of a nomadic origin for the Nordic race than the concepts of obedience and loyalty that this race has developed.[336]

The notion that the relationship between prince and people is based solely

---

[334] See chapter one for what Schultze (Leipzig) says about Bolshevism, which he refers to as a "Tatarized Marxism." When comparing historical accounts of the Hunnic invasions to the atrocities committed by the Bolsheviks, one cannot help but agree with Schultze. Therefore, in this context, reference is once again made to Lothrop Stoddard's work, *The Revolt Against Civilization*, as well as Pitirim Sorokin's *Die Soziologie der Revolution* [The Sociology of Revolution] and General Prince Awaloff's *Im Kampf gegen den Bolschewismus* [In the Battle Against Bolshevism].
[335] Stegemann, *Der Kampf um den Rhein.*
[336] As a very young officer, Joachim-Hans von Zieten defended himself against an attack by his captain with an iron rod, which resulted in his discharge by Frederick Wilhelm I. He never understood the judgment of his king. Similarly, as a young officer, York, later known as Count York von Wartenburg, refused to follow his dishonorable company commander and was therefore dismissed by Frederick II. He, too, never understood this judgment. However, neither of them ever dared to waver in their loyalty to the ancestral royal house.

on a personal mutual obligation has persisted throughout all of German history, although it was only Frederick the Great who made it "socially acceptable" again in modern times. As far as German rulers are concerned, for several centuries of history there was more emphasis on rights than on obligations. Nevertheless, even at the time of Frederick Wilhelm III of Prussia, when a prince died, the gates were hastily closed and the troops immediately swore allegiance to the new lord (Treitschke).

The depth of this sense of connection between master and servant in Germanic societies, until recently, can be observed from the fact that in some churchyards of southern Germany and Tyrol, one can find family graves—even of noble lineages—where, according to their inscriptions, the coffins of old faithful servants are also interred.

Those who have clearly understood the nature of nomadism in relation to warfare and a subjugated population will discover nothing—absolutely nothing—resembling nomadism in the case of the Nordic race.

IX

The Peasantry and Long-Term Marriage as the Biological Foundation of the Nordic Race

I

The establishment of a peasant foundation for the Nordic race, however, is most revealing when discussing the question of the ancient Nordic form of marriage, especially when this question is approached from a more contemporary biological perspective.

We have a relatively good understanding of ancient Nordic marriage. We also know a great deal about the rather unique relationships between the genders within the Nordic race. Despite this, however, many points are still quite unclear to us. In its sexual life and in its ideas about sexuality, the Nordic race is not quite as easy to understand as it is often portrayed today, or as it is often presented with exaggerated enthusiasm. There are often quite glaring inconsistencies in what has been handed down to us. Unfortunately, these inconsistencies have received very little attention, apparently because, depending on the point of view of the person judging, one picks and chooses what seems particularly appropriate at the time. Whatever the case, it should be clear that no race in the world has introduced such a high and noble view of sexual life as the Nordic race. Despite this, there are many aspects of this topic that are difficult for us to understand at first. The patricians of ancient Rome, for example, had a remarkably high view of marriage, this is something that we have already discussed at length in earlier chapters. In ancient Roman marital law, women were free and respected in a way that was nothing short of admirable—the moral purity of women and girls was absolutely not to be questioned and was fully recognized and respected by men. Yet, the ancient Roman patricians did not think of imposing restrictions on themselves with regards to female slaves and servants.

The Spartans present us with even more peculiar contradictions, particularly when viewed from our modern notions of sexuality. There is a well-known story told by Plutarch of ancient Sparta, where the Spartan Geradas tells his guest, "Among us, my friend, there are no adulterers." At the same time, Plutarch also reports that a Spartan could ask another to "attend" to his spouse —older men married to young women did not consider it a disgrace to bring their spouse to a young man and ask him to have a child with her.

The records are just as full of inconsistencies when it comes to the Germanic peoples. We all probably know of Tacitus' account of the purity of Germanic marriage, but the things we hear later about the Franks are markedly different, and the conduct of Emperor Charlemagne the Saxon Slayer with his children is, to say the least, strange to our sensibilities. He surrounded himself with a host of vibrant women from all of the Germanic tribes (all of whom he lawfully married) and allowed his daughters, described by Angilbert as very Nordic in appearance, the pleasure of free and wild marriages. For that matter, the Nordic Edda also grants the following to Freya and the Ásynjur: "The beautifully adorned choose men as they like, it does no harm." Charlemagne the Saxon Slayer's behavior is therefore by no means really un-Nordic, nor does it even suggest a non-Nordic ancestry. In any case, he did nothing more than continue what was customary for Frankish kings. Adam of Bremen states that the Swedes "kept moderation in everything, except in the number of their wives. Each one takes as many as he wants according to his means, and these are said to be legitimate marriages." He then continues,

> Apart from the Scandinavians, polygamy still occurs rather late among the Frankish nobility. King Chlotar I took two sisters as wives, Charibert I had many wives, and Dagobert I had three wives (and innumerable concubines). These were legitimate marriages, established by purchasing the bride, betrothing her, and then taking her home. In addition to these marriages, the Germanic peoples had concubinage, but the concubines had neither the rank nor the rights of wives.

Even so-called test nights were common, at least among some of the Germanic tribes. According to Murrer, the fifty-second law of the Alemanni, in any case, must be interpreted in this way, "Whoever breaks off relations with a bride must swear that he has not tested her out of suspicion of some ailment, nor has he actually found anything of the sort wrong with her."[337] Later we will examine in great detail a certain custom of the Germanic peoples—in this context it will be touched upon briefly. Among the ancient Germanic peoples, it was customary for the honored guest (but not every guest) to receive a man's wife

---

[337] Ploß, *Das Weib in der Natur*.

or daughter for the night.[338] This custom survived in Scandinavia for quite some time. Until recently, vestiges of it were still clearly visible in the fact that the honored guest was put to bed by the housewife or daughter. Murrer informs us of something similar from the Netherlands, citing the following tradition: "It is a custom in the Netherlands that when the host has a dear guest, he offers him his wife in good faith."

The very extensive regulations concerning the position of illegitimate children among the Germanic peoples proves that such regulations were necessary. From our modern point of view, this still does not quite go together with the particularly severe punishments that the Germanic and Indo-European peoples could inflict on an adulteress. After reading these few examples, one must admit that it is not at first possible to find any truly clear and consistent principles in how the Nordic race approached their sexual life.

Those who have a closer understanding of the Nordic race, especially those with a particularly astute comprehension of its original way of thinking, will agree with the author that a great respect for women and their purity runs deep in the Nordic man's blood. But Nordic woman also presupposes this quality in men. Accordingly, she behaves with a freedom toward Nordic men that she could never allow herself with any other race in the world. As is well known, freedom of movement for women does not even extend as far as the Latin states. The true Nordic maiden and the true Nordic woman even find it "degrading" if they are assessed from an exclusively sexual point of view without their personality at least being given equal consideration. They can then become so unconditionally disapproving in their inner feelings that they no longer respect a man who nevertheless looks upon them in this way.

How great this respect for women is, and how uniformly this characteristic appears again and again, may be seen in the following reference. In the Canary

---

[338] It is important to note that the concept of the guest was something different in the past than it is today, and it would be wrong to understand the concept of the guest as synonymous with that of the foreigner per se. Kuhlenbeck provides insight into this matter: 'Fundamentally, the foreigner had no legal rights. Peace, justice, and freedom were, in fact, guaranteed only through membership in a family (*gens*) and within the broader associations (*tribus, populus*) to which it belonged. The foreigner had no role in domestic worship—the presence of a foreigner even desecrated religious rituals. Originally, the concept of the foreigner and that of the enemy were identical. The only exception, the only relief afforded to this fundamental lack of legal rights for the foreigner, was through *hospitium*. Translating this term as "hospitality" is likely to lead to misconceptions—for the ancients, legal protection was the primary concern. *Hostis* refers to the foreigner in a hostile sense, while *hospes* refers to the same person once he has been received as a guest (etymologically, the word "guest" is related to *hostis*). Those who violated the *fides* against their guest-friend were met with infamy. The *hospitium* constituted a reciprocal contractual relationship between members of different nations, aimed at ensuring mutual legal protection. Nonetheless, the *hospitium* did not constitute a legal relationship in the modern sense, sanctified only by religion and custom, and made all the more inviolable precisely for that reason—it was a legal-religious relationship."

Von Amira informs us about the Germanic peoples: 'According to ancient law, a foreigner to the land (Old High German *alilanti*, Middle High German *ellende*) or guest (Germanic *gastiz*, Latin *hostis*), lacked legal capacity (rights) on their own. Similar to how *hostis*, which corresponds to *gastiz*, became the term for enemy among the Latins, among the Germans, the concept of the *elenden* evolved similarly. However, the legal vulnerability of the guest gave rise to hospitality. The foreigner who voluntarily sought the protection of a rights-having associate had the protection of the law mediated to them through the representation of that associate."

Islands, the blond-haired, blue-eyed Guanches were able to preserve this characteristic until the fifteenth century, when they were subjugated and wiped out. Their customs (as we understand them) seem very Nordic, especially concerning the position of women—women were not allowed to be addressed by any man unless they gave permission by means of a sign. In England (at least until the war), it was considered highly discourteous for a gentleman to greet a lady on the street without waiting for her permission, which she would give by a nod of the head. Similarly, in Germany (at least until the war), it was considered highly discourteous to address a lady in public without first waiting to see if the lady actually wanted to be addressed. In these three examples, there is no doubt about what is the common root cause, although the author will not venture to decide in each case what is Phalian and what is Nordic. Furthermore, other generally observable characteristics of the Nordic race in the relationship between the sexes are: the innate chivalry of men toward women, high regard for the matron with many children, long-term marriage, and the need to evaluate marriage from a moral point of view.

To these noble views of sexual life we may now add a counter-example that cannot be easily denied by anyone examining the Nordic race with an open mind. Those who are familiar with our good Nordic farming areas in Germany know that the peasants judge a peasant's daughter who has "fallen in disgrace" far differently from a maiden who has become pregnant—the latter is not taken so harshly. Even the peasant's wife does not hold a particularly big grudge against the peasant if he happens to have a paramour. Anyone who objectively examines our nobility's views on sexual life will find them to be exactly the same as those of our peasants, the plot of *Kabale und Liebe* comes to mind here.[339] The same is true of English society, and it is all quite in keeping with what we know about the patricians of ancient Rome. In short, the central theme in all of these cases is that a man's conduct toward a woman within his estate or group of equals is assessed differently than his conduct toward women or girls outside of it. This is by no means some kind of a one-sided master morality which, out of vanity, demands purity from a woman of one's standing or blood, while absolving the man in all matters. Nordic women, too, unconsciously make a distinction between those fellow women of whom she is jealous and those of whom she is not.[340]

There will be many readers who will want to argue with the author about the existence of a certain double standard on the part of Nordic men, as recognized by true Nordic women. Regardless, this observation has been purposefully cited here. The facts just described can be observed again and again if one observes the world with open eyes. This phenomenon will be all the clearer to us if we bear in mind that, wherever we observe the Nordic race in early history, we find an emphasis on the moral purity of women and girls—we certainly know of many words for this—but nowhere do we hear a man praised for submitting to perfect sexual abstinence. We do not even have a word for male sexual abstinence, and we have always had to add the adjective "sexual" to the term "abstinence" to make its meaning clear. For example, when speaking of a woman, the word loyalty is quite clearly related to a

---

339 Schiller, *Kabale und Liebe*.
340 Ruedolf, *Fluch Unserer Geschlechtsmoral*, 31.

woman's sexual life, but not so when speaking of a man, where something quite separate from sex may be meant—the same is true of the words for steadfastness, virtue, purity, and so on. The only thing we can know with certainty from early Nordic history on this matter is the requirement that the young man abstain from sexual intercourse until he finally becomes a grown man. However, since the physiologically trained animal breeder is also aware of this phenomenon as being necessary in order to not interfere with the maturation process of a male animal, there is no need to immediately think of moral motives for this tradition, and one may assume that similar physiological considerations led to this requirement. Caesar, in any case, says quite clearly,

> Those who have remained chaste for the longest time, receive the greatest commendation among their people; they think that by this the growth is promoted, by this the physical powers are increased and the sinews are strengthened. And to have had knowledge of a woman before the twentieth year they reckon among the most disgraceful acts; of which matter there is no concealment, because they bathe promiscuously in the rivers.

What Caesar says here corresponds word for word to the fact that no horse breeder would ever think of using a stallion for work during the breeding season and vice versa, or of using him prematurely for breeding. Forgive the author for making these zootechnical comparisons, but perhaps they will nonetheless help to clarify some of the things handed down to us from the ancient world. Like all Indo-European peoples in general, the Germanic peoples did not esteem early marriage (we will discuss this later) and believed that the best age for a man to marry was between his thirtieth and fortieth year. This means that Caesar's comments on the sexual relations of young Germanic men can only be referring to their relations with concubines and not to those in lawful marriages.

Even the word "chaste" (*keusch*), which we would use today to mean sexual abstinence, originally had a different meaning. The term chaste was still understood in the Middle Ages to mean a eunuch rather than a morally pure person. There is no doubt that the High German *keusch* is related to the Low German *kuse* (meaning tooth; in a hunting context, a deer's canine tooth), the Swedish *kugge* (meaning tooth), and the High German *kauen* (meaning to chew). In fact, the castration of reindeer used to be carried out by biting the testicles, as is still the case among Laplanders today—the Finnish root *kuoh*, which is found in the Finnish *kuoho* (meaning neutered domesticated animal), may also belong here. Another place where the connection between biting and castrating is clear is the German *schnappen* (meaning snap or snip, such as with scissors) and the Swedish *snöpa* (meaning to castrate). The Latin name for beaver, *castor*, is derived from the Latin *castus* (meaning pure or chaste) and can be traced back to the fable in which a hunted beaver bites off his testicles, using this sacrifice to avoid being captured.

We can see, then, that there are inconsistencies that are not easily reconciled in what has been handed down to us concerning the Nordic race's approach to sexuality. We will in no way resolve these inconsistencies by simply turning a blind eye to certain qualities that do not fit into our modern idea of the Nordic race, as is unfortunately being done by various parties. Where a race feels and acts unconsciously, we are witnessing the genuine genetic effects of race, effects that have gradually evolved over the course of the race's development. We must approach the unraveling of the contradictions in the Nordic race under this guiding principle, or, to express it differently, we must try to bring a biological meaning to what we are witnessing. In doing so, we must be on guard against lazy presuppositions and instead seek an explanation that not only explains how the universally found characteristics of the Nordic race were bred into being, but also resolves the above-mentioned contradictions in the simplest way. It must be emphasized, however, that according to today's moral standards, it is absolutely forbidden to evaluate the things to be discussed here. Our modern view of marriage and sexuality is based on moral-legal and non-biological viewpoints, both of which are a product of their time, just as the ancient Nordic view of marriage and the ancient Nordic view of sexuality were a product of their time. If such things are not taken into account, one can never approach these questions without bias.

2

It has been pointed out a lot recently that the ultimate mysteries of Nordic marriage, as well as the way Nordic people behave toward a population of another race (such as in the Mediterranean basin in early historical times), must have somehow been connected with racial consciousness, and that this conduct served to keep Nordic racial heritage pure. As undoubtedly correct as this idea is, it is also certain that it does not fully grasp the topic. What is overlooked is that Nordic marriage and the effort to preserve the purity of Nordic blood did not first begin as a protective measure against other races in the Mediterranean but had already been in existence beforehand, meaning that its true origin must have been in the ancestral homeland. This means that it is of little utility to stress that this or that caste was formed in early history in order to keep the blood pure. References to the caste system of India or to the patrician efforts to segregate from the plebeians are not helpful because the question then arises—how, then, did those family lines know that interbreeding would be harmful? While this is not the case for India, it can in fact be said that the Nordic conquerors in the Mediterranean did not always encounter such sharp racial differences that a sexual aversion to the women and girls of the subjugated population could be taken for granted on the part of Nordic men. Quite the opposite! In fact, first-generation bastards (half-breeds) tend to exhibit hybrid vigor (heterosis), meaning that they combine parts of their biological inheritance (genetic make-up) from pure-bred but racially divergent parents in such a fortunate way that one might say that they surpass the performance of the two source races. Considering this observation on its own, it is natural to reach the shortsighted and erroneous conclusion that mass inter-breeding can be useful or even advisable. This opinion has even become fashionable today. Unfortunately, the proponents of such views, distorting the facts, tend to rely on certain animal breeding customs. Therefore, it should be briefly stated here that animal breeding does indeed make heavy use of hybrid vigor from half-breeds, but it does not continue to use of these half-breeds for breeding purposes. Instead, it unshakably adheres to pure breeding in the two source breeds that supplied the half-breed. The hybrid vigor of half-breeds is mainly used for the production of animals used in food production and not for breeding purposes. The English aptly refer to the breeding of half-breeds for public consumption as "cross and kill." For these reasons, animal breeders describe this type of breeding process as parallel breeding, because two pure breeds must be kept side by side in order to produce the respective half-breeds.[341] Whoever, therefore, in public life, makes use of the hybrid breeding customs and practices of animal breeders—the "cross and kill" animals of the English—in order to recommend the total inter-mixture of human beings is making a fool of himself and does not know it. In fact, such a person would then logically have to assume that it was only on the basis of some disastrous interactions with mongrels that the ruling Nordic families introduced the practice of preserving Nordic blood purity in the Mediterranean basin. But it is the other way around—the Nordic race already had a very clear awareness of its blood when it appeared in the Mediterranean basin and it maintained this awareness for a while against the temptations of its senses, finally succumbing and then disappearing from history. As a result, the problem of Nordic marriage and the efforts to keep Nordic blood pure are necessarily rooted in the ancestral homeland of the Nordic race, which we may assume to be north-central Europe.

It may be a self-evident hypothesis to modern race science that racial consciousness and race are necessarily linked together. First of all, this is an assumption that cannot be proven because the opposite fact (the tendency to interbreed) is by all means a common phenomenon in the world everywhere we look. Second, human races do not simply fall from the sky, but must first grow out of something that was there before. Third, the world has never had such absolute geographic boundaries that a race could fully develop within those boundaries only to then set out from that ancestral homeland (at least not on the time scale in which the human race developed). Finally—and the author's zootechnical training compels him to unconditionally stick to this view—race is not something fixed and does not have clear boundaries with respect to other races. Rather, it has quite fluid borders, and it is only for reasons of classification that it is assigned clear borders. This means that it is quite impossible that the racial instincts of those who are borderline cases in terms of racial categorization should necessarily be oriented only toward their own race and should not also be inclined to turn in a different direction.

We do not have to just assume this—we can see this with great certainty in Germanic law. According to the *Sachsenspiegel* (mentioned in chapter three),

---

[341] The "Irish Hunters," a type of hunting horse well known in lay circles, are also an example of such utility hybrids. In Germany, this breeding method is primarily employed in pig farming to produce particularly large and fast-growing animals for fattening.

any freeman who married into unfree blood became unfree himself. "The unfree hand draws the free one after itself." The ancient German, with wonderful nonchalance and clarity, annotates this as follows: "If you step on my hen, you will become my rooster." The concern for keeping one's blood pure in Germanic law even went so far as to declare that whoever separated himself from his kind and took up residence among the unfree became unfree himself, stating that "unfree air makes one unfree." These laws by no means applied just to the nobility or to a single caste, they applied to all who were born equal and free, and the *Sachsenspiegel* 1.3, 2.12, and 3.30 explicitly state that it is applicable to burghers and peasants as well. This shows that the Germanic laws of equal birth were a way of achieving pure breeding, not a way of creating class barriers.

As we learn more about prehistory, we continue to recognize that even in the very earliest times we can assume the uninterrupted movement of the human races, or at the very least the presence of distant connections. Questions of power and power shifts determined the destinies of peoples even then, just as they still do today. But how and where did the awareness of the uniqueness of one's own blood develop and how has it been preserved throughout the millennia? The Germanic peoples used to quite clearly and externally mark the unfree by requiring that a cord be worn around their neck, along with different hairstyles and clothing. This would not have been necessary if there had been a definite racial distinction between the free and the unfree. The latter can be proven, for example, for India by means of the Sanskrit language, where the word for concubines, unfree, and the subjugated population is the same (we will return to this point in greater detail below). If the Nordic race is understood simply as a ruling class that migrated into Europe, one might be shifting the fundamental question outside of Europe, but it still remains unanswered, quite apart from the fact that there is no reason to assume a non-European ancestral homeland for the Nordic race. Furthermore, it is entirely implausible that during the occasional internecine wars, the subjugated population did not ever have the same blood as the conquering class. Now, even with the utmost effort, it becomes difficult to determine which racial demarcations would have been used once the external distinguishing racial features between free and unfree ceased to exist.

From a zootechnical point of view, it should also be said that belonging to a race actually says nothing whatsoever about the performance-capability of the person, because the constitutional variations that exist within a race are great. Breeding solely on the basis of the external aspects of a racial type can spoil the racial type just as much as it can also maintain it at a high level.

So there must have been some other reasons behind the Nordic concept of pure breeding that either made the quality of the blood a clearly tangible defining characteristic or clearly demonstrated the value of pure breeding. In fact, such an assumption could be made right now, but in order to see the connections here, one should first familiarize oneself with some zootechnical principles and insights from the evolutionary history of our domesticated animal breeds. Using the history of English thoroughbred horse breeding as an example, we will attempt to outline the basic concept that is central to this discussion. We will first begin with a brief and simplified history of the breed.

Virtually on its own, the age-old passion for horse racing in England gradually resulted in the breeding of a line of performance-capable animals. Over time, the culling of inferior horses consolidated both the horse's ability and type. Breeding selection, when carried out over a long period of time, with a fixed goal or with the consistent culling of undesirable predispositions, always leads to the secure removal of undesirable traits and finally also to the homozygosity (pure heredity) of the desirable traits by means of closing off the blood (with the use of inbreeding). This is a very self-evident principle in animal breeding, but its practical implementation is only possible if, through uncompromising culling, it is ensured that no pathological predispositions can establish themselves within the genetics. In practice, however, this requires a vast amount of source material.[342] Through racing, the English thoroughbred horse was subjected to the toughest constitutional test imaginable. Nothing makes more uncompromising demands on the heart and the lungs—two very subtle physiological indicators of constitutional defects—than flat racing in particular. It was soon found out in England that only a few families of horses remained truly performance-capable and could endure the demands of racing from generation to generation. This, of course, could not be established through genealogical research (pedigree research). It was the memory of the breeders, whose wealth of training and experience on the animals' type allowed them to repeatedly detect among offspring the presence of certain families (bloodlines, we would say today) that were impacting performance. Thus, partly consciously and partly unconsciously, further breeding was limited to these victorious horse families, who gradually grew into a kind of horse aristocracy. By introducing noble horses from abroad, attempts were made to improve the breeding even further (to increase their performance), but the results were often quite unsatisfactory. For example, the curious observation was made that a performance-capable stallion of unknown origin often spoiled things more often than the occasional successes achieved by this method justified. In fact, only three stallions (whose names are very famous today: Byerley Turk, Darley Arabian, Godolphin) have been able to prove their worth. English thoroughbred breeding began in the year 1680, when King Charles II of England began to introduce foreign stallions for his "royal mares."

In 1793, England took an important step and decided to continue breeding only with proven lineages, keeping foreign blood away as a matter of principle. All horses were registered in the so-called "General Stud Book," which is the oldest breed registry in the world. Before that, performance was registered only in the racing records. Recent pedigree research based on the stable books and racing records has shown that the entire horse population recorded at that time could be more or less clearly traced back to those three stallions mentioned above and to about thirty-four foundational mares. Since the establishment of the General Stud Book, no foreign blood has entered English thoroughbred breeding, and anything

---

[342] In 1906, Wright initiated an inbreeding experiment with thirty-five guinea pig families, continuing the propagation through consistent mating of siblings. Today, approximately thirty generations later, only five families remain.

that does not pass the hard constitutional test of the racetrack (or has physical defects) is uncompromisingly chucked out. It is very instructive that after a certain
point it is no longer possible to increase performance—the whole breeding process
is now simply a matter of maintaining performance levels, which is by no means as
easy as it seems.

However, the achieved level of performance is so unrivaled that no other type
of horse is able to match it. This even includes the Arabian thoroughbred, since it is
bred toward a different purpose. But, of course, the English thoroughbred lags
behind the Arabian in the realm of actual performance-capability. Both thoroughbred types—or thoroughbred breeds, depending on how you look at it—are
anomalous breeding achievements within their breeds, and both were initially created exclusively through the culling of inferior specimens as well as an uncompromising performance test involving the entire body and its constitution. For the
English horses it was the racetrack, and for the Arabian, it was the harsh conditions
of the Arabian Desert and the ruthlessness of their masters—the "Arab's love for his
horse" is a pious fairy tale of the Occident. But as soon as such an anomaly of
whole body performance is reached, it becomes possible to lower, but never raise,
this level of performance though the introduction of alien blood. It is not without
reason that the author has just emphasized "relating to the whole body," because
exceptional breeding achievements that exclusively take into account individual
characteristics (such as high milk yield) without keeping an eye on the health of the
whole body can very easily lead to the degeneration of a breed. This can be demonstrated excellently with the help of an enlightening example from modern cattle
breeding. On the one hand, we have the North Americans, who engaged in unrestrained breeding practices that aimed to improve performance and resulted in
some astounding accomplishments. This was done by simplistically transferring
knowledge from plant breeding and uncompromisingly applying Mendelian principles. On the other hand, German cattle breeding proceeded more thoughtfully
and did not lose sight of the general constitution of their animals. German animal
breeding in particular is premised on the idea that the animal body is never a random conglomerate of hereditary factors (genes), but rather it is an organism in
which all the hereditary factors must be in a harmonious relationship with each
other so as to ensure the smoothest possible course of vital activity. In any case, it
seems that success has proven the German breeders right, as some Americans
have already openly admitted that they have been on the wrong track with their
cattle breeding methods. They discovered that their high-yielding dairy cows
could be traced back to about four families of cattle, thus theoretically validating
Mendelism and Johannsen's ideas of "pure lines" and applying them to animal
breeding. At the same time, however, the Americans are not able to get over the
fact that they will not be successful in putting these animals, over-bred solely for
performance, on a useful healthy foundation. In the meantime, German cattle
breeding is slowly but surely coming to the fore, because the performance of its
animals is based on a thoroughly healthy foundation, and because the health of
the breeding animal has been established as the supreme law of performance. On
the other hand, the author has been able to prove from observing Finnish rural
cattle that one-sided selection on the basis of Mendelian principles never has a

harmful effect so long as deliberate or natural circumstances prevent the intrusion of degenerate genetics into the animals with the desired capacities, which can be done by means of an uncompromising culling of unhealthy individuals.[343] In Finland, this would be the result of the fact that the young animals are reared on the natural and therefore healthy soil of a forest pasture, where they stay day and night from spring to autumn. Perhaps our eugenicists should take into account such zootechnical experiences and consider that the unbalanced fostering of certain abilities without maintaining the health of the entire physical constitution is the quickest route to degeneration.

Once such high breeding has been worked out within a breed—whose individual members are of impeccable health and are kept in this state of good health by appropriate circumstances—then one has something much more valuable than a breed per se. For the concept of breed is, after all, generally a flexible one. As self-evident as it is to every layman knowledgeable in animal breeding that the animal breeder only works with purebred animals, in practice, however, modern animal breeding still does not utilize the concept of "purebred" at all. This is not to argue against the concept of breed, only that in most cases it is too broad a concept for the breeder. For this reason, the breeder works with more narrowly defined groupings within the breed. As soon as the animal breeder is engaged in high breeding, all theoretical Mendelism is of no use to him whatsoever, for the preservation of high breeding is possible only through adherence to proven blood, and this is more a matter of health evaluations than of Mendelian considerations. Thus, thoughtless and ill-considered cross-breeding of foreign blood into a highly developed high breed can, under certain circumstances, have the same effect as poison. It is possible to destroy the work of generations of breeders with one single action of this kind, especially if its detrimental nature does not become apparent until some time has passed.

As a matter of fact, in animal breeding, physiology also plays a role alongside Mendelism. Breeding is an art, not a science. Genetics has uncovered for us the limits of the art of breeding, freed us from some superstitions, and has put to rest many a heated controversy. But it has by no means been able to replace the methods of those ingenious breeders of old, such as those produced by England in particular. This is only natural, of course, for just as the best training in anatomy and physiology and the mastery of all the techniques of sculpting do not by themselves make a sculptor—although they are the tools of success for the born sculptor—so too does the mastery of the measuring compass and the knowledge of the laws of heredity do not by themselves make a breeder. It is no mere coincidence that the English have come to realize that Mendelism has played a sifting role in their cattle breeding but not an uplifting role.[344] The latter is only ever conceivable in the case of very elaborate scientific experiments in institutes with considerable government support. At first, practical animal breeding is only indirectly affected by this, in that the special experiments worked out

---

[343] Darré, "Die Einheimischen Rinderschläge Finnlands."
[344] G. F. Finlay, *Cattle Breeding: Proceedings of the Scottish Cattle Breeding Conference* (Edinburgh-London: 1925).

and prepared in the institutes are only later handed down to practical animal breeding. The author asks not to be misunderstood here. He is not speaking against the importance and correctness of Mendelism, he is only discussing its practical applications in the field of animal breeding, especially in the field of breeding large animals. It must also not be forgotten that in large animal breeding, we never get enough offspring from one animal to be able to determine individual hereditary factors with absolute certainty. Only scientific institutes that can approach Mendelian questions free of economic pressures and have extensive source material at their disposal are in a position to resolve individual special questions. These institutes also have the means to perform what is known as mating analysis, that is, the ability to understand an animal's genetic inheritance through inbreeding and skilled evaluation of Mendelian numerical ratios in the case of recessive traits.[345] Although it is a long and arduous path, it is one that nonetheless produces results over time. These difficulties must be recognized if one wants to be able to judge modern animal breeding, or if one is surprised that animal breeders do not make use of Mendelism with the same enthusiasm and urgency as plant breeders. For that matter, it would not hurt at all if some eugenicists—and the author does not mean the official eugenicists in Germany—would dwell a little less on the "backwardness of animal breeders" and instead get to know (or at least improve their knowledge of) the very broad and sometimes rather difficult field of breeding large animals.[346]

Now you can perhaps understand why breeding proven, highly bred bloodlines is governed by a somewhat different set of rules than one would expect from purely theoretical Mendelian considerations. Intentional breeding, or what is known as positive breeding, has been virtually nonexistent. All progress in animal breeding is only ever based on the culling of the inferior and the preservation of proven blood. Only a few gifted artists in the field of breeding have managed to create something new and valuable from different but proven source material. In animal breeding, once you have something truly valuable in your hands, you anxiously guard it

---

[345] The coining of the term and the scientific application of the method, if the author is correctly informed, originated from Professor Frölich (Halle) of the Animal Breeding Institute at the University of Halle-Wittenberg.

[346] In his presentation titled "Organization and Function of a Research Institute for Animal Breeding" at the Fifth International Congress of Genetics (Berlin) in September 1927, Crew (Edinburgh) explicitly highlighted these matters. He stated approximately the following—if one merely extrapolates the research of a Russian scientist on mutations in the wild fruit fly, which involved 239 initial specimens and yielded 150,000 offspring, onto domesticated animals, it becomes immediately apparent how limited we are in research on all fronts, and why animal breeding has thus far seemingly gained so little from the field of genetics. We Germans, however, do not have to wait for the Anglo-Saxons' judgment in this matter. Since 1924, Professor Kronacher (Hannover), among others, has been advocating for the general acceptance of this idea. For example, refer to his thoughts in "Modern Genetics and Animal Breeding" in the second part of his text *Allgemeine Tierzuchtlehre* [General Animal Breeding], and, more recently, in an article published in the special issue of the "Illustrated Agricultural Journal" devoted to the International Congress of Genetics. In this regard, there is nothing to be done but to continue to breed toward an "ideal type" in practical animal husbandry, as has long been done. This process involves the gradual refinement of the collection and the cataloging of existing living animal material in order to gradually supplement or improve upon the ideal type set forth by the breeder.

against unknown blood. Therefore, even the most magnificent and performance-capable horse has no chance of ever being included in the General Stud Book of the English thoroughbreds because it would hardly benefit the genetic make-up of the thoroughbreds, and in all probability would very likely harm it. Another illuminating aspect of English thoroughbred breeding is that the original source material was by no means very uniform, and the differences, even from the standpoint of the systematist, can still be seen today—family characteristics (bloodlines) simply come through again and again. With regard to physiology, however, the English thoroughbred has developed rather homogeneously and can be recognized quite clearly. This physiological unity could be called the "biological effect" of breeding, as opposed to the morphological effect, which is important for systematics. This biological effect has imprinted on the English thoroughbred a certain type—a very certain nobility.

Let us summarize the key points of this history of English thoroughbred breeding. Out of a population of horses that was certainly not uniform, a few performance-capable families emerged through the application of uncompromising performance tests. Over time, they have come to form a kind of true nobility among the horses and can now only be maintained at their level of performance by uncompromisingly preserving the purity of their biological inheritance (their blood). Although these families did not coalesce into a single entity according to systematics, their physiological expressions do form an unconditional unity (as far as their biological effect is concerned) and this stamp of nobility is clearly imprinted on each member. Thus, the philosophy of high breeding is: once a breed has reached a certain level of performance, based on a performance test that takes into account rigorous constitutional tests, the only way to maintain that level of performance is to uncompromisingly keep out any other blood, even blood from the same breed. In the following, this phenomenon will be referred to as the iron law of performance-based high breeding, a term not taken from the technical terminology of animal breeding, but coined by the author in an attempt to find a concise and vivid expression for the rather broad field of thoroughbred breeding. The measures necessary for this are self-evident to the breeder, so there is no need for him to coin a special term.

The author now believes that with this knowledge of the causes of performance-based high breeding, we now also hold in our hands the key to solving the question of Nordic marriage from a biological point of view.

3

To understand the Nordic race, we have to start with the Nordic environment. The environment is always a prerequisite for performance breeding, because, of course, performance breeding is always done with a goal in mind, and this goal must of course be present before breeding. However, the term "environment" should not be understood solely in terms of climate. In the case of the English thoroughbred, for instance, the environment is first and foremost the race course, which can now be found in every major city in the world.

The living conditions of the Nordic environment, with the emphasis on hunting, were bound to produce a noble, capable, and great breed of men, of which more has already been said in chapter six. Perhaps at this point, in order to better understand such questions, one should picture English thoroughbred horses or Russian sight hounds or Malayan fighting cocks in order to visually grasp the fact that all performance breeding that places high demands on the heart and lungs produces small cell, noble forms.

Now we understand the factors necessary to explain the formation of the Nordic breed as such. We can even begin to assume that the above circumstances led to the creation of purebreds by intentionally or unintentionally closing off the blood, thereby establishing the type. But this is far from being performance-based high breeding. The latter presupposes not only the existence of pure breeding, but also within this pure breeding there must also be mating according to selection from year to year (from generation to generation), keeping out the undesirable. It is quite possible, for example, to also achieve pure breeding on matrilineal grounds and thus account for the formation of races, so long as all foreign blood is kept out of a lineage. Selection then takes place only according to the principles of environmental natural selection. However, high breeding never emerges in this way, because it requires a fine-tuning of ability in addition to pure breeding, and this can only be done by deliberately pairing useful individuals—the technical term "*sprung aus der hand*," or "jumping out of the hand" is used by breeders).

Now, could such a view of conscious breeding perhaps be assumed for the Nordic race? In other words, might it be said that the Nordic race not only paid attention to pure breeding, but also had the means of only allowing desirable individuals to marry, excluding the rest? The foundational precondition of high breeding, namely the exclusive mating of offspring that have been continuously selected from generation to generation, would then have to be present. Well, not only is it possible to make such a hypothesis, but we can also give reasons why this is likely the case. The Nordic farm and its right of inheritance, which has passed down undivided family farms from generation to generation, does in fact form such a foundation.

It can be demonstrated that, in some places, the German peasantry has preserved certain physical selection criteria for farm heirs, even to this day. In this manner, the peasant inheritance system of the Nordic race, connected to an individual farm, acquires a highly meaningful significance as a means of culling during the breeding process.

Natural living conditions quickly separate the healthy individuals from the sick without any artificial countermeasures. We can therefore assume that the Nordic race is healthy in this respect. As Ihering had pointed out, under healthy circumstances and in healthy families, the eldest son is also always the strongest and therefore the natural heir to the father. The frequent, although not always observable, fact that the farm passes to the eldest son (majorate) is certainly based on this ancient consideration, which, from a biological point of view, is very understandable. However, we can also say with certainty that the eldest son did not inherit anything if there was any serious concern about him. This has been preserved in some German peasant communities to this day.

Having proven above that the Nordic farm was passed on in an undivided manner to a single heir in a long-term marriage, and that this heir was the product of a natural or deliberate selection among the siblings, we already have all the factors in hand to explain the step from pure breeding to high breeding in the case of the Nordic race.

To reiterate, high breeding presupposes previous pure breeding and requires repeated selection from generation to generation within a closed bloodline, as well as further breeding exclusively within the selected material—all this would be impossible under matrilineal conditions.

Under this principle, a race could be bred upwards as well as downwards, unless, as a further condition, the strictest constitutional examination was incorporated so that only truly perfectly healthy people would be allowed to marry. Majorates and inbreeding did not harm our nobility as long as our simple way of life and strict living conditions prevented the marriage of unfit majorate heirs. Once these unfit individuals are permitted to marry, particularly if defective genes find their way into the marriage, rapid and rampant degeneration can occur.

A Nordic community or tribe had enough time to form a judgment about the value of each boy as they grew up. The Nordic environment was also decisive in allowing doubts about the suitability or unsuitability of individuals to arise. Anyone who has been a frontline soldier, or who has ever had the opportunity to observe dangerous situations in other areas of life, will know how incredibly quickly and unconditionally the moment of danger separates the brave man from the coward. Often this cannot be determined in advance, not even through sport. But the moment a man's life is in danger, his character is revealed with unmistakable authenticity. There are imponderable circumstances at work here that can hardly be put into words. You actually have to have been a soldier yourself to understand the subtle differences at play. But perhaps the following can make the difference clear—the French have always been excellent stunt pilots, but poor fighter pilots, while the case was exactly the opposite with the Germans and the English. The same is true of cavalry, where the Poles and Italians, despite break-neck stunts being popular among their officers and despite equestrian sport reaching a very high level there, do not make for very good cavalrymen. In the field of horse breeding, it is said that a thoroughbred horse differs from other horses because of the "steel" in its blood. What is meant by this is a certain "toughness" that is able to bring strength to victory when the horse itself, from a purely material perspective, should be completely exhausted and drained. This "steel" in the blood of the English thoroughbred would perhaps correspond most closely to that racial imponderability that clearly demonstrates the courage of the true man, and which really only shows itself in the hour of real danger. Life in the wilderness of the Nordic environment, with its abundance of dangerous wildlife, ferocious storms, and other calamitous events, left no doubt as to what a young man's character and physical condition would be during a hunt (it is not even absolutely necessary to think of war). Therefore, we can probably assume that even in the distant past, no one could inherit a farm (marriage, lighting of a hearth fire) who did not meet the general requirements customarily assumed for a man in a Nordic community. In the field of noble horse breeding, this excellent expression is used: "to test a horse's heart and kidneys." The heart represents the horse's courage on the obstacle course and, in a broader sense, its character traits overall, while the kidneys are the litmus test for the physiological process of physical performance. It was probably not very different in the early days of the Nordic race with regard to their growing offspring. Therefore, we can assume that the heir of an estate had to not only be completely healthy, but also represented certain selection criteria in terms of character and physique. The assessment was based on the observation of their development during youth, as well as the qualities esteemed or desired by the community. See chapter seven for further details.

In fact, we have these purely biological and eugenic considerations confirmed by a jurist. Von Amira, for example, says this quite clearly:

> It was the duty of the free man to bear arms. Physical fitness is a requirement for fulfilling this duty. The exercise of the most important rights is conditional on fulfilling them. The free man is therefore called *heerman* (army man) or *hariman*. And since the army consists only of free men, and since, moreover, only free men have legal capacity and rights, only free men constitute the "nation" or the "people." Therefore, they alone bear the special name of their people. In earlier times, the insignia of the free Germanic peoples was hanging hair and (for men) the carrying of common weapons (people's weapons). Unable to wield weapons, women and male youths were deprived of the ability to participate in a *thing*, the ability to testify and take oaths, and the ability to be guardians. In a similar manner and to a similar extent, German laws recognize the limited legal capacity of free persons of abnormal physical condition, in the case of the insane, the feeble-minded, and the leprous.

That in the ancient Germanic world, a legal dispute could also be settled by a duel further demonstrates the unity of physical integrity and full-born legal rights. Von Amira writes,

> The duel was a battle of personal prowess, taking precedence over forms of verbal combat. Personal prowess, however, was the physical prowess of the free man. If he was not able to pass this test, he

acknowledged himself to be a "lesser" man, who deserved a lack of rights and even the name of *neiding*.[347]

Lack of rights, however, also meant total or partial exclusion from the rights of honor, including inheritance and the ability to marry. In other words, it amounted to a very drastic culling.

But once the connection between performance and birth had been recognized, the individual communities and tribes within the Nordic race will have behaved more or less like the English thoroughbred breeders did just before the introduction of the General Stud Book. It was observed that individual performance-capable families pushed themselves to the fore and that while alien blood could very well lower their level of performance, it could rarely raise it. Above all, the extent to which a woman's womb determined the rise or fall of a family line would have been quickly understood. It can be assumed that the next step was to marry only into performance-capable blood, and the step after that was to become more and more fearful and suspicious of foreign blood. Now, the path was clear for the Nordic race to go the way of high breeding, for selective breeding always presupposes the "closing off" of the blood. Soon, the iron law of performance-based high breeding will have ruthlessly prevailed. As the blood became more and more uniform from generation to generation, and its performance more and more refined and balanced (according to the standards of the Nordic race), the only way to maintain this level of performance within the blood was through marriage. This consideration—which can be easily verified in light of comparable phenomena in the development of our domesticated animal breeds—is surely the key to understanding the emergence of a race or breed from a broader and more general population, without having to assume the presence of awkward geographic confinements, an assumption that is unfortunately common in race science today. We can conclude, then, that the nobility of the Nordic race has most likely been the result of narrow selection within the Nordic race (discussed earlier in chapter seven).

The author's hypothesis that the Germanic nobility did not represent a superimposed master race, but rather that its origins can be traced back to the iron law of performance-based high breeding (thereby making the nobility a genuine result of high breeding, rather consciously subjected to exactly the same laws as English thoroughbred breeding), can indeed be substantiated by the following words from von Amira:

> The estate above the common freemen is the nobility (*apal*, meaning quality, descent, or lineage). In the earliest times, nobility was given only by innate nature. That is why both women and men were part of it. Whoever possesses such a nature is called noble: *apiling* (Old Frisian *etheling*, Old High German *edeling* and

---

[347] *Neiding* is an Old Germanic and Norse word for a despicable person, roughly translated to villain, scoundrel, or coward.

adaling). The ancient Germanic noble lineage is a legendary lineage. Divine descent is attributed to the noble family line. The essence of the ancient Germanic hereditary nobility (*geburtadel*) lies in it limiting itself to a closed number of lineages which can only be diminished but never increased. Due to these constraints, this nobility disappears among some South Germanic tribes (including the Franks, Goths, Burgundians, and Alemanni) during, or shortly after, the Migration Period. Among others (such as the Bavarians), this nobility lasts until at least the early Middle Ages. Among the Anglo-Saxons and other North Germanic tribes, where it was limited to the ruling families, it persisted into the sixteenth century only for the Frisians, as a politically privileged class of "lords" or "chieftains," thanks to a distinctive connection with privileged hereditary estates (*ethel*), "noble manors" (*edelen heerden*), or "judicial homesteads."[348]

It is significant that the nobility as a privileged class did not emerge until the Middle Ages, while its distinct breeding separate from the common freemen can be clearly seen as far back as the Migration Period. Since, from a purely racial point of view, Nordic blood can still be found among Franks, Alemanni, peasants, and others centuries later (in which case the old Germanic nobility mentioned by von Amira could not have undergone a denordification in the racial sense), the author considers it proven that the Germanic nobility was nothing more than the genuine product of deliberate high breeding that followed the iron law of performance-based high breeding.

While the development described here likely only took place unnoticed at first, the Nordic race, as soon as it experienced the iron law of performance-based high breeding within its own ranks, had to become blood-conscious, and consequently had to pay more and more attention to preserving the purity of its blood.

In any case, it is remarkable how easy what is said in the historical record concerning the sexual life of the Nordic race can be understood if one does not take the rather broad concept of race as the determining factor and considers instead the iron law of performance-based high breeding as developed here.

It has already been mentioned that in horse breeding, no horse has a chance of being registered in the English General Stud Book (in other words, being listed among the thoroughbreds) if it does not belong there through its ancestors. The English thoroughbred breeder can confidently breed his stallions to non-thoroughbred mares because the resulting foal is always, of course, clearly marked as non-thoroughbred through its mother. On the other hand, he is quite anxious to protect his mares from being bred to a stallion who is not thoroughbred. The reason for this is very simple—no half-breed (meaning horse that is not a thoroughbred) but otherwise noble horse can

---

[348] Amira, *Grundriß des Germanischen Rechts.*

compete with thoroughbreds on the flat track. However, if a thoroughbred breeder is not careful and mates his mare with a half-breed stallion, the resulting foal is inevitably a loser on the race track. Although the breeder may later sell the foal as a very noble half-breed, in terms of performance the foal is pretty much the same as any other foal born that year. But if the breeder does not know the origin of the foal (if he does not know that the stallion was a half-breed) and runs it in the races, the whole thing can become very expensive for him because there is no chance of the animal winning on the racetrack. Furthermore, he may have to face other inconveniences. Now, one can understand why in thoroughbred breeding, dams are anxiously protected from unwanted sires. Likewise, the same is true in dog breeding, where there are also highly developed thoroughbreds. Perhaps this circumstance is the reason why laypeople and some breeders without biological training have confused such necessary measures for the protection of the thoroughbred lineage from telegony.

Once a person becomes familiar with the need to protect thoroughbred lineages, it becomes immediately apparent why the two sexes are judged differently within the Nordic race when it comes to matters of sexual morality. The heart of the entire issue lies in the concept of a long-term marriage coupled with the inheritance of a farm. Admission as a farm heir acted as a eugenic filter. From such a marriage emerged the next generation that would once again be subjected to the selective process. No child who, through its parents, had not indirectly passed through the eugenic filter of long-term marriage and its associated ignition of a hearth fire was capable of becoming the source material for a new generation of heirs to the hereditary estate. Therefore, a man with a concubine could father as many children as he wished, and the community had no undue concerns regarding these half-breed offspring. These "bastards" were never considered for a lawful marriage, as their origin was unequivocally known through their mothers of lesser birth. For these reasons, these bastards always aligned with the lesser family line, which clearly delineated their exclusion from inheritance. In the case of the Nordic race, it simply meant exclusion from a marriage linked to inheritance (in other words, exclusion from the equal born marriage associated with the hereditary estate). The presence of bastards was thus inconsequential to the thoroughbred lineage of the Nordic race as long as the bastard could not enter into a full marriage.

But the situation was quite different for free women. Due to having a mother of lesser birth, the bastard child of a free man was always an obvious matter. The woman of free blood, however, was definitely capable of secretly mixing foreign blood among her legitimate offspring. The birth itself, of course, does not reveal who the father of a child is. Therefore, even in situations where long-term marriage and farm inheritance served as a eugenic filter, a woman could very well smuggle half-breed blood into the strictly guarded thoroughbred lineage of a tribe. Since this circumstance could only be avoided by preventing such a conception, the free Nordic women were left only with the choice between procreation or fornication (*zucht* or *unzucht*),[349] in other words, they were left with the choice of either following through with their blood-duty to breed (synonymous with being *züchtig*, meaning virtuous) or removing themselves from the genetic pool if they should forget themselves (what else could they forget but their task, their destiny!), in which case, quite logically, they were simply fornicators (*unzüchtig*). These things will require a more thorough investigation. Here, however, we can say that it now makes sense why a word for male sexual abstinence was not coined in speech, while we have several expressions for it for the Nordic woman. Von Amira writes, "Adultery can be committed by a woman against a man, but not by a man against a woman."

There may be some readers who will not readily accept the objective application of the concept of breeding to a noble human race of early history. But the author must point out that this is not just an assumption of his—the evidence for it is abundantly available.[350] Even for the author, who is accustomed by his profession to consider questions of breeding as a matter of course, the similarities between the breeding laws of the Nordic race and our present-day zootechnical measures for the preservation of thoroughbred lin-

---

[349] The etymology of the word *zucht* is quite clear, according to Weigand's *Deutsches Wörterbuch* [German Dictionary], the Dutch *tucht* and Old Frisian *tocht* both mean fertility or production, and the Gothic *ustaùhnts* means completion. Old High German *zuhtig* translates to fecund or pregnant. Middle High German *zühtec* fundamentally means fruitful but also well-mannered. The direct connection between the term *zucht* and the act of sexual intercourse is still preserved in the fact that we refer to a rape—the involuntary surrender of a woman—as *notzucht*. In the time of our ancestors, a "chaste maiden" was certainly not someone who completely ignored motherhood and sexual matters, on the contrary, she was a person who consciously embraced the idea of one day presiding over a large brood of children as a mother—in other words, she was a maiden who lived with the conscious intention of preserving the racial heritage and purity of her lineage!

[350] The author would like to emphasize in particular that Tacitus in his work *Germania*, deviates significantly from the framework of ancient Germanic traditions in this regard. One only needs to refer to von Amira (*Grundriß des Germanischen Rechts*) or Schrader (*Reallexikon*) to find confirmation of the accuracy of this assertion. It is much more difficult, however, to determine why Tacitus takes this unique position. Tacitus could hardly have simply made it up. The whole question deserves a thorough investigation. Under no circumstances, however, should Tacitus' *Germania* be taken as the starting point for an investigation aiming to clarify Germanic marriage and breeding laws. Tacitus, with his account, currently stands too isolated in this regard. Nevertheless, the author does not claim that what Tacitus recorded is outright incorrect. This cannot be the case, especially because notable similarities can be observed between the recorded marriage laws of the ancient Roman patricians and Tacitus' description of Germanic marriage. In any case, the author would like to reiterate here that it is inadmissible to approach these ancient records using contemporary moral concepts. If the Roman Tacitus noted the sexual purity of the Germans, it does not prove, for example, that a Germanic man did not engage in sexual relations with a concubine. To the Roman mindset of the time, this behavior was a matter of course. Therefore, if Tacitus had not encountered this practice among the Germans, it would have seemed to him to be remarkable. Tacitus would have undoubtedly mentioned such a peculiar abstention (as it would have come as a surprise to a Roman) had he discovered that Germanic individuals abstained from sexual intercourse with concubines. However, Fehrle (Heidelberg) has suggested to the author that Tacitus is not as far removed from Germanic traditions as it first appears. According to him, Tacitus in chapter 19 is actually in line with what the author presents here, if one interprets Tacitus' emphasis on moral purity in the context of Germanic women rather than as the behavior of Germanic men toward concubines. Tacitus leaves certain aspects unmentioned because his work was intended to serve as a moral reflection on the morally degenerate Romans of the time.

eages are nothing short of astonishing. The Nordic race does not ever think of judging the sexual act as such from the so-called "moral" point of view—it does not even keep the things related to it private out of a sense of shame. We shall see that the Nordic race treats all questions of sexuality very innocently, particularly from the standpoint of loyalty to one's biological inheritance; one is at first a little perplexed when working through this topic, even as an animal breeder.

In the end, when judging such issues, it must be remembered that even in nature, the most magnificent blossom is only ever the manifestation of a plant that has its roots in the earth. Therefore, on the one hand, we can safely appreciate the tender and delicate blossoms of love that the Nordic race has produced in its gender relations, but on the other hand, we need not blame the researcher for trying to shed light on the biological foundation of these blossoms. In this case, one does not cancel out the other—both complement each other to constitute the living reality of the Nordic race.

Therefore, in the case of the Nordic race, equality of birth depended upon the child being born in wedlock, and indeed we have just seen above what conditions this depended upon. This meant that a man could have as many children as he wanted with concubines, as these children posed no threat whatsoever to the genuine thoroughbred lineage by being fundamentally excluded from inheritance (from the hereditary estate). However, it is a mistake to assume that such illegitimate children would carry a stigma in the modern sense. They were kept away from breeding in a very matter-of-fact way, just as a horse breeder who raises thoroughbreds together with half-breeds on his stud farm carefully separates the two in his breeding measures, but nevertheless shows a similar love to all animals. In Euripides' *Andromache* (233), it is said of Andromache that she raised the children conceived by Hector with house slaves at her own breast. For example, Busolt writes,

> Despite everything else, the Spartan oligarchy (which was democratically organized) adhered exclusively to its Spartan origins in terms of civil law. An ancient law forbade members of the royal houses from fathering children with foreign women.[351] Marriages with daughters of helots or *perioikoi* were inherently prohibited, however, extramarital intercourse was quite common. There were many "bastards" in Sparta. The *mothakes* largely consisted of the illegitimate children of Spartans and helot women. They were referred to as "helot children" and were brought up together with Spartan boys, underwent civic education at the expense of their foster father, and as a result regularly received freedom from the state. They did not receive, except in very few exceptional cases, full citizenship, although they probably always

---

[351] From Plutarch's *Agis*: "Lysander, however, who was still ephor, set on foot an indictment of Leonidas by virtue of an ancient law which forbade any descendant of Heracles to beget children by a foreign woman, and ordained that anyone who left Sparta to settle among foreigners should be put to death."

possessed legal rights (*civile*). In other regions of Greece, an extramarital relationship might only involve sexual contact or might take the form of domestic concubinage. Concubinage maintained by a citizen with a freeborn woman—a citizen's daughter—for the purpose of producing freeborn children (like marriage) had been protected by law since ancient times. A legally recognized concubinage of this kind appears in the blood law of Draco.[352] A citizen's daughter entered into this legitimate concubinage through an act similar to *engyesis* (marriage contract). Her family guardian gave her to the suitor. But the act was not *engyesis*, and the concubinage was therefore not marriage. Children born from such concubinage were called *nothoi*, and they had no inheritance rights to the paternal hereditary property. They were also not admitted into the male phratries (the family line of the father). However, in terms of their descent, they were otherwise unblemished and could be fully and legally adopted by their rightful father at any time, especially if he had no heirs for his hereditary estate. On the other hand, children born from relationships with slave women and other unfree women were practically never considered for inheritance.

In the historical records, the judgment of children begotten by a free man with a slave woman varies in many instances. There is no doubt that this depended on the slave's lineage. If the slave woman was of impeccable descent and had only fallen into bondage through misfortune (war, etc.), her children were not fully free but the good descent of the mother was still recognized. Thus, the son born to the noble Castor from a slave woman—whom Odysseus deceivingly claims to be in line 199 of Book 14—is still able to marry the daughter of a nobleman. He also receives a portion of the inheritance, although he must be content with less than his legitimately born brothers. Teucer holds an honorable position among the heroes, despite not being the legitimate son of Telamon, as he was born from a slave woman captured in war. Significantly, however, this slave woman was originally a princess. The historical records give us similar examples for the Germanic tribes. Von Amira writes, "Through her right of cohabitation, as well as by belonging to her husband, the wife differed from the concubine kept in the house."

We should not be surprised, then, that in India, Greece, Rome, and among the Germanic peoples, the sexual freedom of men was preserved in law and custom, while separate laws were applied to women. Ihering writes, "Not every woman taken by a man into his house to live with him becomes his wife; special conditions and formalities are required for this." Children conceived with slave women did enter under his paternal responsibility but only under his sovereign power, Ihering continues,

---

[352] Demosthenes, *Against Aristocrates*, section 53: "If a man kill another . . . in intercourse with his wife, or mother, or sister, or daughter, or concubine kept for procreation of legitimate children, he shall not go into exile as a manslayer on that account."

They are not children in the legal sense (*legitimi*), but merely in the natural sense of procreation (*naturalis*). . . . The legitimate child presupposes the legitimate mother, and the legitimate mother presupposes the legitimate marriage, with the latter being the foundation of the whole Roman family.

Schrader states, "[The German] word *kind* corresponds phonetically to the Latin *gens* and *gentis*, meaning lineage. Thus, its original meaning stems from procreation and lineage, essentially meaning 'what belongs to the lineage.'"

Thus, only the child who came from a marriage of equal birth and whose ancestry was known and acceptable was considered a legitimate child. These ancestry requirements, which can be found in all the traditions of the Nordic race, persisted among us until the eighteenth century in all of our guilds and in certain peasant communities. Even in 1782, a Hannoverian document states that "free people abhor the union with serfs because then the children become serfs." The reasons why the bastard always aligned with the "lesser family line" were discussed above in relation to Nordic land law. In this regard, Germanic law is uniform, regardless of whether one is examining the oral traditions (*weistümer*) of the Anglo-Saxons, Franks, Burgundians, or Danes; see chapter four. However, among the Nordic race, the position of the bastard was never regarded as contemptible in any way. Just as the difference between a wife and a concubine in the realm of sexuality often only consisted of the fact that the wife slept by the husband's side while the concubine had to sleep at his feet, there was no external distinction for the legitimate and illegitimate children of a father, except in matters of inheritance. The husband would never even consider expelling the children born of the concubine, who were not of equal birth, from his house, and his wife could not make any claim to do so either.

The expression "*mit kind und kegel*" has preserved the memory of the shared raising of a man's legitimate and illegitimate children.[353] The concubine never faced any objection, and her commercial exploitation was likely completely unknown to the Nordic race. The latter is a phenomenon that didn't emerged in Germany until the Middle Ages and must presumably be attributed to racially-foreign influences.

The position of the concubine provides revealing indirect evidence (circumstantial evidence) regarding the prehistory of the Nordic race. According to Schrader, in the Indo-European languages, the term for concubine only ever appears in connection with a slave or a foreigner.[354] The most compelling evidence in this regard can perhaps be found in Old Indic *dâsî*, which originally

---

[353] Translator's note: "*Mit kind und kegel*" roughly translates to "with the whole family" or "with everyone and everything." Literally it refers to *kind*, meaning child, and *kegel*, meaning illegitimate child.

[354] This also applies to the Germanic peoples. For example, von Amira states that this is also the case when discussing the unfree and the actual servants (emphasizing that it was natural for the Germanic people to believe that servants were a distinct race, identifiable by their physical characteristics). He writes, "Furthermore, the servant was referred to as a *diener* (Old High German *diu*), related to the Old High German *diorna* and Middle High German *dirne*, meaning slave daughter."

meant "*dâsa* woman," that is, it originally referred to a native female inhabitant of India, and later coming to signify "slave" or "concubine." This is quite revealing because if a word for "slave" and "concubine" is formed from the word for "native female inhabitant" after India had been conquered by the Nordic race, it implies that the Nordic race was previously unfamiliar with such a state of affairs, otherwise, they would inevitably have used a more familiar word for it, and the corresponding word would be found in its root form in all Indo-European languages. From this observation, two conclusions can be drawn—first, the Nordic conquerors of India gained practical experience with a subjugated population only after arriving in India and so were not familiar with this condition in their ancestral homeland. Second, the peasant trek of these conquerors must have reached India from their ancestral homeland without extended stops along the way, or at the very least, they did not become acquainted with subjugated populations during their journey. Since we have now identified the ancestral homeland of the Nordic race as Sweden, it is likely that the migration to India originated from this location or a nearby one in Lower Germany. It is impossible for the Nordic race to have already ruled over a subjugated population as a master race in this ancestral homeland, as Kern suggests. A race of nomadic warriors that first arrived in Europe and then later embarked on a conquest of India would have had sufficient time and opportunity in central Europe to become familiarized with the concept of "slave" and "concubine." Therefore, these terms would not have needed to be developed in India first.

If, however, we go along with the author's assumption that the Nordic race existed as a peasant race without a subjugated population in its ancestral homeland, then everything immediately lines up. It is likely that during their time in the ancestral homeland, breeding selection was already taking place, allowing only select young men and maidens to enter into legitimate marriages on inherited land. This allowed capable family lineages to be cultivated, while the unfit lineages slowly but surely fell further behind. Initially, it may have been the case that the unfit families formed second-tier lineages, eventually descending to the status of serfs if they were particularly incapable. However, among the Nordic race, the serf was certainly no slave.

It is likely that racial tensions were originally not known in the ancestral homeland at all. It is significant, for example, that according to Schrader, the distinction between legitimate and illegitimate children in Indo-European languages only appears once the distinction between free and serf classes becomes apparent. This allows us to initially conclude that when the Nordic conquerors of India left their ancestral homeland, it was at a point in time when the distinction between the free and unfree did not yet clearly exist there. Otherwise, there would have been no need for them to create a word for the unfree in their new home. Furthermore, we can also assert that their migration to India from the ancestral homeland occurred without significant interruptions that would have brought them into conflict with a population of a different race. Otherwise, the word for concubine and slave that they adopted along the way would have been applied to the *dâsa* women, as they indeed did not hesitate to give familiar names to newly encountered tree species.

The most important thing to note here, however, is that all these considerations unequivocally point to the fact that the migration of these Nordic conquerors of India must have taken the form of a genuine peasant trek. Warrior nomads could have only journeyed from northern Europe to India through parasitic war campaigns, much like the Huns did in the opposite direction later. Nomadic war campaigns, of course, are never anything other than the "consumption" of existing civilizations, leaving behind almost nothing, much like a swarm of locusts. A peasant trek, however, either peacefully passes through a territory without undue contact with the local population or fights its way through, as the Cimbri and Teutons did in Upper Italy and Gaul, without any significant non-combat interactions taking place. A peasant trek does not willingly carry unnecessary mouths to feed and places little value on serfs. Drawing from recent colonial history, we can demonstrate that peasant treks who establish themselves in a new territory—as we can confirm for North America and South Africa, for example—initially have no relationship with a subjugated non-peasant population. Taken on its own, this is completely natural, and that is for several reasons. Of course, conquest by a peasant trek does not always involve the outright subjugation of the existing population (unless they encounter established farmers), rather, it often simply results in displacement. Furthermore, the displaced population is motivated to migrate away only on rare occasions—more commonly, they often choose to withdraw to remote areas where they then become a constant source of unrest for the peasants.

This unrest may either manifest as raids on individual settlers or as theft, livestock rustling, etc. They have ample time to scout and identify when and where they can exact revenge on the hated intruders. Therefore, in the beginning, peasant conquerors are generally distrustful of all non-peasant natives and are reluctant to employ them. Their repeated experiences tell them that these individuals are mostly spies who are merely scouting for opportunities to cause petty mischief for the benefit of their own people. It is only when a generation has passed since the initial colonization—when newborns have known nothing other than the existing conditions from birth—that tensions often dissipate with remarkable speed. This is particularly true when there is a significant cultural gap between the two groups and when the martial superiority of the conquerors is completely evident. There are places in the United States of America where just fifty years ago, settlers had little to give a redskin, aside from a shotgun pellet. Nowadays, however, their grandchildren peacefully interact with redskins on university campuses. We can assume the same exact scenario for the peasant conquerors of India. As the author has already demonstrated in chapter four, contrary to popular belief, the Nordic conquerors of India were peasants who encountered a non-peasant indigenous population. The history of the word *dâsî* is sufficient to refute as nonsensical the idea that the Nordic race can be traced back to a nomadic culture or any

other sort of parasitic master class. Otherwise, the Nordic race unquestionably would have already had a word for "slave" and "concubine" before
their invasion of India, precisely because they never hesitated to recognize
the sexual freedom of men.

It is also worth noting that the word for marriage only emerges when the
permanent state of cohabitation with a wife of one's own blood needed to be
emphasized in contrast to the temporary relationship with a slave. This indicates
indisputably that, for the Nordic race, long-term marriage was not an artificially
constructed matter resulting from logic and reason, but rather a condition that
naturally developed in their ancestral homeland, without the aid of intellect.
Originally, there was simply no need to discuss or articulate the customary marriage practices that had existed since ancient times. This would be unimaginable
if we did not already know that even the animals living in the deciduous forests
of central Europe practice monogamy. Once again, we see that Nordic
monogamy is at first nothing more than a natural condition that also occurs in
the wildlife of this region. In terms of biology, the Nordic race is, in every aspect,
most closely integrated with these conditions of life. Consequently, we can draw
the following conclusion, which is significant from the perspective of evolution—the evolutionary history of the deciduous forest region of north-central
Europe also holds the key to understanding the phylogenesis of the Nordic race.

While long-term marriage may have originally been natural and somewhat
instinctual, there is no doubt that a deeper understanding of it eventually developed. In any case, from very early on the protection of the wife plays a prominent role in related Nordic legislation, almost to the point that the husband very
often appears to be almost subordinate. Just consider, for example, the restrictions imposed on the ancient Roman patricians, where the head of a family lineage faced the loss of his entire fortune if he divorced his wife for reasons not
legally foreseen—he even faced the death penalty if he sold his wife. There is not
a single nomadic people in the world with such protective measures for women.
Indeed, the patriarchal conditions of the pre-Islamic Semites can be described as
paternalistic (despite retaining a matrilineal basis) because the woman becomes
the property of the man, who effectively exercises complete control over her.
Nevertheless, there remains an insurmountable contrast between the Semites and
the Nordic race, whereby, in addition to other things, the Semitic patriarch could
sell his wife at any time, whereas the ancient Roman patrician, for example,
would immediately face the death penalty for the same act.

Among the Indo-Europeans, the woman was by no means the property of
the man. In a sense, the wife is entrusted to the husband by the tribal community. The rights of the man over the woman are legally regulated in a clear fashion.
If the husband exceeds his powers of punishment against members of his family,
the community could take uncompromising action against him. Therefore, the
term "paternalistic" is actually incorrect for the Nordic race. Even with regard to
the children, the father did not have arbitrary power at his own discretion (as we
will see later), his powers were also limited in this context. Marriage and child-
rearing were social obligations for the head of a racially-Nordic family. However,
the head of the family also had certain rights that extended beyond those of un-

married tribal members—historical records clearly indicate the head as a faithful steward of the collective. From this perspective, naturally, marriage is conceivable only as a permanent condition. This, the state of permanence, is the hallmark of Nordic marriage, not paternalism. Von Amira writes,

> Ancient Germanic marriage was an aggregate of various legal relationships: the mutual right to cohabitation of the spouses as "domestic partners" and "companions," the household rule of the man (and the associated guardianship over the woman), and the wife's household duties. Through her right to cohabitation and her affiliation to the man, the wife not only differed from the *friedel*, but also from the concubines kept in the house. Insofar as marital authority allowed, the woman (as the mistress) also had command in the house.[355] Thus, in the absence or temporary incapacitation of the man, complete household authority rested in the hands of the woman. Through this "power of the keys," the wife distinguished herself from the free female servant.

Heune (German Dictionary) states, for example, the following about marriage:

> Marriage (*ehe*), meaning legal union of man and woman. From the Gothic *aivs*, related to the Latin *aevum*, the Greek *aiôn* (meaning time or eternity), the Greek *aiei / aei* (meaning always), and the Sanskrit *âyus* (meaning lifespan). It has the temporal meaning of duration and eternity, adhering to the Old High German *êwa*, Middle High German *êwe*, and modern German *ewig*, meaning eternal (in the sense of the Old German *ewigkeit*, meaning eternal God or eternal torment and thus related to the divine and supernatural).

Therefore, in the context of the Nordic race, the term "paternalism," which leads to confusion with the pre-Islamic Semitic patriarchy, should be completely abandoned in the future and replaced by another term. The author currently does not know of a sufficiently concise and descriptive expression because it would need to encompass, on the one hand, a long-term marriage patrilineal in character, and, on the other hand, the social and procreative obligations associated with it vis-à-vis the community, as well as the rights resulting from their position as the family head.[356]

---

[355] *Friedel* refers to female servants of free blood.

[356] The Germanic people referred to the father or the head of the household—as the author convincingly argues in chapter three—as a peasant (*bauer*), and those belonging to the nobility as noble peasants (*adelsbauer*). However, since today we interpret the word "*bauer*" entirely differently, the Old High German *bauer* can no longer be readily employed for this purpose. However, one could aptly paraphrase the core concept of the ancient Germanic (though it would be more accurate to say Old High German) marriage by not referring to patriarchy in an absolute sense, but rather to domestic patriarchy or domestic-patriarchal conditions. In this case, the term "housefather" clearly indicates that for our ancestors, marriage was not just a sexual (or even a purely emotional) bond between a man and a woman.

4

In the following paragraphs concerning the sexual life of Nordic women, we will clearly see how the communal organizations of the Nordic race have always recognized the value and importance of women to the race, in other words, we will see how well they have understood the principles of breeding. Everywhere the Nordic race appears in its original form, there is no valuation whatsoever of the sexual act in and of itself. It did not assume that men should live a sexually abstinent life nor did it demand morality in the modern sense from the women. For the Nordic race, the sexual life of men and women is considered a natural expression of life and is therefore discussed openly, just like eating and sleeping. When one reads through the historical records concerning this matter (despite some things being incomprehensible from our modern perspective), they always seem clear, vivid, and honest. Yet, we never encounter the dull, dirty fantasy of the Orient, which feels right at home needlessly fixating on erotic feelings and sentiments, as well as in the mire of obscenity. No, the love life of the Nordic race has always been open and genuine—only that which stood against their racial heritage was considered immoral.[357] Regarding Sparta, for example, Busolt states,

> It was not considered inappropriate for an elderly man to provide his young wife with a vigorous boyfriend in order to produce desired offspring. Furthermore, it was permitted for a man who did not wish to be intimate with his wife to father children with the wife of another Spartan, provided that the other man also gave his consent. Moreover, it was not uncommon for impoverished brothers who relied on a single hereditary estate (*klêros*) to share a wife and consider the children as their joint offspring. Children conceived by a proxy with one's own wife or by a man with another man's wife could be adopted with a simple declaration before the king and thus receive full citizenship rights and inheritance rights on the hereditary property.[358] In these cases, we are dealing with legitimate sons from extramarital unions between Spartans and women of Spartan origin.

Concerning Greece as a whole, Busolt says the following:

> The state was indeed interested in marriages, but primarily with regard to the creation of offspring. For political and religious reasons, it was very important to the state that the number of households did not diminish and that the worship of each

---

[357] See the story by Gottfried Keller about a nun with seven children, mentioned in Ruedolf, *Fluch Unserer Geschlechtsmoral*, 50.

[358] See: Plutarch, *Lycurgus*, chapter 15 and Herodotus, *The Persian Wars*, Book 6, chapter 57. Without being adopted, they would still receive full citizenship rights but would not be legally entitled to their father's hereditary property.

household's gods continued. Therefore, even in Athens, legal provisions were enacted concerning the fulfillment of marital duty,[359] and in Sparta, one was threatened with punishment for being unmarried. Furthermore, the state displayed a strong interest in the civil legitimacy of the offspring. Thus, it legally established the civil prerequisites for a lawful marriage. The family lines, upon admitting a newborn son into their membership, were required to verify that he was truly conceived in a lawful marriage. However, the state was not actually involved in the marriage itself, the way it is today through institutions like the registrar.

As we have already discussed above, a married woman is very well capable of smuggling bastard blood into a pure thoroughbred bloodline. For this reason, the Nordic race used uncompromising methods to deal with the adulteress and sentenced her to death—it could be said that racial defectives had to be culled as emphatically as possible. Later on, things became a bit more lenient, but the adulteress was generally expelled from the free community and clearly marked as unfit for further breeding through hair cutting (bob cut!). It was originally the case that the older laws only ever recognized sexual infidelity as a matter pertaining exclusively to married women. Consequently, only bastards born from an adulterous wife were initially considered "illegitimate," while those conceived between a married man and an unfree woman remained clearly distinct from this category and did not need to be referred to as such. Such "illegitimate" children born to a married woman are always given names in the records that point to the clandestine (concealment!) nature of their birth, examples of this include "born in secret," "born in a stable" (?!?), "born in a forest," and "bencher," the latter meaning that this was a child conceived on a bench rather than in the marital bed, where the legitimate child was born. The concubine did not need to give birth to her children in secret, since she naturally had nothing to hide.[360]

One might get the impression that these provisions for married women were the products of male vanity, demanding sexual abstinence for women while exempting men from such demands. However, two facts mentioned earlier clearly contradict this assumption by showing how little these provisions had to do with moral reasoning in the modern sense. Firstly, it was mentioned that the wife was made available to an honored guest for the night, and, secondly, that in the case of illness or infertility of the spouse (for example, due to war injury), a procreation assistant would step in. Now, as for the guest, if he was an honored guest, it was of course clear that he is a man of the same blood, or, at the very least, the lineage the man was known and acceptable, thereby posing no threat to the blood-inheritance of the tribe

---

[359] From Plutarch, *Solon*: "Which permits an heiress in case the man under whose power and authority she is placed by law is himself unable to consort with her, to be married by one of his next of kin. Some, however, say that this was a wise provision against those who are unable to perform the duties of a husband. . . ."
[360] Ruedolf, *Fluch Unserer Geschlechtsmoral*, 31.

as a whole. The heir to the property was usually the eldest son and, as such, the continued progenitor of the family lineage. The bride's kin (her clan) had to vouch beforehand that the first child was indeed the child of the legal father. This explains certain customs observed on the wedding night, which will be discussed shortly. With subsequent children, such exactness was no longer necessary. The main concern in all cases remained whether the head of the family could demonstrate the child's lineage before the community, ensuring that the community was not being deceived regarding the child's origins.

This concept of breeding is even more evident in the Germanic variety of the so-called procreation assistant. The community entrusted a virgin to the husband's faithful care so that he could father children with her. And, by means of well-defined inheritance laws, it was ensured that there was a sufficient dietary space for his brood of children. However, if, for any reason, the husband was unable to conceive children, the Nordic race did not want to allot the valuable food-producing land to individuals who would not be raising a family. Instead, it was demanded that the husband make his wife available to another free man, so that the fertility of the woman could be utilized. Dissolving the marriage was out of the question because the husband's position was connected to social rights, and, moreover, he was the owner of the inherited property (the hereditary property). When we are told that adultery did not exist in Sparta while at the same time being told that the practice of exchanging spouses was permitted, these are not contradictions, but rather accounts that correspond exactly to the breeding laws of the Germanic people.[361] Essentially, it has to be taken into account that the Nordic race has always associated the concepts of fidelity and infidelity to biological inheritance and has never thought of linking these questions to sexual intercourse as such.

Even in Athens, the ancient Nordic procreation assistant can still be clearly identified. For example, Plutarch once said the following about the related Solonic legislation:

> That law, too, seems absurd and ridiculous, which permits an heiress in case the man under whose power and authority she is placed by law is himself unable to consort with her, to be married by one of his next of kin.

Plutarch could not possibly have known the source of this ancient Nordic law—which was undoubtedly not created by Solon, but merely preserved by him—and so could not have understood the meaning behind this institution. Therefore, he indulges in moral outrage following the aforementioned passage. However, further down, he adds this enlightening remark: "It is a wise provision, too, that the heiress may not choose her consort at large, but

---

361 Ruedolf, *Fluch Unserer Geschlechtsmoral*, 53.

only from the kinsmen of her husband, that her offspring may be of his family and lineage."

Furthermore, the connection between Solon's legislation and the ancient
Germanic marriage laws is made even clearer in a following passage by
Plutarch, and is therefore mentioned here: "In all other marriages [Solon]
prohibited dowries; the bride was to bring with her three changes of raiment, household stuff of small value, and nothing else."

In the next chapter we shall see that the elimination of the dowry in
marriage is an ancient Nordic principle that can be clearly found in all
Nordic historical records. It is therefore safe to say that the marriage laws
attributed to Solon in Athens are not truly Solon's, but were either simply
adopted by him (or had to be adopted by him) under pressure from the
noble families. It is obvious that in the future, these ancient Greek lawmakers will have to be seen in a similar light to comparable German figures such as Eike von Repgow, who, by compiling the *Sachsenspiegel* did
not of course create any laws, but created a document which has recorded
and passed down to us old established laws. Besides, the fact is that, in
itself, there is actually no contradiction between the aforementioned
"heiress" and the emphasized prohibition of a dowry, as Plutarch seems to
assume. In the case of the so-called heiress, she was simply an heiress's
daughter who was to provide the inheritance (the landed property) with a
large brood of children. If the chosen spouse was prevented from fulfilling this task, a procreation assistant (preferably a person of the same
blood as her husband) would simply step in, thereby keeping her family's
blood alive on the inherited land. The question remains open as to
whether Solon was actually aware of these connections.

These laws about procreation assistants may seem strange to us, but
in the following chapter we will see that girls were often betrothed and
moved into their future husband's household as early as the age of twelve.
However, we will also see that this was not a marriage in the biological
sense, but most likely only a legal guarantee of a girl's future—the girl's
future position as the mistress of a household was secured. However, if a
lawful husband was unable to produce offspring, this by itself was, of
course, not a sufficient reason to disqualify him from the position of husband, which in ancient times was endowed with extensive rights. Since
we know that marriage in those times was primarily for the purpose of
procreation and not for the personal pleasure of the spouses, then it follows that the use of a procreation assistant for reproduction is, in principle, a reasonable emergency measure. It may seem strange to us, but it
will seem logical if one frees oneself from contemporary ideas and thinks
according to the customs and perspectives of the past. If the woman was
completely free to choose the procreation assistant, that is, if she was not
bound to her husband's relatives, then this Solonic tradition could be
associated with vestiges of matrilineal views. But since the procreation
assistant was quite clearly limited to the husband's lineage, this leaves no
doubt about the nature of this emergency measure. Moreover, the fact

that the woman was free to choose among the men of her husband's immediate family cannot be interpreted as laxity in sexual matters, nor can it be explained as even being the faintest echo of matrilineal practices. On the contrary, the author sees this as an emerging sensitivity to female personhood—she was spared the trouble of having to submit to a man she did not love or even hated. Anyone still not convinced should be cognizant of the fact that in ancient Nordic marital law, the wife by all means always remained under the hand (authority) of her husband. Therefore, the freedom granted to her to choose her procreation assistant at her discretion (from her husband's relatives) represents an extraordinary accommodation. Clearly, the procreation assistant was considered an unavoidable breeding necessity resulting from extraordinary circumstances, and every effort was made to mitigate any unnecessary harshness or heartlessness associated with this arrangement.[362]

The Nordic race certainly did not consider adultery to be the sexual intercourse of a married woman with another man, but rather the secret intercourse of the wife with a man unknown to her spouse. If the adulterer belonged to the class of free citizens, different laws applied to him than those mentioned above for the adulteress, and in this case, she was not sentenced to death. In early times, the husband had the right to seek retribution without fear of starting a blood feud. In the Laws of King Alfred (*Dōmbōc*, Law 42.7), we find something striking similar to the Greeks:

And a man may fight without fear of feud (blood vengeance) if he finds another with his lawful wife behind closed doors or under a covering, or with his lawfully-born sister, or with his mother, who was given to his father as his lawful wife.

An Anglo-Saxon law also stipulated that the adulterer of free blood had to provide another wife to the injured person.

Once again, the characteristic feature here is that adultery when committed by a woman is dangerous only when there is the possibility that unknown blood can creep into the community's thoroughbred lineage. When the adulterer is a familiar person and is of free blood, then this danger does not exist, and punishments purely for the sake of correcting poor behavior now follow, quite distinct from the death penalty, for the death penalty is a eugenic provision whose purpose is to cull.

---

[362] Interestingly, it is in Crete, particularly influenced by its pre-Hellenic Cretan population and culture, where the rules regarding heiresses are most relaxed. In particular, heiresses here have greater freedom to choose whom they wish to marry. If there was no one in her clan who could or would marry her, she was free to marry whomever she chose. Here, it appears that the pre-Hellenic population had clear matrilineal influences, ensuring that women were granted the right to choose the person with whom they wished to have a child, regardless of whether the man in question had any connection to their race. This is the complete opposite of the old Nordic concept of the heiress. The Nordic idea, of course, was primarily concerned with nothing more than the preservation of a lineage through inheritance and an heiress, without any intention of considering the sexual preferences and inclinations of the young woman.

Accordingly, the North Germanic people—and the patricians of Rome, for that matter—clearly make a distinction between three types of illegitimate children. Illegitimate children who resulted from an open concubinage with a free woman, illegitimate children who resulted from a secret affair with a free woman, and illegitimate children who resulted from the sexual intercourse between a free man and an unfree woman (concubine).

This threefold distinction of illegitimate children would be meaningless if illegitimacy as such were understood according to contemporary moral standards. Note, however, how finely preserved the eugenic aspects are. Illegitimate children born of open concubinage with a free woman pose no harm whatsoever to the thoroughbred lineage, because their lineage is without blemish, assuming, of course, that they have a free father. Illegitimate children born of secret intercourse with a free woman, however, are very dangerous to the thoroughbred lineage because this situation enables paternity from unwanted blood. There is, in fact, no clearer proof of the fact that the Nordic race did not attach any importance at all to the act of sexual intercourse itself—the descent of the child meant everything to them.

Significantly, children fathered by a free man with concubines were placed in a special class, which can also be understood according to breeding considerations. In these cases, the child's origin was always obvious through their mother. Like with horse breeding, these children could never shake off the fact of being half-breeds.

Unmarried girls, too, were assessed from a breeding point of view rather than according to moral views of sexuality. The virgin had to enter marriage in a state of purity to assure her husband that his first-born child was indeed conceived by him. The clan, not the girl herself, was responsible for the girl's sexual purity. This in turn is associated with various wedding night customs. For example, the tradition of having a guard of honor stationed outside the bridal chamber on the wedding night. Another tradition involves having the marriage consummated in the presence of witnesses. One might say that this was the way they ensured that everything was done properly and that there would be no unjustified objections afterwards. However, it seems that they also relied on evidence of a more concrete nature to prove the bride's chastity. The German ruling families have preserved to the present-day customs which, strangely enough, are also found in some peasant communities in Russia—this indicates that the origin of both customs is likely to be found in the Nordic race. The bride was bathed and then dressed in a snow-white shirt (bridal shirt) for the wedding night. It is known that in those days people never slept in clothing, but always undressed. In Russia, the bridal shirt would be presented to the community on the wedding night, and they would express their joy by vigorously smashing dishes (*Polterabend*). Otherwise, the clan would present the bride with a pot riddled with holes, which was considered a great shame for her clan, but less so for the bride herself.

The custom of saving the unwashed bridal shirt has been maintained by many of our German noble families to this day. The author mentions these two examples because they clearly prove that the purity of the virgin was a matter pertaining to the community or race, related to the laws of pure breeding, and had nothing to do with reasons of an erotic, mystical, perverse, or religious nature. What other races and peoples later made of this custom as they learned of it is not our concern here, as we are concerned only with the breeding laws of the Nordic race.

However, when considering the following, it will become even clearer that questions of chastity were solely evaluated from the perspective of biological inheritance. A virgin of free blood was not required to enter marriage as a chaste woman if the identity of the person who deflowered her was known. Her future husband only needed to be aware of this information, and the girl's clan had to assure that enough time had passed since the incident, so that it could no longer affect the proposed marriage. Namely, it was possible that the daughter of a household had been given to an honored guest; in such a case, the girl was not devalued. Similarly, there was no devaluation from a eugenic standpoint if a girl of free blood conceived a child with a free man in a wild or informal marriage. At most, a punishment was imposed to deter this behavior in the future. The children born of such wild unions between free people were fundamentally free and without fault. Such children were called *winkelkinder* (corner children) by the Germanic peoples.

Von Amira writes,

> Although a *winkelkind* was not considered equal to a legitimate or "genuine" child, they were nonetheless granted a position within the paternal family association whereby they could participate in *wergeld*, perform guardianship functions, and have entitlements to financial support—and even inheritance rights—from the father, or at least receive compensation for such rights.

Among the patricians of ancient Rome, the main distinction between those born in a legitimate marriage and those born out of wedlock was that the latter did not come under the control of their father and were not entitled to inheritance from him or his clan. In Greece, it was possible for free citizens to enter into unofficial marriages, resulting in children whose lineage was nevertheless impeccable; such unions, however, were not well regarded. Importantly, the intentional seduction of a free woman by a free man would result in punishment, although plays such as Menander's *Epitrepontes* and *Samia* depict instances of seduction still taking place.

If, however, a free maiden had become involved with an unfree man, or if she could not identify the father of her child, she invariably faced the harshest punishment. In Athens, the father was allowed to sell his daughter into slavery if she had been convicted of voluntary dishonor. Bonifacius explicitly emphasizes "that the same cruel punishment that befell an adulteress also awaited a girl who defiled her father's house with unchastity." However, only the virgin who was not mindful of her procreative duty (who spoiled her blood) was considered unchaste; the girl who gave herself to a free man out of affection did not receive such a label. The latter situation was considered, in the truest sense of the word, a "private" matter with which the community as such did not concern itself.

In the work of Ida Naumann,[363] under the title "Love Affair" (Sea Saga, Thule 10), we find the following tale, which excellently reflects what has just been said.

At an autumn *thing*, many people came together and a game was organized. Ingolf, Thorstein's son, took part and showcased his agility. One time, when he tried to catch a ball, it so happened that it flew toward Walgerd, Ottar's daughter. She covered herself with her cloak and they chatted for a while. She seemed to him to be a particularly beautiful woman, and every remaining day of the *thing*, he went to talk to her. After that, he visited her constantly.

Ottar was not of the same mind, however, and asked Ingolf not to do anything that would bring dishonor to both of them. He said that he would rather give the girl to him honorably than to disgrace her dishonorably. But Ingolf said that he would continue his visits as he saw fit, and they would not bring him any dishonor.

Ottar then went to see Ingolf's father, Thorstein, and Thorstein said to his son, "Why are you bringing shame to Ottar and dishonoring his daughter? You have evil intentions, and our relationship will come to an end unless you make amends."

Ingolf stopped his visits, but would write love poems about Walgerd and made them known to others. Ottar returned to Thorstein, and Thorstein told him that he had spoken with Ingolf, but had been unable to get anywhere with him.

Ingolf married Haldis, the daughter of Olaf of Habichtskluft. He would visit Walgerd whenever he rode to or from the *thing*. Ottar disapproved of this greatly. Walgerd would also sew the finest clothes for Ingolf. After Ingolf's death, Ottar married his daughter Walgerd to a man from Stangenwald.

We observe that the affair between Walgerd and the married Ingolf, while not looked upon fondly by the Walgerd family, does not in any way prevent her subsequent marriage to another man. Walgerd's behavior was considered less "immoral" and more "mischievous" according to the views of the time. The narrative actually aims only to depict the disobedience of Walgerd and Ingolf toward their respective fathers, rather than serving up a "risqué" story about the sexual relationship of these two.

The word virtue (*tugend*) originally had a connection to suitability and fitness (*tauglichkeit*). Virtuous (*tugendhaft*), originates from the Middle High German *tugenthaft*, meaning capable. Virtuous (*tugendsam*) originates from the Middle High German *tugendsam*, meaning of noble and fine morality. Ihering writes,

---

[363] Naumann, *Altgermanisches Frauenleben*.

Military aptitude is the quality that matters most in a man, it is the virtue of the man just as fertility is the virtue of the woman. The memory of this primeval idea is permanently preserved in the Roman *virtus* and *vir*, as well as the Sanskrit *wira* (related to the Old High German *wair* and the Old English *wer*, from which the compound *wergeld* derives), meaning man, hero, or warrior. It is with *virtus* that the Roman concept of virtue is associated.

It is natural that a polity that viewed marriage as a public service would also value an abundance of offspring along these lines. Ihering writes,

> The polity extends protection to the woman, but in return, it expects her to bear children, preferably as many as possible, and most preferably male. From the *quinque* (fifths) of the *dos* (dowry), it follows that a Roman marriage should bear at least five children. This number, found in the oldest laws, was also maintained for the *jus liberorum* (right of children) in the provinces, while it was reduced to four in Italy and three in Rome. A woman who only gives birth to boys (*puerpera*) is highly esteemed, while a woman who bears more girls than boys or only girls is considered misfortunate, and a woman who did not have children was considered cursed. The proper woman becomes a mother, and therefore, from *mater* comes the designation of marriage as *matrimonium*, and *matrone* as an honorary title for a woman (*matronarum sanctitas*). Correlatedly, the word *pater* is used for wealth: *patri-monium*. The woman takes care of the children, the man takes care of the wealth.

According to Plutarch, violating the honor of a Roman matron was comparable to temple desecration and accordingly punished.

Accordingly, the laws regarding divorce were also regulated from a breeding perspective. We have already heard that among the patricians, a man who sold his wife was subject to the death penalty. Furthermore, if a woman was expelled by her husband without a legal reason, he had to forfeit his wealth. These grounds for divorce can be traced back to Romulus, and therefore undoubtedly have an ancient Nordic origin. Ihering writes,

> A man who sells his wife (Old Latin *voxor*, New Latin *uxor*; from Sanskrit *vaçâ*, meaning beloved) shall be punished with death. He may kill her for adultery or if she becomes intoxicated. He may only divorce her for certain legally specified reasons. If he repudiates her without legal grounds, he shall forfeit his entire fortune, with half going to the wife and the other half to the gens.

From a breeding perspective, it is also significant that a Roman man could kill his wife if she became intoxicated. There has already been quite a bit of musing on this point, but the case itself is clear from a breeding standpoint. The Nordic race has always embraced alcohol. It was customary for the hostess or daughters to serve drinks to the guests. In ancient Nordic runes, Gunnlaug blesses the parents of Helga of Borg, his beloved, as follows: "Eternally do I thank the noble parents / who begot you, you virtuous youth, / the maiden who so delightfully pours the wine." But when a woman becomes intoxicated, she is no longer able to resist a man, considerably increasing the odds that the woman could conceive a child from an unknown or undesirable source.

Plutarch mentions two additional grounds for divorce, and they are the poisoning of the children and the forging of keys. These grounds are somewhat puzzling, as they contain inherent contradictions. However, in a highly astute analysis, Ihering arrives at the following conclusion—there are not two, but three grounds for divorce, and they can be found in the historical record in a garbled and condensed form. The first grounds for divorce is attributing a child to a woman who did not birth it, in other words, the concealment of infertility. The second grounds for divorce is the forging of keys. This cannot be referring literally to keys but must be symbolic since the bride was handed the keys at the time of marriage and had to return them upon divorce. It would have made no sense for her to forge these keys. Ihering, however, believes that the keys should be viewed as a symbol, specifically as a badge of honor for a woman who gives birth easily. Based on our previous considerations, Ihering's assumption must be correct, as we have observed that the selection of a wife by the community relied on the expectation of being blessed with children in the future. If, in this marriage, difficulties arose during childbirth, Ihering suggests that the husband was allowed to simply dissolve the marriage as a result. This idea also falls perfectly in line with the breeding laws that we have discussed so far. The third grounds for divorce is likely less about poison and more about love potions; the Romans called such a love potion *philtrum*. The poet Lucretius took his own life after consuming such a love potion, and Lucullus lost his sanity on a similar occasion. It would therefore be understandable if legal measures were taken against these things.

Ihering was a jurist, and taking breeding into account in his analysis must have been completely foreign to him in his day. But the three grounds for divorce that he developed here are certainly accurate and provide us with another way of understanding the breeding laws of the Nordic race.

It is to Ihering that we owe another study of Roman marital relations that is likely to be of fundamental importance to race science. Nevertheless, it should be noted that Ihering was not able to interpret the records he uncovered and had to be content with their enigmatic nature.

Firstly, Ihering observes that the Laws of the Twelve Tables, imposed on the patricians by the plebeians, brought about a change that affected all of Roman law. He writes,

The idea behind the patrician kinship state was that the individual was just one part of a whole. Marriage, arrogation (adoption of a son), adoption (adoption of a child of either gender), and testamentary matters affected the interests of the entire community and therefore required its involvement. The idea behind the new plebeian system was that the individual was self-reliant, and all three acts depend on his free decision.

In his investigation of the observable differences between the patrician and plebeian views of marriage, Ihering reaches the following conclusion, among others,

The old law presents a quite surprising contrast regarding the legal position of the man in relation to the woman, recognizing two forms of marriage—one in which the woman comes under the *manus* (the authority of the *pater familias* over the woman) of the man through *confarreatio*, and another in which an additional act, *coëmtio*, is required if this is intended. The *manus* is the same in both cases—the difference, therefore, lies only in its origin. But this difference is highly significant. It involves not only a mere difference in form but brings to mind two fundamentally different and contradictory views of the marital relationship, one insisting that the woman must be under *manus*, and the other suggesting that she can be independent. Both views cannot possibly have originated on the same soil, and if, despite this, they are found together in Rome in the historical period among the same people, we are compelled to search for a different origin for each of them. It is not enough to assume a temporal difference. If one had temporally replaced the other, it would not be understandable why, after the emergence of marriage without *manus* (the so-called free marriage), one would still need to employ *coëmtio* to add the *manus*. The only explanation remaining is that this is a contrast between the patricians and the plebeians, and I agree with this opinion (which has been expressed by others). The *confarreate* marriage is of patrician origin, and the opposing one, in which the *manus* can be added or is absent according to agreement, is of plebeian origin. This was the view of the Romans themselves—they trace the legal formation of the *confarreatio* marriage all the way back to Romulus and is among the fundamental institutions of the kinship state created by him. This is also supported by the number of witnesses participating in its establishment.

Ihering then goes on to discuss how this has not solved the puzzle, but merely shifted it. For us, however, the connections are clear. The *confarreatio* marriage is the ancient Nordic one. The plebeians evidently incorporated matrilineal views into the forms of marriage they borrowed from the patricians, which explains the non-*confarreatio* temporary marriage that could later be transformed into a permanent marriage only by the act of *coëmtio*.[364] Ihering proceeds,

> The distinguishing feature of the *confarreatio* form of marriage, as compared to other forms of entering into marriage, lies in the involvement of the Pontifex Maximus, the Flamen Dialis, and ten witnesses.

Ihering is likely correct in recognizing these individuals as those responsible for checking whether those who marry belong to the appropriate "family lines." Ihering continues,

> In the historical period, marriage is dissolvable, specifically *non-confarreatio* marriage. This was possible both through an agreement between the spouses and through unilateral termination. On the other hand, *confarreatio* marriage is only conditionally dissolvable—it requires the act of *diffarreatio* and the participation of the same persons that participated in the *confarreatio*, who were granted the same rights of examination and potential refusal of their consent (the same rights they had initially).

Ihering does not believe that divorce was originally very common in *confarreatio* marriage, given that the first divorce is placed in the sixth century BC.

According to Ihering, the patricians regarded marriage with plebeians as a mixing of noble blood (*contaminare sanguinem*):

> By granting *conubium* to the plebeians through the Lex Canuleia, the patrician kinship-based state was dealt a significant blow. The swiftness with which the contrasts between the two groups were reconciled in public law is primarily attributed to the Lex Canuleia.

---

[364] In terms of racial science, one can conclude from this tradition with a reasonable degree of certainty that the plebeians could not have constituted a population of Nordic origin. It is worth noting that the non-Nordic pre-Hellenic population of Greece also resisted the sexual customs of the Hellenes and attempted to introduce matrilineal perspectives into their sexual practices. Upon closer examination, one must also admit that Nordic monogamous long-term marriage has a biological meaning only if one takes into account how sustenance-providing land was secured by the passing on of genes. Where this is not the case, or is no longer the case, and there is a more or less pronounced separation or independence from the land, it would probably be more biologically correct to affirm matrilineality and consider the man only as the trigger of fertilization. In this case, one must either give the mother full rights over the child or, alternatively, ensure through communal efforts that the children can be raised. Thus, for example, it is entirely consistent that Marxism, which consciously seeks to decouple the individual from all forms of attachment—especially the connection between a family's sustenance and land—should seek to reintroduce matrilineality and leave it to the woman to decide whether and from whom to conceive a child.

In this concise statement, Ihering succinctly identifies the reasons for the eventual decline of Rome, although his intention was not to assert this but rather to explain the transition from an organic to a mechanistic conception of law.

But let us return to the Nordic concept of pure breeding. Women are vulnerable beings, and since the Nordic race placed such value on the preservation of blood purity, special protective provisions for women and girls would have been considered. As a matter of fact, such provisions were largely in place. Of course, we have already discussed the protection of the wife. In early times, the daughter was protected by always remaining under the care of her father—only the son could become a responsible adult (never the daughter). Nevertheless, it was never assumed that the father alone could provide sufficient protection for a girl, so brothers were also held responsible for their sisters. In the ancient Indian family, the brother is explicitly mentioned as the guardian of his sister's virtue, "She seeketh men, as she who hath no brother . . ." This implies that a girl lacking a brother surrenders herself more boldly to a man. This is also praised in the case of Nausicaa, for example:

> Thrice-blessed then are thy father and thy honored mother, and thrice-blessed thy [brothers]. Full well, I ween, are their hearts ever warmed with joy because of thee, as they see thee entering the dance, a plant so fair. [365]

However, there are other considerations that arise practically out of necessity, and they are much more illuminating. Just as in animal breeding, when breeding reaches a sufficiently high level (such as, for example, in English thoroughbred breeding), the biological inheritance of a useful animal for further breeding attains a value that can be entirely beyond any calculation. To give an example, in 1926, the Prussian Stud Administration purchased an English Thoroughbred stallion (Poisoned Arrow) for five hundred thousand reichsmarks. We can apply this idea to the Nordic concept of breeding, where a virgin born into a true, recognized marriage had a hereditary value that could not be attained by a woman from an unrecognized lineage, even if she belonged to the same race. A pure-blooded daughter of the tribe thus became the sole vessel through which a future heir could pass on their blood in a pure form to the next generation. Therefore, this virgin stood under the protection of the entire tribe—her blood (her biological inheritance) was a matter of concern to each individual member of the tribe, and it became the duty of each one of them to preserve and protect her. This included both her physical protection and her virginal purity, for both are of equal importance in the preservation of the biological inheritance. This is perhaps the source of the deep-rooted belief (still held by every Nordic man today) that he must chivalrously come to the aid of a "noble" or "virtuous" girl or woman in distress.

It is easy to understand that as soon as the blood was no longer hermetically sealed (as was the case, for example, with the original true nobility of early

---

[365] Homer, *The Odyssey*, 6.150–160.

medieval Germany), the idea of blood would inevitably recede, with class, the court, and property taking center stage in its place.[366] Eventually, "equal birth" became an entirely superficial matter of social status. Today, when even our high nobility can no longer claim to be thoroughbred, social prejudices have naturally become meaningless. They are nevertheless important and revealing because they are remnants of primordial (atavistic) breeding instincts, which are excellent tools for shedding light on the thinking of the Nordic race in prehistoric times.

However, such an attitude on the part of men toward women of their blood must necessarily have resulted in a certain asexuality of the sensual drives, which, given the pronounced sexual duality of the Nordic race, has always stood out as a peculiar contradiction.

In addition to this, there is the fact that cohabitation under the same roof leads to a certain coldness in the relations between the sexes—something that can, of course, be observed in the individual households that preserved their naturalness, which can be found in any peasant settlement in Germany. It remains debatable whether this occurs out of necessity, to make such close cohabitation even possible, or if constant familiarity with the sight of the opposite sex diminishes sexual allure—the author is inclined to believe the latter. Finland and vast areas of the east are, in parts, not inhabited at all by the Nordic race. However, those who have had the opportunity to witness the casualness with which family members of both sexes bathe together unclothed in Finnish saunas may in fact be inclined to view such questions not only from the perspective of race, but also just as much from the perspective of upbringing and habituation. Furthermore, it should be noted that in farmhouses with healthy family lines, three to four generations of female relatives often live together, with at least the grandmother still alive. Apart from sowing the seeds for the development and preservation of a strong sense of family tradition, this arrangement also leads to the close monitoring of the female youth as they grow. With the thoughts developed here, we surely have the key to understanding the platonic relationship between the Nordic sexes when living together.

Stemming from its peasant and racial heritage, the Nordic race's respect for women—perhaps not so much for women themselves, but for the inheritance of its own noble perfection as preserved in woman—has never been understood by other races, and consequently could never be understood by them without a knowledge of these connections. We repeatedly encounter astonished reports, for instance, that a state like Sparta, which tolerates such "female rule," still nonetheless produced such exceptional warriors. However, Gorgo, the wife of Leonidas, provided a fitting response by stating that "Spartan women are capable of ruling over men precisely because they alone are capable of giving birth to men." A remarkable statement!

---

[366] Dungern, *Adelsherrschaft im Mittelalter.*

5

The Nordic race does not always appear to be completely uniform in its breeding laws. However, the basic ideas—as outlined here—are more or less always clearly discernible. It will have to be left to further research to uncover the reasons for this divergent behavior. Perhaps only our traditions are to blame, either because they have come down to us in a distorted form or because they have been hitherto misinterpreted. The author would like to propose two additional possibilities for consideration.

The author would like to assume, at first, that certain variations in type have also had an impact on the Nordic race.[367] However, since we currently lack any detailed research in this area, there is no point in making any assumptions. Only this much needs to be emphasized—in the field of animal breeding, we do not find a single breed that does not exhibit variations in type. While it often requires a trained eye to be able to discern them, they are definitely there. Whether such differences in type can also be observed in the bone structure (the skeleton) may be doubted in certain cases in animal breeding—at the very least, animal breeders do not entertain the idea of considering the possibility of such skeletal differences.

Differences in type are often more a matter of physiology than of morphology. Although no conclusive explanations have been provided thus far, certain beliefs still persist stubbornly in the field of horse breeding, such as the idea that a relationship exists between skin and hair color on the one hand, and between temperament and performance-capability on the other. Mind you, these are differences of color within a breed, not comparisons of color among members of different breeds. Finally, it must not be forgotten that type does not even represent the smallest unit in animal breeding, but rather dissolves into subtypes, which in turn break down into varieties. Therefore, there would be no biological obstacles in assuming certain subtle physiological differences within the Nordic race that could serve as explanations for the variations present in the historical accounts.

However, it seems more probable to the author that the migration "treks" from the ancestral homeland that took place at different times each embodied different stages of development, though the individual differences need not be assumed to be too significant. Additionally, due to the various foreign influences that impacted each of the daughter colonies, a different interpretation of the original traditions necessarily had to result in each case.

---

[367] For instance, one can readily establish the following two types within the Nordic race. The first consists of individuals that are politically highly gifted, but altogether lacking in artistic disposition (though endowed with a keen eye for bodily forms and physical sculpture) and consistently unmusical (yet possessing a pronounced inclination toward military music). This type we find most pronounced in Sparta, the ancient Roman patricians, Prussia, and especially among Low Germans and Anglo-Saxons. The second consists of individuals that are politically indifferent, but artistically highly gifted and distinctly inclined toward music. This type is most pronounced in Athens, among some southern German tribes, and the Swedes.

Thus, some might assume that the observable differences in attitudes toward polygamy or monogamy among the various peoples of the Nordic race are due either to differences in type or to some form of alien racial influence. However, neither of these possibilities is very likely. This is evidenced by the fact that polygamy persisted in the ancestral homeland of the Nordic race (Sweden) until relatively recently and by the fact that there were always enough concubines available in the daughter colonies to make polygamy unnecessary. The author would instead like to assume that there was no fundamental difference between polygamy and monogamy among the Nordic race, and that it was only we, based on our modern concept of marriage, who introduced a distinction into these marriage traditions. As we have seen, the essential purpose of Nordic marriage was tied to procreation. It is therefore certainly conceivable that, for example, a prince who has demonstrated his noble blood through his office could afford multiple lawful marriages if he had sufficient landholdings. Tacitus, in any case, states quite clearly,

> They are almost the only barbarians who are content with a wife apiece; the very few exceptions have nothing to do with passion, but consist of those with whom polygamous marriage is eagerly sought for the sake of their high birth.

The same factors lead us to a quite different conclusion when considering the patricians of ancient Rome. When the patrician peasant trek eventually settles on the banks of the Tiber and Romulus distributes the land, the number of households corresponded to the number of ignited hearth fires. Since land ownership for the Nordic race is always associated with the family, and since this race was originally unfamiliar with further division of family property, it necessarily follows that only monogamy could prevail on the ancient patrician estates. Nordic polygamy was never polygamy in the sense that several lawful wives presided over a single hearth fire—each hearth fire was tended by one mistress. Nevertheless, the surviving records regarding the Romans are not entirely clear. Namely, it seems that although polygamy was legally permitted in Rome, it was generally not common practice. This would support the aforementioned assumption of the author. For example, during Cicero's time, Plancius was accused of polygamy, which was a moral accusation but apparently not a punishable offense in court. Caesar planned to legally introduce polygamy in Rome for the purpose of procreation. The great Mark Antony married Queen Cleopatra while still married to Octavia. According to Birt, Marcus Valerius Martialis and Seneca also provide further evidence in this regard: *matrimonium vocari unum adulterium* (adultery is nick-named marriage). Concerning Greece, for example, Busolt states quite clearly,

> Polygamy was highly unusual in Sparta. According to Herodotus, the Ephors demanded that King Anaxandridas divorce his infertile wife and marry another so that the lineage of Eurysthenes would not die

out. Since the king did not want to send his wife away, the Ephors and Gerontes demanded that he marry a second woman alongside her. Anaxandridas complied and thus had two lawful wives. King Ariston married three women successively because the first two were infertile.

It is clear, therefore, that monogamy and polygamy are not mutually exclusive if marriage is not understood in the modern sense (as a "private matter" between a man and a woman), but rather as the potential for procreation secured through sustenance-providing land, together with the associated task of preserving a valuable lineage or passing on the genes of a valuable individual to the next generation in the greatest possible abundance and perfection.

A few remarks on inbreeding should be added here, as some readers will certainly assume that the laws of pure breeding, as we have developed them here, will necessarily lead to degeneration. Aside from the fact that our investigation of the breeding laws of the Nordic race is based on the biology of the English thoroughbred and its history (a very tangible example of inbreeding), animal breeding when it comes to certain other breeds has even greater degrees of inbreeding. We have already mentioned the Russian Orlov trotters and the English Shorthorn cattle—one could continue listing these examples almost indefinitely. In the famous Spanish Riding School in Vienna, horses have been propagated for generations within two small families through extremely close inbreeding, and they have maintained their old quality for over a century.

But do not assume that the author is recommending inbreeding per se. We do not currently have the means to employ inbreeding at our discretion. In this regard, we can only establish that inbreeding does not necessarily have to be harmful, but we still do not know in which cases it is harmless and in which cases it is harmful. Therefore, animal breeding warns breeders against the thoughtless application of inbreeding while admitting that almost all breeds have developed on the basis of inbreeding. Skilled breeders, who have a keen eye for the constitution of an animal, never hesitate to make use of inbreeding if necessary, even if it means acting uncompromisingly. Inbreeding is a breeding technique for experienced, accomplished high breeders and not for the average breeder.

In this context, it is worth compiling and mentioning some historical accounts of inbreeding from ancient times, specifically referring to the closest form of inbreeding, namely incestuous breeding. Inbreeding was practiced in antiquity among the Phoenicians, according to Justinus, as well as among the Medes and Persians, according to several other authors. For instance, Herodotus reports that Cambyses married his own sister, Plutarch mentions that Artaxerxes married his daughter, and Curtius Rufus recounts that Sysimithres, the Satrap of Sogdiana, married his mother, without presenting this as a particular exception.

The Egyptians considered it permissible for siblings to be married, and the Ptolemies adopted this custom when they came to power. The first ruler, Ptolemy Lagos, married his children, Ptolemy Philadelphus and Arsinoe (who were full siblings) to each other. The last member of this dynasty, also a product of incestuous breeding, was Cleopatra, a physically and intellectually exceptional personality. Queen Cleopatra was the daughter of a marriage between a brother and sister, and her grandparents were also siblings. She herself was married to her brother and, after his death, married her younger brother.

Among the ancient Greeks, marriage between legal siblings was permitted up until the fifth century BC. Consanguineous marriage was prohibited by the Greeks and Romans relatively late. This prohibition was not due to unfavorable experiences with offspring but solely to prevent the accumulation of large fortunes. It was not until the year 605 that Pope Gregory I made consanguineous marriage religiously forbidden in Christianity.

Even the inhabitants of ancient Peru, especially the kings, were reported by Garcilaso de la Vega (*Comentarios Reales de los Incas*) to practice sibling or half-sibling marriage. The incestuous breeding of the Ptolemies and the Incas is explicitly attributed to eugenic reasons by writers, as these ruling dynasties feared being corrupted by inferior blood. However, it is also possible that correct observations were involved here. It has been found in certain animal breeds that foreign blood can have a poisonous effect in a high breed that has become insensitive to inbreeding (these cases have not yet been conclusively proven). They are mentioned here because the Ptolemies and Incas may have derived their views on inbreeding from correct observations, suggesting a principle based on experience rather than superstition. The commonly held belief in today's public discourse that inbreeding inevitably leads to degeneration is utter nonsense. When tribes or lineages begin to degenerate, other causes are to blame. However, it must be acknowledged that inbreeding can accelerate degeneration in such cases.

In the case of the Nordic race at least, opening their closed thoroughbred lineage to other blood has proven to be detrimental whenever it has been attempted, leading to, among other things, the loss of their instinctual understanding of the iron law of performance-based high breeding. The unrestricted mingling of genders always very quickly turns into a disaster, and moral freedom naturally transforms into its opposite, eventually reaching a highly immoral state. Guglielmo Ferrero excellently details this sudden transformation in his book,[368] to which special reference is made here because we have few works which so clearly prove that not only a woman's womb, but also her mentality and disposition, significantly influence the rise and fall of family lines and states, more so than the abilities or inabilities of men. Of course, the Nordic woman, due to her evolutionary history, does not possess the instinct of women from matrilineal societies who, despite sexual freedom, still always keep the advantage of their tribe in mind. In history, we see that the moment that the asexual moral freedom of the Nordic woman turns into an immoral sexual one, the dissolution of the state follows with almost frightening rapidity. In chapter four, the author was able to present similar causes for the decline of Sparta and provided corresponding evidence. As Sparta began to forget the true meaning of its moral laws (though it did not abandon the moral freedom of will required for the production of fully free children, meaning those born on

[368] Ferrero, *Frauen der Cäsaren*.

hereditary estates were still faultless in their lineage), the Spartan woman remained aware of her breeding duties until the downfall of Sparta. However,
during the decline, it was no longer considered immoral for a Spartan woman
to engage with a man of her choosing for any reason, either before or after fulfilling her breeding task. Preventive measures however, were taken to ensure
that no children would result from such encounters, as the birth of a child under such circumstances from a freeborn Spartan woman was still considered an
extremely immoral act, even during the decline of Sparta. Consequently, Spartan women were perceived throughout Greece as being rather unrestrained and
promiscuous, even sassy and brazen.

6

Nonetheless, one should not derive the customs and practices of Nordic
marriage solely from biological perspectives, but must also consider their
close association with peasanthood, to which they are as inseparable as the
plow is to the field.

    Under the living conditions of northern Europe, which were not par-
ticularly easy, the settlement pattern (especially the later individual farmstead of the Nordic peasant), necessitated a division of labor between men
and women—men took on outdoor duties, while women managed the
household. In the case of natural relationships that persist through generations, the choice of spouse tends to favor those who are best equipped to
handle the tasks that come their way. This would naturally lead to clearly
defined criteria for marital suitability, which can then serve as a benchmark. In the peasantry of the north, the expectations of men were quite
different from those of women. As we noted earlier, the patricians had developed distinctly different concepts of virtue for men and women. Here,
we likely encounter the source of the phenomenon that, in the primeval
times of the Nordic race, fostered this unique sexual dimorphism, which is
possessed only by them and subsequently triggered some of their distinctive
secondary sexual characteristics.

    An old peasant proverb states that a woman, with her apron, can carry
more out to the farmyard than a man can bring in with his harvest wagon.
In other words, even the most capable farmer will come up short if his wife
is inept. Those who have firsthand knowledge of the daily life of a peasant's
wife find this fact entirely natural and understandable. While in earlier
times, women may have remained under the control of their husbands,
once the Nordic farmstead began to take shape, women soon gained
enough influence over the emotional lives of their husbands to mature into
equal personalities alongside the men, at least within their domain. For
example, Laertes avoids interacting with Eurycleia out of fear of his wife's
anger.[369]

---

[369] Homer, *The Odyssey*, 1.433: "He honored her even as he honored his faithful wife in his halls,
but he never lay with her in love, for he shunned the wrath of his wife."

It is worthwhile to cite here a few more words from the aforementioned Professor Beckmann (Bonn), as they quite splendidly characterize the exceptional significance of the ancient rural and peasant woman:

If one wishes to discern the fundamental aspects of the position of the German peasant woman and does not approach it from the perspective of the way of life on the individual farm, but rather from our national German characteristics, then two fundamental questions immediately arise. Firstly, the leading position of the German peasant woman within the farm, and secondly, her significant responsibilities essential for the functioning of the farm. Both aspects stem from the same root, namely, the monogamous marriage on the German estate. This has been a Germanic custom for millennia. From this ancient Germanic institution, we derive the domestic (household) economy as a women's economy. Throughout the Middle Ages, up until around 1850, the household economy remained bound to traditional practices. From the early Middle Ages to the *Capitulare de villis* of Charlemagne the Saxon Slayer to the Peasant Liberation of 1848—that is, for a millennium—we have passed down a continuous bond that sustains the position of the housewife. This is due to two distinct factors—the closed household economy and the system of domestic service. Household management as a way of life and domestic service as a form of labor have been the focus of the household economy for a thousand years.

The goal of the household economy is to produce everything one needs for life on one's own (I am referring primarily to the closed household economy of this millennium). Ideally, all household necessities should be produced internally. In earlier times, household economies were extraordinarily large—they consisted of the immediate family, relatives, servants, domestic workers, and often also craftsmen. If a person desired to make these enormous household economies self-sufficient, it required organizing and creative talents of the highest order. There are still many households today, but these modern households lack a sense of organization, since in today's households the biggest risk is that someone might get a tummy ache, whereas in those days, the priority was simply for everyone to be fed. . . . The second major aspect of the household economy in the early medieval period revolved around the organization of the domestic service. The domestic servants are fully integrated into the household, therefore, they are cared for and trained by the housewife. Today, we find a comparable situation only among the peasantry. As we know, in these cases there is still a sense of community between the workers and owners, where they share the same house and table. If you were to visit a *Landesökonomierat* (a highly renowned and important man with highly modern and exemplary facilities) on his farm, for instance, you would see that he still shares his house and table with all of his staff.

As long as this tight-knit community exists, there is no social antagonism. This only begins once the tablecloth is cut. Thus, in Bavaria, the position of the peasant woman still exists in the old form. . . . Therefore, the archetype of the older peasant woman, benevolent and understanding of life because she has firsthand experience of all the work she demands of others, survived until 1850. She is also attentive to strict order and daily schedule, since punctuality is essential for the farm, even more so than for the household. In addition, she initially views life from an "economic" perspective, because the social status of the peasant woman is tied to her economic success, affecting her reputation and rising and falling accordingly.

One might almost venture to say that mothers who were able to manage such operations also had to give birth to sons who knew how to handle life and all the tasks that came their way.

In ancient Nordic society, the *herrin* (mistress) thus appeared alongside the *herren* (lords).[370] It is certainly no accident that the word *herrin* is derived from *herr*, clearly indicating a subsequent development. The peasantry of the Nordic race was the birthplace of the development of female personhood.

The extent to which this ancient Nordic and traditional peasant idea, which derives the value of a woman from her domestic virtues, still persists among our people, and how clearly this connection still resonates with the nobility can be seen in the fact that the German people consider the late Empress and Queen Louise as particularly "noble" female figures precisely because they epitomized the roles of wife and homemaker so completely. These are views of women that are no longer compatible with modern perspectives, but they are quite illuminating when it comes to unraveling the German national psyche.

It is significant that even today, at the moment of marriage, there is a sudden change in the way that German women are valued. While a young girl was generally allowed to attract the attention of German boys before marriage—indeed, this is even welcomed by all sides—that changes as soon as marriage occurs. From that moment on, it is expected of the bride to prove herself in all areas of domestic virtue. This transformation occurs so abruptly that, in order to understand this fact biologically and not perceive it as a contradiction (but as perfectly logical), one must keep in mind the original concept of marriage associated with Nordic peasant civilization. In addition to this, it is worth noting that the genuine Nordic woman, in fulfilling her domestic virtues, instinctively demonstrates a secondary sexual

---

[370] A lord is someone who commands and someone authorized to command, from the Old High German *hêriro* (meaning the more exalted or distinguished one) and *herrisch* (meaning the one who behaves in the manner of a lord). From Weigand, *Deutsches Wörterbuch*.

characteristic that certainly has an effect on the genuine Nordic man. Such Nordic women have a deep inner need to take care of something. This can be clearly seen by reading Homer, and our own German history also rings brightly with the praise of the domestic virtues of the genuine Nordic woman.

In fact, one only needs to compare the female figures of Nordic legends with the sultry, vivid tales of the Arabian Nights to see the distinct and peculiar way in which Nordic women are valued.

The unity of the Nordic farmstead conditioned the man to look upon his wife as a companion of equal status. It also planted the seed for another characteristic of the Nordic race in the relationship between the sexes. The sense of distance toward subordinates, on the one hand, and the shared concerns, on the other, brought the husband and wife closer together at a human level, allowing the husband to open his heart up to his wife. The Nordic man has a need to reveal himself to his wife, while keeping himself closed off to strangers—in fact, the true Nordic woman demands this openness, for otherwise she would feel neglected.

As we have seen above, marital fidelity was primarily measured according to the loyalty of the spouses to their blood, and not, for example, by the sexual abstinence of the spouse with regard to unfree women and girls. The Nordic woman, therefore, probably never originally considered feeling jealous of the concubine. She would have seen it as a self-inflicted degradation, since it would have inadvertently implied that her value was of a purely sexual nature and in some way denied her biological inheritance. The latter was as foreign to her sensibilities as the notion that a concubine could bear legitimate children. Her marriage was not the result of the husband's beauty-based sexual preference, but the natural consequence of her birth—in this realm no concubine could compete with her, no matter how beautiful the concubine might have been. She was, indeed, the mistress of the house, and that was the sole and essential aspect of her marriage—not the potential sexual preferences of her husband. Significantly, she could only feel offended in her capacity as a wife, and our German language still clearly expresses this when we say that a wife feels "neglected" (*zurückgesetzt*, literally meaning "to move back") by her husband. This clearly and literally conveys that the mistress is "removed" (*weggesetzt*) from her honored place as a housewife, where she belongs, and another is "installed" (*hingesetzt*) in her place. The Gothic word for divorce, *afsateins*, literally means dismissal. Thus, an offense only affected the mistress in her dignity as a housewife or, in some cases, as a mother (if the competence of her children was doubted). This is explicitly emphasized, for example, by Birt for Roman women, who states,

Certainly, the Roman woman was something to behold—a thoroughbred woman, as we imagine her, spirited, capable of ruling, and at times clever as well. It is said that the Roman rules the world, but the Roman woman rules the Roman! However, she was a mother. Cornelia is famous because she was the mother of the Gracchi, and Agrippina is infamous because she was the mother of Nero—you shall know them by their fruits. Whether good or bad, in Rome, the son has been the woman's crowning achievement.[371]

An exceptional proof of the fact that, in the case of the Nordic race, women were primarily valued as housewives and mothers (in other words, in terms of their offspring), and that this played a decisive role in their lives, can be found in the aforementioned booklet by Ida Naumann (*Altgermanisches Frauenleben*). Under the title "Wife and Concubine" (Sea Saga, Thule 6), Naumann recounts the story of Höskuld, his wife Jorunn, and the concubine Melkorka. She presents the story as alleged evidence that the moral purity of the Germanic people was by no means as impeccable as is always claimed today. In the introduction to her book, she directly states, for example,

> The prevailing opinion, which still largely stems from Tacitus, idealizes the relationship between man and woman to an excessive degree. It is essential to improve this view by considering practical aspects, which are decisive, as we will encounter a lack of restraint not only among women but also among children, reminding us of the agricultural milieu at every turn.

Throughout this chapter, we have already thoroughly observed that the sexual life of the Nordic race took place on the basis of a positive sensuality, and that certain aspects would have to be described as extremely "offensive" according to our present-day standards. However, we have also seen that the sexual life of that time was subject to a breeding-oriented philosophy that was focused and avoided aimlessness. It is only in the aimlessness of sexual life that the sensual instincts of humans do not manifest in a way that is constructive to civilization—instead, they lead to its destruction. Modern humans have lost our understanding of our ancestors' original concept of breeding, resorting to an evaluation of "morality" based on entirely different criteria. Therefore, the aforementioned judgment by Naumann is undoubtedly much too harsh, particularly in the case of the story we are about to discuss, where she evidently overlooked the meaning of the traditional legend, completely missing the humor of the entire narrative. Let us present the story itself here:

> Höskuld, the son of Thorgard and Kolls, the granddaughter of Unn, became a follower of King Hakon and married Jorunn, the daughter of Björn from Bjarnarfjord and Ljufa. Jorunn was a beautiful girl and very proud, exceptionally distinguished by her intelligence. She was considered the most eligible match in the entire Westland, just as her

---

father was the foremost *bonde* (Old Norse word meaning landowner) in the entire coastal area.[372] She was betrothed to Höskuld with a large estate, and the wedding was celebrated at Höskuldstadir. Jorunn now took charge of the household with Höskuld.[373] It was soon evident from her behavior that she was clever, capable, and experienced in many matters, but always somewhat proud.[374]

Her cohabitation with Höskuld went well, even though they did not particularly show it in their everyday interactions.[375] Their children were Thorleik, Bard, Hallgerd Langhose, and Thurid.[376]

During his journey to Norway, Höskuld purchased a slave-girl from Gilli for three silver marks. She was mute. Höskuld brought her into his tent and provided her with fine women's clothing.[377] After the king had provided him with building timber and bestowed upon him a golden arm ring and a sword, Höskuld expressed his gratitude to the king for the gifts and honors bestowed upon him, boarded his ship, and sailed to Iceland. He landed at the mouth of the Salmon River and had the building timber transported to his estate.[378]

Then he rode home with a few people and was received well, as expected. The estate had been well managed in his absence.[379] Jorunn asked him who the woman in his entourage was.[380] Höskuld said, "You may think I'm joking with my answer, but I don't know her name." Jorunn said, "Two possibilities exist—either the rumor that was brought to my attention is false, or you have spoken more with her than merely asking for her name." Höskuld did not deny it and truthfully told her everything. He requested that the woman be treated well and expressed his wish that she be allowed to stay in the tent.[381] Jorunn said, "I will not start a quarrel with your concubine, whom you brought from Norway, even if she causes trouble in the

---

[372] In other words, Jorunn had an impeccable lineage.

[373] Jorunn is now the legally recognized mistress of Höskuldstadir, her husband's property.

[374] Put differently, she was an impeccable, albeit perhaps somewhat haughty, housewife.

[375] The characteristic Nordic trait of concealing one's inner emotional world from prying eyes is explicitly emphasized here, suggesting an intention to highlight the impeccable affiliation of the two spouses to their race.

[376] There was clearly no issue with Jorunn's fertility.

[377] What this means is that he did not merely treat her as a prostitute, but apparently granted her a form of domestic authority over his possessions. In any case, he elevated her to the status of his acknowledged lover.

[378] Since there is—even today—no wood in Iceland, we see here that Höskuld had undertaken a business trip to Norway to purchase building timber. Thus, his absence from Höskuldstadir had a very practical reason.

[379] That is to say, Höskuld had no grounds to complain about his wife in any respect.

[380] In the following response, the author requests that the reader pay attention to the narrator's emphasis on Höskuld being unaware of his slave's origins!

[381] In other words, Höskuld has no intention of undermining his wife's role as the mistress of the household—he does not "replace" her. However, he does desire to keep the slave as his lover alongside his wife. This desire does not at all take his wife aback, as we will see shortly, nor does it arouse any feelings of jealousy in her.

house. Under these circumstances, I can only be happy that she is deaf and mute."

After his return, Höskuld slept with his wife every night and had little interaction with the stranger. Everyone nevertheless noticed the stranger's noble demeanor and intelligence.[382]

At the end of winter, the stranger gave birth to a boy. Höskuld was summoned, and they showed him the child. To him, it seemed as if no more beautiful and noble child had ever been seen, and he named him Olaf, as his maternal brother Olaf Feilan had recently passed away. Olaf was an exceptionally splendid child, and Höskuld bestowed upon him all of his affection.[383]

In the summer, Jorunn declared that the stranger must either perform some work or leave the farm.[384] Höskuld determined that the stranger should attend to the needs of the husband and also take care of their son.[385] When the boy was two years old, he could speak fluently and ran about on his own like a child of four years.[386]

One morning, Höskuld saw his son Olaf with his mother near a stream that ran along the slope of the meadow. Suddenly, he knew that she was not mute. She sat down with him on the meadow slope and said, "My name is Melkorka, my father was called Murkjartan, he is the king of Ireland. I came from there as a prisoner of war at the age of fifteen." Höskuld remarked that she had concealed her noble lineage for far too long. He went into the house and told Jorunn about it. However, Jorunn stated that it was uncertain whether she was telling the truth and that she had no regard for such exotic people. With that, they ended their conversation.

After this revelation, Jorunn did not treat her any more kindly, but Höskuld began spending more time with her.[387] Shortly thereafter, when Jorunn went to sleep, Melkorka took off her shoes and stockings and laid them all together on the floorboard. Jorunn took the stockings and used them to strike her on the ears. Melkorka be-

---

[382] The affection between the two spouses was in no way affected by the presence of the concubine. However, it should be noted that now the concubine's ancestry is beginning to play a role in the narrative.

[383] That is to say, the concubine's son exhibits remarkably high hereditary value, indicating a superior lineage.

[384] It is at this moment that Jorunn's jealousy emerges. She begins to sense an "**equality**" in the concubine that is capable of rivaling her own lineage. Hence, she makes the significant demand of her husband to either remove the concubine from the household or assign her a position so conspicuously inferior that Jorunn's own status as wife and mother is publicly and unmistakably clear and secure.

[385] What this means is that while Höskuld does not comply with his wife's either-or demand, he does assign a place to the concubine within the household that unequivocally positions her *beneath* the wife. Thus, the dignity of the wife is not compromised. Nevertheless, the indirect acknowledgment of the concubine's hereditary value is certainly evident in Höskuld's refusal to grant his wife's wish as well as in his careful upbringing of their son Olaf.

[386] Put differently, this was an an exceptionally well-developed child.

[387] Note how the *certainty* of Melkorka's impeccable lineage now changes the whole situation.

came angry and punched her in the nose, causing her to bleed.[388]
Höskuld arrived and separated them. He then allowed Melkorka to
leave and gave her a dwelling in the upper valley of the Salmon River.
There, Melkorka set up her house. Höskuld provided her with everything she needed, and their son Olaf moved there with her.[389] It was
soon evident that Olaf, as he grew up, would surpass other men in
attractiveness and chivalry.[390]

This story of the concubine Melkorka is nothing more and nothing less than a
tale told in a most concise form with a moral lesson on heritability and breeding. Melkorka, the Irish princess of the noblest lineage, finds herself in captivity through no fault of her own (due to war) and loses her freedom as a result.
She feigns muteness, apparently in order to avoid answering humiliating questions—proud and silent, she resigns herself to her fate. By chance, she ends up
in Iceland, where she becomes the concubine of a local noble peasant. However, it is through her son that she demonstrates her lineage and ancestry! The
purpose of the narrative is to demonstrate that no human folly or fate was able
to extinguish this royal blood. Its noble nature inevitably prevails, defying all
external constraints and demanding recognition. The nobility of the blood
inevitably comes to light in her son.[391] Her fate (an aristocratic princess ending
up as the unfree lover of a noble peasant), which must have been a most bitter
humiliation for Melkorka, paradoxically becomes the beginning of her new-
found freedom. As a fully recognized woman and mother, she spends the rest
of her life at her own hearth.

This is, from an ancient Nordic perspective, the story of the Irish princess
Melkorka!

There is no denying that the narrative, despite its laconic brevity, is depicted with astonishing force. Each sentence seems to have been crafted and hewn
with a rough but steady hand, as if a Nordic peasant were chopping wood with
his axe in order to assemble a log cabin solely on the basis of impeccable join-
ery, without the need for nails or other binding elements. Note how securely
the personality of proud Jorunn is portrayed and how clearly she presents herself as the mistress in her domestic realm. It is also noteworthy how little is
actually reported about Melkorka, yet the noble lineage of Melkorka becomes

---

[388] It is not clear what actually triggered Jorunn's anger, but apparently, the narrator only wants to
emphasize Jorunn's carefully restrained jealousy through the baselessness of the occasion. It is also
noteworthy that Melkorka abandons the humble position of a servant and simply strikes back.
Melkorka thus now sees herself as entirely equal to Jorunn and regards the treatment she receives as
an indignity, a mentality to which she is not entitled to as a dependent servant.

[389] At the very least, this means that Höskuld granted her freedom. It is more likely, however, that
it is meant to express that Höskuld made Melkorka his second wife and that she ignited her own
hearth in the Salmon River valley for this reason.

[390] In other words, the reference to Olaf's noble blood at the end served to justify Höskuld's actions to some extent and underscores Melkorka's impeccable lineage once again.

[391] One cannot help but think of the famous words from Goethe: "It has always been denied, and
rightly so, that nobility can be learned." From his *Ballade vom Vertriebenen und Zurückkehren-
den Grafen* [Ballad of the Exiled and Returning Count].

increasingly apparent to the reader. Jorunn's behavior is used as a benchmark to illustrate Melkorka's increasingly obvious worthiness.

As long as Melkorka was only the husband's concubine, she was of no importance to Jorunn. With considerable indifference, Jorunn also allows the concubine to share her husband's bed. However, as her husband begins to fully acknowledge the concubine's son as his own, her attitude toward Melkorka gradually and steadily changes. Jorunn's pride is struck by Melkorka's mother-hood, causing her to eventually forget all lordly restraint. The idea of competition in the sexual sphere for the favor of her husband was far removed from the mindset of a housewife ruling as a mistress in her husband's household, the saga therefore does not weigh the personalities of Jorunn and Melkorka against each other at all. However, the son (the hereditary significance of lineage) becomes the yardstick for assessing a female's worth. Thus, we find in this saga the same attitude toward women that Birt describes with regard to the Roman patricians. This, of course, is an attitude that stands in stark contrast to today's, let's say, "modern" perception of women.

Höskuld's position between the two women is described with a certain humorous serenity. With calm assurance, Höskuld always stands above the women and holds the reins of household authority firmly in his hands. He is and remains the lord of Höskuldstadir, and the women must submit to his decisions. However, the matter-of-fact way in which he manages to uphold the role of his actual wife, despite all his affection for Melkorka and her son, is actually quite pleasing to him. Indeed, it is clear that despite Jorunn's impeccable qualities, despite Höskuld's unwillingness to violate the domestic supremacy of his lawful wife, and despite Melkorka's emphasized restraint, the concubine's royal lineage still insistently asserted its rights.

The author cannot refrain from quoting Ida Naumann's analysis of the story. She states,

> Höskuld also had Melkorka, the mother of his son Olaf, with him as a concubine. It is not very amusing to see how his wife Jorunn gets along with Melkorka, and how Höskuld sometimes shows more interest in one woman, and then in the other woman, all according to his whims and fancies.

Ida Naumann's judgment here is absolutely correct from the perspective of modern sensibilities that emphasize the individual's self-centered emotional world and measure the value of individual human experiences based on that. In that light, however, the story of Höskuld and his two wives takes on a completely different appearance. Höskuld is then nothing more than an unfaithful adulterer, who, by virtue of his marital rights as the head of the household, is also cold-hearted enough to force his wife to tolerate the presence of the concubine. His affection fluctuates between the two women, a condition that may seem entirely plausible to our modern writers, who have long since stopped depicting real men in their stories and only consider the male psyche when deconstructing it through psychological analysis. The outcome of the sexual struggle between the two women for Höskuld's favor culminates in a decidedly bourgeois scuffle in Jorunn's bedroom that concludes with the wife receiving a bloody nose but preserving her domestic power as the mistress and the moving out of the concubine, who was granted a special property somewhat resembling the establishment of a "*pavillon d'amour*" in Iceland.

These words in no way detract from Ida Naumann's otherwise excellent study of women's lives among the Germanic peoples. The author felt it necessary to juxtapose here the ancient Nordic perspective with a modern one in order to demonstrate the fundamental differences that can arise in the interpretation of ancient Nordic traditions when the Nordic concept of breeding is not taken into account in the relationship between the sexes.

The Nordic peasantry and its relation to the Nordic system of marriage also explains a certain peculiarity that will be mentioned here as a final thought. The clear division of labor between the genders has led, among other things, to the exclusive involvement of men in community affairs. It is likely that the Nordic *thing* originated from this practice.

As intimate and responsible as the Nordic man's coexistence with his wife may be, and as highly as he regards and values her as a person, he does not have a tradition of allowing her to appear in public. Given the high regard in which women were held, this would be an incomprehensible contradiction were it not for the peasant roots of this phenomenon, which required a clear division of labor. There is really only one exception to this attitude of Nordic men toward women in public, and that is in the case of female sovereigns. However, this is entirely consistent with those cases where the Nordic peasantry allowed succession by daughters when a male heir was not present. To reiterate, it should be emphasized once again that the Nordic race regarded the farm merely as the land necessary to sustain a new generation of children, and in this respect the principle of inheritance was less important than the coming together of equivalent blood through marriage on a farm.

At the end of this chapter (a chapter which has touched on many subjects), we would like to present, as a final summary, a charming description by J. Müller of married life among the German peasantry.[392] In Müller's words, we can clearly see that, as a whole, the marital laws of the Nordic race must have emerged from a peasant foundation. Reading through the following lines, one is compelled to realize that in our old peasant marriage laws, we have before us the biological foundation of the Nordic race:

The question "should I get married?" is very easily answered by the peasant. If he has a farm or can find one, the question is answered with an unconditional yes. Right here, we can see that land ownership plays the key role—for what is a peasant without land? If the foundation of land is not guaranteed, genuine peasants are most vehemently opposed to marriage. The peasant does not take into account general human feelings—he is unwilling to tolerate

---

[392] Müller, *Mann und Weib*, 3:8, 357.

proletarians who burden the community with their children, and no amount of humanitarianism can persuade him that starting a family is a universal human right. But when someone takes over a farm, it goes without saying that a wife must be part of it. The wife is absolutely indispensable for the peasant. The peasant's wife is always a companion in her husband's work, a relationship that is seldom the case with the other classes. Man and woman work on the farm together like two business partners or two brothers running the same company. It is evident how this strengthens the bond between the two and brings honor to the woman. The rebuke "I must provide for you," does not apply to the farmer's wife unless she completely neglects her own duties. While the husband works the field, the wife tends the barn. The proceeds that she earns from the milk, butter, and eggs that she brings to market belong to her, just as the proceeds from grain and livestock fall within the husband's economic sphere. This has been the case since time immemorial, and no civil code needs to regulate it.

And since the farm and its demands are the determining factor in all of the peasant's affairs, the other question, "when should I marry?" is also easily answered. The peasant has time and patience for all things. He waits until his parents leave him the farm or, if he is the younger son, until he acquires enough money to marry into another family. And the daughter does the same. She saves her earnings year in and year out, spinning and weaving her linen wardrobe together. She knows very well that one day some son will need a wife because he is taking over the family farm (or because he needs a daughter-in-law on the farm), and if everything else otherwise falls into place, she will be up for consideration and will eventually be chosen. Sentimental fantasies do not enter her mind in the meantime, for she does not even read novels. Hard work takes up enough of her thoughts.

The fact that the farm plays the main role in all considerations is also very important when choosing a bride. The father explains to the young couple the intricacies of the future matrimony, dryly and soberly, in the presence of all the family members. Love plays a minor role here. The peasant is coarse, as might be expected, and not sentimental. He knows that a woman is there for life and that resources are necessary for living together. Therefore, financial circumstances are taken into account above all else. Besides, there is no aristocrat more strongly insistent on equal birth and opposed to *mésalliance*[393] than the peasant in the context of his children. It is also

---

[393] *Mésalliance* is a French term originating in the seventeenth century that refers to a marriage between people of unequal social ranks, considered inappropriate or disgraceful by societal standards. The word combines *més* (a pejorative prefix akin to mis- in English) with *alliance* (meaning union or marriage).

of great importance to the peasant that the potential housewife is economical and fits into the household well. The peasant rarely marries a non-peasant woman, for what use can he make of a non-peasant woman? Because of this, the girls who work as seamstresses or in similar trades in the countryside do not easily find a provider, no matter how inviting their personal qualities may be.

Marriage itself among the peasant class is characterized by solidity and firmness. Divorce is not common and is considered a disgrace. The joint work, joint thinking, and joint feeling makes differences and incompatibilities of character much rarer than in the city. When they do occur, the peasant, by virtue of his healthy nerves, deals with them far better than our modern generation, which is delicately composed.

Religious seriousness shapes the peasants' views on marriage and family. You won't hear jokes about marriage from a peasant, he doesn't talk about its intimate aspects, and he displays a more confident tactfulness than many city dwellers. His religious seriousness also prevents mixed marriages, which he feels would bring a foreign element into the household. Relations between men and women in the countryside are on a fairly equal footing, according to custom. Joint cooperation is the foundation on which the peasant household rests. The peasant household is not the same as the modern, narrow version of family, where not even the grandparents—let alone unmarried members of the family—are accommodated. It is still the comprehensive household, along the lines of Riehl, where brothers, sisters, uncles, and aunts do not feel like strangers. When the eldest son takes over the farm, siblings who cannot find accommodation elsewhere are not a burden to him—they work with him after all. Even the elderly are gladly received. They can all be useful, even if it is only to watch over the children. And everyone has a voice when it comes to household matters. This closeness of all the members of the family gives the peasant household a charm of its own, which is lacking in today's narrow-minded cultural life.

When Riehl says "the future of Germany lies in the peasant," he is not only referring to the economic role of agriculture for the Reich, but also to the fact that the peasant is a refuge of customs and morals, a preserver of the good old tradition, and a reserve of strength in moral and religious matters.

May he also be a model and example to the other classes in this regard! What we call national character (*volkstum*), folk art (*volkskunst*), and folk wisdom (*volkweisheit*) is largely peasant character, peasant art, and peasant wisdom. It is this character of integrity and resilient vitality that is inherent to anything produced by the peasantry, while whatever is in fashion in the city is forgotten within a few months.

If sexual matters and reforms now occupy the urgent interest of the educated world, it is indeed worthy of their importance to weigh them against the sound judgment of the peasant. It is as if they are being put to the test by nature. The glaring contrast between today's genuine peasant culture and superficial urban civilization is best highlighted by this.

X

Some Additional Health Measures
Taken by the Nordic Race

I

The questions to be discussed here simply take the ideas developed in the previous chapter and bring them to a resolution. This chapter is primarily concerned with measures that indirectly served the Nordic breeding concept by maintaining the health of the race. The material on this subject is quite incomplete and does not allow us to form a coherent picture, which is why the author discusses these questions in their own chapter. Despite this, there should be no harm in trying to piece together the fragments that do exist.

In the previous chapter, much attention was paid to how important the health of the individual is for breeding. There is no point in discussing breeding issues unless all the issues of maintaining the health of a breed have been addressed. For this reason, it is said in the field of animal breeding that, as a general rule, questions of animal care must always precede those of animal breeding. This fact cannot be stressed enough.

There is no doubt that the Nordic race originally lived in an environment where only the healthy were guaranteed to survive. At the very least, it seems to have been recognized very early how important physical health was for the growth of the race. Otherwise, it would be difficult to explain the existence of certain measures taken in this domain. The best-known example in this regard is certainly the famous and widely cited provisions concerning the abandonment and exposure of sick and weak newborns.

Now, it is revealing to the author that in almost all the works dealing with national racial improvement, these Nordic abandonment provisions are mentioned alongside moral asides, depending on the ideological sympathies of the author—but up to now hardly any physician or biologically-trained researchers have placed these provisions in the appropriate biological context. Namely, it appears that today's generation considers it perfectly normal for deformed, crippled, and weak children to be born. Therefore, people tend to not give any additional thought at all to these peculiar abandonment provisions implemented by the Nordic race. To the physiologically-trained animal breeder, however, these abandonment provisions are a genuine mystery. When breeding is based on uncompromising constitutional tests and reproduction takes place from generation to generation in accordance with the principle of selection, sick, weak, and crippled offspring are an exceedingly rare occurrence. In no case—or in only the rarest of cases—are children born that are so obviously unfit that their future unsuitability for breeding or complete uselessness can already be determined at birth. There is no reason for why this should not have also been true for the Nordic race in its early history. For the few defective individuals that may have been born, the Nordic marital laws discussed in the previous chapter would have been more than enough to prevent them from breeding further. This would not have required special and detailed abandonment provisions, for abandonment was by no means left to the arbitrary discretion of the father—it was a communal matter and the father merely acted on behalf of the community in abandoning the child (we will discuss this in more detail below).

Now, it is certain that every newborn child was subjected to some sort of test. But it is equally certain to the author that there must have been much more subtle reasons at play for such a culling than we are currently assuming. At least given the circumstances, it is impossible that such a large number of deformed children would have been born to require and justify such elaborate measures clearly regulated by law, as we see in the historical records of the Nordic race.

We only know that the child was not considered part of the family or the community until it had been picked up by the father. Though a lot has already been written on this point, most of it misses the mark significantly. It has been said that this was the father's way of protecting himself from having a child falsely attributed to him. But in the previous chapter, we saw that the Nordic race deals with this problem in a preventative manner, namely at the time of conception. Furthermore, it is certainly doubtful that one can just look at a newborn child and know with absolute certainty from whom it descends. It has also been explained that the act of picking up the child merely represented a legal act to establish paternity publicly. That may well be true. But given all we have learned in the previous chapter about the legal forms of marriage and their eugenic rationales, these are all very insignificant observations. The legitimate child cannot exist without the legitimate mother, and the legitimate mother cannot exist without the legitimate marriage. Thus, with the act of marriage, the legal aspect of the issue has already been taken care of. Still, there must have been a sensible rationale behind this practice of picking up the newborn. This practice is obviously related to the abandonment provisions. But what kind of pediatrician today would dare to judge whether, say, a newborn child with no physical defects will grow up to be physically strong or weak? Hardly any! Now try doing that with individuals as healthy as those exhibited in the early history of the Nordic race. It is simplistically assumed that every single father was capable of telling whether a newborn child would later grow to be healthy or not.

Thus, unless the house father had at his disposal a finely-tuned method of testing, such notions of a fitness test for newborns by the father must be abandoned. It is still possible, however, to assume the existence of such a test, but this assumption should be taken with caution—it is only presented here for the sake of discussion. It would, in fact, be possible to connect it to baptism, and to a certain extent this has already been done. Unfortunately for us, however, what we see in the historical record is simply not clear cut enough for us to make a conclusive statement. What is certain, however, is that according to some traditions, the newborn was immersed in cold water immediately after birth. Von Amira writes,

> In pagan times, the legal relationship between father and child was not determined simply by the birth of the child in marriage and by the father's recognition of the child. It was done in a visible way by the father picking up the newborn from the ground and accepting what was offered to him. That being said, the naming of the child and the first acts of caring for the child, namely pouring water over the child (erroneously called water consecration in recent times) or feeding the child, could also be used for formal recognition, given that from then on the father was no longer allowed to abandon the child. It was not until the arrival of Christianity that the right to abandon children, which was already limited, was completely suppressed. But even after that, fragments of this pagan tradition continued to exist, such as with baptism being a condition for inheritance in Visigothic and East Norse law.

Just think of the enormous difference in temperature that the little body suddenly had to compensate for when cold water was poured over it. One must admit that the newborn had to perform a rather impressive physiological feat. This measure, in any case, would have been a constitutional test of the highest order. It seems that they were able to draw certain conclusions from the way the newborn reacted to this treatment. We have reason to assume that a healthy child would respond to such a measure with a rather persistent cry. If that is true, certain other traditions could be explained in a way that is both natural and, above all, biologically understandable (such as the tradition that a newborn had to cry under the gable of a house before it was recognized).

When a father decided to abandon his child, this act was by no means dependent on his will alone. The patricians of ancient Rome categorically forbade the abandonment of a healthy boy. The father who did so anyways could be severely punished. If a patrician wanted to abandon his son, he had to present him to five witnesses before doing so. This law goes back to Romulus[394] and is certainly of ancient Nordic origin, as proven or at least implied by all other Nordic traditions with similar provisions. Plutarch says of Sparta,

> Offspring was not reared at the will of the father, but was taken and carried by him to a place called Lesche, where the elders of the tribes officially examined the infant, and if it was well-built and sturdy, they ordered the father to rear it, and assigned it one of the nine thousand lots of land; but if it was ill-born and deformed, they sent it to the so-called Apothetae, a chasm-like place at the foot of Mount Taÿgetus, in the conviction that the life of that which nature had not well equipped at the very beginning for health and strength was of no advantage either to itself or the state. On the same principle, the women used to bathe their new-born babes not with water, but with wine (!!!), thus making a sort of test of their constitutions. For it is said that epileptic and sickly infants are thrown into convulsions by the strong wine and loose their senses, while the healthy ones are rather tempered by it, like steel, and given a firm habit of body.[395]

However, the practice of closed inheritance on hereditary estates is incompatible with the decree that Plutarch speaks of here. Busolt writes,

> This decree presupposes that the state always had a large number of hereditary estates at its disposal. E. Meyer believes that although it was no longer in practice in the fourth century, it still bore the stamp of an authentic, ancient, long-lost statute that preserved the memory of the legal right of each Spartan to own a "lot" of land (a hereditary estate). However, this seemingly ancient statute is not just incompatible with the hereditary nature of each estate, but also with the call for a general redistribution of land that appeared during the time of Tyrtaeus. It is reasonable to assume that there is much truth in the tradition that only strong children should be allowed to become the lords of a hereditary estate.

Once again, we see that it is quite incorrect to speak of paternalism as such when we speak of the Nordic race. Again and again, the head of the family appears to us only ever as the trustee of the whole, presiding over the smallest kinship unit, namely the family. The best way to understand this relationship—in a figurative sense, of course—is to think of our company commanders (or battery commanders, or squadron commanders) before the war. The smallest military unit was entrusted to them by their sovereign. They had to

---

[394] Dionysius of Halicarnassus, *Antiquitates Romanae*, 2.15: "These he did not forbid their parents to expose, provided they first showed them to their five nearest neighbours and these also approved."

[395] Here the connection between baptism and a physiological constitutional test is quite clear.

dedicate their person completely to the unit entrusted to them. But in return, they were given a certain amount of punitive power. Within their sphere of influence, they could freely manage things as they saw fit, but outwardly, despite their great freedom of action, they were still clearly and firmly integrated into the military as a whole.

While we are on the subject of child abandonment, we should take this opportunity to mention a peculiar phenomenon in Rome that could possibly shed a lot more light on the issue of denordification. When the plebeians forced themselves into the laws of the patricians via the Twelve Tables, the provisions regarding the abandonment and exposure of newborn boys suddenly changed. Whereas the old law of Romulus required that every boy be raised unless five witnesses authorized his abandonment, the Twelve Tables explicitly limited abandonment to weak or deformed children. On the surface, there appears to be no difference whatsoever between the law of Romulus and those of the Twelve Tables. However, the explicit limitation to deformed and obviously weak children stands out, because one would think that before the Twelve Tables, only these very reasons would have been justification for abandonment. However, the author suspects that the real reason for this limitation is as that the old law of the patricians, as has been said, permitted the abandonment of boys in certain cases, provided that five heads of household gave their consent. It appears that it was left to the discretion of the father and the five witnesses to determine the reasons for the abandonment. However, since the plebeians had now achieved social equality with the patricians through sheer obstinacy (by means of the Twelve Tables), and since marriage between a patrician and a plebeian had now become possible, the following case could have occurred, given the old law of abandonment: a patrician married a plebeian for the sake of domestic convenience, either by choice or by force. This was, after all, not only a private matter between these two people but also, at the same time, a matter of land ownership. The inevitable result would be that the plebeian blood on the mother's side would find its way into the next heir of the farm—the plebeians, in the truest sense of the word, would have taken root within a patrician lineage.

Compare this with what was said in earlier chapters about the connection between marriage, the lighting of the hearth fire, and sustenance-providing land, for it will allow us to understand the significance of plebeian blood finding its way through the eugenic filter of legitimate marriage. But if a patrician had married a plebeian woman out of necessity, the old abandonment provisions still allowed for him to coordinate with the heads of five patrician families to abandon all of his children. There is no reason at all to doubt that accomplices from within the ranks of the patricians would have always been available for this purpose. It is highly probable that in such a case, patricians would have even disregarded the old law of Romulus stipulating that all healthy boys were supposed to be brought up. If this patrician-plebeian marriage remained childless because all of its boys were abandoned, the inheritance would revert to a patrician who was able to enter into a marriage that was faultless in terms of breeding. The plebeians then had the short end of the stick. The marriage of a plebeian to a patrician, in any case, did not benefit them much. At least in the case of a patrician *confarreatio* marriage, the woman left her family unit and became completely integrated into her husband's. Moreover, if one of these marriages remained childless, the plebeians gained nothing whatsoever. It seems that they feared something along these lines, or that similar experiences had already occurred, which led to the Twelve Tables explicitly limiting abandonment to deformed children. In this way, the healthy half-breed could no longer be abandoned—plebeian blood could now take root in patrician family lines.

In the case of daughters, the abandonment provisions were fundamentally different. Among the Indo-Europeans, for example, the only obligation was to allow the first-born daughter in a group of children to live. On the other hand, the father was free to dispose of the remaining girls as he wished (to either raise or abandon them). We have quite clear records of this among all peoples of the Nordic race. In the case of the ancient Roman patricians, we have exact knowledge of the relevant laws that were in place, and in the case of the Greeks, the following passage may be mentioned: "Many a man raises his sons even when he is poor, and abandons his daughters even when he is rich." The same is true for the Germanic tribes, despite Tacitus reporting the contrary (see Schrader).[396] In the Attican phratries, legitimate daughters were admitted through an initiation sacrifice, but this merely signified that the father recognized the daughter as legitimate. Verification by the phratries, on the other hand, took place only in the case of daughters who were to be heiresses—for the other girls it was sufficient proof that the father had recognized them.

There is nothing in the Nordic historical records that is a better example than this to prevent the researcher from introducing an idealized romanticism into the relations between the sexes among the Nordic race. Taken on its own, it would appear that there are irreconcilable contradictions in what has been handed down to us regarding the abandonment of daughters. So far, we have seen in all the laws a respect for the female comparable to what no other race has thought of or desired—with the possible exception of the Phalian race. Suddenly, we are confronted with an indifference toward the life of a female newborn that at first seems to be almost shocking. And yet, even here, everything is very easily explained, provided that we do not lose sight of the breeding laws set forth in the previous chapter and the peasant background of the Nordic race.

For the Nordic race, the daughter of free blood was, at its most basic level, only the vessel through which the family or the lineage was to be propagated in a pure manner. Land, or the farm, provided sustenance for such a breeding

---

[396] From chapter 19 of *Germania*: "...to limit the number of their children, to [abandon] any of the later children is held abominable, and good habits have more force with them than good laws elsewhere."

In the Ludwig Wilser German translation (Leipzig: 1923), the translator adds, "Here the report is not quite accurate—miscarriages, cripples, and bastards were allowed to be abandoned before they had been fed and named. By lifting them from the ground, the father recognized the child."

practice. Therefore, there were only ever as many marriages as there were farms (hearth fires!). Since the farms were inherited in an undivided manner, it was more than enough for each head of the family to keep one daughter alive. It, of course, follows that there were always the same number of daughters available as there were farms. Therefore, it is safe to assume that there was a wife on each farm.

Now, for those who believe that such a small number of girls could not possibly have been enough to provide the necessary number of wives, it must be borne in mind that healthy peoples under natural and healthy conditions do not experience the same rates of child illness and defectiveness that we do now. The predispositions to illness that we are accustomed to today would have been unknown back then. Historical evidence could even be provided in support of this fact. Recall, for instance, the famous words of Cato the Elder, who purportedly declared that the flourishing of medical science was merely proof of the decline of the people, and that Rome would only rule so long as doctors had no voice.

However, if a daughter in a Nordic community actually happened to fall ill or die, or if a family did not have daughters, an arrangement was made with another head of household who had a second or third daughter to keep this child alive. To secure the future of such daughters—although it would probably be more accurate to say that they were securing the biological future of the farm—the child was immediately engaged to a farm heir in front of witnesses. Such guidelines are clearly evident in the laws of the ancient Roman patricians, and they can also be demonstrated just as well among other Nordic peoples.

Of course, it must be remembered that in some cases, a daughter who could not marry was a great burden to her family. While this may not have been true in economic terms, it was certainly true in breeding terms. The father and brothers were held accountable by the community for ensuring that their daughter or sister did not engage in romantic relationships that would have to be regarded as a breeding disgrace. In those chaotic times, however, that may have been easier said than done. Therefore, it was generally just left to the father's free discretion whether or not he wanted to raise his daughters. The Nordic race has always been a race that thinks very clearly and logically, within a "causal" framework. It has never hesitated to subordinate personal feelings to a measure when it was deemed necessary.

Apart from that, single daughters posed a certain danger to the whole community at that time. Back then, of course, intimacy was still understood in a natural way. The reputation of married women could be indirectly undermined by the presence unmarried daughters, since the implication existed that these children were born of a wild union between a married freeman and an unmarried woman. Such a situation, however, would have been utterly repugnant according to the Nordic race's outlook on marriage and the position of the wife. Therefore, there seems to have been no hesitation to protect the moral foundations of marriage by the somewhat ruthless measure of abandoning daughters.

Still, it can definitely be assumed that the father's personal feelings, among other factors, kept far more daughters alive than there were hearths available. What measures would then be in place to compensate for the surplus of girls? We know from the German Middle Ages that nobles would summarily send their unmarried daughters to a convent. This, as we all know, is what allowed the nunneries to flourish. It would be worth considering whether this custom arose because Christianity had prohibited the traditional practice of abandoning surplus daughters. With these Christian nunneries, the daughters excluded from inheritance could now be accommodated somewhere. The institution of marriage in the Middle Ages was, of course, still heavily dependent on land ownership. Is the phenomenon of the Vestal Virgins not a mechanism for the Roman patriciate to accommodate the surplus girls of equal birth, a phenomenon analogous to the placement of noble maidens in monasteries in the German Middle Ages? One could argue in favor of this idea by citing a number of things. Certain accounts of Germanic women (including accounts of chaste priestesses) might then begin to make more sense without reference to religious sexual norms. The idea that the daughters of noble families who do not marry should somehow devote themselves to public service is still very much with us today, and so is the view that such service requires unconditional sexual abstinence on the part of the woman, since one cannot rightly "serve two masters."

However, there is another conclusion that can be gleaned from these thoughts which has the potential to be highly enlightening. If, as with the Nordic race, a daughter of pure blood derived her value primarily from her biological inheritance and looked upon marriage as a duty (a service to the collective), then this girl would not have had to employ any kind of technique or manipulation to gain a man's favor. While a Nordic girl had every reason to be healthy, to blossom, and to develop, she did not have to fight for a husband, as she was self-evidently guaranteed one by birth, provided that she was healthy and chaste (meaning faithful to her blood inheritance). In fact, even today it is impossible for the truly Nordic maiden to master all of those "arts" that the women of other races use to flatter men's senses. Nordic women believe that they are "humiliating" themselves by using such measures, and they often make blunders when employing these tactics because they lack the natural instinct for this behavior.

An excellent example reveals the root cause of this within the sexual instincts of Nordic women, even today. There is no nation in the world which has so sure a sense of gentlemanly dress (corresponding to the Nordic sense of posture and appearance) quite like the Anglo-Saxons—but there is also no nation in the world whose women are so often allowed to go about in public so devoid of any sense of femininity quite like them. As long as Nordic blood set the tone in English society—this must be emphasized here unfortunately—the Englishwoman never succumbed to Parisian fashion. On the contrary, she often walked around in outfits that one could describe as comfortable and practical but certainly not beautiful. Yet, the Englishwoman had a very refined taste when it came to proper formal attire—at least when she was in an environment where people were socializing "among their own." Even here in Germany, there are clearly vestiges of similar ideas. A lady is expected to adorn herself and make herself beautiful within a circle of equals, but at the same time she is expected to not look at or pay attention to strangers outside that circle. Otherwise, she has *vergibt* (given away) something, which quite literally means that she possesses something that she has no right to give out in the first place. Certainly, this has nothing to do whatsoever with a so-called "societal double standard," as it is often maliciously portrayed. Rather, one can perhaps see it as the now obscure remnants of ancient Nordic breeding measures, where it was understood that the woman was considered a sexual being within a circle of equals, but kept the woman away from foreign blood. The central theme of breeding has been very clearly preserved in some peasant customs. For example, traditional dress clearly distinguishes between married and unmarried women, and the uniformity of the traditional dress also reveals an unsexual attitude toward girls.

The Nordic race by all means went beyond just implementing clear breeding laws and rigorously culling newborns to maintain the achieved level of performance. As a matter of fact, the entire life of each individual was governed by the idea that a civilization could only be maintained at its height by weeding out the inferior (culling). Within Germanic society, individuals deemed cowardly, unsuitable for warfare, or possessing a despicable physique were promptly submerged in the swamps. These measures are thus especially illuminating, as the death penalty, intended solely as a deterrent, was administered by hanging. This means that the only people they submerged in the swamps were those who needed to be weeded out for eugenic reasons (those who needed to disappear from the surface of the world), so it was presumably not meant to be a punishment in the legal sense in any way. When the Nordic race got rid of "breeding defectives" by drowning them (today we have the possibility of sterilization),[397] this was in principle no different from the animal breeder that entrusts his culled animals to the butcher.

Perhaps some readers will perceive it to be somewhat crude that cowards and those unfit for battle used to be summarily put to death. However, it is important not to evaluate such matters from a modern perspective. If a nation

---

[397] It unfortunately still needs to be pointed out, even to educated individuals, that sterilization and castration are not the same—sterilization and emasculation (castration) do not have the same meaning. While emasculation (castration) involves the destruction of the bodily organs required to procreate, resulting in the lamentable side effects seen in eunuchs that were castrated during their youth, sterilization is something entirely different. In the case of sterilization, a minor incision performed by a physician in an outpatient setting adjusts the position of a valve in the seminal duct, redirecting the semen during sexual intercourse. While it may seem as if the semen wishes to be ejaculated, due to this redirection, it is emptied into an intracorporeal space where it can be reabsorbed. Sterilization is essentially an internally applied contraceptive method, and its association with an individual's sexual life and sexual sensation is as little or as much as any externally applied contraceptive method.

It is an act of rudeness or a lack of empathy to still resist the legal implementation of sterilization, thus preventing genetically burdened individuals or criminals from liberating themselves from the curse of their inheritance for a lifetime. Our children will look back upon this resistance to the means of sterilization for genetically burdened individuals with the same bewilderment with which we currently regard certain incomprehensible aspects of the past.

can only assert itself through the affirmation of struggle, then it has no choice but to subordinate its feelings and sensibilities to the necessities of this struggle. The notion that cowards should face a military tribunal has held true as long as the spirit of our army has remained healthy. Nevertheless, some people would prefer to see this practice as the exclusive "invention" of soldiers. It would be wise for such people to examine the history of lynching laws in the United States of America. The harsh reality of existence and the uncertainty of life there required that unsuitable personalities be eliminated without any kind of sentimentality. In the country of the author's birth, Argentina, the law used to be—or perhaps still is—that any person who enters a fenced property or a house uninvited, without identifying himself or explaining his purpose, could be shot with impunity by either the home owner or someone with a definitive relationship to the property. There are, of course, some legal reservations about such simplified legal procedures. However, they undoubtedly serve to provide a reasonable amount of safety for people in unsafe areas or times. If we take into account such facts—which we are still able to see in modern times—and if we consider not only the phenomenon itself, but also its relationship to the circumstances in which it occurred, then these culling regulations implemented by the Nordic race appear logical in a community of people where the highest law was to preserve the health of one's own kind. This enabled it to assert itself in the struggle for survival.

It is not so easy, however, to understand why people of despicable physique were also culled in this manner. First of all, it is highly unlikely that such people were born in large numbers, and second, it is equally unlikely that they would not have been culled as newborns. Either these were deformities that did not appear until later in childhood, in which case the measure seems unjustifiably harsh, or the accounts are inaccurate and refer less to the body and more to the character. To put it another way, people whose character had been found to be unsuitable were culled. In this context, it is worth mentioning Günther. He writes,

The Old Germanic legal system can serve as an exemplary model for us with its many basic ideas. It was more lenient toward what was done in passion, anger, and haste, but regarded as serious everything that appeared as *neidingswerk*, that is, everything that was an expression of a vile state of mind. The *nithing* was considered a degenerate, and a repeated offense was regarded as a sure sign of degeneracy. The clan would then try to purify themselves of the *nithing* through the death penalty. This basic understanding of *neidingswerk* as a sign of degeneration opens us to an understanding of the reasoning behind the Germanic peoples' practice of public executions. These public executions had nothing at all to do with retribution, and certainly nothing to do with any of the charges that contemporary philosophies associate with public punishment. Through public executions, society wanted to cull as vigorously as possible all which was out of character. Public executions thus arose out of a desire to keep the race pure.

He then quotes the following from von Amira: "The people's desire to keep the race pure came together with the divine requirement that the race that originated from it be kept pure." Günther then continues,

> Among other peoples of Nordic origin, the criminal was also considered a degenerate. The Hellenes saw criminal acts as an expression of malice, and the Romans saw the criminal as a monstrosity to be eliminated.

2

It is very peculiar that the Nordic race gave the utmost consideration to a practice that, with the exception of animal breeders, is likely to go completely ignored today. This practice is the art of evaluating the healthy body in terms of its suitability for breeding. In the field of animal breeding, this forms the fundamental basis on which the actual evaluation of performance in relation to breeding value is established. In order to give the reader an overall view of this somewhat multifaceted field, a few remarks will be included here.

In recent times, doctors have gradually come to recognize that the human body functions as a unified entity, and any evaluation of its performance-capability must inevitably begin from this unified entity. It is likely that this shift in medical opinion could have been initiated by sports medicine, which focuses on the evaluation of the healthy body—the sickly body only concerns this field in a secondary way, if at all. In the case of illness, it is enough for a doctor to just locate the site of the disease. But if one wants to evaluate the performance of the whole organism—and a correct evaluation of performance is, of course, the basis of any eugenic evaluation—not much progress will be made by assessing the individual parts of the body. Medical knowledge of each part of the body is nothing more than a tool to be used in service of a theory of evaluation. This, however, is itself still dependent on the ability of the assessor to correctly evaluate the interplay of all of the parts, thus making it essentially a question of sight or observation. In the past, the budding young animal breeder was trained exclusively through "visual exercises" to learn to evaluate the "type" and "constitution" of an animal. However, since such a method of evaluation requires a certain innate talent for observation—not to mention the ability to actually evaluate performance—and since the assessor, more than anything else, must have an infallible and unerring memory of biological types, this kind of approach has always remained somewhat unfair (it was a certain unfairness that hinged on the personal aptitude of the individual assessor). It was not until Dr. Disselhorst (Halle) began to combine the old observational training of animal breeders with modern knowledge of anatomy and physiology that a new path was opened for animal breeding in terms of a theory of evaluation. Despite this, the main focus of zootechnical evaluation training is still placed on the trainee's sense of sight. To underline the importance of this fact, a few remarks by Disselhorst from the introduction to his work on state-of-the-art zootechnical evaluation theory will be quoted here. Disselhorst first mentions the value of assessing the skeletal structure and the muscular structure, as well as physiological exercise. He then goes on to say,

> In addition to the knowledge of all these things on the part of the assessor, however, this type of assessment really only requires one skill, namely visual ability. This is certainly indispensable and can be greatly improved by regular training. Anyone who does not possess this ability or is unable to acquire it is useless as an animal breeder. . . . In the lessons that I teach in evaluation theory, which is obviously the foundation of any training in animal breeding, I absolutely prioritize a knowledge of the skeleton and its mechanical relationships. That is not all, of course—this merely provides a solid foundation. As already mentioned, the most important thing (the practical application of this knowledge for the purpose of assessment) can only be obtained through frequent observation of live animals. Here, so-called "visual geniuses" will easily become superior to others. But since the assessment according to this method does not involve the memorization of images, but rather the determination of the relationships of distinctive, immovable bone points protruding on the surface, the mutual relationship of which is known, anyone equipped with normal eyesight and adequate background knowledge can become a competent assessor through practice. The breeder must have a solid framework for visual assessment and a solid understanding of the skeletal structure, and must have acquired a highly-trained sense of sight in order to be able to distance themselves from the unfortunate and almost universal nonsense opinion and widespread belief that equates breeding hobbyism with breeding expertise. . . . The ability to scrutinize the breeding value of an animal potentially requires extensive, multi-year experience with a wide variety of material. It also requires nothing less than the almost divinatory (prophetic) eye of the natural breeder, which is granted to few and ultimately cannot be learned. A thorough knowledge of the skeletal structure is also indispensable, although in some cases it may have to take a back seat to other factors.

The author has intentionally prefaced the following analysis with these remarks by Disselhorst. The reason for this is that we cannot avoid first making a few fundamental remarks on contemporary racial assessment procedures before we can address the evaluation training apparently implemented by the Nordic race. Related to this, it is also necessary to say a few words about the way in which the concept of race is sometimes treated in human race science today.

Anyone who has been trained in the principles of modern zootechnical assessment and has personally experienced how only continuous self-education and constant practice on living specimens sharpens the eye and makes it reliable for

breed assessments can hardly look upon what is often called the "racial evaluation" of today's human race science with any great esteem. If a breed or race
could be evaluated solely by the measuring compass and a mathematical calculation of its ranges of variation, then animal breeding would indeed be a very simple matter. In fact, it seems to the author to be nothing short of a great misfortune that race science appears to have allowed itself to be pushed into the domain
of so-called "scientific objectivity" and considers it a sign of scientific rigor if an
"appraisal" of a race is avoided. From a zootechnical point of view, it is not really
possible to agree with race science on this point. In animal breeding, breed or
race and its meaning is primarily a practical matter for practical use. Academic
disputes about classification or the phylogeny of a breed are of no immediate
value to the breeder. For instance, according to the most recent research, it is
probable that the Schleswig heavy workhorse and the English thoroughbred
horse share a common evolutionary ancestor. This hypothesis is likely to be of
paramount importance for science, particularly for inheritance biology. However,
anyone who thinks that any of this will cause the horse breeder to suddenly look
at the two breeds differently is very much mistaken. The breeder and breeding-
assessor is concerned only with the present reality, and he works with this reality
into the future. In this case, the difference between the English thoroughbred
and the Schleswig workhorse is their biological reality, and breeders really have
no choice but to just accept this difference and work with it (in other words, they
have to decide what they really want and which breed they want to work with).
In contrast, zootechnical scientists have a completely different field of work.
They, on the other hand, investigate how the biological reality came to be and
how the interrelationships within that reality work—particularly whether knowledge of these interrelationships can yield clues for practical application. But only
when the zootechnical scientist can approach practical breeders with truly tangible suggestions does he do so, and only then does the fruitful interplay of science
and practice emerge. This may be shown by another example. Inspired by work
done in England, a Hamburg physician by the name of Axel de Chapeaurouge
turned his attention to bloodline research in the context of horse breeding. He
became the founder of German scientific bloodline research, although it was
actually Frölich (Halle) who first conceptualized something that was useful for
general practice.[398] For example, in the course of his research, De Chapeaurouge
was able to demonstrate to a northwest German horse breeding association that
the relentless decline in their prosperity was due solely to the use of unsuitable

---

[398] The literature compiled by Axel de Chapeaurouge is quite extensive, rendering it futile to present
specific excerpts here, as everything consistently addresses the same underlying concept. Given that a
scientific exploration of the question of bloodlines in animal breeding has only emerged since the
conclusion of the World War, this domain has remained largely unfamiliar to the public. In Germany,
the Animal Breeding Institute at the University of Halle-Wittenberg (directed by Professor Frölich)
has taken the lead in the field of bloodline research and numerous doctoral theses on bloodlines have
been published there in recent years. Geneticists and medical professionals with an interest in these
matters might find it most effective to directly contact the institute.
     The author gives this information because it is considered necessary that future animal breeders
and eugenicists do not continue their research in parallel and without coordination, as has unfortunately been the case up to now.

bloodlines—moreover, he was also able to identify for the association the blood responsible for their old glory. At that time, the association had the wisdom to follow his advice and shortly reinstated the old type and blood as a breeding objective. The association managed to save its breeding operation and is once again at the top of Germany's leading horse breeding associations.

For this reason, scientific animal breeding has recently gone so far as to refrain from any scientific definition of "breed" whenever it cannot be reconciled with the concept of breed that has proven to be useful and unambiguous in the context of practical animal breeding. The scientist should be limited to shedding scientific light on the concept of breed as it is used in practice, but preferably in a way that does not disrupt practice. The representatives of scientific animal breeding take the standpoint that their science is only there to serve practice, not to oppose it—scientific animal breeding does the latter only when it believes it has indisputable evidence. This is why, for example, it rejects as unjustified and dangerous any concept of breed that has the potential to break down the concept of breed that has proved useful in practice. Furthermore, scientific animal breeding takes the position that it is more important to do something useful with the living facts of reality than to dismantle and beat these facts to death in academic disputes over definitions. This position was expressed as a guiding principle by Professor Walther (Hohenheim) at the spring meeting of the German Society for Breeding Science in Berlin on February 1, 1928.

The author felt compelled to include these remarks here because it appears that racial science is well on its way to becoming very unscientific due to excessive scientific rigor. One can be a very great scientific systematist and hereditary biologist and still be a layman or be unsuccessful in the field of practical breeding, and vice versa. Professor Baur (Berlin-Dahlem), the well-known hereditary biologist, once began a lecture to animal breeders at a conference with the following words,

> I suppose you will allow me a word *pro domo* first! I am fully aware that at least 90 percent of you know more about practical animal breeding than I do myself. Yet, if I am speaking here, it is because I certainly understand more about heredity science than 90 percent of you. Further, I also know very well that it is extraordinarily difficult to put theoretical knowledge into practice. In fact, people generally do more stupid things by attempting practical application with too much science than they do with too little. Precisely because I have quite a bit of experience in another field of breeding, plant breeding, one might even say that I am extremely skeptical about the practical application of all science.

The beginning of the beloved professor's speech, which was received with great enthusiasm, has been reproduced here by the author in full detail because it is intended to show the reader that the art of breeding assessment and the establishment of a breeding objective are matters that are only indirectly related to scientific systematics and hereditary biology.

Breeding primarily involves the evaluation of existing realities with a view to the future. Breeding without a breeding objective is a complete contradiction of itself. It does not matter whether this objective is directed toward an ideal type or simply aims for the culling of the unfit according to a specific plan. Therefore, in all matters of breeding, the breeding objective is more important than the current state of biological reality, which one (of course) intends to improve or modify through the breeding objective anyway. The simple observation of racial or hereditary-biological reality initially belongs exclusively to the realm of pure systematics and only becomes relevant to actual questions of breeding or of the racial improvement of a people when continuously assessing them against an established breeding objective.

From a zootechnical point of view, for example, Günther did the only right thing in human racial science when, based on the experience of German history, he gave our people a breeding objective in his "Nordic idea."[399] Anyone who disagrees with Günther's breeding objective must establish another one, provide a rationale for it, and then defend it.[400]

The animal breeder initially identifies a target image in order to establish a breeding objective—the reference point for breeding. They then completely align themselves with it and continuously evaluate their breeding stock against it. If, as a result of practical experience, it becomes apparent that certain elements of the target picture are better left out, or if, based on proven performance, certain previously unnoticed characteristics need to be added to the breeding target image, then the breeder does so. From a zootechnical point of view, it would be absurd if one were to abandon a breeding objective simply because all of the preliminary genetic-technical questions had not yet been answered. Indeed, the history of German animal breeding is replete with examples where it is shown that it is the will of the breeder that gives a breed its purpose and allows it to flourish. The will

---

[399] Günther, *Der Nordische Gedanke*.

[400] During the Fifth International Congress on Genetics in September 1927 in Berlin, Hammond (Cambridge) addressed similar phenomena in animal breeding. He also countered the tendencies present in animal breeding to rely solely on precise experimental approaches. He emphatically cautioned against attempting to exclusively pursue a strictly "scientific" approach in large-scale animal breeding. Instead, he advised scientific animal breeders to do what observant and thoughtful practical breeders have always done—engage in selection based on an ideal type. Notably, German animal breeding can proudly state that it has never deviated from this inherently self-evident principle. Professor Fröhlich (Halle), a pioneer in introducing Mendelian thoughts into German animal breeding, never allowed himself to be removed even a hair's breadth from the sound direction of the traditional practical breeder. He continually emphasized to his students (including the author) that "learning to see" must remain the foundation of every breeding measure and that without a conscious training of young animal breeders in observing the ideal type, the entire field of animal genetics could never achieve success.

The present attitude of some German specialists in the field of racial studies toward the Nordic idea put forth by Günther—in the sense that Günther presented a breeding model for the German people in the Nordic individual—often appears quite perplexing to those well-versed in animal breeding. Such a reaction initially demonstrates that these individuals seem to lack an understanding of the basic fundamentals of breeding matters. The author, who is a student of Valentin Haecker (Halle) in genetics, a student of the paleontologist Walther (Halle) in biological developmental history, and a student of Frölich (Halle) and Kraemer (Gießen) in animal breeding, can likely permit himself to form a judgment in this regard without fearing being dismissed as a mere "layperson" by certain "specialists" in racial studies. *Cucullus non facit monachum.*

of the breeder, of course, cannot create something new out of thin air. However, shaping the existing genetic stock into a successful breed with practical results is solely a matter of will. A breeder must simply know what they want and the means by which the goal can be achieved. There is no better way to undermine a breed than by stripping it of its breeding objective. A classic example of this can be found in the Mecklenburger horse, which was once a leading breed half a century ago but began to waver and lose direction in terms of its breeding objective. In a short time, the once thriving and world-renowned breed was reduced to a mere afterthought. Today, especially in the post-war period, the situation has changed. The author has chosen this example from the many applicable cases precisely because the rapid decline of the Mecklenburger horse in the second half of the last century is always cited in animal breeding as a so-called classic example that demonstrates how quickly a breed can decline once it begins to waver in its breeding objective. It goes without saying that a breeding objective must remain within the realm of achievable possibility. The task of science is to improve the breeding objective implemented by practical breeders (if necessary), whether by removing a sub-goal deemed impossible or by adding a previously overlooked trait.

Nevertheless, science never has the right to oppose a breeding objective simply because it does not yet understand the circumstances of its genetic inheritance within the breed in question. In general, it remains an empirical fact that even the most ambitious breeding objective can never have as detrimental an effect as not having an objective at all. Stable master von Oettingen, a practical breeder who truly has the right to pass judgment on breeding matters, has an important message to all those prominent critics who focus on insignificant details in the realm of purposeful breeding. His words, originally expressed in his invigorating German, hold significance for us here as well: "The fear of mistakes, especially obvious mistakes that any fool can see and criticize, has a paralyzing effect on breeding, just as it does in all aspects of life, be it politics or science."

There have been practical animal breeders who have had no knowledge of hereditary biology, and yet managed to made ground-breaking advances in the field of animal breeding.

All this must be emphasized, for otherwise the reader might begin to wonder how the Nordic race could have had racial-scientific evaluation training and a breeding objective in its prehistory, considering that the public did not know about "Mendelism" until the year 1900 AD.

To sum up, the author would like to say that from a zootechnical point of view, it is not possible to evaluate a breed without taking into account its physiological circumstances and without establishing a breeding objective. In particular, physiological conditions that can only be determined through the life and movement expressions of an organism, which are imponderables that can only be grasped by training one's eye (and certainly not with instruments alone). From a zootechnical point of view, the best scientific description of race may be the one offered by the anthropologist Scheidt (Hamburg): "a race is a group of hereditary traits selected within a species." This definition allows for enough flexibility to include physiological racial characteristics that can only be captured through observation of a living organism of the respective race.

At least in the case of German animal breeding, the situation is such that a breeding evaluation cannot be made if the body as a whole is ignored (if only certain details are given attention). This is simply because the animal organism is an interplay of various forces, and its health is first and foremost nothing more than the smoothest possible functioning of this interplay. The health of the individual being is, after all, the foundation of any breeding consideration. In the future, a theory of human evaluation in the context of racial improvement will not be able to avoid placing similar perspectives at the forefront of its thinking. Just like animal breeders, they will have to learn that individual organs and organ parts cannot be evaluated without considering their physiological interplay. Just as one can only evaluate a machine's performance by studying its gradual construction from individual parts and observing the machine during its operation (as a whole), one can only obtain a clear image of an animal or human organism by assembling its individual components into a whole and then observing their collaboration.

It can now be argued against the author that man also has a spirit and that in all matters of racial improvement, certain things in addition to the body should be considered in a breeding evaluation. It has also been argued against the author that it is unjustified to place too much emphasis on the body in an evaluation theory of humans. In response to that, it can be said that the entire realm of human intellectual capabilities cannot be adequately addressed from a biological-breeding standpoint, and, in consequence, everyone is certainly free to consider a person's intellectual abilities in addition to a physical assessment, if that is what they wish to do. However, the author suspects that the relationship between the human mind and body is similar to that of a steam engine. Steam power cannot reach its full potential when acting upon a poorly constructed mechanism, just as a good mechanism cannot operate at full strength when it lacks sufficient steam power. The old saying *mens sana in corpore sano* (a healthy mind in a healthy body) likely holds a deeper meaning than our sports-obsessed and record-seeking era is willing to acknowledge. In the breeding of noble horses, for example, it is often the case that the horse inherits the temperament and will to win, but lacks a sufficiently robust physical structure to fully manifest these gifts. The horse then quickly wears out or exhausts itself, and in such cases, the horse breeder says that its "galloping capacity" has surpassed its foundations. If one examines the biographies of some great minds, such as the poet Heinrich von Kleist, one often suspects that their galloping capacity exceeded their foundations (in other words, their mind did not find sufficient support in the body and therefore struggled to come to terms with itself and its environment). The author mentions this here only to encourage those who still wish to neglect the body in favor of the mind to reflect on this matter, and also to awaken an understanding that the body as a whole must be given attention if we want to approach the question of racial improvement in greater detail in the future. A very important horse breeder, the late Schwarznecker, disagreed with all those who, when evaluating a breeding animal, preferred to focus on the performance of individual details without considering the whole organism. His words are relevant for our analysis—figuratively speaking, of course—and are therefore quoted here:

> However, I do not believe that Lessing's statement that "Raphael would have become a great artistic genius even if he were unfortunate enough to be born without hands" can be extended to the point that Kincsem would have become a great racehorse even if she happened to have been born with three legs. Performance is to some extent dependent on the mechanical structures in which and through which it can manifest and express itself.

The Nordic race has never separated body and mind—at the very least, this coupling has not harmed the mind or spirit of the Nordic race. It seems that the youth were deliberately educated to learn how to evaluate a body as a living whole, in terms of its individual parts and its expression of movement. However, as already explained earlier, one can only learn to evaluate a body over time through instruction and continuous practice on living individuals. That is why the Nordic race made sure that people could get to know each other as God created them. This applied not only to the interactions between the genders but also in their evaluations of the opposite gender. For example, we know that among the Germanic peoples, girls were required to praise and criticize the young men during contact sports. Since all of these contact sports were performed naked, this account only makes sense when connected with a body assessment. Those educated in this way were trained to understand the expression of movement of a body and draw certain conclusions from it. This absolutely aligns with zootechnical experiences, as the way an animal moves or carries itself often allows one to draw far-reaching conclusions about not just its constitution, but also its biological inheritance. There are preeminent animal breeders who primarily focus on these aspects before assessing the skeletal structure and other details.[401] The correct sequence of a zootechnical evaluation is, of course, first an evaluation of the overall body, then the expression of movement, and finally the small details.

But the clearest proof that there was a conscious education in the evaluation of the human body among the Nordic race comes from Spartan accounts, particularly regarding the legislation of Lycurgus. The legislation of Lycurgus explicitly states that the youth should be educated in the evaluation of the human body from a eugenic point of view. Plutarch writes,

---

[401] With show horses, it is often quite surprising how they suddenly and unexpectedly express traits associated with one of their ancestors, such as in the way they approach fences or exhibit other characteristics. These cases can be quite enlightening for breeders. However, in addition to having the personal aptitude required to even perceive these aspects along with an unwavering memory—because you can rarely place the ancestor next to the horse you are observing—it is also necessary to gain insight by immersing oneself in all matters pertaining to breeding. Acquiring these skills does not happen overnight.

In the matter of education, which he regarded as the greatest and noblest task of the law-giver, he began at the very source, by carefully regulating marriages and births. . . . He made the maidens exercise their bodies in running, wrestling, casting the discus, and hurling the javelin, in order that the fruit of their wombs might have vigorous root in vigorous bodies and come to better maturity, and that they themselves might come with vigor to the fullness of their times, and struggle successfully and easily with the pangs of child-birth. He freed them from softness and delicacy and all effeminacy by accustoming the maidens no less than the youths to wear tunics only in processions, and at certain festivals to dance and sing when the young men were present as spectators. There they sometimes even mocked and railed good-naturedly at any youth who had misbehaved himself; and again they would sing the praises of those who had shown themselves worthy, and so inspire the young men with great ambition and ardor. For he who was thus extolled for his valor and held in honor among the maidens, went away exalted by their praises; while the sting of their playful raillery was no less sharp than that of serious admonitions, especially as the kings and senators, together with the rest of the citizens, were all present at the spectacle.

Nor was there anything disgraceful in this scant clothing of the maidens, for modesty attended them, and wantonness was banished; nay, rather, it produced in them habits of simplicity and an ardent desire for health and beauty of body.

It gave also to woman-kind a taste of lofty sentiment, for they felt that they too had a place in the arena of bravery and ambition.

Moreover, there were incentives to marriage in these things—I mean such things as the appearance of the maidens without much clothing in processions and athletic contests where young men were looking on, for these were drawn on by necessity, "not geometrical, but the sort of necessity which lovers know," as Plato says. Nor was this all; Lycurgus also put a kind of public stigma upon confirmed bachelors. They were excluded from the sight of the young men and maidens at their exercises, and in winter the magistrates ordered them to march round the market-place in their tunics only, and as they marched, they sang a certain song about themselves, and its burden was that they were justly punished for disobeying the laws. Besides this, they were deprived of the honour and gracious attentions which the young men habitually paid to their elders.

Even in his concluding reference to the confirmed bachelors, it is clear that the Spartans' practice of nudity was for breeding purposes as a kind of training in evaluation. As an aside, the author cannot help but point out that this reference to confirmed bachelors contradicts Plutarch's previous (implausible) claim that there were only as many boys as there were "lots" of land. There must always have been a surplus of young men who, if they married, could only do so in the form of the so-called extended family. This passage is controversial in the first place. For example, Busolt writes this about it,

According to chapter five of Plutarch's *Agis*, the Spartans maintained the number of lots established by Lycurgus until the Law of Epitadeus. Therefore, inheritance went to a single son, as described by Plato.[402] However, this statement is influenced by political assumptions. The assumed indivisibility, as noted by Pöhlmann,[403] is confirmed by the equal and unchangeable number of measures that the helots of all hereditary estates (*klêroi*) had to deliver to the owner of their respective estate (*klêros*). It is then said by Plutarch that Lycurgus considered this measure to be sufficient for the maintenance of a family. The legislator thus acted according to Plato's teachings.[404] Therefore, the interpretation of the yield of the hereditary estates absolutely does not imply, as some have argued, that the determination of the amount itself stemmed entirely from speculation. This passage also assumes a single owner of the hereditary property; Xenophon agrees with this in *Hellenica*.[405]

However, the possibility of shared ownership of Spartan hereditary estates (*klêros*) is not excluded. According to the Gortyn code, properties were inherited undivided by all the sons. Nevertheless, only one was regarded as the lord of the helots. Something similar can be assumed for Sparta, where occasionally several brothers contented themselves with a common wife, and the children born to her were considered communal. Therefore, they must have also had shared ownership, from which the hereditary estate was hardly excluded.

The author suspects that Plutarch (to whom the concept and meaning of the ancient Nordic inalienable family property was apparently unknown) confused the farm heirs and future family heads with the younger brothers who were excluded from marriage—the "*jung-gesellen*" (young assistants), as our German language still clearly expresses. Farm heirs and future family heads, by contrast, were obliged to marry. Alternatively, Plutarch may have simply extended to all

---

[402] Plato, *Nómoi*, 5.740: "The allotment-holder shall always leave behind him one son, whichever he pleases, as the inheritor of his dwelling, to be his successor in the tendance of the deified ancestors. . . ."

[403] Pöhlmann, *Geschichte der Sozialen Frage*, 76.

[404] Plato, *Nómoi*, 5.737: "First, we must fix at the right total the number of citizens; next, we must agree about the distribution of them—into how many sections, and each of what size, they are to be divided; and among these sections we must distribute, as equally as we can, both the land and the houses. An adequate figure for the population could not be given without reference to the territory and to the neighboring States. Of land we need as much as is capable of supporting so many inhabitants of temperate habits, and we need no more. . . . These matters we shall determine, both verbally and actually, when we have inspected the territory and its neighbors. . . ."

[405] Xenophon, *Hellenica*, Book 3, chapter 3, section 5, trans. Carleton L. Brownson, Loeb Classical Library ed. (Cambridge: Harvard University Press, 1918), "...and of all who chanced to be on the country estates belonging to Spartiatae, while there would be one whom he would point out as an enemy, namely the master..."

male Spartans the laws regarding the heirs to a farm, which he was more familiar with.

Plato does not express himself quite as clearly and definitively regarding the education of youth for eugenic evaluation.[406] Nevertheless, he does state in no uncertain terms,

> Each *phyle* (group of family associations) shall organize two sacrificial celebrations monthly, one solemn and solely dedicated to the service of the deity, and one festive, meant for the joys of social gathering. The families within the *phyle* must get to know each other well, if only so that they may enter into suitable marriages with one another. For the same purpose, we will organize dances of boys and girls, so that they may see each other and develop mutual affections. They will perform these dances naked, without compromising modesty and shame.[407]

In any case, the Nordic race consciously ensured that both genders got to know each other as they were created. The Nordic race has never appreciated any kind of concealment, in any domain, and it knew very well why it educated its youth to become accustomed to the sight of the naked body. If necessary, it took measures to prevent any harm from arising out of the natural interaction between the sexes. When one often hears today that this ancient Nordic habituation to the unclothed body of the opposite sex was merely an expression of an untouched, innocent, "natural people," that is partially correct insofar as it can be said that any natural thinking considers nudity as natural. But this explanation does not quite apply to the Nordic race in the essence of the matter, for there is no doubt that the Nordic race quite consciously used habituation to nudity for the purpose of eugenic evaluation training—this must be emphasized.[408]

With this in mind, the stories of tremendous physical feats by some Nordic women and young maidens begin to make a great deal more sense. After all, it was only natural that a healthy generation that had undergone such deliberate

---

[406] Carl Vering, *Platons Gesetze: Die Erziehung Zum Staate* [Plato's Laws: State Education] (Frankfurt: 1926).

[407] Günther, *Platon als Hüter des Lebens*.

[408] With these remarks, the author does not intend to defend the "nudism movement," which is becoming more and more widespread and which often seeks to create the conditions for the existence of certain erotic cults. In this field, however, one should learn to differentiate and approach a healthy affirmation of the body with an open mind so as to not throw out the baby with the bathwater, so to speak. The film "*Wege zur Kraft und Schönheit*" (Ways to Strength and Beauty) has shown that there are ways and means to restore the German people's awareness of their bodies and to educate them in the art of judging a healthy physique without violating the dictates of decency. In this book, it is appropriate to draw attention to the health risks of the unfortunately widely favored "bathing costumes," as it represents perhaps the most senseless invention ever conceived. On the one hand, it recklessly exposes bodily shapes to the public, rendering its use essentially an act of hypocrisy. On the other hand, it exposes the body to excessive heat loss after bathing, particularly in its most sensitive areas (back, kidney region, and stomach), due to the evaporative cold of the wet fabric. Moreover, this fabric, like no other, retains moisture. In our climatic regions, there is rarely, if ever, weather that would justify withdrawing such quantities of warmth from the body as the wet bathing costume does in open air. Many instances of anemia and lifelong physical debilitation may have originated here.

training will have also necessarily produced a healthy female physical strength. It is unfortunate that in the modern public life of our people, the worn-out figure of Gretchen from Faust is still held up as the ideal Nordic maiden. The author would even doubt that sculptures such as the Venus de Milo or the Venus of Knidos actually give us a correct impression. It is much more likely that Michelangelo's statue of the Dawn in Florence captures the essence of the ancient Nordic maiden. Her female body displays a wonderful muscular form and the noblest of dimensions, and yet it still has tremendous femininity, albeit more heroic than sweet. Of course, it takes the masterful hand of a Michelangelo to create a body like this out of marble. In any case, such a maiden is more likely to have the strength of a Brunhild, who sang and played catch with King Gunther of the Burgundians on her wedding night. But you do not even have to delve into the realm of Nordic legend in order to become familiar with powerful female figures. Just read Ida Naumann's *Altgermanisches Frauenleben* (The Life of Ancient Nordic Women). In it, you will read about female figures who perform feats that are quite inconceivable without considerable physical strength and endurance.

Teutonic women utilized swords and axes against both fleeing and pursuing enemies at Aquae Sextiae, preferring death over enslavement, just like the Germanic women captured by Caracalla. The Germanic maidens were endowed with extraordinary physical strength—Tacitus describes them as *validae*, meaning strong, and *pares*, meaning equal to the young men—and of exceptional strength of character. During a Germanic incursion into Raetia during the reign of Marcus Aurelius, bodies of armed women were found on the battlefield (as claimed by Dio Cassius). According to the account of Flavius Vopiscus, ten Gothic women, fighting in male attire, were taken captive, while many others perished. Three hundred Nordic shieldmaidens fought in the Battle of Brawalla, and Atli maintained a female bodyguard, like the King of Dahomey. The Valkyrie saga, which finds clear echoes in the myths of both Pallas Athena and Artemis, as well as the Amazons (who posed a danger even to Achilles himself), essentially dominates the German and Nordic heroic sagas, crystallizing in a gem of a certain dark splendor in the character of Brunhilde. The modern perception of her as a black-haired, dark-eyed beauty is certainly wrong, completely un-Germanic and completely unfounded. Rather, we should attribute to her reddish-gold, flowing hair and blue, defiant, sparkling eyes. The Sigurd songs of the Faroese (translated by Willatzen) depict her as a Lorelei-like character: "She leans in her chair / and combs her hair / and it is as fine as silk / and wonderfully golden." So not brunette or dark-haired, but extremely blonde. This presumably corresponds with the statement in the Wilkina saga during the quarrel of the queens, "This enraged Brunhilde so much that her entire body turned as red as freshly spilled blood."

In the Volsunga saga, the verbal dispute between Sigurd's two lovers, which brings the dramatic plot to a disastrous conclusion, takes place during a bath in the Rhine, which could certainly inspire a great painter to depict two royal bodies full of passion instead of modern harlots and dancers.[409]

The concerns expressed by some gynecologists (such as Sellheim)[410] regarding women's sports, stating that sports might be detrimental to female muscle development and could have harmful effects on the female body, do not seem to have arisen during the early historical period of the Nordic race. It would be worth considering whether racial differences can also be observed in this field over time. The multi-award-winning German champion in athletics, Miss von Bredow (Charlottenburg) is a purely Nordic figure.

Originally, the denial of the body was entirely alien to the Nordic race. It was only when, from the east, the rising shadow of asceticism (the monastic way of life), hostile as it was to beauty, ushered antiquity into a cultural solar eclipse that moral concepts began to be distorted, eventually allowing one to see only sin in the body. Even in our country, the Germanic people did not give up their delight in the body until the Middle Ages. In time, however, evidently non-Nordic tendencies gained the upper hand, banishing the body from the public sphere or transforming the joyful ancient Nordic embrace of the body into the modern non-Germanic, cheerless, sensual sexuality. What a tremendous difference exists between those Germanic maidens (women who bathed daily) and a pious figure like Queen Elizabeth, who, out of sheer sanctity and body denial, refrained from washing altogether, resulting in a scent that made it somewhat challenging for sensitive noses to deal with her holiness.

The emergence of body denial in the Nordic race is undoubtedly due to the Orient. This circumstance is very important because it puts us on a track that is very significant from the point of view of race science. One will hardly find among any truly nomadic people anything corresponding to the affirmation of daily physical exercise as developed by the Nordic race. It is even less likely to witness nomads encouraging their women to engage in public physical exercises. On the contrary, some Semitic peoples even set their ambitions on having the fattest women possible. To meet their beauty standards, the Moors and Tuaregs, for example, fatten up girls of marriageable age with camel's milk. Once again, there is such a striking difference in the perception of women between the Semitic peoples and the Nordic race that evolutionary grounds must be sought to understand these contrasts.

The author believes that the nomads' views on women, which are so alien to our sensibilities, can be traced back to their nomadic lifestyle.

The nomad, in his parasitic way of life, is faced with the predicament of either having slender wives while on the move or fat ones in places where he finds ample food and can parasitize. After all, nomadic women only work when they have to—the less she has to work, the better her situation appears, and the more powerful her master and ruler must appear to be (as he can keep slave women for her). Therefore, when Tuaregs fatten their girls up with camel's milk, it reveals a pronounced need for ostentation. Additionally, it reflects the fact that the Tuaregs are true desert nomads, as camels are only found in the desert and are the pre-

---

[409] Grosse, *Die Schönheit des Menschen.*
[410] Sellheim, *Das Geheimnis vom Ewig-Weiblichen.*

ferred domesticated animals of the Semitic peoples.

This brings us closer to the question of body denial itself. The constant wandering of the nomad naturally ensures that the body receives the necessary movement for maintaining health. For such nomads, there is therefore no reason at all to pay attention to these things. In contrast, a settled person who wants to maintain military readiness is virtually required to engage in daily physical exercises. This is at least one of the reasons why one occasionally finds great natural dexterity among nomads, but never the inclination to strengthen themselves through daily physical exercise.

It has already been pointed out in detail in the previous chapters that the ancestral homeland of all nomads is the steppe or the desert, and that the latter is the geographic outcome of sunlight-intensive conditions and a severe lack of water. In such an environment, it is impossible to wander around without clothing. The lack of clouds in these regions also causes a significant and abrupt difference in temperature between day and night, making it impractical to move around unclothed in deserts or steppes. Out in the open, the nomad only ever sees a woman's face, because her body is constantly veiled.[411] This explains why all nomads have a curious enthusiasm for women's faces, and why Oriental tales and folklore describe women's faces in such a way. Similarly, the face veil of Muslim women probably originated from these circumstances. In the traditions of the Nordic race, in any case, we do not find the enthusiastic Oriental descriptions of women's faces—we are also unable to sympathize with the face veil worn by Turkish women.

Even in pre-Islamic times, Arab women wore the veil. However, according to Jacob,[412] when they wanted to seduce a man, they would remove their veils. In accordance with the Semitic love for the face, great attention was paid to its embellishment. They used a preparation called *kohl* (an antimony-based substance) to darken their eyelids to a deep blue color. In order to emphasize the mouth particularly clearly and to make the white teeth stand out quite vividly in contrast, the lips were given a coral red coloring with red indigo, known as Ludbeard, Persio, Persian red, or coral red. Face painting is an ancient Semitic pastime that can be traced back to the most ancient of times. It makes sense, then, that makeup would also be involved in the religious ceremonies at Semitic engagement and wedding celebrations. It is worth noting that the Semites explicitly associate makeup with arousing the sensual passions of the bridegroom. In addition to makeup, perfume has also played an important role since ancient times, both for the bride and the groom.

Thus, the nomad only knows the female body when he sees it in an intimate setting and through the lens of sexual desire. Of course, bathing and washing are not possible in the nomad's homeland, where water is scarce, and it can be said that there is hardly ever a reason for a non-sexual nudity. The naked female body

---

[411] The term odalisque (Ottoman harem concubine), for example, originates from the word *ôdalik*, which in turn derives from the Turkish word *ôda*, meaning room. Therefore, it originally referred to a chamber companion, which later evolved into the concept of a concubine and harem slave.
[412] Jacob, *Arabisches Beduinenleben*.

thus seems to always coincide with memories or ideas of sexual arousal in the sensual world of the nomads. This probably explains the strong sexual imagination that is always present among nomads, who love to indulge in fantasies about the possible appearance of a beloved woman or adorning their thoughts with sexual images. In fact, this disposition could be considered a genuine "breeding result" of the nomadic lifestyle.

In this way, it can also be understood why all Oriental descriptions of the female body are strangely limited to descriptions of sexual details. In Arab songs and hymns, love is purely physical—love, for an Arab, is simply sexual intercourse. Winckler and Jacob state that while Arab love songs occasionally exhibit very tender poetry, the descriptions themselves are limited to purely sensual descriptions of the female body, while the character traits of the woman, on the other hand, are almost not mentioned at all.[413] As an example, consider the following poem:

It denies the breasts, the fullness of the loins to the delicate dress / to nestle the body and to cling to the back. / When the evening breezes blow toward her, they arouse anguish of jealous, astonished, envious glances.[414]

Conversely, in Nordic traditions, one will always find an emphasis on the nature of the woman or the female body—explicit sexual references are almost non-existent. This would also explain why the body-denying asceticism originating from the Orient always directed its wrath particularly harshly toward the Nordic embrace of the body and constantly sought to depict nudity as offensive. In the nomadic realm of fantasy and emotion, the female body and sexual arousal seem to be coupled together as a single entity.

The author has delved into these matters in more detail because it appears that once again the insurmountable contrast between the Nordic race and the nomads emerges. Furthermore, it should be shown that the evaluation training, as we have come to know it in the Nordic race with regard to the human body, must naturally be connected to an affirmation of the body that is understandable according to the life conditions of this race.

3

To conclude our analysis, we should also consider another breeding measure that must have been of far-reaching importance for the preservation of the health and the progressive racial improvement of the Nordic race.

First of all, let us recall something emphasized several times in the previous chapter. It was noted that the system of permanent marriage on a

---

[413] The minnesingers of the Middle Ages often adopted (sometimes even slavishly imitated) the customs of the ancient Arabs. This fact merits closer examination, particularly to avoid misconceptions about the sexual life of the Nordic race.

[414] The last sentence becomes clearer when rearranged: "So they arouse the torment of jealous glances and the amazement of envious glances."

hereditary farm was important because it acted as a eugenic filter for the Nordic race. Related to this, it is highly significant that almost all accounts of the Nordic race (Germanic, patrician, and Greek) specify the optimal age of marriage for men as being between thirty and forty. This high age for marriage is so strikingly common in all accounts of Nordic peoples that it cannot be a mere coincidence. Late sexual development is not something one has to worry about in this age range. Indeed, as we have already seen, it was required of the young man that he abstain from concubines only until his twentieth birthday.[415] It was more honorable for a young man to prove himself as a man among men than seek the approval of women.

To some extent, the late age of marriage for men is certainly related to external reasons. Being the head of a household was an office that came with many rights, but also an equal number of responsibilities—not only toward the family, but also toward the community. It is understandable that such a burden, which, as mentioned, also extended deeply into the public law of community life, was not willingly placed on all-too-young shoulders. A family head had to be able to fully exercise his practical and legal authority if the entire institution of the head of household was to have any meaning.

However, in this regard, we must acknowledge a certain late maturity in the Nordic man. The Nordic man is undoubtedly sexually mature at the end of his second decade of life, but he is still far from being physically fully developed and mentally mature. Based on certain observations from my time in the military, I would argue that the Nordic man often only reaches his proper shoulder width in his mid to late thirties. This phenomenon cannot simply be attributed to a Phalian trait, as even in the predominantly Nordic English society, broad shoulders with narrow hips and well-positioned legs are highly regarded in men. Of course, it requires extensive physical activity to bring out the full potential of the shoulders. Furthermore, it seems that Nordic people only reach a certain level of mental maturity in their late thirties. When the people of Württemberg say, albeit jokingly, that a man becomes "wise" only at the age of forty, this can only be understood in the sense of a completed mental development, corresponding to the full mental strength of a mature man.[416] In judging such matters, one should not be distracted by the precocious works of a few geniuses. The questions under discussion here concern the whole personality of the Nordic man and his character, not any individual talents that he may have. Simply put, there are always exceptions in life. Even if Field Marshal

---

[415] From *Commentarii de Bello Gallico*: "They think that by this the growth is promoted, by this the physical powers are increased and the sinews are strengthened." Original Latin: *"Hoc ali staturam ali vires nervosque confirmari putant."*

[416] Dr. Blendinger, veterinarian, has written several thought-provoking essays based on certain observations in animal breeding regarding the inverse relationship between physical and intellectual maturation. Unfortunately, the essays available to the author are no longer accessible to the public. However, the author believes that the ideas developed by Blendinger are significant enough to warrant attention from the field of human medicine in order to better understand the Nordic race.

Graf Wrangel led a regiment and held the rank of colonel only at the age of twenty-nine, this in no way disproves the principle that in peacetime, the company commander (captain) should ideally be over thirty.

Indeed, even today, Nordic communities still appreciate a certain "greyhound time" for their adolescents and do not value precocious and quickly maturing men. At the very least, they prefer to see young people "let the wind blow around their noses," meaning that they would prefer that young people gain experience before assuming positions and titles. There is no difference between the English sending their sons out into the world before they take up serious work and our former guilds sending their apprentices on journeys before they could become masters. In both cases, a young man is not at all expected to be "mature" in a hurry. Nowadays, however, we educate our youths less to become mature men and more as workers, whether it be in manual labor or in intellectual pursuits. In this regard, the currently prevailing Taylor system of education, which aims to shorten the training period as much as possible and focus on practical knowledge applicable to professions, is undoubtedly ideal. However, the Nordic race did not originally set out to create irresponsible workers, it preferred innately grounded and rooted individuals. Trust was given only to those who possessed the abilities of a full-fledged free man and future leader. One must bear this in mind when trying to understand the traditions surrounding the high age of marriage among the Nordic race. Hence, it is not appropriate to impose contemporary notions of "competence" and "usefulness" on the original worldview of the Nordic race.

One should take the time to study the portraits of German and English aristocrats in their youth. It is truly astonishing how late their faces often acquire their distinctly masculine features. The author has made similar observations only among certain peasant families in northwestern Germany.

For these reasons, the author would like to propose the following hypothesis—the traditionally high age of marriage among Nordic men was partly due to the desire to wait and see how the young man would develop and mature. If this assumption is correct, it would be another indication of the existence of breeding selection among males. In any case, the Nordic race did not originally follow a mechanical system of inheritance where the eldest son automatically succeeded the father simply by virtue of being the eldest. Instead, succession and its associated marriage always depended on the consent of the community. In this context, it is quite enlightening when von Amira points out that in Norwegian law, the word for "hero" in German, *held* (from *holdr*), originally referred to an individual who had inherited a hereditary estate (*èðdal*) or could assert a claim to it. This inheritance entitlement distinguished the "hero" from the common freeman.[417]

---

[417] This same ancient Germanic principle has now been reintroduced by Regent Horthy in Hungary—see chapter four.

This once again proves not only the peasant origins of the Nordic race but also the significance of breeding selection in the peasant laws of inheritance.

At this point, it is necessary to mention a circumstance intentionally left untouched by the author until now. We have seen that in marriage, one was expected to have as many boys as possible, and we just saw that admission to marriage was based on selection. So, what happened to the younger brothers of the heirs? First of all, it should be considered that losses (hunting!) and wartime events always resulted in a certain reduction. In fact, one can safely assume a casualty rate of 50 percent—this is, by the way, a very high percentage, as even in the bloodiest of all wars, the World War, the losses among eligible German men was only about 20 percent. Even with a casualty rate of 50 percent during the early history of the Nordic race, a sufficient number of men remained that could be selected as heirs of a hereditary estate and who could bestow life upon a flourishing brood of children. For example, when we hear about Ohm Kruger, the famous Boer leader, being reported to have had nine sons and seven daughters with his second wife, Susanne du Plessis, we have a very nice example at hand for judging the fertility of a healthy farming community. We can confidently assume such an abundance of children during the early period of the Nordic race.

The question here is what happened to the surviving younger brothers who were not allowed to marry. The author believes that a custom was prevalent in this regard since ancient times, a practice that we can still see in our more recent history. The word *kadett* (cadet) originally referred to the younger son of a noble family, later evolving to mean a young nobleman exclusively trained for military service. The word originated from Old French *capdet*, which is synonymous with the Latin *capitettum*, a diminutive form of *caput*, meaning head. Therefore, it referred to the smaller part of the head, or in this case, the younger brother of the head of the family. Therefore, in the history of this word, we can see that the concepts of the younger brother and of exclusive dedication to military service are intertwined. This is natural and reasonable, especially in an inheritance system like the one the Nordic race had in place. Obviously, there was a kind of division of labor, where the heir, as the worthiest among the siblings, was responsible for perpetuating the family line, while the non-inheriting brothers were responsible for the defense of the community. This is also consistent with what was mentioned in chapter three about the "uncles." In this context, the followers of the Germanic princes, known as the *hagastalde* (from which the term *hagestolz* derives, meaning older bachelor) or berserkers (meaning weapon-bearers), whose sole profession was warfare, appear to have been the direct precursors of our cadets or the peasant "uncles." It is noteworthy that Tacitus explicitly states that these *hagastalde* had no house or property, but were hosted by everyone. Whether an army is supported by quartering in a community or by levying taxes to sustain the army is essentially irrelevant. Tacitus' assumption that these *hagastalde* lived independently of home and property because of a personal desire or because of their warlike character and disposition is probably incorrect. Rather, it is more likely that their existence was due solely to the logical necessities of a healthy peasant inheritance system that designated surplus sons for the profession of arms to defend the community and to prevent the sustenance-providing land of a marriage from being diminished. In this context, one must also keep in mind that the Germanic tribal alliances established explicit defensive boundaries by maintaining a wide strip of uncultivated land (wasteland) along the border. This fact strongly indicates a certain state of governmental permanence, with defense being the decisive factor. Nomads are not usually inclined to do such things, for there would be no point whatsoever in them doing so. If the unmarried entourage of a Germanic chieftain would occasionally relieve their boredom with a small military expedition, such behavior is ultimately understandable. It is also understandable that it occasionally led to larger disturbances as a result. However, this is by no means a reason to associate the Germanic *hagastalde* with nomadism, or even to infer a nomadic nobility in Kern's sense. See chapter three for more on this subject.

From the peasant inheritance system that was just described, with its implications for non-inheriting younger sons, we also gain the key to understanding many phenomena in Germanic, especially German, history.

In war or in any other conflict, the fact remains that those who want to stand together in battle must also be able to rely on each other—otherwise, a collectively sustained fight is not possible. In this regard, an either-or situation arises. The most important and cleverest person is worth no more than a shot of gunpowder to a soldier if, in times of danger, they prioritize their "self" and abandon their comrades. This is absolutely true, and anyone who refuses to believe it must be told that he has apparently never had the opportunity to experience the value of comradeship in moments of true life-threatening danger. Tartuffes[418] do not thrive among soldiers as long as Mars rules the hour. Therefore, wherever struggle must be affirmed and sustained by a voluntarily formed fighting community, comradeship necessarily arises.[419] After all, it is only on the basis of such loyalty that a fighting community can be maintained. However, this type of fighting community also requires individuals that are aware of its value and can therefore act voluntarily and responsibly. When war is not an affirmation of struggle, but merely theft through violent means—as is the case with nomads—the concept of loyalty is unknown. That kind of fighting requires the unconditional subordination of the individual will, firstly because this situation is required by the nature of the struggle (robbery), and secondly because the consciousness of the nomad, trapped in purely materialistic

---

[418] Tartuffe refers to a character from the play *"Tartuffe, ou l'Imposteur"* [Tartuffe the Impostor] by Jean-Baptiste Poqueli, better known as Molière. Tartuffe is an insincere and duplicitous character who feigns religious piety and moral superiority in order to manipulate others.
[419] The motto of Felix Count Luckner and his lieutenant Carl Kircheiß (Hold fast, men!) is more than enlightening in this context.

(greedy) thinking, simply allows for no other possibilities. These robbers have no intention whatsoever of coming to the aid of a comrade in distress—they only associate with each other for the sake of self-seeking expediency. Anyone who wants to control such a gang and get anything done with them can only do so by imposing his will with iron determination and displaying animalistic cruelty toward defectors for the sake of deterrence (one ought to study the Russian Cheka carefully in this regard). But this warband, born and maintained out of predatory instincts, contrasts like night and day with the voluntary warbands of the Nordic race, which were based on the consciousness of one's own personal worth. The difference here is absolute. But in recognizing this difference, we also hold the key to the mystery of Nordic "loyalty." The armed fellowship of the Nordic race, based on loyalty, was the only possible way to ensure the defense of one's own ethnic community, or more accurately, tribal community. In the opposite case (when self-interest takes precedence), the defense of the community and a mutual trust among the men designated to defend it becomes impossible, because logically each individual must act in a way that corresponds to his own advantage. This entails the dissolution of a community unless it can be held together through uncompromising punishment and persecution where, in a sense, the selfish advantage lies in not exposing oneself to such punishments and persecutions. Here, the advantage lies only in the sense of settling accounts, not in the monetary sense, but in the figurative sense.

All military alliances or organizations hitherto established on the foundation of defending the homeland have never been able to dispense with the concept of an "oath," that is, these warbands were linked to a higher purpose beyond self-interest. In the history of war, all military defense organizations that allowed oaths to be violated have always disintegrated very quickly. Only armies intended for looting or destruction are kept together without an oath—they are held together exclusively by the promise of spoils. Hence, we consistently find these army structures among nomadic groups, who do not hesitate whatsoever to even involve slaves in their plundering military campaigns, since these slaves cannot run away and the plunder also benefits them. Interestingly, we also find this nomadic mentality among today's political condottieri, as they have no other choice and their existence is essentially always due to the dissolution of a community, and thus to conditions that bring forth expedient and self-centered individuals to the forefront.

There is no worse way to misunderstand the morally unique concept of Germanic warrior loyalty than to conflate it with the predatory instincts of the nomads.

Now, the Germanic warrior who entered Roman service becomes much more understandable. According to Germanic tradition, he could take this step without hesitation if his people did not necessarily need him to defend their homeland. Indeed, such a step was even considered entirely appropriate, as it offered the younger son without inheritance rights the opportunity to achieve prosperity abroad and kindle their own hearth (to be able to marry), which would have been denied to them in their homeland. This ancient Germanic view has, by the way, survived to the present day,[420] the only difference being that available opportunities for younger sons have expanded into various domains and are no longer limited exclusively to military service. The fact that the heir to the farm remains a peasant while the younger brothers (depending on the favor of luck and fate) often rise to the highest positions of public life is a phenomenon that can still be observed in many good rural areas of Germany. The author can support this with an example from his maternal family, where his grandfather's older brother remained a simple peasant on the hereditary farm (Öland Island), while one of the younger brothers became mayor of Stockholm, and another became a shipowner and a consul in Spain. If the ridiculous prejudice against our peasantry were not so prevalent in Germany, and if so, many men were not ashamed of their origins, one might soon be astonished to discover how many of our most important figures in German public life are little more than the younger, non-inheriting sons of peasants.

That the Germanic tribes initially only recognized the younger brother (who devoted himself to the craft of warfare) and the farm heir was ultimately disastrous in terms of their historical development. This circumstance, combined with their notions of loyalty (originally derived from a completely different worldview), was bound to prove disastrous the moment that Germanic individuals began to enter Roman military service and were subsequently used against the Germanic peoples. Although in itself correct and necessary, the idea of loyalty to arms was to some extent misdirected. The whole question of the *landsknecht* system and the "masterless swords" of our medieval nobility can be understood naturally and understandably through this, but it does not prevent us from often wishing that our German history had developed differently. It was only with the rise of the monasteries that a breach was made in this peasant-noble *landsknecht* system, namely through the creation of an estate that could accommodate the non-inheriting freemen without requiring them to relinquish their allegiance to the freemen's estate. In principle, of course, the idea had existed

---

[420] During the Middle Ages in Germany, closed inheritance law was adhered to in the establishment of its cities. Urban inheritance law did not permit a marriage to take place unless the dietary space necessary for sustaining a family was secured. Originally, the dietary space of each urban family was secured by providing the household with agricultural land—later, this evolved into only allowing apprentices to become masters (and to marry) if they could guarantee the family's subsistence through their manual labor. For this reason, a city only admitted as many masters as there was available income for them. From the perspective of contemporary economics, one may lament the constraints on economic development imposed by such guild and marriage laws, but it cannot be denied that only under such protection could the heartfelt flourishing of the old German urban family culture develop.

It is significant, by the way, that Malthus' population theory was not accepted in Germany until the first third of the last century, when efforts were made to abolish the urban guild system. It was then pointed out with horror that the possibility of unrestricted marriage would lead to overpopulation, making the problem of feeding this mass of people an almost impossible one. At the time, these objections were laughed off, but they persisted throughout the nineteenth century. The present day shows us that those concerns were justified.

before, in that the priesthood was reserved exclusively for freemen. However, there were not enough priestly positions to solve the issue solely through this institution. This was only achieved with the emergence of monasteries, and this new institution became comprehensible to the Teuton through the old concept of divine service. Originally, the monastery owed its existence to a completely non-Nordic philosophy originating in Egypt. But its cultural-historical significance for the Germanic peoples lies in the fact that it provided a home for the sons of Germania who were not entitled to inherit—and who would not have married anyway—and gave these men, otherwise born only for the rapier, a new profession, namely the field of science. To engage in the field of science was now considered as worthy of a free individual as riding in the retinue of a great lord. The actions of many abbots in the German Middle Ages, who were as adept at intellectual debate as they were at wielding their swords, become more understandable from this perspective. When the era of the monasteries had run its course, the path was now clear for Dr. Martin Luther.

Even today, it is customary in England for younger sons of noble families to devote themselves to the clergy. This circumstance did as little to denordify England as the monasteries did in the Middle Ages. In fact, it can be said that the reason that the English nobility has never become estranged from the people it leads is in no small measure due to this custom. In this respect, the Protestant nobility of Germany has certainly failed, although its behavior can be understood within the unique historical development of German Protestantism. Nevertheless, the House of Hohenzollern did manage to redirect the question of non-inheriting sons in two other directions. Under Frederick William I, a bureaucracy imbued with a Nordic spirit was established, and Frederick II nurtured his officer corps on similar principles. In essence, he did nothing more than return the ancient Germanic concept of *hagastalde* to its original purpose, the defense of the homeland.[421] Thus, the Germanic warrior's concept of loyalty, which was originally rooted in his tribe and had deviated from its true path during the German Middle Ages, was transformed by the two Hohenzollern rulers

---

In essence, it was Hardenberg's reckless negligence that caused the guild system to be thoughtlessly abolished without regard for the immense treasure of cultural value that was also being discarded. With ardent zeal, though unfortunately in vain, Baron vom Stein opposed Hardenberg's actions. While he also believed that a reform of the guild system was in order, he had clearly recognized the cultural disadvantages associated with the dissolution of the guilds. For him, technological progress was of little importance compared to the moral development of the people, which he saw as the true purpose of the state.

While in the field of industrial policy we have indeed repaired some of the damage done a century ago by overzealous liberalism, we have almost blindly overlooked the fact that the old German guild system succeeded in extending the healthy foundations of peasant life to urban areas. In doing so, it provided the opportunity for the moral development of the Germanic institution of marriage within the city. In the last century we have ignored this fact. Now, we find ourselves amidst the ruins of Germanic family culture, amazed at the moral decay that grips the German people today.

[421] Historically, it is undoubtedly more accurate to attribute the formation of a native officer corps to Frederick William I. However, it is also a fact that it was Old Fritz's victories that instilled in this officer corps a proud sense of duty deeply rooted in the land. One might therefore argue that the structure of the Prussian officer corps can be traced back to Frederick William I, especially if one takes into account the foundations already laid by the Great Elector. Nevertheless, it was only Frederick the Great who breathed life into this framework.

(Frederick Wilhelm I and Frederick II) and infused with a dutiful spirit of loyal service to the state. This is why the Prussian state creation stands so uniquely in the world—it is no coincidence that Mussolini has literally described his fascism as "Prussianism."

4

The key to the development of this state is the Nordic peasantry and its peasant inheritance laws. Had the Stein-Hardenberg agrarian reforms been consistently pursued, the German people in the nineteenth century could have successfully undertaken the task of providing the non-inheriting sons of peasants with new ways of sustaining a family (in other words, by transitioning them into logically structured industrial and commercial bourgeoisie and working classes closely tied to agriculture). Grounded in Germanic peasant inheritance laws, the German people have been able to shape history for a millennium and a half. They effortlessly overcame the immense bloodletting of the most horrific wars imaginable and even discovered the strength to further their own development. Throughout world history, this is an unprecedented occurrence that directly challenges all theories about denordification through war. Only with the modification of peasant inheritance customs through the rural inheritance laws of the German Civil Code (BGB) did the German people, for the first time, strike a blow to the root of their ethnic identity, thereby—and this can be said without hesitation—severing the lifeblood of the Nordic race within the German national body.

For that matter, it may also be historically unfounded to attribute the demise of the old medieval nobility to denordification by war. Similarly, this denordification is connected to peasant inheritance laws—only in the opposite direction. While the medieval nobility retained its ancient Nordic peasant inheritance laws, they committed the mistake of severing the land from the idea that it should strictly serve as the provider of sustenance for one marriage, instead linking it to the idea that it was a means of acquiring power. This paved the way for the creation of so-called dynastic power through the consolidation of estates (hearths). This policy of dynastic power, which the House of Habsburg mastered like no other, inevitably and continuously diminished the number of opportunities for kindling hearth fires. As a result, a so-called high nobility emerged ever more clearly, continuously diminishing the actual available land for sustaining Nordic families. On November 9, 1918, this development came to its conclusion.

In conclusion, the author would like to say once again that today's view of denordification through war obviously misses the heart of the matter. With sound land laws and healthy marriages, warfare has never harmed the Nordic race in the biological sense. It is only when there is a departure from peasant life and marriage is no longer seen as a collective responsibility (but rather as a business transaction, for personal pleasure, or a matter of house power politics) that wars begin to have a "denordifying" effect. Under such circumstances, the number of children necessarily decreases, and the previously insignificant percentage of casualties begin to have a devastating effect. This also affects biological selection among heirs, as the pool of selection gets smaller and smaller. Furthermore, it should be mentioned at this point that if Nordic bravery always had to lead directly to heroic

death, then the "Old Dessauer" would never have reached old age, and
Albert Leo Schlageter would not have needed to be executed by the French
on a sandpile.[422] As a former soldier, I often have the feeling that the currently popular notion of denordification through war is overly "academic"
in its analysis.[423] The author must also express concern that such viewpoints are inclined to obscure the central aspect of actual denordification,

---

[422] "Old Dessauer" refers to Leopold I, Prince of Anhlat-Dessau. He distinguished himself in the
War of the Spanish Succession and the Great Northern War and is best known for his drilling and
training reforms, which are believed to have laid the groundwork for Prussia's later military dominance.

[423] Colonel Marx published in Military Weekly (No. 32: 1928) a revealing compilation of the percentage of former active officers that were lost to heroic deaths in the World War. The percentage stands at
33.59 percent for infantry, 18.3 percent for pioneers, 16.4 percent for field artillery, 15 percent for
cavalry, and 13.8 percent for foot artillery. These figures are especially valuable due to the fact that proponents of the theory of denordification through war have often leaned on the losses suffered by our
active officer corps in the previous World War. The provided numbers are undoubtedly substantial, yet
in relation to the total number of men who engaged in combat in the last war, they are relatively low.
For instance, the English have recently revealed that they expended 480,000 tons of artillery ammuni-
tion in the first nine weeks of the Battle of Ypres. It can hardly be denied that the officers returning from
the war and their maturing children would have been more than sufficient to replenish the population
in biological terms. Of course, this assumes that the returning individuals and the growing youth were
provided with the opportunity to enjoy healthy marital conditions under healthy circumstances.
    Above all, one should refrain from using the heroic struggle of our student corps near Ypres in
1914 (remember the charge accompanied by the German national anthem) as an argument for the so-
called denordification theory. In this context, the question arises whether it was even necessary to form
entire regiments from youths intended to be future officer replacements. Furthermore, it should be
considered whether it wouldn't have been more sensible to create a sufficient reserve of replacements
during peacetime and to distribute the young volunteer students, destined to become future officers,
among all the regiments.
    Moreover, let us put it bluntly—as bright as the glory of the Ypres assault will continue to shine in
German history, from the point of view of the responsible military leadership at the time, there is little
reason to be proud of this charge. This is not the place to discuss this matter, but it is worth noting that
there is no reason to use the Ypres assault as a basis for questions of denordification.
    Another example of how casualty figures are not always as authoritative as they are often made out
to be (particularly in connection with the question of denordification) is the following—of the ninety-
nine students enrolled at the German Colonial School in Witzenhausen at the outbreak of war in 1914
(the author was one of these enrollees), thirty-three were killed in action, exactly one third. Considering
that admission to the Colonial School was only open to those students who could produce a medical
certificate certifying their suitability for tropical military service, it becomes clear that these ninety-nine
students represented a physical elite. This was due to the fact that the requirements for so-called tropical
service military fitness were much higher than those for general military service. Moreover, if we consider that admission to the school was subject to the same intellectual requirements as other similar institutions of higher learning, we must admit that these students stood out not only physically, but also in
terms of a certain active energy. Before the war, those with more leisurely inclinations had ample opportunity to choose a more contemplative course of study at the university rather than entering foreign
colonial service, which often required more vigorous effort on the part of the applicant.
    These ninety-nine students were undoubtedly a selection of enterprising young men who could
hardly be accused of lacking a Nordic blood-heritage. Accordingly, all of them—all ninety-nine of them
—were stationed at the very front of the frontlines throughout the entire 1914–1918 war. The significant loss rate of 33 percent, which is comparable to the casualty rate of active infantry officers, is therefore understandable. Furthermore, this example also proves that a 33 percent loss among the students of
the Colonial School would in no way indicate "denordification" if the remaining sixty-six students who
returned from the war had been able to enter into healthy marital relationships and, for example, settle
in the east.
    Additionally, the author would also doubt that any other student organization or institution of
higher learning had as high a loss rate in their 1914 class as the 33 percent rate of the Colonial School.

peasant inheritance law.[424]

But let us return to the breeding measures taken by the Nordic race. Another circumstance of great importance for breeding was that the virgin did not bring a dowry into the marriage. Spousal selection was based solely on biological factors. One should not be deceived here by child betrothals, which may seem to prove the opposite. In a well-developed and thoroughbred stock where the physical health of individuals is preserved, the biological selection of a girl can be made based on the capability of her father. In horse breeding, for example, it is customary in the pedigrees of both thoroughbreds and half-breeds to only indicate the names of the sires. "Welser from Wels, from Adeptus XX, from Julianus, from Nero," simply means that Welser comes from a horse named Wels and a mare who was sired by Adeptus XX, whose dam was a daughter of Julianus, who in turn mated with a daughter of Nero. This type of ancestry record assumes that one is aware of the biological inheritance of each sire. If that is the case, constructing the pedigree becomes quite easy. Such a horse breeding practice proves to us that in ancient Nordic marriage, the selection of brides based on the capabilities of their fathers was by no means exclusively a matter of family politics, as it is often portrayed today, but originally may very well have been connected with breeding considerations.

Only the "heir daughters" stand somewhat apart here. Since they still inherited their father's genetic material, this practice was solely a breeding measure to pass on the blood of the estate's family line through the daughter in cases where there were no more sons—it was not a matter of property rights. For this reason, the heir daughter had to marry a relative of her father, and it was particularly desirable if this relative was as closely related to her father as possible (such as the father's brother or the son of a father's brother). Moreover, daughters had no inheritance rights. Daughters were entitled only to a stipend and, if she married, potentially an endowment. The lord of the estate on which she was born was obliged to do this, whether the lord was her father, brother, or brother-in-law.

Frequently, in historical records, the aspects of breeding and health come distinctly to the forefront in all matters related to marriage. According to Icelandic law, the father of the bride had to legally pledge to the groom that the bride was without any physical defects. According to ancient Indian law, the father had to inform the groom of any defects in the bride, otherwise, he would be punished and the marriage would be invalid. Thus, among the Nordic race, be-

---

[424] Anyone who, prompted by these suggestions from the author, wishes to gain a brief yet comprehensive understanding of German land law, is directed to the pamphlet "*Bodenrecht, Siedlung und Besteuerung*" [Land Law, Settlement, and Taxation] authored by Privy Councillor Gerstenhauer and published by the *Reichslandbund* (now *Reichsnährstand*). This publication can be obtained through the Reichslandbund's distribution center at Dessauer Straße 26, Berlin SW 11, for a price of forty reichsmarks. A proper understanding of German land law is essential if one is to not be misled by the Marxist and un-German nature of contemporary land reform (such as that of Damaschke). In this context, while not exclusively related to land law, the concise and affordable publications produced by the most distinguished German scholars and published by the Society of the German State in Jena are recommended, as they are reasonably priced and inexpensive. However, one must also mention the journal *Nationalwirtschaft, Blätter für Organischen Wirtschaftsaufbau* [National Economy, Papers for Organic Economic Reconstruction], which attempts to guide the worker masses detached from the soil towards a rational land-based way of life.

trothal was not merely a contract but the act of establishing a marriage.

There may be some readers who, based on the ideas developed here, could come to the conclusion that the ancient Nordic marriage must have been characterized by something remarkably impersonal. However, in reality, this might not have been entirely the case, at least not in general terms. By ensuring sustenance-providing land and with the further precondition that only healthy individuals could enter into marriage, the material foundation for a happy marriage was there. Furthermore, it should also be noted that the two people entering into marriage were so similar (by virtue of being of the same race and having a comparable upbringing) that any potential differences in character between them could not have caused too much friction. It should also not be forgotten that marriage was entered into from a public service perspective and was considered a duty to the collective, thereby preemptively cutting off all melodramatic emotional acrobatics—these are unfortunately encouraged by modern romantic literature. Furthermore, it should be noted that marriage was not only accompanied by responsibilities but also carried extensive rights. It seems that in ancient Nordic communities, only the husband was the bearer and executor of public authority. Similarly, a girl could only attain a social position through marriage, whereas an unmarried girl of free blood could never escape from the authority of her paternal household. It can hardly be denied that, as a result, almost all the reasons and causes that make marriage a "problem" nowadays were eliminated from the outset. Therefore, one may well assume that these marriages, seemingly contracted on very pragmatic considerations, actually unfolded in a much more radiant and happier manner than our present-day "emotion-driven" marriages—consider the divorce rate of recent years.

As soon as dowry becomes prevalent in a Nordic community and marriage ceases to be driven by biological expediency (instead becoming a transaction in monetary terms), the preservation of pure blood and Nordic civilization usually comes to an end very quickly. The reasons that led to the implementation of dowries may not have always been the same throughout the history of the Nordic race, but the effect was the same in all cases. As early as 550 BC, Theognis depicts this process quite elegantly and accurately,

> When it comes to oxen, cattle, or horses, we act rationally and choose according to their utility and value, and select, without fail, animals from a sound and faultless lineage. But when it comes to marriage, the price always determines the outcome—men marry for gold and daughters are given away. The scoundrel, the fool, who swims in gold, can now unite his child with the oldest lineage. Thus, everything mixes, noble and base! If you, therefore, find us to be a degenerate mixed breed in manners, form, and spirit, do not wonder, my friend! The reason is clear, and it would be futile to lament the consequences.

It should be mentioned in this context that, according to historical records, the marriageable age for Nordic girls can be set at around twenty years old. The records are not consistent in this regard, but the differences are not significant.

The girls were allowed to marry only after reaching full maturity. In addition, it may not be biologically appropriate to marry women at an early age if they are expected to remain fertile for a long time.[425] The role of a housewife also required a certain dignity and versatility in domestic affairs—someone who is too young would not have been able to meet these requirements.

Legally, however, the marriage age for girls was lower, at around twelve years old. But these are not child marriages in the true sense. Therefore, we may assume that it was merely a way to allow a girl to enter the family of her future husband at the age of twelve, if that were necessary. However, this does not mean that the child actually married at such a tender age. Such provisions were probably more about the legal requirements of taking over the personal protection of the girl. Of course, we have seen that the raising of a young maiden involved great obligations for the father and brothers. Thus, it seems that the idea was that the protection of virginity should also be exercised by the clan that would ultimately benefit from the young maiden preserving sexual abstinence until marriage. This would explain the somewhat peculiar age of twelve years—it represents the end of childhood for Nordic girls but still precedes the earliest onset of physical maturation. In any case, Plutarch states, "The Romans married their daughters at the age of twelve, and often even earlier, in order to hand them over to the groom in a purer and less corrupted state, both in body and soul." However, Plutarch's view is obviously due to a misunderstanding of the nature of the custom handed down to him.

We have come to the end of our analysis on the marriage and breeding laws of the Nordic race. Due to the nature of the subject, the author could only provide an overview. There is one thing, however, that the author believes he can say with absolute certainty. If at first it may have been natural biological causes that shaped the Nordic race in all of its glory, later in its development it was certainly a clear will and clear breeding laws that carried it to its cultural heights. Therefore, let us conclude with a word from Schiller, which the Nordic race, like no other race in the world, has understood how to realize

Art is to chisel out of marble
Venus and Apollo.
Higher art is to shape the human
As he should become.

---

[425] Incidentally, it is also not in accordance with zootechnical principles to breed dams too early if they are to remain fertile for a long time.

Appendix A

SS-Order – A – No. 65

The *Reichsführer-SS*.

Munich, December 31st, 1931.

1. The SS is an association of German men certified to be of Nordic descent and selected according to particular criteria.
2. In accordance with the National Socialist worldview and in recognition of the fact that the future of our people rests in the selection and preservation of good blood in terms of race and hereditary health, I hereby introduce the "Marriage License" for all unmarried members of the SS, effective January 1, 1932.
3. The desired goal is the creation of a German clan that is both certifiably Nordic and hereditarily healthy.
4. Marriage licenses are granted or denied solely on the basis of racial and hereditary health considerations.
5. Any SS man who intends to marry must obtain a marriage license from the *Reichsführer-SS*.
6. Members of the SS who marry despite being denied a marriage license will be expelled from the SS; they are free to leave.
7. The proper processing of marriage requests is the responsibility of the "Race Office" of the SS.
8. The Race Office of the SS manages the "SS Clan Registry," in which the families of SS members are recorded once the marriage license is granted or the application for registration is approved.
9. The *Reichsführer-SS*, the Chief of the Race Office, and the advisers to this office are sworn to secrecy on the basis of their honor.
10. The SS is aware that with this order it has taken a step of great importance. Mockery, scorn, and misunderstanding do not affect us; the future is ours!

The *Reichsführer-SS*

Signed, H. Himmler.

Appendix B

The Reich Hereditary Farm Law (*Reichserbhofgesetz*) of September 29, 1933[426]

The government of the German Reich aims to preserve the peasantry as the lifeblood of the German people while safeguarding ancient German customs of inheritance.

Farms are to be protected from undue indebtedness and fragmentation in inheritance, ensuring that they remain permanently in the hands of free Peasants as family inheritance.

Our goal is to work toward a healthy distribution in the sizes of agricultural properties, because the best guarantee for the preservation of the health of the people and the state is a large number of viable small and medium-sized farms, distributed as evenly as possible throughout the entire country.

Therefore, the German government has passed the following law. The fundamental principles of the law are:

1. Land designated for agricultural or forestry activities between a minimum of one *ackernahrung*[427] and a maximum of 125 hectares shall be classified as a Hereditary Farm (*erbhof*), provided that it is owned by an individual that meets the criteria to be a Peasant.
2. The owner of the Hereditary Farm shall be referred to as a Peasant.
3. To qualify as a Peasant, one must hold German citizenship, be of German or kindred blood, and demonstrate respectability.
4. The *Erbhof* passes undivided to the heir.
5. The rights of co-heirs are limited to the remaining assets of the Peasant. Descendants not designated as heirs are entitled to receive vocational training and provisions commensurate with the capabilities of the farm. In the event that they find themselves in hardship through no fault of their own, they shall be granted Home Refuge (*Heimatzuflucht*).[428]
6. Closed inheritance (*anerbenrecht*) may not be suspended or restricted through testamentary disposition. The Hereditary Farm is fundamentally inalienable and may not be surrendered.

---

[426] Wilhelm Saure, *Das Reichserbhofgesetz. Ein Leitfaden zum Reichserbhofrecht* [The Reich Hereditary Farm Law: A Guide to Reich Inheritance Law] (Berlin: Neudetsche Verlags und Treuhandgesellsch, 1933).

[427] *Ackernahrung* is defined in §2 of the Reich Hereditary Farm Law and is similar to other measures of a land's ability to sustain a family (such as the *pflugland* or plowland) discussed in chapter three.

[428] *Heimatzuflucht*, or home refuge, is defined in §30 of the Reich Hereditary Farm Law.

The law is hereby proclaimed:

Section I
The Hereditary Farm (*Erbhof*)

§ 1. Definition

(1) Land designated for agricultural or forestry activities is considered a Hereditary Farm if it:
    1. Meets the size requirements outlined in §2 and §3, and
    2. Is under the exclusive ownership of an individual that meets the criteria to be a Peasant.
(2) Farms that are continuously utilized through leasing are not Hereditary Farms.
(3) Hereditary Farms are entered *ex officio* into the Registry of Hereditary Farms (*Erbhöferolle*). Entry into this registry has a declaratory, not a legal, significance.

§ 2. Minimum Size

(1) The Hereditary Farm must be at least the size of one *ackernahrung*.
(2) *Ackernahrung* shall be defined as the amount of land necessary to feed and clothe a family independent of market conditions and the general economic situation and to maintain the economic viability of the Hereditary Farm.

§ 3. Maximum Size

(1) The Hereditary Farm may not exceed 125 hectares in size.
(2) It must be possible to cultivate it from a single farmstead without outbuildings.

§ 4. Establishment of Hereditary Farms through Division

The formation of multiple Hereditary Farms through the division of larger estates is permitted, provided that:
    1. Each individual farm meets the requirements outlined in §1 to §3.
    2. The cumulative value of the owner's debts, including any encumbrances in rem on the property to be divided, does not exceed 30 percent of the last taxable assessed value determined prior to the division.

§ 5. Establishment of a Hereditary Farm through Special Authorization

(1) The Reich Minister of Food and Agriculture is authorized to grant exceptions to the requirements of §3 following consultation with the District Peasant Leader and the Regional Peasant Leader.

(2) Nevertheless, a size exceeding 125 hectares shall generally only be permitted:

1. When it is deemed necessary due to the soil type or climate.
2. If it is an economically self-sufficient farm with consolidated lands that has demonstrably been in the ownership of a peasant family for more than one hundred and fifty years.
3. If a German who has rendered exceptional service to the overall well-being of the German people is to be honored, either personally or through their descendants.
4. If the family residing on the farm has created valuable assets there (such as buildings of artistic or cultural-historical significance) that, with a farm size not exceeding 125 hectares, lack a sufficient economic basis for their maintenance.

(3) The requirement that the Hereditary Farm must be operated from a single farmstead without outbuildings shall only be disregarded in cases where specific operational circumstances necessitate the presence of such outbuildings.

§ 6. Wine, Vegetable, or Fruit Cultivation

(1) The regulations of §1 to §5 also apply to properties utilized for the cultivation of wine, vegetables, or fruit.

(2) In the case of wine cultivation, a farm is considered one *ackernahrung* if its own production of wine grapes is adequate to sustain a family.

(3) For vegetable or fruit cultivation, a farm is considered one *ackernahrung* if the utilized land would still be considered one *ackernahrung* in the sense of §2 para. (2), even when converted to a different type of agricultural use.

§ 7. The Hereditary Farm

(1) The Hereditary Farm encompasses all the properties owned by the Peasant that are regularly cultivated from the farmstead, along with any farm accessories owned by the Peasant.

(2) Temporary leasing or similar temporary use of farm properties, such as *altenteilsland* for example,[429] does not disqualify it.

§ 8. Farm Accessories in Detail

(1) Farm accessories primarily encompass livestock, agricultural and domestic equipment (including linens and beds), existing stocks of fertilizer, and agricultural products and supplies essential for cultivation on the farm.
(2) Farm accessories additionally encompass documents related to the farm, family letters from previous generations, pictures of sentimental value, antlers, and other memorabilia associated with the farm and the peasant family residing on it.

§ 9. Insurance Claims and Repayment Credits

The Hereditary Farm also includes any claims resulting from insurance acquired for the farm and its accessories, including the corresponding compensation amounts, as well as accrued repayment credits related to a farm debt.

§ 10. Determination of Hereditary Farm Status by the Inheritance Court

In cases where the qualification of a farm as a Hereditary Farm is uncertain, the matter shall be resolved by the Inheritance Courts upon the request of the owner or the District Peasant Leader.

---

[429] Translator's note: *Altenteil* or *altenteilsland* refers to a portion of land set aside on a farm so that the peasant and/or his spouse has a place to stay when the farm is handed over to the heir.

Section II
The Peasant

§ 11. Definition

(1) Only the owner of a Hereditary Farm shall be referred to as a Peasant.
(2) The owner or holder of other land utilized for agricultural or forestry purposes shall be referred to as a farmer (*landwirt*).
(3) The use of alternative names for owners or holders of land utilized for agricultural or forestry purposes is prohibited.
(4) The professional designation of landowners in the Land Register shall be changed gradually to align with these definitions.

§ 12. Requirement of German Citizenship

The status of Peasant is limited to individuals with German citizenship.

§ 13. Requirement of German or Kindred Blood

(1) The status of Peasant is limited to individuals of German or kindred blood.
(2) To be of German or kindred blood entails the absence of Jewish or colored blood among one's ancestors on either the paternal or maternal side.
(3) The requirement stipulated in para. (1) must be proven back to at least January 1, 1800. If there are any doubts as to whether the requirements of para. (1) are met, the Inheritance Court shall decide at the request of the owner or the District Peasant Leader.

§ 14. Exclusion through Incapacitation

A person shall be ineligible for Peasant status if he is legally incapacitated, provided that any action for nullification has been legally dismissed or not raised within the legal period of notice.

§ 15. Respectability and Qualifications of the Peasant

(1) The Peasant must be honorable. He must be capable of managing the farm properly. Lack of maturity alone is not a valid exemption.
(2) In the event that the conditions of para. (1) are not met, or if the Peasant acquires excessive debt obligations in a manner that would have been possible for him to avoid with proper farm management, the Inheritance Court may, upon the request of the Regional Peasant Leader, permanently

or temporarily transfer the administration and usufruct of the Hereditary Farm to the Peasant's spouse or to the individual who would be the heir in the event of the Peasant's death.

(3) In the absence of a spouse or heir, or if the spouse or heir are not eligible to be considered a Peasant, the Inheritance Court, upon the request of the Reich Peasant Leader, may transfer ownership of the Hereditary Farm to a designated individual who meets the criteria to be a Peasant. If suitable relatives of the Peasant are available, the Reich Peasant Leader shall propose one of them.

(4) Ownership of the Hereditary Farm is transferred upon the legal enactment of the resolution for transfer. The Inheritance Court is to request that the Land Registry record *ex officio* the new owner. The regulations of §419 of the German Civil Code apply accordingly.

§ 16. **Consequences of Losing Peasant Status**

If the Peasant loses his Peasant status, he may no longer call himself a Peasant. His ownership of the farm, subject to §15, as well as the hereditary status of the estate shall remain unaffected.

§ 17. **Joint Ownership and Legal Entities**

(1) A Hereditary Farm cannot be included in marital joint property or otherwise be jointly owned by multiple individuals.

(2) A Hereditary Farm cannot be owned by a legal entity.

§ 18. **Verdict of the Inheritance Court Regarding Peasant Status**

If there exist any doubts as to whether a person is qualified to be a Peasant, the Inheritance Court shall decide upon their request or at the request of the District Peasant Leader.

Section III
Succession under Closed Inheritance

§ 19. Succession on the Hereditary Farm

(1) Upon the death of the Peasant, the Hereditary Farm constitutes a distinct component of the inheritance with respect to legal inheritance and estate division.
(2) The Hereditary Farm passes undivided to the heir by law.

§ 20. The Order of Heirs

The heirs are designated in the following sequence:
1. The sons of the testator. In the place of a deceased son, his sons and grandsons succeed.
2. The father of the testator.
3. The brothers of the testator. In the place of a deceased brother, his sons and grandsons succeed.
4. The daughters of a testator. In the place of a deceased daughter, her sons and grandsons succeed.
5. The sisters of the testator. In the place of a deceased sister, her sons and grandsons succeed.
6. The female descendants of the testator and their descendants, provided that they are not already eligible in Nr. 4. The person closest to the testator's male line takes precedence over distant descendants. Otherwise, priority is given to the male gender.

§ 21. Specific Regulations with Regard to the Order of Heirs

(1) Anyone who is not qualified to be a Peasant shall not be eligible to be an heir. The Hereditary Farm passes to the individual who would have been appointed if the unqualified individual had not been alive at the time of the inheritance.
(2) A relative is ineligible for succession as long as a relative of a higher category exists.
(3) Within the same category, whether priority will be given to the eldest or the youngest will depend on the local custom. If no specific custom exists, then the right of the youngest prevails. If there is any doubt as to whether such a custom exists, or which custom exists, the Inheritance Court shall decide upon the request of one of the parties.

(4) Among the sons, the sons of the first wife take precedence over other sons. In the case of brothers and sisters, full siblings take precedence over half siblings.

(5) Children legitimized by a subsequent marriage shall be deemed equivalent to legitimate children born after entry into marriage. For children legally declared as belonging to the father, the same order applies as for legitimate children; illegitimate children of the mother simply follow after legitimate children.

(6) Persons adopted in lieu of children are not entitled to succession.

(7) If there are no sons or grandsons at the time that the farm becomes a Hereditary Farm by virtue of this law, heirs of the fourth category shall be appointed ahead of those belonging to the second and third categories.

§ 22. Exchange of a Hereditary Farm

(1) If the heir already has a Hereditary Farm, he is no longer considered eligible to be an heir. The Hereditary Farm passes to the individual who would have been appointed if the ineligible individual had not been alive at the time of the inheritance.

(2) Nevertheless, this shall not apply if the heir formally declares to the Inheritance Court, either through publicly certified means or by writing to the administrative office, his intention to assume ownership of the inherited farm within six weeks of becoming aware of the transfer.

(3) If the conditions outlined in para. (2) are fulfilled, ownership of the heir's existing farm shall legally transfer to the next designated heir of the testator. The latter can renounce the transfer. The regulations of the German Civil Code regarding the acceptance or renunciation of an inheritance apply accordingly.

(4) The Inheritance Court shall determine the extent to which this subsequently designated individual is obliged to release the heir from the liabilities of the estate.

(5) The regulation of para. (4) shall also apply to the personal liabilities of the heir associated with the transferred farm. To the extent that the Inheritance Court obliges the acquirer of the farm to bear these costs, he is also liable to the creditors.

§ 23. Multiple Hereditary Farms

(1) If the Peasant leaves behind multiple Hereditary Farms, the heirs may each choose one Hereditary Farm in the order of their appointment, so that no one receives more than one Hereditary Farm.

(2) The selection must be declared to the Inheritance Court in publicly certified form or by writing to the administrative office. At the request of a subsequent person entitled to choose, the presiding closed inheritance authority shall set a reasonable deadline for said person to declare their selection. If the selection is not made before the deadline expires, the person entitled to choose shall yield precedence to other persons entitled to choose.

(3) Each person entitled to inherit shall acquire ownership of the farm he has selected upon completion of the selection. Upon the final selection, the next person appointed will immediately become the owner of the remaining farm.

§ 24. Testamentary Dispositions

(1) The testator cannot, by virtue of the closed inheritance, prohibit or limit succession through testamentary disposition.

(2) The regulation of para. (1) does not preclude disposition over individual accessories that are not required for the management of the farm, provided that they are not farm documents or the special items referred to in §8 para. (2).

(3) Dispositions restricted under closed inheritance include dispositions made upon death by which a charge is imposed on the farm or the remaining estate is disposed of in such a way that it is no longer possible to adjust the liabilities of the estate in accordance with the regulations of §34.

§ 25. Designation of the Heir by the Testator

(1) The testator may designate an heir within the first category,
   1. If closed inheritance was not customary in the region when this law came into force.
   2. If free determination by the Peasant was customary in the region when this law came into force.
   3. In other cases, with the consent of the Inheritance Court, if there is good cause.
   4. In cases of doubt, the Inheritance Court shall decide whether the requirements of nos. 1 and 2 are met.

(2) In the absence of legitimate sons or grandsons, the testator may, with the consent of the Inheritance Court, appoint an illegitimate son of whom he is the father as an heir. Before making its decision, the Inheritance Court must consult the Regional Peasant Leader.

(3) With the consent of the Inheritance Court, the testator may determine that a person of the fourth category shall become an heir before persons of

the first, second or third categories. The Inheritance Court shall give its consent if there is good cause.

(4) The testator may designate the heir within the second and subsequent categories. He may also skip one or more categories with the consent of the Inheritance Court.

(5) If there are no persons of the categories specified in §20, the testator may designate the heir. If the heir designated by the testator is not qualified to be a Peasant, or if the Peasant makes no designation, the Reich Peasant Leader shall designate the heir. Preference should be given to relatives or in-laws of the deceased who are qualified to be a Peasant.

§ 26. Administration and Usufruct for the Father or Mother of the Heir

The testator may order that the father or mother of the heir be entitled to the administration and usufruct of the farm beyond the age of majority, but not beyond the age of twenty-five.

§ 27. Use of the Farm Name

The testator can specify that the heir use the name of the farm as an addition to his name.

§ 28. Form of the Testator's Instructions

The testator may only make the instructions provided for in §25 to §27 by means of a will or inheritance contract.

§ 29. Renunciation

(1) The heir may renounce the transfer of the Hereditary Farm without renouncing inheritance of the remaining assets. The regulations of the German Civil Code concerning the renunciation of inheritance apply accordingly to this renunciation.

(2) The renunciation must be declared to the Inheritance Court. The deadline for renunciation begins at the time at which the heir becomes aware of his appointment as heir. If the appointment is based on a testamentary disposition, not before the pronouncement of the disposition.

(3) If the person appointed as heir is not a German national, his resignation as heir (§21 para. (1) and §12) shall not initially take effect. However, it is deemed to be a renunciation of the transfer if he has not applied for

German citizenship within the period specified in para. (2) or if his application is rejected.

§ 30. Providing for the Testator's Descendants and Home Refuge (*Heimatzuflucht*)

(1) The descendants of the testator, provided they are co-heirs or entitled to a legitimate portion, shall be appropriately supported and educated on the farm until they reach the age of majority.
(2) They shall also be trained for an occupation appropriate to the status of the farm, and after they become independent—this also applies to female descendants upon their marriage—they shall be provided for, insofar as the resources of the farm permit. The provision may specifically also consist of the granting of funds for the procurement of a homestead.
(3) If they find themselves in hardship through no fault of their own, they may also seek refuge on the farm at a later date in return for appropriate work assistance (home refuge). This right is also available to the parents of the testator if they are co-heirs or entitled to a legitimate portion.

§ 31. *Altenteil* for the Spouse

Provided that they are a co-heir or entitled to a legitimate portion and they waive all claims to which they might have against the estate, the surviving spouse of the testator may demand from the heir lifetime support on the farm customary in such circumstances, insofar as they cannot support themselves from their own assets.

§ 32. Settlement of Disputes

In the case of disputes arising from §30 and §31, the Inheritance Court will make the necessary arrangements, taking due account of the circumstances of those involved, in such a way that the farm remains viable. It may revoke or limit the entitlement to financial support if the beneficiary is otherwise financially secure, or if the obligated party can no longer be reasonably expected to provide support, especially if it exceeds the resources of the farm.

§ 33. The Remaining Estate

The Peasant's assets other than the Hereditary Farm are inherited according to the regulations of general law.

§ 34. Liabilities of the Estate

(1) The estate liabilities, including the mortgages, land charges, and annuity debts resting on the farm, but excluding other encumbrances (*altenteil*, usufruct, debt relief annuity, etc.), are to be settled from the assets available outside of the farm provided that they are sufficient for that purpose.

(2) In cases where the estate liabilities cannot be settled in this manner, the heir is obliged to bear them alone and relieve the co-heirs of them.

§ 35. Division of the Remaining Estate

(1) If there is a surplus remaining after settling the estate liabilities, it is to be distributed among the co-heirs of the heir according to the regulations of general law.

(2) The heir can, if he is entitled to a share in the remaining estate according to the regulations of general law, only demand a share of the surplus in excess of the unencumbered earning power of the Hereditary Farm. The earning power is determined by the net proceeds that the farm can sustainably provide based on its existing economic abilities.

§ 36. Liabilities in the Case of Multiple Hereditary Farms

(1) If the estate includes multiple Hereditary Farms (§23), those entitled to support in accordance with §30 and §31 can choose which farm they want to receive support from. The obligation to provide professional training and provisions is borne jointly by all heirs, in proportion to the value of the farms relative to each other.

(2) The heirs shall bear the estate liabilities in proportion to each other based on the value of the farms.

(3) If a dispute arises regarding the application of sentence 2 of para. (1) or regarding para. (2), the Inheritance Court shall make the final determination.

Section IV
Restrictions on the Sale and Encumbrance of the Hereditary Farm and Matters Pertaining to Foreclosure

§ 37. Sale and Encumbrance of the Hereditary Farm

(1) The Hereditary Farm is fundamentally inalienable and not subject to encumbrance. This does not apply to sales of accessories that are made within the scope of proper farm management.

(2) The Inheritance Court can approve a sale or encumbrance if there is good cause. Approval may also be granted conditionally.

(3) The Inheritance Court shall grant approval for the sale of a Hereditary Farm if the Peasant intends to transfer it to an heir entitled to inheritance who would be the immediate successor in the case of inheritance or could be designated as the heir by the testator according to §25. The Inheritance Court should grant approval if the transfer agreement does not burden the Hereditary Farm beyond its capacity.

§ 38. Protection against Enforcement

(1) There shall be no enforcement upon a Hereditary Farm on account of a pecuniary claim.

(2) There shall also be no enforcement upon the agricultural products produced on the Hereditary Farm on account of a pecuniary claim, except as outlined by the provisions of §39 and §59.

§ 39. Enforcement Due to Pecuniary Claims under Public Law

(1) Enforcement upon the agricultural products produced on a Hereditary Farm on account of public levies, on account of a claim arising from public charges, or on account of another type of pecuniary claim under public law is permitted insofar as these agricultural products are not part of the farm's accessories and are not necessary to sustain the Peasant or his family until the next harvest.

(2) Enforcement under para. (1) shall only commence if the creditor has served the District Peasant Leader one month in advance with the order for enforcement and a declaration that he intends to initiate foreclosure proceedings against the Peasant.

(3)　Within the time limit, the District Peasant Leader may, provided that he is authorized to do so by the Reich Food Society (*Reichsnährstand*),[430] make a written declaration to the creditor stating that he will assume the debt on behalf of the Reich Food Society. By virtue of this declaration, the Reich Food Society is obliged to satisfy the creditor upon delivery of the enforcement order and provide him with a publicly certified receipt. The creditor can no longer assert the claim against the Peasant.

(4)　Insofar as the Reich Food Society satisfies the creditor, the creditor's claim shall be legally transferred to it. The Reich Food Society may enforce the enforcement order against the Peasant in accordance with the restrictions stipulated by §38 and §39 para. (1).

(5)　The regulations of para. (2) to (4) are not applicable if the claim and costs do not exceed the amount of 150 reichsmarks without interest.

---

[430] Editor's note: Until Darré's retirement in 1942, he concurrently served as the Reich Minister of Food and Agriculture, the Reich Peasant Leader, and the leader of the Reich Food Society (*Reichsnährstand*).

Section V
Inheritance Authorities

§ 40. Principle

(1) To carry out the specific duties of this law, Inheritance Courts, Hereditary Farm Courts, and the Reich Hereditary Farm Court shall be established.

(2) Matters referred to the Inheritance Authorities for judgement under this law may not be brought before the ordinary courts.

§ 41. The Inheritance Court

(1) The Inheritance Court shall be established by the State Justice Administration (*Landesjustizverwaltung*) at the local district court. The State Justice Administration may designate a different district; in particular, it may stipulate that one Inheritance Court may be established for multiple local court districts.

(2) The decisions of the Inheritance Court shall be made by a panel consisting of a presiding judge and two Peasants.

(3) The chairperson and their permanent deputy are appointed by the State Justice Administration, usually for the duration of the calendar year. They are required to be familiar with the inheritance customs of the Peasant population.

§ 42. Local Jurisdiction of the Inheritance Court

(1) The Inheritance Court with jurisdiction over the farmstead of the Hereditary Farm shall have authority.

(2) In cases of uncertainty, the President of the Hereditary Farm Court will determine the responsible Inheritance Court.

§ 43. The Hereditary Farm Court

(1) A Hereditary Farm Court shall be established for each federal state by the State Justice Administration at a higher regional court of its own determination. A joint Hereditary Farm Court can be formed for several federal states by the federal states involved. Several Hereditary Farm Courts can also be formed in one federal state.

(2) The decisions of the Hereditary Farm Court shall be made by a panel consisting of a presiding judge, two additional judges, and two Peasants.

(3) The regulations of §41 para. (3) apply accordingly.

§ 44. Appointment of the Peasant Assessors

The Peasant Assessors of the Inheritance Court are appointed by the State Justice Administration upon the recommendation of the Regional Peasant Leader, the Peasant Assessors of the Hereditary Farm Courts, or the Reich Peasant Leader. In addition to the assessors, the necessary number of deputies shall also be appointed.

§ 45. Legal Status and Compensation of Peasant Assessors

(1) Regarding the legal status and compensation of Peasant Assessors, the existing regulations applicable to lay judges under the Judiciary Act §31 to §33, §35 nos. 1 and 5, and §51 to §56 shall apply accordingly, with the provision that the public prosecutor's office need not be involved.

(2) With regard to the supervisory complaint specified in the final sentence of the Judiciary Act §55, the President of the Regional Court shall make the final decision in cases overseen by Inheritance Courts and the President of the Higher Regional Court in cases overseen by Hereditary Farm Courts.

(3) If it subsequently becomes known that a requirement for appointment as an assessor has not been met, or if a requirement subsequently ceases to apply, the assessor shall be removed from office by the authority which appointed him; the assessor shall be granted a defense before a decision is reached. The decision is final.

§ 46. Proceedings

(1) Proceedings before the Inheritance Court and the Hereditary Farm Court are regulated by a decree of the Reich Minister of Justice and the Reich Minister of Food and Agriculture in accordance with the principles of proceedings in matters of voluntary jurisdiction.

(2) The decree enables preliminary decisions by the chairperson and the collection of evidence by individual members of the court.

§ 47. The Reich Hereditary Farm Court

(1) The establishment, proceedings, and seat of the Reich Hereditary Farm Court shall be regulated by a decree of the Reich Minister of Justice and the Reich Minister of Food and Agriculture. In this regard, the verdicts of the Reich Hereditary Farm Court shall be subject to confirmation by the Reich Minister of Food and Agriculture.

§ 48. Immediate Appeal

(1) An immediate appeal may be lodged against the verdicts of the Inheritance Court. Appeals must by lodged within a period of two weeks.
(2) An immediate appeal may also be lodged by the District Peasant Leader against verdicts made by the Inheritance Court on the basis of §10, §15 para. (3), §18, § 21 para. (3), §25, and §37 para. (2). The Inheritance Court shall deliver *ex officio* the aforementioned verdicts to the District Peasant Leader.
(3) The Hereditary Farm Court shall decide the appeal.

§ 49. Immediate Further Appeal

(1) An immediate further appeal may be lodged against the verdicts of the Hereditary Farm Court. The period for lodging the appeal is two weeks.
(2) If the verdict of the Hereditary Farm Court relates to one of the decisions mentioned in §48 para. (2), this appeal may also be lodged by the Regional Peasant Leader. The Hereditary Farm Court shall deliver *ex officio* the aforementioned verdicts to the Region Peasant Leader.
(3) The Reich Hereditary Farm Court shall decide the further appeal.
(4) Further appeal is only admissible if the verdict of the Hereditary Farm Court contains new independent grounds for appeal. This does not apply to an appeal by the Regional Peasant Leader provided for in para. (2).

§ 50. Enforcement of Decisions

Enforcement shall take place upon the final verdicts of the Inheritance Courts, the Hereditary Farm Courts, or the Reich Hereditary Farm Court in accordance with the provisions stipulated by the Code of Civil Procedure.

§ 51. Costs

The fees and costs for the proceedings before the Inheritance Authorities are regulated by a decree of the Reich Minister of Justice and the Reich Minister of Food and Agriculture.

Section VI
The Registry of Hereditary Farms and Land Register

§52

(1) The Registry of Hereditary Farms (§1 para. (3)) shall be kept at the Inheritance Court.
(2) The registration of Hereditary Farms shall be free of charge.
(3) The establishment of the farm registry and the registration procedure is regulated by a decree of the Reich Minister of Justice.

§ 53. Entry in the Land Register

(1) At the request of the chairman of the Inheritance Court, the entry of the properties belonging to a Hereditary Farm that has been entered into the farm registry must also be recorded in the Land Register. Entry shall be free of charge.
(2) Properties belonging to the Hereditary Farm shall be entered on a special page in the Land Register. The Land Registry should do its utmost to ensure that the Peasant has them combined into one property by means of a corresponding entry in the Land Register.

Section VII
Final Provisions

§ 54. Local Jurisdiction of the District and Regional Peasant Leaders

The local jurisdiction of the District and Regional Peasant Leaders is determined by the location of the Hereditary Farm.

§ 55. Exemption from the Inheritance and Land Acquisition Tax

An heir does not have to pay any inheritance tax or land acquisition tax on the transfer of a Hereditary Farm.

§ 56. Rules of Interpretation

If any doubt arises as to the application of this law, the judge shall decide in accordance with the purpose of the law as stated in the introductory words.

§ 57. Commencement

(1) This law comes into effect on October 1, 1933.
(2) It shall apply to inheritances that occur after that date.

§ 58. Transitional Provisions for §23 (Multiple Hereditary Farms)

If the testator owns multiple Hereditary Farms, he may by will or testamentary contract, and in derogation of §23, stipulate that in the first case of succession occurring after the commencement of this law, a total of two Hereditary Farms shall be allotted to one heir if the heir is a son or grandson and both farms together do not exceed 125 hectares.

§ 59. Transitional Provisions for §§ 38 and 39 (Enforcement)

The regulations of §39 regarding enforcement against agricultural products produced by the Hereditary Farm shall also apply to enforcement with regard to pecuniary claims under private law until another regulation is adopted and implemented by way of ordinance.

§ 60. State Laws

(1) Upon the commencement of this law, state regulations concerning inheritance rights become void.

(2) State law regulations on closed inheritance remain unaffected in the case of estates formed on the basis of the laws regarding the dissolution of fideicommissa (in particular forest estates and estates on reclaimed land), provided they do not become Hereditary Farms, and in the case of hereditary leasehold estates.

§ 61. Regulations for Implementation

(1) The Reich Minister of Justice and the Reich Minister of Food and Agriculture are authorized to jointly issue the statutory ordinances and general administrative regulations necessary for the implementation of this law.
(2) To the extent that they deem it necessary to achieve the purpose of this law, they may also issue regulations of a supplementary or deviating nature, particularly including the repeal or amendment of the regulations specified in §60 para. (2).

Berlin, September 29th, 1933.

Reich Chancellor

Adolf Hitler

Reich Minister of Justice

Dr. Gürtner

Reich Minister of Food and Agriculture

R. Walther Darré.

Bibliography

Aereboe, Friedrich. *Allgemeine Landwirtschaftliche Betriebslehre* [General Agricultural Management]. Berlin, 1917.

Adametz, Leopold. "Herkunft und Wanderung der Hamiten Erschlossen aus ihren Haustier-rassen" [Origin and Migration of the Hamites Inferred from their Livestock Breeds]. *Osten und Orient* [East and Orient], Wien, 1920.

Adametz, Leopold. *Österreichische Molkerei-Zeitung* [Austrian Dairy Journal], 1904.

Almquist, E. *Archiv für Rassen und Gesellschaftsbiologie* [Archive for Racial and Social Biology].

Almquist, E. "Die Nordische Rasse beim Untergang des Wotankults" [The Nordic Race at the Fall of Wotanism]. *Archiv für Rassen und Gesellschaftsbiologie* [Archive for Racial and Social Biology] 4, no. 15.

Amira, Karl von. *Grundriß des Germanischen Rechts* [Outline of Germanic Law]. Straßburg, 1913.

Antonius, Otto. "Die Abstammung der Hausrinder" [*The Ancestry of Domestic Cattle*]. *Naturwissenschaften* [Natural Sciences], vol. 7 (1919).

Antonius, Otto. *Stammesgeschichte der Haustiere* [Phylogeny of Domesticated Animals]. Jena, 1922.

Arndt, E. M. "Einige Leichte Bemerkungen zu Cäsars und Tacitus Berichten über die Feldordnung und den Ackerbau der Alten Germanen" [Some Light Comments on Caesar's and Tacitus's Reports on the Field Organization and Agriculture of the Ancient Germanic Peoples]. *Zeitschrift für Geschichtswissenschaft* [Journal of Historical Science] 3 (Berlin: 1845): 231–255.

Augstin, Max. *Die Entwickelung der Landwirtschaft in den Vereinigten Staaten von Nord-Amerika* [The Development of Agriculture in the United States of North America]. Munich-Leipzig, 1914.

Baur, Erwin, Eugen Fischer, and Fritz Lenz. *Grundriß der Menschlichen Erblichkeitslehre und Rassenhygiene* [Outline of Human Heredity and Racial Hygiene]. 3rd ed. Munich, 1927.

Below, Georg von. *Der Deutsche Staat des Mittelalters* [The German State in the Middle Ages]. Leipzig, 1914.

Birt, Theodor. *Römische Charakterköpfe* [Distinctive Features of the Romans]. Leipzig, 1916.

Breune. *Süd-Afrika* [*South Africa*]. Morawe u. Scheffels, 1926.

Buschan, Georg. *Das Deutsche Volk in Sitte und Brauch* [The German People in Custom and Tradition].

Cabanis, Pierre J. G. *Rapports du Physique et du Moral de l'Homme* [Relationships Between the Physical and Moral Aspects of Man], trans. L. Jacob. Halle, 1804.

Caesar, Gaius Julius. *Commentarii de Bello Gallico* [Commentaries on the Gallic War]. Translated by W. S. Bohn and W. A. McDevitte. Harper & Brothers, 1869.

Caldecott, Alfred. *English Colonization and Empire*. London, 1897.

Clauß, Ludwig. *Rasse und Seele* [Race and Soul]. Munich, 1934.

Curtius, Georg. *Grundzüge der Griechischen Etymologie* [Principles of Greek Etymology], 5th ed. 1879.

Darré, R. Walther. "Die Einheimischen Rinderschläge Finnlands" [The Native Cattle Breeds of Finland]. *Deutsche Landwirtschaftliche Tierzucht* [Journal of German Agricultural Animal Breeding] 31, no. 44.

Darmstädter, Paul. *Die Vereinigten Staaten von Amerika* [The United States of America]. Leipzig, 1909.

Darré, R. Walther. "Das Finnische Pferd" [The Finnish Horse]. *Deutsche Landwirtschaftliche Tierzucht* [Journal of German Agricultural Animal Breeding] (1926): 836.

Darré, R. Walther. "Das Schwein als Kriterium für Nordische Menschen und Semiten" [The Pig as a Criterion for Nordic People and Semites]. *Volk und Rasse* 2, no. 3 (1933).

Darré, R. Walther. "Innere Kolonisation" [Internal Colonization]. *Deutschlands Erneuerung* [Germany's Renewal] 10 (1926): 152.

Demangeon, Albert. *Das Britische Weltreich* [The British World Empire]. Berlin, 1926.

"Die Schwangerschaftsverhütung als Sozialmedizinisches Problem" [Contraception as a Socio-Medical Problem]. *Zeitschrift für Volksaufartung, Erbkunde und Eheberatung* [Journal for National Racial Improvement, Hereditary Science, and Marriage Counseling] 6, no. 3 (Berlin: A. Metzner).

Diodorus Siculus. *Library of History*. Translated by C. H. Oldfather. Loeb Classical Library ed. Cambridge: Harvard University Press, 1933.

Dungern, Otto von. *Adelsherrschaft im Mittelalter* [Noble Rule in the Middle Ages]. Munich, 1927.

Fehrle, Schweizer. *Archiv für Volkskunde* [Swiss Archive for Folklore], vol. 26 (1926), 260.

Ferrero, Guglielmo. *Die Frauen der Cäsaren* [The Wives of the Caesars]. Stuttgart: J. Hoffman.

Fleischmann, Wilhelm. *Cäsar, Tacitus, Karl der Große und die Deutsche Landwirtschaft* [Caesar, Tacitus, Charlemagne, and German Agriculture]. Berlin, 1911.

Froude, James A. *The Earl of Beaconsfield*. London: J.M. Dent, 1905.

Gaius. *Gaii Institutionum Iuris Civilis Commentarii Quatuor* [*Elements of Roman Law*], Translated by Edward Poste. Oxford: Clarendon Press, 1771.

Gilbert, Gustav. "Der Staat der Lakedaimonier" [The State of the Lacedaemonians]. In *Handbuch der Griechischen Staatsaltertümer* [Handbook of Greek State Antiquities]. Leipzig, 1881.

Grant, Madison. *Untergang der Großen Rasse* [The Passing of the Great Race]. Translated by Rudolf Polland. Munich, 1925.

Grosse, Johannes. *Die Schönheit des Menschen* [The Beauty of Man]. Dresden, 1912.

Günther, Hans F. K. *Adel und Rasse* [Nobility and Race]. 12th ed. Munich, 1927.

Günther, Hans F. K. *Der Nordische Gedanke* [The Nordic Idea]. Munich, 1927.

Günther, Hans F. K. *Platon als Hüter des Lebens* [Plato as the Guardian of Life]. Munich, 1928.

Günther, Hans F. K. *Rassenkunde des Deutschen Volkes* [Racial Studies of the German People]. 12th ed. Munich, 1927.

Dade, Heinrich. *Arbeitsziele der Deutschen Landwirtschaft nach dem Kriege* [The Work Goals of Post-war German Agriculture]. Berlin, 1918.

Hansen, Joseph. "Der Englische Staatskredit unter König Eduard III und die Hansischen Kaufleute" [English State Credit under King Edward III and the Hanseatic Merchants]. *Hanseatische Geschichtsblätter* [Hanseatic History Papers] 37, 1910.

Herodotus. *The Persian Wars*. Translated by A. D. Godley. Loeb Classical Library ed. Cambridge: Harvard University Press, 1920.

Heyne, Moriz. *Deutsches Wörterbuch* [German Dictionary]. Leipzig, 1890.

Hilzheimer, Max. *Natürliche Rassengeschichte der Haussäugetiere* [Natural Breed History of Domestic Mammals]. Berlin-Leipzig, 1926.

Ihering, Rudolf von. *Geist des Römischen Rechts auf den Verschiedenen Stufen Seiner Entwicklung* [The Spirit of Roman Law at Different Stages in its Development].

Ihering, Rudolf von. *Vorgeschichte der Indoeuropäer* [Evolution of the Indo-Europeans]. Leipzig, 1894.

Isocrates, *Panathenaicus*, section 179, trans. George Norlin, Loeb Classical Library ed. (Cambridge: Harvard University Press, 1929)

Jacob, Georg. *Arabisches Beduinenleben* [Arab Bedouin Life]. Berlin: 1897.

Jung, Erich. *Deutsche Geschichte für Deutsche* [German History for Germans]. Langensalza, 1925.

Kayser. "Berufstand und Staat" [Profession and State], *Deutsches Volkstum* (June 1926).

Kerckerinck zur Borg, Engelbert Freiherr von. *Beiträge zur Geschichte des West-fälischen Bauernstandes* [Contributions to the History of the Westphalian Peasant Class]. Berlin, 1912.

Kern, Anton. *Ursprung und Artbild der Deutschen* [Origins and Breed Pictures of the Germans]. Munich, 1927.

Kern, Fritz. *Stammbaum und Artbild der Deutschen* [Family Tree and Breed Pictures of the Germans and their Kin]. Munich, 1927.

Kossinna, Gustaf. *Ursprung und Verbreitung der Germanen in Vor- und Frühgeschichtlicher Zeit* [Origin and Spread of the Germanic Peoples in Prehistoric and Early Historical Times]. Berlin-Lichterfelde, 1927.

Kraemer, Hermann. *Allgemeine Tierzucht* [General Animal Breeding], vol. 1. Stuttgart, 1924.

Kraemer, Hermann "Zur Ältesten Geschichte der Pferde" [On the Earliest History of Horses]. *Biologie und Rassengeschichte* [Biology and Breed History] 1.

Kremer, Freiherr von. *Kulturgeschichte des Orients unter den Kalifen* [Cultural History of the Orient under the Caliphs].

Kuhlenbeck, Ernst. *Die Entwicklungsgeschichte des Römischen Rechts* [The History of the Development of Roman Law]. 13th ed. Munich.

Kynast, Karl, *Apollon und Dionysos* [Apollo and Dionysus]. Munich, 1927.

Leist, Burkhard W. *Alt-Arisches Jus Civile* [Ancient Aryan Civil Law]. 1896.

Leutwein, Theodor. *Die Kämpfe mit Hendrik Witboi 1894 und sein Ende* [The Battles with Hendrik Witboi in 1894 and His End]. Leipzig, Voigtländer.

Malsburg, V. D. "Die Zellengröße als Form- und Leistungsfaktor der land-wirtschaftlichen Nutztiere" [Cell Size as a Shape and Performance Factor for Livestock]. *Arbeiten der Deutschen Gesellschaft für Züchtungskunde* [Works of the German Society for Breeding Science] 10 (Hannover: 1911).

Merk, Walther. *Vom Werden und Wesen des Deutschen Rechts* [On the Development and Essence of German Law]. Langensalza, 1926.

Meitzen, A. *Siedelung und Agrarwesen der Westgermanen und Ostgermanen usw.* [Settlement and Agriculture of the West and East Germanic Peoples, etc.], vol. 1. Berlin: 1895.

Mielke, Robert. *Die Siedlungskunde des Deutschen Volkes* [The Settlement History of the German People]. Munich, 1927.

Mucke, Richard. *Urgeschichte des Ackerbaus und der Viehzucht* [Prehistory of Agriculture and Animal Husbandry]. Greifswald, 1898.

Müllenhoff, Karl. *Deutsche Altertumskunde* [German Classical Studies]. Berlin, 1900.

Müller, Josef. *Mann und Weib* [Man and Woman]. Union Deutsche, "Die Beiden Geschlechter Innerhalb des Bauernstandes" [The Two Genders within the Peasantry].

Münchhausen, Börries Freiherr von. "Die Grafen von Beaumanoir" [The Count of Beaumanoir].

Naumann, Ida. *Altgermanisches Frauenleben* [The Life of Ancient Germanic Women]. Jena: Eugen Diederichs.

Nietzsche, Friedrich. *Human, All Too Human*, trans. Helen Zimmern. Edinburgh-London: T.N. Foulis, 1909.

Oettingen, Burchard von. *Die Zucht des Edlen Pferdes* [Breeding the Noble Horse]. Berlin, 1908.

Peters, K. J. *Deutsche Landwirtschaftliche Tierzucht* [Journal of German Agricultural Animal Breeding].

Paudler, Fritz. *Die Hellfarbigen Rassen* [The Light-Colored Races]. Heidelberg, 1924.

Pira, Adolf. *Studien zur Geschichte der Schweinerassen, Insbesondere der Schwedens* [Studies on the History of Pig Breeds, Especially Those of Sweden], trans. Spengel. Jena, 1909.

Ploß, Hermann H. *Das Weib in der Natur und Völkerkunde* [Woman in Nature and Ethnography]. Leipzig, 1891.

Pöhlmann, Robert von. *Geschichte der Sozialen Frage: Antiker Kommunismus und Sozialismus* [History of Social Questions: Ancient Communism and Socialism].

Ritter, Kurt. "Geschichte der Landwirtschaft der Welt" [*History of World Agriculture*]. In *Handbuch der Landwirtschaft* [Handbook of Agriculture], 1. Berlin, 1928.

Ruedolf, Richard. *Fluch Unserer Geschlechtsmoral* [*Curse of Our Sexual Morality*].

Rümker, Kurt von. *Tagesfragen aus dem Modernen Ackerbau* [Current Issues in Modern Agriculture], 9th ed. Berlin, 1922.

Saborsky, Paul. *Das Wallisische Schwarze Rind* [The Valais Black Cattle]. Vienna, 1913.

Schiller, Friedrich. *Kabale und Liebe* [*Intrigue and Love*]. 1784.

Schrader, Otto. *Reallexikon der Indogermanischen Altertumskunde* [Encyclopedia of Indo-European Archaeology]. Berlin-Leipzig, 1917–1923.

Schuchhardt, Carl. *Alteuropa, eine Vorgeschichte unseres Erdteils* [Ancient Europe, A Prehistory of Our Continent]. Berlin-Leipzig, 1926.

Schuhmacher, Karl. *Der Ackerbau in Vorrömischer und Römischer Zeit* [Agriculture in Pre-Roman and Roman Times]. Main: 1922.

Sellheim, Hugo. *Das Geheimnis vom Ewig-Weiblichen* [The Mystery of the Eternal Feminine], 2nd ed. Stuttgart, 1924.

Skalweit, Bruno. *Die Englische Landwirtschaft* [English Agriculture]. Berlin, 1915.

Strabo. *Geographica* [Geography]. Book 7, chapter 5, section 7. Translated by Horace L. Jones. Loeb Classical Library ed. Cambridge: Harvard University Press, 1923.

Stegemann, Hermann. *Der Kampf um den Rhein* [The Battle for the Rhine]. Berlin-Leipzig, 1924.

Stoddard, Lothrop. *The Revolt Against Civilization: The Menace of the Under Man*. New York, 1922.

Strabo. *Geographica* [Geography]. Translated by Horace L. Jones. Loeb Classical Library ed. Cambridge: Harvard University Press, 1923.

Treitschke, Heinrich Gotthard von. *Deutsche Geschichte im Neunzehnten Jahrhundert* [Nineteenth Century Germany History], vol. 1.

Ulmansky, S. *Die Andalusische Rinderrasse* [The Andalusian Cattle Breed]. Wien, 1918.

Valentin, Veit. *Kolonialgeschichte der Neuzeit* [Colonial History of Modern Times]. Tübingen, 1915.

Weigand, Friedrich L. K. *Deutsches Wörterbuch* [German Dictionary]. Gießen, 1909.

Weisheit, Friedrich. *Devons und South Devons* [Devons and South Devons]. Vienna, 1914.

Wettstein, Friedrich von, *Wie Entstehen Neue Vererbbare Eigenschaften* [How Do New Inheritable Traits Arise], *Züchtungskunde* [Breeding Science] (1927).

Williamson, James A. *A Short History of the British Expansion*. London, 1922.

Wittich, Werner. *Die Grundherrschaft in Nordwestdeutschland* [The Manorial System in Northwestern Germany]. Leipzig, 1896.

Wittich, Werner. *Die Frage der Freibauern* [The Question of Free Peasants] (Weimar: 1901).

Wolff, K. S., *Rassenlehre* [Racial Doctrine]. Leipzig: Mannus-Bibliothek, 1927.

Wundt, Max. *Staatsphilosophie* [Philosophy of State]. Munich, 1923.

Xenophon. *Anabasis*. Book 4, chapter 5, section 25. Translated by Carleton L. Brownson. Loeb Classical Library ed. Cambridge: Harvard University Press, 1922.

Zorn, William. *Haut und Haar als Rasse- und Leistungsmerkmal in der Landwirtschaftlichen Tierzucht* [Skin and Hair as Breed and Performance Characteristics in Agricultural Livestock Breeding].

ENJOYED THIS BOOK?

TO READ MORE, VISIT US AT

ANTELOPEHILLPUBLISHING.COM

www.ingramcontent.com/pod-product-compliance
Lightning Source LLC
Chambersburg PA
CBHW030914140626
46545CB00016B/1298